Interwoven

Exploring Materials and Structures

Interwoven

Exploring Materials and Structures

Maarit Salolainen

**with contributions by Maija Fagerlund, Anna-Mari Leppisaari, Kirsi Niinimäki,
Tiina Paavilainen, Emmi Pouta and Aalto University alumni and students**

photographs by Eeva Suorlahti

CONTENTS

2 TO THE LOOMS—WEAVING AND EXPERIMENTING 119

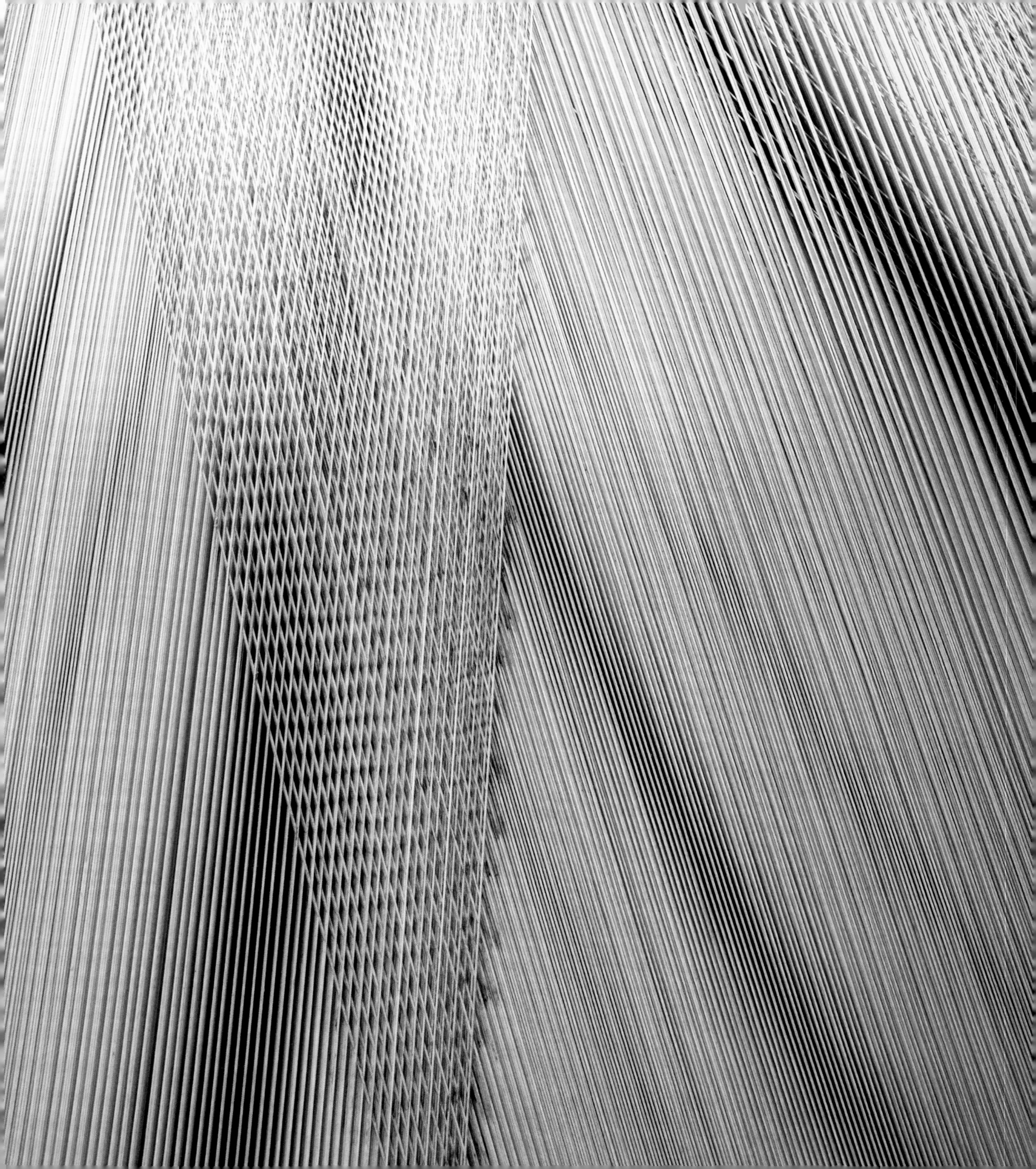

Foreword

by Helena Hyvönen

Interwoven is a testament to the pioneering work that Maarit Salolainen has done in the field of design, particularly in textile design, and shares this expertise with a wider audience. This book is designed to inspire the reader to think creatively through textiles and encourages the development of technical and design skills by emphasising the importance of materials and structures in textile design. *Interwoven* thus not only introduces the reader to woven textile design, but promotes a more immersive approach; *textile thinking*.

I have worked in textiles—textile art, textile design—and more broadly in the field of design for almost my entire life since my teenage years. In that time, I have worked in every design industry role imaginable: artist, product designer, head of collections, teacher, entrepreneur, and director. Throughout my career I have seen the restructuring of the textile industry as well as the heavy burden that the textile and fashion industry place on the environment. Experiencing these challenges first-hand sparked questions: What would remain in Finland, and how to promote the industry here? What potential could be uncovered in interdisciplinarity, in dialogue with other fields, and by exploring design practices from different disciplinary contexts or traditions? These questions led me to a career in higher education. I started work in 1998 at the University of Art and Design Helsinki, and was later appointed Principal. When the University became a part of Aalto University, I was appointed the Dean of Aalto University's School of Arts, Design and Architecture, a post from which I retired in 2014.

Guided by my background in industry, my goal in higher education was to collaborate with the fashion design faculty to weave the Textile and Fashion Studies programmes closely together. We asked what role textiles and fashion could have in design teaching and recognised the challenge of moving beyond siloed thinking towards a comprehensive and shared design approach. A significant leap towards this type of interdisciplinary learning was taken by investing in fashion and textile studios, and developing the curricula towards learning by making.

Since then crossdisciplinarity, opening the textile workshop doors to all students of the design department, developing new textile teaching methods as well as combining textile studies with other disciplines, has brought the field closer to shared design thinking. Design, like many other disciplines, was caught in its own silo at the time and its quest for reform was only beginning to take shape and find new patterns for collaboration. Central to the teaching approach was to focus student time on the essential; teaching design thinking, producing

← Jacquard harness

content and weaving a narrative, as well as developing technical skills in an efficient way. Testament to this approach are the various successful careers our students have gone on to have in the textile industry and international fashion houses, not to mention the BA Programme in Fashion and MA Programme in Fashion, Clothing and Textile Design which reached the top of the Business of Fashion Ranking in 2019.

It was as these ideas around teaching textile design were taking shape, that I met Maarit Salolainen in the beginning of the 2000s following her return to Finland after a long stretch of working abroad. From our first meeting, I knew that I had met a colleague and kindred spirit. We had gathered similar work experience in the textile industry and field of industrial design. We began a collaboration with a purpose to answer a series of questions: How to teach the fundamentals of textile design; fibres and yarns as well as textile structures in the simplest and fastest way possible? How to provide sufficient time for thinking, for developing fundamental *textile thinking*? How to open doors for everyone interested, and thereby strengthen the future and development of textile design? *Interwoven* provides answers to these questions and invites the wider public to experiment with textile materials and structures. The book shares the secrets of woven fabrics, yarns and finish with a large audience of diverse learners, from experts to novices, by developing a multidisciplinary way of working and seeking methods for shared learning by doing. *Interwoven* is not a woven fabrics textbook for a small group of specialists in the field; instead it introduces a pedagogical model which can be applied to other teaching as well. The book has grown from Maarit's own learning experiences, expertise gained in professional practice, and passion for challenging oneself as a teacher. The pedagogical platform introduced in the book makes *Interwoven* a tool for woven design teaching, which helps create a multi-disciplinary learning environment

equally for those dipping their toe in as for students specialising in textile design. It opens up the terminology of woven fabrics and weaves, the qualities of fibres and yarns, introduces the process of design and visual research, as well as principles of collection design which are key to designing textiles. The book places emphasis on experimentation and gives excellent tips on how to do this, without forgetting the importance of mastering technical skills all the way up to computer-aided design. The book does not shirk away from addressing environmental concerns, which should be considered regardless of field, but which are particularly fundamental to the future of textiles and fashion.

However, *Interwoven* is also much more than this. It is an uncompromising account by a beloved and respected teacher. It raises the all-important question; where are we coming from and where are we going? Human memory is woven with a thread and needle. It is a story of technological innovations in textile manufacturing well before the age of computers. Without fabric we would not be human. Maarit's teaching is a part of a deeper narrative, one which very much overlaps with her teaching methods. The students learn *textile thinking* through creating stories and weaving them. In doing so, the students weave themselves into the story of humanity. Without students there would be no book. Testament to this are the contributions in this book by Maija Fagerlund and Anna-Mari Leppisaari, both proteges of Maarit's teaching methods, who are now taking their turn to develop textile teaching methods even further.

Technology, business and art meet at Aalto University. This phrase summarised our belief as the founders of Aalto University, in solving the grand challenges of the world with multidisciplinary collaboration across programmes, national borders, and together with industry. What proved most difficult was learning to communicate across the artistic and scientific ways of thinking and working.

To me Maarit's book also embodies this ethos; *Interwoven* brings art, technology and science to the wider public. The book is grounded in design pedagogy and the principles of learning design by doing. Studying woven textiles is a process of learning ways of thinking as well as expression. The current literature in the field has a tendency to leave out much of its potential audience. It consists of pattern handbooks, crafts publications or industrial weaving manuals. With its high-quality images and engaging layout, *Interwoven*, originally published by Aalto ARTS Books in 2022, was enthusiastically received by designers and design collaborators alike. One aim of the book is to add to the international debate on design pedagogy–designing as learning.

I am thrilled, that with this revised edition, Thames & Hudson brings *Interwoven* to new audiences across the world, spreading the wonder and wisdom on crafting cloth.

A warm thank you for my friend Maarit for this book!

15 July 2024, Helsinki

Helena Hyvönen
Doctor Honoris Causa of Arts
Professor Emerita
Aalto University

↑ Maarit Salolainen and Maija Fagerlund guiding students in experimenting with woven structures.

Acknowledgements

I dedicate this book to all the talented, wonderful students with my complete gratitude to your endless creativity and for all your beautiful fabrics and interwoven stories which inspired me to write this book. You amaze me and without you this book would never have been written.

Writing this book has taken a village! It has been a journey shared with many insightful colleagues, students and collaborators. First, I want to thank Maija Fagerlund for sharing the passion for textile design and being my comrade in arms in opening up the fascinating field of woven textiles to the students of Aalto University, School of Arts, Design and Architecture. The chapter *Jacquards – Boosting the Patterns*, written by Maija, elaborates on the development she has done on the methodology and pedagogics in this complex and fascinating area.

I thank Anna-Mari Leppisaari, for the information on studio teaching methods for textile finishing in the section *Searching for the Final Hand and Look*. Anna-Mari's insight on fashion design has greatly influenced teaching approaches for textiles for fashion at Aalto University, as demonstrated by her subsequent article *The Hybrid Practice of Combining Textile and Fashion Design*.

Tiina Paavilainen, without your help and support throughout all these years of writing there would be no book. Your skill in selecting the best image among a pile of photographs and in simplifying difficult concepts to clear charts and structural drafts is astonishing.

Tiina also shared her skills in creating unique three-dimensional textiles with fil coupé technique in her article *Floating and Clipping*.

Textile designer, photographer, Eeva Suorlahti has captured the soul of each fabric with her miraculous photography. Likewise, my immense gratitude is owed to designer Minna Luoma for the stunning book design and for making sense of its multilayered structure. Eeva and Minna, your artistry makes this book shine.

Maija, Tiina, Anna-Mari and Eeva, as your former teacher it is my greatest success to work alongside you and watch you promote textile design, each in your own way bringing the world of textiles to a new generation of students.

Kirsi Niinimäki, thank you for lending your leading expertise in the field of sustainability to this book. Thank you, Emmi Pouta, for your help and guidance in framing the introduction to the revised section *Textile Thinking towards Multidisciplinay Futures*, and for the forward-looking article based on your research on eTextiles.

This book's explorations in materials and structures are interwoven with works by talented students at Aalto University, collected throughout a decade of woven fabrics studio courses and student generations. Most of you have graduated and are working in various jobs in the design, textile and fashion industries, thank you for giving permission to share your woven path in this book. A special thanks to all dear former students Nora Bremer, Venla Elonsalo, Petra Haikonen, Leonardo Hidalgo-Uribe, Yuki Kawakami, Hanna-Kaisa Korolainen, Josh Krute, Helmi Liikanen, Heta Vajavaara, Sandra Wirtanen and Aoi Yoshizawa for the articles describing your passion for textiles and the processes you developed to break boundaries and create new ideas.

Thank you, weaving studio masters Tiina Saivo and Päivi Kokko-Vuori, as well as all the wonderful studio assistants over the years, for creating an open and supportive learning atmosphere in the weaving studio through decades of changes and pedagogic development.

I owe immense gratitude to the team at Aalto ARTS Books – Annu Ahonen for providing your guidance and experience throughout the project, editors Pia Alapeteri and Maija Lähteenmäki – and best-ever editor Essi Viitanen for your unrelenting support in making the miracle finally happen. Maria Rehbinder, thank you for your expert support. Thank you Oldouz Moslemian for your editing help and guidance throughout the challenges of the second chapter. Heidi Paavilainen's guidance at the beginning of the writing process helped me find the best practices for handling the multilayered complexity of the manuscript and source material.

I am grateful to Helene Boström from the art bookstore Konst-ig in Stockholm, for the enthusiastic nudge starting this book's journey at Thames & Hudson. Thank you, Francesca Vinter and the T&H team for taking it up from there.

I also want to acknowledge the reviewers, especially Marja Rissanen on textile engineering and Karina Grömer on textile archaeology as well as my colleagues at Vanelli who took the time to provide insight on their specific field of expertise and give astute recommendations that have improved both text and content. I am also grateful to the various individuals, museums and institutes across the world who generously provided images for this book.

I am indebted to the Türkün Family, for their encouragement and support, the beautiful view of the Bosporus, which was a tranquil backdrop for writing, and the company Vanelli for their valuable contribution.

Special recognition is owed to Helena Hyvönen. Her initiative on this book in addition to her friendship and continuous support throughout my two decades at Aalto University and over the years of writing this book has been elementary.

Finally, but not least, my gratitude is owed to my family for enduring the labour of this book alongside me. Thank you, Timo for your love and support, meals and endless pots of green tea, which have supported me during years of stitching this book together. Thank you, Emmi and Oskari, I promise to lock up my computer and spend the next summer holiday with all of you on the pier. Much of my writing was accompanied by the late Sissi's calming presence next to my desk and the rest of the four-legged team all helped by grounding the mind and providing long walks to clear the mind.

The team behind this book is indebted to funding from Aalto University Department of Design as well as to Finnish Cultural Foundation and The Arts Council of Finland for the grants which enabled the writing of this book.

27 July 2024, Helsinki
Maarit Salolainen

Preface

by Maarit Salolainen

In woven textiles, what seems to be a surface, is in fact a multidimensional world made up of two interlacing systems: the warp and the weft. The craft of drafting woven structures is a perfect example of a binary system – these two variables can form a complex multilayered construction or the simplest interlace.

My first encounter with these woven textile constructions was in a classroom with no textiles. The teacher presented us with structural drafts, diagrams of black and white squares on point paper. The assignment consisted of designing a warp for a set of hand towels, setting it up on the loom and weaving it.

I still remember the puzzlement I experienced dealing with this task. I was desperate to realise my ideas of how I wanted the fabric to look, feel and function, but felt paralysed by all the information. The first step was to choose yarns for the warp and weft, and a simple structure. However, it seemed impossible to figure out the best possible materials or structures without understanding the process. Finally, I chose a picture of a nice looking fabric from a weaving book and decided to weave linen towels using that structure. The weave structure, executed using a set-up of block draft on twelve shafts, turned out to be rather complicated for a beginner. Challenged by the complexity of the weave, I slowly began to understand the correlation between the draft images, the structure, and the resulting cloth. The actual learning process happened at the loom, lifting the shafts and little by little understanding how woven constructions work. It took me years to gain enough experience of different types of warps, textile fibres, yarns and woven structures to feel confident in my ability to design woven fabrics.

Later when I was working as the design director of a weaving mill, I was approached to develop textile and surface design courses for Aalto University's School of Arts, Design and Architecture. My approach to textile design came from within the industry and business, and I sought to bring the design practices

← Collection *Precious Treasures* 2020, Vanelli

↑ Maarit Salolainen and the Vanelli 2020 fabric collections

of a professional design team to the textile studios of the university. Most of all, I wanted to introduce endless possibilities for expression and storytelling through textiles: the tacit interplay of materials, textile fibres, colours and structures, and the huge potential of a wider application of textile practices to a great variety of different design disciplines.

My experiences as a student were clear in my mind as I started to rework the woven textile design courses in 2006. The methods employed in teaching weave structures and woven textile design had not changed since the time I had graduated. I had to find a way to help the students plunge head first into the wonderful world of fabrics, to inspire them with the expressive as well as functional properties of different textile fibres, yarns, weave structures, and finishes. I wanted to encourage students to fearlessly tackle technical information as they learn by doing and—most importantly—utilise this knowledge to understand the complexity of the environmental impact of textiles in order to work towards new solutions for sustainable textile futures.

This new pedagogical approach to woven fabric design enables quick advancement

from learning the fundamentals to designing advanced shaft weaves and jacquards. The potential of studio practices for *textile thinking*, material experiments and structural 3D surface creation is emphasised over the artisanal production of handwoven cloth. Students learn to use basic weaves as well as the most important derivative weaves, including multiple weft and warp systems and double weaves, and to utilise these together with an array of yarns to create a versatile woven fabric collection. The method utilises pre-set warps, which differ in threading plan, tie up, sett and yarn materials. Each warp introduces new aspects of weave structures and properties of textile fibres. The learning process is driven by the will to tell tactile stories through an exploration of materials and structures. Practical knowledge of textile fibre properties and yarns, as well as their behaviour and relationship to different weave structures, grows by creating a versatile fabric collection right at the beginning of woven textile design studies. The students learn to use different structures, fibres and yarns to influence the properties and appearance of the finished fabric. In this way the practice-led research process is integral to textile technology studies. Students advance quickly to combined weaves and jacquards to innovate, implement and apply their skills in textiles, fashion or other domains.

For me the very essence of textile design lies in cooperation and multidisciplinary applications. Textiles are commonly implemented as materials or components for a variety of purposes: clothing, interiors, medicine, architecture and technical applications among others. This book supports the development of a designer who has "hybrid" skills. The ability to imagine new sustainable design solutions is encouraged, and priority is given to skills which go directly to the essence of textile design—the interplay of different materials, structures and techniques—around a strong conceptual core of artistic and visual research. The aim is to communicate the knowledge to a

wider audience. Learning the basics of textile techniques efficiently enables swift progression to more advanced studies and beyond – to implement and apply the acquired skills to fashion design work or to the wide range of other disciplines.

It might seem contradictory to present a specialised textbook on the area of woven textile design while intensively stressing a multidisciplinary approach to textile design as a path to innovations. Immersed in the current newsfeed of novel innovations linked to high tech, it is easy to forget the roots of human innovation. The eye needle ranks alongside the taming of fire as one of early humanity's most revolutionary innovations.[1] Textiles are a central part of human consciousness. Modern textile practices are linked to an ancient chain of tradition and development. Throughout the history of different cultures, cloth has played important roles in social, political and economic life. Weaving appears as an important part of archetypical mythical stories, it holds important symbolic meanings and serves as metaphor for core psychological, cultural and political ideas. In our individual lives, memories of fabrics store deep, tactile feelings.

I have experienced that discussing our individual and human stories interwoven with the art of making cloth, offers a foundation and inspiration for creative work and helps create an atmosphere of openness and sharing in the weaving studio. Through the art of weaving, sitting at a loom for the first time is linked to a long chain of textile innovations. The puzzlement over new information on weave structures and fibres is brushed aside by the joy of experimenting, while the potential of rich and textured storytelling through materials and structures and the practice-led research process lead to innovative thinking.

Textile design is a specialist area, but its treasures can be seized faster by forgetting the conventions of traditional teaching methods. The transmitted theoretical information should be practice-driven to support the design

process and innovative thinking. This book and the method it explains update the way in which textile design has been taught and help open up the essence of techniques as well as craft and design practices. Grasping this basic alphabet of the field is necessary for textile and fashion designers–but also when grappling with issues of sustainability in textiles, or collaborating with textile specialists on inter-disciplinary projects.

Whether used to form the simple interlacing system of the plain weave or a complex multilayered construction, this book too comes down to two variables: the warp and the weft. These variables have facilitated innovation for millennia: adjusting to new fibres and applications, spurring technological innovation and challenging human thinking. At the beginning of the 19th century, Joseph Jacquard's invention of the jacquard loom stored information for the first time in binary format on its perforated cardboard cards, and laid the ground for automatic information processing, computers and data networks. Today, as society

evolves–textile structures and materials are given new medical applications, electronics are incorporated into woven textiles and new fibres reshape the future–textiles remain at its core. I see textile professionals and connoisseurs as important members of international, interdisciplinary research and design groups. Even now, we might be on the verge of a new era, resembling the revolution which the invention of the jacquard loom started.

With these words and through sharing this new way of teaching, learning and *textile thinking*, I want to invite you on a journey into the world of textile design. I encourage all readers to take a seat at the loom–even in your imagination–and tell your stories.

Introduction

Interwoven: Exploring Materials and Structures introduces a successful path to learning woven textile design from basic and derivative weaves to multilayered structures and digital jacquard design, from handwoven explorations to industrially manufactured, finished fabrics, and on to coordinated collections and textiles for fashion, interiors, and multidisciplinary applications. The book is a textbook, multilayered storybook and an inspiring treasure trove which interweaves the story of textiles, deeply intertwined in the very essence of humanity, with learning woven fabric design.

This book is for everyone wanting to explore the wonderful world of textiles, plunge into this domain where technical understanding lays the foundation for creative skills and practice. The book is organised in a way that guides the reader into the world of textile materials and structures, and on to woven fabrics, advancing to jacquards, textile finishes and applications. The first chapter *1. Interwoven – On Textiles and Humans* presents the fundamentals of woven fabrics: fibres, yarns, structures, looms and production processes, and guides the reader into *textile thinking*. The chapter begins with a brief introduction to fibres, the building blocks of textiles, and expands to discuss related sustainability issues in *Environmental Impact of Fibres* written by Kirsi Niinimäki. Furthermore, the reader is introduced to textile structures and the development of textile production processes, looms and spinning tools to reveal the fundamental role of textile innovations in human advancement and culture. The summary presented on the history of woven textiles, and the vital cross-cultural roles and metaphorical and mythical meanings that textiles hold, is written to encourage readers to study more and see the omnipresent nature of textiles. The chapter discusses the ways in which textile making, throughout history, has catalysed and changed human thinking, and focuses on the loom and practice of weaving as a creative means for embodied thinking. The capacity of textiles to demonstrate identity and belonging, evoke memories, express feelings, and tell stories is explored in the final section of the first chapter, and demonstrated by emotionally rich, textured fabric collections made by students.

In its quest to appeal to a wide audience – like a cookbook that allows you to taste the perfect imaginary meal from the comfort of your own sofa – the second chapter *2. To the Looms – Weaving and Experimenting* offers a selection of ten predefined warps and sample fabrics woven on them. The vividly illustrated sample fabrics are accompanied by technical information on fibres, yarns and weave structures, guiding anyone regardless of their previous level of knowledge of the field, with or without access to a weaving studio, to grasp the myriad of possibilities and modifications that woven textile design on shaft looms allows. Hands-on advice is given on varying the design and experimenting through the interplay of different yarns

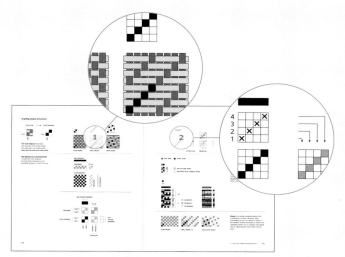

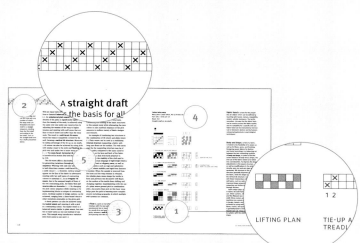

↑ The way structural drafts are arranged varies geographically and according to traditions. The manner of drafting used in this book is explained at the beginning of Chapter 2. The weave information helps visualise the interlacement and movement of ends and picks within the structure (1). The lifting plan as well as the treadling and tie-up information are included for each sample warp (2).

↑ The ten sample warps in the second chapter all introduce particular weave structures, fibres and yarns. The set-up features information for treadle looms as well as dobby looms (1), computer-assisted dobby looms or table looms. The various threading draft types are featured at the top of the page (2). Further information appears on an off-white background (3). Each sample warp includes information on the yarns used, the yarn sett and reed on a light grey background (4). The sample warps, weave structures and yarn materials are introduced from a practice-led perspective (5).

↑ Chapter 2 has a multilayered structure. Each section introduces a weave structure and features images of industrially woven samples (1). Fabric trade names are included on a beige background (2). Examples and variations of the weave, woven by students on the sample warp, include the cloth diagram and pick sequence along with details of the yarns' fibre composition. (3). These examples are enriched by the students' inspiration material including images (4) and texts (5).

Colour codes

Further information and **examples** are on an off-white background

Articles and **collection stories** are on a light grey background

Fibres and **yarns** are introduced on a light pink background

Fabric samples and **names linked to each weave structure** are on a light beige background

Instructor's notes and **texts on studio teaching** are on a light green background

Assignments are on a light blue background

and structures. Readers are thus invited to adjust the materials and structures according to availability and preference–to add salt and vary the spices–and learn how this affects the properties of the resulting cloth. Students in particular, whether advanced or novice and coming from textile design, fashion design or other design fields, will find the experimental and adaptable approach to textile practices useful to their studies, especially in regards to design processes and material design.

This book allows readers to explore different aspects of fibres, yarns and textiles made of them, providing a platform for initial discovery and allowing students to build skills further. The assignments interspersed throughout the book inspire designers to push bound-aries, tackle technical skills, innovate–and most importantly–tell stories through woven samples. This chapter is interwoven with an abundance of sumptuous woven samples that demonstrate creative storytelling.

The third chapter, *3. Jacquards–Boosting the Patterns* written by Maija Fagerlund, further broadens the possibilities of woven fabrics by advancing to patterning and designing for

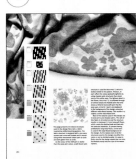

↑ Instructions in this section provide information on creating a jacquard design in Photoshop. First, the drawing of basic weave structures (1) and the method of filling them in with a surface pattern (2) is introduced. After that, a method of creating structures with multiple weft and/or warp systems is explained (3). Example pages of jacquard fabrics present surface patterns and weave structures as well as the information of yarns' fibre composition (4).

jacquard looms. The chapter introduces the reader to the design of jacquard fabrics starting from concept and initial sketching to drafting pattern repeats and finally to preparing digital production files. It gives easy steps for designing simple damasks as well as elaborate patterns and multilayered constructions using Adobe Photoshop as a tool, a practical solution to drafting woven structures. The detailed instructions are brought to life through examples of real woven fabrics and elaborated by student's stories.

The fourth and final chapter, *4. Finished Fabrics – into Fashion, Interiors and Beyond*, features two sections written by Anna-Mari Leppisaari. *Searching for the final Hand and Look* expands the design skills of woven fabrics into finishes, while *The Hybrid Practice of Combining Textile and Fashion Design* applies these to designing for fashion. The chapter ends with uplifting glances to textiles in interiors, commercial collections and multi-disciplinary research, introducing visionary work by graduates whose journey into woven fabrics has been guided by the methodology presented in this book. From the looms into the wider world and into use, these examples illustrate the diverse applications of textiles and demonstrate how the skills gained at the looms in the preceding two chapters can blossom into collections, and technological innovations and be applied to a variety of uses and contexts. Circling back to the themes of Chapter 1, these examples demonstrate that textiles are still integral to the everyday lives of humans.

For teachers and studio masters, in addition to providing assignments that guide the learning journey, the book includes information on the warps used as well as additional advice on organising a woven fabrics studio course in which technical study content is interlinked to conceptual thinking, storytelling and hands-on making. This study content is applied to fashion and collection design studies, as well as to practices in the textile industry.

This book encapsulates a method which guides towards professional textile design practices and processes, keeping in mind the needs of budding design professionals. The practice of weaving is a tool for experimenting and creating new design ideas and a shortcut to understanding drafting information, weave structures as well as fibre and yarn properties. The focus is in creative work that acknowledges the "unity of mind and body, hand and thought"[1] instead of production of handwoven pieces as such. There already exist detailed books on weave structures and plenty of craft books on weaving, as well as textbooks on textile engineering with a comprehensive overview of technical topics such as fibres, yarns, and finishes. That said, most of the existing books on woven fabrics are focused clearly on the theory of weave structures, while craft books give practical advice for hand-weavers. On the other hand, the books focusing on textile engineering – fibres and materials, constructions, processes and machinery – rarely include the creative aspects of textile design. Though offering a unique entry point into tactile learning and *textile thinking*, this book is not intended as an alternative to existing literature. Those readers wishing to take their textile journey beyond the pages of this book will find a wealth of recommended reading material in the appendix.

There is a compilation of useful titles at the end of this book, categorised according to their scope, for those interested in deepening their skills, setting up their own warps, learning more about the technical aspects of textiles or otherwise deepening their understanding of the vast domain of textiles and their technical and creative design.

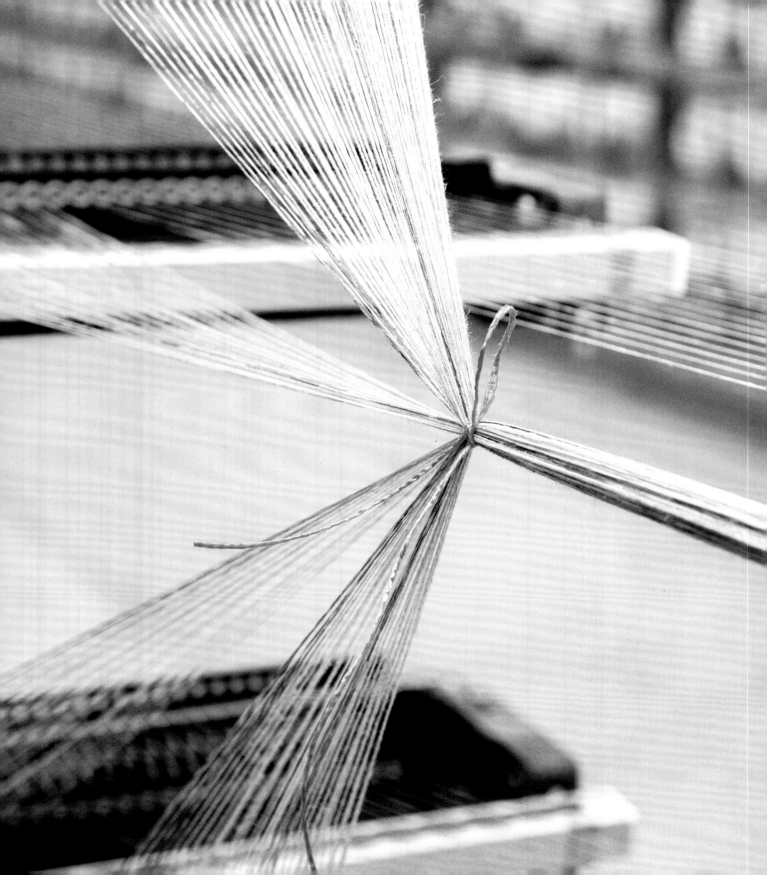

1. Interwoven – On Textiles and Humans

The world of textiles evolves from **fibres**–the building blocks–and **structures**– the interlacing of fibres and **yarns**. The development of production **processes** and **tools** for making textiles, fundamentally interrelated to the innovations and advancements in fibres and yarns, reflects the evolution of human thinking and achievement.

This chapter introduces the reader to the basics of textile fibres and structures, and advances to reflect on the development of looms and other tools used to produce yarns and woven cloth. Pivotal points in textile – and human – history illustrate the integral nature of fibres, yarns, and cloth to human technological and social development. Fabrics and techniques have travelled throughout the ages and had a profound impact on the world in a multitude of ways –from fuelling the global economy and industries to showcasing functional and aesthetic properties that subtly shape our everyday lives. This journey through textile history leads the reader to the pressing contemporary challenges of the industry, namely the environmental impact of fibres. Sustainability in textiles is a system-related and overarching theme. By broadening the reader's understanding of the field, and its basic concepts, practices and processes, this chapter begins to unravel the complexity of the problem and endeavours to encourage the seeking of new sustainable design futures.

The practice of weaving, closely linked to the loom and its mechanism, makes visible how tools and technology catalyse our thinking and making. The chapter ends with a transition from the broader viewpoint of weaving and human history to *textile thinking*, weaving personal (hi)stories and exploring materials and structures. The rich past of textiles is the industry's great resource and inspiration for constant re-creation. Cloth and weaving are an abundant source of metaphors and myths, they demonstrate identity and belonging. The capacity of textiles to tell stories, evoke memories and express feelings is demonstrated here, as well as throughout the book, by the emotionally rich textured fabric collections created by students. At the looms, exploring materials and structures, vibrant personal narratives are interwoven.

A Spun yarns made of natural staple fibres wool and cotton

1.1 Fibres – The Building Blocks

Fibres are the initial raw material of textiles. Throughout the history of textiles, exploiting the key characteristics and properties of fibres has challenged the boundaries of engineering and design. During the past century these boundaries have been pushed at an increasing speed creating new fibres with the potential to turn millennium-old textile technologies into powerful tools for creating materials designed for novel purposes.[1] The quest remains to apply and create fibres that are both sustainable and functional, and thus adapted to the challenges of today's world.

Fabrics are constructed either directly of fibres or yarns made of fibres. Yarns can be made of one type of fibre or they can be blends of many fibre types. The types of yarns, and their fibre composition and fibre characteristics such as fibre chemistry, structure, length and shape, together with the fabric structure, the construction method used to form the textile, influence the properties and performance of the resulting fabric. They determine the fabric's absorbency, thickness, strength, elasticity, texture and softness. Understanding this interrelation helps align fibres, yarns and fabrics for specific end-uses and users. Building on this core fibre knowledge, yarns and their manufacturing processes are further expanded upon throughout Chapter 2.

Fibres are either **natural** or **man-made**. They are small threadlike, fine and flexible structures of long chain molecules which have a definite preferred orientation and a high ratio of length to thickness. There are two main kinds of fibres: **staple fibres** and **filaments**. While staple fibres are of relatively short length, filament fibres are of indefinite length.

Yarns are created from fibres by twisting or laying them together. Staple fibres are spun to create **spun yarns** (A). **Continuous filaments** (B) are generally **combined** and **twisted** to

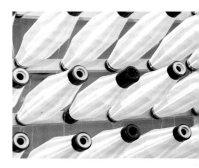

B Man-made synthetic continuous-filament yarns

← Preparing the creel and yarn bobbins for warping at the Vanelli weaving mill. See pp.74–75 for more images of warping in today's industry.

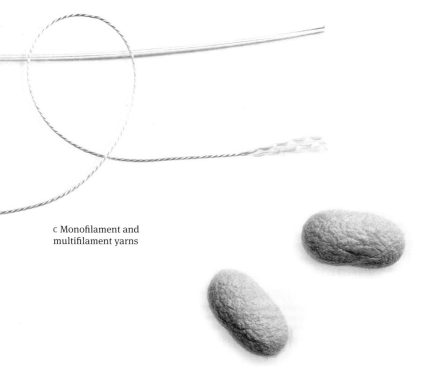

C Monofilament and multifilament yarns

E Silk cocoons

D Flax fibre

form **multifilament** yarns, whereas **monofilament** yarns are composed of only one fibre (C). Synthetic and regenerated filament fibres can also be **cut to short lengths** to create **spun yarn**, which imitates natural fibre yarn. Fibres can be used on their own or mixed with other types of fibres to combine properties and enhance the quality of the end-product or to affect its price.

Natural textile fibres come either from plant, animal or mineral sources. The key fibres used in textiles from prehistoric times up until the first half of the 20th century were natural fibres: wool, cotton, silk, hemp and flax. **Cellulose** is the main component of **plant fibres**, also referred to as **natural cellulose fibres**. The categories of natural cellulose fibre include **seed fibres** such as cotton and kapok, **bast fibres** such as jute, flax (D), ramie and hemp, **leaf fibres** such as sisal and abaca, and **fruit fibre** such as coir. Characteristics shared by all these **staple fibres** are good water absorbency, a tendency to wrinkle easily, resistance to alkalis and organic solvents, and high flammability.[2]

Animal fibres or **natural protein fibres** are divided into fibres from hair follicles composed of **keratin** and **secreted** fibres. Wool, cashmere, mohair and camel hair are examples of keratin **staple fibres** whereas silk, the only **natural continuous filament**, is a secreted fibre excreted by various moth larvae (E). Animal fibres have excellent moisture absorbency, which makes them comfortable in most environmental conditions. Other common characteristics are moderate strength, sensitivity to alkali, elasticity and resiliency against wrinkling. They are also naturally flame resistant.[3]

Man-made fibres are manufactured in an industrial process from either **synthetic polymers**, **natural polymers** or **inorganic materials**. The use of one material to imitate another is a prominent feature in the development of man-made textile fibres. The fibre's chemical properties can be modified on the molecular level, and physical characteristics such as lustre and colour, length, shape, and diameter can be controlled during the fibre spinning process[4]. Manufactured fibres can be engineered into either silk-like **continuous filaments**, or cut into staple fibres imitating yarns made of natural fibres such as cotton or wool, and then further twisted to generate **spun yarns**.

The first man-made fibres were **regenerated cellulose fibres**, made from natural cellulose, predominantly wood pulp. Developed in the late 19th century in a quest to imitate silk, their industrial production only really started in the early 20th century. These **man-made cellulose fibres** (MMCFs) include wet-spun fibres produced with the viscose method, resulting in viscose (rayon) and modal, and the more sustainable **lyocell method**, used to produce lyocell. Cupro, manufactured from cotton linter, is another regenerated cellulose fibre with a small market share. Acetate is a **cellulose ester fibre**, mainly used for non-textile applications. The properties of most cellulosic fibres resemble those of cotton and other natural cellulosic fibres. They are soft, well-draping, breathable and absorbent, and have relatively poor elastic recovery and resiliency against wrinkling. However, acetate is a thermoplastic fibre with properties similar to synthetic fibres.[5]

In a quest for more sustainable solutions, a new generation of man-made cellulose fibres is entering the market. The share of these

F

G

In order to convert synthetic or natural polymers or inorganic materials into fibres suitable for yarns, they undergo a **fibre-extrusion spinning** process in which the polymer fluid is extruded through nozzles to form continuous filaments. There are various **fibre-extrusion spinning technologies** grouped according to the method of forming the molten polymer solution and bringing the fibres to their solid state after the extrusion phase.

Melt-spinning is the most popular method, largely due to its speed and cost efficiency. The process is used for manufacturing polyester, polyamide and polypropylene. These thermoplastic synthetic polymers are heated to form the molten solution, extruded while simultaneously attenuated by drawing, and subsequently cooled to their solid filament state.

↑ Dry-jet wet spinning process of man-made cellulose fibres – spinning of Ioncell. The images feature the Ioncell dope, or cellulose-ionic liquid spinning solution, being extruded through a spinneret (F)

In **wet-spinning** the polymer is **dissolved** into a solution of sufficient viscosity to permit the extrusion through a spinneret into a spin-bath solution consisting of a polymer non-solvent, which then coagulates the polymer chains into continuous solid filaments. This method is used for polymers which do not melt – or thermally degrade rather than melt – or do not dissolve in a volatile, evaporating solvent. This includes regenerated cellulose fibres such as viscose, lyocell, modal and cupro, as well as synthetic fibres such as acrylic, modacrylic, and polyurethane (elastane).

into water (G), where it coagulates and forms Ioncell fibres. An image of the final Ioncell fibre and details of its development currently ongoing at Aalto University can be found on pp. 38 and 155.[6]

Another widely used method is **dry-spinning**, which uses a volatile, easily evaporating solvent to dissolve non-meltable polymers. The resulting viscous solution is then extruded into a heated atmosphere to solidify the polymer through solvent evaporation while stretching the filament by means of drawing. Fibres manufactured by dry-spinning are the cellulose ester fibre acetate, and synthetic fibres: acrylic, modacrylic and polyurethane.[7]

GLOBAL FIBRE PRODUCTION (MILLION METRIC TONS)

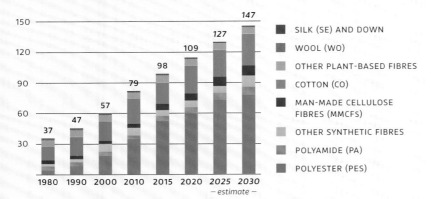

Legend:
- SILK (SE) AND DOWN
- WOOL (WO)
- OTHER PLANT-BASED FIBRES
- COTTON (CO)
- MAN-MADE CELLULOSE FIBRES (MMCFS)
- OTHER SYNTHETIC FIBRES
- POLYAMIDE (PA)
- POLYESTER (PES)

Values: 1980: 37, 1990: 47, 2000: 57, 2010: 79, 2015: 98, 2020: 109, 2025: 127, 2030: 147
2025, 2030 – estimate –

↑ Global fibre production has almost doubled over the past two decades, reaching a record of 116 million tons in 2022. Production is further escalating and is expected to increase by another 30%, to an estimated 147 million tons in year 2030 if business as usual continues, posing serious concerns regarding sustainability. This places pressure to develop more sustainable fibres and increase circularity (p.38). Following the increasing demand for fibres, the production of man-made cellulose fibres (MMCFs)–mostly viscose–has more than doubled in the past 30 years and is expected to grow in the coming years.[12] However, as a result of the increase in the production of polyester, the market share of MMCFs has been shrinking since the early 1980s.

GLOBAL FIBRE PRODUCTION IN 2022

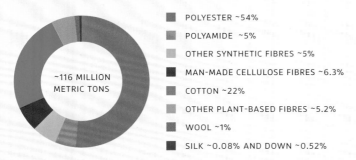

~116 MILLION METRIC TONS

- POLYESTER ~54%
- POLYAMIDE ~5%
- OTHER SYNTHETIC FIBRES ~5%
- MAN-MADE CELLULOSE FIBRES ~6.3%
- COTTON ~22%
- OTHER PLANT-BASED FIBRES ~5.2%
- WOOL ~1%
- SILK ~0.08% AND DOWN ~0.52%

↑ Synthetic fibres have dominated the fibre market since the mid-1990s, when they overtook cotton volumes. In 2022, this fibre category accounted for 65% of the market share. Polyester is the most widely produced fibre with a market share of over half of all global fibre production. Plant fibres had a combined market share of around 27% of the global fibre market. Cotton is the second-most important fibre in terms of volume. At about 25 million tonnes, it had a market share of approximately 22% of global fibre production in 2022. The market share of cotton covered by programs recognized by the 2025 Sustainable Cotton Challenge increased again from 25% in 2020/21 to 27% in 2021/22. The market share of animal fibres was 1.6%. While global wool production has been declining over the years, the market share of wool programs is increasing.[13]

MMCFs from **recycled raw materials** is estimated to be around 0.5%, but with the amount of ongoing research and development, the share is expected to increase significantly in the coming years. These new innovations, such as *Ioncell* (p.155) and the **cellulose carbamate** fibre *Infinna*[8] can contribute to the circular economy through **chemically recycling** cellulose waste material such as post-consumer textiles (see p.38). Another novel cellulose-based man-made fibre innovation is *Spinnova*[9], made from wood pulp or cellulose waste by treating the pulp mechanically–with minimal water use and without any harmful chemicals–in order to create microfibrillated cellulose mixed with water. The fibre is formed as this suspension is extruded through nozzles, and the water evaporates.

Natural protein can be used as raw material for **man-made protein fibres** produced from sources such as milk casein, corn and soybean. The tensile strength of these fibres is low and their use marginal. Moreover, protein is an important source of nutrition and employing protein fibres for textiles presents an ethical problem.

Production of man-made fibres has changed the global fibre production scene since the invention of **synthetic fibres**, developed in the late 1930s. They are based on substances such as coal and petroleum. The burgeoning production of synthetic fibres took off after the Second World War with polyamide, which was taken over in popularity by polyester in the 1970s. Other synthetic fibres include acrylic, modacrylic, polylactide, elastomeric fibre elastane (composed mostly of polyurethane), and polyolefin fibres polypropylene and polyethylene. The properties of synthetic fibres differ greatly according to their molecular properties and how they have been engineered on the molecular, microstructural or macrostructural level.[10]

In addition to the aforementioned fibres, there are **high-performance fibres** with special properties such as high tensile strength, excellent resistance to chemicals or to heat. These manufactured fibres are either of synthetic or **inorganic** origin. Examples of such fibres include the flame-retardant fibre aramid, used in firefighter uniforms. As further examples, carbon fibres and glass fibres possess high tensile strength combined with low density, qualities which are utilised to create light-weight and strong composite materials. **Metallic fibres**, with good electrical and thermal conductivity, are used in heat-pro-tective garments, but they are also used to make decorative metallic yarns (p. 159).

As described in *Environmental Impact of Fibres* (p. 36), sustainability issues are increasingly pressing. Sustainability must be considered when refining engineered fibres and developing new-generation fibres, as well as when making fibre choices for fabrics and textile products. The areas in fibre development which are gaining more importance – in addition to sustainability issues – include nanotech-nology, high performance, multifunctional, and technical applications and develop-ments in microfilament production.

Fibre mechanical recycling is a mechanical process for disassembling used textile products, extracting fibres and incorporating them into a new textile product or other application. **Thermo-mechanical recycling** is a process that melts a polymer to permit recycling. **Chemical recycling** is a process that converts waste materials into feedstock by changing their chemical structure to be used in the production of new materials, divided into **polymer recycling** (e.g. polymer dissolution and re-spinning) and **monomer recycling** (e.g. polymer depolymerizing).[11]

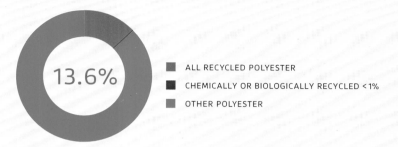

SHARE OF RECYCLED POLYESTER IN 2022

13.6%

■ ALL RECYCLED POLYESTER
■ CHEMICALLY OR BIOLOGICALLY RECYCLED < 1%
■ OTHER POLYESTER

↑ Polyester is the most widely produced textile fibre worldwide. It is a synthetic fibre made from crude oil. With the demand for sustainable solutions, the share of recycled polyester (rPET) is gradually growing. Today, 99 % of rPET is thermally recycled from PET plastic bottles, i.e. chips made from bottles are heated and extruded into filaments. Amid increasing demand for postconsumer bottles within the packaging industry, competition for feedstock is increasing. Scaling up textile-to-textile recycling will be key to reducing green-house gas emissions. New operations for commercial production of chemically or biolog-ically recycled polyester are starting and the low market share (< 1%) of this virgin-polyester quality recycled fibre is expected to grow in the coming years. It is also possible to manufacture polyester from bio-based raw materials but production is limited at the moment.[14] For more information, see pp. 36–39 and p. 155.

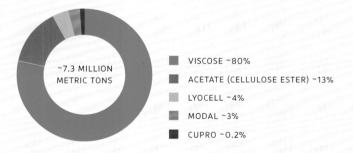

SHARE OF MAN-MADE CELLULOSE FIBRES (MMCFS) BY TYPE IN 2022

~7.3 MILLION METRIC TONS

■ VISCOSE ~80%
■ ACETATE (CELLULOSE ESTER) ~13%
■ LYOCELL ~4%
■ MODAL ~3%
■ CUPRO ~0.2%

↑ In 2022 **viscose** accounted for approx-imately 80 % of all MMCFs produced globally. **Acetate** had the second largest share of MMCFs. Out of all regenerated cellulose fibres almost 5.8 million metric tons were viscose, while only some 300,000 metric tons were lyocell fibres with a market share of around 4 %.[15] The new-generation lyocell manufacturing process, using a recyclable NMMO solvent, can be considered more sustain-able than the viscose method (see p. 37).[16] MMCFs are currently primarily produced from wood. Less than 1 % is made from recycled or other alternative feedstocks. The market share of "recycled" MMCFs increased from an estimated 0.47 % in 2021 to 0.49 % in 2022 and is expected to increase significantly in the coming years. For more information on viscose and lyocell, see p. 155.

Textile Fibres – Classification and Abbreviations

Natural Protein Fibres

Keratin Staple Fibres

WO   wool
WP   alpaca
WA   angora
WS   cashmere
WK   camel
WL   lama
WM   mohair
WG   vicuna
WY   yak
HZ   hair

Secreted Fibres

SE   silk
      (silkworm cocoons)

Natural Cellulose Fibres

Seed Fibres

CO   cotton
KF   kapok

Bast Fibres

JU   jute
LI   flax
RA   ramie
HA   hemp

Leaf Fibres

SI   sisal
AB   abaca
      (manila hemp)

Nut Husk Fibres

CC   coir

Mineral Fibres

inorganic
ASB   asbestos

Textile terminology is often confusing. The intertwined history of textiles with its many parallel traditions results in disparate terms being used for the same concepts (e.g. honeycomb vs. waffle weave p.274). Trade names are frequently mistaken for fibre terms. Wool, chenille, satin and Nylon, for example do not on their own define a particular fabric. Wool is a fibre, chenille a type of yarn, satin a weave structure and Nylon a fibre brand name (p.170). In this book, basic terminology is explained, interchangeable terms are explicitly stated and overlapping terms specified.

MANUFACTURED FIBRES

Regenerated Fibres

Man-made Cellulose Fibres

CV   viscose
CLY   lyocell
CMD   modal
CUP   cupro

**Man-made Cellulose
Ester Fibres**

CA   acetate

Man-made Protein Fibres

(protein source: soybean,
  milk casein, corn...)

Synthetic Fibres

PES   polyester
PA   polyamide
PAN   acrylic
MAC   modacrylic
PP   polypropylene
PO   polyoleofin
PLA   polylactide
      (polylactic acid)
EL   elastane (spandex)
PU   polyurethane

Inorganic Fibres

GF   glass fibre
MTF   metallic fibres
CF   carbon fibres

↑ Generic classification of the main textile fibres grouped in categories according to their origins and chemical structure. The abbreviations are included in this chart as reference points for later chapters, where they are used throughout the structural drafts.[17]

Other Abbreviations used in this book

PI   paper yarn
TR   mixed fibres / unspecified composition
ME   metallised (fibre, yarn)

A Compilation of Textile Performance Concepts and Properties[18]

General Fibre Properties	
Fibre length	The length of **staple fibres** varies greatly depending on their source and is typically between 2 and 50 cm. Fibre length greatly influences the appearance and other properties of the staple yarns and fabrics made out of them, including strength, evenness and hairiness. **Filaments** are of indefinite length and can be made into yarns with little or no twist, generally resulting in a smooth, silky appearance (see effects of fibre shape below).
Fibre shape	**Natural fibres** come in a range of shapes. **Synthetic fibres** can be manufactured in almost any shape. Similarly to fibre length, the shape of the fibre greatly influences the appearance, care and comfort of the final textile product. Fibre shape can refer to: • the longitudinal shape: smooth or rough and uneven. Man-made fibres can be texturised to alter their properties. • the cross-sectional shape: the common types being round, dog-bone shaped, trilobal, multilobal, serrated, and hollow.
Fibre diameter (fineness)	Thinner fibres have a greater surface-to-weight ratio and are generally more flexible, drapeable and have a softer handle than thicker fibres. **Natural fibres** usually are irregular and their diameter varies over their length, while man-made fibres, extruded through a spinneret, have a consistent diameter. Fibre diameter is measured in **microns** (wool) or in terms of **linear density** i.e. weight per unit length (silk and many synthetic fibres), such as denier or tex (see p.127). More information on measuring yarn fineness can be found on p.126. Information on the fabric weight categories is on p.231.
Colour and lustre	The colours of **natural fibres** vary depending on the source. **Filaments** are usually white when manufactured but can also be coloured by incorporating colouring matter in the polymer prior to extruding the filaments (dope dyeing). The colour and surface characteristics have a major effect on fabric appearance including lustre, the sheen created by light reflection.
Colourfastness	The ability of a fibre to retain colour when exposed to certain environmental or chemical conditions such as sunlight and other weather conditions.
Dye affinity	The receptivity of individual fibres to colouration by a particular dyestuff. This property is dependent on the chemical structure of the fibre and its absorbency.

Textile performance

The textile industry provides textiles for **clothing and apparel, interiors** as well as numerous **technical** uses. Technical textiles—engineered to meet precise performance specifications—are applied in uses ranging from highway stabilisation to intricate medical appliances. However, the performance requirements of these highly specialist textiles increasingly overlap with the main use categories. Technical requirements for clothing such as protective gear are high, as are the specific needs in textiles for interiors. Throughout the application categories, high performance properties such as abrasion resistance, flame-retardancy, chemical or light resistance, and antibacterial properties are needed.

Making appropriate textile choices requires knowledge of the factors which influence their performance properties. The choice of material—fibre composition—is fundamental. Taking into account the **performance concepts and properties** of textiles requires evaluating the chemical and physical properties of the fibres used, and the type and characteristics of the yarns which they form. These choices are important to make the beginning of the design process as they influence decisions regarding the fabric structure, later development stages and the functionality of the finished fabric. The choice of fabric construction is essential. Fabric construction, along with material choice, bindings and finishes as well as special treatments, influences the fabric properties permanently.

→

Understanding the **hygroscopic** and **thermoplastic** qualities of a fibre as well as properties and concepts such as **durability, comfort, care, appearance** and **safety** are important in evaluating performance. These performance concepts help assess the suitability of a particular fibre, yarn, or fabric to its designated end use.

In order to assist the reader through later chapters of this book, here is a list of important textile concepts. Some of the terms are related only to fibres or yarns while other concepts apply to fabrics.

Fabrics are specified by defining the following characteristics: fibres, yarn-type, construction (e.g. woven, knitted), weight (g per m²), finishing, dye and/or print, and finally any other special characteristics and test results relevant to the fabric's end use (e.g. Martindale test result and pilling test result for upholstery fabrics, or resistance to sunlight for outdoor fabrics). Environment standards can be added. **Care labeling** is necessary information for all fabrics. For washable fabrics, information on shrinkage can be added.

A Compilation of Textile Performance Concepts and Properties[18]

Properties related to comfort and care	
Moisture absorbency	The way in which fibres respond to moisture • **Hydrophilic** fibres absorb moisture easily • **Hydrophobic** fibres absorb moisture less easily or not at all • **High-regain** fibre / high heat of sorption: a fibre which absorbs moisture and generates heat until saturated • **Hygroscopy**: the ability of a fibre to absorb water vapour without feeling damp • **Absorption**: the soaking up of water into the fibre or fabric • **Adsorption / Wicking**: the ability of a fibre or fabric to accumulate moisture to its surface
Electrical conductivity	The ability of a fibre to carry or transfer an electrical charge • **Electrical conductor**: A fibre or fabric with the ability to transfer electrical charges • **Electrical insulator**: A fibre or fabric with the ability to build up electrical charges
Properties related to comfort and care	
Thermal properties	The response of fibres to heat • **Thermoplastics**: fibres which soften and then melt at higher temperatures • **Non-thermoplastics**: fibres which tend to char and become brittle rather than soften or melt at high temperature Properties of **thermal conductivity.** The thermal insulation or conductivity of fabrics is influenced more by the type of yarn and fabric construction (amount of air trapped in the fabric) than by the type of fibre. • **Thermal conductor**: A fibre or fabric with the ability to transmit heat from the body • **Thermal retainer** (insulator): A fibre or fabric with the ability to hold heat next to the body
Chemical reactivity and resistance	The vulnerability of the fibres on a molecular level in interaction with acids, alkali, oxidising agents, solvents, enzymes, bleaches etc.

A Compilation of Textile Performance Concepts and Properties[18]

Properties of Durability	
Tensile strength	The resistance of a fibre to breaking when stretched
Elongation / extension	The degree to which a fibre may be stretched without breaking
Flexibility	The ability of a fibre or fabric to bend repeatedly without breaking. This property affects the drape and **fabric hand**. Flexibility of the fibre results in drapability of the fabric.
Elasticity	The ability of a fibre or fabric to stretch and recover to its original size and shape
Resiliency	The ability of a fibre or fabric to recover its original position after it is bent, twisted or compressed. The property relates to wrinkle recovery. A high elastic recovery is associated with good resiliency.
Dimensional stability	The ability of a fibre to retain a given size and shape through use and care (shrinkage)
Tenacity (strength)	The ability of a fibre, yarn, or fabric to resist stress
Abrasion resistance	The ability of a fabric to withstand rubbing without yarns breaking or mass loss
Pilling	The forming of tangled fibres on the surface of the fabric
Properties of Safety	
Flame resistance	Burn-properties of a fibre or fabric • **Flammable,** or **Inflammable,** fibres ignite and burn easily (cellulose fibres) • **Flame retardant** fibres burn but self-extinguish when removed from flame (protein fibres) • **Flame resistant** fibres burn and melt. They often self-extinguish when removed from flame (synthetic fibres) • **Non-flammable,** or **flameproof,** fibres do not burn. These fibres will not ignite (mineral fibres) Analysing burn properties aids in the identification of fibres.

Fabrics made of spun yarns might have problems with **pilling**, which refers to the formation of small balls of tangled fibres on the surface of the fabric. In applications prone to wear, such upholstery fabrics, the issue of pilling must be considered, and tested, from the beginning of the design process. Pilling is often especially disturbing when formed from protruding ends of man-made staple fibres, and worsened by other fibres or substances sticking to them. Although similar tiny bobbles appear on natural-fibre fabrics, their innate staple-fibre shape with soft, thinner ends results in softer and less prominent pills. The pilling problem can be tackled by engineering the fibres and their staple length, altering the twist, type or composition of the yarns, changing the weave structure, yarn density, and through finishes.

Fabric hand refers to a consumer's instinct to use the sense of touch when choosing a fabric; to describe and assess the fabric quality and its suitability for a specific end use. The way that the fabric feels, a tactile sensation, is described as its handle or 'fabric hand'. Fabric hand can be evaluated by mechanical or electronic devices and by users with psychophysical or psychological techniques.[19]

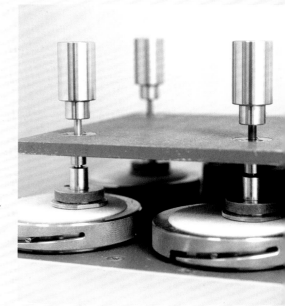

→ Martindale abrasion and pilling tester. The instrument is used to measure abrasion resistance and pilling in textiles. A circular test piece of the fabric is placed in the test clamp base and then rubbed against a standard abrasive wool material at a low pressure in looped and curved figures. The test result given in Martindale cycles after comparing the amount of abrasion or pilling against standard parameters.

→ Polyester is a by-product of the petroleum industry. While it is not renewable, it is possible to recycle it. Currently, most recycled polyester originates from PET bottles and not from recycled polyester textiles.

↑ Cotton picking in Fergana, Uzbekistan. The traditional cultivation of cotton is highly water intensive and requires large quantities of pesticides and fertilisers.

ENVIRONMENTAL IMPACT OF FIBRES   by Kirsi Niinimäki

When discussing the **textile lifecycle**, all phases must be considered: fibre cultivation, material manufacturing, yarn spinning, weaving, dyeing and printing processes, different finishing options, and logistics phases, as well as the use and the end-of-life stages. It is hard to determine which material is best when evaluating the overall environmental impact of a textile, as every material has its own environmental weaknesses. It is also good to remember that natural fibres are not always better than man-made ones. For example, the cultivation of cotton requires intensive consumption of water and large quantities of pesticides and fertilisers. Cotton therefore has a higher environmental impact during its cultivation compared to the production phase of polyester. On the other hand, polyester is a by-product of the petroleum industry and it is not renewable which increases its long-term environmental burden.[1] Polyester production, because of its use of raw fossil materials, has a 63% higher energy consumption than the production of cotton, but the amount of water needed for polyester production is less than 0.1% of water necessary for cotton cultivation.[2]

The cultivation of organic cotton uses less chemicals (pesticides and synthetic fertilisers) than traditional cotton, yet it might consume more water than traditional cotton farming. Although entirely dependent on where the cotton is cultivated, as well as the method of irrigation, research suggests that the water usage in organic cotton cultivation can be up to three times more than in traditional cotton farming.[3] Flax, jute, hemp, and ramie are all plant-based natural fibres that use less water during cultivation than cotton. They are also easily grown crops and need less fertilisers. They grow in nearly all climate conditions and might even be pest-resistant (e.g. flax).[4] Examples of manufactured fibres made out of plant-based raw materials include viscose, cupro and acetate. Polyester, polyamide, acrylic, and spandex are petroleum-based raw materials. The reduction of oil supplies might lead to some problems in the production of petroleum-based fibres in the future, generating the need to develop new material sources. Regenerated sucrose-based polyesters can be made out of maize or sugar beet.[5] Plant-based fibres are renewable, and in some cases even biodegradable, although this is not recommended for textile products. Recently, more environmentally friendly fibres have been developed to substitute cotton. These include the lyocell fibre Tencel, which is a regenerated cellulose fibre manufactured from fast-growing eucalyptus wood using the lyocell process.[6] The lyocell production method is considerably simpler and uses much less energy than the viscose process. As opposed to the toxic chemicals used in the viscose process (p.155), non-toxic chemicals are used to manufacture lyocell. Furthermore, the process is a closed-loop procedure. This means that all chemicals are reused, which keeps them away from waste waters.[7]

Greenwashing

The use of misleading arguments to highlight environmental benefits that may be entirely untrue, also known as greenwashing, is quite common in the fashion and textile sector. These arguments are adopted to attract consumers who are interested in environmental issues within the textile industry. Bamboo is a good example of the controversial issues in evaluating environmental benefits of textiles. Bamboo is often marketed as an ecological choice but is actually a man-made fibre produced through viscose process, which has a high environmental impact due to its extensive use of water and toxic chemicals. As bamboo grows quickly, it is possible to harvest it several times during the growing period. Moreover, it is renewable and pest-resistant, and thus in this way better than many other fibres. However, it cannot be claimed to be an eco-fibre because of its harmful industrial process. Bamboo viscose is also a soft material that provides a good fabric hand, but this property might shorten the use time of the product.

Table 1. Environmental impact of different fibres

Fibre	High environmental impact	Low environmental impact
Cotton	Water and chemical use during cultivation Water consumption during production Use of chemicals in production Waste waters from production Possible use of harmful formaldehyde finish	Low greenhouse gas emissions Renewable, Biodegradable
Linen	Use of chemicals in production Waste waters from production	Low environmental impact of cultivation Renewable, Biodegradable
Wool	Use of pesticides High methane (greenhouse gas) emissions High ecological footprint (depending on the type of sheep-farming) Use of chemicals (depending on production method) Water consumption during production Waste waters from production	Life-cycle impact (i.e. self-cleaning properties during use phase) Renewable, Biodegradable Excellent fibre for fibre mechanical recycling
Viscose	Energy use during fibre production More water use than in polyester production Use of toxic chemicals Waste waters from production Greenhouse gas emissions	No pesticides used Biodegradable Raw materials from renewable sources Less water use than in cotton cultivation
Polyester	High energy use Greenhouse gas emissions Raw materials from non-renewable sources Microplastics emissions	Low water consumption during fibre production Pesticides are not used Reduced waste water from production Possible to use recycled raw material (PET)
Polyamide	High energy use High greenhouse gas emissions Raw materials from non-renewable sources Microplastics emissions	Pesticides are not used Low waste water from production
Acrylic	Use of chemicals High energy use High greenhouse gas emissions Raw materials from non-renewable sources Microplastics emissions	Pesticides are not used

↑ Ioncell is a technology that turns used textiles, pulp, and even old newspapers into new textile fibres sustainably and without using harmful chemicals.[13]

↑ This fabric is dyed with old European indigo plant woad (*Isatis tinctoria*), which it is possible to cultivate even in northern countries. It generates a natural indigo colour. This photo includes the woad seed, which can also be used in dyeing.

Textile manufacturing processes

Fibres are made into yarns through spinning, which may contribute to increased health risks for the workers, for example through dust pollution. Yarns are woven or knitted into textiles, but prior to this stage, yarns are bleached, mercerised, and dyed. These processes can also be done at the fibre stage. Starch is applied to the warp yarns during the weaving process, and needs to be washed off the fabric after weaving. The textiles are then treated with different finishing processes to improve their properties. All these procedures use chemicals and water, and increase the environmental impact of the textile industry. In general, it can be supposed that while aiming for high quality products, more treatments, water, and chemicals are expended.[8] It is estimated that as much as 200 tons of water is consumed to produce a ton of textile, making the textile industry a highly water intensive sector.[9] Furthermore, the textile industry's waste water is not always appropriately purified from harmful chemicals, especially in developing countries. These chemicals can end up in the water system, blending with the marine ecosystem and even ending up in the food chain. Chemicals from the textile industry can also pollute ground waters, destroying drinking water for large groups of inhabitants. For example, the use of metal complex dyes is forbidden in most Western countries, but they are quite commonly used in developing countries. A recent study identified 72 toxic elements from textile manufacturing. Of these toxic elements, 42 can be purified but only partly in commonly used waste water treatment plants, and 30 elements cannot be treated at all by current waste water treatment processes.[10] The newest waste water purification technologies are costly, and therefore not used when low cost is prioritised over environmental concerns. The considerable and irresponsible use of harmful chemicals is a risk not only for the environment but also for the textile industry workers and even for the end users with toxic chemicals remaining in the textiles. As noted, legislation restricts the use of toxic chemicals in textile products in Europe and most Western countries, and textile exporters are responsible for the products meeting these regulations.

Closing the loop

Closing the loop indicates that materials can be reused or recycled after their first use phase. The premise is that a product is initially designed to include several life cycles and enable the recycling of all materials at the end of a product's life. McDonough and Braungart presented the principles of the **cradle to cradle** approach, which separates the products' end of life path into a biological or technical cycle.[11] The biological cycle, or composting, is not possible for textiles that mix synthetic and natural fibres and include many chemicals. However, technical recycling is possible. This allows separating, or processing materials within the same system. Currently products made from mono-materials, with all layers and parts made of the same generic fibre type, appear easier to recycle than blends of polyester and cellulose fibres, or products with fibre mixtures (p.227).

Currently much of the research around sustainability is conducted around textile recycling, especially on **upcycling** textile waste into high quality new fibres rather than down-cycling textiles into lower value products such as filling materials (see the EU's New Cotton project)[12]. In **fibre mechanical recycling** fabrics and yarns are shredded and spun into new yarn, using methods that are traditional in wool and even in cotton recycling. This type of recycling process needs mainly mono-materials. The other option for recycling is **chemical dissolution** and **regeneration of fibres** from old post-consumer textiles. This method can be used on cotton and viscose type fibres.

Recycled polyester is already well known, but is currently mainly made out of thermomechanically recycled PET bottles rather than

← One fifth of water pollution caused by global industry is due to textile dyeing and the synthetic chemicals used in the process. Natural dyes can decrease the environmental impact of dyeing if the mordant chemicals used are non-toxic. Furthermore, plants fix CO_2 through their roots into the soil and can contribute to slowing down climate change. In the Biocolor 2019–2025 project, research is conducted into how natural colours can be used in industrial processes and how design can add eco-luxury values in the context of bio-economy.[15] The photo presents a garment design by Arttu Åfeldt, and textile design by Kirsi Niinimäki.

chemically recycled polyester textiles (p.31). Producing polyester from waste uses 70% less energy compared to virgin polyester production, but always needs some virgin polyester to maintain the high fibre quality.[14] In general, the challenges of recycling are to keep the fibre quality high, to expand the process to an industrial scale, and to sort and separate the different materials before the fibre recycling process. Blends, mostly using cotton, viscose, and synthetic fibres, are problematic from a recycling perspective. Only a few materials seem to be suitable for chemical recycling. Currently, nearly all textiles (especially in the garment sector) are made from blends, which are hard or impossible to recycle. Moving towards a closed loop perspective, we have to critically consider what materials are suitable to be used in the textile industry if all materials and products need to be recyclable.

Good design, quality according to lifetime

One of the biggest problems in the textile sector is the huge amount of **textile waste** especially in all Western countries. This reflects the very short use time of textiles – especially fast fashion – and also their low quality. To avoid this, designers play a key role in choosing materials for textiles which are best suited to their intended use and to the intended lifetime of the product. It is good to remember that the best way to influence the environmental impact of textiles is to extend the use time of a product, which can be done through informed design decisions on two levels: technical and aesthetic. Technical quality means attributes and functionalities that are most suitable for the product's predetermined use. High quality products are intended for long use time to avoid early disposal. Here it is advisable to select materials that age aesthetically; products and materials that look good even after long use. Yet, in some cases it is better to estimate the real use time of the product and optimise its quality accordingly. It is good to use recyclable materials if the intended use time is average or shorter. Aesthetic quality from the environmental viewpoint signifies not only long-lasting and classical design, but also design which makes the user fall in love with the product and establish an emotional bond with the item, which is cherished and maintained well to extend its use time.

See also pp.438–440.

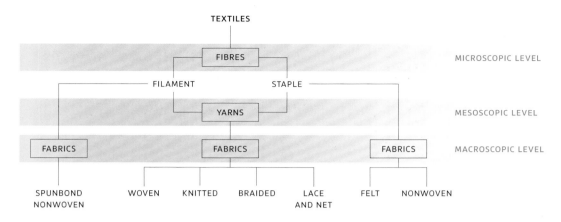

TEXTILES

FIBRES — MICROSCOPIC LEVEL

FILAMENT — STAPLE

YARNS — MESOSCOPIC LEVEL

FABRICS — FABRICS — FABRICS — MACROSCOPIC LEVEL

SPUNBOND NONWOVEN — WOVEN — KNITTED — BRAIDED — LACE AND NET — FELT — NONWOVEN

↑ The hierarchical levels (major production steps) and main types of textile structures.[21]

1.2 Structures – Interlaced, Intertwined, Intermeshed

All textile materials have an internal three-dimensional structure of fibres and, usually, yarns. This architecture of cloth – a flexible, interlaced, intertwined or intermeshed universe – can be constructed through the techniques of **weaving**, **braiding**, **knotting** or **knitting**, or the fibres can be **bonded** and **interlocked** together by other means to form nonwoven structures. Fabrics range from lightweight nets and sheers to heavy velvets, thick felts and rigid carpeting.

Though this book is dedicated to woven fabrics, it is important to note the broader context of textile constructions and comprehend the role of the constant rethinking of structures, as well as the related techniques, in the evolution of textiles. This section briefly introduces the different ways of constructing textiles and the fundamental characteristics of the resulting structures.

When working with soft and flexible fibres and yarns, the application of **tension** by hand, machine or through anchoring the yarns is necessary. As well as being an elementary

feature of the tools used in the manufacturing process of fabrics, applied and released tension – and control over this process – is an important element of textile structures contributing greatly to fabric texture. The invention of a tensioned warp, which enables the technique of weaving, is assumed to have developed from using a fixed and stretched "warp" as a base for twining.[20]

In **weaving**, two sets of threads, the **warp** and the **weft**, are interlaced to form a structure. The warp threads are held parallel to each other, stretched and **tensioned** on a **loom**. They run down the length of the fabric, while weft is worked across the fabric, row by row, over and under the warp threads. The process of weaving requires **shedding**, separating the warp yarns for weft insertion, and **beating-up**, pushing the inserted weft yarn into the new fabric. Woven constructions range from the simplest plain weave with alternating "over one, under one" interlacing (A) to complex multilayered structures, and can be woven in any width from narrow tapes and ribbons to

← A Woven structure released from loom tension

← B Caned chair seat with a triaxial weave structure

→ C Basketwork

↔ D Basket and shoes made from birch bark. These items are examples of 3D structures.

→ D Roof in Kerala, South India made of interwoven palm leaves attached to the wooden construction with palm fibre rope. Basketry and matting techniques of interweaving, twining and plaiting materials found in nature have been and still are commonly used to build shields, roofs and ground coverings.

wide technical fabrics of over ten metres in width. Today weaving is used in far more applications than any other textile manufacturing method.

Woven constructions can also consist of three or more sets of yarns. In a simple **triaxial** (B) weave the three sets of yarns, interlacing at 60 degrees with each other, are interlocked and all the yarns are compacted tightly at each intersection. Consequently, the structure has a high material stability which makes it suitable for applications requiring light weight, high structural integrity and good ventilation such as seat backings.[22] A traditional example of this type of construction are caned chair seats.

A primary example of ancient non-tensioned weaving is **basketwork** (C), incorporating at least one of the components firm enough to manipulate in a free state and therefore not requiring a loom. The interlocking of a basket's elements can thus be done by hand. The ancient arts of basketry and matting also incorporate various twisting, plaiting and finger-weaving techniques and enable construction of free forms for dwellings and three-dimensional objects (D). No machine has replaced the practice of making baskets by hand.[23]

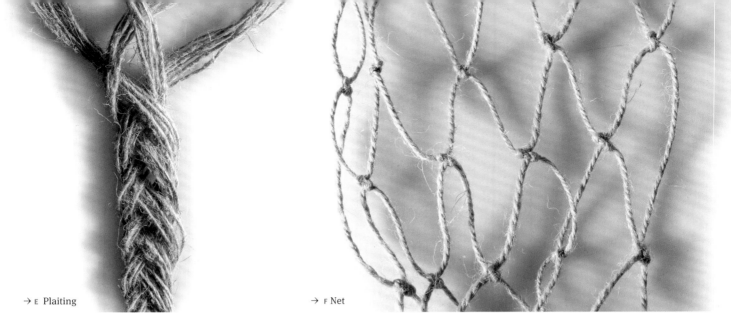

→ E Plaiting

→ F Net

In contrast to weaving, which uses two sets of multiple threads, **plaiting** (E), or braiding, is a simpler means of fabric formation. Plaited structures are made by interlacing three or more strands so that they cross each other in diagonal formation. All of the strands are interchanged in every cycle during the process. The simplest braided structure is that of a hair plait made of three strands. Braided items include solid and flat one-dimensional products, such as shoe laces or tubular braids, which can be used as cover for electric wires and hoses. Due to manufacturing issues, braided structures have a limited width.[24]

Different types of **nets** (F), **lace** (G) and **macrame** (H) are examples of the many variations of fabrics made by **looping**, **twisting** and **knotting**. Macrame is a heavily knotted fabric, while nets and laces are low density openwork fabrics. Provided the material is strong, the ancient technique of netting is firm yet flexible whether linked, as in a chain-linked fence, or looped. It can be very closely worked or widely spaced, always retaining its inherent elasticity. **Crochet** (I) is a type of knotted fabric with a structure more stable than knitted fabrics due to interlooping that connects loops to both the previous row, as in knitting, and to loops in the same row. The "knotless netting" or **nålebinding** technique uses one needle, relatively short lengths of thread and the fingers of a hand to form a strong and durable construction. Nålebinding predates knitting as a means to make close-fitting small items such as socks, mittens and hats. Textiles made with this ancient technique have a strong resemblance to knitted items.[25]

↓ G Lace

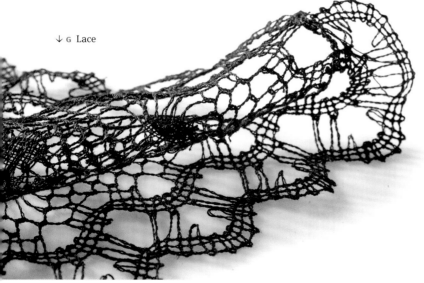

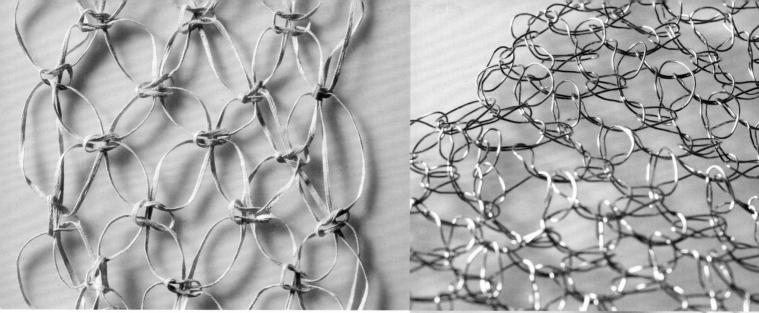

Knits (J) are constructed from a series of intermeshing loops from a continuous length of yarn, by hand using needles or by machine. In hand knitting, the movement of the wrists and fingers performs a series of complex actions nearly impossible to simulate mechanically. Therefore, the mechanical process of forming loops on a knitting machine with its own needle for each individual loop, differs significantly from that of hand knitting. There are two distinct types of industrial knitting technologies, weft knitting and warp knitting, which produce vastly different fabrics for specific applications. The properties of knitted fabrics differ substantially from those of woven fabrics. Knits are less stable, but more flexible and generally have a better drape than woven structures. Knitting is traditionally a technique used for producing ready-made clothing. The technique enables seamless construction of garments, minimizing waste, as described on p. 442. Its ability to stretch and insulate enabling warm, close-fitting garments has been an important feature through its evolution. These qualities combined with minimal creasing have made it popular for modern casual and sportswear.[26]

↑ H Macrame

↑ I Crochet
↓ J Knit

Nonwovens are structures of staple fibres, continuous filaments (spunbond), or chopped yarns which have been bonded together e.g. by spray bonding, needlepunching or calender bonding, or by using technology originating from the paper making process. They are highly porous and permeable and widely used in diverse consumer, medical and industrial products such as absorbent hygiene products, crop covers or as interlinings in clothing.[27] **Wool felt** is the earliest form of nonwoven fabric. It is manufactured directly through the compression of fibres by applying pressure to hot, wet fibres, resulting in the fibre scales becoming interlocked.

There are endless variations and combinations of the different techniques discussed above. **Leno weave** (p. 225), first found in ancient Chinese textiles, is a combination of tensioned-warp loom-weaving and twisting. In this technique, weft yarns are locked in place by warp twists to form a lace-like gauze (see p. 225). This is related to old finger-weaving and basket-making techniques where pairs of warps (or wefts, in weft twining) are twisted around each other as the opposing element is inserted.[28] **Tablet-weaving**, discussed on p. 60, is another variation of tensioned-warp weaving. In the making of **hand knotted** carpets, the yarn pile is tied and knotted to the warp threads while the base is woven.

As described, all textile materials have a third dimension: depth. Depth is created through the internal architecture consisting of fibres or yarns. Woven fabrics are generally produced as flat or sometimes cylindrical two-dimensional sheets. However, in some cases the ultimate shape of the product is three-dimensional. It can either have an overall three-dimensional form similarly to items made with basketwork techniques (p. 42 D), a layered internal three-dimensional structure (K) or both (L).

Three-dimensional woven, braided, knotted or nonwoven structures are often referred to as **3D fabrics**. Historically the origins of such products lie in the need for close-fitting and elasticated coverings for the body,[29] such as hand-knitted socks, knitted in-the-round on multiple needles and turning at the heel. Today, one large consumer market for such products is garments and apparel knitted in one piece (see seamless-knitting technology, p. 442). In addition to knitwear, macrame and crochet can be used to make ready-shaped garments and accessories, including hats and bags.[30] **Interwoven fabrics** (p. 206), layered woven structures, offer the potential to form **woven 3D textiles**, used in the development of advanced fibre-reinforced composites,[31] and in the integration of interactive functionalities into woven textiles, as described on pp. 470–473. Interchanging double-weave layers offer the potential of expanding to form **woven textile forms** (K, L) and **3D-woven garments**, as illustrated in the intriguing project *I Weave Dogs and Clothes* on p. 442.

↑ L 3D-woven Dog, 2024. See pp. 442–443 for more information on the experimental woven textile-form project by Venla Elonsalo

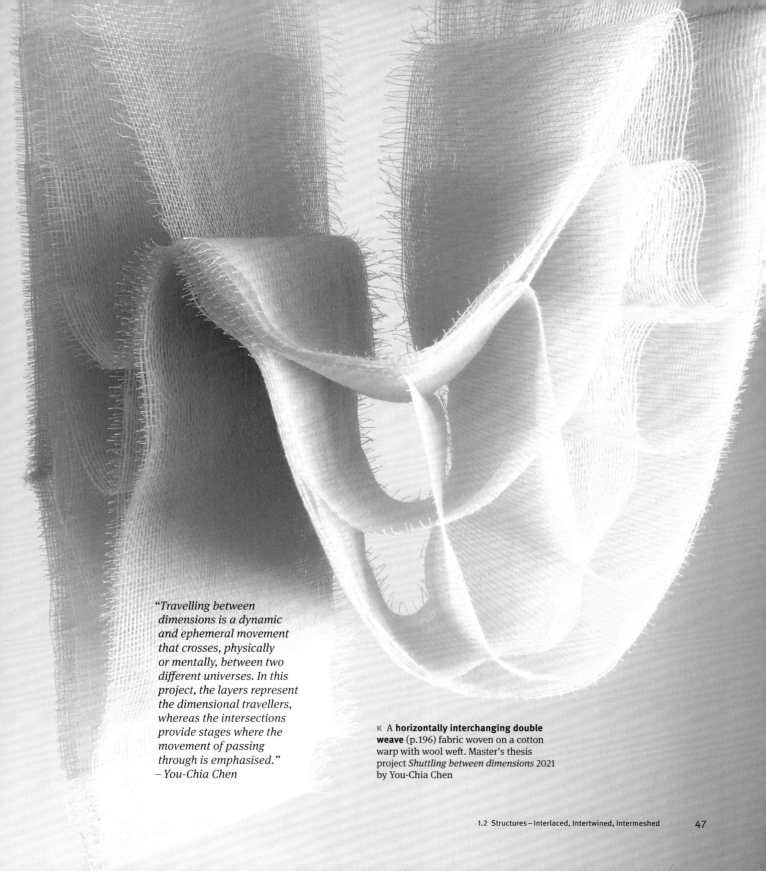

"Travelling between dimensions is a dynamic and ephemeral movement that crosses, physically or mentally, between two different universes. In this project, the layers represent the dimensional travellers, whereas the intersections provide stages where the movement of passing through is emphasised."
– You-Chia Chen

ᴋ A **horizontally interchanging double weave** (p.196) fabric woven on a cotton warp with wool weft. Master's thesis project *Shuttling between dimensions* 2021 by You-Chia Chen

The field of textiles is diverse, with countless materials, techniques and applications.[32] Textile design practice is about both **creating** and **using** materials, the scale varying from microscopic to architectural. In this chart, the various types, or decision levels, of textile product design are divided into four groups according to the stage in which design or selection of the textile material enters the design process, and based on what type of textile decisions and activities the designer deals with. Textile decisions might consist of merely creating a specification for a material and handing it over to someone else to finalise, or selecting an existing fabric for a product. On the other hand, a textile material can be designed in extreme detail, requiring great textile specific expertise—as in engineering a man-made fibre. The first group of textile product designs featured in the chart relates to these fibre material decisions as well as textile construction, and forms the core of a textile designer's expertise.[33]

TEXTILE DESIGN DECISIONS DURING THE TEXTILE PRODUCT DESIGN PROCESS

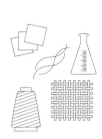  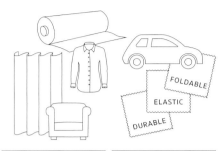

	MATERIAL CONSTRUCTION	MATERIAL ALTERATION	MATERIAL SELECTION	MATERIAL SPECIFICATION
ACTIVITY	**Core textile design and engineering expertise:** textile designers, textile engineers, chemical engineers, material scientists, electrical engineers, computer scientists...	**Core textile design and engineering expertise:** textile and fashion designers, textile engineers, chemical engineers, material scientists, electrical engineers...	textile and fashion designers, architects, industrial designers, engineers, medical doctors, scientists...	concept designers, architects, industrial designers, engineers... **specifying a type of material or set of properties for products or other functional purposes.**
EXAMPLES OF PROFESSIONS	**Examples of textile techniques:** fibre spinning, yarn twisting, weaving, knitting, felting, warp knitting, rapid prototyping, bioengineering...	**Examples of textile techniques:** dyeing, printing, basic finishes, functional finishes, embroidery, laser cutting, pleating, virtual technologies, smart technologies...	**For:** interiors, clothing and fashion, architecture, automotive, aerospace, technical, industrial, military, medical and biomedical applications...	**Examples of specifications:** foldable, elastic, durable, conductive, biodegradable, circular, recyclable...

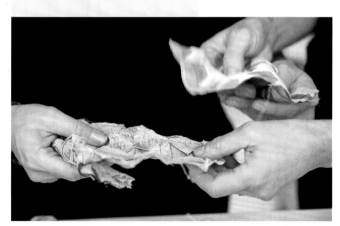

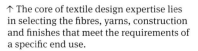

↑ The core of textile design expertise lies in selecting the fibres, yarns, construction and finishes that meet the requirements of a specific end use.

↑ Designing woven textiles incorporates sampling on looms. In this type of textile product design process, the fibre content, yarn type and weave structure are designed in detail for the fabrics to match the requirements of a specific product.

Interlacing Molecular Threads [34]

When textile structures are adapted to architectural or microscopic scale, the point of view changes from interlacing fibres and yarns to two- and three-dimensional structures comprised of materials outside of the textile realm. An intriguing example of how knowledge of textile structures can inspire science is demonstrated in the work of Yuzhong Liu and her research team in their **molecular fabric** analogue, developed in a quest for new, more elastic materials. The research group was able to emulate the design concept of "inherently flexible woven fabrics" in extended chemical structures by weaving chains of two- and three-dimensional molecular structures using metal-organic frameworks. Utilizing the woven structure increased the elasticity of the material 10-fold. [35]

→ Exploring three-dimensionality in a woven surface through the interplay of materials and structures. Fabric from Master's thesis project *Unfold* 2020 by Mithila Mohan

"Without delay they set up the twin looms in different places and stretch them with the fine warp. The web is bound to the beam, reed separates the thread, the woof is threaded through the middle with sharp shuttles, which their fingers help through, and once led between the threads, the notched teeth pound with the hammering sley. Both hasten along, with their mantle girded about their breasts they ply their skilled hands, their eagerness making the labour light."
– Ovid, Metamorphoses 6[36]

1.3 Looms and Other Tools

As a form of interlacement, woven structures pre-date the invention of spun yarns and looms. Basketry and matting techniques of twining and plaiting materials found in nature, such as fibrous roots, grasses, branches and strips from the inner bark of trees were used by hunter-gatherers to build everyday articles such as mats, bags and components of early forms of dwellings, shields, roofs and ground coverings (p.42). These constructions, though employing weave structures, are made of rigid elements interlaced by hand without a frame to apply tension on the components.[37]

When working with soft and flexible fibres and yarns, application of tension, by body weight, machine, or through anchoring the yarns, is necessary. While there are many variations among looms throughout history and different cultures, all of them serve the same basic function: to hold the warp threads in parallel and under tension while the weft threads are inserted. While the basic concept has remained the same throughout ages, developments in loom design have made the weaving process easier and increased its speed. Technological advancements propelled production and textiles took a leading role in the Industrial Revolution, with manual processes being gradually taken over by mechanised spinning and weaving machines.

The development of weaving technology is one of human innovation and engagement. It not only charts developing technical innovation, but equally mankind's economic, political, and cultural currents. At its best the development of looms reflects the evolution of human thinking and use of tools. Furthermore, the **binary code** – derived from the notation of woven structures with two variables, the warp and the weft – has become the means for humans to interact with machines.

The art of weaving evolved independently around the world as developments in fibres and advances in making more refined yarns drove technical innovations such as ways to adjust the warp tension, adding shafts to enable a growing variety of different weaves, and mechanisms for shedding. The expanding international textile market and its need for quantity influenced and pushed new manufacturing methods further and revolutionised the way goods are produced.

← Automatised weaving in today's industry. Shaft looms at Lodetex s.p.a., Italy

String revolution

↑ Greek painting on a terracotta oil flask from ca. 550–530 BCE showing various stages of wool fabric production – weighing wool, preparing loom, spinning yarn with a drop spindle, weaving at a vertical warp-weighted wool, and folding the finished cloth. The fragmentary and discoloured state of most excavated textiles makes literary references and visual evidence – such as this depiction of textile making – particularly valuable.[38]

Greater awareness for subtle findings of perishable artefacts – such as an indentation of a fishing net preserved on clay – has altered the field of archaeology dramatically during the past decades. This and recent novel scientific methods for determining age and raw material composition have contributed to research and revealed the central role of textile inventions in the success of mankind. The point of view has broadened from Stone Age men in furs hunting mammoths with spears to women, children and elderly people working with textiles.[39]

Archaeologist and linguist Elizabeth Barber uses the term **string revolution** to describe what happened during the **Palaeolithic** period when our ancestors learned how to make cordage, twist and plait short fibres into continuous yarn. According to Barber, this invention "opened the door to an enormous array of new ways to save labour and improve the odds of survival" and suggested that it may well have been the "unseen weapon" that enabled humans to populate virtually every niche they could reach. In addition to being integral for netting and weaving, "string can be used simply to tie things up – to catch, to hold, to carry".[40]

Barber's theory has been supported by findings from various archaeological sites. 30,000-year-old twisted and pigmented bast fibres, as well as worked bone artefacts including a perforated needle, were found in the Dzudzuana cave located in Caucasus, Georgia.[41] The prevailing belief that Palaeolithic people survived mainly through men hunting mammoths and other large wild animals was pushed aside when archaeologists Olga Soffer and James. M. Adovasio found imprints of fibre artefacts, nets and interlacing structures made from wild plants on clay at the 26,000-year-old archaeological site of Dolni Vestonice I in Moldovia, present day Czech Republic. Based on other finds at the site, the nets and baskets were likely to have been used as traps for smaller animals such as rabbits and birds that must have provided the majority of people's daily calorie intake. The bone and antler objects which were long thought to have been used in hunting were discovered to be in fact parts of fibre-related tools such as awls, net gauges and weaving battens. These findings suggested that at these early times, late Ice Age people of Eurasia were well along in the string revolution. The hunter-gatherers must have been twining, making cordage, netting, finger weaving, sewing and making free-standing basketry for a very long time to have developed such ability, diversity and sophistication of technique. Women, children and the elderly of the prehistoric world, named the "silent majority" by Soffer, were all actively involved in sourcing food with the help of textile structures.[42]

All of this historical evidence indicates that string was a principal springboard for significant human achievement. From sewing to seafaring, thread, yarn, cord, and rope were fundamental to the very formation of societies, making possible efficient hunting and herding, shelter and storage, exploration and migration, and the aesthetic expressions vital to cultural cohesion, namely individual adornment and outward affirmations of group beliefs and identity.[43]

INVENTING—FARMING, SPINNING, SHEDDING

Fibre cultivation

The textile fibres in use today have been cultivated and used by humans for millennia. Advancements in textile technology and the growing need for textile fibres resulted in organised cultivation of wild fibre plants such as **flax** and **hemp** as the early **Neolithic** peoples began to settle in permanent dwellings and to farm and domesticate animals. Flax, referred to as **linen** when made into textiles, grown widely for fibre in the Near East since ca. 7000 BCE,[44] was one of the first domestic crops and the earliest known domesticated fibre, with cultivation coinciding with the invention of pottery[45]. Flax fibre processing was based on thousands of years of experience of using tree bast fibres.[46] Some of the oldest surviving woven fabrics are plain-weave linen cloth fragments woven with finely spun plied thread found at excavations in the Pre-Pottery Neolithic village of Çatalhöyük, located in present-day Turkey, dating from 6300 BCE and plain-weave linen fabrics from the Nile Valley dating from 5000 BCE, with yarn density of 12 by 9 threads per cm.

Sheep and **goat** were kept often simultaneously with flax cultivation in mixed farming economies and by pastoral nomads, and their hair was used for weaving and felting.[47] However, the use of sheep and goat hair as fibre does not seem to have been important until the end of the Neolithic era, which is several thousand years after the domestication of flax.[48] Representations of woolly sheep became more numerous around 3000 BCE and wool fabrics grew popular in a wider area

↖ Field of blooming flax. The invention of processing plant fibres started with tree bast and later flax. Bast fibre is regarded as one of the major natural vegetable fibre resources in the world. It has played an important role from prehistoric times up to the textile industry of today.

↗ Sheep were kept in early
farming cultures and by
pastoral nomads as sources
for both food and wool. The
progress in breeding sheep
types with wool better suited
for spinning yarn grew hand
in hand with technological
advancements.

of the Near East and Europe.[50] **Sheep wool**
became the most important fibre for Central
European prehistory, when Neolithic bast-
culture was replaced by Bronze Age "wool-
culture".[51] Meanwhile in South America **llamas**
and **alpacas** were domesticated for **camelid
wool**. An example of European Bronze Age
wool fabrics from 2000–1600 BCE is discussed
later in this section.

Cotton cultivation, spinning and weaving
first developed in the Indus Valley in the period
of 5000 BCE to 3000 BCE. Early finds of cotton
seeds date to around 5000 BCE and the earliest
fragments of cotton textiles to around 3000 BCE
in what is today Pakistan. Independently,
during the same prehistoric time span, cotton
was cultivated in the Western Hemisphere in
present-day Peru, Mexico, and other parts of
the Americas as well as in Eastern Africa. In
Peru – the earliest center of cotton cultivation in
South America – archaeologists have excavated
cotton fishing nets dated to 2400 BCE and
cloth fragments from around 1600 BCE. The
Mesoamerican cotton industry was similarly
early, with evidence of cotton being planted
as early as 3400 BCE. Techniques in weaving

and dyeing in the Americas were more and
more refined as evidenced by finds of Chavin
cotton textiles created during the period of
1000–600 BCE.[52]

Sericulture, the rearing of silkworms and
the production of cocoons for **silk**, developed
in China before 3000 BCE[53] and has been
regarded since as a highly valued textile
fibre. Fine and sophisticated silk fabric was
produced from early times. The earliest woven
silk fragments found to date come from the
period between 2860 and 2650 BCE. Although
these examples were in plain weave, it is
supposed that patterned fabrics followed
soon after. A tomb find from Machan in what
is today Hubei province from a later period,
dating to about 300 BCE, reveals astonishing proof of the range of textile patterning
techniques of silk fabrics. The loom-patterned
textiles include both warp-patterning and weft-
patterning techniques with designs ranging
from geometric diamond shapes to hunting
scenes with chariots and wild animals. The
fine, continuous-filament silk threads also
enabled weaving delicate patterned gauzes[54].

Spinning

Compared to matting and basketry, weaving on a tensioned warp requires long and flexible materials. No filament produced by nature, however, is long, strong, and flexible enough to be easily used for weaving. Soft and flexible wool fibres, hairs, and most individual vegetable fibres are too short and breakable to be used without somehow being combined and twisted into one long continuous thread (see yarns p.126, spun yarns p.132). Even silk, the longest natural filament is too fragile to be used as a single filament. The early Neolithic invention of the **spindle** (A) and with it **spinning** (B), the twisting of several single and usually short fibres to form strong continuous yarns resistant enough to be set under tension and undergo the mechanical process of weaving, was a pivotal moment in the chain of human innovation. It guided technological–and in this case also agricultural–change, setting the scene for further developments.[55]

The **spinning wheel**, a much later technological spinning invention dating back 1000 years, and still used in rural communities[56], formed the basic idea for the breakthrough industrial yarn production advancements of the Industrial Revolution (p.71).

← A **Hand spindle** with still intact spun lime tree bast from the wetland settlement Arbon Bleiche 3 ca. 3370 BCE in what is today Switzerland. The spindle consists of a wooden **spindle shaft** and a symmetrical weight, called the **whorl**, made of fired clay. A spindle can be used to both **twist yarns** from loose fibres and to **ply** the twisted yarns. Prehistoric spindle whorls vary in shape, size, and weight according to different functions (e.g. spinning and plying), the use of different fibres (e.g. plant bast and wool) and cultural traditions. Comparisons of spindle whorls from excavation sites can be used to identify immigration of both people and technology thereby illuminating mobility and innovation in prehistoric Europe.[57]

↓ B The image features the basic spinning technique for a single wool yarn. During spinning the spindle is set in rotation while holding the wool fleece and end of the thread in the other hand. The weight of the spindle facilitates thread formation by drawing the thread downwards in a rapid rotation. The fibre material is drawn from the mass, and by pulling and twisting gently, the rotation shapes loose fibre material to thread. After reaching the desired length of twisted yarn, the thread is wound on the spindle, the end of the thread secured to the spindle, and the spinning process is repeated.[58]

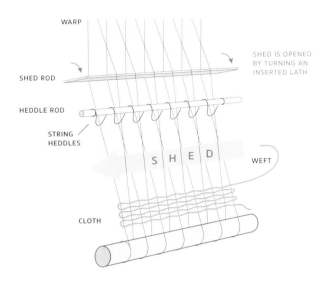

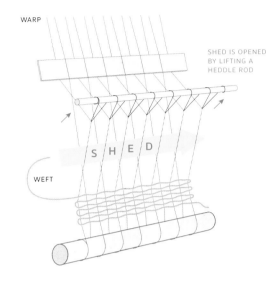

↑ The images feature the basic principle of simple hand-operated shed and countershed formation using a heddle rod with string heddles and a shed rod.

Shedding

The Neolithic invention of **shedding** in the loom was a ground-breaking advancement in weaving technology. Instead of using the basketry technique of finger-weaving, individually picking suspended warp threads with fingers to insert weft materials, the new invention enabled passing of the weft straight through a "tunnel" or **shed** of the tensioned warp threads in which some are raised and others lowered.

At least two sheds are required in weaving. The simplest form of shedding is the **natural shed**, with warp yarns laying alternately above and below a **shed rod**, an inserted thin lath. The shed is opened by turning the lath up on one edge to form a space for the weft to be passed through. The **countershed**, called the **artificial shed**, is obtained by lifting a **heddle rod** with simple string **heddles** attached to the set of warp yarns under the shed rod.

All **looms** – from the simplest handlooms to industrial weaving machines – are designed to tension, organise and control warp yarns in order to create a shed. A **shuttle** inserts the weft yarn through the shed.

The type of shedding mechanism on the loom determines the size and scope of fabrics, weave structures and designs that can be woven on it. **Mechanised shedding** enabled thousands of warp threads to be raised or lowered with a single movement by means of the shed rod and heddle rod. With the introduction of more advanced shedding devices, shuttles and weft-insertion techniques, weaving took a mega-leap in speed and quality of production, making it the most widely used method of making fabric.

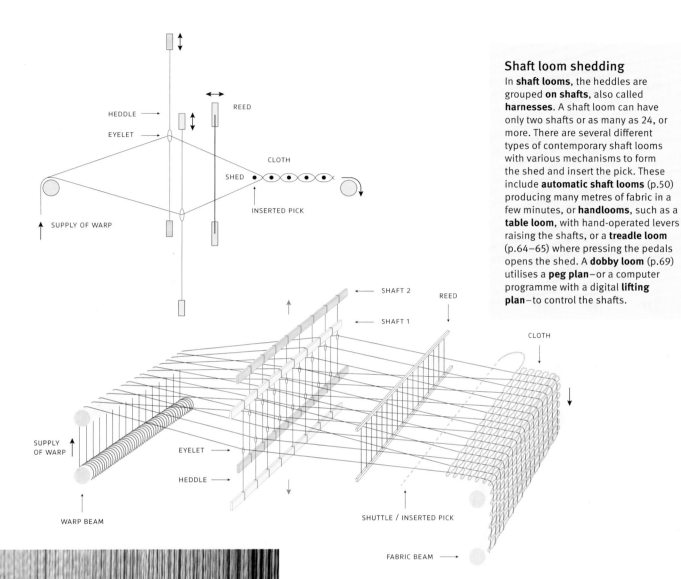

HEDDLE
EYELET
REED
CLOTH
SHED
INSERTED PICK
SUPPLY OF WARP

SHAFT 2
SHAFT 1
REED
CLOTH
SUPPLY OF WARP
EYELET
HEDDLE
WARP BEAM
SHUTTLE / INSERTED PICK
FABRIC BEAM

Shaft loom shedding

In **shaft looms**, the heddles are grouped **on shafts**, also called **harnesses**. A shaft loom can have only two shafts or as many as 24, or more. There are several different types of contemporary shaft looms with various mechanisms to form the shed and insert the pick. These include **automatic shaft looms** (p.50) producing many metres of fabric in a few minutes, or **handlooms**, such as a **table loom**, with hand-operated levers raising the shafts, or a **treadle loom** (p.64–65) where pressing the pedals opens the shed. A **dobby loom** (p.69) utilises a **peg plan**–or a computer programme with a digital **lifting plan**–to control the shafts.

← Warp ends drawn-in through the heddle (heald) eyelets on a shaft loom. The heddles are mounted on the shafts, which rise and fall to form the shed for pick insertion.

↑ The images feature the basic principle of conventional **shaft loom weaving** with warp yarns wound on a beam and each end threaded through the eyelets of the heddles mounted on shafts. The weaving process includes releasing the tension of the warp beam, shedding, feeding the pick through the shed, beating the fabric up with the reed or comb, and winding the cloth onto the fabric beam. In shuttle looms, the weft is inserted with a **shuttle** (pp.63–67, 70) and in contemporary shuttleless looms (p.73) by other means. The shafts are moved up and down according to the weave structure, thus forming the shed.

The story of early European wool fabrics

The study of textile history depends greatly on the chance survival of materials inherently prone to decay.[59] All early finds of actual cloth are extremely rare and depend on favourable archaeological conditions. Hundreds of surviving fragments of exceptionally well-preserved early fabrics have been unearthed from the prehistoric salt mines of Hallstatt and Dürrnberg in Austria.[60] Karina Grömer from the Natural History Museum Vienna has examined these fine and intricate fabrics for evidence of a long prior process of experimentation and practice highlighting the interrelation of material and technical innovation. These early textiles demonstrate extensive, refined traditions of spinning and weaving done by experienced practitioners.

The development of textile technology in Central Europe from the **Bronze Age** in the 2nd millennium BCE to **Early Iron Age** 800–600 BCE, also called **Hallstatt period**, demonstrates how available materials guide textile innovation. The finds of finer and more diverse wool fabrics from the Hallstatt period in comparison to earlier Bronze Age textiles illustrate a remarkable range of structures, patterning and colour. The progress in breeding sheep types with wool more ideal for spinning yarn grew hand in hand with technological advancements in wool spinning, yarns and weave structures. An example of how sheep breeding during the Iron Age was led by aesthetic decisions of the people, is the growing preference of light-coloured wool. Early sheep had brown wool but the breeding of sheep for light wool allowed dyeing the wool yarns in bright colours, such as blue, red and yellow.[61]

Textiles which reflected an innovative weave type or patterning had a different and softer wool type, evidencing creative choices in the selection of raw materials. Hand in hand with wool development, new weaving and patterning techniques were used. Among the main Bronze Age textile culture of simple **plain weaves** and **plain-weave derivatives**, finds of **twill-weave** fabrics woven of fine wool yarns demonstrate early innovation in loom development–a warp-weighted loom equipped with multiple shafts developed for weaving of twills–constituting one of the largest changes in weaving technology before the invention of the treadle loom.[62] In addition to enabling decorative possibilities, the supple twill weave (p. 249) structure completely changes the character of a wool fabric from stiff plain weave to a more elastic and dense fabric, hence twill can be assumed to have been invented at the time wool became popular.[63]

In textile art throughout ages, design of patterns is closely linked to the type of tools used to produce the textile. The fabric designs are based on the technique of shaft weaving with patterning resulting from the interplay of weave structures with bands of coloured yarns in warp and weft direction.[64]

The textiles from the Hallstatt salt mine demonstrate the value and importance of skill and creativity in textile production within the social context of Central European prehistory. Although tradition and functionality play a great role in producing textiles, visual and haptic creative decisions are evident, and the resulting material and technical transformations guide and drive an aesthetic and conceptual shift.[65] To the textile designer of today, this story of early European wool fabrics offers a fine example of the interdependence of tools, materials and structures driven by technological innovations. It highlights the importance of raw material in design innovation–striving to advance textile quality, appearance and performance–and process thinking in textile production. Delightfully, it also shows the truly evergreen nature of textile design: the steadfast faithfulness of plain weave and the versatility of its derivatives, the classic nature of twill patterns, checks and stripes and the play with yarn twist direction. This invigorating palette of features is still being varied by today's designers linking the ancient past to present-day design practice and industrialised textile production. The excellence needed now and then in handling the complex textile production process from fibre cultivation to yarn production, weaving, finishes to craft fine textiles have remained much the same.

Sections 2.1. and 2.7. guide in experimenting with these versatile weaves with a long history.

Textiles from the Hallstatt salt mine (pp. 59–60), dating 800–600 BCE, demonstrate the boom of Innovation and Creativity in Early Iron Age. The collage of fragments features a variety of textile qualities, colours, stripe and check patterns, different weaves and twill variations. The fabrics are woven on vertical multiple-shaft warp-weighted looms of fine wool threads with yarn density up to 40 threads per cm. Multicoloured rib-weave bands are woven with rigid-heddle type looms, and elaborately designed trimmings are made with tablets. By the Hallstatt period, wool fibres were of a higher quality, prepared better and the wool combed prior to spinning. Better raw materials enabled exploration of differences in spinning direction in woven fabrics for subtle textural effects and spin patterning.[66]

A Fragment of a fine 2:2 **basket-weave** (p. 136) wool fabric in density of 40 by 18 yarns per cm, with a subtle textural **spin pattern** created by alternating pairs of **Z- and S-twisted** single yarns. In addition to adding texture, spin patterning stabilises the fabric and counteracts rolling up and deformation (pp. 126 and 415).[67]

B Fragment of a chequered 2/2 **chevron twill** (p. 254) wool fabric woven with z-twisted single yarns in a pointed sequence with yarn density of 14 by 10 yarns per cm. The reversing point of the draft is set in the middle of the band of darker warp yarns.[68] As the featured fabric fragments do not include the selvedge, the weave structure can only be assumed to be a **vertical pointed twill** and thus woven on a warp with a pointed threading instead of a **horizontal pointed twill** (p. 251) achieved by the lifting sequence.

A

75814

B

75473

C

D

78552

1   5 cm

E

c Two fragments of a chequered 2/2 **diamond twill** (p.256), or lozenge twill, wool fabric woven with z-twisted single yarns and density of 13 by 13 yarns per cm. The striped colour repeat does not correspond with the wale direction sequence of the lozenge twill. The smaller sample shows the back of the fabric with its narrow strip of plain weave. Finds of fine diamond twill patterns prove that both twill wale reversing techniques, **pointed threading** and **reversing the lifting sequence** (p.251), were known to the weavers of the Hallstatt period.

D Fragment of a chequered 2/2 **chevron twill** wool fabric woven with z-twisted single yarns on an irregular pointed draft with yarn density of 14–12 yarns per cm. The colour repeat of the check pattern made of bands of light and dark threads does not coincide with the pointed twill sequence[69] thus resulting in irregular textural patterning of the stripes (p.182).

E Fragment of a chequered 2/2 chevron twill wool fabric woven with z-twisted yarns and density of 11–12 yarns per cm in both warp and weft directions.[70] The pointed draft sequence and the colour repeat are not coinciding thus resulting in an irregular appearance of the **colour-and-weave** patterning (p.258).

F A narrow **warp-faced rib-weave** wool band woven on a dense warp of 30 ends per cm of alternating plied yarns in contrasting colours arranged in a sequence resulting in a multicoloured chessboard pattern. The blue colour is identified to be dyed with **woad** (p.38) while the source of the yellow and red dye is unidentified.[71] Rib-weave bands were used as starting borders for weaving or on hems and borders of garments. In this function these strong, dense bands of plied yarns were not only decorative but strengthened the areas of the garment exposed to most wear. Such bands requiring only two shafts were possibly woven with rigid heddle looms.[72]

G A complicated multicoloured **tablet-weave** meander-pattern border woven with 21 four-holed tablets displays extensive skills in the art of tablet weaving. The multicoloured warp made of z-and s-twisted plied wool threads and woven with a horsehair weft[73]. Complicated and colourful patterns can be produced on tablets (H) with simple

means–without a loom or weaving frame– only the tablets and two fixed attachment points suffice. Moreover, tablet-woven textiles are particularly durable as the warp strands usually consist of four threads twisted together. Consequently, tablet weaves have been used as trimmings for garments and as belts since prehistoric times.[74]

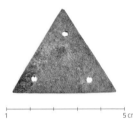

H Archaeological finds of weaving tablets from Carnuntum, ca. 100 CE

In **tablet weaving** the weaving process, technique of combining warp and weft threads, is based on rotating tablets with warp threads led through holes in the tablets' corners. Rather than intersecting the warp and weft by raising and lowering a heddle rod, the weft is passed through a gap between the upper and lower threads.[75] (I)

→ I Tablets for tablet weaving and belt of wool yarns in progress

↑ A Bhutanese weaver
at a backstrap loom

LOOMS

Very complex work can be produced on the
simplest of **looms**. A good example of this is
the ancient **backstrap** or **body tension loom**
(A), also called the belt loom, still in use in
many parts of the world. At one end the warps
are attached to a fixed beam or post and at the
other to a breast beam held to the weaver's
body by a belt or strap. On the backstrap loom,
the tension of the warp threads is controlled
through the movements of the weaver's body
and the shafts are raised by a shed lath and
simple string heddles attached to a shaft.
Although simple, this loom is used to produce
a large variety of weave structures and support
elaborate decoration techniques. Backstrap
looms are effective only for weaving fabrics
the width of the weaver's reach. Vertical looms
and horizontal looms are necessary for wider
textiles.

Also ancient in origin, the **vertical
warp-weighted loom** (B) was the most
commonly used type of loom in prehistoric
Northern and Central Europe. The warp tension
in this loom is achieved through weights made
of stone or baked clay attached to hanging
warp threads on two sides of a fixed shed rod.
This loom type is also closely associated with
Greek wool weaving, appearing in Greek vases

VERTICAL WARP-WEIGHTED LOOM

CLOTH BEAM

1 METRE

POSITION OF WARP THREADS:

HEDDLE RODS ON BRACKETS

NATURAL SHED

← HEDDLE RODS →

from the sixth to fourth centuries BCE. The
warp-weighted loom generally requires two
standing weavers to manipulate the heddle
rod and pass the weft. Beating the weft up
against gravity makes the task more difficult.
During the early centuries of the Christian
era the warp-weighted loom was gradually
replaced by the vertical and horizontal
two-beam loom in most of Europe.[76]

↑ B The mechanism of
a vertical warp-weighted loom.
Although gradually replaced
by other loom-types in most
of Europe, the warp-weighted
loom has remained in use in
Scandinavia and Iceland until
recently[77].

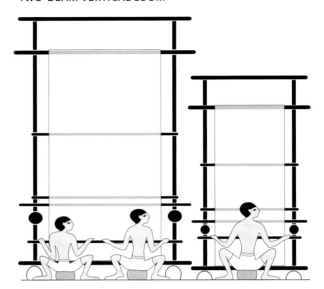

→ C Egyptian tapestry loom as depicted on a wall-painting from the tomb of Thotnefer at Thebes, Egypt ca. 1500 BCE

For weaving densely-beaten tapestry and rugs, a **stable frame** is needed and the warp must be tightly stretched. Hence, a **tapestry loom** usually has a rotating beam at the bottom and another beam for the warp. The two-beam **vertical loom**, appearing in Egyptian wall paintings c. 1500 BCE (C) is markedly similar to the European tapestry loom in use since the Middle Ages and to the tapestry and **rug looms** still used today in Africa, Near East, Mediterranean and by the Native people of the American Southwest.[78]

The loom type which has seen most development in the course of history up to the modern industrial looms is the **horizontal loom**, depicted on Egyptian drawings as early as 4000 BCE (D) and used for weaving **linen**. Complete pieces of fine linen woven on **horizontal ground looms** in width of up to 1.5 m and length of 20 m have been found in mummy bindings of ca. 2000 BCE. This type of ground loom has a warp stretched between two **beams** held in place by four pegs hammered into the ground. Weaving of larger widths is

→ D Egyptian type horizontal ground loom featured on a pottery bowl of the Badarian Civilisation ca. 4000 BCE in present-day central Egypt[79]

done by two people sitting on either side of the warp and beating the weft in while lifting and lowering a heddle rod to change the shed. Narrow widths can also be woven by a single weaver. As the weaving proceeds, the weavers change their positions and the positions of the rods. The beams and sticks of a horizontal loom can easily be packed for transport, thus similar horizontal ground looms are still used by nomadic weavers of today (E).[80]

To enable weaving longer pieces of fabric on the loom, systems of **tubular** or **circular warp** (F) have been used in various cultures and created with different types of looms.

HORIZONTAL GROUND LOOM

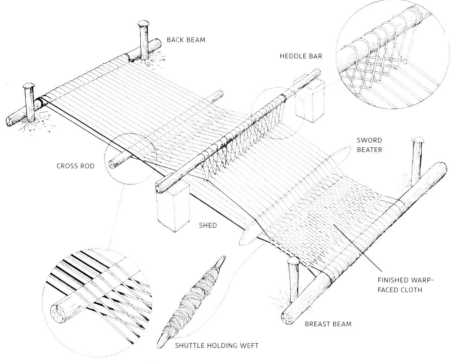

BACK BEAM

HEDDLE BAR

CROSS ROD

SWORD BEATER

SHED

FINISHED WARP-FACED CLOTH

DETAIL OF WARP CROSSING

SHUTTLE HOLDING WEFT

BREAST BEAM

TUBULAR WARP

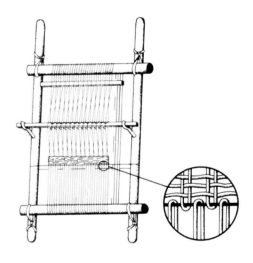

↑ F Schematic drawing of a two-beam vertical loom with a tubular warp. A warp of this type enables weaving of round-woven garments, such as a tubular skirt or peplos.

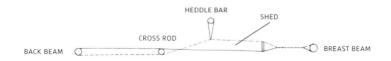

HEDDLE BAR

SHED

CROSS ROD

BACK BEAM

BREAST BEAM

↑ E Schematic drawing of a type of loom still used by the Bedouins on the Arabian Peninsula[81]

→ G A Finnish weaver
at a counterbalance-
type treadle loom in
1925. The roller beams,
warp beam and the
fabric beam, allow
weaving long pieces
of fabric.

64

COUNTERMARCH TREADLE LOOM

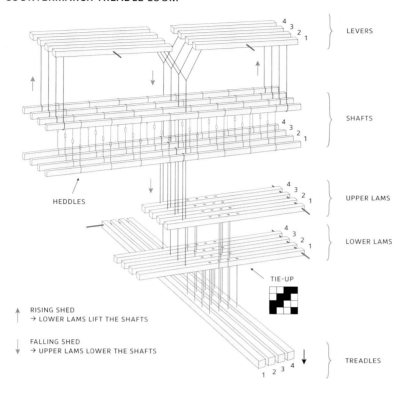

LEVERS

SHAFTS

HEDDLES

UPPER LAMS

LOWER LAMS

TIE-UP

↑ RISING SHED
→ LOWER LAMS LIFT THE SHAFTS

↓ FALLING SHED
→ UPPER LAMS LOWER THE SHAFTS

TREADLES

A ground-breaking improvement is the invention of the **roller beam**. Winding a long warp up on a **warp beam**—and the final woven fabric on a **fabric beam**—allowed weaving far longer pieces than any other warp feeding method had allowed (G). The roller beam paved the way for further developments in weaving technology, which enabled weaving of longer pieces and it remains a standard feature of modern-day weaving machines.

The **treadle loom**, originated in Asia, was another revolutionary invention, with which the variety of combinations of risen shafts became easier to handle, thus multiplying the possibilities for varying the interlacement of the warp and weft yarns.

The new invention was introduced into India sometime between 500 BCE and 750 CE, and into China—by silk weavers—in 200 CE.

Countermarch treadle looms (H) and **counterbalance treadle looms** (G) are still widely in use in the cottage industry as well as in design studios, schools and universities.

As versatile and practical as the treadle-operated looms are in catering for the weaver's needs, the number of sheds remains limited not only by the number of individual shafts but also by the amount of pedals. A long row of pedals requires space and brings challenges to operating the loom. Achieving a greater diversity of sheds to enable a wider variation of weaves would require time to change the tie-up between weave areas. In some cases wider variation can also be achieved by a shed that can be raised using two pedals. Though available, these alternatives pose limitations to efficiency and variation.

↖ H Schematic illustration of the operating system of a countermarch treadle loom. The ability to control both the rising and falling of each shaft, thus allowing for a perfect shed even with a large number of shafts, has made the countermarch treadle loom popular among hand-weavers. The treadles, or pedals, are connected to the shafts through two sets lams. Pressing a pedal raises or lowers an individual shaft depending on the **tie-up** connecting it to either to the shafts or the levers at the top of the loom.

DRAWLOOMS

The need for more elaborate patterning led to the development of looms with mechanical appliances, which enable the weaver to control specific warp ends or groups of ends according to a pattern repeat. Historically, silk weaving has played an essential role in these loom and weaving technology advancements. Fine silk threads and the desire for patterning led to the use of the **drawloom**, and with it the idea of operating two warps, a patterning warp and a ground warp, simultaneously. The sheds linked to cords were sometimes pulled in sequence by up to four "drawboys", positioned somewhere aloft in the great looms, while the weaver inserted the weft. This invention, developed by silk weavers in China and in the Middle East and the Byzantine Empire–with Constantinople as the centre of silk cloth production for the late Roman Empire and for early Medieval Europe–was adapted by Italian and French silk weavers resulting in the richly patterned damasks introduced in the course of the 15th century.[82, 83]

A variety of drawloom patterning mechanisms evolved to suit different weaving techniques and traditions. Silk fabrics have been preserved in collections and museums and evidence of the stunning designs can be seen in paintings depicting textiles from these eras, but much of the history of the looms–details and evidence of the mechanical appliances–has not survived. However, the effect of these inventions on weaving technology was revolutionary, eventually leading to the invention of the jacquard loom.[84]

↖ Illustration featuring a miniture model of the French drawloom "Métier a la grande tire" showing a binding harness and a drawloom figure harness. This type of loom was in use in the silk weaving centres of France and Italy from the 16th to 18th century. The complex system of harnesses and cords was replaced by the Jacquard loom (p.67).

← A Chinese drawloom from the *Tiangog Kaiwu* encyclopedia published in 1637 showing a silk weaver at a drawloom with a "drawboy" pulling cords to open the pattern sheds.

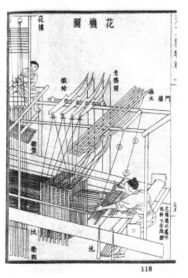

The invention of the **jacquard machine** (L), the jacquard shedding device, by master silk-weaver Joseph Marie Jacquard in 1804 transformed the weaving industry and greatly speeded up production by enabling automatic shedding control in manufacturing patterned fabrics. In shaft-loom shedding the heddles—and with each heddle a warp yarn—are attached to shafts and hence raised according to their shaft. The distinctive difference to the shed control mechanism on a **jacquard loom**—and to some extent its predecessor the **drawloom**—is the capability to raise each individual warp yarn separately thus allowing for a bigger repeat size and with it large-scale patterning.

Controlled by a binary code stored on punch cards or—after the introduction of electronic jacquard machines in 1980s—a computer programme, the heddles with the warp ends of a jacquard loom can be individually risen and lowered thus forming the shed.

Jacquard shedding

In **jacquard shedding**, as opposed to shedding on shaft looms (p.57), the **heddles**—and with them the warp yarns—are controlled individually based on the number of **hooks** in the machine. See pp.346–347 for information on the jacquard repeat.

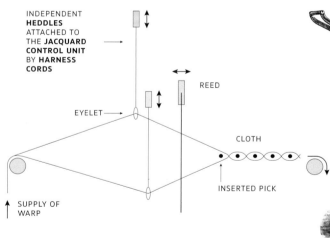

INDEPENDENT **HEDDLES** ATTACHED TO THE **JACQUARD CONTROL UNIT** BY **HARNESS CORDS**

REED

EYELET

CLOTH

INSERTED PICK

SUPPLY OF WARP

↑ The basic principle of jacquard shedding, where individual warp yarns are raised according to the lifting plan.

JACQUARD LOOM

↑ L Early jacquard loom. The jacquard shedding device with punch cards is mounted on top of the loom to lift the individual heddles and warp threads in a configuration of four repeats.

↗ Jacquard card making

↑ o Jacquard punch card used to store information in binary format

Jacquard's invention of using perforated cardboard cards with binary code to control shedding in a jacquard loom precedes the use of the binary code–dobby chain–on a shaft loom. For more information, see Chapter 3. *Jacquards – Boosting the Patterns.*

Jacquard's invention is based on the fact that woven structures include two variables, the warp and weft. The placement of these two variables in relation to each other–either warp yarn above or below the weft yarn–forms the basis of the **binary notation system** of weaves (see p.124). Based on this fundamental principle, Joseph Jacquard's invention stored information for the first time in binary format on perforated cardboard cards (o). Inspired by the jacquard machine, mathematician and mechanical engineer Charles Babbage had the idea to use punch cards to create a calculator that would read a set of sequential instructions. Babbage and his assistant mathematician Ada Lovelace described what is now recognised as the first algorithm, and created the **Analytical Engine**,[85] a programmable calculator with memory. This basis of modern computing laid the ground for automatic information processing, the invention of the Turing machine and the birth of modern information technology.

The story of the invention of the jacquard machine is a prime example of how textile inventions have contributed to the evolution of human thought, reflecting and informing human innovation on multiple levels.

DOBBY LOOM

DOBBY CHAIN (MECHANICAL)
→ PEG PLAN CONTROLS THE SHAFTS

COMPUTER (CAD)
→ LIFTING PLAN CONTROLS THE SHAFTS

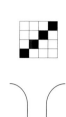

CAD (COMPUTER AIDED DESIGN)

BINARY CODE
DEFINES RAISING OF
EACH INDIVIDUAL SHAFT

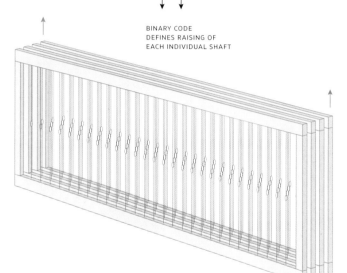

SHAFTS

↑ I The image shows details of an early six-shaft dobby loom with a dobby chain and flying shuttle system (pp.67, 70) with three shuttle boxes and the sley which carries the reed. Similar to the punch cards used in early jacquard looms, a binary code is used to store weave information and programme the loom. The dobby chain– wooden slats with holes–is programmed by placing pins in the holes. The chain is then circulated through the dobby head which reads the program. Wherever there is a pin, a shaft is raised. The combination of raised shafts creates the weave of the cloth.

← J Schematic illustration of the basic principle of the dobby system in shaft loom weaving with the binary code, a dobby chain with a peg plan or a computer programme with a digital lifting plan, controlling the shafts.

As a further result of Jacquard's invention, the limitations of the treadle-operated shaft loom, described on p.65, were surpassed by the invention of the **dobby loom** at the end of the Industrial Revolution in the mid 19th century. This invention boosted the potential of shaft weaving and resulted in dobby looms quickly taking over the industry. A **binary code** defines the raising of each individual shaft in a dobby mechanism. The shaft selection for each pick is operated by a mechanical **dobby chain** (ɪ) or–recently–a **computer** (ᴊ, ᴋ). As opposed to the limitations of treadle looms, the advantage of the dobby loom lies in the ease of adjusting the shedding sequence.

→ ᴋ Student weaving on a computer-assisted manually operated dobby loom with a flying shuttle. The flying shuttle system is composed of a track along the front of the beater for the shuttle to run on, and boxes at each end containing a mechanism to thrust the shuttle to "fly" from one side of the loom to the other. See p.70 for more information on this notable advance in weaving technology.

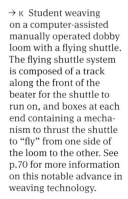

→ B Women plying silk thread on their spinning wheels. The spinning wheel, used to spin and ply yarns, had remained fairly unchanged over the centuries until the Industrial Revolution.

EXPANDING INTO AN INDUSTRY

A vast increase in the global demand for textiles, especially **cotton** goods, drove the **Industrial Revolution** in the 1700s to 1800s by applying pressure on the means of production. The increasing speed of technological innovations, with water and steam harnessed for power, spurred the industry and set textiles at the forefront of the Industrial Revolution. It set in motion a gradual shift which saw weaving workshops taken over by factories focused on increasing the productivity of labour. A series of carding, spinning and weaving inventions in England mechanised fabric production and set in motion the Industrial Revolution.[86]

The first half of the 18th century marked the start of a period of great technical innovation. John Kay's invention of the **flying shuttle**

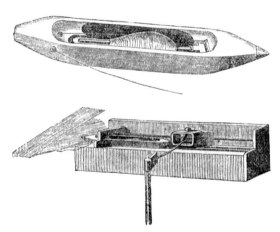

↑ A Power-loom shuttle box and flying shuttle with its bullet-shaped and metal capped ends

← D Spinning mule room. The mechanisation of textile production replaced skilled artisans with wage labourers. The advancements in spinning technology improved production speed significantly, allowing one person, even children, to spin over one hundred threads at once.[89]

(see ʞ p.69, ᴀ p.70) halved the amount of labour needed to weave wide cloth, thus greatly speeding up the weaving process and propelling the need for innovations in other stages of the textile production process.[87] Hand spinners, each on their own spinning wheel, could not meet the growing demand for yarn (ʙ). The invention of the **spinning jenny** by James Hargreaves in 1764 transformed the production of wool and cotton yarns by multiplying the amount of thread which could be spun by one spinner, thus being an instrumental kick-starter for the boom of the cotton industry (ᴄ). Hargreaves' invention was suitable for spinning soft weft yarns, but it did not produce strong enough thread for warp yarns. This was rectified by Richard Arkwright's invention of

the **water frame**, patented in 1769, a spinning machine powered by water, which spun coarse and strong cotton yarn. Finally, the capstone of the spinning inventions, Samuel Crompton's **spinning mule** (ᴅ) invented in 1779, produced yarn which was strong, yet soft and fine, thus combining the advantages of the preceding inventions and rivalling the finest hand-spun yarns. The mule, also known as the muslin wheel, could be used to produce threads for fine fashionable fabrics which so far had been of Indian import, and it remained the most common spinning machine of the 19th century.[88]

↓ ᴄ The spinning jenny is a multiple-wheel system which could be worked from a single power source and which could also be used in the home.

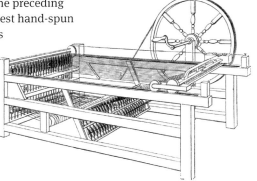

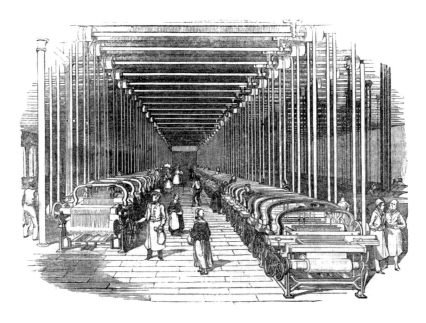

↑ E Cotton factory with power looms

quality made cotton products increasingly popular for clothing as well as interiors.

Cotton fabric was a major commodity, which was traded for enslaved people in Africa. The textile trade had tied together Asia, the Americas, Africa and Europe in a complex globe-spanning capitalist system fuelled by slavery. As Sven Beckert notes in his book *Empire of Cotton*, "Never before had the products of Indian weavers paid for slaves in Africa to work on the plantations in the Americas to produce agricultural commodities for European consumers".[93]

Another technological invention, along with ideal climate conditions and large areas of available land, shifted the spotlight to the Americas making the continent the cotton heartland of the world. Though cotton had been cultivated since prehistoric times, the invention of the mechanised **cotton gin** in 1793 by American inventor Eli Whitney lowered the cost of production and made cotton quickly a major cash crop and source of wealth for the plantation owners and cotton manufacturers in the American South.[94] Before Whitney's invention, cotton fibres were separated from cotton seeds by hand in a time-consuming and tedious process. Mechanised separation allowed a fifty-fold daily increase of processed cotton.[95]

The new innovations in part boosted production and propelled economy and trade, but the increased scale of production came at a social, moral and ecological cost. The craze for cheap cotton from the Americas grew the need for a workforce for cultivating, picking and processing cotton, and the planters and merchants of the Southern US Colonies, West Indies and South America exploited the labour of enslaved people to propel their economy.[96]

The availability of cheap cotton increased the ramifications for workers around the globe. Indian cotton farmers and weavers lost their income from exports, and cheap cotton replaced European flax, throwing farmers, spinners and weavers out of work. The changes

With spinning no longer slowing down production, the need for development shifted to weaving.[90] First came a boom in home-and workshop-based weaving, which by the mid-1800s was replaced by industrialised weaving in mills and factory halls filled with power looms (E). John Kay's invention of the flying shuttle had not only enabled a faster weaving process, but the mechanism also allowed for further inventions, leading to the development of mechanised weaving with waterpower harnessed to speed up the process. A water-powered loom, patented in 1785 by Edmund Cartwright, started the development of automatic **power looms** (F), further refined during the following decades to cater for the ever-growing needs of the booming cotton industry.[91]

Cotton was not grown in Europe, so the expanding industry's essential raw material had to be brought from far-flung locations. In the beginning of the 1800s, before the heyday of the new machines and revolution of textile production in England, cotton fabrics in Europe were mainly imported from India.[92] The bright colours, superior design, and

were reflected in the wool and silk trade as well, which faced sharp inroads. This dislocation of the sector seemed to endanger profits and threaten the social stability of the European manufacturing industry. The growing amounts of affordable raw material from the Americas, combined with the flourishing market for easily washable and comfortable cotton goods, made replacing Indian cotton cloth imports with domestic production in England a lucrative goal to aspire to.[97] The natural advantages of a wet climate and waterpower made Manchester and its surroundings the centre of the English factory system and brought it to the forefront of the Industrial Revolution. The labour force was plentiful. The new factories were staffed with workers unwillingly turned from rural cultivators or artisans into wage labourers. Inequality grew while textile industrialists and cotton farmers, now able to boost production with new machines, cheap labour and exploited workers, became increasingly wealthy.[98]

The expansion of the newly mechanised textile industry with its **factory system** set the stage for the global textile industry of today. Since the Industrial Revolution, economic and political development, and continually growing demand for textiles, raw materials and cheap labour has once again shifted the

↑ F Schematic image of the mechanism of a power loom with two shafts and flying shuttle system

epicentre of the textile industry back to Asia. However, the fraught period of the Industrial Revolution remains yet another example of the interrelated advancement of fibres and yarns, production technology, consumers' preferences and global trade. The textile industry has remained one of the largest industries in the world. The business has continued to shift power, money and capacity–and alongside them, cheap labour and raw materials, and environmental and social problems–around the globe.

The machinery and processes in today's weaving mills are optimised for astounding efficiency, automatised and digitally controlled. The basic principles of weaving have to a great extent remained the same in shaft (dobby) and jacquard weaving, and within these categories there exist special applications for purposes such as carpet weaving and velvet weaving. Shuttle looms have for the most part been replaced by **shuttleless weaving machines**, with more efficient technology for transferring the pick through the shed. Among these are **rapier machines** with rapiers that grip the weft yarn and carry it to the receiving rapier–similar to passing the baton in a relay race–at speeds of up to 400 ppm (picks per minute), while even faster **air-jet** weaving machines shoot the weft at speeds of up to 1000 ppm with help of compressed air blown by air-nozzles.

The textile industry now is mainly fed by synthetic fibres–primarily polyester, the cheap fibre of today. Therefore, developments in weaving technology and machinery have centered around weaving synthetic filament fibres and the extreme precision in production these require. The emerging more sustainable man-made fibres, sustainable cultivation of natural fibres and quest for circularity– with novel solutions for recycling textiles–will hopefully continue to drive development in the future and mark the next great transformation of the global textile system.

A   B

Standardised industry

↑ Spun warp yarns running from the **bobbins** on a **creel** (A, B). As the featured **sectional warping process** produces a dense warp consisting of thousands of ends, the warp yarns are organised into yarn bands and wound on a **warping drum** (c) into sections determined by the number of bobbins prepared on the creel (p.26), the warp density and width. The tension of the warp sections is precisely set and continuously monitored as the yarns are wound perpendicular to the drum.

As textiles have grown into a global industry, the **factory system** – influenced by economic and political forces in global trade – has encouraged standardization and streamlining throughout the process, from fibres to machinery and the final products' parameters. Weaving machines are standardised in order to produce quality fabric in widths that are acceptable in the international markets. At a weaving mill, the sourcing and stocking of yarns for continuity and uniformity of the production is a significant effort and cost. Preparation of the yarns and the process of warping as well as setting the looms are time consuming and labour-intensive stages. The weaving and finishing stages also need to be taken into account, with various types of machinery and capacities needed for fabrics of differing fibre composition, type, and end-use. For these reasons, weaving mills are usually

specialised in certain types of fabric qualities, production widths, warp and weft yarns, warp thread counts, and fabric weights. Driven by the need for an efficient production process, production at a mill usually takes place on **standard warps**, with possible edits to warp colours and stripe warp patterns. New warps are designed to fit in the mill's portfolio of setts and qualities. Therefore, for textile designers working in an industrial setting, understanding the production technologies and capacities at a mill is essential along with the ability to work creatively within these limitations. There are endless possibilities for creating the desired look, feel, design and texture to the fabric by varying the weave structures, weft materials and colours, weft thread count, and finishes. Restrictions in the production process can be seen as a source of inspiration (see pp.464–465).

← Winding spun warp yarns on a warping drum (c). The ends in each yarn band are organised using **warp-cross** equipment, a **leasing device** that splits the yarns onto layers (d). The yarns then run through a **warping reed** (e) into the density of the final warp and are wound strictly parallel on the warping drum. To ensure the equal length of each warp yarn, the drum and carriage move with every section. After winding the warp sections on the warping drum, the warp is **beamed** on the **warp beam**. In the beaming process, the complete warp in its whole width and with all its ends is unwound from the drum to the beam. Controlled winding and beaming of the warp prevents yarn breaks during the weaving process.

C

D

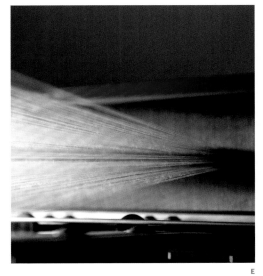

E

There are two different types of warping, the featured **sectional warping** and **direct warping**. In the latter process the yarns are directly warped from a creel onto a beam. The warping process requires strict parallel organization of the warp yarns and careful control of yarn tension. In today's industry, warping machinery includes equipment such as precision direct drive, advanced electronics, and programmable breaks.

All images on pp.74–77 are from the Vanelli textile mill in Turkey. The mill manufactures interior fabrics ranging from lightweight lenos and sheers to upholstery fabrics.

→ **Sizing** a spun yarn warp for weaving (F). The sizing process strengthens the ends by fixing the slubs and individual fibres of the warp yarns together with starch or another agent adapted for the particular yarn type. Sizing prevents the entanglement of the warp yarns and consequent yarn breaks during the weaving process, which mechanically stresses the warp due to abrasion within the lamella and reed (H) as well as through rapidly changing tension forces during shedding (J). Warps with fine natural and man-made **staple fibre yarns** such as texturised yarns and microfibres undergo an additional sizing process to prevent abrasive damage that these yarn types are susceptible to during weaving.

↑ Producing **fancy yarns** (p.156) for weaving (G). Bouclé yarns and other fancy yarns are made on specially dedicated machinery. The machine loops the effect yarn around the core yarn and twists the binder yarn around them. At a weaving mill, design and production of fancy yarns offers a myriad of possibilities for variations in fabric textures and hand.

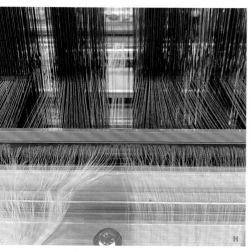

↑ **Drawing-in** process at a weaving machine (H). Each end is drawn into the **drop wire** (lamella), **heald** (heddle), and **reed**. Drawing in a new warp on a weaving machine is a labour-intensive process requiring individual insertion of each warp yarn manually or with special automatic drawing-in machinery.

Standardised warps, produced in great lengths and running continuously, are preferred in the industry as **machine knotting** of the subsequent warp with an identical number of ends allows for an efficient warp change process resulting in minimum down time of the weaving machine.

↑ Leno weaving on a **rapier** (p.73) **shaft loom** fitted with a **leno harness** (doup) (I). The leno equipment shifts the doup ends attached to it alternately from right to left, crossing the ground ends before the insertion of each pick. The resulting figure-eight loops in the leno weave hold the picks in firmly place (p.225). In the weaving process the **heald frames** (heddle frames) are lifted according to the lifting plan to form the sheds in which the pick is inserted by the rapiers (J). After each insertion the weft yarn is beaten to the fabric with the reed. The pick density is regulated by the warp feeder.

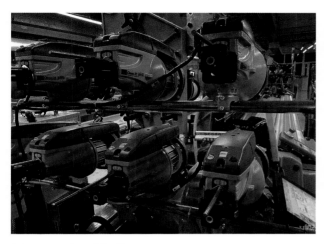

↑ An automatic **weft feeding system** ensures consistent tension of the weft yarns (κ). The **weft feeders** (weft accumulators) regulate yarn tension throughout the yarn insertion process from the bobbin to the rapier.

↑ **Bobbins** with weft yarn waiting to be inserted at a **jacquard loom** (ʟ). In the contemporary textile industry, jacquard control units with punch cards have largely been replaced by automatic,

digitally controlled jacquard machines (м). The weave designs are created on computers and digitally transferred from the design department to the jacquard control unit. A jacquard loom in fact consists of two machines, the **weaving machine** and a **jacquard machine** built on top of it, which need to work seamlessly in unison. **Production planning** at a weaving mill is a demanding task which entails managing a complex production flow and handling demanding supply chain issues. As discussed earlier, the weaving industry produces predominantly on standard warps designed according to the specialisation of the mill. In large production facilities which often have more than a hundred looms from several different manufacturers, the machines are dedicated to weaving certain types of qualities (see p.74). Same standard warps might be woven on both dobby and jacquard machines. Allocation of weaving work to the various machines depends on the suitability of the machine and the overall production flow, which might on occasion result in weaving dobby designs on jacquard machines.

"*When an axe or a sheath knife is being used, the skilled user does not think of the hand and the tool as different and detached entities; the tool has grown to be a part of the hand, it has transformed into an entirely new species of organs, a tool-hand.*" – Juhani Pallasmaa[99]

1.4 Tools, Practice and Materiality

Tools and technology catalyse changes in how we think and what we do.[100] The practice of weaving, closely linked to the loom and its mechanism, forms an interesting reference point to this. Several anthropologists and ethnographers believe that millennia ago, the thought processes which resulted in the development of tools for making fabrics have had a notable impact on the human brain and human advancement. According to this view, textiles long ago became essential models of cognitive processing. Despite the machinery and techniques involved in manufacturing textiles, they are able to communicate with us. Throughout history, textiles–from simple basketry to complex jacquards and the practices involved in making them–allow our subconscious to intuit a vast range of concepts from emotions to the binary code and speak to our ability to grasp these big ideas. Weaving is something we share as humans. It has offered tangible advantages for human survival and provided a way for storytelling which extends beyond its historical context. Manipulating materials not only trains **haptic perception** and **embodied thinking**, but also the eyes.[101] This goal of learning to "think through making" can be seen in the weaving studio filled with students weaving their way to material meanings and narratives using traditional wooden treadle looms alongside new computer-assisted dobby and jacquard looms.

These embodied thinking processes form the core of the **learning-by-doing studio methods** described in this book. The approach inspires the telling of tactile stories through structural and material exploration, whilst the **practice-led research processes** demonstrate how tightly the creative and technical aspects of textile design are intertwined. The scope of technical knowledge, such as understanding textile fibre and yarn properties, their behaviour and relation to different weave structures, grows through the process of experimenting and weaving on looms. An embodied perspective to the repetitive practice of weaving helps master the creative and technical textile design process. It also allows the weaver to understand the limits and possibilities within woven textiles whilst letting cloth speak. From a pedagogical point of view, this close involvement with materiality can be expanded from learnings in textile design and applied to a diverse range of other disciplines, such as fashion design (pp. 437–449), furniture design (pp. 450–453) and acoustics (pp. 454–457). The potential in creative adaptation of textile practices is further described in *Textile Thinking towards Multidisciplinary Futures* (pp. 467–473).

In a world of computer screens and a culture disconnected from the making of cloth, the history and context of woven textiles deserve to be revived. The contemporary industrial production system has radically reordered the role of textiles in society. High-velocity turnover has deflated the value of textiles as a domain for expression and transferred the making of cloth somewhere out of sight, available quickly with discounted prices, and sustainability out of mind. As a counteraction, there is a desire to reacquaint ourselves with textiles and move away from the textiles produced in masses to more personal, intimate readings and weavings.[102]

"Our predisposition for art has long ensured that we have grown up in and constructed our own especially enriched environments. For tens of thousands of years our play with the intense patterns of intricate arts like weaving and carving, song, dance, verse and story, has enticed us to repeat 'practice' events and so remodelled human minds." – Brian Boyd[103]

The weaving studio – creating on looms

There are several types of **handlooms** in use in textile designers' studios and weaving studios in schools and universities. The studios are often equipped with **treadle looms** and **looms with a computer-assisted dobby mechanism**. Hand-operated table looms have been popular in educational settings for their small size, but are rather slow to operate. For development and proto-typing of jacquards, studios are equipped with **hand-operated electronic jacquard sampling looms** (p.336), such as the TC2 loom. Furthermore, industrial weaving machines, found in some institutions, are an asset in strengthening the learning path from artisanal to industrial scale and adapting handwoven samples for industrial produc-tion (pp. 82, 84–85, 338–339).

Exploring the principles of shaft weaving on both treadle looms and dobby looms is beneficial for learning. During the *Woven fabrics studio course assignment* (p.122) students are familiarised with the concept of a tie-up on treadle looms, a lifting plan (peg plan) in dobby weaving, and are thereafter ready to proceed to more advanced exercises and learning about jacquard weaving.

Weaving on a treadle loom within the limits of its tie-up guides students in their first steps to understand the fundamentals of weave structures and their derivates. Weav-ing on a hand-operated computer-assisted dobby loom then reinforces the grasp of shaft weaving, and enables more flexibility in combining weaves and patterning, espe-cially in twills and satins as described on pp.244–245, 303–304. Dobby looms and jacquard looms are used in the industry. Hands-on experience on manually operated looms provides knowledge that the students can use in designing for the industry.

Students are taught to draft weaves for shaft looms using **weave design software** (eg. WeavePoint, PointCarré). The same software is used for the loom control of the computer-assisted dobby looms. Working at the dobby loom – drafting, weaving and experiment-ing – furthers the learning process. In Chap-ter 3, students also learn to use Photoshop software to draft jacquard designs.

The hands-on role of the instructor and workshop master, and the pre-arranged sample warps, are elementary for the type

The **structural drafts** for each sample, including **threading**, **treadling**, **tie-up** and the **pick sequence** and **end sequence** (p.124), are drafted on conventional weave design software. Learning to document the technical details of a sample on a product card is an important learning outcome.

"I still remember the day I started in the weaving studio. First I felt lost. The theory, drafts and mechanisms of the loom seemed incomprehensible. The eureka moment occurred when I sat at a loom and started to weave. It was the moment I found the lost piece to the puzzle. I positioned myself at the right angle to observe the world of woven fabrics."
– You-Chia Chen

of learning-by-doing concept introduced in this book. Working on existing warp set-ups not only saves students' time in their crowded curricula, but also facilitates creative problem-solving and acts as a link to industrial weaving.

Studio teaching allows for learning and exploring in a group. Mixed groups work well, with students from different design disciplines as well as beginners and more advanced weavers sharing and learning from each other. Students are encouraged to engage with each other's explorations, and to discuss and share the creative possibilities. As additional practical advice to instructors, in order to enable seamless switching between the looms with different warps and set-ups, it is advisable to have the same amount of looms set up as there are students in the group.

See Chapter 2, section *Sample warps* p.121 and *Assignment* pp.122–123 for more information.

The **handwoven samples** presented in chapters 1 and 2 are created on countermarch treadle looms (some with a double-beam system) and hand-operated computer-assisted dobby looms on ca. 20 cm wide warps. A narrow **sample warp** eases weaving by controlling the pick density, keeping the selvedges straight and the beating even. Weaving the square samples is not too time consuming and the size is sufficient for exploring the effects of the yarns and weaves.

For the *Woven fabrics studio course* (p.122), each loom and warp is named and numbered (p.474). Intriguing samples woven on the warp invite the students to start weaving and exploring. General information on each warp can be found on a **warp card** (p.476) at the loom. The infor-mation on treadle looms includes a structural draft with suggestions for treadling sequences. The sample warps on computer-assisted dobby looms include suggestions for the lifting plan.

The **midway critique** is an important milestone on the *Woven fabrics studio course*. Its focus is on tech-nical aspects. The fabrics are taken off the looms and reviewed together, warp by warp. Ideally, at this point, the students have woven at least one sample on each warp. Learnings and observations on weave structures and yarns are shared among the students. The instructor facilitates the discus-sion, points out special features in each warp – highlighting the students' findings – and offers advice for further explorations. At the end of the course, in the **final critique**, the focus is on each student's collection, storytelling and artistic expression.

→ The weaving studio at Aalto University School of Arts, Design and Architecture.

Designing collections

A well-rounded **textile collection** requires a variety of different fabric weights and qualities. Weaving on a range of warps adds versatility to the collection and helps manage a balanced set of qualities and fabric weights for different end-uses in a commercial set-up. A designer creating interior textile collections or selecting fabrics at a fashion house builds a textile collection from a variety of fabric qualities – often produced by textile mills around the world specialised in those particular types of fabric. In the pedagogical approach of this book, the sample warps described in Chapter 2. *To the Looms* can be seen as an analogy for warps at weaving mills. While learning the basics of woven textile design by weaving on the sample warps, the students are guided to compose their stories from a variety of cloth qualities.

"Learning a skill is not primarily founded on verbal teaching but rather on the transference of the skill from the muscles of the teacher directly to the muscles of the apprentice through the act of sensory perception and bodily mimesis." – Juhani Pallasmaa[104]

← Exploring yarns, weaves, **fil coupé** (p.419) ideas and colours on the handloom. *Experiments* by Pilvi Waitinen

Handloom prototyping

The industrial loom is a relevant tool in today's design process, and production trials on the industrial machine are an important development stage. However, much of the design development and prototypes for industrial weaving is still done on handlooms, often on computer-assisted dobby looms or jacquard sampling looms. Furthermore, there is an increasing need to engage with the textiles and their design on a personal haptic level. Manual weaving allows designers and weavers to experiment with weave constructions, patterns, and yarns before committing to an idea, while experimenting on mecha-nised looms allows less room for errors. See p.468 on prototyping complex func-tional textiles.

→ Maheshwar Handloom Sari production in Madhya Pradesh, India. A **sari** is an unstitched garment, a length of fabric created on the loom. Its interwoven qualities help maintain the form of the sari when it is worn. Patterning, the weave structure, and weave density are varied between the inner part, body, outer end-piece and borders, which provide drape, strength and weight. The length and width vary greatly from area to area as the wearing style of the sari depends on the community. Sari weaving in India is associated with strong local traditions. The Maheshwari Saris, woven on silk warps with cotton wefts, are known for their fine dual tone check and stripe patterns.[105]

Handloom production

Although mechanised looms have for the most part replaced handlooms in production, many fabrics are still woven by hand. These include intricately patterned brocades, unique haute-couture fabrics with very open and loose weaves, as well as fabrics produced with fancy yarns too delicate for industrial machines. Similarly, traditional silk saris, tapestries as well as carpets and customised home textile items such as table mats, are still woven by hand. In countries such as in India or Indonesia, where skilled artisans and a flourishing **cottage industry** exist, a substantial part of commercial production both for the domestic and the export market is still handwoven. Handweaving workshops still play a part in textile production across the world. **Harris Tweed** (p.253) is a Scottish example of contemporary handloom production based in the artisans' houses.[106]

⭥ Handloom and warp preparation at Arte della Seta Lisio Foundation in Florence. The workshop nurtures the Florentine art of handwoven silk, gold and silver brocades and velvets and produces authentic handwoven fabrics for historical interiors, and museum settings. In addition to production, the foundation is involved in handing down disappearing hand weaving skills.[107]

→ **Brocading** a silk ground with gold and silver threads at the Lisio Foundation. Each individual brocaded motif is woven with its own set of shuttles. Authentic brocade fabrics can only be woven by hand, although the fil coupé technique can be used to imitate some of their qualities in industrial manufacturing.

See also p.397 on handwoven warp-pile velvet production at the Lisio Foundation.

"In the same way that the boundary between the hammer and the hand disappears in the act of hammering, complicated tools such as musical instruments merge with the user's body; a great musician plays himself rather than a separate instrument."
– Juhani Pallasmaa[1]

EMBODIED THINKING IN HAND WEAVING PRACTICE

by Helmi Liikanen

Hand weaving is a highly creative, intuitive and innovative medium for designing woven fabrics. Hands-on design practices, be it weaving, tailoring or ceramics, are a powerful way of understanding our environment through the sense of touch. Craft holds a special meaning in a world that is largely experienced through the digital and immaterial.

In a recent project, I designed a set of woven textures by means of hand weaving for production at Lapuan Kankurit, a Finnish weaving mill. I used a sixteen-shaft loom to create textures that combine a pleasant hand-feel with a contemporary look. Despite the production happening at the speed and scale of industrial machines, hand weaving was an elementary part of my design process. The physicality of the weaving process provided me with plenty of design ideas and with a multi-sensory understanding of the linen material I used.

While weaving by hand the designer's ability to alter structures and observe the changes from a close proximity increases the intuitiveness of the design process. Design variables, such as weight of the material or the surface structure of the fabric, can be assessed through the sense of touch. The designer almost becomes another physical part of the loom, adding their mental and embodied capacities into the design process. In my project the making process itself functioned as a source of inspiration, as observations about material behaviour often sparked new design ideas to be tested.

The physicality of the weaving process is its strength. Through the close contact between the designer and their materials, an intimate connection is created. This emotional connection instils a human quality to the designs, as the designer creates things with care and time. We are living in an increasingly digitised world, where there is growing need for products that embrace the multisensorial human experience. The multi-sensorial quality of hand-weaving practice is an asset when it comes to designing soft and tactile experiences and products. These concepts of haptic experience and the embodied design process have been comprehensively examined by Pallasmaa[2].

In the act of making, the designer employs their whole bodily being in the thinking process. Much of the knowledge related to design processes is learnt and realised in an embodied way. The French philosopher Maurice Merleau-Ponty saw the body as the primary site of understanding the world. His theory of embodied knowledge claims that perception through the senses is key to knowledge formation as human cognition is never independent from its interaction with its surroundings.[3] The working hands of a designer, plunged into the material, are key to their knowledge formation through the sensory experiences that the body provides. The designer, working in an embodied contact with their medium and observing action from a close

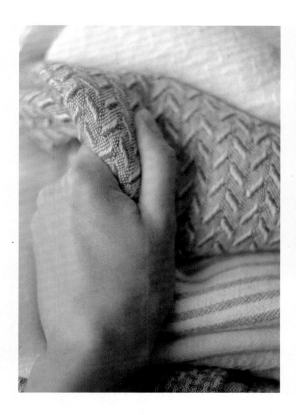

↑ Fabrics from a collection
of linen products for Lapuan
Kankurit

*Ranta – Embodied thinking in hand weaving
practice.* Master's thesis collection 2019 by
Helmi Liikanen

distance, comes to understand the process
in depth.

While the physical design studio continues to be well-established in art and design
education, the professional landscape of
designers and artists is changing. Due to the
introduction of online platforms and social
media as extensions of design practice
(and of everyday life), our perception of
materiality is changing. Platforms such as
Instagram or Pinterest, used as part of the
creative practice, have enabled designers
to see creative practices and art around
the world, providing them with sources of
inspiration beyond the limitations of their
local environments. Nevertheless, profound
design goes well beyond appearances and
communicates with its viewers in nuanced,
tacit and multisensory ways. In the physical
design studio, the designer's multi-sensory
first-hand observations form a vital part of
the creative practice.

At the beginning of my design project I
had difficulties understanding the behaviour
of the linen yarns, which I had not used
much before. However, through several
days of weaving and observing I began to
understand the design possibilities of the
material. The repeat size of the design on a
shaft loom is small, which means that a new
design cannot be created by simply altering
the pattern, as can be done with a jacquard
loom. The designer working on a shaft loom
is almost forced to innovate with the weave
structures in order to create new designs. In
the hand weaving project, the physicality
and proximity with the tools functioned as
a source of inspiration and learning. The
manual design tools bring the maker and the
material together, and thus demand more
human innovation.

In my opinion, hand weaving practice is
beneficial for the designer's ability to understand materials and their properties in more
depth. The bodily contact with the materials
and tools facilitates intuitive and embodied
thinking in the design process, giving way
to innovation and higher attention to detail
in the design process. If we are to create
something new to this world that is already
filled with 'stuff', let it be something that
elicits feelings of warmth and joy. Something
designed with care and attention that gives
comfort amongst the countless hours spent
touching and looking at computer screens.
These are product qualities that physical,
hands-on design methods are capable of
creating.

1.5 Weaving Human Stories

"The weaver-god, he weaves; and by that weaving is he deafened, that he hears no mortal voice; and by that humming, we, too, who look on the loom are deafened; and only when we escape it shall we hear the thousand voices that speak through it."
– Herman Melville, Moby Dick

Made from the raw materials of the environments we live in and shaped by our innovations, textiles are major components of our material culture, reflecting eras of history and representing value systems and societal change. Textiles are products of technology and items of trade. Cloth has functioned as the backbone of many national and global economies and deeply affected the course of global trade and the history of nations and cultures.[108] Textiles are cultural symbols, works of art and markers of status and power. They are a means of communication and group building, both in our tribal past and in our contemporary urban subcultures. The rich historical repertoire, designs, knowledge and technological innovations travel with textiles, connecting and transcending space and time.[109]

Daily chores involving spinning and weaving have disappeared from our everyday life, but words associated with the long history of making cloth have stayed in our language: metaphorically, poetically, and as ways to define abstract concepts.[110] We speak of the web of life, the need to unravel our thoughts and put a new spin on ideas. The essence of fabric's materiality, the interwoven organisation of the warp and weft, refers to grids, constructs, and systems. To weave is to unite, to interlace and to bind–a straightforward act which requires no explanation. Weaving the fabric of society brings into play notions inscribed into the collective memory, gestures that allow us to grasp social organization, while simultaneously demonstrating a possible, or desirable, way to conceive of life in society.[111] Weaving unites what must be unified. Woven cloth evokes ideas of connectedness and tying, wrapping provides protection from malevolent forces, be they spiritual or from the natural environment.[112]

Stories were woven long before they were written. The act of weaving is one that binds the weaver to the tactile history of mankind. In this section, as we move to the looms, we take the learnings of human innovation and technical advancements and interweave these with various other entry points into the intimate human relationship with textiles–emotions, identity, narratives, metaphors and myths. The rich cultural-historical canon of textile stories set an inspiring stage for weavers to delve into.

This book introduces a cognitive method of learning which encourages the reader to take their place at the loom and weave their own (hi)stories into the tactile narrative continuum. The woven stories presented in this section were created by students weaving their way through the warps and the study assignment (p.122) introduced in Chapter 2 or crafting textiles for a more in-depth collection project.

An extensive list of reading on these subjects can be found in the Further Reading section of this book.

← Drawing *Kangaspuiden ääressä* [At the Loom] by Hugo Simberg. Ateneum Art Museum, Helsinki

IDENTITY AND BELONGING

Cloth carries with it immense social, political, and cultural significance. Throughout time, in the form of clothing and adornment, as cherished heirlooms, or stocked for trade, textiles have been used by social groups for the purpose of differentiation and to achieve autonomy or advantage in their interaction with others.[113] Fabrics take on many roles, adapt to various forms and shapes, and fulfil a multitude of functions. They serve our everyday needs – literally from birth to death – but they can equally be worn or displayed in a way that carries great symbolic weight and significance.[114]

Through the range of textile techniques, with their endless variation in textures, decoration, and use of colour, cloth has an almost limitless potential for communication. Cloth can convey identity, complex moral and ethical issues as well as the wearer's ideological values and claims.[115] The patterns and colours of fabrics have served to distinguish individuals and groups, acting as markers for social rank, gender, age, occupation and status.[116] As in the case of Islamic rug patterns, the understanding of the intricacies of patterns and their meaning bound together cultural groups, whilst simultaneously setting them apart from those who could not decipher them.[117]

Cloth can become a symbol for global intercultural and political exchange and a representation of national identity. Mahatma Gandhi in India demonstrated its potential to unify a large and diverse society of various ethnic and language groups. Gandhi elevated khadi, homespun cotton cloth, and the peasant woman's spinning wheel as the central, unifying symbols of economic nationalism and the struggle for liberation from British rule. Through its aesthetic imagery and identification with the poor, khadi dissolved the boundaries that divided Indian society. Distinctions of region, religion, gender, and rank were overcome by a simple textile as Gandhi, himself a lawyer educated abroad, summoned up the oldest and most humble craft traditions of the subcontinent.[118]

Textiles continue to mark identity and belonging in contemporary societies across the globe, as for each of us. At the loom, interlacing our own markings on the warp gives us the opportunity to weave our way to the roots of our own identity and communicate the themes which have united fabrics and humans throughout history.

→ The ornate patterning in *Heirloom* by Tiia Sirén is done with weft-faced rib weave, often used to decorate traditional textiles.

TRIBES

Tribes / Gangs
Woven fabrics studio course assignment 2012
by Tiia Sirén

The story of textiles is interwoven with the history of humans. Fabrics of different eras and geographical locations map a visual timeline of our changing societies and highlight our inherent need to belong to a pack. Textile patterns have been used in cultures throughout the world to mark belonging and one's status within a group. Tiia Sirén's complementary collections, *Tribes* and *Gangs*, draw on this rich social history. The collections are a study in collective identity taking inspiration from both early fabrics and contemporary textiles. The themes of the collections offer a snapshot of the lived experience in different times and environments. *Tribes* takes its motifs from the natural environment of early collectives whilst *Gangs* is inspired by the urban milieu and its subcultures. Though different in materials, structures and motifs, the collections mirror one another, demonstrating that gangs are simply the tribes of today's cities. In these collections, done on the *Woven fabrics studio course* during her first encounter with weaving, Tiia Sirén reflects on identity and belonging through textile storytelling (see assignment p.122).

→ Collection *Tribes*, fabrics from top to bottom: *Heirloom* (p.89), *Man's best friend*, *Nature, Life, Luck Charm, Community* (p.142), *Coins* and *Talisman*

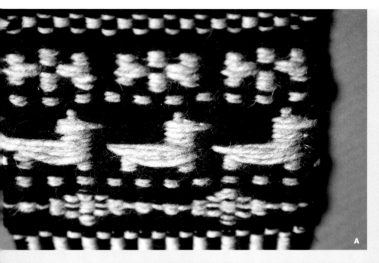

↖ The ornate patterning in *Man's Best Friend* (A) is done with weft-faced rib weave, often used to decorate traditional textiles.

Life and Nature (B), *Luck Charm* (p.150) (C) and *Talisman* (D) from collection *Tribes*

Tribes takes its inspiration from early fabrics that brought together groups of people and acted as markers of a shared identity. Coarse wool yarns in warm natural hues of beige and off-white, combined with thick cotton and metallic yarns, form striking patterns on a black background.

GANGS

Tribes / Gangs
Woven fabrics studio course assignment 2012
by Tiia Sirén

While *Tribes* pairs natural materials and colours with black, *Gangs* combines the black base colour with bleached shades of white. As the sample titles such as *Tarmac*, *Skyline* and *Fences* suggest, *Gangs* visualises the contemporary urban landscape and its synthetic materials.

→ Collection *Gangs*, fabrics from top to bottom: *Skyline*, *Beat* (p.200), *Graffiti 1*, *Tarmac*, *Fences*, *Together*, *Alleys*. The structures used in this collection are largely similar to the ones used in *Gangs*, but the choice of yarns and material combinations gives the collection its contemporary edge.

"Together we are stronger"

"They can't keep us away"

"This is what we want to say"

"Never hold back"

Together (A), *Graffiti 1* (p.181) (B), *Graffiti 2* (C) and *Fence* (D) from collection *Gangs*

← The *Graffiti 2* sample's fuzzy and glittery tactility is created with a mix of fancy yarns.

→ A Navajo woman weaving a blanket under a cottonwood tree with a canyon wall in the background

↑ Navajo rugs from the Hubbell Trading Post National Historic Site, Arizona USA. The dominating motif of Navajo blankets is a cross representing the Spider Woman, a reminder of her wisdom and teachings to avoid pride and perfectionism. The Spider Woman is not of this world and her spirit should not be entrapped, therefore in some Navajo weavings, the cross will have an actual hole.

MYTH AND METAPHOR

"I shall weave the fabric of my life,
I shall weave it white as a cloud;
I shall weave some black to it;
I shall weave dark maize stalks into it;
I shall weave maize stalks into the white cloth;
Thus I shall obey divine law."
– Kogi prayer [119]

Myths related to fabric and weaving are widely known in all cultures. They are shared figures of thought widely used by cultures and civilisations – repeated, modified and revived over time.[120] Cloth-making is seen as a generative or life-giving activity in many of humankind's creation stories, allegories and fairy tales. Goddesses of fertility are often portrayed as spinners and weavers, frequently associated with the sun, or other cosmic elements and with life-giving fire, farming, and healing. The Spider Woman of the Navajo people instructs the women how to weave. The myth describes her loom with cross poles made of sky and the structure supported with cords of earth, the warp rods made of sun rays, the heddles of rock crystal, and beater from the halo of the sun.[121]

In ancient Greek mythology Zeus, at the mythical dawn of time, stood before a loom to weave a rich mantle, resplendent with Ocean and Earth, for his bride. Weaving emerges as a metaphor as rich with promise and possibility as Zeus's gift.[122]

Many age-old societies consider weaving skills to derive from a mystical deity or ancestor, transmitted through dreams or revelations. The weaver, bound to cultural rituals and taboos, not only demonstrates respect for these sacred sources, but also infuses their product with spiritual value, sanctifying the raw materials, the techniques and the emerging cloth.[123] For the Kogi people in the Amazon rainforest this is most pronounced. The Kogi understand their place in the cosmos as part of the great weaving of a sacred cloak over the

Great Mother. Everything they do is conceived of as a fabric, and everything begins and ends with the loom. The act of spinning is akin to thinking, with each journey and each thought likened to threads. Their wanderings are likened to weavings as each seasonal migration becomes a prayer for the well-being of the people and the entire earth.[124]

The ancient Greek myth of the master weaver Arachne, who is turned into a spider by her rival weaver Athene, warns against overconfidence and hubris. In Navajo weaving tradition, moderation is encouraged as a cure against the *excess of craft*.[125] A Native American legend is a reminder that life must be lived in balance, explaining why generations of Navajo, Hopi and Pueblo weavers have carefully woven mistakes into their traditional blankets. Like the Greek Arachne, the Weaving Woman of Native American legend becomes too enamoured with her talent, and as a punishment disappears into her loom, redeemed only when the Spider Woman pulls out a strand to release her. Since then, the weavers have promised to make "spirit trails", openings somewhere within their blankets, and to prevent pride from becoming the master of their spirits.[126]

Textiles are metaphorically equated with life and mythically linked to time.[127] This rich history of myths and metaphors inspires us to join the long line of weavers that have come before us to renew, reinvent and revive cultural roots and ancestral stories at the loom.

Warp and weft – union of opposites

In classic texts of ancient Greece and Rome, the areas of application in which the metaphorical and poetic use of weaving and fabric are common and most concrete, are those of political thought, social relations and marriage.[128] The fundamental gesture of weaving – the interlacing of warp and weft – readily symbolises the union of opposites. The union of the warp and weft has permeated our imagination and language. In ancient Greek the rigid warp *stemon* or *mitos*, both words being masculine, and the weft, the feminine *kroke*, formed a union symbolic of that between man and woman. The meaning of the term *connubium* (marriage) is precise: the prefix *co-* indicates that the bride and groom are *together* beneath the *veil*.[129] Similarly, among the Temang in Nepal, women are depicted as the interweaving weft yarns in contrast to men, symbolised by the continuous warp threads. Temang women exchange cloth at marriage thus binding together the new family lines. Balancing cloth against writing, the men's texts record the divine oaths that give continuity to ancestral lineages.[130]

What makes woven fabric the symbol of marriage, are precisely its material properties, transformed into metaphors of conjugal relations. The symbolism extends beyond the linguistic. In an Indonesian marriage ceremony a tubular uncut fabric binds the bride to the groom. For the Etruscans and Romans holding a woven cloth over the bride and groom was a symbol for their union.[131]

↙ Rumpelstiltskin and the Miller's daughter illustrated by Walter Crane. Cloth-making can conjure a magical process of transforming ordinary substances from nature into valued commodities. In the Rumpelstiltskin fairy tale a young girl bargains with an elf who can spin straw into gold. The association between making thread and making life carry the story to its devastating end where the first-born child is offered as the ultimate price for completing the transformation. This[132] story is related to many other folktales that feature malevolent spirits heightening the perils of spinning.[133]

FOR BETTER

For Better / For Worse
Woven fabrics studio course assignment 2014
by Kaisa Kantokorpi

The starting points for my two collections
were weddings and funerals, and therefore
I named them *For Better* and *For Worse* after
the traditional wedding vow. Those themes
might at first seem opposites to each other.
We think of weddings as something light
and happy, as funerals are dark and filled
with sorrow. But both occasions involve
mixed feelings. Someone's death can make
others very happy, just as other people's
love can break someone's heart. With all the
traditions, beliefs and social relations, the
two events have also a level of comedy. Each
sample has a story written in the form of a
wedding or funeral announcement. Like in
real-life announcements, only a couple of
words tell a life-long story. One just has to
read between the lines.

I study interior architecture and furniture
design so weaving was really a step into
an unfamiliar area. The assignment (p.122)
encouraged us to tell stories using textiles,
translating abstract concepts into a tactile
language that I was then unfamiliar with.
But I think my lack of experience actually
worked to my advantage. I was free from
all expectations and rules: every time I sat
down in front of a new warp, I started my
work just by trying different things, even in
unorthodox ways.

*"She was about to marry
the man of her dreams.
For the fourth time."*

← *For Better* starts with the white
and fluffy sample *The Bride*.

← The Engagement is light-coloured and stands for the hope you feel when you are starting a new phase in your life. After engagement there is *Summer Wedding* (p.223) which has the feeling of a beautiful, clear summer day. *Weekday* and *The Five-Year Crisis* are what happens after the wedding. *The Five-Year Crisis* is a piqué weave with a zig-zag pattern, the lines represent the struggle you have deciding whether you should stay in your current relationship or move on.

"Only fools fall in love but some are even more stupid and marry those idiots."

← Weekday is a grey-toned plain weave with golden stripes; monotonous everyday life with glimpses of happiness in between. As well as arguments and boring family life, there are also good times: *Plain Joy* refers to the satisfaction of waking up next to the partner you love. *Silver Lining* (p.209) shows how on the other side of obstacles, there is always a positive way of looking at things.

"You are the same as you were yesterday but I love you even more."

For Better
Kaisa Kantokorpi

And They Lived Happily Ever After

*Because some people just deserve it.
Those lucky bastards.*

"Because some people just deserve it. Those lucky bastards."

← The wedding collection ends with the sample *And They Lived Happily Ever After*. The golden plain weave symbolises real love and the possibility of finding it.

FOR WORSE

For Better / For Worse
Woven fabrics studio course assignment 2014
by Kaisa Kantokorpi

The first sample of the funeral collection *For Worse* drew inspiration from a black-and-white photograph. The sample is called *Tracks* and it imitates footprints in the snow left by people visiting the graveyard.

In the sample *At the Cemetery* (p.283) I replicated a picture of a misty graveyard where tombstones stand in endless lines. *Ashes to Ashes* (p.224) is woven with a yarn which gives the sample an ash-like feeling; it is soft yet heavy and has the colour of burned coal. *Sorrow* (p.255) is a twill weave with a serrated pattern that depicts the agonising, continuous pain caused by the loss of your loved one.

"At the funeral there were some unwanted guests."

↑ *The Mistress* is a sample made with a silk and a lace-like yarn. When weaving that particular sample, I had an image in my mind of a beautiful and seductive femme fatale who arrives at a funeral surprising all the guests.

*"Only the priest
and gravedigger
were present but
at least his soul
was saved."*

← *The Unknown Deceased* is a more
graphic swatch. The motif woven with
a dark wool yarn refers to the line of
simple gravestones without a name or
identity.

For Worse
Kaisa Kantokorpi

Until Death Do Us Part

*"He Was my North, my South,
my East and West,
My working week and my Sunday rest,
My noon, my midnight, my talk, my song;
I thought that love would last for ever:
I was wrong.*

W. H. Auden

↖ *Until Death Do Us Part* is the last
sentence of the wedding vow and also
the final piece of the funeral collection.
Its black and white stripes show the strict
line between life and death: one moment
we stood together and now we stand
apart.

"Too soon–Why?"

← *Too Soon* gives you a feeling of sorrow
and sadness. The piece is uneven and
ruffled, woven with thin metal wire weft
yarn spaced at uneven intervals.

See assignment p.122

TELLING TACTILE STORIES

*"We are, as species, addicted to story.
Even when the body goes to sleep, the mind
stays up all night, telling itself stories."*
– Jonathan Gottshall[134]

The softness and ultimate fragility of textile materials capture the ambiguity and vulnerability of the human experience. Their structure encases the tactility of emotions, lived moments and relationships, making them an ideal medium for storytelling. Homer's description of Penelope weaving her wedding blanket by day but then unravelling the same fabric each night–seeking thereby to halt time and neither mourning her husband Odysseus nor marrying a suitor in his absence–encapsulates this profoundly humane notion in a deeply tactile way.[135]

The pedagogical approach of this book uses the basic human need for storytelling[136] as a method of cognitive learning. The desire to tell stories invites us to engage with tactile, multilayered and rich world of textiles. Cloth is near to us all, we are literally and metaphorically wrapped within it. The act of weaving and composing cloth has the potential to reveal personal memories and emotions and encourage expression whilst acknowledging cultural and historical context and meanings. The tactile stories interwoven throughout this book illustrate the potential and scope of woven narratives to convey thinking and emotions.

→ *Memento* from the collection *Escape* (p.104–105) by Heta Vajavaara reflects on escaping into memories and nostalgia.

↘ Collection *Sorrow* by Heta Vajavaara presented on p.102–103.

Texere−Text

Weaving occupies a primary role among the metaphors that have been used to describe linguistic activity. Verbal weaving conveys tactility, materiality and structure, and the value of hand-made, the lexical memory of which has been maintained by Indo-European languages. The basic connection between the two realms is built into the language. The word *text* itself derives from the Latin *texere*, "to weave", commonly used in classic texts in the sense of "composing a written work". As any other "weaving", or written work, a poem can be a "fabric". Rediscovering the etymology of the words "text" and "texture", having the connotation of a "basic structure" as in "the texture of society" leads to the history of this archaic metaphor, reminding us that it designates well-constructed language or poetic creation.[137]

Sorrow / Escape
Woven fabrics studio course assignment 2015
by Heta Vajavaara

It is interesting how something as abstract as emotions can have such concrete effects on our daily lives. When I create something, I always start with a personality trait or an emotion and it gives me the direction for the design. I can then start to think what would that emotion smell, feel, look or sound like. My interest in textiles is very much linked to my interest in emotions. Every material and every touch creates different sensations in us. The tactile sense is, in my opinion, very underestimated, when it could be a way of communicating feelings for so many people.

For this collection of woven fabrics I started with an emotion that was at that time very familiar to me: sorrow. My grandmother, in my eyes the matriarch of the family and my lifetime role model of a strong, kind and independent woman, got into an accident and her health took a turn for the worse. It felt only natural to deal with the situation by translating my own and my family's feelings into textiles. Sorrow is usually depicted as something black, hard and desolate. I see it as something soft, grey and irregular. It is messy and erratic. At first, it takes control of your whole life, then constantly alters and diminishes, until slowly, day by day, it becomes part of your everyday life. These thoughts became guidelines for choosing the yarns and structures for the collection.

"Sorrow grows secretly and takes over every aspect of your life, it covers you like a heavy rug and secludes you from the rest of the world. Over time the isolation becomes the only safe and secure place you know."

"It's almost inexplicable, you feel all the emotions in the world at the same time and they become so mixed that you have no idea how you feel or how you should feel. You're not even sure if you feel anything."

Sorrow
The collection starts with a sample called *Sorrow Taking Over*. It is like a thick, heavy rug that covers you whole and secludes you from the rest of the world. *Mixed Feelings* is also heavy and soft, with a gradient of grey mohair yarns that are as mixed and messy as your feelings. The lumpy, uneven surface of *Irregular Emotions* (p.101) tells the same story: you feel all emotions possible at the same time but you have no idea how you should feel. You're not even sure if you feel anything. The next sample, *Volatile Feelings*, is already lighter. But it is still uneven, up-and-down, and as delicate and vulnerable as you. Slowly, you start to see little glimmers of hope.

Sorrow Taking Over

Sadness Within (left)
and *Grief* (right)

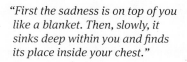

"First the sadness is on top of you like a blanket. Then, slowly, it sinks deep within you and finds its place inside your chest."

Sadness Within has the depth of sadness in the waffle weave, but shows hope in the glitter yarns woven inside the structure. *Emotional Waves* depicts how you can ride the wave and feel like you're on cloud nine, but suddenly hit rock bottom.

Mixed Feelings

↑ *Emotional Bursts* and *Grief*

Finally the samples start to be more even and flat. In *Emotional Bursts*, with its regular plain weave, ordinary everyday life goes steadily on. But the fil coupé tufts bursting from the plain surface illustrate how the sorrow you once felt can still sometimes take over. As the last step in experiencing sorrow, *Grief* seems at first to be a black plain-weave cloth: simple, familiar and steady. Yet, when you look closer, you can see small weft-faced rib-weave stripes here and there. You are living your normal life, but it's not like it was before: sorrow is an inseparable but benign part of it.

Volatile Feelings

ESCAPE

Sorrow / Escape
Woven fabrics studio course assignment 2015
by Heta Vajavaara

If one doesn't face the sorrow and try to live through it, the immediate and very human response is to escape it. As a counterpart for the *Sorrow* collection I started thinking about the ways in which people escape reality. One person might go shopping for something new, shiny and comforting. Another would live a life through movies, stories or in an imaginary world of their own. Yet another might try to bury themselves in nostalgia and memories of the good old days. All of this is escaping from reality into something better, imaginary and unreal. It is artificial and won't last, but brings momentary joy to a person in despair.

Escape
The *Escape* collection opens up with *Fantasy Fur*. It is a puffy, three-dimensional sample made from glimmering plastic yarns. Wearing the fur of a fantasy animal that does not even exist is the height of escapist luxury. *Memento* is wavy and see-through, delicate like a fleeting memory.

↓ *Fantasy Fur*

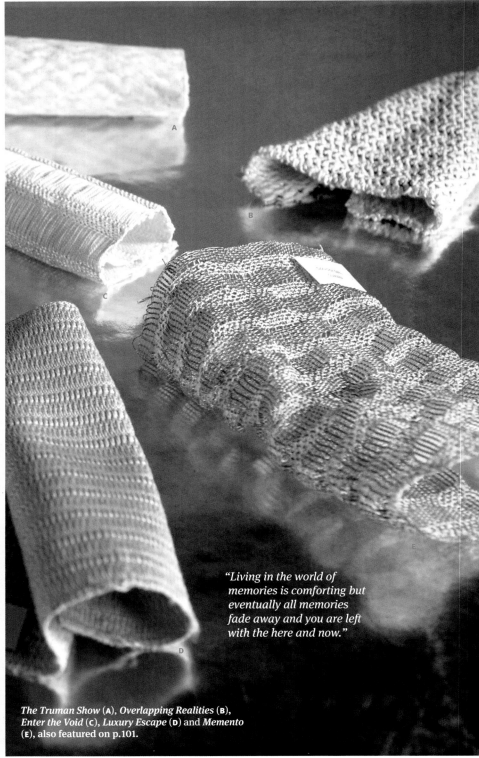

"Living in the world of memories is comforting but eventually all memories fade away and you are left with the here and now."

The Truman Show (A), *Overlapping Realities* (B), *Enter the Void* (C), *Luxury Escape* (D) and *Memento* (E), also featured on p.101.

glitter dimension
heta vajavaara

ornament mirage
heta vajavaara

← *Ornament Mirage*
and *Glitter Dimension*

Desperate for salvation from the dreariness of sorrow, you long for something different, exotic, out-of-the-ordinary, but as you seem to get there, it vanishes. It is not real. *Ornament Mirage* depicts this with an waffle weave with oriental glitter stripes that glimmer like a mirage on the horizon. *Glitter Dimension* is a luminous world, another dimension where everything is glitter and gold.

OVERLAPPING REALITIES

← *Overlapping Realities*

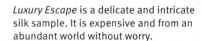

luxury escape
heta vajavaara

↑ *Luxury Escape*

Luxury Escape is a delicate and intricate silk sample. It is expensive and from an abundant world without worry.

The movie *The Truman Show* tells the story of a person living in a made-up world. A sample named after it is a plump white piqué weave with a cloud-like pattern. Escape is like another realm, another layer on top of this world. *Overlapping Realities* has these two layers: a black and brown striped warp and a wavy white weft pattern on top of it. Finally, *Enter the Void* is also about layers of different dimensions. With warp-faced rib weave stripes, it illustrates the everyday world slightly visible under the floating yarns of the imaginary better world.

ENTER THE VOID

worlds beyond this
who seek

← *Enter the Void*

See assignment p.122. *Life of Garments* by Heta Vajavaara pp.446–447

FLORIDA

Finland / Florida
Woven fabrics studio course assignment 2012
by Tiina Teräs

Memories can form a strong emotional background for the process of structural and material exploration. The two collections created by Tiina Teräs during the *Woven fabrics studio course* feature woven memories. (See assignment p.122)

I decided to base my collection on personal memories. The samples weave the story of my life while the tactile qualities of the textiles capture the subjectivity of memories. My two collections depict different periods in my life: one portrays my current home and adulthood in Finland, while the other reflects on my childhood in Florida. The contrast is intentionally large between the two collections. A hazy, subtropical atmosphere of blurred childhood memories found in faded photographs of family albums is set against sharp memories of the texture of newly fallen snow on the road in front of the bus stop. The two parts represent not only different stages of life, but also the difference between distant memories and the clarity of present experiences. The *Florida* collection is saturated by playfulness and imagination, whereas in *Finland*, pragmatism and minimalism are more dominant. It was a delightfully new experience to delve into memories as well as to analyze the present through weaving.

The following samples from these collections are presented in detail in Chapter 2: *Palmtree* (p.140), *At Sea* (p.180), *Reeds* (p.219), *Incipient Winter* (p.300).

↑ Collections *Florida*, with *Dress up* (p.185) on top, and *Finland*, with *Fresh Snow* (p.199) on top.

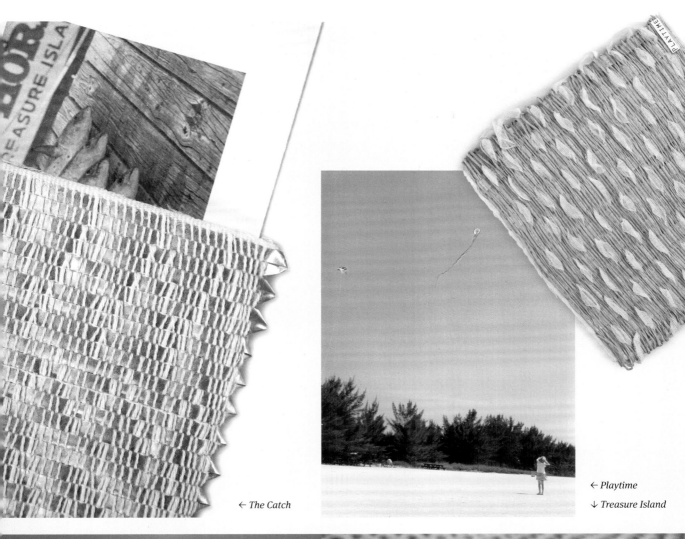

← The Catch

← Playtime

↓ Treasure Island

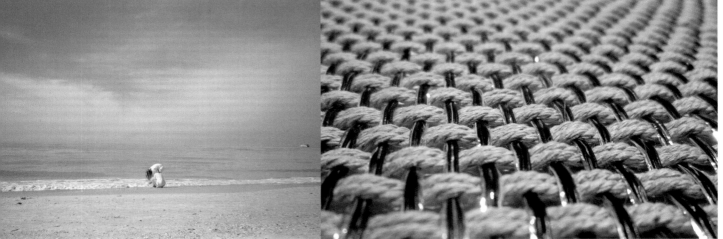

Finland / Florida
Woven fabrics studio course assignment 2012
by Tiina Teräs

↑ *Yesterday's Snow*
↓ *Winter Wind*

TALVI TUULI

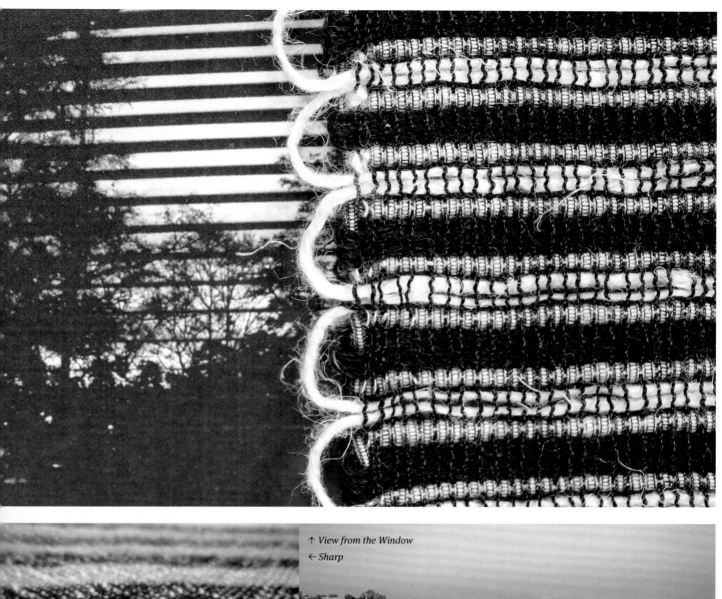

↑ *View from the Window*
← *Sharp*

Hefty
Woven fabrics studio course assignment 2013
by Salla-Maaria Syvänen

The given assignment (p.122) was to explore the contrast between two concepts. My structural exploration was guided by inspiring images on two mood boards that played an important role in the design process. I based my collections on the contrast between *Hefty* and *Light*. For me *Hefty* evoked connotations of something tiresome and dull. *Light*, on the other hand has a bubbly and loose look and feel. I began my design process by exploring eras and genres of art that would resonate with the themes. I decided to pair *Hefty* with 1960s' space age and combine *Light* with surrealism. To contrast the collections even further, I chose a monochrome palette: *Hefty* predominantly in white and *Light* in black. Through a process of visual research, I compiled a mood board for each collection and selected the yarn materials to match each story.

The mood board images and corresponding samples from the collection *Hefty* are presented on these pages.

I have a background in both design and textile engineering. As a designer, I find a process-orientated approach is helpful when compiling material for my mood boards. I usually tend to search for images that give me clear inspiration for the yarns, structure and pattern. Though I knew the theory of woven structures from my earlier studies, as a weaver I was a beginner. Advancing to the looms, I took a photo from my mood board, placed it next to me, selected suitable weft yarns, and tried to find a way to weave the structure or feeling I saw in the photo. I wove a swatch for both themes of the collection, *Light* and *Hefty*, with each loom. I added three adjectives to each sample to further explain their concept.

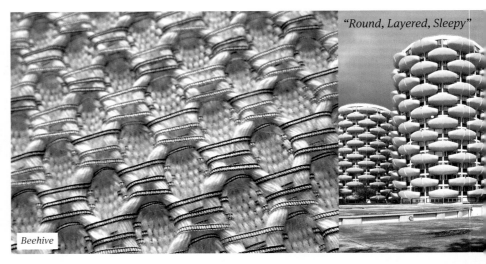
Beehive

"Round, Layered, Sleepy"

"Sensitive, Careless, Shallow"

Weal

Brisk

"Intense, Crispy, Eager"

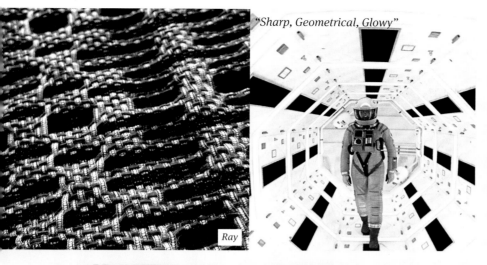

"Sharp, Geometrical, Glowy"

Ray

A good example of this method is *Beehive*. It is a direct interpretation of the photograph of the building *Les Choux de Créteil* that inspired it. The image pushed me out of my comfort zone and encouraged me to expand my knowledge of weaves.

The film *2001: A Space Odyssey*, by Stanley Kubrick (1968 MGM) was an important thematic and visual inspiration for the collection. The Astronaut scene inspired me to weave *Ray*, exploring the possibilities of grouped weft distortion and patterning with contrasting picks.

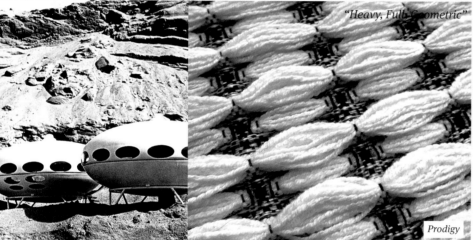

"Heavy, Full Geometric"

Prodigy

An image of the iconic *Futuro House*, conceived by architect Matti Suuronen (1968), triggered me to weave *Prodigy*. I modifed the weave in order to achieve white elliptical shapes on the black wool warp with pointed draft set up for waffle weave (p. 278).

I wove *Weal* on a warp with bands of black and ecru ends set-up on a computer-aided dobby loom with sixteen shafts. I had not envisioned any kind of striped or chequered twills as a part of the collection, so I decided to push my skills and the predefined balanced-twill structure to the hide stripes in the warp. I modified the lifting plan through re-arranging the pick sequence and wove the swatch using two alternating yarns, a very fluffy but thin mohair blend and a thick wool yarn. My approach resulted in a cork-screw-twill structure, which made the swatch appear wavy rather than stripy (see p. 267 for the cloth diagram).

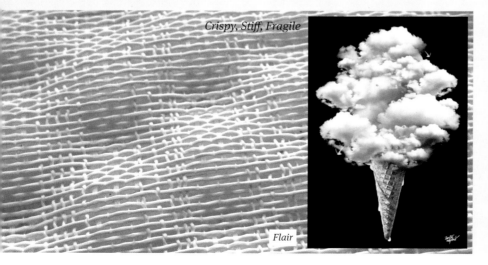

Crispy, Stiff, Fragile

Flair

During the weaving process I took a photo of each swatch and placed it next to the inspiration photo on my collection board. Viewing the collections as a whold, I noticed that the *Hefty* collection still was missing a airiness. I solved the problem by weaving an additional very light and see-through swatch *Flair* to round up the collection.

Escape (p. 183) from the collection *Hefty* and *Play* (p. 279) from the collection *Light* are presented in detail in Chapter 2.

VISUAL RESEARCH—
CREATING AND NARRATING A CONCEPT

Visual research creates the elements of a story. Designers see the method often as an intimate process, guided by their personal preferences and needs. Visual research helps designers collect thoughts and ideas. Having the concept, theme and narrative featured in a visual presentation of colours, forms, textures, materials, patterns and images helps the designer create meaning and navigate through the design process to a solid outcome. The visual research book or mood board is formed by collecting and curating a large amount of visual and tactile material, and often includes very detailed information. Visual research is vital when communicating the concept and explaining an upcoming or finished project. For this reason, it is important to realise which parts of the concept work are interesting from a personal point of view, and which add meaning and interest to others.

In the commercial design process an initial concept, often in the form of a design brief, marks the beginning. Visual research assists in outlining the premises of the design work and aids in communicating the deliverables. It helps others understand the work throughout the process. At the end of the design and development process, visual research material can be presented next to the final outcome and used to further elaborate the story. In a commercial context this method is often used in marketing the final collection or product.

A concept has an enduring element, which in a commercial, or a textile and fashion context, can be seen as the identity of the designer or brand: their vision, aesthetics and philosophy. Consecutive collections and their mood, inspiration, materials, and colours can be seen as storylines; changing and evolving elements. The individual pieces of a collection form the narrative. A concept is not solely shaped by the designer's own values and wishes, but it is also a product of its time and place, reflecting prevailing standards and ethics. Visual research is not static. The elements of a concept need to be flexible, and even the fundamental qualities need to be able to evolve and grow with the creator. Keeping the aspect of storytelling alive helps one look beyond the restrictions of an initial concept–or given brief–and to cope with it flexibly and on one's own terms.[138]

The mood board is part of a visual and tactile portfolio, a road map guiding the design and selection of fabrics throughout the collection design process. The images on these pages feature the initial visual material, the mood board and colour palette, next to samples of the final fabrics from a sheer and curtain fabric collection industrially produced using recycled polyester yarns. At a textile mill where the design and development process arches over multiple stages and involves a group of designers, from pattern designers to weave designers, print designers, technical designers, and colourists, setting a clear and comprehensible creative direction is essential. A well-defined overall concept specifying the function, weight and type of the final fabrics—with yarn types, weave structures and techniques to use— as well as a visual story with precisely defined colours and colourways— including exact directions for their use, relations and combinations—are essential tools when coordinating design work done by a team. Collection *Living Spaces* 2020, Vanelli (MS).

↑ Images of spreads from the diary which gathered the family stories. Left: story *Mojarra in Taganga*, right: story *The Golden Hour*

CREATING STORYWORLDS FOR STRUCTURAL DESIGNS

by Leonardo Hidalgo-Uribe

Storytelling is a sensitive and useful tool to ideate designs for woven fabrics. Similar to textiles, stories evoke emotions and sensations that surround us in both physical and intangible realms. Here, I want to focus on how designers are able to create stories and translate them into woven, structural designs by developing the notion of a storyworld.

Storyworlds are composed of interrelated pieces such as geographies, inhabitants, places, characters, amongst many others, that build the world of a story. Crafting a storyworld requires the creation of one or several atmospheres that permeate the characters and spaces where stories take place. The function of the atmosphere is to bring a sensorial and emotional direction to the storyworld, which determines the look and feel of the designs. During the process of worldbuilding, every colour, material, sketch, drawing, woven structure, yarn selection and

the final designs will contribute something to the feeling and expression of the story.

For my collection, *Geographies of Memory and Nostalgia*, I created a narrative based on my family by conducting a series of one-to-one interviews, collecting different stories about places and characters, which subsequently were transformed into written fiction. These stories are based on the memories of my mother, her parents and grandparents, who lived together in the same house for decades and travelled around Colombia during different periods of time.

The stories were gathered into the form of an atlas using the structure of a diary written in first person. The diary contains all the stories and illustrates their worlds by combining text with visual material. It also serves as an encyclopedia that permits the reader to navigate through diverse kinds of places, characters, atmospheres and memories of the storyworld, as well as to find inspiration to create various types

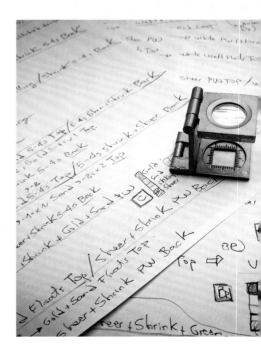

Visual research material and final industrially woven fabrics from *Geographies of Memory and Nostalgia*, Master's thesis collection 2020 by Leonardo Hidalgo-Uribe for Vanelli

of textile collections. I used collage as a method to juxtapose different media, such as photographs, drawing and writing, while constructing a narrative. This approach brings material, visual and emotional dimensions within the expression of the story, which is fundamental for later steps in the creation of structural designs.

The process of building the pages of the diary helped me to start sketching the material dimension of each story, and guided me to decide what kind of yarns and woven structures to explore in the later stages of design and prototyping. On each page, I used combinations of images and materials to experiment with colour, scales, yarn interactions, weights and drapes amongst many other elements that could provide the look and feel for each story. This way, the expression of the storyworld gradually transforms a narrative into surfaces, yarns and weave structure selections.

↑ From left to right fabrics *Delirium, Crescendo, Andante* and *Lento* from the story *The Golden Hour*

↑ From left to right, the fabrics *Affable, Incessant, Meticulous* and *Timid* from the story *The Meditation of My Father*

↑ From left to right, the fabrics *Daybreak, Ripples, Mojarra* and *Radiant* from the story *Mojarra in Taganga*

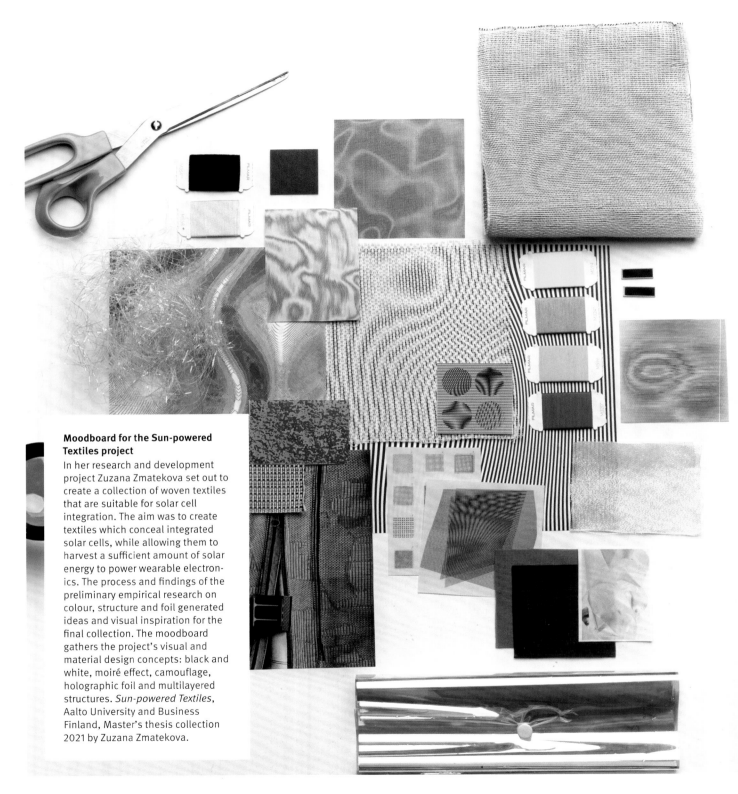

Moodboard for the Sun-powered Textiles project

In her research and development project Zuzana Zmatekova set out to create a collection of woven textiles that are suitable for solar cell integration. The aim was to create textiles which conceal integrated solar cells, while allowing them to harvest a sufficient amount of solar energy to power wearable electronics. The process and findings of the preliminary empirical research on colour, structure and foil generated ideas and visual inspiration for the final collection. The moodboard gathers the project's visual and material design concepts: black and white, moiré effect, camouflage, holographic foil and multilayered structures. *Sun-powered Textiles*, Aalto University and Business Finland, Master's thesis collection 2021 by Zuzana Zmatekova.

Hubris (and Defiance), Bachelors' thesis collection 2019 by Nora Bremer. Creation was guided by the *Textile collection design course* assignment (p.435).

HUBRIS (AND DEFIANCE) — A PROCESS OF VISUAL RESEARCH

by Nora Bremer

The process of creating a comprehensive visual world for a collection of textiles is always exciting for me. It is a process of contrasts, which keeps the work dynamic and interesting. There has to be balance between active and passive working, between esoteric and familiar, between serious and light-hearted. The process of visual research I have developed for myself is one fit for my own personality—observant and easily distracted. I allow myself to go down rabbit holes and dwell on research for extended periods of time, one hyper-fixation leading to another. This immersion requires time and a constant ability to be interested in one's surroundings.

I usually have an immaterial theme that I want to build the visual world around before I start thinking of how it can manifest in the form of colours, textures and structures. My collection *Hubris (and Defiance)* had its name before it had its visual depiction. An abstract idea of confidence, identity and defiance had been brewing in my mind for a while and was waiting for the right visual outlet. In my process I call this stage passive working and it can go on for months or years, slowly gaining enough traction before finally getting an outlet. Historical references to Greek mythology, Victorian dandies and stories of heroes all swirled in my mind at this stage as the visual and narrative material evolved. This process requires space to breathe and reflect.

The passive working allowed me to uncover unexpected influences, which lead to active research of archives of 1970s commercial menswear. There was a wealth of visual material to draw from, and most importantly, it sparked my enthusiasm and ignited the engine that drives the active work of browsing, printing, cutting, drawing, painting and selecting.

I always endeavour to find a counterpoint to my main visual imagery, something from another world, to make the whole concept more unique and to give more integrity to the final outcome. Having more than one source is an opportunity for more contrasts. I enjoyed the idea of having a fun and colourful, whimsical main theme of glossy 70s overconfident male models as my main source of inspiration. However, I needed something else to add credibility: something more traditional and more anchored that would focus on method. For this I usually look to textile-related crafts, i.e. techniques that have existed for thousands of years and bear a great amount cultural importance. In this case I researched embroidery techniques from around the world. Having this element as a part of my visual research gave it a sensory dimension. It also brought textile materials into a book of images, paintings and paper cut outs, tying together the visual research with the textile collection.

Part of the charm of a finished project is that its story will inspire following collections. The themes might change and the focus shift, but experience and research from past projects will always influence the next.

This chapter serves as a guide to all readers, both within and outside of the classroom setting, who want to work at expanding their knowledge and imagination of the unlimited potentials of woven structures, yarns, and textures.

The sample warps provide inspiration for warp set-ups. Some require a double-beam loom. The ideas can be adapted broadly to other yarn types as well. An existing warp might be utilised for a tie-up inspired by the sample warps. There are no boundaries, the ideas in this chapter can be explored by various means and materials.

See p.80 for more information on the studio practices and the type of looms used by students to create the presented samples.

2. To the Looms – Weaving and Experimenting

Weaving is a way of three-dimensional modelling through constructive exploration of structures and materials. It is a practice-led design process where thinking takes place through hands-on making. The beauty of creating textiles lies in the expressive potential of their tactile, visual, and even auditory messages, as well as their associations with personal and shared historical and cultural connotations.

This chapter is designed to act as a guide to the experimental design process of producing textiles on ready-made sample warps. Building on the grounding provided in Chapter 1, it offers various design ideas to explore and provides the relevant information on weave structures and their variations, as well as the fibres and yarns used. The woven samples presented with each warp demonstrate the endless possibilities of a single warp set-up, and can be used as inspirations to create even more variations. The fabric sample descriptions point to important lessons on the path of comprehending the interplay between materials and structures.

The resulting textiles can offer ideas for applications in fashion, interiors, architecture, as well as other fields. Nevertheless, at this stage, beyond designing fabrics for specific purposes, the goal of this practice-based exploration process is to serve as a guide to *textile thinking* – understanding how the interplay between materials and structures affects the properties of the resulting construction and recognising the enormous potential of fabrics for storytelling, evoking emotions, and communicating meanings and ideas.

This chapter introduces the sample warps, demonstrates designing on shaft looms, and goes on to present the process of combining weaves and designing patterns. The surface of a woven fabric always has a texture, which can be observed as a small-scale pattern. However, a woven fabric is generally considered patterned, as the colour-and-weave effect or the combination of weaves form a more distinctive pattern design on the surface. The path from textures to patterns is further elaborated upon in the section about combining weaves and moving to jacquard design. The chapter concludes by discussing colour in woven fabrics.

← Student using weave design software to draft structures at a computer-assisted dobby loom.

The **woven samples** accompanying each warp showcase the explorative practice-led design process of students. The desire to explore stories in their work motivated students to research the interplay of materials and structures, and to push the creative boundaries offered by each warp to its limits. Each woven sample is part of a collection created by the student, and is accompanied by both the name of the fabric and the name of the collection it belongs to. The **course assignment** that inspired these textiles can be found on p.122.

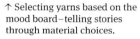

↑ Selecting yarns based on the mood board – telling stories through material choices.

↗ Examining the collection in the final critique.

Understanding **woven structures** and their close interrelation to the incorporated **materials**, **fibres** and **yarns**, is relevant both within and outside of the textile field. The sample warps presented in this chapter introduce a diverse range of textile fibres and yarn types. The warps, made in advance, are designed to guide the students towards a broad range of experimentations with materials and structures and to help them understand textile practices as well as the basics of constructed textile technology. The warp yarns have been selected and tested to be strong enough to undergo uneven tensioning and other problems that inexperienced weavers might face, thus avoiding potential demotivating difficulties caused by complications such as breakage and entanglement of warp yarns. In the weft direction more challenging material choices, fibres and yarn types can be integrated and experimented with.

The weave structure plays an essential role in the finished fabric's appearance and its other properties including stability, strength, and weakness. Fabrics that can be woven on the warps presented in this chapter include all three basic weave structures, namely plain weave, twill, and satin, as well as derivative weaves and combination weaves. This provides a solid foundation for novice weavers to learn about the properties of woven constructions by weaving different variations of the structures and exploring the effects of different yarn materials.

As described in Chapter 1. *Looms and Other Tools* (p.51), control of the **warp tension** is an imperative element in the practice of weaving. Furthermore, the effect of tension is dependent on the properties of the yarn. Experiments with different warp tensions and yarn materials lead to recognition of the potential of this substantial factor as a textural design element affecting the appearance of a woven fabric. To guide this process further, some sample warps consist of two differing warp yarns. These warps are set on double-beam looms and enable more control in altering the tension of specific sets of warp yarns during weaving.

Colour, as a familiar design element in woven structures, often overshadows other forms of expression and storytelling. Colouration of woven fabrics requires experience as the final appearance is greatly dependent on the interwoven mixing of warp and weft, used structures, yarn sett, and yarn type. Hence, basic knowledge of techniques, materials, and structures is essential to tackle this topic.

While weaving a path to the world of constructed textile design, a restricted scheme of black, white and unbleached neutral colours shifts the focus from colour to other design elements–to explore the interplay of an array of different yarn materials and weave structures and their expressive and performative qualities. This neutral colour palette still provides enough colour contrast to explore the colour effects within different weave structures and materials. The use of a more versatile and bolder colour palette is introduced after a basic understanding of the concepts behind woven fabric design have been established (p.327).

A list of supplementary literature on weave structures, technical information on hand weaving, and different methods of planning the warp and setting up the loom is included at the end of this book.

Sample warps

The method of **studio teaching** introduced in this book requires an array of versatile warp set-ups to be prepared in advance by the instructors (p.80). As discussed on p.74 working with standard warps in manufacturing is a common practice within the textile industry. Therefore learning to work creatively on prearranged warp set-ups is an asset to the students, and in fact these restrictions facilitate creative problem-solving and push the boundaries of what is possible. The warp serves as a blank canvas that guides the process of thinking through weaving. If setting up the warps is a preferred element of the first course, one of the sample warps could be collectively set up by the study group.

The warps serve as a guide to understanding how the interplay between materials and structures affects the properties of the resulting fabric. There is no suggested order in which the sample warps should be woven. The students are encouraged to start their weaving explorations on a warp set-up that they find inspiring or challenging, or as often happens in a class setting, on a warp that is available at the moment. In order to highlight this concept further, the warps presented in this chapter are named according to the interplay of yarns and weaves. In this book, the order in which the sample warps–and with them, learning content–are presented, follows a sequence of factors related to weave structures, fibres, and yarns.

Alongside weaving and exploring on the looms, students are introduced to theoretical content on weaves and taught to create structural drafts on conventional weave design software. By using this same software on the computer-assisted dobby looms, students are familiarised with the lifting plan and digital loom control.

Students first encounter the world of woven textiles by weaving on a loom, which is followed by short theory lectures. Importantly, theory content is expanded through practice. Students take notes as they weave and draft the structures and other technical information to form a product card which accompanies each sample.

See pp.80–82 for more information on studio teaching.

A compiled list of the ten sample warps and an example of the warp card can be found in the Appendix pp.474–476.

Assignment: Woven fabrics studio course

Preliminary Assignment

A.

past – present,
traditional – contemporary,
countryside – city,
familiar – strange,
everyday – celebrations,
inside – outside,
surface – depth,
chaos – order,
my native country (city) – my current
environment

What thoughts do these contrasting word pairs evoke in you? What is your relationship with identity and traditions, everyday life, celebrations and ceremonies, memories, the past – or modern cities? What about familiar materials and structures, or strange ideas and environments?

Choose a word pair and make two contrasting visual research boards. You can also create your own combination of contrasting topics. The possibilities of variations are endless.

The two mood boards are best done as a collage, by cutting and pasting images and other visual materials. Study the yarn materials in the weaving studio and include some in your presentation. Keep your presentation tactile, it should not be presented in a digital format. The two mood boards should showcase the two different facets of your visual research.

B. If you are currently working on visual research for your fashion collection or other design or artistic project and want to continue with the same concept, one of the mood boards can show your concept or a facet of it. The other mood board should show a different facet or a completely new, contrasting angle of your concept.

See *Weaving Human Stories* (pp.87–117) for inspiration and guidance on visual research and weaving tactile stories.

Course Assignment

Expand the story of your two mood board concepts through weaving on each of the 10 sample warps – exploring with materials and structures. Start by selecting the yarns that you find suitable to portray each of your stories. Use only yarns in natural, unbleached colours and other neutrals: beiges, black, white and grey yarns.

Design two collections of woven fabrics, each including 8–10 samples, based on your two contrasting concepts. Using the provided weave design software, make a structural draft for each sample and design a **product card** for each sample. Collect the samples and the product cards in two boxes according to their collection. Archiving your samples and the related reference materials methodically will help you to refer back to them later, maybe in order to reproduce the samples as full width fabrics, or for them to serve as a starting point for new explorations.

Research and design process in the woven fabrics studio

Weave two to three samples per loom. Aim to finish a sample, try not to get stuck on small test pieces. You can evaluate the texture better when you have a large enough sample. Pay attention to the pick density as you weave and try to keep the edges of your samples as neat as possible. The width of the sample warps on the looms is 20 cm. The shape of the final woven samples should be a square. You will notice that depending on the warp yarns, weft yarns, and applied structures the actual metric sample size will change when the sample is removed and is no longer under the loom tension. Document these findings as well as other discoveries that come to your mind during your weaving process.

Switch to different looms, do not get stuck on one loom either. Learn from your peers. Follow the processes of your colleagues and share your findings.

After you have woven all your swatches and the fabrics are taken down from the looms, collaborate with the other students to glue, cut and separate the individual samples. Finish the samples by neatly brushing the edges with diluted white wood glue and then by cutting the warp ends to finalise the square sample. Fabrics with slippery synthetic yarns might need a different type of glue. Then make the final selection of eight to ten samples for each collection.

← Gluing and cutting the samples

↑ Examining the product card and sample in the final critique

The content of the product cards

- The title of your sample and the name of the collection it belongs to.
- A structural draft of one repeat, created on weave design software, including the treadling, threading, and tie-up as well as the pick material repeat. Do not copy this from the warp information sheets as this draft needs to specify your particular sample. The structure should be in its reduced form, with the number of shafts reduced to the minimal count necessary to weave the sample.
- A cloth diagram in which the repeating of the weave structure or pattern can be seen (without the treadling, threading, and tie-up).
- The name of the weave or combination of the structures used in the sample.
- Material information. This should include the composition of the material e.g. 100% CO, pick density, and warp yarn sett.
- A photo of the swatch. Photograph your sample in a way that best fits your storyline.
- A short text about every swatch. The text can be about variety of subjects such as technical findings, a memory, a poem. However it should be fitting to your original concept and backup your story. Whichever text style you decide upon, your choice should be coherent throughout both collections and samples.
- You can also include images of your visual research and other references, as well as samples of the warp and weft yarns utilised in your sample.

The course set-up and the weaving studio as a space for learning is discussed on pp.80–82.

Drafting weave structures

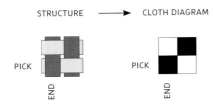

STRUCTURE → CLOTH DIAGRAM

PICK

END

The cloth diagram illustrates the structure of the woven fabric. In this **binary notation** system for weaves, the warp yarns are marked with black and the weft yarns white.

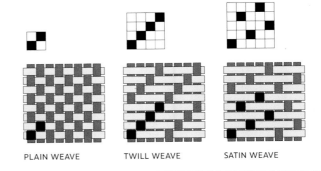

PLAIN WEAVE   TWILL WEAVE   SATIN WEAVE

The elements of a structural draft include the cloth diagram, the threading (drawing-in) and treadling sequences and the tie-up.

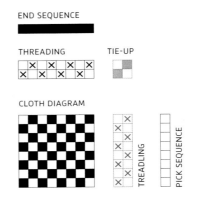

END SEQUENCE

THREADING   TIE-UP

CLOTH DIAGRAM

TREADLING

PICK SEQUENCE

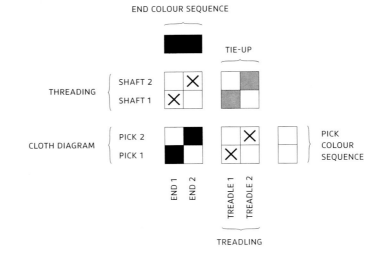

END COLOUR SEQUENCE

TIE-UP

THREADING { SHAFT 2 / SHAFT 1 }

CLOTH DIAGRAM { PICK 2 / PICK 1 }

PICK COLOUR SEQUENCE

END 1 END 2

TREADLE 1 TREADLE 2

TREADLING

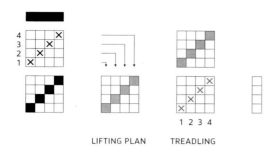

4
3
2
1

LIFTING PLAN   TREADLING

1 2 3 4

Loom type specific drafting of warp presentations employed in this chapter are shown in this example diagram, which presents a four shaft twill 1:3. To accommodate for different loom types, in this book, the lifting plan that is used in **table looms, dobby looms**, and **computer-assisted dobby looms** is included and illustrated next to the treadling and tie up information required for **treadle looms**. The provided structural drafts are illustrated with colour codes and are marked out in ways that help understanding the content of each particular section.

■ TAPE YARN   ■ SPIRAL YARN

□ WO/PA (LOOP YARN)
□ PES/CO/PU (FLAT CHENILLE YARN)

■
CO

Draft information next to the woven samples represents the details relevant to the learning content.

The example draft presented here is retrieved from the sample *Crosswalk*. Understanding the actual colour effects in a fabric through examining the structural draft can be challenging. More details about the sample and an image showing the interlacement of yarns and the actual colour effect in the fabric can be found on p.143.

× 10

× 2

□ CO (WHITE)
□ CO (BLACK)
□ CO (GROUND)

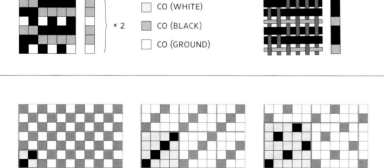

PLAIN WEAVE   TWILL WEAVE 1:3   5-END SATIN WEAVE

A repeat is an entire complete pattern that is repeated in a fabric structure, print, embroidery or lace. In a weave, it refers to the number of yarns necessary to make each repeated pattern.[1] As an example, the repeat size of a plain weave is two ends and two picks.

Yarns

Yarn classification

Yarn is a continuous strand of staple fibres, filaments, or materials in a form that can be used to make fabric.[2] As described on pp.27–28 yarns are classified into **spun yarns** and **filament yarns**. Spun yarns are made from staple fibres. Filament yarns are made from continuous filaments. **Stretch yarns** can be produced through texturizing thermoplastic continuous-filament yarns. **Fancy yarns,** also referred to as **novelty yarns**, are often a combination of both main categories, spun and filament yarns.[3]

Yarn structure

The major aspects of the yarn structure include its visual appearance and its internal layer. The yarn structure depends mainly upon the properties of the **raw materials**, **spinning process**, and **twisting levels**. The yarn structure influences the properties of the yarn such as its handle, strength, insulation capacity, and wearing comfort among others. By changing the parameters in the yarn-making process, it is possible to achieve considerable variations in yarn made of a particular fibre. The yarn structure can be altered so that the unwanted fibre properties are diminished while preferred properties are strengthened or integrated within the fibre.

Spun and **filament yarns** are either **single** or **ply yarns**. Single yarns are the result of twisting the fibres into a single yarn (A). The properties of single-spun yarns are greatly influenced by their twisting levels. A **low-twist**, **soft-spun** yarn is weaker and less elastic and has a fuzzier and softer hand. In contrast, a **high-twist**, **hard-spun** yarn is more compact, stronger, harder, more elastic, and smoother in texture, but generally provides less insulating properties. Yarns can also be **over-twisted**, or crêpe-twisted to add more elasticity, drape, and resiliency.

Plying yarns to **multiple-ply yarns** increases strength, uniformity, and elasticity in the yarn. Similar to single yarn, the construction and **direction of twists** of a plied yarn has a

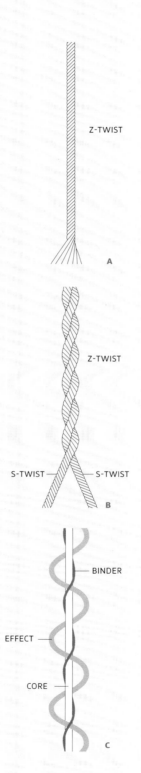

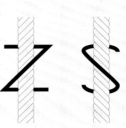

notable effect on its textural appearance and performance, and hence the resulting fabric. A **two-ply yarn** with two **S-twist** yarns plied together in **Z** direction with a balanced number of turns per centimetre creates a smooth and lustrous **balanced yarn** (B). In contrast, using yarns made of singles in the same direction as they were spun, such as S singles into S two-ply yarn, can be used to create puckering effects in fabrics. Combining S-twist and Z-twist yarns in a woven fabric is discussed on p.415.

Core-spun yarns are generally produced to strengthen or add elasticity in natural fibre combinations. They are **composite yarns** (p.159), in which one type of fibre in the centre of the yarn, usually a filament, is wrapped with soft staple fibres.

Fancy yarns, or novelty yarns mostly consist of three parts, namely the core, the effect ply, and the binder (C). Various types of novelty yarns are described on pp.156–159.

Cord yarns or **cable yarns** are strong yarns of two or more plies that are twisted together.

The yarn size or yarn count is a number that indicates the **yarn fineness**. It describes the relation of the yarn's mass to its unit length. Understanding yarn count is essential in communication with yarn spinners and fabric manufacturers and enables evaluation of the hand, weight, and fineness of the fabric that can be produced. There are international and industry-specific variations in the use of different yarn counts in the textile industry. The units differ between filament yarns (p.155) and spun yarns (p.132), as well as between the basic natural fibres. Yarn count cards and online converter applications can be used to assist the calculation of conversions between the different systems.[4]

The **Tex system** is an international standard used for both spun yarns and filament yarns. It is a **fixed length, direct numbering system** with which the mass per unit length, the linear density of the yarn, is measured. The coarser the yarn, the bigger the number. The unit indicates the weight in grams of 1000 metres of fibre or yarn.

Spun yarns use a **fixed weight system**, which is an **indirect numbering system** resulting in finer yarns having a higher yarn count. The **Metric Count (Nm)** is used for wool yarns and blends. The unit describes the number of kilometres of the yarn per kilogram. The **English Cotton Count (Ne)** is used for cotton yarns and refers to the number of 840 yard lengths in one pound. **Linen Count (Nl)** enumerates the number of 300 yard lengths in one pound and is used for flax yarns.

For **continuous-filament yarns** a **fixed length system** is used. The **Denier (den)** yarn count unit specifies the weight in grams of 9000m yarn.

Furthermore, the figure following the yarn count number indicates the number of single yarns in a ply yarn. The yarn size in the metric count is expressed in the reverse. As an example, the cotton seine twine warp yarn presented in the following section is marked with Ne 12/18. Here, the **Ne** refers to the **cotton count**. The first number, 12, stands for the **yarn count of the singles**. The second number, 18, indicates the **ply**, referring to the number of strands twisted together to form the yarn. The tex number of the same yarn is tex 50 × 6 × 3. The first number, 50, stands for the tex count of the singles, the second number, 6, indicates the ply number of each of the 3 plies twisted together to form the twine.

In this book the **tex standard** is marked next to the industry-specific yarn numbering system commonly used in the yarn-production and weaving industry.

It is recommendable to stock as many different yarns as possible for the weaving experiments. The restrictions in use of colour, as described in the assignment (p.122), shift the focus to experimenting with a wide variety of different fibres, yarn types and counts. The warp yarns recommended in this chapter can easily be varied.

Refer to p.132 for spun yarns, p.155 for filament yarns and pp.156–159 for fancy yarns. For information on Textile fibres refer to *Fibres—the Building Blocks* p.27.

Cotton Twine Warp

PLAIN WEAVE
BASKET WEAVE
UNBALANCED PLAIN WEAVE
WEFT-FACED RIB WEAVE
COMBINING WEAVES
CRÊPE WEAVE
EXTRA-WEFT PATTERNING
AND KNOTTED PILES

FIBRE AND YARN INFO:
COTTON
SPUN YARNS

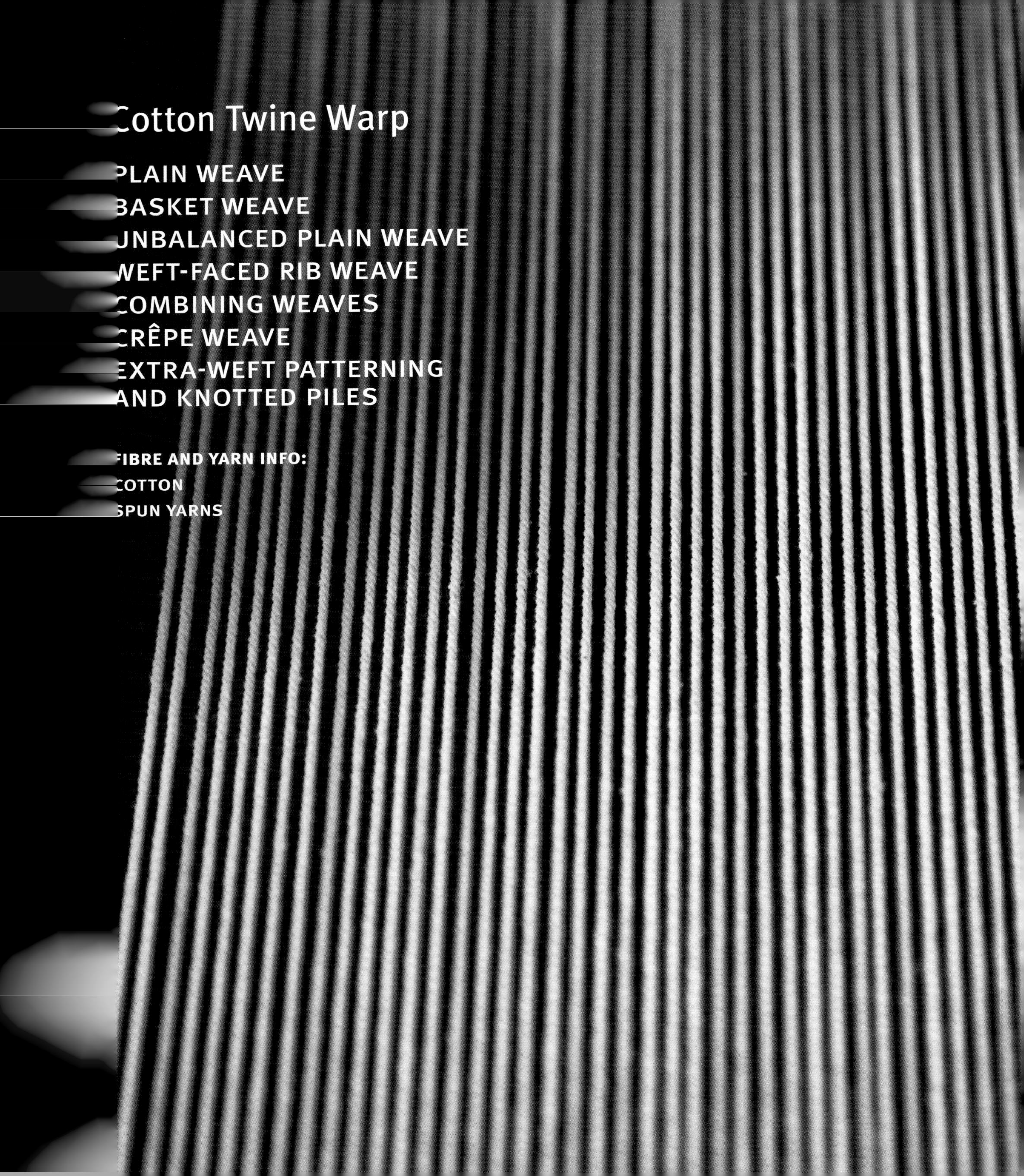

2.1 Simple, Bold and Beautiful

The warp of unbleached cotton seine twine with a low **yarn sett**–referring to the number of **ends per centimetre** or **warp density**–encourages weavers to probe **plain weave** and its **derivative structures**. The set-up of the sample warp is a **straight draft** on six shafts. In other words, the warp ends are threaded onto each shaft in a straight sequence, starting from the first shaft and ending in the sixth shaft. The **threading plan**, or **drawing-in draft**, on six shafts enables the **tie-up**, or **lifting plan**, to accommodate further modifications in addition to the simple over one under one plain weave, which only requires two shafts. This includes a three-to-three as well as two-to-four variant, resulting in a number of design options with derivative structures, namely **basket weave** and **weft-faced rib weave**, as well as additional combinations of these.

As demonstrated by the examples woven on this warp, both the **yarn properties** and the **pick density**, density of the weft yarns, have an essential influence on the appearance of the final fabric. Hence, a wide variety of weft yarns with contrasting colours, different fibres and **yarn counts**, and varying twists and textures should be explored.

Cotton / CO is a cellulose fibre separated from the seed of the plant. It is the most popular natural fibre, production accounting for around 90% of all natural fibres. Its matte appearance and comfortable skin contact as well as its easy care, moderate cost, good durability, and high affinity for dyes make it ideal for clothing, interiors, and many other industrial products. Cotton feels comfortable due to its soft hand, high moisture absorbency, and good heat conductivity. On the other hand, cotton products feel wet and uncomfortable in cool and wet conditions. Cotton has poor elastic recovery and consequently stays elongated in areas of stress. It becomes stronger when wet, so it is an ideal fibre for goods that need to be washed regularly or for products requiring high durability in humid conditions. Cotton fabrics shrink, especially when washed in hot water. The fibre is flammable and burns rapidly. Many of the fibres' properties can be manipulated by variations in yarn type and size as well as fabric construction and finishes. Therefore, fabrics produced from cotton range from soft and sheer batiste to sturdy, strong denim. Due to its characteristics and high consumer demand, cotton is popular in blends. Often man-made fibres are engineered to imitate it.[5] Consumers generally view cotton, a natural fibre, as sustainable. However, although cotton is a renewable resource, its farming and production bear significant environmental impacts (p.37).

General information on plant fibres can be found on p.28. History of cotton is discussed on p.54 and p.70.

Warp yarn:
Cotton seine twine is a strong unbleached spun cord yarn made of several plies of cotton tightly twisted together. This type of yarn has traditionally been utilised as warp to weave rugs and tapestry and in fishing to make seine nets. Due to its high twist and limited stretch, it is very strong and can withstand high tension.

A **straight draft**
is the basis for all
threading plans and
can be used with any
number of shafts.
The warp ends are
threaded onto each
shaft in a straight
sequence, starting
from the first shaft
and ending in the
last shaft, such as
the straight draft over
four shafts presented
above.

With an equal yarn sett, the warp and weft can form a classical **balanced plain weave** cloth (A). An **unbalanced plain weave**, in which the density of the picks is significantly higher than the density of the ends, is achieved using the same over one under one construction by adjusting the tension of the warp to higher tension and weaving with weft yarns that are finer or much looser and softer than the warp ends. The result is a **weft-faced rib weave**, where the warp is completely covered by the weft, forming a **vertical rib structure**. Moreover, by taking advantage of the tie-up on six shafts, a rib weave can also be achieved by using picks with similar count to the ends and **floating** the pick over and under two or more warp ends (C, D). The **warp-faced**, **horizontal rib** weave is introduced in the section *End and End Fancy* (p.153).

The rib weave offers a fascinating playground for generating variations through **pick colour sequence**. Weaving with only one weft yarn in both directions creates a weft-faced rib in a solid colour (C, D). However, vertical stripes appear on the face of the fabric by alternately weaving with two weft yarns of contrasting colours or materials (E). In an **irregular rib weave**, due to the unequal length of floats of the two contrasting picks, the fabric **face and reverse side** are dissimilar (D, E). By changing the pick colour sequence while weaving or by implementing blocks or stripes of contrasting yarns, exciting number of design options can be achieved, ranging from a chess-board check to other variations attainable on the given grid.

A check pattern can also be achieved using the **basket weave** and weaving it with a pick in a contrasting colour. Basket weave is a **balanced weave** similar to plain weave, but uses two or more yarns as one unit instead of one yarn. This sample warp introduces a variation with three yarns in one unit (B).

In addition to patterning through experimentation with different colours and yarns, a woven fabric can be patterned by interchanging the different structures. Combining and mixing of the basic structures in this sample warp while alternating the yarn colour or yarn material sequence of the pick amounts to endless variety of fabric designs and textures.

An example of combining two structures is the combination of rib weave and plain weave (F). Plain weave can be used as a stabilising **internal structure** supporting a fabric with long yarn floats on the surface. The weft yarns used for the supporting structure may be of finer quality compared to the yarns used for the floats on the face and back of the fabric. Integrating a firm structural armature is essential for the stability of the cloth and to control the seam slippage of lightweight fabrics with long floats or slippery yarns, as well as interior fabrics such as rugs and upholstery fabrics, where stability and rigid form fastness is needed. When the sample is removed from the loom and the warp tension is released, the reliable plain weave keeps the textile in form and prevents the decorative weft floats on the surface of the textile from shifting and clumping together. Experimenting with the use of a plain weave ground pick in combination with a decorative float pick on this basic warp helps pave the path to learning more complex weaves including jacquards, in which multiple weft systems are common.

A **float** is a pick or end which does not interlace with the next adjacent yarn, thus passing over two or more yarns. A **warp float** is a result of an end passing over two or more picks, whereas a **weft float** is created by the pick passing over two or more ends.

Cotton twine warp

Warp yarn: Cotton twine, Ne 12/18 (tex 50 × 6 × 3) | 100% CO
Yarn sett: 3 ends per cm
Reed: 30:1
Straight draft on six shafts

Catch yarns, left unthreaded, are recommended in the selvedges

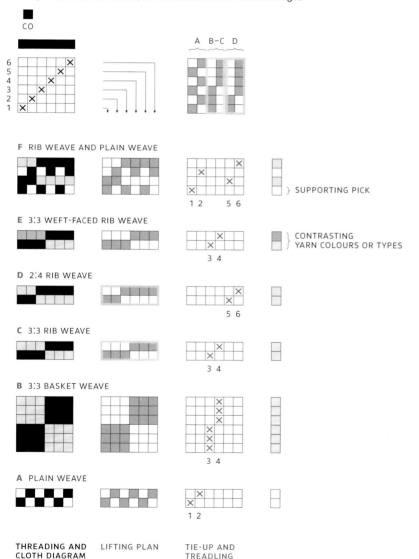

F RIB WEAVE AND PLAIN WEAVE

} SUPPORTING PICK

1 2   5 6

E 3:3 WEFT-FACED RIB WEAVE

} CONTRASTING
} YARN COLOURS OR TYPES

3 4

D 2:4 RIB WEAVE

5 6

C 3:3 RIB WEAVE

3 4

B 3:3 BASKET WEAVE

3 4

A PLAIN WEAVE

1 2

THREADING AND   LIFTING PLAN   TIE-UP AND
CLOTH DIAGRAM   TREADLING

Fabric hand is a term for the properties of a fabric which can be defined by touching with hands: texture, drapability, stretch, wrinkle resistance. The tactile sensation—the way that the fabric feels—can be used to assess the fabric quality and its suitability for a specific end use. Fabric hand can be evaluated by mechanical or electronic devices and by humans using psychophysical or psychological techniques.[6]

Body and drape, or fall of a fabric, is linked to the flexibility of its weave as well as its fibres, yarns, and finishing. Designing woven fabrics for fashion and home furnishings is a balancing act between the two contrasting qualities of **body and drape**. In order to find the correct balance of body versus drape, the end use of the fabric needs to be taken into consideration. To improve the drape, adjustments in the weave structure, as well as modifications in the pick density, yarn size and yarn type might be necessary. Rib structure in the horizontal direction generally improves the body of the fabric, while the drape is improved in the vertical rib structure. Looser weaves with fewer intersections of warp and weft yarns, such as satin and twill, have improved drape properties. The draping properties can further be improved through finishes.

Fabric drape plays an important role in fabrics for both fashion and interior use. Sheer curtains, often woven on light and fine filament yarn warps on double width (three metres and over) weaving machines are a good example. Variations in design, texture, and colouring are achieved by using weft yarns in different fibres, counts, and qualities. Since drape is generally better in the direction of the heavier yarn set, these sheers are sewn to curtains with the width forming the drape.

Spun yarns

Wool and cotton along with all other natural fibres except silk are **staple fibres**, which through the process of **spinning** are fashioned into **spun yarns**, also called **staple yarns**. In comparison to yarns made of continuous filaments, spun yarns generally have a fuzzy and dull surface and a slightly irregular look. This is due to their internal structures with fewer parallel fibres, protruding fibre ends, and variations in the number of fibres along the yarn. Man-made continuous filaments can be crimped and cut to staple fibres to create spun yarns that imitate a natural-fibre look.

Spun yarn manufacturing methods are used to form yarns from natural or staple fibres.

In order to achieve finer yarns and add uniformity, smoothness, shine, and strength to the yarn, the staple fibres are combed to remove short fibres and to make the staple fibres more parallel. The resulting **worsted yarns** and **combed yarns** are usually produced from long fibres with medium or higher twist. Worsted yarns refer to wool or wool blends whereas combed yarns describe cotton and cotton blends. Worsted wool is soft and stretchy and combed cotton smooth and shiny. The extra process of combing and carding adds cost to both the yarns and the resulting fabrics.

Yarns made from shorter staples that have not undergone the combing procedure are referred to as **woollen yarns** for wool or wool blends, and **carded yarns** for cotton and cotton blends. Compared to the medium to high twist combed yarns, carded and woollen yarns are produced with medium to low twist and are bulkier, less regular in size, and fuzzier with protruding fibre ends. These yarns are generally more sensitive to abrasion and have an increased pilling tendency.[7]

Wool yarns: woollen and worsted

woollen wool yarn

worsted wool yarn

Cotton yarns: carded and combed

carded cotton yarn

combed cotton yarn

→ This image demonstrates the difference between a woollen yarn with shorter fibres (left) that has not received the additional combing process, and a combed yarn made of longer staple fibres (right).

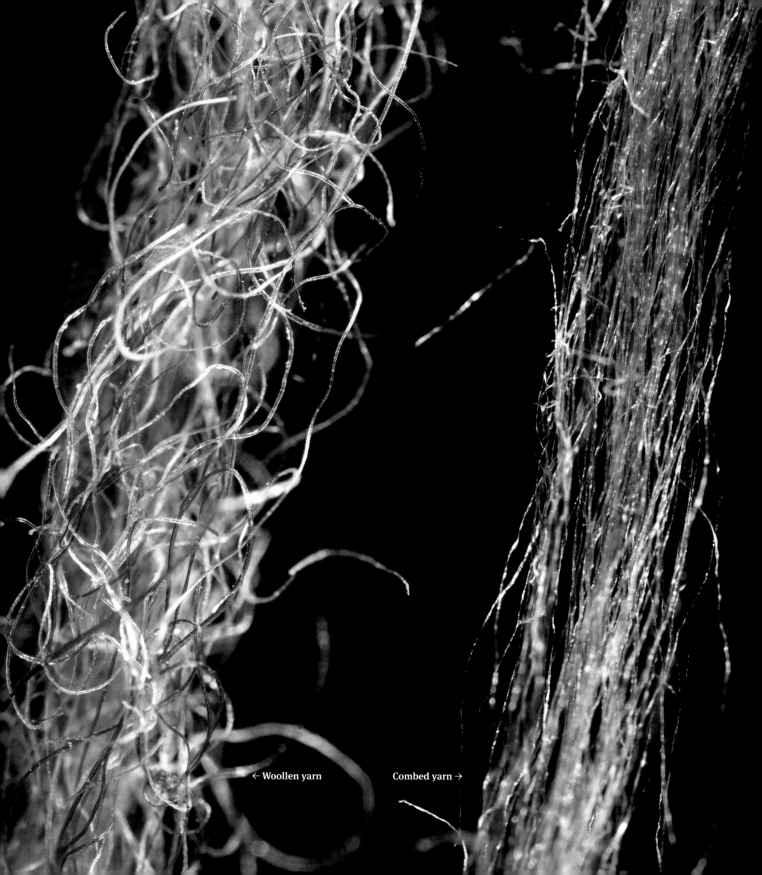

← Woollen yarn   Combed yarn →

PLAIN WEAVE

PLAIN WEAVE

As the wide array of fabric names suggest, **plain weave**, or **tabby**, is the oldest and among the most commonly used basic weave structures and amounts to about 80% of all woven fabrics.[8] Plain weave can be woven using only two shafts, but often four or more shafts are used to avoid crowding of heddles and ease opening of the shed. In a **balanced plain weave**, the ratio of ends to picks is one-to-one, denoting that the number of ends per cm is equal to the number of picks per cm. An unfinished plain-weave fabric has no particular face or back and both sides look the same. The repeat size of the plain weave is the smallest possible weave structure that consists of two picks and two ends interlacing in an over-one under-one construction, and hence encompassing the **maximum number of intersections**. As they are closely bound, balanced plain-weave structures are generally strong and resist slippage, such as the hemp upholstery fabric featured here. They have an excellent abrasion resistance and good dimensional stability but have less elasticity and drape. For more information on fabric properties see pp.33–35. However, similar to all other weaves, the inherent properties of a plain weave fabric linked to its construction can be greatly adjusted by the choice of yarn quality. Plain-weave samples or samples with plain weave in combination with other weaves can be found across Chapter 2, woven on all presented sample warps.

Fabric trade names, along with **weight** and information on the **fibre content**, are used in the textile and fashion industry to **identify fabrics**. Fabrics can be named for their **weave structure**, as in Herringbone (p.252), or method of colouration as in gingham or pinstripe. The differences in **yarn twist** (p.126) define the fabric identity of voile, a plain-weave woven with hard twisted yarns, while batiste utilises softer yarns. **Yarn type** is the defining factor in naming fabrics such as chenille and bouclé (p.157). Sometimes fabrics are named for their **origin**, such as the silk fabric shantung named after a province in China. Fabrics can also be distinguished by their **finishes** such as flannelette or chintz, or **method of dyeing** such as batik.[9]

Fabric names: plain weave

batiste, bengaline, cambric, chambray, calico, challis, chiffon, crêpe de chine, gauze, georgette, gingham, grosgrain, lawn, muslin, madras, organza, organdie, pongee, shantung, sheeting, voile, tapestry, flannel…

134

This simple and beautiful balanced plain-weave surface is woven on the 18-ply cotton seine twine warp using **picks identical to the ends**. The structural friction in this tight over one under one interlacement keeps the sturdy, coarse yarns in place. The result is a strong and stable fabric with a crisp and dry hand.

↓ *Fishing Net* from collection *Rely on Familiar* by Lotta Köhler

■
CO

■■
□

◧ ▫ □ CO

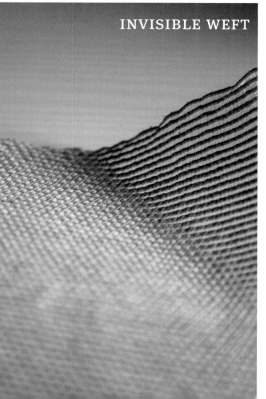

INVISIBLE WEFT

"In this sample, the materials and structures are exhibited clearly, simply, and honestly. Transparency builds trust. Trust makes things indestructible."

← *Honest* from collection *Finland* by Tong Ren

As a consequence of using a thin, smooth, and transparent polyamide monofilament fishing line pick, this simple balanced plain-weave fabric with an **invisible weft** reveals the bold upright rows of the cotton seine ends. Despite the pick being much thinner than the ends, the stiffness of the fishing line keeps the one-to-one ratio of the yarns and produces a balanced plain-weave structure. The smoother appearance and hand of this fabric differs greatly from the grainy *Fishing Net* sample. Filament yarns are discussed on p.27 and p.155.

■
CO

■
□

◧ ▫ □ PA

BASKET WEAVE

↑ This **soft and flexible** three-to-three basket weave is woven using a 18-ply cotton seine twine for both weft and warp. The yarn materials are identical to the yarns used in the sample *Fishing Net* (p.135). However, there is a notable difference in their hand and stability resulting from the looser over three under three interlacement here. This results in longer floats and consequently the yarns are not tightly kept in place.

Basket weave is a derivative structure of the plain weave. In comparison to the one-to-one plain-weave, the repeat of a basket-weave structure has a multiple-yarn configuration. Most common ratios of the basket weave are two-to-two and four-to-four. Compared to the strong and tightly bound plain weave, the outcome of a basket weave is a balanced and loosely bound fabric due to fewer yarn intersections. A commonly used variation of the basket weave is the **half basket**, where the ratio of yarns is two-to-one, which consequently results in an unbalanced thread count. However, the balanced basket appearance is often maintained by using

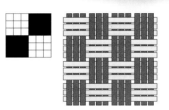

3:3 BASKET WEAVE

warp yarns thinner than the weft yarns, as in Oxford cloth (A), which is a traditional cotton shirting cloth. Basket weave is softer, more elastic and wrinkle resistant than plain weave, but has less strength, dimensional stability, and abrasion resistance.

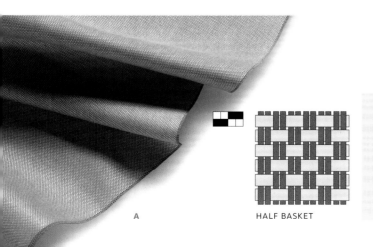

A

HALF BASKET

Fabric names: basket weave

duck, hopsack (B), oxford (A), oxford chambray, canvas, monk's cloth, panama, sailcloth...

B

STABILITY THROUGH PICK DENSITY

Tightly packed thick soft weft yarns provide stability to this basket-weave variation. Alternating four-pick units of coarse dark grey carpet wool with a loosely twisted white cotton yarn reveals the unbleached seine twine warp yarns and emphasises the bulky dot pattern. As a result of the **uneven** two-to-four lifting plan and use of **alternating pick units** in contrasting colours, the face and reverse of the sample differ.

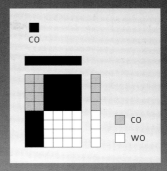

↓ *Home* from collection *Malaysia* by Jonathan Ho

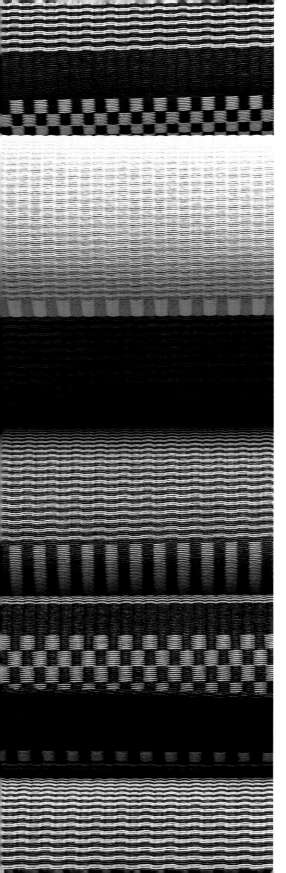

UNBALANCED PLAIN WEAVE
WEFT-FACED RIB WEAVE

Unbalanced plain weave or **rib-weave** fabrics fall into two categories of warp-and weft-faced, depending on which set of yarns covers the other. A **weft-faced plain weave** can usually be identified through a pronounced rib in vertical direction, whereas the **warp-faced plain weave** has a horizontal rib structure. Industrially woven unbalanced plain weave fabrics are mostly horizontal ribs. Vertical ribs are common in interior products such as carpets and place mats. Rib weaves typically have an over one under one construction similar to balanced plain weaves. However, they contain at least twice the number of yarns in either the warp or the weft yarn sets. Alternatively, a **weft-faced rib weave** is created by warp yarns thicker than weft yarns, or by adding multiple adjacent ends to one shaft or tie-up unit as in the featured drafts. The same logic can be applied in reverse to the weft yarns, and thicker or multiplied weft yarns result in a horizontal **warp-faced rib weave**. The drafts on this page illustrate a three-to-three (A), and two-to-four (B) weft-faced rib weave. Similar to their balanced counterparts, rib weaves are tightly woven and are generally strong and durable. Nevertheless, the **unbalanced ratio of picks and ends** has an effect on the fabric's performance. Horizontal rib weaves have substantial body, emphasising shape and structure over drape, whereas vertical warp-faced plain weave fabrics have better drape qualities. The yarns covering the ribs are exposed to wear, which may reduce the fabric's abrasion resistance. This property can be compensated for through utilisation of hard twisted yarns as used in poplin, a popular warp-faced fabric. The featured Woodnotes paper yarn carpets are a good example of the patterning possibilities of rib weaves (c).

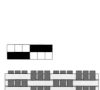

A 3:3 RIB WEAVE

B 2:4 RIB WEAVE

← **C** Woodnotes weft-faced rib-weave paper yarn carpets

Fabric names: weft-faced rib weave

pincord, dimity, ripstop, limbric...

For fabric names of horizontal rib weaves, see p.160.

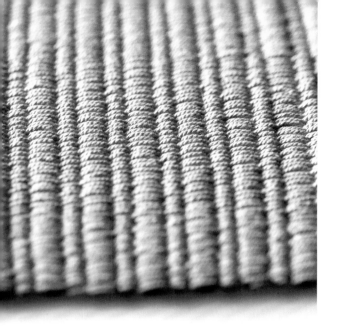

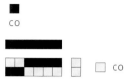

← The two-to-four **weft-faced, vertical rib weave** is woven using cotton seine twine for both weft and warp. In contrast to plain weave and basket weave, the weft-faced rib weave structure enables the weft to completely cover the warp.

CO

CO

FROM BALANCED TO UNBALANCED PLAIN WEAVE

The **ombre-effect** displayed in this sample is a result of gradually increasing the number of cotton strands per shed and subsequently demonstrating the route from a **balanced** to an **unbalanced plain weave**, a **weft-faced rib** in which the weft completely covers the warp. This path of gradual integration generates an optical 3D-illusion on the surface.

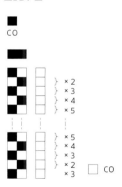

CO

} × 2
} × 3
} × 4
} × 5

} × 5
} × 4
} × 3
} × 2
} × 3

CO

"During the first years in Finland as an outsider, I felt that I was gradually becoming an outsider from my home country China, too. Matters became clearer from a distance, from the outsider's perspective. Although still an outsider, I was simultaneously integrating more and more in Finland and felt as if was walking towards her. Gradually I got increasingly involved in the local society."

→ *Outsider* from collection *China* by Tong Ren

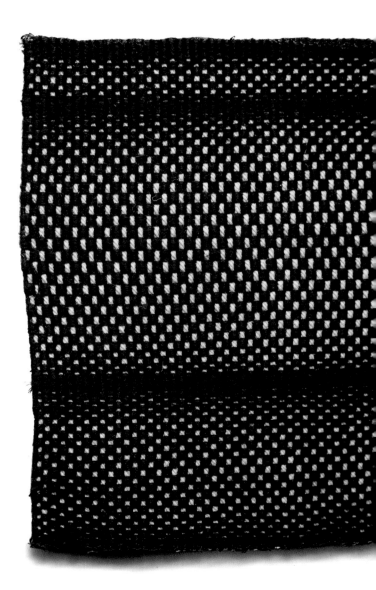

↑ *Home* from collection
Everyday Life by Anna Sorri

"I chose Everyday life *and* Party Time *as the themes for my two contrasting collections. I wanted the* Everyday life *fabrics to feel homey with a modern twist. The differences between the collections are subtle, as I wanted to eliminate our usual perspectives of everyday life as boring and mundane, and instead, to think of how we can celebrate every moment of life.*

To grant a central role to materials, many simple constructions were adopted and more complex structures were used as highlights in the collection. My mood boards were a significant source of inspiration and the materials were chosen to capture the feeling of the images."

CONTRASTING VERTICAL STRIPES

Here, the alternation of **contrasting weft picks**, hairy mohair and stiff polyurethane further emphasises the differences between the two sides of the of this **uneven**, two-to-four vertical rib structure. On the face of the fabric, the mohair pick has a prominent presence, running over four ends, while the alternating polyurethane pick, running over two ends, plays a minor role. The opposite occurs on the other side, resulting in varying appearances on face and reverse of the fabric. Since the cosy mohair yarn is substantially bulkier than the plasticky polyurethane yarn, the effect of structural dominance is reduced on the backside of the fabric, and a more balanced interplay between the two materials is illustrated.

CO

☐ PU
▨ WM

VERTICAL RIB REVEALING THE WARP

A stripy unit of three contrasting white cotton yarns and three unbleached jute yarns thrown in the same shed patterns the **vertical ribs** of this **weft-faced weave**. The thin black polyurethane yarn, fed as a unit of two yarns in the alternating shed creates gaps that reveal the rows of the underlying two cotton **warp ends**. This fabric is structurally close to a **basket weave**, however, as a result of the contrast between the thin pick and the bulgy cotton and jute combination, the vertically ribbed appearance prevails.

→ *Palmtree* from collection *Florida* by Tiina Teräs

CO

} × 2
} × 3
} × 3

▨ PU
☐ JU
☐ CO

A

CONTRASTING PICKS AND REVEALED ENDS

This fragile piece veiled by an **alternating pick sequence** of a transparent polyamide slit-film yarn (A) and a unit of four fine hairy acrylic yarns **reveals** slipping groups of underlying warp ends flowing as if without interlacement. The overall movement of the fabric structure is allowed by loosely woven long weft floats of shiny, smooth weft yarns, which let the warp yarns freely shift after releasing the loom tension. Although structurally similar and woven on the same warp as the other samples on this page, this elegant foil-glazed, furry sample represents the unexpected potential of the *no frills* look of the plain cotton twine warp.

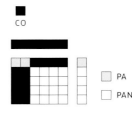

CO

PA

PAN

"In late spring snow and ice start to melt and everything appears to be glimmering in the sunrise."

← *08* from collection *Spring* by Miisa Lehto

↑ *Community* from collection *Tribes* by Tiia Sirén

COLOUR BLOCKS:
PICK COLOUR SEQUENCE

Alternating the **colour sequence** of coarse black and white wool yarns in units of eight picks creates a prominent chessboard pattern identical on both sides. The point of reversal is assigned to where the picks of the same colour repeat. The tightly woven **weft-faced** over three under three **rib structure** covers the warp yarns completely. This gives the weft yarns complete control over the fabric's look as opposed to a similar black and white design *Old Town* (p.145), where the basket-weave lets both the warp and weft to pattern the surface.

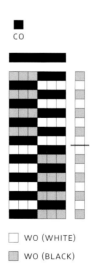

CO

☐ WO (WHITE)

▨ WO (BLACK)

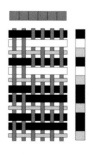

Colours in structural drafts

are used to demonstrate the different structural parts of the weave. In the simplest form and as a basic rule, black is used to represent the warp ends and white is used for the picks. Thus mere observation of the draft makes understanding of the actual colour effects in the fabric challenging.

In order to demonstrate the formation of the concrete colour effect, this image, while showing the actual interlacement of the yarns, reveals how the contrastingly coloured weft yarns form the colour pattern of the weft-faced rib weave sample *Crosswalk*. The plain weave ground weft is marked with light grey, while white and black demonstrate the two colours of the cotton float picks. The warp is marked with dark grey.

Similarly to *Community*, this **weft-faced** fabric plays with an alternating black and white pick colour sequence. However, in contrast, the uneven two-to-four **rib weave** results in a dissimilar face and reverse. Additionally, due to the long floats of thinner, smoother, and more slippery cotton yarn, the support of a **stabilising internal structure** is necessary to firmly maintain the clear division between the black and white areas. A hidden **plain weave** ground armature with fine, high-twist cotton pick keeps the loosely sett warp ends in straight rows after the warp tension is released. Consequently, the patterning weft yarns can securely float in their decorative function. The rib-weave sample on p.139 shows the appearance of the intersection of rib-weave floats without a supporting plain-weave structure between the floats. See more on combining weaves on the following page.

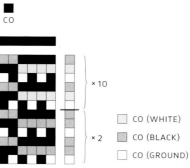

CO

× 10

× 2

☐ CO (WHITE)
▨ CO (BLACK)
☐ CO (GROUND)

↓ *Crosswalk* from collection *City* by Kristiina Hansen-Haug

u vain
lkoisille.

143

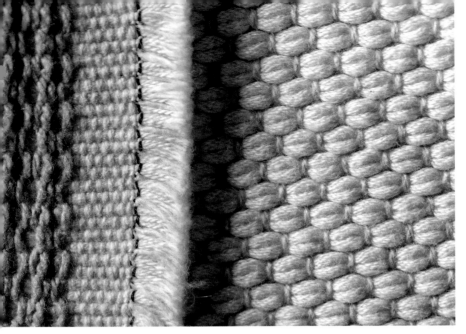

COMBINING WEAVES

↑ A Cotton upholstery fabric, compound weave with weft-faced rib weave on the face and a stabilising plain weave ground

↗ B Linen blend curtain fabric combining plain weave and basket weave, Vanelli

The choice of weave depends on the function of the fabric – the need for stability or flexibility, compactness or transparency, texture, or decoration. Combining the structural properties of different weaves in one fabric – floats and areas of tight interlacement – is about a play of balance between hiding and revealing, exposing a yarn on the surface, blending it or covering it up. Combining structures on shaft looms is more restricted than on jacquard looms, which offer a wide range of possibilities in weave combinations and patterning that are examined in more depth in Chapter 3.

In cases in which weaves are combined due to the necessity for a supporting structure, the weave with longer floats is upheld with a supporting weave, usually plain weave, which forms the internal structure of the fabric. This stabilising structure is often woven with a separate set of thinner weft yarns, as demonstrated in some of the prior samples such as *Old Town* (p.145), *Crosswalk* (p.143), and *03* (p.146) as well as the featured cotton upholstery fabric (A). The supporting weave

layer can also have an additional set of ends or picks or both, as in a **double-cloth** structure and other **interwoven fabrics** (p.206). These types of weave combinations are called **compound weaves** (p.314).

An effective way of **patterning** with a small number of shafts is to combine weaves in horizontal stripes. Due to the unique properties of each weave structure, this technique generally leads to striped, or textural surfaces. The design effects of these structural combinations can also be emphasised – or diminished – by alternating the yarn material, yarn colour, or pick density. Loosely sett warps often lead to grainy textural surfaces, while stripes might be more evident in finer denser warps. With a higher number of shafts, a **block draft** (p.190) can be applied and structures can be combined vertically. The featured grey linen blend curtain fabric combines plain weave and basket weave in a block draft pattern (B). Combining weaves for patterning is further elaborated on in the section *From Textures to Patterns* on p.314.

BASKET-WEAVE VARIATIONS WITH A SUPPORTING GROUND PICK

A three-to-three basket weave check pattern is woven on the unbleached cotton warp with weft yarns in contrasting black worsted wool. The nearly invisible polyamide monofilament **ground pick** for **plain weave stabilises** the structure and prevents the cotton warp from clumping together after the warp tension is released.

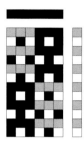

CO

WO

PA

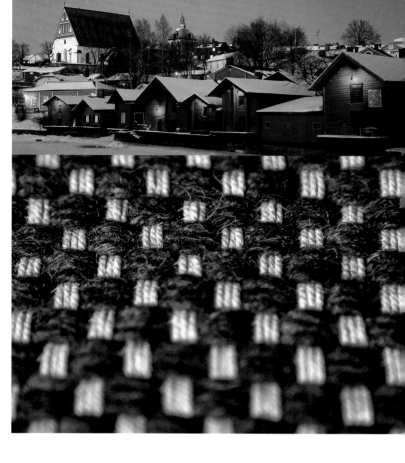

"Blanketed in snow and illuminated by warm light, old houses line the riverbank of the old town in Finland."

→ *Old Town* from collection *Finland* by Yumi Kurotani

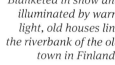

"Narrow streets in the old town in Japan are lined by traditional buildings and shops."

The sample is woven with alternating pick units of six coarse unbleached sisal and jute yarns, thus creating a geometric, layered carpet texture. Similar to the *Old Town* sample, a supporting polyamide mono-filament **ground pick** is used for the plain weave, which maintains a rigid order in this two-to-four basket-weave variation.

CO

× 3

× 3

SI

JU

PA

← *Old Town* from collection *Japan* by Yumi Kurotani

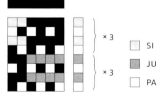

GLASSY FLOATS REVEALING ENDS

Groups of weft floats woven with transparent thin polyamide slit-film yarn and black mohair yarn are framed by a mohair yarn plain-weave ground and result in rows of glassy windows **revealing** the underlying warp threads. The pick sequence of the floating groups is alternately changed.

"More and more high-rises are built in my hometown these days. Behind each window of a building live different people and families. One window represents one unit of the society."

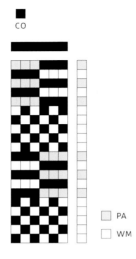

CO

PA

WM

→ *Windows* from collection *China* by Tong Ren

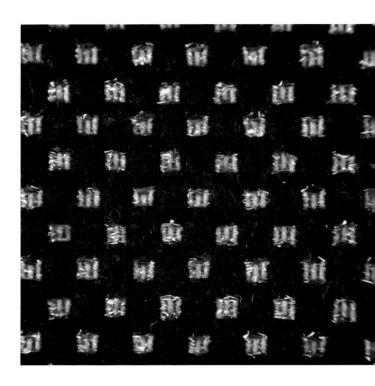

VERTICAL RIB WITH REVEALED SUPPORT

"In the spring the snow gets increasingly heavy on top of the pine trees."

A heavy, thick carpet wool yarn weft is woven densely over four under two. In between the floats, a black mohair yarn weft in one-to-one **plain weave adds stability** to the fabric. As a result, in contrast to the hidden internal structure in the sample *Crosswalk*, the dotted stripes of **plain weave** with black mohair yarn pick and cotton weft are visible.

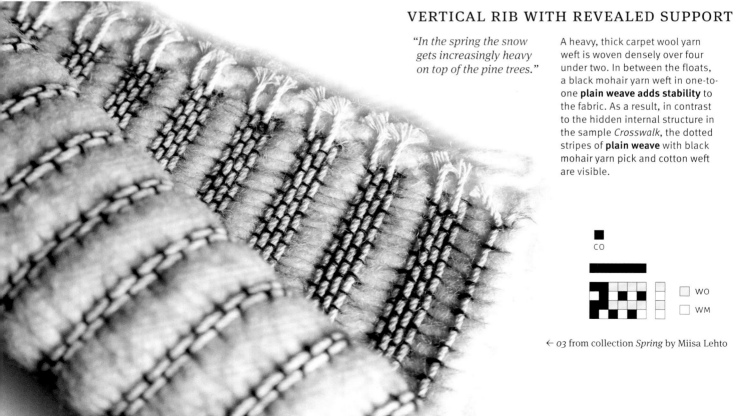

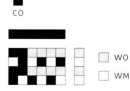

CO

WO

WM

← *03* from collection *Spring* by Miisa Lehto

CONTRASTING WEFT YARNS

The **cramming and spacing** character-istics of **plain weave** and **weft-faced rib weave** are further demonstrated in this fabric. The sample is woven with six units of two-to-four rib weave with a slit-film polyester **raffia-type** yarn (p.156) that alternates with one monofilament plain weave unit. The transparent pick reveals the cotton ends grouped in units of four and two. Moreover, pressure applied by the closely bound plain weave to the stiff monofilament yarns creates a gap between the two picks, thus pushing the groups of crammed raffia floats apart from each other.

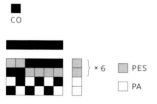

CO

} × 6   PES   PA

"Lying on the beach with a basket full of cold ginger ale, life is good"

→ *Saint-Tropez* from collection *Lucent* by Grace Rubaduka

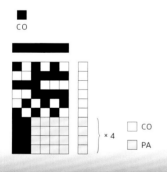

CO

} × 4   CO   PA

This bulgy texture combines two **contrasting weft yarn materials**. The sample is woven using soft knitted polyamide tape yarn for floats that alternate with six picks of high-twist cotton twine in a grainy combination of the available structures. The cotton pick traps the block of polyamide tape yarns and crams it into spongy bubbles.

↓ *Keyboard* from collection *System* by Anni Raasmaja

"The sample reminds me of bubblegum bits. My next step is to develop this idea on a different warp to a finer fabric suitable for fashion. Plain weave between the tape yarn floats would increase stability of the structure."

← This grainy textured **crêpe weave** fabric is woven on the cotton seine sample warp with the same yarn as weft. The non-directional surface structure is achieved by combining rows of stabilizing plain weave with alternating rows of three-to-three and two-to-four floats.

CO

CO

CRÊPE WEAVE

Small-scale all-over **textured weaves**, which are derived from or combine basic weave structures to form grainy, non-directional repeat patterns, are called **crêpe weaves**. A simple way of combining two basic weaves to form a crêpe weave is by alternately weaving a row of each weave. Two different weaves with unequal repeat sizes can be combined by drafting layers of the repeating weave units on top of one another. Crêpe weaves can also be derived from basic weave structures by adding or eliminating stitching points, or by rotating the repeating basic weave units.

Crêpe Fabrics

As a fabric name, **crêpe** refers to a general classification of fabrics with a broad range of crinkled or grained surface effects. Hence, a **plain-weave fabric** can also be a **crêpe fabric** when woven with **crêpe yarns**, over-twisted Z-twist and S-twist yarns (p.126). Crêpe yarns can be used in either weft or warp, or in both weft and warp directions. The grainy effects of these crêpe fabrics are emphasised through finishes (see p.415). See also crêpe finish. p.421.

Due to their textural intrigue and excellent drape, both types of lightweight crêpe fabrics, the ones that have a crêpe-weave structure and the ones where the effect is achieved through over-twisted yarns, are popular dress and suiting fabrics. The examples here include a white crêpe-weave wool crêpe (B) as well as two blue plain weave silk georgette samples and a black and red plain weave silk crêpe de chine (A).

orgette

Crepe de chine

A

Crepe de Chine

Crepe georgette

Overtwisted yarns tend to be difficult to handle for unexperienced weavers, and hence are not suggested as warp yarns for the sample warps in this chapter. It is however recommended to explore the integration of overtwisted yarns in the weft direction.

B

The concept of **cramming and spacing** is essential in woven fabric design and the theme is therefore carried along throughout the book. Its effects on other **textured weave structures** are discussed in the following sections: **crêpe weave**, **seersucker** p.172, **mock leno** p.218, **grouped weft distortion** p.230 and **waffle weave** p.274.

ADDING TEXTURE AND THREE-DIMENSIONALITY

The groups of multiple over three under three fancy yarn floats and over four under two stiff jute yarn floats used in this fabric exaggerate the voluminous **three-dimensional character** of this bold, grainy **crêpe weave** texture. Plain weave is used to acquire the necessary stability in the fabric. The contrasting **cramming and spacing** properties of the two weave structures become evident as a four-ply unit of black linen twine is squeezed within the rice-grain stitches dotting between two identically interwoven over one under one jute yarns.

"Vaskiluoto is an area in my hometown where my friends grew up. It's cosy and idyllic. The buildings are old wooden houses and you can hear the sound of children of different ages playing together echoing between the houses. It is a kind of a place where families gather around the fireplace to drink hot chocolate and laugh together. The textile Vaski-luoto is warm like the atmos-phere in this area. The natural colours and materials are familiar, soft, and kind. The structure is irregular, just like the logs in the wooden houses and the laidback attitude of the families."

← **Vaskiluoto** from collection *Home* by Kajsa Hytönen

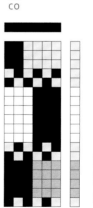

■ CO

☐ PES/CV

▨ LI

☐ JU

EXTRA-WEFT PATTERNING AND KNOTTED PILES

A free-floating **supplementary pick** can be added to a structurally firm **ground weave** for decorative reasons. This method of **extra-weft patterning**, also referred to as **brocade** or **broché**, is commonly used to decorate woven shaft weaves and jacquards (p.83). A similar concept can be implemented in the warp direction by using a supplementary warp.

The essence of broché fabrics is in the use of the extra-threads to merely decorate without forming a constituent part of the fabric. The threads are brought to the face only at isolated spots. See also *Floating and Clipping* p.460.

BROCADE

An extra-weft can be woven in by hand using the brocading techniques that can be traced back to historical fabrics. In this **hand-crafted** sample, the decorative pattern of long floats of soft mohair yarn and flat metallic strips is supported by the plain-weave ground that is woven with a thin metallic wire weft.

CO

∘ WM + ME (EXTRA WEFT)

☐ MTF (GROUND WEFT)

↑ *Luck charm* from collection *Tribes* by Tiia Sirén

"How to create a colourful collection without using colours? I started by thinking what a certain colour means to me. What is the mood of the colour? And how to create the same mood without the colour?

The design 'Yellow' needed the same soft and warm feeling that you have on a sunny summer day. The little black weft floats resemble the beams of light. Yellow is such a joyful colour that I wanted to add some spirited details to the design.

'Fuchsia' is a colour that wants to stand out. So, the design also had to be bold and the highlight of the collection. In this design, I have gathered together almost all the different yarns that were used in the entire collection. I felt that there should rather be too much material than too little in this design."

→ *Yellow* from collection *Colour Blocking* by Terhi Laine

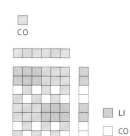

CO

LI
CO

In this fabric, contrasting **extra-weft floats** in black linen twine run as streaky rows on the **plain-weave ground**. The cotton knit tape yarn used for the ground picks adds a soft stretchiness to the cloth.

This sample warp also allows for the exploration of crafted samples, which can be used as highlights in collections. In this sample, long piles of fancy yarns are **hand-knotted** in splashes around the warp ends on the cotton chenille yarn plain-weave ground.

CO

∘ PA, WO, WM, CO, SE (PILES)
☐ CO/PES (GROUND WEFT)

← *Fuchsia* from collection *Colour Blocking* by Terhi Laine

II End and End Fancy Yarn Warp

UNBALANCED PLAIN WEAVE
WARP-FACED RIB WEAVE
SPACING THE WEFT

FIBRE AND YARN INFO:
POLYESTER, VISCOSE
FILAMENT YARNS, FANCY YARNS, METALLIC YARNS, COMPOSITE YARNS

2.2 End and End Fancy

This dense **end and end warp** is set in a straight draft on a **double beam loom** with two alternating **fancy yarns**, flat white viscose polyamide tape yarn and thin black viscose polyamide spiral yarn. Warps consisting of two different types of yarns, or alternatively sets of warp ends that form different structures require winding on two separate beams (see seersucker p.170, double weave p.188, and piqué p.288). Consequently, the tension of each of the yarn types or warp sets can be adjusted separately, thus taking the different elasticity properties of the yarns or interlacement of the weaves into account. In **horizontal rib weaves**, such as here, unequal tensioning of the beams can be used to further emphasise the rib effect by using thicker weft yarns while weaving on the loosely tensioned set of warp yarns.

Due to its high density, the warp dominates the weft, resulting in an **unbalanced, warp-faced plain-weave** cloth (p.160). Although plain weave generally needs only two shafts, the high density of the ends in this warp-faced weave requires spreading warp yarns over four shafts. This practice prevents problems such as clinging ends and over-crowding of heddles on the shafts, and thus eases the shed forming.

Furthermore, this end and end warp allows for demonstration of a variation of the warp-faced rib weave by introducing two contrasting yarn types in the weft. In the warp, the flatter and broader white tape yarn ends form a dense layer covering the weft, while the thinner black spiral yarn ends leave gaps revealing the underlying weft picks. Therefore, introducing two contrasting colours or materials or both in the warp and weft directions, in combination with a basic weave structure such as plain weave, provides extensive potential for exploring **colour-and-weave** effects. For example, by inserting a pick in a contrasting colour, the black warp end

---

Novelty yarns, introduced on pp.156–159, subdivided to **fancy yarns** and **metallic yarns,** are designed for decorative purposes and are mostly used as effects in fabric to add attributes including texture and shine. In some cases, such as warp knitted tape yarn for fashion knitwear or slub yarns for decorative curtain fabrics, the entire fabric is made from a fancy yarn. However, fancy yarns mostly are assigned a decorative role, while regular **staple yarns** or **continuous-filament yarns** are used as warp yarns or as ground weave ends and picks to support the structure.[10]

The classification to different types of yarns is not always straightforward. Some yarns can be classified in two or even more categories. Furthermore, yarns within one category can be further developed in order to achieve different looks as described in the section on *Chenille yarns* (p.157) and *Metallic yarns* (p.159). The main goal of this section is to demonstrate the variety of the techniques employed in producing these novelty yarns and the consequent broad palette of effects achieved. As well, it provides a tool to better understand the naming of the yarns.

Warp yarns:

A **viscose polyester combination spiral yarn** (A) and **viscose polyamide tape yarn** (B) are the alternating ends in this fancy yarn warp. Information on viscose and polyester fibres can be found on the following spread. Information on polyamide can be found on p.169. For more information on **tape yarns, spiral yarns** and other **fancy yarns,** see pp.156–158.

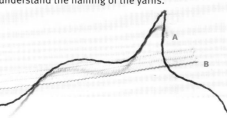

End and end fancy yarn warp

Warp Yarns:
Viscose polyester spiral yarn, Nm 15 (tex 66) | 95% CV 5% PES
Viscose polyamide tape yarn, Nm 4.6 (tex 217) | 80% CV 20% PA
Yarn sett: 10 ends per cm
Reed: 50:2
Straight draft on four shafts on a double beam loom

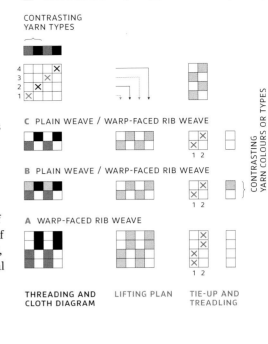

TAPE YARN (BEAM 1)   SPIRAL YARN (BEAM 2)

CONTRASTING YARN TYPES

CONTRASTING YARN COLOURS OR TYPES

C PLAIN WEAVE / WARP-FACED RIB WEAVE

B PLAIN WEAVE / WARP-FACED RIB WEAVE

A WARP-FACED RIB WEAVE

THREADING AND CLOTH DIAGRAM   LIFTING PLAN   TIE-UP AND TREADLING

floats can be exposed or hidden on a black weft ground. This sample warp not only allows texturing with colour, but also explores the interplay of different yarn types.

The dominance of the dense warp and limitations of only working with two alternating sheds urges the weavers to explore ways in which these presets would work in favour of the collection-in-process. The characteristics of the fabric can be trialled by altering the colour, thickness, and pick density, by weaving several picks in the same shed (A), or by using fancy yarns and contrasting yarns with distinctive characters (B).

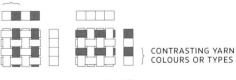

D CONTRASTING YARN COLOURS OR TYPES

CONTRASTING YARN COLOURS OR TYPES

END AND END   PICK AND PICK

An **end and end warp** is an arrangement of warp yarns with two alternating colours or two types of yarn. The same method in the weft direction is referred to as **pick and pick** (D).

End and end warps are commonly used in the industry as warps for shaft weaves to add colour, texture and character to the fabric. A well-known example is the so called **Fil-à-fil,** or **end-to-end** shirting fabric (E, structure F1) with two alternating light and dark yarns forming a heathery effect typical to this type of small scale **colour-and-weave effect**.

The featured images illustrate the formation of small-scale colour-and-weave effects in plain-weave fabrics (F). Refer to *Checks–Colour and weave* (p.258) for examples of this effect in twill weaves.

F1

F2

F3

COLOUR-AND-WEAVE EFFECT (PLAIN WEAVE)

E

Polyester / PES is a **man-made synthetic fibre**. It is the most widely produced textile fibre worldwide with a production volume double than that of cotton (p.30). Polyester is mostly produced as a filament fibre, amounting to about twice the volume of polyester staple fibre produced. Among the various types of polyesters available, thermoplastic polyester, PET, is the most widely used synthetic polymer. It is used in the textile sector as well as for products such as plastic bottles, films, and LCD-screens. PET polyester is thermo-mechanically recyclable. Pilot manufacturing projects of chemically recycled virgin-quality polyester are gradually being scaled up to commercial operations (pp.31, 39).

Polyester fibres display excellent tensile strength and dimensional stability and polyester fabrics resist creasing and abrasion. Due to its aforementioned properties as well as its easy-care attributes such as quick drying, wrinkle-resistance, and negligible shrinkage, the fibre is extensively utilised in clothing and interior textiles. As a durable, all-weather and chemically resistant fibre, polyester is often used for functional wear such as protective clothing. The fibre's abrasion resistance makes it a favourable choice for upholsteries and carpets, while its sunlight resistance also makes it a widely used material for curtains. Moreover, due to its multitude of functional attributes, it is broadly utilised in technical textiles, such as tyre cords, seat belts, and conveyer belts just to name a few.

In home furnishings and clothing, polyester is a preferred fibre in spun yarn **blends** with cotton, viscose, wool, and acrylic. Similar to **polyamide** (p.169), polyester is often used as a component in combination yarns (p.227) and novelty yarns, such as the spiral yarn and tape yarn in the end and end sample warp featured in this section.

The fibre can also be engineered to encompass additional tailor-made material attributes including flame retardancy and antimicrobial properties, thus enabling its application in areas where these specifications are required. An example from the interior contract textiles sector, textiles for public spaces, is the inherently flame-retardant polyester *Trevira CS®*.

From the sustainability standpoint, production of polyester consumes considerably less energy in comparison to the production of other synthetic fibres such as polyamide. However, as the fibre is not biodegradable, it has major environmental implications. Currently, a significant topic of discussion is the microplastics released in the oceans. New developments focus on manufacturing biodegradable polyester from bio-based raw materials (p.31, 36–39).[11]

Viscose / CV and lyocell / CLY are **man-made cellulose fibres (MMCFS)**. The predominant source of pulp for these fibres is wood. Other MMCFS include acetate, modal and cupro. The fibres' characteristics such as lustre, length, and diameter are engineered during production. The fibres can be silk-like continuous filaments, or cut into staples resembling natural fibres, which can be further twisted to generate spun yarns. As pure cellulose-based fibres, their properties resemble those of cotton and other natural cellulosic fibres. They are silky, soft, well-draping, breathable and absorbent. The fibres have relatively poor elastic recovery and resiliency, hence viscose products wrinkle easily and stretch out in areas prone to wear.

Viscose, or **rayon** (US), developed in the late 19th century, is the first man-made fibre. As it is produced from renewable resources and not petroleum, consumers often view it as ecologically friendlier than synthetic fibres such as polyester. However, manufacturing viscose consumes much energy and more water than manufacturing synthetic fibres (but less than cotton cultivation) and requires substantial amounts of toxic chemicals such as carbon disulphide. At the moment, viscose counts for around 80% of the global production of MMCFs (p.31).[12]

The new-generation **lyocell** manufacturing process is considerably simpler and faster, and can be considered more sustainable. Chemical modification of pulp is not necessary before dissolving, and the solvents used are nontoxic, biodegradable and recyclable in the process. Furthermore, lyocell-type regenerated fibres have technical advantages such as a higher tensile strength. In addition to the well-known lyocell fibre *Tencel*, there exist promising new developments such as **Ioncell**[13] that is currently under development at Aalto University.[14] Moreover, new research utilizing cellulose-based textiles as a raw material for chemical polymer textile-to-textile recycling is paving the way to circular economy ecosystems (pp.31, 38).

As viscose on its own is a weak fibre, it is often engineered into **blends** or **combinations** (p.227) with other fibres to achieve more durable yarns, such as the warp yarns in this section and many viscose-blend weft yarns in the showcased samples. On the other hand, viscose and lyocell contribute to blends by adding sought-after qualities. With the trend to use more bio-based materials, absorbent, soft blends of wool and lyocell have become popular in functional wear. Well-draping blends of linen and lyocell are used for fashion as well as interior textiles.

Filament yarns are made from continuous extruded fibres. These dense, compact, and strong yarns allow production of durable fabrics made of fine yarns. **Standard continuous filament yarns** are known as **flat** or **smooth-filament yarns**. On the other hand, **textured-filament yarns** refer to yarns in which the filaments have been altered for stretch or for bulk, introducing textures such as crimps or waves.

Monofilament yarns are made of a single extruded continuous fibre.

Multifilament yarns are a collection of parallel bundles of filaments that lie close to one another and are grouped together either with or without a twist. For more information on fibres and filament yarns refer to sections *Fibres—the building blocks* (p.27), *Yarns* (p.126).

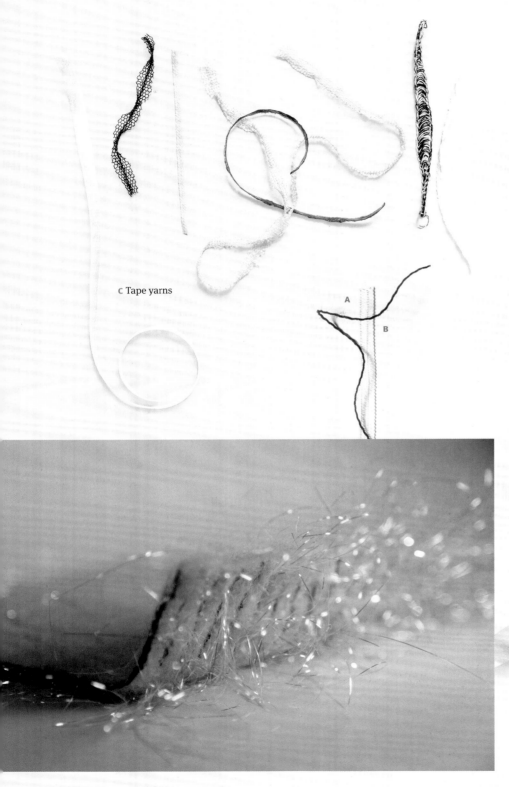

c Tape yarns

Novelty Yarns
Fancy yarns

Spiral or **corkscrew yarns** (A) are textural plied yarns composed of a smooth spiralling of a looser component around a tighter core yarn. The black spiral yarn in the *End and End Fancy* sample warp (p.152) features a soft viscose multifilament yarn loosely spiralling around a fine and resilient polyester multifilament core. The same type of yarn is also used in the striped warp presented on p.169.

Tape yarns (B, C) are flat yarns produced through various methods. They can be braided or woven, or be in the form of cut tapes made of non-woven materials, or be made of knitted narrow ribbons, such as the warp knitted lacy white viscose polyamide yarn used in the sample warp.

Instead of using **fibre-extrusion spinning technology** (p.29) to generate filament yarn (p.155), the synthetic polymer is squeezed out in a form of a thin wide sheet, which is then slit to produce a type of tape yarn called **slit-film yarn** (D). This type of yarn is used in acoustic curtain fabrics and sheers (p.458). A transparent slit-film yarn is presented in *08* (p.141) and *Windows* (p.146).

Raffia-type yarns that imitate the tropical **leaf stalk fibre raffia**, used in products such as hats, bags and furniture coverings, are a type of matte slit-film yarn produced from a film of regenerated cellulose or synthetic polymers such as the pick in *Saint-Tropez* (p.147).

D

← Slit-film yarn pile in *Rug* from collection *Canary Islands* by Riikka Buri

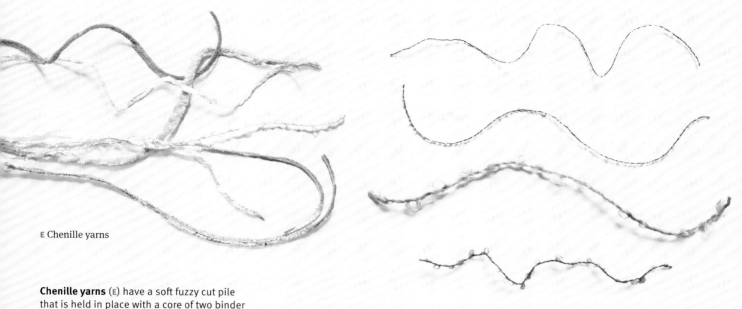

E Chenille yarns

G Loop yarns

Chenille yarns (**E**) have a soft fuzzy cut pile that is held in place with a core of two binder yarns. The yarns are produced either out of cut strips of **leno-weave fabric** (p.225) or by special machinery. Chenille yarns range from thick, bulgy yarns to thin yarns with a short pile. These yarns are commonly used in interior and apparel fabrics to produce soft velvet-like textiles.

Similar to all other yarns, chenille-type yarns can also be finished to create novelty yarns such as the "rubbery" flat-pressed and polyurethane coated tape yarn pick (**Q**) used in *Data* (p.161) and *Baltimore* (p.164).

Bouclé yarns (**F**) are ply yarns composed of a wavy texture effect yarn looping around the ground yarn and held in place by a binder. These yarns often feature contrasting colours in the ground ply and effect ply such as in the *Landscape of China* (p.175). Both bouclé and chenille yarns often generate fabrics in which the yarn dominates the texture of the fabric to an extent that the fabric is named for its yarn type, as **bouclé fabrics** or **chenilles**.

Loop yarns (**G**) are yarns with prominent circular loop projections on the surface. Loop yarns consist of core yarns and a binder yarn, which entrap the looping effect yarn. Refer to *Baltimore* (p.164) and *Snowfall* (p.177).

Marl yarn (**H**) is a ply yarn made by twisting two different coloured strands to a two-ply yarn. The two yarns could also be of different types, such as the metallic slit-film yarn plied with a spun yarn presented in *Wings* (p.177).

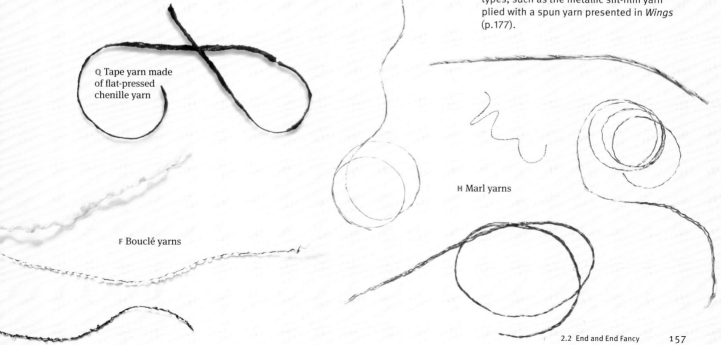

Q Tape yarn made of flat-pressed chenille yarn

H Marl yarns

F Bouclé yarns

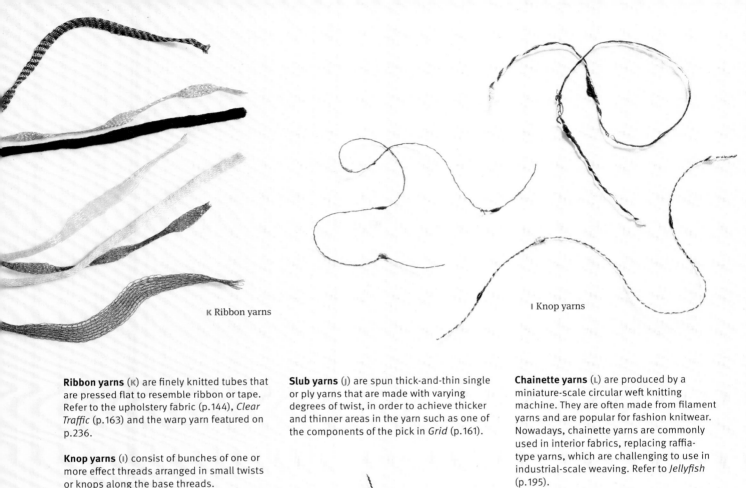

K Ribbon yarns

I Knop yarns

Ribbon yarns (K) are finely knitted tubes that are pressed flat to resemble ribbon or tape. Refer to the upholstery fabric (p.144), *Clear Traffic* (p.163) and the warp yarn featured on p.236.

Knop yarns (I) consist of bunches of one or more effect threads arranged in small twists or knops along the base threads.

Slub yarns (J) are spun thick-and-thin single or ply yarns that are made with varying degrees of twist, in order to achieve thicker and thinner areas in the yarn such as one of the components of the pick in *Grid* (p.161).

Chainette yarns (L) are produced by a miniature-scale circular weft knitting machine. They are often made from filament yarns and are popular for fashion knitwear. Nowadays, chainette yarns are commonly used in interior fabrics, replacing raffia-type yarns, which are challenging to use in industrial-scale weaving. Refer to *Jellyfish* (p.195).

L Chainette yarns

J Slub yarns

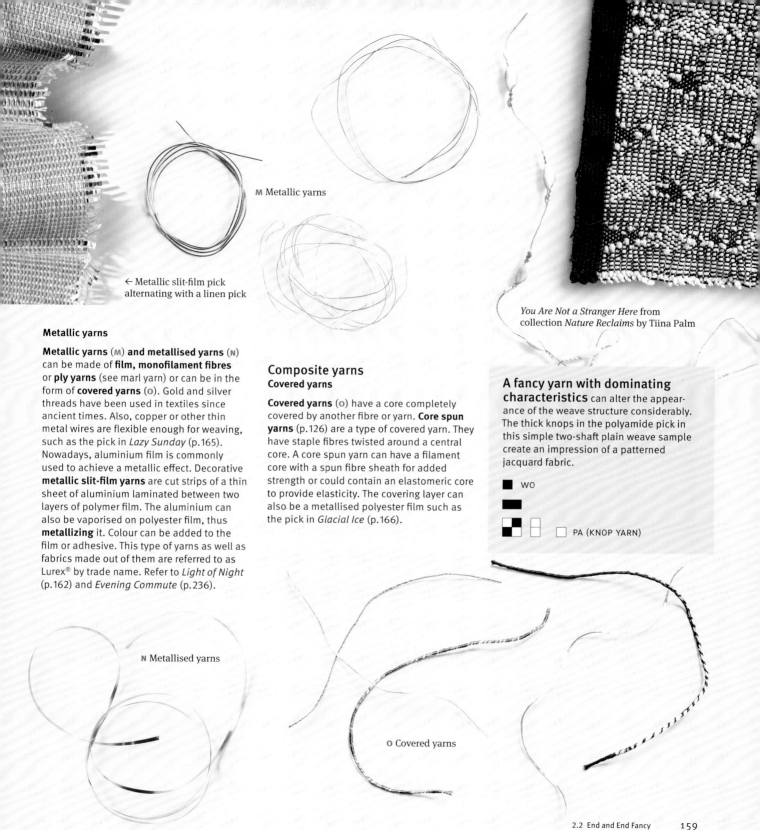

M Metallic yarns

← Metallic slit-film pick
alternating with a linen pick

You Are Not a Stranger Here from
collection *Nature Reclaims* by Tiina Palm

Metallic yarns

Metallic yarns (M) **and metallised yarns** (N)
can be made of **film, monofilament fibres**
or **ply yarns** (see marl yarn) or can be in the
form of **covered yarns** (O). Gold and silver
threads have been used in textiles since
ancient times. Also, copper or other thin
metal wires are flexible enough for weaving,
such as the pick in *Lazy Sunday* (p.165).
Nowadays, aluminium film is commonly
used to achieve a metallic effect. Decorative
metallic slit-film yarns are cut strips of a thin
sheet of aluminium laminated between two
layers of polymer film. The aluminium can
also be vaporised on polyester film, thus
metallizing it. Colour can be added to the
film or adhesive. This type of yarns as well as
fabrics made out of them are referred to as
Lurex® by trade name. Refer to *Light of Night*
(p.162) and *Evening Commute* (p.236).

Composite yarns
Covered yarns

Covered yarns (O) have a core completely
covered by another fibre or yarn. **Core spun
yarns** (p.126) are a type of covered yarn. They
have staple fibres twisted around a central
core. A core spun yarn can have a filament
core with a spun fibre sheath for added
strength or could contain an elastomeric core
to provide elasticity. The covering layer can
also be a metallised polyester film such as
the pick in *Glacial Ice* (p.166).

**A fancy yarn with dominating
characteristics** can alter the appearance of the weave structure considerably.
The thick knops in the polyamide pick in
this simple two-shaft plain weave sample
create an impression of a patterned
jacquard fabric.

■ WO

▬

▨ ▢   ▢ PA (KNOP YARN)

N Metallised yarns

O Covered yarns

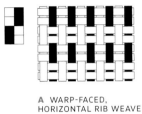

A WARP-FACED,
HORIZONTAL RIB WEAVE

UNBALANCED PLAIN WEAVE

↗ **B** Linen blend upholstery
fabric by Limonta

Unbalanced plain-weave fabrics (p.138) are either warp-faced or weft-faced. Weaving with alternating pick colours or weft yarn types affects the texture and pattern of a weft-faced rib weave. Similarly, an **end and end warp** with two alternating warp colours offers a variety of patterning options in a **warp-faced rib weave** (A). The linen blend upholstery fabric featured here is a good demonstration of how the horizontal rib structure affects the **drape and body** (p.131) of this warp-faced rib-weave fabric (B).

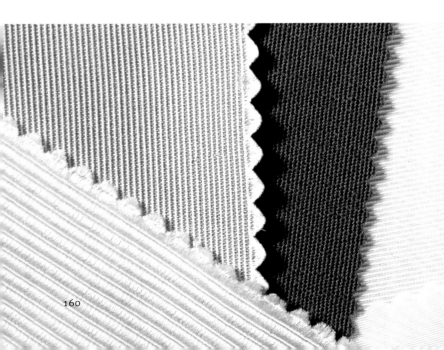

**Fabric names:
warp-faced rib weave**

*broadcloth, ottoman, taffeta,
poplin, faille, bengaline,
repp, rep*

SMALL-SCALE UNBALANCED PLAIN-WEAVE TEXTURES

The textural potential of the **colour-and-weave effect** in the **end and end** sample warp is beautifully demonstrated in this simple **unbalanced plain-weave** fabric. Woven with a thin black viscose linen blend **slub yarn pick** plied together with a thin **metal yarn**, the warp yarns are bound in a moldable tight texture, dotted by occasional flecks of the weft picks.

■ TAPE YARN   ■ SPIRAL YARN

□ CV/LI (SLUB YARN) + MTF (METALLIC YARN)

↑ *Grid* from collection *Digital Patterns* by Laivi Suurväli

In this fabric, densely woven white polyurethane-coated tape yarn picks alternate with picks of thin black **spiral yarn** identical to the warp thread. As a result of the **colour-and-weave effect** with two contrasting colours and yarns in both warp and weft, this compact texture exhibits a vertically striped appearance on the face of the fabric. The appearance of the reverse side of the fabric differs from the face side and displays stitched rows of the black spiral yarn pick.

■ TAPE YARN   ■ SPIRAL YARN

□ PU/CO/PA (FLAT-PRESSED YARN)
□ CV/PA (SPIRAL YARN)

↑ *Data* from collection *Space* by Ilona Hackenberg

↑ Night view of the Earth showing South Korea, Japan and the Sea of Japan.

"Japanese cities glow in a cooler blue-green luminance than other regions of the world. Newer developments along the shore of Tokyo Bay are characterised by orange sodium vapor lamps, while the majority of the urban areas have light green mercury vapor lamps."

→ *Light of Night* from collection *Japan* by Yumi Kurotani

WARP-FACED RIB WEAVE

Alternating a coarse weft pick with a fine pick in an **end and end warp** forms horizontally draping **warp-faced rib weave**. This effect can also be achieved by multiplying the number of picks per shed. Fabrics woven on an end and end warp with unequal stripe widths or contrasting colours display differing colour-effects on the face and reverse sides of the fabric. Small-scale textures and patterns are achieved using fine weft yarns, whereas thicker weft yarns enlarge the scale and emphasise the contrast in the pattern. Refer to the section on weft-faced rib weave p.138 for similar effects in vertical direction.

↑ Here flat and plasticky polyamide filament weft picks alternate with a fine, iridescently glittering metallised polyester slit-film yarn, woven in a dense warp constituting flexible yarns. As a result, the fabric **drapes horizontally**, thus demonstrating the concept of **drape versus body** (p.131), a feature that depends on the direction of the rib in unbalanced plain weaves. The thin black warp yarn floats loosely dot the surface of the fabric letting the lurex glow. Because of the two different weft yarns, the **face and reverse of this warp-faced plain weave vary,** as the stiffer monofilament pick allows for longer warp end floats than the flexible lurex yarn.

■ TAPE YARN   ■ SPIRAL YARN

□ PES ME (LUREX YARN)

□ PA (FILAMENT YARN)

"In Finland the tram route maps are simple; despite the occasional snow storms, traffic is generally in a good condition and it is quite empty."

Similarly, this horizontal rib fabric drapes in the direction of the heavier weft yarns. Picks of black thick cotton **ribbon yarn** are woven in with the black ends lifting, while the white coarse **woollen** yarn picks are woven in with the white warp yarns lifting. As a result, the face of the fabric showcases a clear contrast between the black and white **horizontal stripes**. On the other hand, due to the mixing of the contrasting colours of the ends and picks, the opposite effect happens on the reverse side as the stripes blur together.

■ TAPE YARN   ■ SPIRAL YARN

☐ CO (RIBBON YARN)
☐ WO

⇕ *Clear Traffic* from collection *Finland* by Yumi Kurotani

"I imagine it is crowded in Baltimore and that people are an anonymous mass. So, Baltimore is a small-scale texture. In my mind the city is harsh and a little chilly. The stripes in the textile resemble the skyscrapers of downtown Baltimore."

In contrast to the pick and pick weft sequence in *Clear Traffic* and *Light of Night*, this sample is woven with alternating plain weave units of two black wool polyamide **loop yarn** picks and two black flat-pressed polyurethane coated picks, which result in a **similar uneven stripy texture** on both sides of the fabric.

■ TAPE YARN   ■ SPIRAL YARN

□ WO/PA (LOOP YARN)
□ PU/CO/PA (FLAT-PRESSED YARN)

→ *Baltimore* from collection *On the Way to Uncharted Grounds* by Kajsa Hytönen

MULTIPLYING PICKS

Variations of the ribbed warp-faced texture can be achieved through **multiplying** the amount of picks in each shed. In this horizontal rib, a unit of two thick unbleached cotton twine picks alternates with a single pick generating soft rhythmic stripes of weft floats. As a result of the alteration of picks per shed, the two sides of the fabric differ from one another.

■ TAPE YARN   ■ SPIRAL YARN

 CO

← *Clothes Line* from collection *Gentle* by Anastasia Poljatschenko

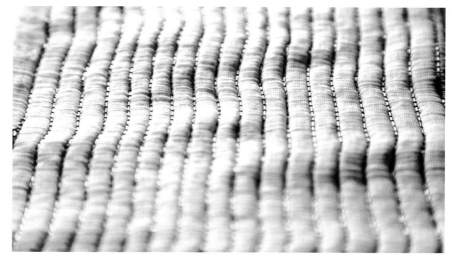

"Lazy Sunday *is organic and manually bent into shape. It is comforting and precious with a free forming effect.*

Morphology *is a woven collection consisting of two parts:* Human Metaphors *and* City Metaphors. *Inspired by two cities, Helsinki and Istanbul,* Morphology *explores how different cities shape us and how we are affected by our everyday urban lives. Through tactile and visual metaphoric textiles, the work expresses how our modern ways of living affect us culturally and personally.*

Human Metaphors *explore how the physicality of the city is connected to our lives and wellbeing. The collection is a tangible manifestation of human emotions and conceptual ideas surrounding daily life.*"

↕ *Lazy Sunday* from collection *Morphology –Human Metaphors* by Erin Turkoglu

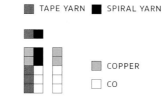

■ TAPE YARN ■ SPIRAL YARN

■ COPPER
□ CO

In this sample, a unit of three thick cotton twine picks alternates with a unit of two copper yarn picks. The reverse side of the fabric reveals the floats of the textured **spiral yarn** ends on the white cotton ground, while on the front side the multiplied cotton twine bulges softly under the flat **tape yarn** ends. The material contrast of the heavy cotton pick and the bending **metal yarn** forms gently waving horizontal stripes.

VARIATIONS TO PICK SEQUENCE

This glittering icy texture is woven with two fancy yarns, a composite yarn consisting of a polyamide slit-film yarn interlaced with cotton viscose tape yarn and a silvery covered yarn with a viscose core. The horizontal ribs covered by the matte tape yarn swell between the tightly woven units of three plain weave picks.

▨ TAPE YARN ■ SPIRAL YARN

☐ CO/PA/CV (COMPOSITE YARN)
▨ CV/PA ME (COVERED YARN)

← *Glacial Ice* from collection *Harsh* by Anastasia Poljatschenko

▨ TAPE YARN ■ SPIRAL YARN

} × 8

▨ WO
☐ PAPER YARN

This stripe repeat is achieved by weaving groups of contrasting picks, a stiff paper yarn and a thin black wool yarn. Integrating a bundle of paper yarns in the same shed adds a rib between the stripes.

→ *Traditional Door* from collection *Finland* by Yumi Kurotani

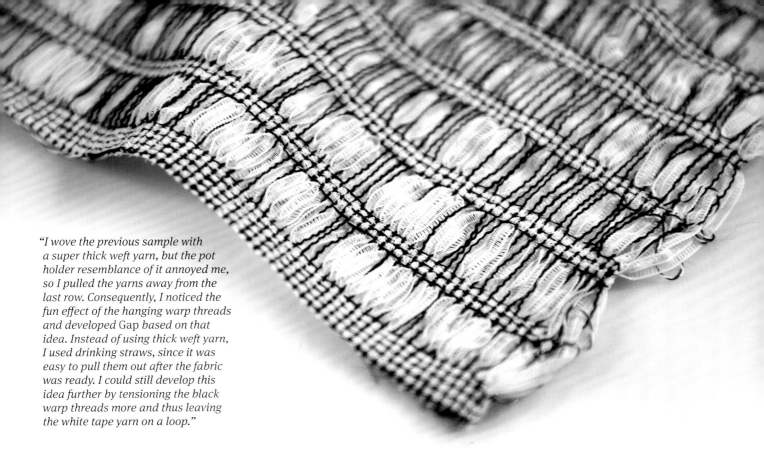

"*I wove the previous sample with a super thick weft yarn, but the pot holder resemblance of it annoyed me, so I pulled the yarns away from the last row. Consequently, I noticed the fun effect of the hanging warp threads and developed* Gap *based on that idea. Instead of using thick weft yarn, I used drinking straws, since it was easy to pull them out after the fabric was ready. I could still develop this idea further by tensioning the black warp threads more and thus leaving the white tape yarn on a loop.*"

SPACING THE WEFT

Plain weave can be varied through modifications in the pick density or the yarn sett. Textured or hairy warp and weft yarns keep their positions in a tightly interwoven plain-weave structure, which allows for repeats of tighter and more loosely set areas. However, a spacing device is needed in between the densely beaten weft picks to allow for the open space.

Structural cramming and spacing, and skip-dent fabrics are further discussed in *Tension, Texture and Transparency* p.169 and *Sheer, Parched and Perforated* p.215.

FREE-FLOATING ENDS

This plain-weave structure with gaps of **free-floating warp end**s is woven with a twisted thin hairy wool acrylic blend pick, which clings firmly in place within the plain weave interlacement. Here, a spacer is used to leave a gap between the stripes of five tightly woven plain weave picks. The free-floating warp ends mix randomly between the plain weave stripes.

■ TAPE YARN ■ SPIRAL YARN

□ SPACER (REMOVED)

□ PAN/WO

↑ *Gap* from collection *Random* by Anni Raasmaja

III Striped Monofilament and Spiral Yarn Warp

SEERSUCKER
TRANSPARENCY—PLAIN-WEAVE SHEERS
CRAMMING AND SPACING
TEXTURING—REPEAT, YARN SETT, AND STRUCTURE

FIBRE AND YARN INFO:
POLYAMIDE
MONOFILAMENT, SPIRAL YARN

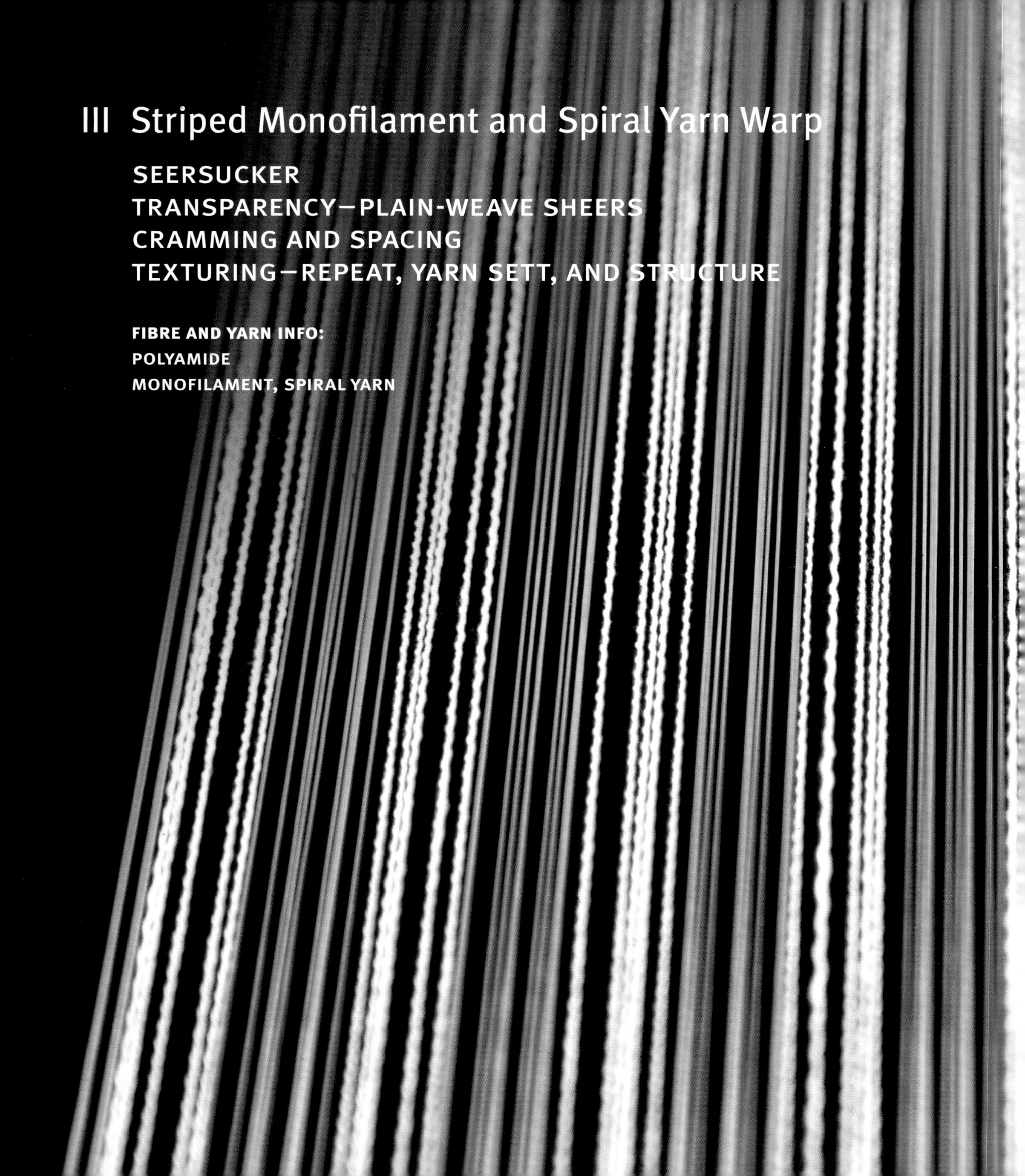

2.3 Tension, Texture and Transparency

This warp with a stripe sequence of ten transparent polyamide monofilament yarns and five white viscose polyamide spiral yarns is set in a straight draft on a double beam loom, using one beam for each yarn type. The **yarn sett**, density of the yarn in the reed, varies between the two sets of warp yarns. In the **reed set-up**, the monofilament ends have a tighter sett with two yarn ends placed in one **dent**, while the spiral yarn ends have a looser sett with each yarn placed as one end per dent of the reed. Furthermore, as each set of warp yarns is wound on a separate beam, **uneven tensioning** of the two sets of warp yarns enables the exploration of **slack-tension** weaving. **Seersucker**, a slack-tension woven fabric with puckering vertical stripes, can be woven on this warp by keeping the set of ground ends under regular tension and the puckering set of ends under light tension.

Polyamide / PA is a strong and elastic fibre with excellent abrasion resistance and elastic recovery. Due to these properties, items such as parachute fabrics, and airbags and safety belts in cars are exclusively made from polyamide. It has low moisture absorbency, and hence dries fast. The smooth, dense fibres pack closely together and result in dense fabrics that are excellent for wind and water resistant jackets, parkas, tents, and umbrellas. Sportswear items, such as tights and swimsuits, make use of nylon's good comfort and stretch. Popular interior textile applications of the fibre include carpets and pile-weaves. Polyamide is also used as a monofilament in applications requiring high tensile strength of a single fibre, such as fishing line.

The abrasion resistance of polyamide is eight times better than cotton and twenty times better than wool. For this reason, core-spun yarns often have a polyamide core, and polyamide filament is commonly used as the ground ply in fancy yarns, such as in the spiral yarn in the sample warp. Polyamide enhances the tensile strength in combinations with wool and adds resiliency to cotton, viscose, and other cellulose-based fibre combinations.

Although polyamide encompasses many desirable qualities, its production and consumption encompass various problems. The deficiencies of polyamide fibres include static build-up and poor sunlight resistance. In fabrics made of spun yarns with staple fibres, pilling can be an issue. Polyamide is processed from petroleum which raises concerns linked to the oil industry. Its production also consumes more energy in comparison to manufacturing polyester. Other example of the environmental impact of polyamide is the discarded fishing nets that cause numerous environmental hazards for marine life.[15]

For more information on environmental impacts of fibres refer to p.36. Refer to section *Fibres – the Building Blocks* p.27 for general information on textile fibres.

Warp yarns
Two contrasting filament yarns are used in this warp sample. One warp yarn set is a transparent, stiff, and strong thin fishing-line type uv-protected **polyamide monofilament**. Due to the fibre's poor sunlight resistance, uv-protection is necessary for the polyamide monofilament in such applications. The other warp yarn set is a textured, soft, and flexible **spiral yarn** (p.156), which is created by corkscrewing a soft viscose multifilament yarn around a fine and resilient polyamide multifilament core. The combination of these warp materials is well suited for the strains of slack-tension weaving.

Striped monofilament and spiral yarn warp

Warp yarns:
Polyamide monofilament (uv-protected), den 750 (tex 83) | 100% PA
Viscose polyamide spiral yarn, Nm 6.8 (tex 147) | 95% CV 5% PA
Yarn sett: monofilament yarn:10 ends per cm | spiral yarn: 5 ends per cm
Reed: 10 yarns monofilament 50:2 | 5 yarns spiral yarn 50:1
Straight draft on four shafts on a double beam loom

Catch yarns, left unthreaded, are recommended in the selvedges

It is noteworthy to mention the first commercial success of the polyamide fibre that was marked with the production of the revolutionary transparent **Nylon®** stockings in 1939. *Nylon®* is a well-known trade name for polyamide. However, it is important to distinguish between **fibre names** and **brand names for fibres**. It is preferable to use the names of the fibres instead of their trade names when discussing fibre properties and compositions of yarns and fabrics. Other examples of commonly used trade names are **Lurex**, a metallised slit-film yarn, and **Tencel**, which is a brand name for the regenerated wood-based fibre lyocell (p.155).

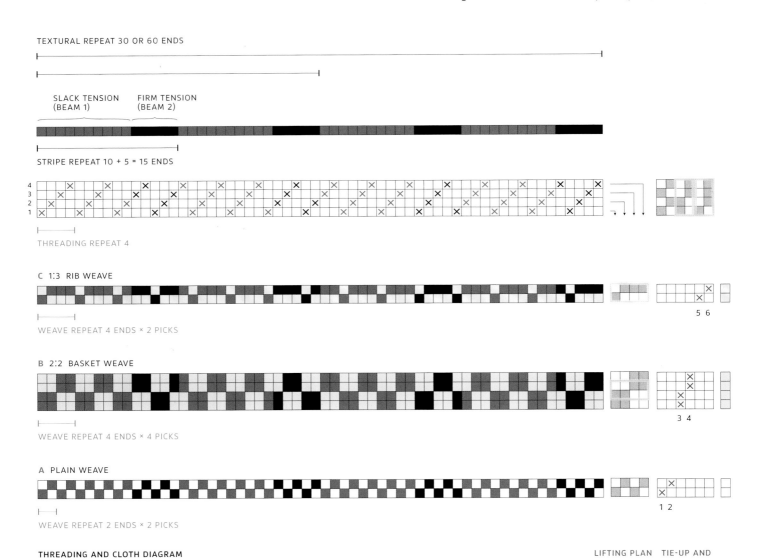

TEXTURAL REPEAT 30 OR 60 ENDS

SLACK TENSION (BEAM 1)   FIRM TENSION (BEAM 2)

STRIPE REPEAT 10 + 5 = 15 ENDS

THREADING REPEAT 4

C 1:3 RIB WEAVE

WEAVE REPEAT 4 ENDS × 2 PICKS

5 6

B 2:2 BASKET WEAVE

WEAVE REPEAT 4 ENDS × 4 PICKS

3 4

A PLAIN WEAVE

WEAVE REPEAT 2 ENDS × 2 PICKS

1 2

THREADING AND CLOTH DIAGRAM

LIFTING PLAN   TIE-UP AND TREADLING

The set-up of the sample warp is a straight draft on four shafts, and the tie-up includes **plain weave** (A), two-to-two **basket weave**, two-to-two **rib weave** (B), and one-to-three **rib weave** (C). Plain weave can emphasise the puckering of the stripes by firmly holding the picks in place and forcing them into a tight interlacement with the normally tensioned ends of the stable areas. The impact of the weave structure on the intensity and type of puckering is more evident whilst weave structures with fewer interlacements are integrated adjacent to the plain weave.

The differing yarn sett of the alternating bands of warp ends and the contrasting shrinkage properties of the slippery monofilament and the soft viscose polyamide spiral yarns, add additional layers of complexity to the material behaviour and provide extensive possibilities for further research into tension and interlacement. The stiff monofilament yarn puckers stubbornly generating big waves on the surface, while the flexible and soft spiral yarn adapts and interlaces tightly.

In addition to the features discussed above, the striped sample warp is a wonderful playground for studying key concepts related to woven fabrics design, such as **cramming and spacing**, **opacity and transparency,** and **texture**, at both yarn and cloth level. The visual contrast between the two warps, densely sett translucent polyamide monofilament ends and sparsely sett matt white spiral yarn ends, provides further inspiration to convey a story by creating textural patterns through exploration and implementation of different weft yarns, variations in pick density and structural interlacements. Utilizing any combination of the three different design areas (A, B, C) and choosing the appropriate weft yarn materials bestows additional opportunities for texturizing.

Furthermore, the **stripe repeat size** of the warp ends and the interrelated repeat size of the **yarn sett** (15 ends, which are **indivisible** to the repeat size of the weave structures (A: 2 ends, or B and C: 4 ends), set the scene for exploring the upscaling of the textural pattern repeat size in shaft-weave fabrics (p.182). This alludes to the importance of taking the potential of various colours, structures, and pattern repeats into account while designing more complex structures and **jacquards**.

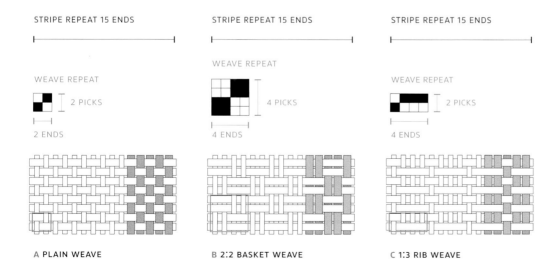

STRIPE REPEAT 15 ENDS

WEAVE REPEAT

2 PICKS

2 ENDS

A PLAIN WEAVE

STRIPE REPEAT 15 ENDS

WEAVE REPEAT

4 PICKS

4 ENDS

B 2:2 BASKET WEAVE

STRIPE REPEAT 15 ENDS

WEAVE REPEAT

2 PICKS

4 ENDS

C 1:3 RIB WEAVE

A

B

SEERSUCKER

Seersucker is a textured weave generated through **slack-tension weaving**, a process that requires two sets of warp yarns and two warp beams. While the ground ends are woven under ordinary tension, the crinkle ends are woven slack and are placed under a looser tension, creating permanent vertical puckering or a pile (A). Slack-tension pile weaving is further discussed in the section on pile weaves (p.210).

Plain weave, with its tight interlacement structure, holds the weft firmly and thus enhances the puckering effect. Seersucker is an easy fabric to care for as it requires no ironing after washing. The classic seersucker fabric is a plain-weave lightweight cotton summer suiting fabric with a blue ground and puckering narrow white stripes, formed from the loosely tensioned white ends (B). Its cooling properties, the airy crinkles that allow air to circulate and prevent the fabric from clinging to the body in heat and humidity, made seersucker a popular suiting fabric in the warm-weather conditions of former British colonies.[16]

Seersucker type fabrics can also be made by weaving with yarns with different shrinking properties, as demonstrated in the sample warp in this section, and in the plain-weave samples woven on the wool and linen yarn warp (p.268). Additionally, seersucker type fabrics can be created by using special shrinking, elasticated, or high twist yarns, such as in the featured sheer curtain fabric (c). The effects achieved by using alternating shrinking yarns can be intensified through **finishes** (pp.415–417). Furthermore, in addition to creating crinkles during the weaving process, similar effects can be achieved through chemical finishes such as **crêpe finish** and **cloqué printing** (p.421).

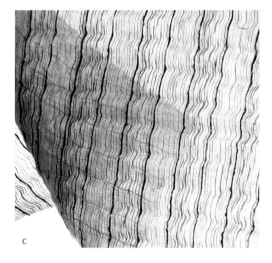

C

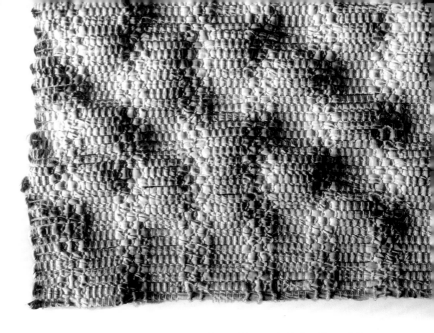

"People, society, how can we be so ignorant? How can we be so blind? Why do we let them rule us? Why do we just complain when we can actually choose?"

This stiff, densely woven plasticky **plain-weave** fabric is woven with strips cut from polyvinyl chloride (PVC) imitation leather, which is a non-recyclable synthetic plastic polymer often used in inexpensive, fast-fashion garments with a short life span. **Puckering** is achieved by keeping the spiral yarn ends under firm tension while the filament ends are slack. The difference in the properties of these two warp yarns emphasises the effect.

↑ *Society* from collection *Order* by Ellen Rajala

■ MONOFILAMENT YARN (PA) ■ SPIRAL YARN (CV/PA)

SOCIETY ☐ PVC

TYRE ☐ CO/PU

Similar to the sample *Society*, this **plain-weave** fabric is woven with the spiral yarn ends under tight tension. However, in contrast to the tightly woven rigid PVC pick in the previous sample, here the flexible flat-pressed and polyurethane coated pick is lightly beaten in, letting the monofilament ends form **soft waves**. The white spiral yarn ends form vertical dash lines on the black rubbery surface.

← *Tyre* from collection *Revealed* by Teija Vartiainen

"In deep space, there are no molecules to produce sound waves. This fabric is making waves just because it can."

PUCKERING PLAIN WEAVE AND FLOATS

Silky viscose polyester filament yarn picks form dense rows of alternating units of tight **plain weave** and **weft floats** in this fabric. The areas woven in plain weave hold the interlacement firmly, enabling **puckering effects** in the monofilament warp while the float areas texturise the fabric into a sparkling grid.

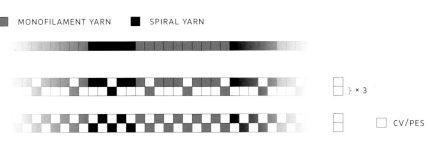

■ MONOFILAMENT YARN   ■ SPIRAL YARN

} × 3

☐ CV/PES

↕ *Sonic* from collection *Surface* by Netta Törmälä

SLIPPING CRINKLES

A seersucker-type effect in both warp and weft directions can be achieved utilizing four differing yarns. Here alternating bands of soft slipping picks and stable picks interwoven in the slack-tensioned warp with two different sets of ends result in a rolling check-pattern of bulges on the lacy surface.

In this sample several picks of **plain weave**, woven with a soft bouclé yarn plied with polyamide monofilament, frame alternating groups of **rib weave** and plain weave of dense bouclé-only picks that are woven without the added support of the rigid monofilament. The combination of a plain-weave structure with the plied monofilament-bouclé yarn positions the ends and picks in a stable grid. In contrast, the surrounding bands of the bouclé-only picks are unable to hold the bulging monofilament ends firmly and let them slip from the interlacement.

■ MONOFILAMENT YARN ■ SPIRAL YARN

BOUCLÉ

BOUCLÉ + PA (MONOFILAMENT)

↓ *Landscape of China* from collection *China* by Lu Zeng

TRANSPARENCY—PLAIN-WEAVE SHEERS

Silk organza above and cotton batiste below

Plain-weave structures, with their maximum number of intersections between warp and weft yarns, resist slippage and thus maintain the spaced grid of the picks and ends in gauzy transparent fabrics. Sheer, lightweight plain-weave fabrics originating from the silk-weaving tradition, today often replaced with man-made **continuous filament yarns**, are woven on warps with fine, **hard-twisted** or **over-twisted** multi-filament yarns. The type and direction of twists in the yarns gives the fabrics, such as **chiffon** and **organza**, their distinct look.

Lightweight plain-weave fabrics originated from the cotton-weaving tradition including **voile**, **batiste**, and **gauze**, are woven on fine **spun-yarn warps**. Unlike strong, fine filament yarn warps, a warp made of fine spun yarns requires undergoing **warp sizing**, a strengthening process in which starch or another chemical is applied onto the warp to protect the yarns from breakage during the weaving process. Refer to *Mock Leno* (p.218) and *Leno weave* (p.225) for further information on gauze type fabrics.

"As on a dragonfly."

TRANSLUCENT SHINE AND TEXTURE

These light and transparent **plain-weave sheer** samples from two complementary collections are loosely woven with soft, fine picks while keeping all the warp yarns under equal tension and thus eliminating the possibility of a seersucker effect. *Snowfall* is woven with a matt and flaky polyester loop yarn pick, while *Wings* is woven with a marl yarn pick in which the metallic ply adds glitters to its surface. In both fabrics, except for the slight gliding of the very fine shiny yarns around the slippery transparent monofilament ends in *Wings*, the plain-weave interlacement firmly holds the picks in place and creates the illusion of weft yarns floating without interlacement.

↑ *Wings* from collection
Party Time by Anna Sorri

→ *Snowfall* from
collection *Everyday Life*
by Anna Sorri

MONOFILAMENT YARN   SPIRAL YARN

SNOWFALL ☐ PES

WINGS ☐ PA/PES ME

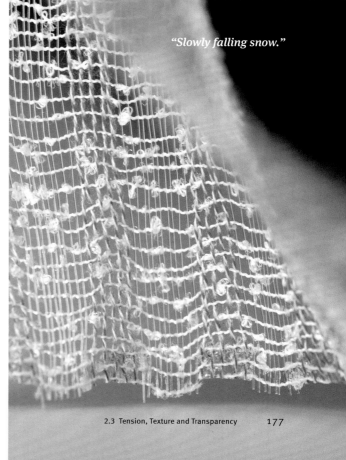

"Slowly falling snow."

2.3 Tension, Texture and Transparency   177

Plain-weave linen viscose blend sheer curtain fabric featuring opaque areas of viscose raffia bunches

CRAMMING AND SPACING

As established earlier, plain weave enables **spacing** and producing open gauzy structures. In contrast, weaves with less intersections have a tendency for **cramming** yarns, thus leading to more compact textures. The characteristics of the yarn types perform a significant role in this interplay. Therefore studying the phenomena of cramming and spacing – opacity and transparency – is key to comprehending the complexities and challenges of woven fabrics design. These investigations include altering the density of the picks, assisted by structural features of the different weaves and yarns, as well as taking into consideration the characteristics of both the ends and picks, and the warp sett and tension. Refer to **Mock Leno** (p.218) for further information on structural features that support cramming and spacing.

Experimenting with **control of warp tension** is necessary to understand the conditions required to achieve the seersucker effect. However, it is important to differentiate and recognise other wavy and puckering effects in fabrics that can be generated without unequal warp tensioning. The samples featuring transparency and opacity, presented on p.177 and pp.180–183 as well as the sample *Bird* (p.185), are all woven while keeping both warps under equal tension. The wavy textures of these fabrics result from the contrasting elasticity of the warp yarns rather than unequal tensioning of the two warps and requires a tight structure keeping the intersections of picks and ends firmly in place. Further examples of this type of fabrics can be found in the section *Checks, Stripes and Camouflage Twill* (p.243).

Utilising combinations of yarns with different thicknesses or other contrasting characteristics, such as combination of slick filament ends with soft spun-yarn picks, result in slippage within the interlacement as showcased in *Landscape of China* (p.175). Under these circumstances, unequal tensioning of the two warps might cause loose hanging ends and hinder the weaving process. Moreover, releasing the resulting fabric from loom tension can lead to the tense warp ends getting pulled out of the interlacement and potentially ripping the fabric.

Weaving a **plain-weave check pattern** by implementing two yarn types with varying characteristics, in both warp and weft directions, offers a fascinating base for exploring ways in which material interplay triggers **cramming and spacing**. Here two plain-weave units of transparent polyamide monofilament pick interlace with similar stiff monofilament ends. Hence the picks are kept steady within the firm, spaced grid of a balanced weave and create rows of small rectangular windows. In contrast, the loosely sett softer white spiral yarn ends let the monofilament picks slip within the interlacement. Moreover, both the spiral yarn and the monofilament ends allow the thin and flexible iridescent polyester slit-film yarns to cram together and cover the warp, generating dense prismatic bands on the surface.

↑ *Entertainment* from collection *China* by Tong Ren

"The neon lights on the streets are fun, mysterious, and entertaining."

■ MONOFILAMENT YARN ■ SPIRAL YARN

} × 2 □ PA (MONOFILAMENT)

} × 35 □ PES

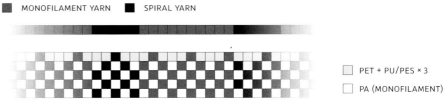

"*This sample is reminiscent of the vast amount of plastic waste found drifting in the seas.*"

TRANSPARENCY AND OPACITY

↖ *At Sea* from collection *Florida* by Tiina Teräs

Similar to *Entertainment*, here two **plain-weave units** of stiff monofilament yarn generate rigid, transparent areas. The bulging stripes of plasticky pick **floats**, woven with bunches of polyurethane coated black yarn and strips of thin plastic bags, are kept separated by the plain-weave units.

■ MONOFILAMENT YARN   ■ SPIRAL YARN

☐ PET + PU/PES × 3
☐ PA (MONOFILAMENT)

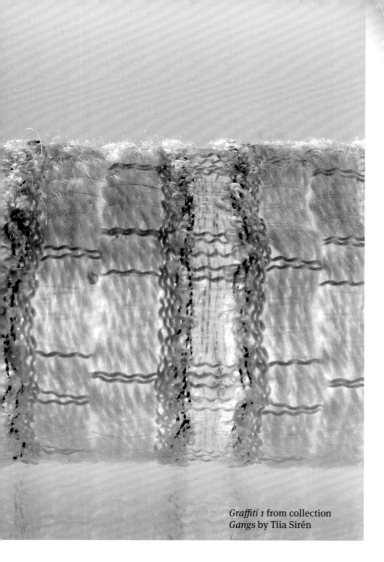

Graffiti 1 from collection
Gangs by Tiia Sirén

The fabric stories of collections *Florida* and *Finland* by Tiina Teräs are presented on pp.106–109.

This sample integrates pick **floats** of a variety of furry yarns including a unit of multiple soft, white worsted wool yarns, a unit of loop yarns, and a unit of spiral yarns identical to the warp ends. The pick units alternate with translucent stripes of **plain weave** that are woven with a shimmering polyester slit-film yarn.

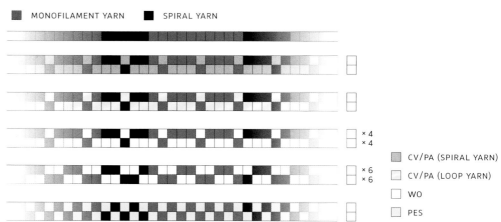

■ MONOFILAMENT YARN ■ SPIRAL YARN

× 4
× 4

× 6
× 6

■ CV/PA (SPIRAL YARN)
□ CV/PA (LOOP YARN)
□ WO
□ PES

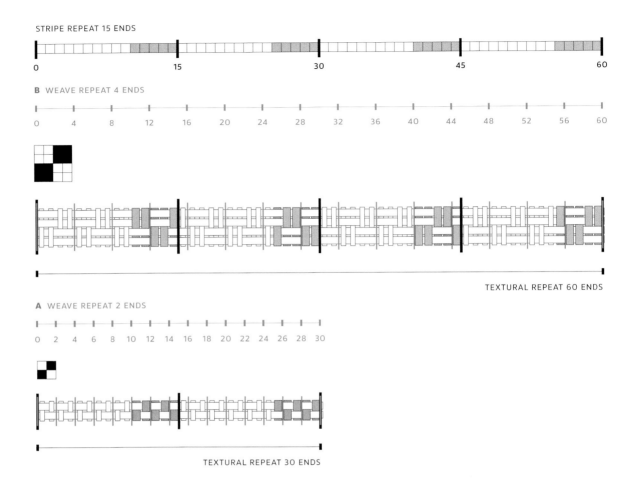

STRIPE REPEAT 15 ENDS

0   15   30   45   60

B WEAVE REPEAT 4 ENDS

0 4 8 12 16 20 24 28 32 36 40 44 48 52 56 60

TEXTURAL REPEAT 60 ENDS

A WEAVE REPEAT 2 ENDS

0 2 4 6 8 10 12 14 16 18 20 22 24 26 28 30

TEXTURAL REPEAT 30 ENDS

TEXTURING—REPEAT, YARN SETT, AND STRUCTURE

Weft-faced rib weave enables tight cramming of the pick, resulting in a vertical rib structure in which the weft covers the warp (p.139). Variations in the yarn sett, the density of the ends per dent in the reed, and alternating bands of contrasting types of warp yarns can also add diversity to the resulting striping.

Learning to navigate design work with different **weave repeat sizes** (p.125) of weaves, colours, and patterns is essential for advancing towards designing more complex structures and jacquard fabrics. As discussed in the sample warp introduction (p.171), the stripe repeat size of the warp ends and the interrelated repeat size of the yarn sett (15 ends) is indivisible with the repeat size of the weave (2 or 4 ends). This discrepancy expands the **textural repeat size** of this warp to the smallest common denominator between the two numbers, which in the case of a repeat with 2 ends is 30 ends (A) (two warp stripe repeats) and in a repeat with 4 ends is 60 ends (B) (four warp stripe repeats).

A similar concept of interplay between warp-stripe and weft-stripe repeats and weave structures is described on p.154 in the section *Colour and Weave* (p.258).

"Ponderous, Bubbly, Conundrum."

Here a loosely twisted cotton mop yarn is woven in plain weave alternates with bulky rib-weave units of multiple picks, thus forming a chequered texture that is bound into bumpy stripes by the strong filament yarn ends of the sample warp. Again, the sixty ends wide repeat of **irregular vertical striping** demonstrates the interplay of the weave structures with the two contrasting types of warp yarns and the method of denting in the reed.

↑ *Escape* from collection *Hefty* by Salla-Maaria Syvänen

■ MONOFILAMENT YARN   ■ SPIRAL YARN

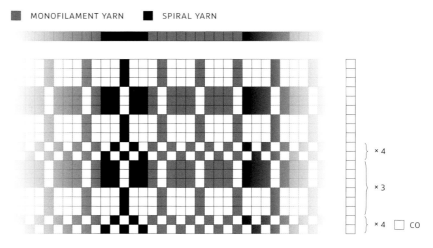

× 4

× 3

× 4   ☐ CO

IRREGULAR VERTICAL STRIPES: WEFT-FACED RIB WEAVE

The fabric is woven with two **contrasting picks**, a fine black mohair yarn and a prismatic metallic polyester slit-film yarn, which create fine, glittering pinstripes on a fuzzy, black ground. As in all the samples presented on this page, the **irregular stripe pattern**, resulting from the interplay of the weft-faced rib weave and the striped warp with two contrasting warp yarns and the differing yarn setts, amounts to four warp stripe repeat units. Furthermore, this weft-faced fabric displays the mohair-yarn dominating the fabric face, while the metallic yarn creates a more shimmering reverse side with the yarns floating over three ends. For more on this phenomenon, see the uneven vertical rib weave samples, *Home* (p.140), and *Crosswalk* (p.143).

↑ *Night Sky – Stars and Fireworks* from collection *Party Time* by Anna Sorri

■ MONOFILAMENT YARN   ■ SPIRAL YARN

■ PES
□ WO

CHEQUERED TEXTURES

This fabric is also patterned by groups of thicker and thinner **vertical ribs**. However, due to weaving only with one pick, the face and back of the fabric are identical. The picks, consisting of plies of a silvery polyester slit-film yarn and a polyester blend spun yarn, cover the warp in sparkly ripples. In addition, narrow **horizontal dents** of plain-weave are woven between bulgier areas of longer weft floats and dice the ribbed areas into a glittering chequered texture. The interplay between the contrasting elasticity of the two warp yarns generates a slight waviness on the fabric surface.

↑ *Dress Up* from collection *Florida* by Tiina Teräs

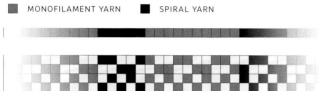

■ MONOFILAMENT YARN ■ SPIRAL YARN

} × 5

} × 2 □ PES/PA + PES ME

PATTERNING WITH CONTRASTING COLOURS

The potential of the striped monofilament and spiral yarn warp are demonstrated in this graphic **colour-and-weave** (pp.154, 258) pattern. The voluminous black cotton jersey yarn picks compose a contrasting background in comparison to the sound-wave like pattern created by the two warp yarns and the silvery bouclé picks.

■ MONOFILAMENT YARN ■ SPIRAL YARN

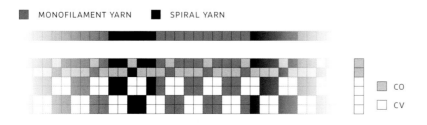

□ CO
□ CV

"If liberty sang a song, little, as the larynx of a bird, nowhere would there remain a tumbling wall."

Song of the Greatest Wish[17] *by Ahmad Shamlou*

↑ *Bird* from collection *The Moments* by Ali Zamiri

End and End Spun Yarn Warp

FIBRE INFO:
WOOL
WORSTED WOOL YARN, MERCERIZED COTTON YARN

2.4 Layers, Pleats and Blocks

This end and end warp set-up consists of white worsted wool and mercerised cotton yarns, or alternatively black and white worsted wool yarns.

Wool / WO is a **protein fibre** derived from different breeds of sheep. It is among one of the earliest fibres made into fabric, either through felting or by spinning the fibres into yarns and weaving (p.53). The textile properties of wool are excellent. This nature's spectacularly functional fibre has attained remarkable levels of efficiency and performance through evolutionary selection. Spring-like proteins in wool cause its crimp, which contributes to the flexibility, elasticity, and resilience of the fibre. Other wool fibre proteins have a more amorphous structure that enables wool to absorb relatively large amounts of moisture without feeling wet. Consequently, spun yarn wool has excellent bulk and insulation properties, and wool fabrics feel comfortably warm and dry next to the skin. Furthermore, wrinkles and creases in the material recover easily. Wool has self-cleaning properties, hence considerably less water and chemicals are required during use. It is inherently flame retardant and strong, which also makes it an ideal fibre for furnishing fabrics.

The breed of sheep and their breeding environment has a great impact on the properties of the wool. As a result, wool varies from super fine **Merino wool** to the high lustre wool of English breeds to coarse hairy wools. The distinct properties of the different wool types are best utilised by processing them into appropriate end products. Innovations in the processing and production of the material, as well as developments in its new blends with other natural and man-made fibres, have extended the applications of wool and improved the technical performance range and trans-seasonal appeal of wool textiles, including a wide range of softer, lighter-weight fabrics for casual and sportswear items.

Consumers generally view wool as an environmentally friendly and sustainable material as it is a renewable resource. However, its production encompasses environmental impacts such as overgrazing, waste-contaminated runoff and emissions of methane, a greenhouse gas, caused by rumination (p.37). On the other hand, the environmental impact of wool depends greatly on the method and policies used in sheep herding and fibre production. As an example, the washing process can be environmentally harmful, if using organic solvents and releasing contaminated water into nature, or sustainable when recycling the water and saving refinable lanolin and salts.[18]

Wool is excellent for fibre mechanical recycling (p.38). The environmental impact of recycled wool production is notably less than virgin wool, saving on the emissions and

Warp yarns

The two sets of warp yarns, the fine and elastic two-ply **worsted wool** ends and the shiny two-ply **combed mercerised cotton** ends, offer an intriguing starting point for exploration into double-weave variations. The mercerised cotton warp forms a firm and reliable base, while the adaptable wool ends are well-suited to achieve effects like pleats and puckering through experimentations with uneven warp tensioning.

The warp set-up and samples in this section present an alternative end and end warp with **black and white worsted wool yarns**.

For information on Cotton refer to p.129. Mercerisation, a process in which an alkali finish is applied to cotton threads and fabrics, is discussed on p.417.

water consumption linked to sheep breeding, and reducing the use of energy, water and chemicals in the later production phases.

Refer to p.28 for general information on animal fibres. For information on the history of wool fabrics, see p.53 and p.58.

All samples presented in this section are woven with the featured set-up with **blocks** in a **divided-draft** (p.288) arrangement on a **treadle loom**. Studying double-weave structures on a treadle loom can help novice weavers better understand the complexities of the structure. Variations transpire by merely altering the pedalling sequences and exploring different yarn qualities.

End and end worsted wool and mercerised cotton yarn warp

Warp Yarns:
Warp 1: Worsted wool yarn, Nm 2/36 (tex 28 × 2) | 100% wo (white)
Warp 2: Mercerised combed cotton yarn (white), Ne 8/2 (tex 76 × 2) | 100% co or worsted wool yarn (black)
Yarn sett: 14 ends per cm
Reed: 70:2

SET-UP I: TREADLE LOOM
Block draft on eight shafts on a double beam loom with the two blocks in a divided-draft arrangement in warp-wise groups.

THREADING AND CLOTH DIAGRAM

TIE-UP AND TREADLING

WHITE WOOL COTTON WARP   **OR**   BLACK AND WHITE WOOL WARP

WARP 1: WO (BEAM 1)   WARP 1: WO (WHITE)

WARP 2: CO (BEAM 2)   WARP 2: WO (BLACK)

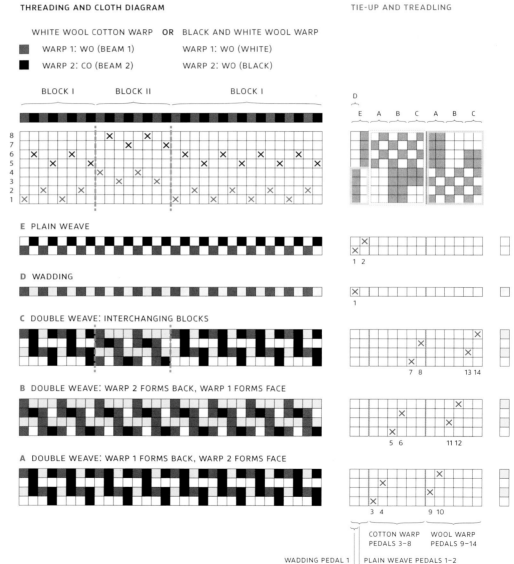

BLOCK I   BLOCK II   BLOCK I

D

E A B C A B C

E PLAIN WEAVE

1 2

D WADDING

1

C DOUBLE WEAVE: INTERCHANGING BLOCKS

7 8   13 14

B DOUBLE WEAVE: WARP 2 FORMS BACK, WARP 1 FORMS FACE

5 6   11 12

A DOUBLE WEAVE: WARP 1 FORMS BACK, WARP 2 FORMS FACE

3 4   9 10

COTTON WARP   WOOL WARP
PEDALS 3–8   PEDALS 9–14

WADDING PEDAL 1 | PLAIN WEAVE PEDALS 1–2

The warp is set on a double-beam loom with a tie-up for a **double weave**, with two horizontally interchangeable plain weave layers (A and B). In addition, **vertical interchange** of the two layers is enabled by the **block draft** (C). **Wadding yarn** can be used to fill in the weave pockets by separating both fabrics (D).

A **double weave** has two separate layers of cloth woven at the same time. The structural draft showing the two layers "flattened" to a draft sequence is often considered challenging to understand and is taught at later stages of studies. However, investigating this structure while weaving on the loom makes it understandable even for novice weavers and sheds light on the logic of the draft. This exploration is made even more intriguing by the vast possibilities offered by the double-weave structure such as patterns, pleats, puckering, and pockets with or without wadding yarn.

As described in the two previous warp descriptions (pp.153 and 169), in cases where the warp is comprised of two different yarns employing **two warp beams** is preferable. In double-weave structures such as the one described in this section, two warp beams are needed in order to maintain the **individual warp tension** in each double-weave layer. The potential to handle each layer separately with the two beams allows for experimentation with pleats and puckering effects.

Wool, as a flexible material, is well-suited for pleats and puckering effects while the mercerised cotton warp forms a reliable base structure. The wool layer may shrink notably after the warp tension is released, hence intensifying the abovementioned effects. See also section *Quilted Layers* p.287.

A double-weave structure, with its two sets of picks and ends, enables the design of **two distinct colour areas**. Therefore, choosing two differing colours for the two warps is a viable alternative. Two sets of warp yarns with different compositions also enable further explorations with materials and structures. The warp set-up and samples featured in this section showcase fabrics woven on both a warp with white wool and cotton yarns and a warp with black and white wool yarns.

For the treadle loom, in order to assist the comprehension of the structural draft, the threading of the **blocks** is a **divided-draft** arrangement with each warp set threaded in groups of neighbouring shafts (SET-UP I). Subsequently, the treadles are in units of two for the position of each individual plain weave cloth layer, and the tie-up exhibits neatly arranged **blocks of plain weave** for each of the four-shaft units. Weave variations can be easily explored by changing the treadling sequence. The warp set-up for dobby looms is featured on the following page (SETUP II).

Warp 2 forms the face cloth (A, white pick) and warp 1 is woven on the back cloth (A, blue pick). The roles are **horizontally interchanged** when warp 2 ends move back (B, white pick) and warp 1 ends are woven on the face (B, blue pick). Furthermore, plain weave can be integrated for tight interlacements in between pleats or to add textural effects (E).

Understanding the logic of a block draft paves the way to designing jacquard fabrics described in Chapter 3. *Jacquards – Boosting the Patterns*. Narrow vertical stripes of warp 1 appear on the face in block II (C, blue pick) while warp 2 appears on the face in block I (C, white pick). Applying any combination and repeat size of the three different design areas (A, B, C) as graphic elements provide further room for patterning.

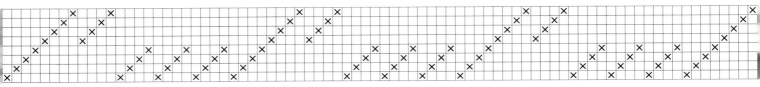

In a **block draft**, or **grouped draft**, the shafts are divided into two or more blocks, each appointed to a different weave structure in the tie-up or the lifting plan. The threads for each weave structure are drawn on their own set of shafts.

Block draft on eight shafts on a double beam loom with the two blocks in a straight-draft arrangement.

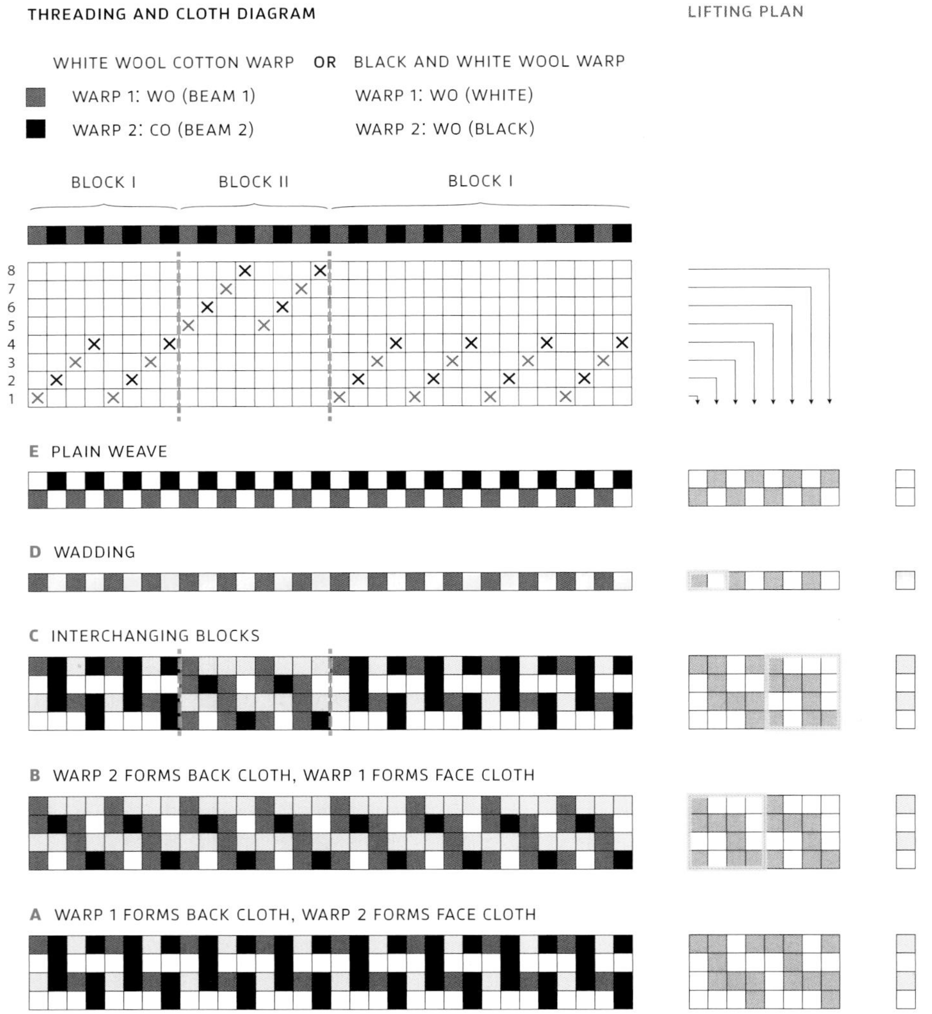

THREADING AND CLOTH DIAGRAM

LIFTING PLAN

WHITE WOOL COTTON WARP   **OR**   BLACK AND WHITE WOOL WARP

▪ WARP 1: WO (BEAM 1)   WARP 1: WO (WHITE)

■ WARP 2: CO (BEAM 2)   WARP 2: WO (BLACK)

BLOCK I   BLOCK II   BLOCK I

E PLAIN WEAVE

D WADDING

C INTERCHANGING BLOCKS

B WARP 2 FORMS BACK CLOTH, WARP 1 FORMS FACE CLOTH

A WARP 1 FORMS BACK CLOTH, WARP 2 FORMS FACE CLOTH

BLOCK I   BLOCK II   BLOCK I

8
7
6
5
4
3
2
1

C INTERCHANGING BLOCKS

B WOOL WARP FORMS FACE CLOTH

A COTTON WARP FORMS FACE CLOTH

B II   B I   B II   B I   B II   B I

A COTTON WARP ON TOP

A {

B WOOL WARP ON TOP

B {

A + B HORIZONTAL STRIPE PATTERN

B {
A {

C VERTICAL STRIPE PATTERN

C {

Examples of the block-draft designs in the sample warp

STRUCTURAL DRAFT   STRUCTURAL DRAFT WITH   SECTION VIEW
                    END AND PICK SEQUENCE

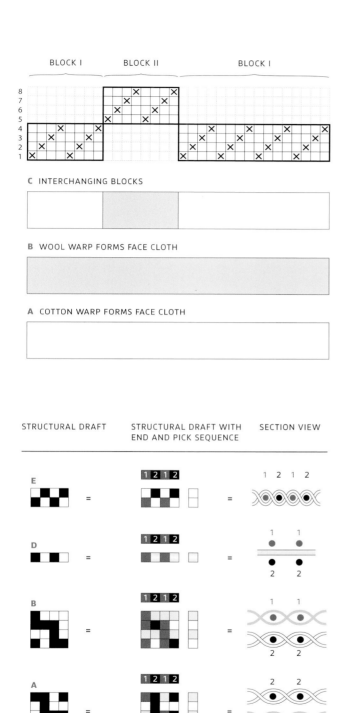

E   1 2 1 2   1 2 1 2
  =   =

D   1 2 1 2   1   1
  =   =   2   2

B   1 2 1 2   1   1
  =   =
                   2   2

A   1 2 1 2   2   2
  =   =
                   1   1

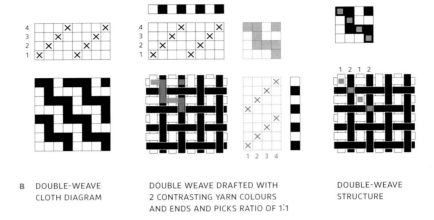

B   DOUBLE-WEAVE
CLOTH DIAGRAM

DOUBLE WEAVE DRAFTED WITH
2 CONTRASTING YARN COLOURS
AND ENDS AND PICKS RATIO OF 1:1

DOUBLE-WEAVE
STRUCTURE

DOUBLE WEAVE

The **double-weave** structure consists of two
layers of fabric woven simultaneously (A). Both
layers, the **face cloth** and the **back cloth**, have
their own set of warp yarns and weft yarns.
Plain-weave double weave can be woven with
only four shafts by appointing two shafts for
each warp (B).

The two warps can be simultaneously woven
on top of each other without any interlacement
(C), resulting in **two separate fabric layers** with
separate selvedges, as illustrated in the drafts
and the example woven on the black and white
warp with a white pick weaving the white ends
and a black pick weaving the black ends (D).

Depending on the number of shafts available, other basic weave structures can be used.
It is also possible to use yarns of varying size
in both weft and the warp. In addition, the
ratio of the yarn sett in both layers can vary, in
other words, the cloth layers can have different
densities in either yarn system.

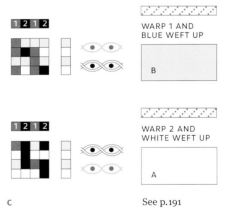

WARP 1 AND
BLUE WEFT UP

WARP 2 AND
WHITE WEFT UP

C

See p.191

**Fabric names:
double weave**

*pocket weave,
pocket cloth,
matelassé*

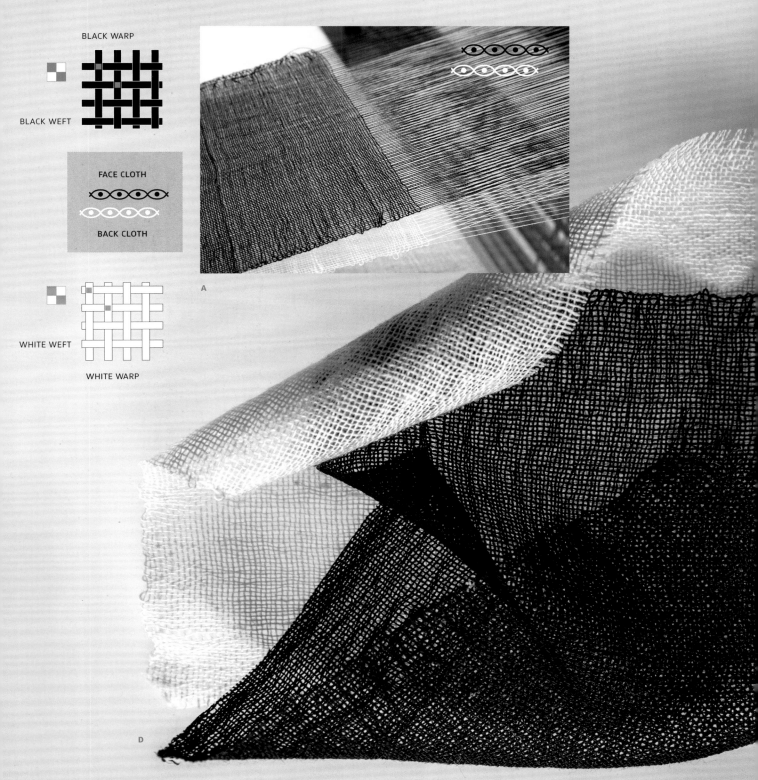

BLACK WARP

BLACK WEFT

FACE CLOTH

BACK CLOTH

WHITE WEFT

WHITE WARP

A

D

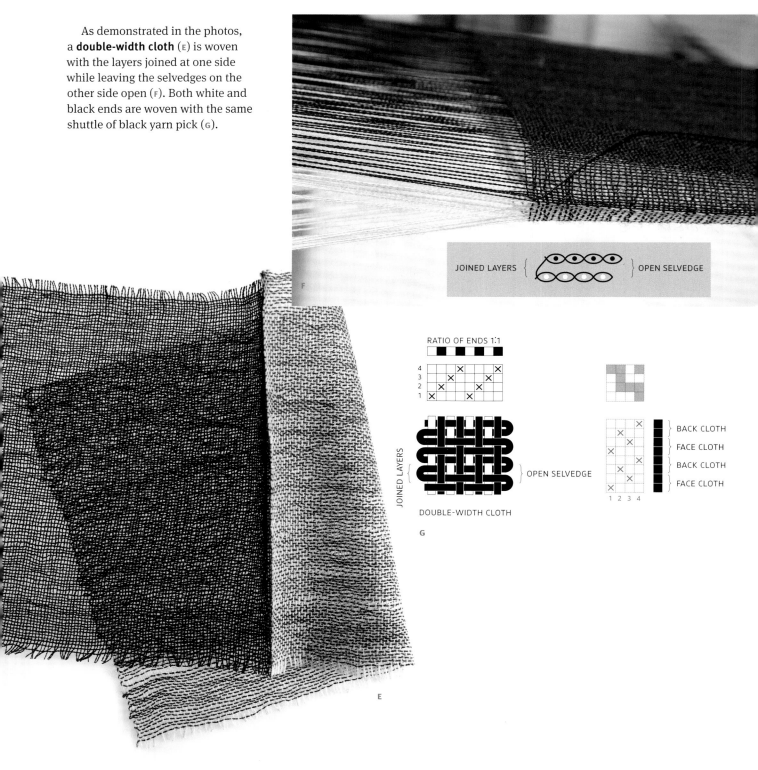

As demonstrated in the photos, a **double-width cloth** (E) is woven with the layers joined at one side while leaving the selvedges on the other side open (F). Both white and black ends are woven with the same shuttle of black yarn pick (G).

JOINED LAYERS { OPEN SELVEDGE

RATIO OF ENDS 1:1

JOINED LAYERS

OPEN SELVEDGE

DOUBLE-WIDTH CLOTH

G

BACK CLOTH
FACE CLOTH
BACK CLOTH
FACE CLOTH

1 2 3 4

F

E

Alternatively, the fabric is woven to create a **tube** with the layers joined at both sides of the selvedges, as presented in *Gucha Gucha* and *Jellyfish*. Weaving a tube is good practice for getting familiarised with the double weave and the logic of its draft before moving on to pocketing and pleating.

A double-weave tube woven on the black and white wool warp with a soft viscose polyamide bouclé yarn.

■ WO (WHITE)
■ WO (BLACK)

A

□ CV/PA

↑ *Gucha Gucha* from collection *Samu* by Elisa Defossez

"Gucha Gucha (Japanese onomatopoeia)– sometimes things seem complicated. Actually they are not."

In this sample, a pick unit of a transparent blue polyamide filament chainette yarn and grey bouclé yarn joins the two separate layers of cloth together at the selvedges. Additionally, rows of plain weave at both ends of the sample combine the two warps, resulting in a big, soft, glimmering, and transparent pocket. In contrast to the loosely woven back cloth in which lack of control lets the warp yarns shift and group into bunches, the top layer of the pocket is woven in double pick density.

← *Jellyfish* from collection *Soft Feels* by Pei-Nung Lee

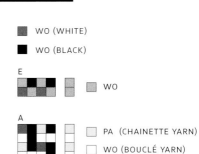

■ WO (WHITE)
■ WO (BLACK)

E

□ WO

A

□ PA (CHAINETTE YARN)
□ WO (BOUCLÉ YARN)

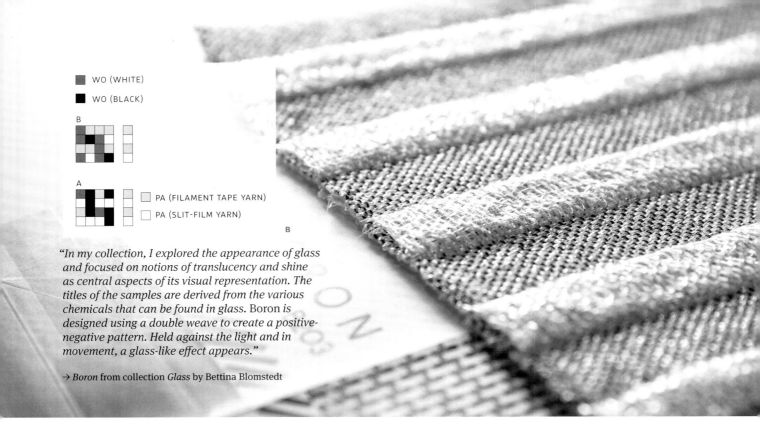

WO (WHITE)

WO (BLACK)

B

A

PA (FILAMENT TAPE YARN)

PA (SLIT-FILM YARN)

B

"In my collection, I explored the appearance of glass and focused on notions of translucency and shine as central aspects of its visual representation. The titles of the samples are derived from the various chemicals that can be found in glass. Boron is designed using a double weave to create a positive-negative pattern. Held against the light and in movement, a glass-like effect appears."

→ *Boron* from collection *Glass* by Bettina Blomstedt

POCKETING—HORIZONTAL INTERCHANGE

↑ This glossy fabric created on a black and white wool warp is woven with two transparent weft yarns. A transparent polyamide slit-film pick weaves the white warp and a lacy poly-amide filament tape yarn is utilised for the black warp. The **horizontal interchange** of the warp layers intro-duces transparent tubes across the fabric.

A pocket weave, or double weave interchange, can be formed by interchanging the posi-tions of the face and the back cloth at regular intervals and hence stitching the two layers together (A). This produces a compound fabric composed of two interwoven layers. Changing the lifting plan on a dobby loom, or alterna-tively adding an extra set of pedals linked to the appropriate tie-up on a treadle loom, **interchanges** the fabric layers **horizontally**, resulting in a **railroaded fabric** with rows of pocketing tubes across the fabric. (B)

Double-weave fabrics are well suited for creating patterned fabrics with **distinct colour areas**. End and end warps with contrasting colours, such as the black and white warp

in *Boron* presented on this page, make clear the differences between the two layers. These variations are reinforced through the choice of pick colours. This concept is further discussed in Chapter 3 in the context of jacquard design.

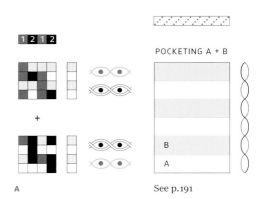

1 2 1 2

+

A

POCKETING A + B

B

A

See p.191

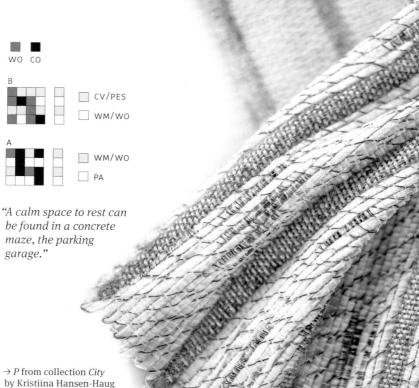

POCKETING STRIPES AND TEXTURES

In this graphic textured fabric, woven on a white wool and cotton yarn warp, the two plain weave layers **interchange** and generate pocketing **horizontal stripes**. The wool warp is woven on the face using a black and white fasciated viscose polyester combination fancy yarn. The cotton warp is woven with a shimmering knitted polyamide tape yarn on the backside of the fabric. As a unifying element, grey wool yarn pick is interwoven as narrow stripes in both warps.

WO CO

B
CV/PES
WM/WO

A
WM/WO
PA

"A calm space to rest can be found in a concrete maze, the parking garage."

→ *P* from collection *City* by Kristiina Hansen-Haug

This double-weave fabric with **horizontal stripes** features experimentation with three **contrasting weft yarns**; a coarse linen yarn, a textured cotton yarn, and a transparent polyamide monofilament. The three picks are alternately woven in all the positions of the **pocket weave** structure, while keeping the **yarn repeat independent of the structural repeat** of the interchanging cloth layers. The transparent monofilament exposes the warp ends and reveals the layer beneath it.

WO CO

B

A
 PICKS: 1. LI, 2. CO AND 3. PA

"The melting snow reveals what is hidden under the snow."

← *Melting Snow* from collection *Finland* by Tong Ren

PLEATS

The double-weave structure allows for **horizontal pleats** to be woven into the fabric. One of the warps is used to create the pleat while the other warp forms the ground cloth. To achieve pleating, the tension of warps has to be controlled separately, thus it is necessary to set each warp on a different beam. After weaving both the ground cloth and the pleat layer to the desired height of the stripe, the cloth layer, which is to be pleated, is independently woven higher. Subsequently, the tension of the pleat warp has to be sufficiently released for the end of the woven pleat to meet the ground cloth. Both layers are then woven tightly together using a plain weave to ensure that the pleat is firmly held in place. A stick can be used in between the two layers to equate the warps before weaving the two fabrics together. The featured draft illustrates the formation of horizontal pleats in a double-weave (A). The industrially woven samples showcase pleated effects in interior fabrics (B, C).

Puckering effects and pleats in double-weave structures can be further explored and intensified through finishes explained in Chapter 4 (see *Cables* and *Frill* p.416).

C ↑ Pleated cotton polyamide mixture upholstery fabric, Backhausen

B ← Pleated cotton polyester mixture curtain fabric from F&F collection *Chandni Chowk* (MS)

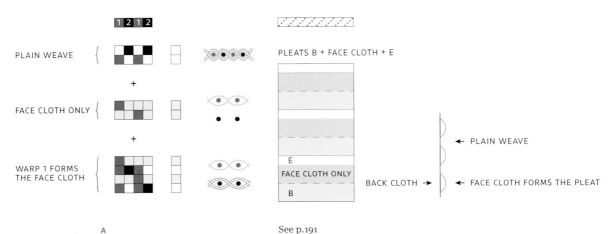

PLAIN WEAVE

FACE CLOTH ONLY

WARP 1 FORMS THE FACE CLOTH

A

PLEATS B + FACE CLOTH + E

E

FACE CLOTH ONLY

B

See p.191

BACK CLOTH →

← PLAIN WEAVE

← FACE CLOTH FORMS THE PLEAT

The flexible wool warp is suitable for rounded soft pleats and puckering effects, while the mercerised cotton warp creates a firm and reliable **ground cloth**. In this fabric, polyester loop yarn pick interlaces with the wool ends to form **textured pleats** on the face of the fabric. A soft polyester filament tape yarn entwines the fabric layers together and produces a firm ground cloth with the cotton ends.

WO CO

E

  PES (FILAMENT YARN)

FACE CLOTH

B

PES (LOOP YARN)

PES (TAPE YARN)

"Let's roll up our sleeves."

↑ *Overtime* from collection
Everyday Life by Anna Sorri

WO CO

E

FACE CLOTH

A

LI

PAN

LONG, HEAVY LAYERED PLEATS

In contrast to *Overtime*, the pleats in this sample are created utilizing the cotton warp instead of the wool warp. Woven with a fluffy polyacrylic pick, the pleats are longer and heavier and hence fall flat on one side and generate **overlapping**. The wool warp, woven with a fine unbleached linen pick, produces the ground cloth.

↑ *Fresh Snow* from collection *Finland* by Tiina Teräs

The collections *Finland* and *Florida* by Tiina Teräs are presented on pp.106–109.

TRANSPARENT PLEATS

The irregular shifting of the smooth mercerised cotton ends of these glassy pleats is triggered by using a slippery thin polyamide monofilament as pick. Due to the **transparent pick,** the warp yarns convey the impression of running freely without interlacement. The contrasting stripes in the ground cloth woven alternately with three different yarns shimmer through the semi-transparent layer of pleats. Similar to fabrics *Overtime* and *Fresh Snow*, a narrow strip of two plain weave picks separates the pleats from one another.

WO   CO

E

FACE CLOTH

A

   ALTERNATING STRIPES OF
1. WO, 2. PAN AND 3. PES

PA

↕ *Beat* from collection *Gangs* by Tiia Sirén

*"Can you hear the music?
Can you see the sound waves?"*

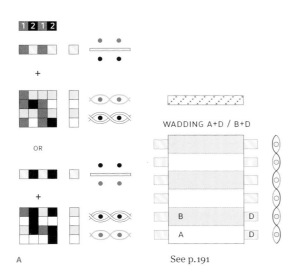

1 2 1 2

OR

+

A

WADDING A+D / B+D

B | D
A | D

See p.191

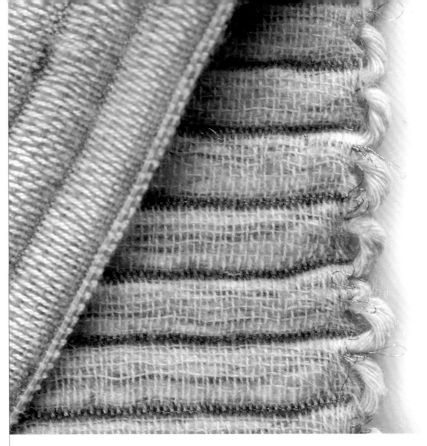

WADDING

Double weave can be padded by inserting **wadding yarns** or **batting** in the pockets between the face and back cloth. After both layers are woven to the desired length, all the yarns of the face cloth are lifted up to allow room for the wadding pick to be inserted. (**A**)

Refer to p.385 for wadding in the context of jacquard design.

PADDED EFFECT

Both the wool and cotton warp are loosely woven with a thin two-ply mohair pick and reveal the **wadding pick**, which consists of bundles of thick cotton mop yarn and strands of metallic yarn. Plain weave woven with a thin coppery metallic polyester-core yarn pick joins the two layers together.

WO   CO

E
PES ME

D
CO + PES ME

B
WM
WM

↑ *H* from collection
Autumn by Miisa Lehto

"I am intrigued and inspired by double weave and especially the idea of yarns floating freely in between the two fabric layers. This fabric is inspired by the autumn; when nature turns into different shades of yellow and copper, and the feeling of the first autumn breeze makes you want to wear layers and layers of warm wool."

B → Pleated cotton polyamide upholstery fabric, Backhausen

POCKETING—VERTICAL INTERCHANGE

Vertical interchange with lengthwise running stripes can be created by utilising a **block draft** (p.190) with an additional set of shafts (A). Varying the colours and yarn types of the picks in the two interchanging layers further enhances the design options. The featured industrially woven fabric demonstrates vertical interchange of two alternating independently striped blocks (B).

Fabrics with lengthwise running stripes are referred to as **up-the-roll** fabrics, as opposed to **railroaded fabrics** (p.196).

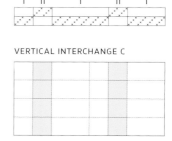

VERTICAL INTERCHANGE C

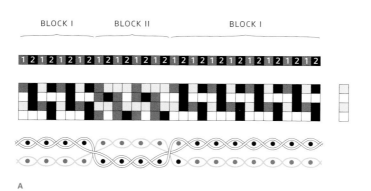

A

↑ *Latu–Ski Track*
from collection *Finland*
by Tiina Paavilainen

See p.191

← **Vertical interchange** of the two double-weave layers creates lengthwise running stripes. On the face of the fabric, white wool ends woven with a black wool yarn appear as narrow stripes, while the cotton warp ends woven with white polyamide pick form the broader stripes. The reverse effect appears on the backside of the fabric.

WO   CO

C

WO

PA

EXAMPLES OF BLOCK-DRAFT DESIGN IN THE SAMPLE WARP

| B II | B I | B II | B I | B II | B I |

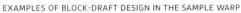

A + C PATTERN

C

A

B + C PATTERN

C

B

C

C

A + B + C PATTERN

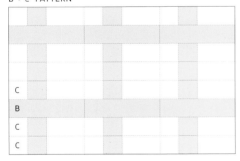

C

B

A

C

FURTHER PATTERNING

Block and check designs and other patterns can be generated by combining both horizontal and vertical interchange in double weave (c). A double-weave structure with its two sets of picks and ends enables the design of distinct colour areas, which makes it a favoured structure for patterned fabrics woven on dobby looms and jacquard looms. Refer to p.380 for double-weave constructions in jacquard fabrics.

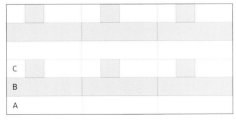

↖ Tightly pocketing patterned double-weave upholstery fabric, Torri Lana

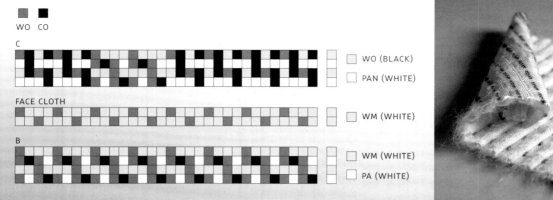

WO CO

C

WO (BLACK)
PAN (WHITE)

FACE CLOTH

WM (WHITE)

B

WM (WHITE)
PA (WHITE)

BLOCKS HIDDEN IN PLEATS

Vertically interchanging blocks, speckled by a set of two fluffy black wool picks, flutter behind wales of soft white **horizontal pleats** woven with fuzzy soft mohair yarn. The reverse side of the fabric features a graphic pattern of horizontally and vertically interchanging plain weave layers that are textured with the strikes of black wool pick and a contrasting selection of shiny, hairy and smooth yarns.

↕ Sample from collection *Sunlight* by Hanna-Maaria Sinkkonen

↕ *Adulthood* from collection *Life* by Julia Trofimova

MIXING BLOCKS, CHECKS, STRIPES, AND PLEATS

Layers and pleats with an **assortment of yarn types** with varying counts in colours ranging from black to white through shades of grey, pattern this explorative sample of horizontal and vertical double weave interchange.

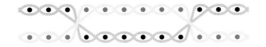

A
DOUBLE WEAVE (POCKET WEAVE)
2 SETS OF WARP AND WEFT YARNS

B
BACKED WEAVE (DOUBLE CLOTH)
2 SETS OF WARP AND WEFT YARNS

LAYERED STRUCTURES — INTERWOVEN FABRICS

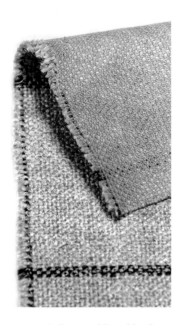

C A chequered linen blend backed-weave upholstery fabric with two sets of ends and picks, Lauritzon

Double weave, **double cloth**, **backed weave**, and **double faced fabric** are names for variants of **interwoven fabrics**. **Piqué**, introduced in the section *Quilted Layers* (p.290), also belongs to this type of **multilayered structure**. It is important to note that often within textile terminology, different interpretations and terms are used to refer to these fabrics. These differences in terminology are industry specific, region specific, and craft-tradition specific. The same notion applies to some of the other weaves introduced elsewhere in this book (e.g. honeycomb p.274). Hence, one might encounter contradictory explanations for the terms double weave and double cloth. However, rather than engage in semantic discussions, it is predominantly important to understand the structural differences between these distinct types of double fabrics, and consequently be able to adapt to the different traditions.

Double cloth, sometimes referred to as **backed weave**, is an **interwoven fabric** with the face and back fabric layers woven together. Similar to double weave, both sides of the fabric contain separate warp and weft systems. The main difference between double weave and double cloth is in the manner in which the two layers are stitched together. In a **double weave** (A) the fabric layers interchange positions between back and face, creating pockets between them.

In contrast, in a double-cloth fabric the warp sets do not swap positions and the **stitching yarns**, ends or picks linking the two fabric layers, are preferably not noticeable on the opposite side. The fabric look of double-cloth

structures can notably differ on the face and the reverse side. The distinctions may be in colour or colour sequence, yarn texture, yarn sett, weave structure, or any combination of these.

Within the textile industry, the term **backed weave** is often used for double-cloth fabrics with two sets of ends and picks, in which the two layers are stitched together by interlacing the back ends to the face picks or alternately back picks to face ends at regular intervals. These interlacing stitching yarns can be kept invisible by disguising them behind the floats of the surrounding yarns (B). This type of a backed-weave structure is often used in upholstery fabrics. In the featured furniture fabric, a loosely sett plain weave with linen blend bouclé ends and picks is stitched to a more structurally stable and densely set backing layer of thinner yarns on the reverse side. The thin yarns are hidden behind the floats of the thicker yarns (C).

The term **double cloth** is mostly assigned to interwoven fabrics with five sets of yarns; two sets of warp yarns and two sets of weft yarns and an additional set of either weft or warp yarns. This extra set of **binder yarns** weaves into both face and back side and is used to bind the layers together (D). Thick fabrics such as Kersey, which is used for winter coats, are produced using this method with the extra set of weft yarns that generate an insulating wadding between the two layers (E). Double cloth with binder yarns can also be designed to be later cut into two separate fabrics, as in **velvet** (p.212).

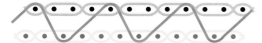

D

DOUBLE CLOTH
2 SETS OF WARP YARNS AND 3 SETS OF WEFT YARNS

F

DOUBLE FACED FABRIC
1 WARP AND TWO SETS OF WEFT YARNS

The third type of interwoven fabrics, **double-faced fabrics**, are made with three sets of yarns; either two warps and one set of weft yarns, or one warp and two sets of weft yarns (F). These fabrics include **diagonal ribs** (p.265) and double-faced **satin** and **twill** fabrics (G), in which both sides of the fabric are lustrous because of the finely woven warp-faced configuration on the face and back of the fabric, with the weft yarns interweaving the warp sets together in the middle[19].

The potential in multilayered woven structures for forward-looking applications, such as eTextiles, is described in the article *Layered Approaches – Woven eTextile Explorations through Applied Textile Thinking* (pp.471–473). Moreover, double-cloth and double-weave

structures can be expanded to 3D-woven garments and objects by cutting between the interchanging and interwoven layers to release the unfolding form, as illustrated in the project *I Weave Dogs and Clothes* (pp.46, 443). A similar approach has been adopted in the three-dimensional structures featured in *Floating and Clipping* (pp.460–461).

Double-weave and double-cloth structures are discussed in the context of jacquards in *Jacquards with Multilayered Structures* (p.380) and *Jacquards with Multiple Weft Systems* (p.364).

E ← A double-cloth wool coat fabric, Kersey, with two sets of warp yarns and three sets of weft yarns. The zoomed-in image highlights the white binder yarn that interweaves the two layers of fabrics together.

G → Double-faced silk fabrics featuring two sets of warp yarns and one set of weft yarns.

A handwoven double-cloth fabric with two sets of ends and picks; a sheer silk fabric layer and an interwoven layer of thin cotton gauze. The cotton layer stitches into the silk fabric at regular intervals thus interweaving both layers together.

For Better
Kaisa Kantokorpi

Silver Lining

*In sickness and in health,
on rainy days and on sunny ones,
I have been there for you
and always will.*

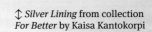

↕ *Silver Lining* from collection
For Better by Kaisa Kantokorpi

INTERWOVEN LINING

The two layers of this **double cloth** are
skilfully stitched together by allowing every
third thin silvery pick of the back cloth to
weave over the alternating wool ends of the
face cloth. The matt, lacy polyamide yarn
pick on the face cloth hides the stitching
points.

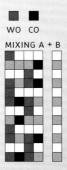

WO   CO

MIXING A + B

☐ PA

☐ CV/PES

A ← The image demonstrates the process of manufacturing corduroy. In the lower half of the fabric, columns of extra-weft are cut into pile, which forms the wales of corduroy after further finishes.

B → The finished cotton corduroy fabric and a blue baby-cord fabric

PILE WEAVES

Fabric names: weft-pile fabrics

velveteen, corduroy, pinwale corduroy (B)

Woven-pile fabrics are **pile-weave** structures produced with an extra set of yarns either in warp or weft direction. In these fabrics, the set of yarns forming the pile are called **pile yarns**, and the regular warp and weft yarns are identified as **ground yarns**. The ground structure of pile weaves is usually plain, rib, or twill weave. These pile weaves should not be mistaken with hand-knotted fabrics such as *Fuchsia* (p.151).

Weft-pile fabrics

Fabrics in which an extra set of weft yarns is used to form the pile are referred to as **weft-pile fabrics**. These fabrics are produced by weaving an additional layer of extra-weft floats over a ground weave. The floating pile yarns are then cut at the centre of the float to produce the cut-pile surface. The extra-wefts can be placed lengthwise in columns to produce **corduroy**, with its distinct wale-effect characteristic (A and B). In order to produce an even surface, as conveyed in **velveteen**, the extra-wefts can also be arranged randomly. Extra-weft patterning is further discussed on pp.150 and 319. Also refer to **corded weaves** on p.290 and **fil coupé fabrics** on pp.419 and 460.

Warp-pile fabrics

Fabrics in which the pile yarns are generated using an extra set of warp ends are called **warp-pile fabrics**. Weaving a warp-pile fabric requires separate tensioning of the pile yarn ends. The piles are cut to produce a **cut-pile weave**. A warp-pile fabric can also be left uncut to form an **uncut-pile weave** with loops on the surface of the cloth. This type of fabric is also called a **loop-pile fabric** (c).

A method utilised to produce both cut warp-pile fabrics and uncut-pile fabrics with loops is to raise the extra set of pile yarns over a rod. After securing the loops in place, through weaving a sequence of **ground weave** and raised pile yarns, the rods are removed from the pile yarns and create a loop-pile fabric.

To form a cut-pile fabric, a blade on the edge of the rod cuts the pile yarns as it passes, creating two rows of fine cut pile. This method produces one piece

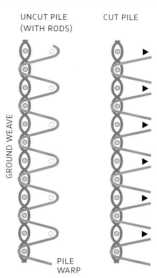

C LOOP-PILE FABRIC
2 SETS OF WARP AND 1 SET OF WEFT

UNCUT PILE   CUT PILE
(WITH RODS)

GROUND WEAVE

PILE
WARP

of pile fabric at a time. This system has many technical variations, but the same basic principle is applied to most warp-pile weaving processes. The technique is also adapted to weaving pile carpets. On hand-operated looms (p.213), or with special industrial machinery, cut and loop pile can also be integrated into the same fabric to form decorative patterns.

Terry cloth, an absorbent **loop-pile cloth** used in towels, is created by **slack-tension pile weaving** (see slack-tension weaving, seersucker p.169). During slack-tension pile weaving, the ground yarns are held under tension while the pile yarns are allowed to relax or slacken. The looped piles are generated as the picks are beaten into the fabric. Loops may appear on one or both sides of the fabric.[20]

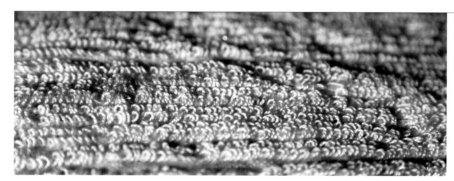

↑ *Special* from collection *Passivity* by Siiri Raasakka

"I explored weaving a woven-pile fabric with the wool warp looping on a ground weave. I figured out the required interlacement quickly, but faced technical difficulties in dealing with the loose warp ends. Through practice, I found the correct way to weave this."

The pleating warp is left unwoven to create a **loop-pile surface**. In this fabric, the wool warp forms the **pile warp** and the cotton warp is used as the **ground warp**. As a stable and tight structure, plain weave is a suitable weave for the ground. When experimenting with **woven-pile fabrics** on a handloom, rods can be used to keep the pile loops on the surface while weaving, and help avoid any loosening of the warp tension. The rods are ultimately removed after securing the pile yarns within the ground cloth.

WO   CO

● ALTERNATING
CO AND PES + PAN/PA

↑ E Silk velvet fabrics

Fabric names: warp-pile fabrics

velvet, velour, épinglé, frieze, terry cloth, chiffon velvet, panné velvet, plush

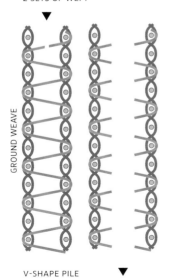

**D CUT WARP-PILE FABRIC
3 SETS OF WARP AND
2 SETS OF WEFT**

▼

GROUND WEAVE

V-SHAPE PILE   ▼

In contrast to the loop-pile weaving process explained on p.211, **cut warp-pile fabrics** such as **velvet** are made from a **double cloth** (p.206), in which pile warp yarns are used to connect and interlace between the two layers. After weaving, the double cloth is split into two separate fabrics by cutting between the face cloth and the back cloth, and leaving the interlacing pile yarns to form the cut pile surface as demonstrated in the graph (D). Hence, this method produces two pieces of velvet at the same time. Velvet fabrics range from plains (E) to elaborate multicoloured decorative velvets woven on jacquard looms (F).

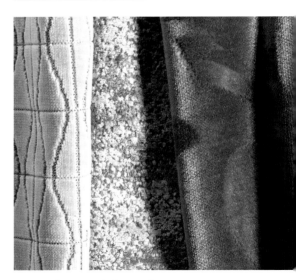

F Jacquard woven upholstery velvets

212

The Arte della Seta Lisio foundation in Florence nurtures the disappearing art of handwoven silk jacquard warp-pile velvet production. The images depict how the decorative patterns are formed by combining cut and loop pile on a ground weave as in the method described on p.211. The pile warp consists of silk ends, each on a separate roll to allow individual slacking for loop-formation (G). The ends are raised over a rod (H) according to the pattern and the loops are either cut with a special knife or left uncut to form loop pile areas (I, J).[21]

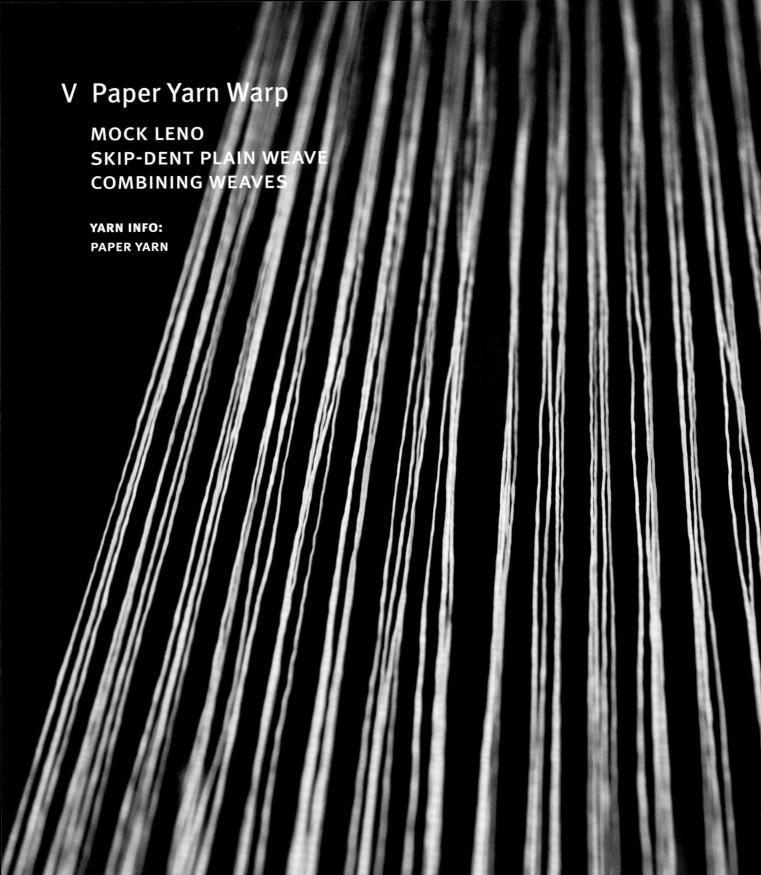

V Paper Yarn Warp

MOCK LENO
SKIP-DENT PLAIN WEAVE
COMBINING WEAVES

YARN INFO:
PAPER YARN

2.5 Sheer, Parched and Perforated

The paper yarn warp with the **mock-leno** set-up presented in this section enables explorations of **yarn distortions** and showcases methods to further emphasise such effects through **reeding** and **varying the pick density**. The set-up of this warp is a straight draft on eight shafts. The ends are grouped into units of four yarns and are placed in one or two adjacent dents with **skipped dents** between the groups.

Mock leno is a **plain-weave derivative** that belongs to the **open weave structures**. This weave provides an excellent platform for examining a number of aspects, including structural triggers to **warp and weft distortions** as well as **cramming and spacing**, which are essential for mastering woven fabric design.

The distorted-yarn effect is a structural phenomenon in which yarns are displaced from their regular linear path in the warp, or weft, or both directions.

    Grouped warp and weft distortions are created by assigning units of **differing weave structures** next to one another. This phenomenon is discussed in the section *Undulating Pick* (p.227).

Warp yarn
Paper yarn / PI is made from a narrow strip of thin twisted paper, moistened with water containing adhesives or other additives. The properties of paper yarn depend on the type and properties of the paper used in making the yarn. The material's strength is reduced when wet, making it sensitive to damage. The yarn used in the sample warp is tightly twisted and is therefore strong and rigid enough to be used as warp ends and woven into a fabric. Paper yarn is used in woven carpets (p.138), furniture fabrics, and wall panels in residential interiors.

Shifu, the Japanese craft of making yarns by folding, cutting and spinning hand-made mulberry plant paper, has traditionally been used to weave household textiles and everyday clothing.

Paper yarn warp
Warp yarn: Paper yarn Nm 3.9 (tex 256) | 100% PI
Yarn sett: 4 ends per cm
Reed: 20:4,0
Straight draft on eight shafts

Catch yarns, left unthreaded, are recommended in the selvedges

REED PLAN | 4 | 0 | 4 | 0

PI

E PLAIN WEAVE

1 2

D 4:4 WEFT

3 6

C 1:2:1 AND 1:2:1

4 5

B MOCK LENO

3 4 5 6

A MOCK LENO

3 4 5 6

THREADING AND
CLOTH DIAGRAM

LIFTING PLAN

TIE-UP AND
TREADLING

The structure of mock leno is a grid formed of alternating units of three or more ends and picks grouped together, inverting the interlacement of their adjacent units (A, B). The lacy appearance is created by the horizontal and the vertical lines of inverted interlacements (red lines), in which the **internal structural friction** pushes the units of similarly bound yarns apart from one another. The empty spaces in the reed emphasise this perforated effect in the warp direction (vertical red line). A similar effect in a horizontal direction is generated by controlling the impact of the beater on **the fell of the cloth** at the line of inverted interlacements (horizontal red line). A spacing device can be used to control the density of the picks (p.167).

The lifting plan includes a four-end unit **mock leno** (A and B) and **plain weave** (E). Furthermore, sections independent of the mock-leno structure, one-to-two (C) and four-to-four (D) **weft-faced rib weave**, can be explored individually or integrated within other weave combinations.

Plain weave provides a stable ground for observing the effects of **skipped dents** in the reed within the resulting fabric. Alternatively, adding rows of plain weave between stripes of mock leno offers the opportunity to compare the textural effects of cramming and spacing in both weaves.

The stiff paper yarn warp complements the overall organised rigidity of the weave, especially when woven with weft yarns with similar properties. Using firm ends and picks restrains the horizontal spacing of the open structure and helps overcome the challenge of regulating the pressure when beating the weft into place, a task often difficult for novice weavers. Experimenting with weft yarns with different composition, yarn count, type, and texture offers various approaches with which **opacity and transparency** effects can be adjusted based on the pick choice. Utilizing varying types of weft yarns, for each of the two structural areas of the pick interlacement, either emphasises or diminishes the spaced-out appearance of mock leno leading to further textural variations.

Grouped weft distortions are discussed in the section *Undulating Pick* (p.227).

Reducing the number of shafts

In order to broaden the possibilities of exploration, the sample warps in this book are designed to facilitate variations to the presented weaves. Plain weave is included in all warps to enable integration of closely bound areas or supplementary picks that resist slippage. Hence, the warps are set up on more shafts than required for individual weave types. Therefore, should there be fewer shafts available, their number can be reduced but at the expense of reducing the number of potential variations.

The number of shafts is determined by the number of alternative interlacements for each end (A). Similarly, the number of required treadles is established by the number of interlacement options in the horizontal, pick, rows of the draft.

As illustrated below (A), the four-end unit mock-leno structure presented in the sample warp can be woven on a loom with fewer shafts by employing a **block draft** (p.190). However, it is necessary to increase the number of shafts to eight to allow for integration of rows of plain weave between the mock-leno areas (B). As a substitute, a three-end unit mock leno including plain weave only requires four shafts (C).

The subject of evaluating the required shafts and treadles is essential to understand the boundaries of weave options in shaft weaves.

REDUCING THE NUMBER OF SHAFTS

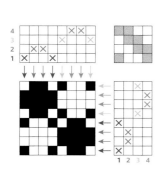

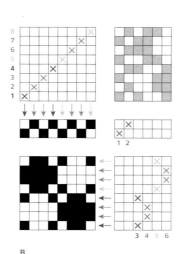

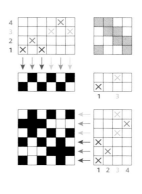

A
4 SHAFTS AND 4 TREADLES REQUIRED

B
8 SHAFTS AND 6 TREADLES REQUIRED

C
4 SHAFTS AND 4 TREADLES REQUIRED

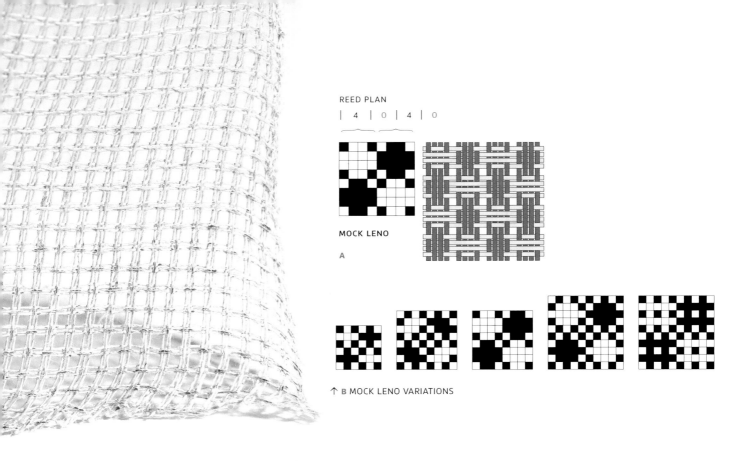

REED PLAN

| 4 | 0 | 4 | 0

MOCK LENO

A

↑ B MOCK LENO VARIATIONS

MOCK LENO

↑ c Mock-leno linen sheer, Larsen Fabrics

Fabric names: mock leno

canvas weave, huck lace, huck-a-back, huck, imitation gauze, Swedish lace, bronson lace

The gauze-like texture of the **mock leno**, also known as **canvas weave**, **etamine** or **imitation gauze**, is a plain weave derivative composed of two inverted adjacent structural units. The yarns in each unit of similarly interlacing ends and picks group together. On the other hand, the sharp contrast between these groups causes maximum internal friction thus triggering separation of the groups and forming a perforated open area. The lacy appearance of the fabric, caused by the abovementioned **warp and weft distortions**, can be emphasised by varying the yarn sett on the reed (A).

The structural repeat is typically divided into four units, with two alternating opposing structural units of three-, four- or five- or more ends. The cloth diagrams of mock leno variants showcase the units of similarly interlacing yarns opposed to areas of inverted interlacement (B).

Due to the complementary symmetry of the warp and weft floats in the weave, mock-leno fabric has a similar appearance on its face and reverse sides. The intricate play of opacity and transparency makes these fabrics a popular choice for applications such as shirting, blouses, dresses, and lightweight curtains (c).

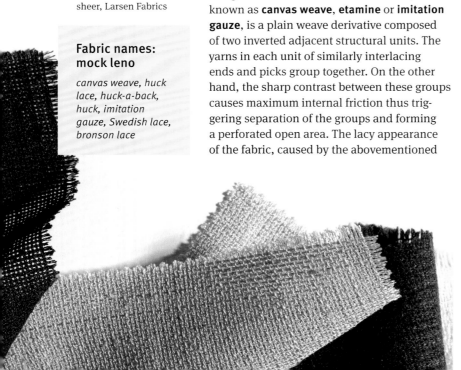

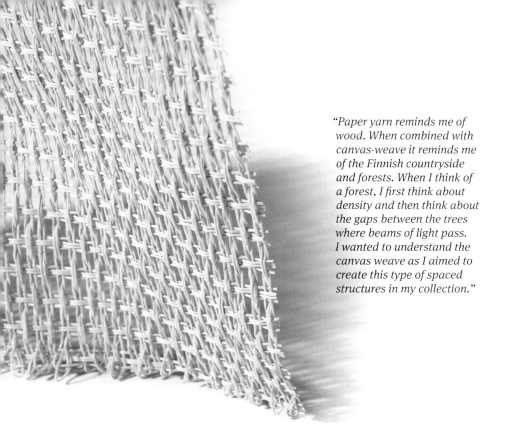

"Paper yarn reminds me of wood. When combined with canvas-weave it reminds me of the Finnish countryside and forests. When I think of a forest, I first think about density and then think about the gaps between the trees where beams of light pass. I wanted to understand the canvas weave as I aimed to create this type of spaced structures in my collection."

This archetypal four-end unit **mock-leno** sample is woven with a paper yarn pick identical to the warp yarn. The weave in the pick direction is carefully spaced, and hence retains the symmetry of the weave.

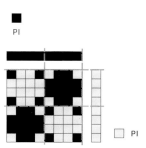

← *Woods* from collection *Nature, Order, Seasons* by Nur Horsanali

CONTRASTING PICKS

Contrasting weft yarns alter the spaced out appearance of mock leno. In this fabric bunches of loosely spun coarse jute yarn picks are constrained in place by stiff linen yarn picks. Large gaps highlight this dry and rough texture revealing the intriguing differences caused by the choice of yarns.

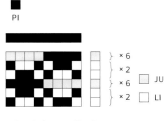

← *Reeds* from collection *Florida* by Tiina Teräs

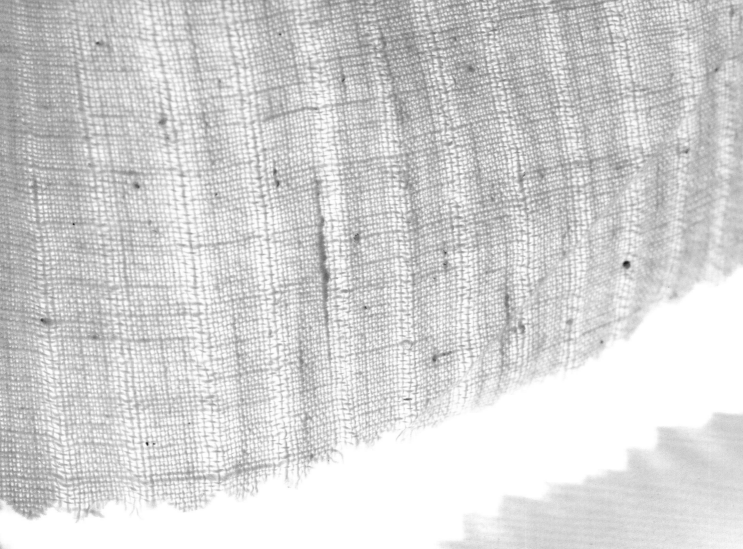

SKIP-DENT PLAIN WEAVE

↑ Skip-dent linen
curtain fabric

Spaced-out vertical, **up-the-roll** stripes can be formed through varying the density of the ends in the reed. These so-called **skip-dent fabrics** are woven on warps where the ends can be crammed in a number of reed dents while other dents are left empty. In the horizontal orientation, the pick direction, a spacing device can help in generating and keeping the gaps in place. Apart from slight unavoidable shifting, plain weave as a stable, closely bound construction keeps the yarn sett in place in skip-dent fabrics. Furthermore, the type and texture of the warp and weft yarns affect the stability of the cloth. Yarns with a hairy, clinging structure, such as wool, secure the placement in the weave. Skip-dent fabrics are often finished by washing, which further stabilises the yarns in their places. Refer to pp.167 and 178 on cramming and spacing in the weft direction.

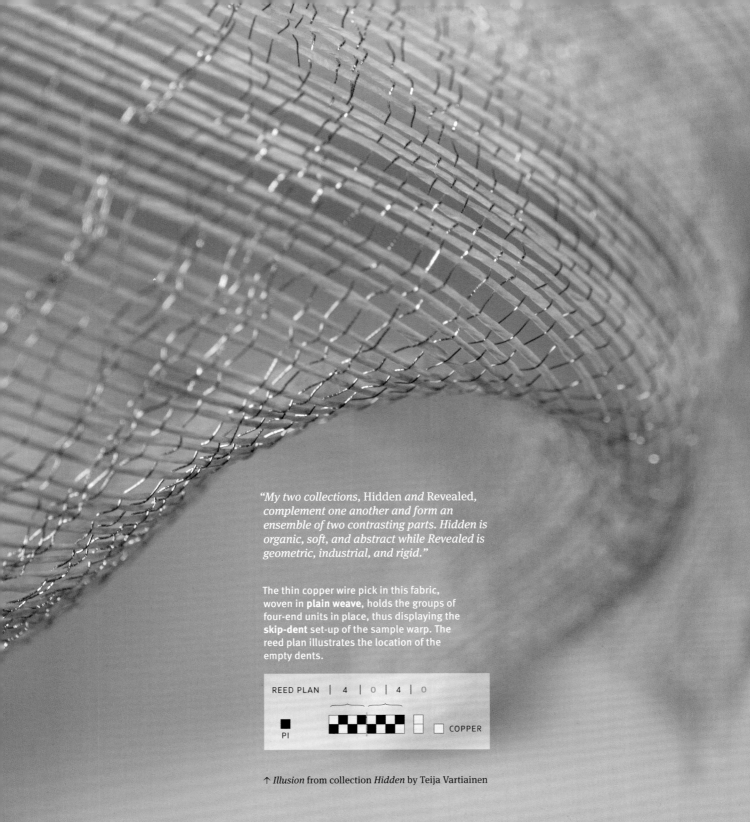

"My two collections, Hidden *and* Revealed, *complement one another and form an ensemble of two contrasting parts.* Hidden *is organic, soft, and abstract while* Revealed *is geometric, industrial, and rigid."*

The thin copper wire pick in this fabric, woven in **plain weave**, holds the groups of four-end units in place, thus displaying the **skip-dent** set-up of the sample warp. The reed plan illustrates the location of the empty dents.

| REED PLAN | 4 | 0 | 4 | 0 |

PI

COPPER

↑ *Illusion* from collection *Hidden* by Teija Vartiainen

↑ Jacquard-woven mock-leno
polyester sheer. Lodetex (TP)

← Jacquard-woven linen sheer
combining mock leno and plain
weave, Vanelli

COMBINING WEAVES

Mock leno is frequently set in a block draft
on shaft looms, or woven on a dobby loom
or jacquard loom to enable vertical stripes,
blocks, and other lacy patterns within other
less transparent ground weaves. Sheer
curtains and other lightweight fabrics often
feature **mock leno alongside plain weave.**

PI

MOCK LENO JOINS PLAIN WEAVE

In this fabric a silky viscose filament pick softens the rigid rows of paper yarn ends, creating a pattern with lacy horizontal mock leno stripes against a **plain-weave ground**.

← *Wood* from collection *Finland* by Yuki Kawakami

☐ CV

For Better
Kaisa Kantokorpi

Summer Wedding

It was the only sunny day in that June.
It had to be a sign.

PI

"It was the only sunny day that June. It had to be a sign."

Two contrasting picks, a smooth white cotton polyamide yarn and a silvery acrylic metal effect plied yarn, are woven in a sequence of **floats** alternating with **plain weave**. The rigid paper yarn ends maintain their straight rows while letting the thin picks slip and draw together forming a lacy, breezy veil.

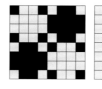

☐ PAN/PES ME
☐ CO/PA

← *Summer Wedding* from collection *For Better* by Kaisa Kantokorpi

PLAIN WEAVE, FLOATS AND CONTRASTING PICKS

Here a unit of **plain weave**, woven with a rubbery flat black polyurethane coated pick that is hidden under dense **weft-faced rib weave** floats of flat-pressed black chenille-type yarn, results in a perforated velvety texture.

PI

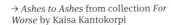

☐ CO/PA (FLAT-PRESSED CHENILLE YARN)

☐ PU/CO (COATED YARN)

→ *Ashes to Ashes* from collection *For Worse* by Kaisa Kantokorpi

"Although I have your ashes in an urn on the mantelpiece, I still can't believe you are gone. The house is so quiet. Finally, I can hear my own thoughts."

PI

☐ WM (LOOP YARN) OR PA (MONOFILAMENT)

☐ WM (LOOP YARN) + PI (FLAT PAPER YARN)

☐ PI (FLAT PAPER YARN)

A random sequence of **contrasting picks**, a brittle raffia-type flat paper yarn, a stiff and transparent monofilament, and scattered picks of soft mohair loop yarn create this dry and airy texture. The stiffer yarns aid in keeping the spaces open at points of inverted interlacements.

← *Winter* from collection *China* by Lu Zeng

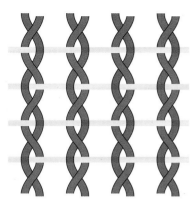

A LENO WEAVE

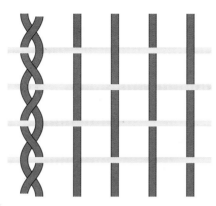

B LENO SELVEDGE WITH PLAIN WEAVE

Leno weave

The gauze-like structure of mock leno resembles the appearance of **true leno fabrics**. Therefore, it is important to draw a difference to this open and stable fabric, known as **leno weave** (A), giro inglese, or full gauze weave, that is created on a loom fitted with a **leno harness**, or doup. The harness alternately shifts the doup ends attached to it in a right- and left-hand direction, crossing the ground ends before insertion of each pick (p.76). The resulting figure-eight loops in leno weave firmly hold the picks in place and prevent any shifting in warp-direction, and thus enable transparency, firmness, and strength superior to other fabrics of similar count. Mock leno's weave structure stability in relation to its openness does not measure up to the stable open structures that can be produced with a true leno weave. Filament yarns or hard-twist yarns, commonly used in leno, further enhance the fabric's strength.

Leno-weave fabrics include sheer curtains such as marquisette, mosquito netting, and see-through apparel fabrics. The prospect of producing strong, spaced out fabrics with less material makes leno weave fabric a popular choice for industrial and packaging purposes, such as fruit bags. Similar stable and slippage resistant net fabrics can also be produced with warp knitting machines. Leno weave is also utilised in the production of **chenille yarns** (p.157).

In industrially woven fabrics produced through shuttleless weaving, the edges of the material are fringed. Integrating a leno selvedge into these fabrics reinforces the fringes and prevents unravelling[22] (B).

Fabric names: leno weave

grenadine, marquisette, English gauze, giro inglese...

↑ Leno weave sheer curtain fabrics. The use of spun yarns gives these polyester fabrics their natural-fibre hand and appearance, Vanelli

VI Tape Yarn Warp

GROUPED WEFT DISTORTION
VARIATIONS—REVEALING THE FLOATING ENDS
SHRINKING WEFT YARNS

FIBRE, YARN AND FABRIC INFO:
BLENDS, COMBINATIONS, MIXTURES
ELASTANE
FABRIC WEIGHT CATEGORIES

2.6 Undulating Pick

The sample warp in this section offers insight into **grouped weft distortion**, a weave type created by **blocks of opposing interlacement**, resulting in curved shapes forming within the fabric. In a grouped weft distortion, the **pattern pick** units consist of blocks of closely interlacing **plain weave** and blocks of **warp yarn floats** woven alongside one another. A unit of plain weave **ground pick** woven across the fabric frames the areas of pattern pick, thus curving into the loosely woven areas and creating medallion-shaped indentations. Since a structural draft fails to reveal the undulating effects of the distorted weave, oval markings highlight the location of the notches in the featured cloth diagram.

Warp yarn
The **viscose polyamide combination tape yarn** used in the sample warp is a flat warp-knitted yarn. The black-and-white effect of the ends adds textural intrigue to the resulting fabrics. A warp-knitted yarn is fairly elastic, and hence facilitates maintaining adequate warp tension with textured weave structures. More on fancy yarns on pp.156–159.

Blends, combinations and mixtures
A **blend** is an intermingling of different generic fibres spun together throughout the yarn. Fabrics woven of such intimate-blend yarns are also referred to as blends.

A **combination** yarn is a ply yarn composed of filaments or strands of different generic fibre types. Many fancy yarns, such as the viscose polyamide tape yarn featured on this page, are combination yarns. Fabrics woven with yarns of this type can also be referred to as combination fabrics.

A **mixture** refers to a fabric with yarns of different generic fibres woven together. As an example cotton yarns might be used for the warp, and wool yarns for the weft. A warp itself can also be a mixture, as featured in the sample warp (p.243) composed of two sets of yarns, wool yarns and linen yarns.

Fibre blends, combinations, and mixtures are often composed in a way that one fibre supplements the performance of another fibre. As an example, weak fibres such as viscose can be engineered to blend with other more durable fibres such as polyester and polyamide to increase strength and abrasion resistance while maintaining the comfort of the cellulose fibre.

Blends, combinations, and mixtures can also be created to enhance the texture and appearance of yarns and fabrics, or to reduce their cost. Special effects, such as bulging can be engineered in yarns by combining strands of fibres with different shrinkage properties. Furthermore, unique colour effects are made possible through cross-dyeing.

Refer to Chapter 4 (e.g. pp.421, 424, and 430) for information on ways in which different properties in the fibre composition of the yarn can be used in the finishing phase of the fabric design process. The section *Closing the loop* (p.38) provides Information on the environmental aspects of fibre blends, combinations and mixtures.

Tape yarn warp
Warp yarn: Viscose polyamide tape yarn Nm 45 (tex 22) | 78 % CV 22 % PA
Yarn sett: 4.5 ends per cm
Reed: 45:1
Block draft on eight shafts

Catch yarns, left unthreaded, are recommended in the selvedges

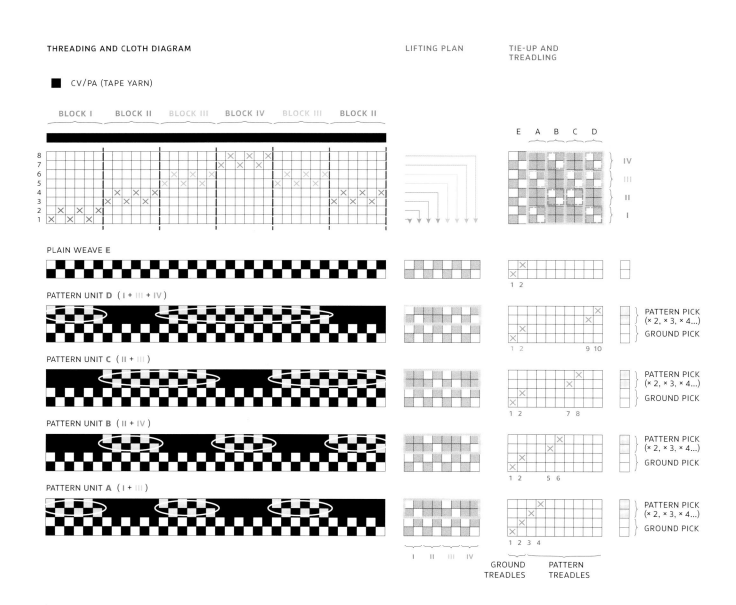

THREADING AND CLOTH DIAGRAM

LIFTING PLAN

TIE-UP AND TREADLING

■ CV/PA (TAPE YARN)

BLOCK I BLOCK II BLOCK III BLOCK IV BLOCK III BLOCK II

PLAIN WEAVE **E**

PATTERN UNIT **D** (I + III + IV)

PATTERN UNIT **C** (II + III)

PATTERN UNIT **B** (II + IV)

PATTERN UNIT **A** (I + III)

PATTERN PICK (× 2, × 3, × 4...)
GROUND PICK

GROUND TREADLES   PATTERN TREADLES

The set-up of the viscose polyamide tape yarn sample warp is a block draft. The warp is set in four blocks on eight shafts in a **pointed sequence** enabling the versatile creation of designs through combinations of the four different pattern units (A, B, C, D). In addition to patterning and texturing through combining the pattern units, rows of plain weave can be added between the curving lines (E). Block numbers and colours are included in the tie-up and the lifting plan in order to help understand the way in which the four threading blocks have been allocated to the pattern units.

Utilising differing weft yarn types and varying yarn colours for the ground pick and the pattern pick maximises the three-dimensional textural effects and accentuates the outlining curves. Depending on the yarn choice, the tightly woven plain weave notches remain more or less trapped between the undulating ground pick. Weaving two samples with the same yarns but in the opposing structural areas opens up a fascinating correlation between yarn materials and weave structures.

In order to allow space for the ground pick to undulate in the fabric, adequate slack should be given to the inserted yarns. As well, the warp should be held under fairly loose tension in order to allow the outlining ground picks to curve into the float areas. Fairly elastic and flexible warp yarns, such as the warp-knitted tape yarn in this sample warp, support the regulation of a suitable warp tension, adapt well to different types of weft yarns, and allow for more prominent notches.

To avoid slacking of the yarns in the warp direction, it is crucial to pay attention to the balanced alternation of areas of floats and tight interlacements. For example, a chequerboard pattern consumes the warp material equally (A+B).

Finally, in this textural structure, as in **waffle weave** (p.274) and **piqué** (p.290), it is especially important to consider the shrinkage of the fabric after it is released from the loom

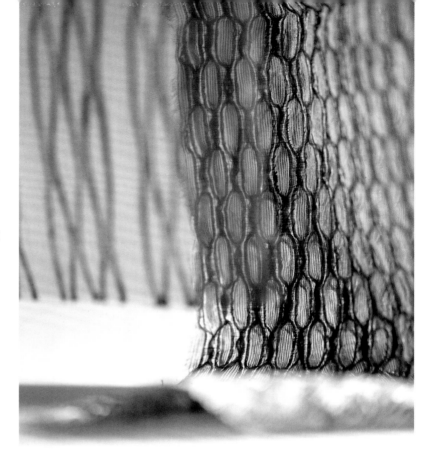

↑ Lightweight polyester sheer fabrics featuring grouped weft distortions. Lodetex (TP)

tension. While the relaxation of the warp and weft deepens the notches and enhances the three-dimensional effects, it also considerably shortens the woven fabric.

For the distorted-yarn effect, refer to the previous section *Parched and Perforated* (p.215).

Exploring the shrinkage in different weave types and yarn materials is an important lesson covered in the teaching aims of this book. Fabrics shrink when released from the loom tension. The assignment (p.122) specifies that the shape of the final woven samples should be a square. Achieving this requires attention to the elasticity of the yarn materials and structures.

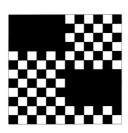

GROUPED WEFT DISTORTION

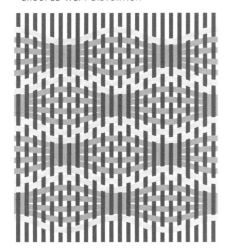

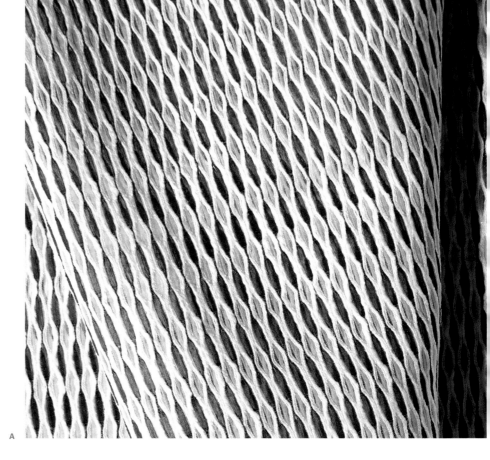

A

GROUPED WEFT DISTORTION

↗ A Flame retardant
polyester Trevira sheer
with a grouped weft
distortion structure,
Vanelli

The three-dimensional surface of a **grouped plain-weave weft distortion** is created by contrasting weave structures: blocks of plain weave and blocks of floats. The plain weave **ground pick** forms closely interlaced layers across the fabric while the **pattern pick** is interwoven to blocks of plain weave alternating with blocks of warp floats on the face of the fabric. Once released from loom tension, the warp yarns contract resulting in a reaction in the outlining plain weave rows. The ground picks slip next to each other in an attempt to cover the warp yarns floats (A).

Two sets of contrasting picks are commonly used to emphasise the depth-effects in this textured weave. Often a thick fancy yarn or a contrastingly coloured yarn is woven as the ground pick. Depending on the weft yarns,

the tightly woven plain weave cells remain more or less trapped between the undulating wefts.

Grouped weft distortions create fabrics that have a curved structural effect on the face side and are dominated by weft floats on the reverse side. In contrast, distorted-yarn structures, such as mock-leno fabrics, have an identical face and back. Grouped weft distortion textures are often seen in shirting and dress fabrics, as well as in interior fabrics such as the sheer textures presented on this spread.

In some weaving traditions, the distorted weft structure is referred to as **honeycomb**. However, within the textile industry honeycomb weave commonly refers to the **waffle weave** (p.274).

↑ Lightweight polyester sheer fabrics featuring grouped weft distortions. Lodetex (TP)

BASIC FABRIC WEIGHT CATEGORIES

WEIGHT G/M^2 (GSM)	CATEGORY	APPLICATION EXAMPLES
UP TO 130 GSM	VERY LIGHTWEIGHT	LINGERIE, SHEERS...
~ 130–200 GSM	LIGHTWEIGHT (TOP WEIGHT)	SHIRTING, SHEERS, CURTAINS, BED LINEN...
~ 200–350 GSM	MEDIUM WEIGHT (TOP AND BOTTOM WEIGHT)	TROUSERS, CURTAINS, SUITING...
~ 350–400 GSM	HEAVY WEIGHT (BOTTOM WEIGHT)	WORKWEAR, JACKETS, DRAPES...
OVER 400 GSM	VERY HEAVY WEIGHT	COATS, UPHOLSTERY, BLANKETS...

← This chart offers an approximate guide. The weight ranges differ regionally and by industry. Application examples are also dependent on the fibre composition as well as other parameters.

CONTRASTING PICKS

This fabric with a chequerboard pattern is woven with two **contrasting weft yarns**, a soft and furry dark grey mohair yarn for the undulating ground pick and a thin, straw-coloured viscose filament yarn for the pattern pick. The flexible mohair yarn adapts easily to slack insertion of the pick, resulting in soft, round forms accentuating the shiny viscose yarn notches.

■ CV/PA (TAPE YARN)

PATTERN UNITS A + B

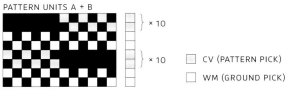

} × 10

} × 10

□ CV (PATTERN PICK)

□ WM (GROUND PICK)

← *Lacy Dreams – Touch Me* from collection *Party Time* by Anna Sorri

As opposed to *Lacy Dreams*, here the three-dimensionality is flattened by reversing the roles of the furry mohair yarn and the thinner filament yarn. The ground weave of tape yarn ends and thin filament picks encloses the tightly woven mohair pattern pick to soft, furry ovals on the face side. The back of the fabric is dominated by furry mohair yarn floats.

■ CV/PA (TAPE YARN)

PATTERN UNITS A + B

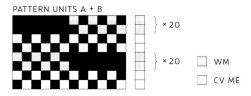

} × 20

} × 20

□ WM

□ CV ME

"A cocoon is protective and soothing; a rare feeling in the urban environment where people are constantly between places."

← *Cocoon* from collection *Morphology – Human Metaphors* by Erin Turkoglu

The contrast between the soft and flexible wool pattern pick and the stiffer two-ply cotton viscose ground pick adds an irregular puckering effect to this tonal texture, created using all four sample warp pattern units. The effect has been emphasised by steaming the fabric lightly.

■ CV/PA (TAPE YARN)

PATTERN UNIT D
} × 3

PATTERN UNIT C
} × 3

PATTERN UNIT B
} × 3

PATTERN UNIT A
} × 3

□ WO
□ CO/CV

"Just imagine the streets dusted with snow, slowly melting, revealing the pavement stones below"

↓ *Winter Is Coming* from collection *Finland* by Yuki Kawakami

RIGID PICK

In this rigid three-dimensional texture, both the ground pick and the pattern pick are woven with a paper yarn. The contrast between the two is achieved by **multiplying the yarn** in the ground weave. The elasticity of the tape yarn ends compensates for the stiffness of the paper yarn pick and adapts to the bulges formed by the undulating multiplied paper pick, thus enhancing the wavy three-dimensionality of the fabric.

The samples featured on these pages all shrunk notably when released from warp tension.

■ CV/PA (TAPE YARN)

PATTERN UNITS A + B

□ PI
□ PI × 3

CREATING WAVE PATTERNS

Here, weft-faced plain weave alternates with medallion-patterned bands framed by two wavy stripes. Floats of the glittering grey pattern pick on the reverse reveal that both the wave rows and the areas of the medallions are structurally identical. However, in the wave pattern, the black wool polyamide ground pick is replaced with the shiny grey yarn in every other ground weave unit. As a result, only the outlining black parallel waves are highlighted and the grey ground pick blends with the identical pattern pick.

See pp.318–319 for more fabric stories from *Earth* and *Space*.

↔ *Grapes* from collection
Earth by Ilona Hackenberg

■ CV/PA (TAPE YARN)

PATTERN UNITS A + B

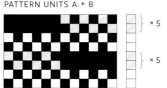
} × 5
} × 5

I MEDALLIONS

PATTERN UNITS A + B

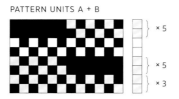
} × 5
} × 5
} × 3

II WAVES

PLAIN WEAVE E

} × 25

□ WO + PES ME
□ WO/PA

III PLAIN WEAVE

Grouped weft distortion lends
itself to attractive patterning
also in heavier weights, such
as this upholstery fabric
by Vanelli.

CITY / LAPLAND

City / Lapland
Woven fabrics studio course assignment 2014
by Kristiina Hansen-Haug

"The city, filled with people and cars moving at a fast pace, can be distressing. The City *collection is an interpretation of daily urban life, which portrays even the busiest moments of the day in a harmonious and meditative way. The inspiration comes from mundane man-made elements found in a city such as crosswalks, car parks, and street lights, as well as the materials they are made of like concrete."*

■ PA (RIBBON YARN)

PATTERN UNITS A + B

☐ CO

☐ PES + PES ME (LUREX YARN) × 3

The distorted-weft fabrics of these two complementary collections, *City* and *Lapland*, are woven on a white polyamide ribbon yarn warp (Nm 7, 100% PA, Reed 30:1) (A). The showcased samples both share the same thick black knitted cotton ribbon yarn pattern pick. *Evening Commute* is woven with a glittering ground pick of a thin polyester yarn plied with a metallised yarn, whereas in *Aurora Borealis* a lacy white polyamide tape yarn ground pick (B) forms the undulating pattern. A variation of the basic distorted-weave structure in *Evening Commute* hinders the formation of the plain weave medallion pattern and lets the warp yarns float in lengthwise stripes along the fabric. In addition to the slight differences in the weave structures, each of these

"Pause for a moment to watch the buzz of the traffic."

A

samples implement varying types of yarns as ground picks. As a result, the textural pattern generated in the final fabrics is completely different.

More fabric stories from *City* and *Lapland* collections by Kristiina Hansen-Haug can be found on pp.143 and 197.

↑ *Evening Commute* from collection *City*

↑ *Aurora Borealis* from collection *Lapland*

"*Lapland, its nature is simultaneously raw, peaceful, and magical. The* Lapland *collection celebrates the beauty of details. It draws inspiration from natural phenomena such as the northern lights and the enchanting landscape of Lapland with its bogs, juniper trees, and deadwoods.*"

■ PA (RIBBON YARN)

PATTERN UNITS A + B

□ CO

□ PA

"*Glowing like fox fur, northern lights illuminate the sky. If you catch a glimpse, you will gain luck and prosperity.*"
– Lappish mythology

B

"The weft yarn is very thin. I spent hours weaving this swatch, like a worker in a factory assembly line repeating the same task day after day."

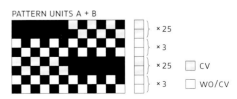

VARIATIONS—REVEALING THE FLOATING ENDS

↑ *Calculation* from collection *China* by Tong Ren

The fabrics on this spread feature variations on the distorted weave, achieved through the choice of weft yarns and the degree of slack they are woven with as well as the degree of warp tension. Instead of being hidden under the undulating ground weft yarns, in these samples the warp yarn floats are visible.

In this glimmering three-dimensional texture, the shiny and fine viscose filament pattern pick is tightly packed, triggering the equally densely woven plain weave units of thin wool viscose blend ground picks to slip. As a result, the blocks of warp yarn floats are revealed and suspended over the grooves.

■ CV/PA (TAPE YARN)

PATTERN UNITS A + B

} × 25
} × 3
} × 25   □ CV
} × 3   □ WO/CV

238

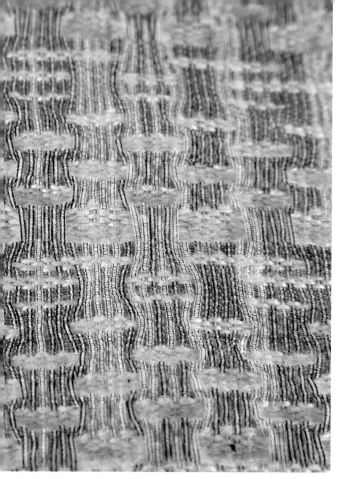

← *Living in China* from collection *China* by Lu Zeng

TEXTURING WITH CONTRASTING PICKS

The soft mohair yarn pattern pick forms furry indentations on a ground of the black-and-white tape yarn ends invisibly interwoven with a thin and transparent polyamide monofilament ground pick. The bare ends reveal the often hidden **distortions** occurring in the **warp direction**.

■ CV/PA (TAPE YARN)

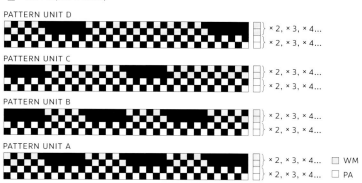

PATTERN UNIT D
} × 2, × 3, × 4...
} × 2, × 3, × 4...

PATTERN UNIT C
} × 2, × 3, × 4...
} × 2, × 3, × 4...

PATTERN UNIT B
} × 2, × 3, × 4...
} × 2, × 3, × 4...

PATTERN UNIT A
} × 2, × 3, × 4... □ WM
} × 2, × 3, × 4... □ PA

This flat, silvery, striped texture is woven with an alternating pick sequence of black and silver yarns, concealing the distorted weave appearance behind the more dominant colour-and-weave effect. Vertical black and silver stripes are created on the face of the fabric while the back side is dominated with the weft floats.

■ CV/PA (TAPE YARN)

PATTERN UNIT D
} × 3

PATTERN UNIT C
} × 3

PATTERN UNIT B
} × 3

PATTERN UNIT A
} × 3

ALTERNATING PA/PES ME, WO/PA AND CV

↑ Sample from collection *Moonlight* by Hanna-Maaria Sinkkonen

COMPUTER DREAMS

In this sample, a pattern pick of
alternating black cotton yarn and
white polyester yarn creates blocks
of vertical rib weave. Tightly woven
strips of shrinking ground pick
squeeze the blocks to black-and-
white striped bulges. The back of the
fabric features floats of pattern pick
next to rib-weave bumps.

■ CO

PATTERN UNITS A + B

} × 10
} × 2
} × 10
} × 2

■ CO
□ PES
■ PES/EL
(SHRINKING YARN)

Both fabrics are from
collection *Computer Dreams*
by Leevi Ikäheimo

Elastane fibres
are elastomeric
fibres, containing
by mass 85% or
more polyurethane
and encompassing
up to 99% elastic
recovery and high
extensibility. Elastane
fibres are always used
in combination with
other fibres, either as
filament yarns or as
the core in **covered
yarns** (p.159).

SHRINKING WEFT YARNS

Shrinking yarns can be added to the weft yarn
palette whilst advancing in studies of woven
structures. These engineered yarns shrink
notably during the finishing process, when the
fabric is heated by steaming or in hot water.

To examine the effects of yarn shrinkage in
a woven structure, it is advisable to use the
shrinking yarn in a repeating pick sequence
alternating with conventional yarns or to
assign it to a particular structural area within
the weave. A grouped weft distortion structure is well-suited for experimentations with
shrinking yarn. The effects of yarn shrinkage
in the closely interwoven plain-weave ground
pick areas lead to intriguing puckering effects
in the adjacent areas. Layered structures are
equally well-suited as the shrinkage of one
layer is juxtaposed with a stable layer.

Related phenomena, caused by differences
in the elastic properties of the yarns, based on
weave structures, and by varied warp tension
in a double-beam configuration are discussed
in the sections on *Tension, Texture and Transparency* (p.169), *Layers, Pleats and Blocks*
(p.187) and *Quilted Layers* (p.287), as well as
in the following section *Checks, Stripes and
Camouflage Twill* (p.243).

The two featured grouped weft distortion
fabrics, *Stack Overload* and *Judder*, are woven
on a warp of grey mercerised cotton (100% CO
Nm 34/2, reed 40:2). In both samples, shrinking polyester elastane ground pick units form
compressed bands in the fabric. Additionally,
the ground picks were woven under higher
tension to maximise the shrinkage and elasticity. The samples have shrunk notably during
the steam finish.

The main focus of this chapter is to study the properties of yarns and weave structures without the added complexity of finishes. However, with proper instructions, **shrinking yarns** can be included at this stage. In addition to the yarn featured on this page, there also exist 100% polyester shrinking yarns, without elastane, that can be easily utilised as weft yarns. Similar effects can also be achieved with over-twisted yarns (p.126).

The theme of shrinking and finishes is further explored in the section *Searching for the Final Hand and Look* (p.411).

"Outside of virtual reality,
Judder is significant shaking."

Here, a broad warp-knitted black polyamide tape yarn pattern pick is tightly packed forming heavy, dense puckering plain weave areas between a rhythmic pattern of visible warp floats. The shrinking yarn ground pick pulls the texture together resulting in bulging tape yarn floats on the back of the fabric.

■ CO

PATTERN UNIT C

} × 4

PATTERN UNIT B

} × 4
} × 1, × 3

PATTERN UNIT A

} × 4
} × 1, × 3

□ PA
■ PES/EL (SHRINKING YARN)

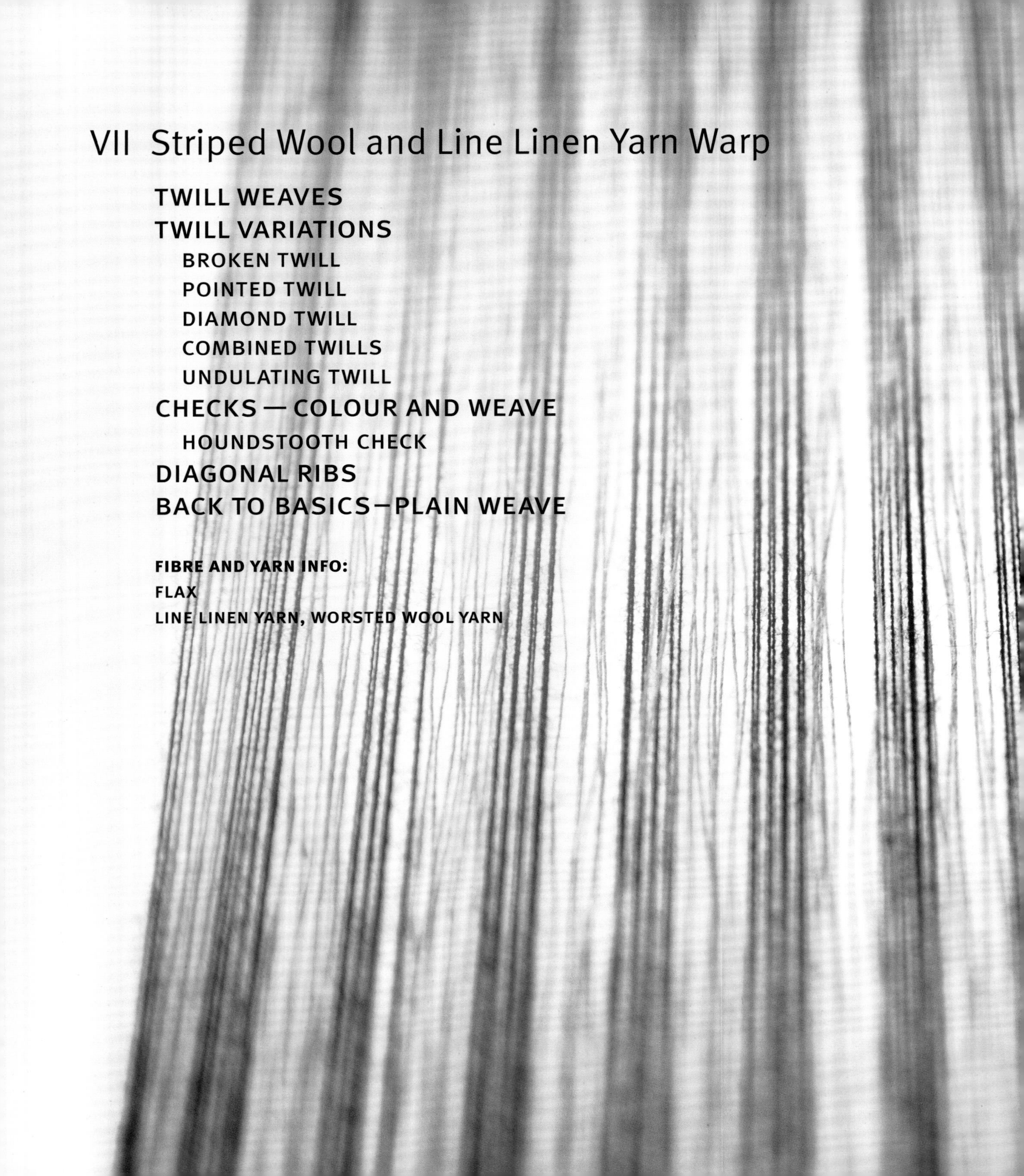

VII Striped Wool and Line Linen Yarn Warp

2.7 Checks, Stripes and Camouflage Twill

This section introduces **twill weave**, one of the three basic weaves alongside plain weave (p.134) and satin weave (p.306). Twills are recognisable by a diagonal **twill line**, yarn floats shifting sideways in each successive pick and running across the fabric. The yarn intersections in a twill weave are less frequent than the intersections in a plain weave and generally result in a more compact, closely woven fabric. The sample warp, a mixture with alternating bands of eight black worsted wool ends and eight unbleached linen ends, provides an example of the interrelation between the characteristics of the weave and the yarn properties – the soft, flexible wool yarns and the strong, stiff linen yarns. In addition, the striped warp allows for weaving **chequered** twill patterns and exploring the **colour-and-weave effect** (pp.154 and 258).

Flax / LI is a bast fibre and among one of the oldest textile fibres (p.53). Yarns and fabrics made from flax are called linen. Linen yarn is strong and lustrous and has an irregular slub-texture. Linen fabrics have low elasticity and poor resiliency, and therefore tend to wrinkle. They have a comfortable hand due to high moisture absorbency and good heat conductivity. These properties make linen excellent for summer clothing and household applications such as towels and bed linen. Flax, **hemp**, and other bast fibres are becoming increasingly popular in composite materials, replacing materials such as glass fibre. The strong, coarse, and rigid bast fibres are lighter and biodegradable in comparison to glass fibre. Composites made of bast and biodegradable plastic are used in cars and in construction applications such as acoustic or decorative boards.

Compared to other cellulosic fibres, the price of flax is relatively high and it is hence commonly used in blends with cotton, viscose, and polyester staple fibres. Incor-porating a small portion of flax endows the yarns and fabrics with a linen-like hand and look. On the other hand, the introduction of cotton or viscose to a linen blend makes the yarns softer.

In comparison to cotton, flax has less environmental impact as its cultivation requires fewer chemicals and less irrigation. However, bast fibre contains lignin and other non-cellulose matter. Retting and degumming processes are needed to separate this non-fibrous matter before spinning the fibres to yarns. Retting in water is environmentally harmful if done in natural waters such as rivers and lakes. When done in water tanks so that waste water is treated properly, the environmental impact of this process is low. The latest enzyme technologies and novel practices such as microbial degumming have accelerated the process, providing an alternative to the environmentally harmful practice of degumming by chemicals, with less damage to the fibres and reduced water pollution.[23]

Warp yarns

The striped mixture warp with stiff **line linen**, and fine and elastic **worsted wool** ends offers an intriguing starting point for explorations of yarn properties and weave structures.

The sample warp's unbleached line linen yarn is a strong wet spun yarn of high-quality line flax (long fibre flax), making it particularly suitable as a warp material. This type of yarn has traditionally been used to make home textiles such as table and bed linens, curtains, and furnishing fabrics. In its sizing information, NeL 16/1, **NeL** stands for **linen count**, number 16 represents the yarn count of the strand, and number 1 indicates the number of strands, thus specifying a **single yarn**. For information on wool and worsted wool yarn see pp.187 and 138.

Striped wool and line linen yarn warp
Warp yarns:
Line linen yarn, Nel 16/1 (tex 103) | 100% LI
Worsted wool yarn, Nm 2/36 (tex 28 × 2) | 100% WO
Yarn Sett: 10 ends per cm
Reed: 50:2

Here two alternative set-ups are suggested: straight draft on eight shafts (SET-UP I) and straight draft on sixteen shafts (SET-UP II). The wool and linen yarns are beamed separately, enabling independent tensioning of each set of ends. The suggested twill variations include a 4/4 and a 2/2 **balanced twill** (I A, II C). Woven on the striped sample warp with an equally striped light and dark pick sequence, the 4/4 alternative showcases a variation of the familiar **colour-and-weave effect** in which the prominent twill line is camouflaged behind the **houndstooth check pattern** (I A). This effect is best explored when the weft yarns are identical to the warp ends. **Pointed twill** (I B) and **broken twill** (I C) can be studied on a treadle loom by changing the direction of the treadling progression, or on the dobby loom by reversing the lifting plan. The effects of a **pointed draft** (p.272) can be experimented with by dividing the straight draft into two sets of eight shafts and mirroring the weave. **Diamond twill** (II B) can be achieved by additionally mirroring the weave in the weft direction. Other explorations include uneven, **warp-faced twill** (II D) and combined twills, such as a 3/1 **warp-faced twill** with 1/3 **weft-faced twill** (II E).

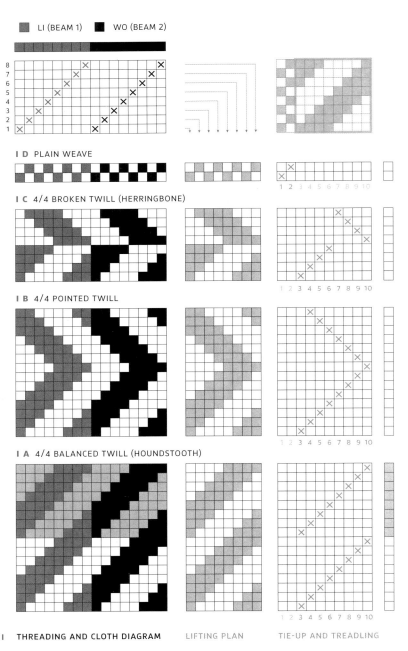

■ LI (BEAM 1)   ■ WO (BEAM 2)

I D PLAIN WEAVE

I C 4/4 BROKEN TWILL (HERRINGBONE)

I B 4/4 POINTED TWILL

I A 4/4 BALANCED TWILL (HOUNDSTOOTH)

I   THREADING AND CLOTH DIAGRAM   LIFTING PLAN   TIE-UP AND TREADLING

Studying twills on a computer-assisted dobby loom rather than on a treadle loom with its restricting tie-up supports flexible switching between various twill patterns, altering the direction of the twill line in both warp and weft directions, and combining weaves. The samples presented in this section are woven on a sixteen-shaft **computer-assisted dobby loom** with both lifting plans I and II as a starting point.

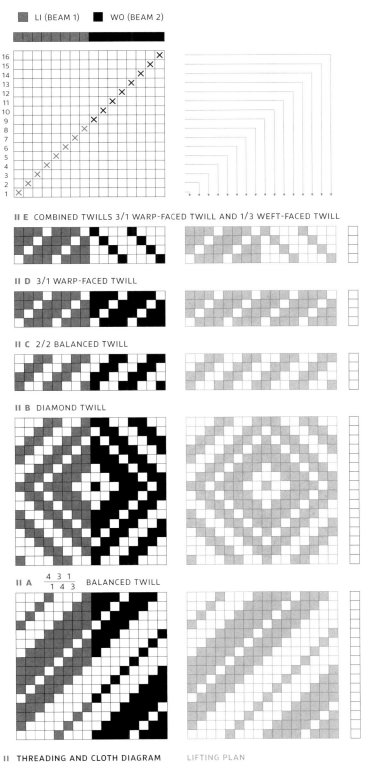

LI (BEAM 1)   WO (BEAM 2)

SET-UP II: DOBBY LOOM
Straight draft on sixteen shafts on
a double beam loom

The samples and diagrams featured in this section present additional twill patterns. The endless variety of twill effects include **fancy twills**, **corkscrew twills**, and **interlocking twills** just to name a few. Furthermore, the angle of the twill line can be altered, and even made to undulate by altering the ratio of ends and picks while weaving.

Experimenting with weft yarns of different composition, yarn count, type, and texture offers insight into the interplay of materials and structures. It is especially intriguing to weave different yarns in a striped sequence, forming a chequered pattern, and to study their interlacement with the two contrasting bands of wool and linen ends. Additionally, attention should be given to regulating the pressure when beating the weft into place while weaving. Attempting to keep the diagonal twill lines at a 45° angle during the first twill weaving trials is recommended.

Besides the twill variations, the sample warp set-up includes plain weave (ı D). As discussed in *Combining weaves* on p.144, a supporting plain weave ground of finer weft yarns can be woven between long patterning twill floats. Moreover, seersucker type (p.172) effects requiring tight interlacement can be explored by weaving plain weave samples.

→ In addition to the featured variations, the lifting plans of set-up ı can also be explored here.

II E COMBINED TWILLS 3/1 WARP-FACED TWILL AND 1/3 WEFT-FACED TWILL

II D 3/1 WARP-FACED TWILL

II C 2/2 BALANCED TWILL

II B DIAMOND TWILL

II A $\frac{4\ 3\ 1}{1\ 4\ 3}$ BALANCED TWILL

II THREADING AND CLOTH DIAGRAM   LIFTING PLAN

2.7 Checks, Stripes and Camouflage Twill   245

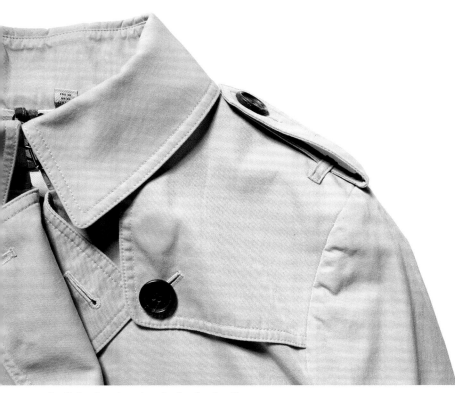

TWILL WEAVES

All twill weaves can be recognised by the **twill line**, or **wale**, a diagonal line running across the fabric. In basic twills the twill line is formed by yarn floats shifting to the right or left by one end in each successive pick. Equal density of picks to ends, using the same yarn count, will produce a **regular twill** with a twill line at a 45° angle. Most twills are of this type. The angle can be altered by adjusting the yarn thickness or density of the picks as compared to the ends (A). The angle of a **reclining twill** is less than 45° and a **steep twill** has an angle more than 45°. As the angle of the twill contributes to a higher yarn density, a steep twill structure is often used for fabrics requiring higher durability. A classic and well-known example of a steep twill fabric is **gabardine**, a fabric originally developed for raincoats (B).

↑ B Cotton trench coat made of a 1/2 gabardine.

**Fabric names:
twill weaves**

cavalry twill, chino, chevron, denim, drill, tweed, foulard, gabardine, galatea, glen plaid, houndstooth check, herringbone, jean, tartan, surah...

STEEP TWILL

REGULAR TWILL

RECLINING TWILL

A

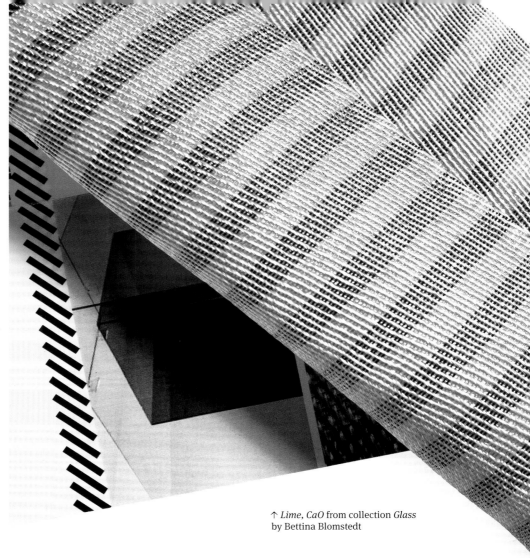

↑ *Lime, CaO* from collection *Glass* by Bettina Blomstedt

In this glassy 4/4 twill sample the high density of the thin translucent raffia-type viscose yarn makes the **twill angle recline**.

"Lime *is a shiny twill. Despite the densely sett pick,* Lime *is translucent and lets light through. The swatch keeps its rigidity when stretched in the warp or weft direction, but contorts when pulled diagonally.*"

LI   WO

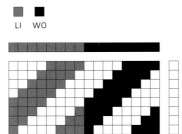

☐ CV (RAFFIA-TYPE YARN)

4/4 BALANCED TWILL

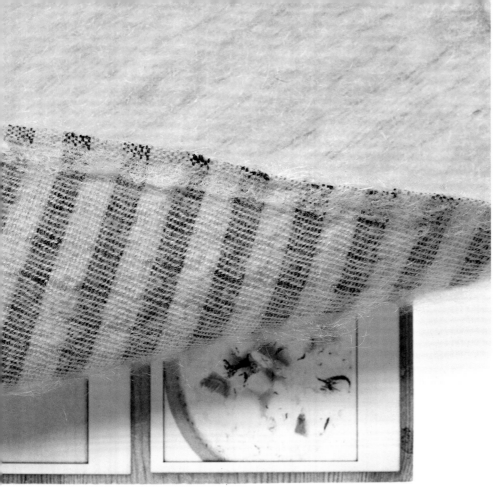

A twill weave can be **balanced** or **uneven**. In a **balanced twill**, also referred to as **even-sided twill**, the warp and weft floats are the same length and both sides of the cloth are identical. Uneven twills are either **warp-faced** or **weft-faced**. Due to the unbalanced ratio of floats, the face and back of the cloth differ. The back of the warp-faced twill fabric features the majority of the picks.

↑ *Salmon soup–Creamy, Thick and Rich* from collection *Maku–Finland* by Nina Chen

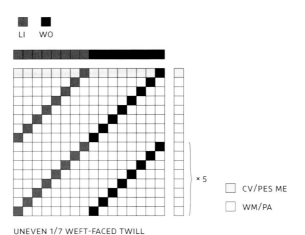

LI   WO

× 5

CV/PES ME

WM/PA

UNEVEN 1/7 WEFT-FACED TWILL

This **uneven**, 1/7 **weft-faced** twill represents a reclining twill diagonal of less than 45° angle due to the higher density of picks than ends. The long floats of over seven ends lead to the cramming of the picks and the furry mohair polyamide combination yarn dominates the fabric face while only the fabric back reveals the stripy warp. A shiny golden pick scattered between the closely woven groups of mohair pick creates subtle glittering dots within this smooth texture.

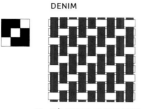

DENIM

C 2/1 WARP-FACED TWILL

The yarn intersections in a twill weave are less frequent than those of a plain weave. The increase of the overall float length results in a more compact, closely woven durable fabric with a high thread count. Furthermore, the yarns can move more freely, which results in a greater degree of internal adjustability and thus higher resistance to tearing. The pliability of a twill-weave fabric can be altered through the length of the yarn floats.

Compared to plain-weave fabrics, twills are more flexible and have a better drape and lustre. In comparison to basket-weave fabrics (p.136) with similar float length, the twill structure contributes to elasticity combined with better overall stability. As a result, twill fabrics wear well and have a better air and water resistance, which makes them popular for workwear, outerwear, and for all types of suiting. An iconic example of a twill weave fabric is **denim**, a 2/1 warp-faced cotton twill woven on an indigo blue warp with white picks (c, D).

The direction in which the twill line of a fabric runs on the face of the fabric is described as **right-handed** or **left-handed** (E). Traditionally, twills made of silk or wool were right-handed whereas cotton twill fabrics were left-handed. Today, most twills are of the right-handed type. The directions of both the twill line as well as the twist of the yarn (p.126) have a notable influence on the prominence of the wale.

↑ D Denim trousers, 2/1 warp-faced twill

E BALANCED LEFT-HANDED 2/2 TWILL

BALANCED RIGHT-HANDED 2/2 TWILL

4/4−1/3 combined twill

2/2 pointed twill

4/4 twill

4/4 broken twill

2/2 diamond twill

TWILL VARIATIONS

↑ Twill variations from left to right woven on the striped wool and linen sample warp with cotton, wool, and linen picks.

As the previous pages indicate, variations of the twill weave are countless. Due to the diversity of twills, the following pages are constructed to include the essential aspects of this versatile weave and provide a pathway for creating further modifications.

The featured table with variations of a 2/2 twill tie-up demonstrates how the direction of the twill line and consequently its pattern change by altering the threading plan and the lifting sequence (A).

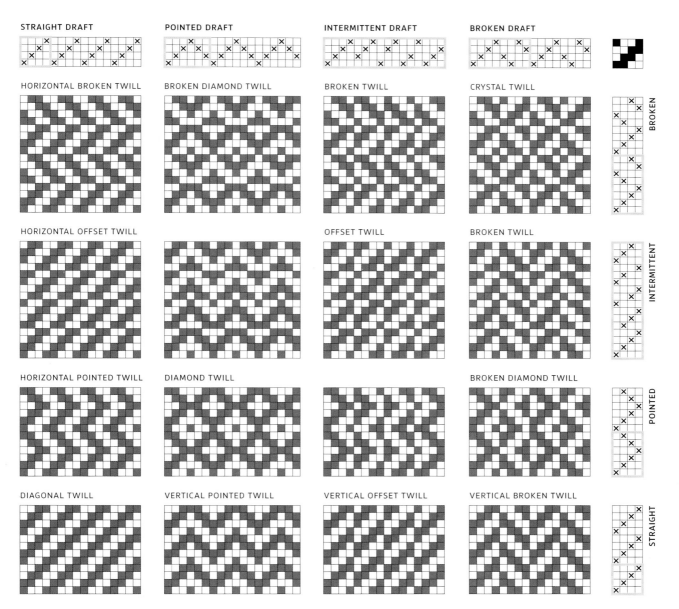

STRAIGHT DRAFT   POINTED DRAFT   INTERMITTENT DRAFT   BROKEN DRAFT

HORIZONTAL BROKEN TWILL   BROKEN DIAMOND TWILL   BROKEN TWILL   CRYSTAL TWILL   BROKEN

HORIZONTAL OFFSET TWILL   OFFSET TWILL   BROKEN TWILL   INTERMITTENT

HORIZONTAL POINTED TWILL   DIAMOND TWILL   BROKEN DIAMOND TWILL   POINTED

DIAGONAL TWILL   VERTICAL POINTED TWILL   VERTICAL OFFSET TWILL   VERTICAL BROKEN TWILL   STRAIGHT

A VARIATIONS OF 2/2 TWILL ON 4 SHAFTS

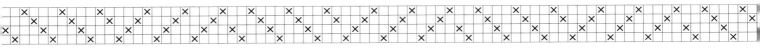

In a **broken draft**, one group of threads is drawn in a straight sequence in one direction and then another set of threads is threaded in the opposite direction. At the point of reversal, the first thread of the new series is started higher or lower than the last thread of the preceding set. The threading plan featured on this page showcases a broken draft as in the herringbone wool suiting fabric (A).

The **intermittent draft** featured in the table on p.251 is a variation of the straight draft, but with the difference that at short intervals, depending on the weave to be used, a number of shafts are skipped.

Broken twills are generally more practical in use than **pointed twills**, as the long floats that occur next to the points of the pointed twill are eliminated by the break-points of the broken twill.

B BROKEN TWILL 1/3

Broken twill

The diagonal twill line of a **broken twill** is interrupted and reversed. As demonstrated in the table on the previous page, changes in the twill sequence can be done by either changing the threading pattern, or the pick progression. If the threading plan is a **broken draft**, the break lines are vertical. Whereas, weaving with a **broken lifting sequence** or changing the direction of the treadling on the treadle loom reverses the pattern and breaks it horizontally. The classic **herringbone** pattern, also called the **dornick twill**, is a broken twill (A).

A commonly used broken twill variation is the four-shaft 1/3 version that results in a smooth warp- or weft- faced appearance without a prominent twill line, and is therefore frequently substituted for a satin (B) as described on p.307.

↑ A Woollen Herringbone tweed

The word **tweed** began to be used to denote woollen twill-weave cloths from Scotland during the first half of the 19th century. Although it sometimes has been assumed that tweeds are directly named after the river Tweed flowing through the Scottish Borders region, closer inspection reveals that the name derives from the Scottish word *tweel*, a term for twill weave. Scottish wool textiles has predominantly featured the twill structure since before the 18th century, in contrast to the English wool industry which largely specialised in fine broadcloths made in the plain weave.[24]

Named varieties of tweed include the well-known **Donegal Tweed** and **Harris Tweed**. Handwoven from pure virgin Cheviot wool spun on the woollen system (p.132) by islanders in their homes in the Scottish Outer Hebrides, Harris Tweed is a heavy handwoven suiting or interior fabric in mainly twill or broken twill constructions. Legal and trademark protection has been vital in supporting the Harris Tweed industry and its unique production system, enabling it to hold its distinctive position in today's global market. The plain weave such as in classic Donegal Tweed, characterised by its structure and the pepper-and-salt effect with knops of felted wool spun into the coarse yarn, has played a notable secondary role alongside twill weaves.[25]

Design exchange between Scottish and French wool fabrics during the past century has influenced the development of *novelty tweeds* for womenswear. The famous *fantasie tweeds* by Chanel are woven with bouclé, knop yarns, slub yarns and other novelty yarns (p.158).[26]

LI WO

4/4 BROKEN TWILL

CO/PAN

This 4/4 **broken twill** is woven using a white and shiny 2-ply cotton acrylic blend as pick. The herringbone appearance is disguised behind the colour-and-weave effect created by the combination of the striped warp with bands of contrasting ends and the long floats of the balanced twill.

↓ *Nurkka* from collection *Hidden* by Teija Vartiainen

Pointed twill

In a **pointed twill**, or **chevron** pattern, the wale reverses and forms a zigzag pattern. When woven on a **pointed draft** set-up the twill pattern reverses vertically across the cloth, whereas weaving with a **pointed lifting sequence** turns the pattern into a horizontally reversing zigzag, as demonstrated in the table on p.251.

The pointed twill samples on these pages are woven by changing the direction of the pick progression. As a result, the twill pattern runs **horizontally**.

See also p.59 for information on Early Iron Age fabrics featuring pointed twills.

↓ Linen blend pointed-twill suiting fabric

For Worse
Kaisa Kantokorpi

Sorrow

[sor-oh, sawr-oh]
noun
*1. (a cause of) a feeling of great sadness:
The sorrow she felt over / at the death of
her husband was almost too much to bear.*

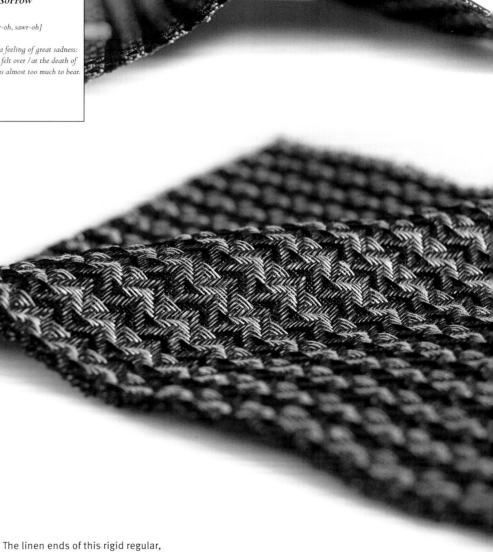

LI WO

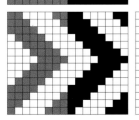

☐ PU/CV/CO

4/4 POINTED TWILL

The linen ends of this rigid regular,
pointed twill fabric reveal the sharp
edges of the vertically running
reversing twill lines woven with a
stiff dark polyurethane coated yarn.

↑ *Sorrow* from collection *For Worse*
by Kaisa Kantokorpi

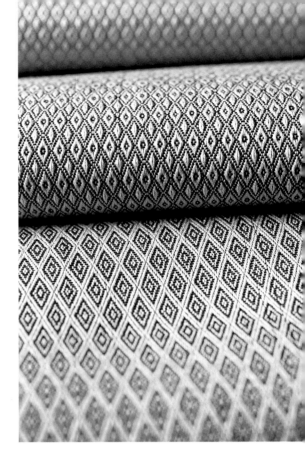

Diamond twill

In a **diamond twill**, or **lozenge twill**, both the threading and the lifting sequence are pointed. Similar diamond-shaped patterns can also be achieved by interrupting and reversing the twill line as in the broken twill. Refer to the table on p.251 for examples on both types of patterns as well as combinations of them.

See p.59 for archaeological findings of early lozenge-twill fabrics.

→ Mercerised cotton diamond twill fabrics

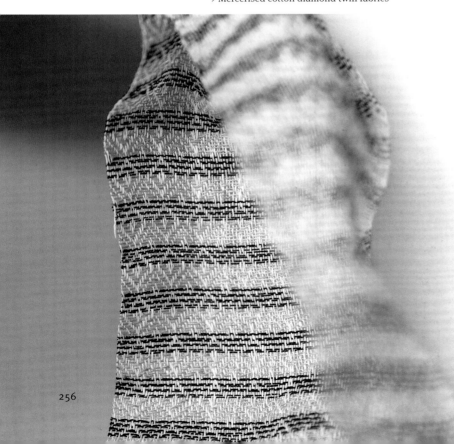

This diamond twill fabric woven with a white linen pick on the striped sample warp features the decorative patterning formed by a pointed draft sequence in both warp and weft direction.

LI   WO

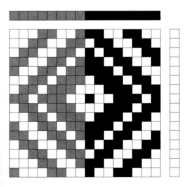

LI

DIAMOND TWILL

← *Babushka* from collection *Moscow* by Helmi Liikanen

Combined twills

Different types of balanced twills and uneven twills can be **combined** horizontally, vertically, or in blocks, depending on the number of shafts available and the order of threading. Various twill weaves ranging from weft-faced twills to warp-faced twills are often used in jacquards in order to distinguish between the different colour areas (see p.354). When weft-faced and warp-faced twills are combined, sharp breaking of the weaves with one another is an essential feature. This is achieved by running the twill line of the warp and weft weaves in opposite directions (A). See also damask p.310.

A Cotton linen blend fabric with a block-draft pattern of warp-faced and weft-faced twills

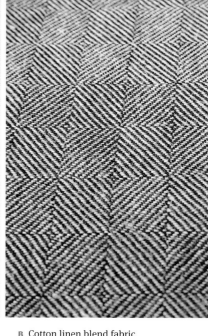

B Cotton linen blend fabric with a block-draft pattern combining right-handed and left-handed 2/2 twills

Warp-faced and weft-faced twills create a **chequered pattern** with alternating bands of four light grey and four black worsted wool picks. Consequently, the fabric exhibits multiple shades.

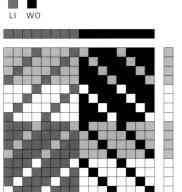

LI   WO

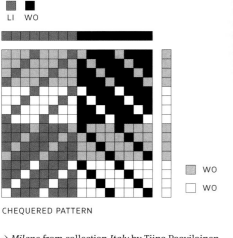

WO
WO

CHEQUERED PATTERN

→ *Milano* from collection *Italy* by Tiina Paavilainen

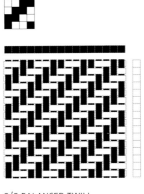

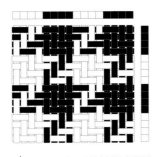

2/2 BALANCED TWILL

2/2 TWILL, HOUNDSTOOTH CHECK

A

↑ B Chequered worsted wool 2/2 twill suiting fabrics, the upper fabric showcases the houndstooth check

CHECKS—COLOUR-AND-WEAVE

Colour-and-weave is an effect using alternating bands of yarns in contrasting colours in both warp and weft directions in combination with a weave structure such as plain weave, basket weave, or twill. The contrast in colours disguises the appearance of the weave. Plain-weave derived examples of this effect have been discussed in the fabrics *Data* (p.161) and *Bird* (p.185). The illustrated draft (A) demonstrates how the modification of the colour sequence, using alternating bands of four light and four dark threads in both warp and weft directions, affects the visibility of the diagonal twill line and alters the overall appearance of

the regular, balanced 2/2 twill, generating a houndstooth pattern. Twills with colour-and-weave effects, such as the classic **houndstooth check**, or **pied-de-poule**, are popular in suiting fabrics (B). Another well-known pattern is **glencheck**, which can be identified by the houndstooth pattern in one of its colour-and-weave areas (C, D).

Ways in which the pick sequence influences the pattern in rib weaves are demonstrated in *Community* (p.142) and *Crosswalk* (p.143). Colour and weave effects in end and end warps in plain-weave fabrics are discussed on p.154.

2/2 TWILL

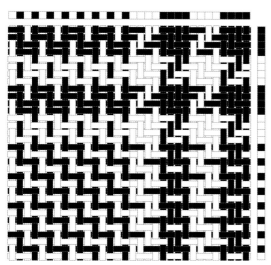

C The draft illustrates the way in which alternating pick and end colour sequences form patterns in a 2/2 twill glencheck

D Worsted wool 2/2 twill glencheck-patterned fabrics on the left and colour-and-weave suiting fabrics on the right

Houndstooth check

This fabric features a **balanced, regular twill** with an identical face and back, The equal ratio of ends and picks per cm forms a 45° angle in the **twill line**. In this fabric the diagonal line is disguised by the colour-and-weave effect with alternating bands of light linen threads and dark wool threads in both warp and weft directions. Observing the interlaced combination of two yarns made of different fibres – with varying elasticity properties – offers further insight into the interplay of materials and structures. This chequered pattern displays the various yarn combinations of wool with wool, linen with linen, and linen with wool. The loose 4/4 twill structure lets the flax yarns pull loose into slight waves while the wool yarns keep the structure intact.

→ *Roosters' Song* from collection *Cream* by Riina Heinonen

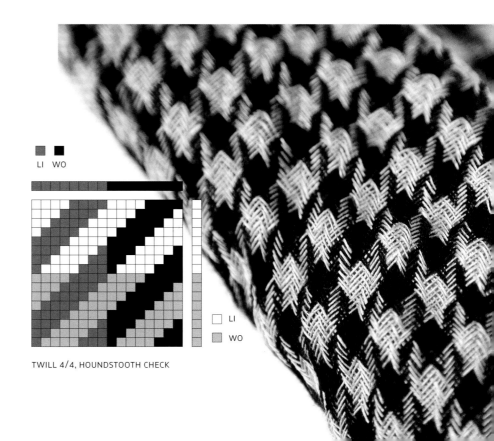

TWILL 4/4, HOUNDSTOOTH CHECK

CAMOUFLAGED ZIG-ZAG

Utilising two **contrasting** black **picks**, soft fluffy acrylic yarn and thin cotton yarn, in alternating units of two to seven picks camouflages this slightly undulating **pointed twill** pattern. The difference between the two warp materials is visibly demonstrated as the flax yarn ends bulge to form loose waves while the flexible wool ends interlace more closely with the picks.

LI   WO

ALTERNATING PAN AND CO

$\frac{4\ 3\ 1}{1\ 4\ 3}$ POINTED TWILL

↑ *Ke Jia Stir-Fry – Tossed, Colourful,*
Textured and Shiny from collection
Taste – Taiwan by Nina Chen

COMBINING WEAVES

Alternating horizontal stripes of **plain
weave** and **twill** as well as the surprising
and unconventional material composition
bring textural variety to this seemingly
classical chequered fabric. Plain weave,
woven with thin wool yarn between the
twill-weave stripes of transparent polyamide slit-film yarn and shiny grey monofilament, stabilises the fabric structure.

LI   WO

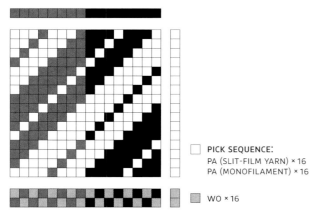

☐ PICK SEQUENCE:
PA (SLIT-FILM YARN) × 16
PA (MONOFILAMENT) × 16

▨ WO × 16

$\frac{4\ 3\ 1}{1\ 4\ 3}$ BALANCED TWILL AND PLAIN WEAVE

↑ *Light My Fire* from collection
Doors by Marjo Hanhisalo

In this **steep twill** sample woven on the
striped sample warp, the light linen ends
create flame-like **colour-and-weave patterns**
on the contrasting black background. The
loose 4/4 twill structure woven with a thick
cotton pick is held in place by **plain weave**
woven with a thin wool polyamide combination pick.

LI   WO

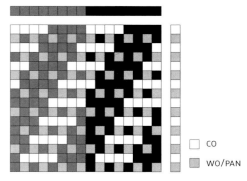

☐ CO

▨ WO/PAN

4/4 BALANCED TWILL AND PLAIN WEAVE

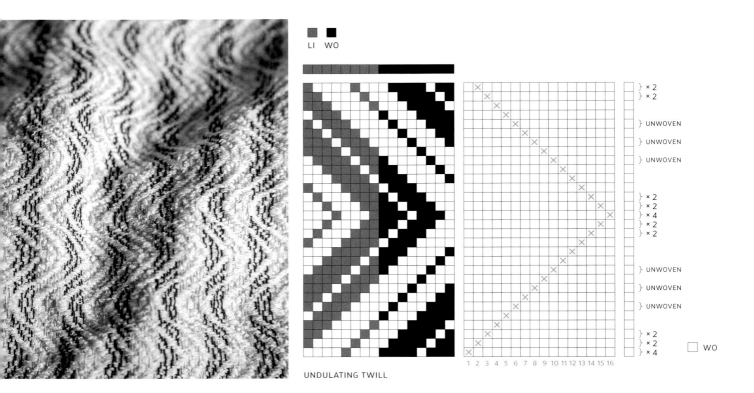

LI WO

```
             } × 2
             } × 2
             } UNWOVEN
             } UNWOVEN
             } UNWOVEN
             } × 2
             } × 2
             } × 4
             } × 2
             } × 2
             } UNWOVEN
             } UNWOVEN
             } UNWOVEN
             } × 2
             } × 2
             } × 4
```

□ WO

1 2 3 4 5 6 7 8 9 10 11 12 13 14 15 16

UNDULATING TWILL

Undulating twill

A **curved** or **undulating twill** is a **distorted twill** generated through irregular offsetting of floats in each successive yarn. Changes in the angle of the twill line can occur in either the weft, the warp, or both directions. The angle of the twill line can be curved through irregular reeding in the warp direction or through irregular grouping of picks per shed in the weft direction, as presented in the sample on this page. Another method of distorting the twill line is weaving with alternating bands of fine and thick yarns exemplified in the sample *The View* on the opposite page. The twill line can also be modified in the weft direction by altering the sett of the picks through adjusting the pressure of the beater as showcased in the sample *10* on the same page.

In this undulating-twill fabric the distortions of the twill line occur through **irregular grouping of picks** per shed. The fabric is woven on the striped wool and linen sample warp with a straight draft on sixteen shafts using a grey wool pick.

↖↑ Undulating twill fabric design by Essi Lehto

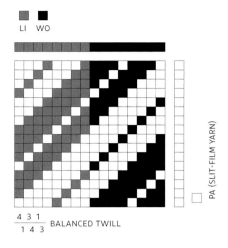

LI WO

4 3 1
─── BALANCED TWILL
1 4 3

PA (SLIT-FILM YARN)

Altering the sett of the pick results in an undulating twill line. Modifying the pressure applied to the beater changes the density of the picks. Exerting higher pressure on the beater increases the pick density and reclines the twill line angle, whereas applying less pressure decreases the pick density and generates steeper twill line angles. Here the transparent, stiff polyamide slit-film yarn keeps the irregular sett in place.

Weaving with alternating **bands of contrasting weft yarns**, a flat lacy tape yarn and a thin shiny viscose yarn, creates a curved twill line.

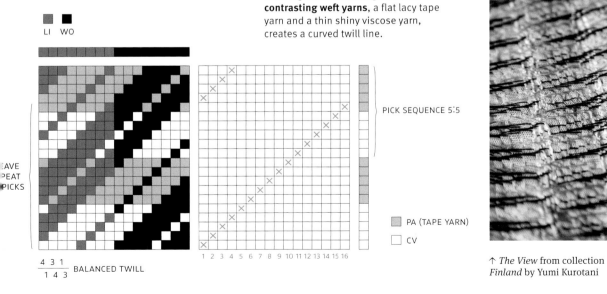

LI WO

WEAVE REPEAT PICKS

4 3 1
─── BALANCED TWILL
1 4 3

1 2 3 4 5 6 7 8 9 10 11 12 13 14 15 16

PICK SEQUENCE 5:5

PA (TAPE YARN)

CV

↑ *The View* from collection *Finland* by Yumi Kurotani

Decorating through threading patterns

The method of **decorating woven surfaces through threading patterns** has traditionally been utilised in cases where creating elaborate weave patterns on a limited number of shafts is desired. The structures are rib or twill weaves. Often the drawing-in pattern is repeated in the treadling sequence, thus generating both vertically and horizontally mirroring designs. For more on the impact of threading on pattern design see pp.320–325.

↑ Handwoven linen towels with an undulating pointed drawing-in pattern repeated in the lifting sequence.

← Sample cuttings and structural drafts showing elaborate threading and treadling patterns on eight shafts.

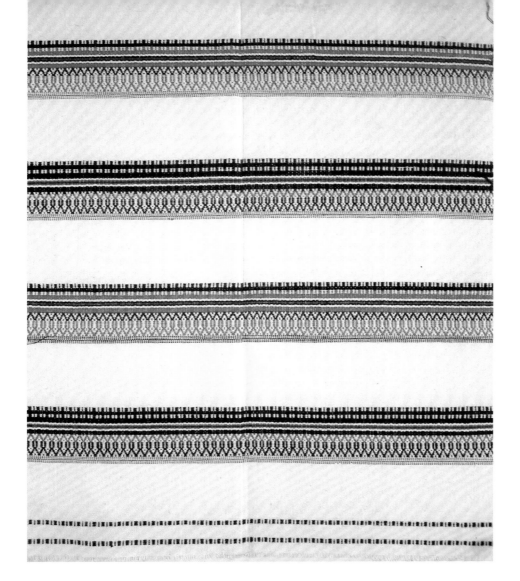

DIAGONAL RIBS

Diagonal ribs, also called **corkscrew twills**, are **twill derivatives**. They are **double-faced** (p.207) structures of either warp- or weft-faced type. These weaves are generally heavier than other twills, due to their layered, double-weft, or double-warp system, with two picks or ends nesting together and taking up the space of a single yarn. Diagonal ribs can be reversed, deflected, or undulating and are often woven by alternating two yarns of different colours, as featured in the fabric *Screen*. Due to their thick, insulating structure, diagonal-rib weaves are often used in fabrics for coats. This decorative weave and its variations have been popular in carpet and fabric traditions around the world (A). Threading drafts with reversing patterns are frequently adapted in these folklore designs.

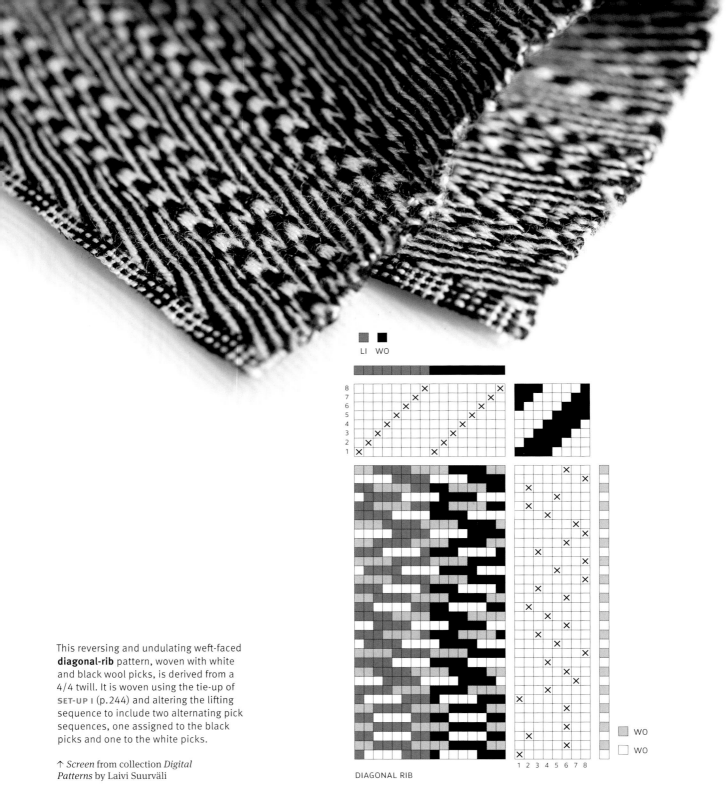

This reversing and undulating weft-faced **diagonal-rib** pattern, woven with white and black wool picks, is derived from a 4/4 twill. It is woven using the tie-up of **SET-UP I** (p.244) and altering the lifting sequence to include two alternating pick sequences, one assigned to the black picks and one to the white picks.

↑ *Screen* from collection *Digital Patterns* by Laivi Suurväli

LI   WO

DIAGONAL RIB

WO
WO

LI   WO

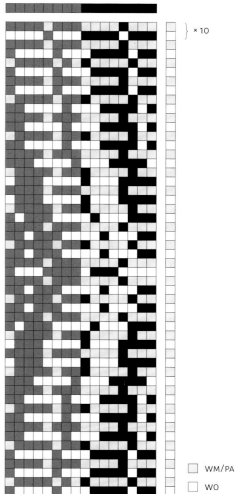

} × 10

WM/PA

WO

DIAGONAL RIB

This soft and furry fabric woven with two
alternating picks, a thick 4-ply worsted
wool and a thin mohair combination
yarn pick, features a **diagonal-rib** variation of the sample warp's balanced twill
pattern SET-UP II A (p.245). As a result
of the unequal yarn count of the two
alternating picks, the fabric's face and
back are dissimilar.

← *Weal* from collection *Hefty*
by Salla-Maaria Syvänen

↑ *High-rise* from collection
Aggressiveness by Siiri Raasakka

LI   WO

GRADIENT-EFFECT
PICK SEQUENCE

☐ LI

☐ WO

Plain weave–the simplest of weaves–is added to all sample warp set-ups featured in this chapter. In addition to enabling exploration of the effects of a basic weave in different material combinations, a supporting plain weave ground can be integrated to stabilise other weaves with floats throughout the sample warps, as discussed in *Combining weaves* on p.144. Inclusion of plain weave highlights how the properties of the warp yarns, different fibres, yarns types, and yarns' twist direction as well as the yarn sett can influence the appearance and performance of a weave structure.

BACK TO BASICS—PLAIN WEAVE

The mixed warp with separately beamed bands of linen and wool ends allows us to see how interlacement brings out the effects of yarns of differing elasticity properties. Moreover, the tight interlacement of plain weave enhances the **seersucker-type** puckering effects that can be achieved by combining yarn materials with differing properties. Refer to the section *Tension, Texture and Transparency* (p.169) for more information on this type of double-beam techniques.

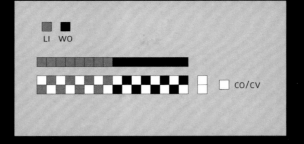

LI WO

CO/CV

PUCKERING PLAIN WEAVE

The featured plain-weave fabrics on the left
and below exemplify the puckering effects
that are created due to the different elasticity
of the bands of wool and linen ends. *Sauna* is
woven with a cotton blend pick, and *High-rise*
is woven with a gradient pick sequence of
unbleached line linen and black worsted wool
yarns. In both fabrics, the elastic wool ends
allow for firmer tensioning on the loom in
relation to the linen ends, further intensifying
the puckering effects. Moreover, the effect is
amplified by steaming the fabric.

↓ *Sauna* from collection *Everyday Life* by Anna Sorri

VIII Worsted Wool Yarn Warp

WAFFLE WEAVE
MAXIMUM 3D-DRAMA
PATTERNING WITH WAFFLE
STRUCTURAL EXPLORATIONS—MODIFYING WAFFLE

YARN INFO:
WORSTED WOOL YARN

2.8 Going 3D

The worsted wool sample warp introduced in this section enables exploring the **waffle weave**, a derivative of the twill (p.246). This **textured weave**, also called **honeycomb**, is a symmetrical weave structure with **groups of opposing interlacements**–squares of warp and pick floats framed by plain weave. When released from the loom tension, the floating ends and picks contract and the tightly interlaced plain weave areas bound into deep notches.

The choice of both warp and weft yarns notably alters the extent of the three-dimensional effect that can be achieved in the fabric.

The wool ends of the sample warp are flexible, which intensifies the effect of released loom tension. When wool yarn is also chosen as pick, the structure contracts into a thick, insulating three-dimensional honeycomb structure. Experimenting with weft yarns of different composition and type offers insight into their influences on the textile's three-dimensionality when the warp tension is released in this structure. Rigid picks, such as paper yarn, which do not shrink in weft-direction are stacked into horizontal ridges by the contracting wool ends. Furthermore, the warp tension can be regulated in order to adjust the influence of the warp.

Warp yarn
Worsted wool yarn accommodates the strain of tension build-up which is resolved as the fabric is taken out of loom tension. Steaming and wash finishes shrink the yarns and further emphasise the three-dimensional effects in waffle. More on wool and worsted yarns on pp.132 and 187.

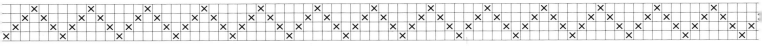

In a **pointed draft** the warp ends are threaded in a straight draft from front to back, reversing at the last shaft of the sequence and thereafter threaded from back to front. The point of reversal receives only one thread while the other shafts each have two threads in the threading repeat. The thread at the point of reversal is called the point thread. Examples of a pointed draft in a twill can be found on p.251. When the reversal skips one or more positions as in herringbone twill, the threading pattern is a broken draft p.252.

Worsted wool yarn warp
Warp yarn: Worsted wool yarn, Nm 2/18 (tex 55 × 2) | 100% wo
Yarn Sett: 8 ends per cm
Reed: 40:2

Catch yarns, left unthreaded, are recommended in the selvedges

SET-UP I: TREADLE LOOM OR DOBBY LOOM
Pointed draft on eight shafts

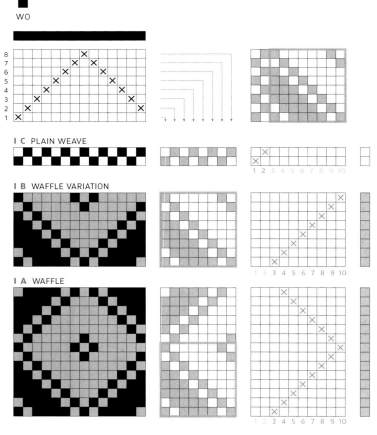

WO

I C PLAIN WEAVE

I B WAFFLE VARIATION

I A WAFFLE

I   THREADING AND CLOTH DIAGRAM   LIFTING PLAN   TIE-UP AND TREADLING

Here two alternative set-ups are suggested: a **pointed draft** on eight shafts (I) and a straight draft on sixteen shafts (II). In the latter set-up the effects of a pointed threading are achieved by dividing the straight draft into two sets of eight shafts and mirroring the weave. The length of the floats impacts the three-dimensionality of the fabric; the longer the floats, the deeper the indentations in the cloth. Set-up II features a waffle weave with fifteen-end and -pick floats (II B). A sixteen-shaft pointed threading enabling even longer floats is presented on p.278. With such long floats, depending on the yarns, the risk of the collapse of this wonderfully three-dimensional loom-tensioned structure into a pile of loose

The samples in this section are woven on the worsted wool yarn warp on either an eight-shaft treadle loom with a pointed draft (I), or a sixteen-shaft computer-assisted dobby loom with a straight draft (II). The samples on pp.278–280 are woven on a sixteen-shaft pointed threading. Studying the waffle weave on a table loom, dobby loom, or computer-assisted dobby loom, instead of a treadle loom with its restricting tie-up, encourages flexible switching between various waffle patterns as well as composing other variations of this intriguing weave.

yarns is high. The problems caused by overlong floats can be avoided by adding some extra binding points in the middle of the longest floats (II A, I A), or by weaving in thicker yarns. Set-up II suggests a smaller sized regular waffle (II C) and an irregular waffle featuring a modified distribution of plain weave areas (see page 460). A triangle shaped variation can be woven with a straight treadling sequence (I B). Studying the effects of the structural phenomena causing disparity of tension between the opposing areas can lead to further experiments–waffle weave modifications can be composed on a dobby loom by arranging distinct shapes of warp and weft floats on a plain weave ground. Finally, as in all the sample warps, the set-up supports plain weave, and encourages exploring this simplest of structures on yet another warp material (I C, II E).

Waffle is a **balanced weave**, the ratio of ends to picks is one-to-one. Hence, attention should be given to regulating the pressure when beating the weft into place while weaving, particularly when aiming for the regular waffle chequered with rows of symmetrical squares. Moreover, in this **textured weave** structure, as in grouped weft distortion (p.230) and piqué (p.290), it is important to consider the shrinkage of the fabric after it is released from loom tension. While the relaxation of the warp and weft deepens the notches and enhances the three-dimensional effects, it also considerably shrinks the woven fabric.

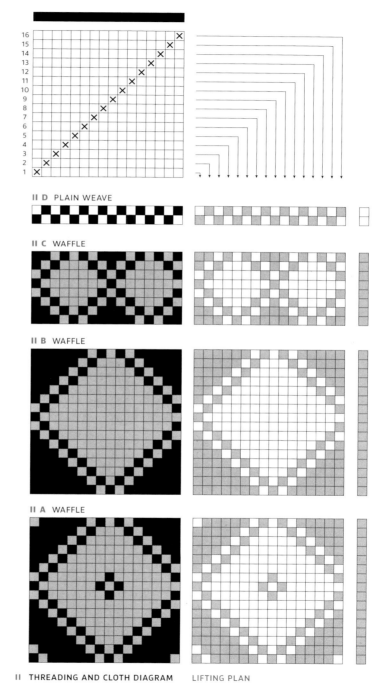

SET-UP II: DOBBY LOOM
WO   Straight draft on sixteen shafts

II D PLAIN WEAVE

II C WAFFLE

II B WAFFLE

II A WAFFLE

II   THREADING AND CLOTH DIAGRAM   LIFTING PLAN

WAFFLE WEAVE

Both the **waffle weave**, also called **honeycomb**, and the grouped weft distortion (p.230) are based on the interplay of two opposing types of interlacement: loose warp and weft floats, and tightly interlaced plain weave. The groups of warp and weft floats are stabilised by an outlining plain weave. The symmetrical diamond shaped structure of the waffle weave is woven as a balanced weave with ends identical to picks. The fabric has no particular face or back and both sides look identical.

As a result of the disparity of tension between the opposing areas, the fabrics change dramatically when taken out of loom tension, when the threads are free to settle in their most stable configuration. The long floats contract, pushing the plain weave areas down to form honeycomb-like notches (A). The dimensions of these depressions in the cloth depend on the length of the floats as well as the elastic properties of the fibres used in the yarns, the yarn type and count (B). Stitchers can be added halfway to tie down the longest floats, as demonstrated in the black wool waffle fabric (C). Steaming and wash finishes further emphasise the three-dimensional effects in waffle weave. The highly insulating bulkiness makes the weave type popular for blankets. Moreover, due to their three-dimensional structure, waffle weave fabrics absorb moisture well, making them ideal for towels and other bath textiles.

In some weaving traditions, the **distorted weft structure** (p.230) is referred to as **honeycomb**. However, within the textile industry the name commonly refers to the waffle weave.

B ← Cotton, wool and linen waffle fabrics

→ Cotton waffle kitchen towels

274

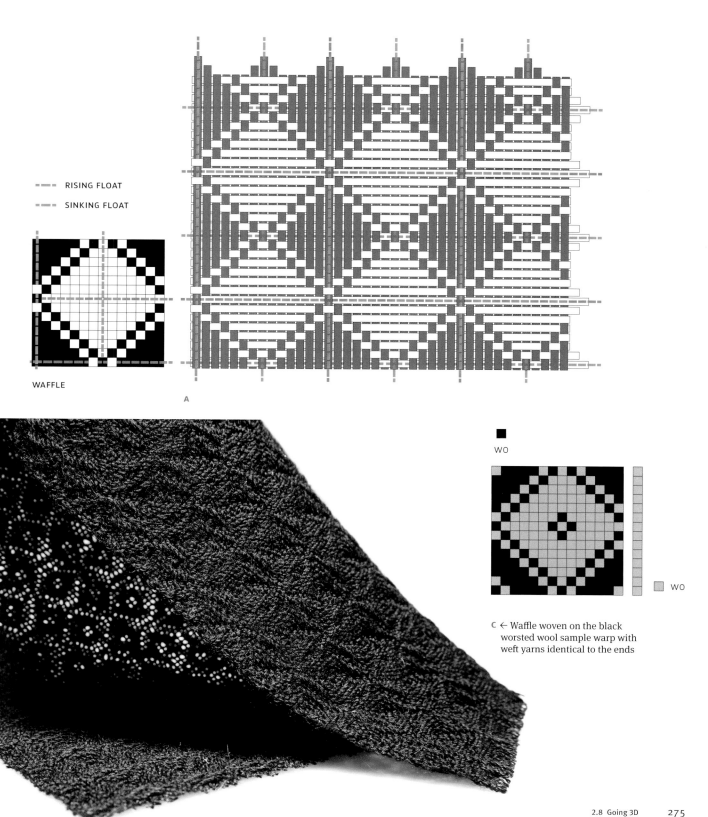

RISING FLOAT

SINKING FLOAT

WAFFLE

A

■
WO

□ WO

C ← Waffle woven on the black
worsted wool sample warp with
weft yarns identical to the ends

↑ *Laika* from collection *Space*
by Ilona Hackenberg

THIS IRREGULAR WAFFLE CAN BE
WOVEN WITH SETUP II

Waffle weaves can also be constructed in an
asymmetrical manner, with depressions that
are not lined up. The soft, three-dimensional
sample woven with a wool weft similar to
the warp is distinguished by long floats and
deep notches forming an intriguing maze.
In one corner of this soft darkness, embroidered with metallic threads, floats a lone dot.

More fabric stories from *Earth* and *Space*
by Ilona Hackenberg can be found on pp.161,
234, 298 and 318–319.

VARIATIONS WITH PICK

On the face of this puffy fabric, black, soft
knitted-tube yarn picks are arranged into
bulgy horizontal ridges of weft floats.
Consequently, the rows with thinner wool
warp floats are pushed to the grooves.

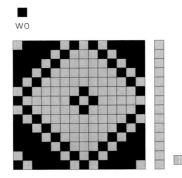

"In the darkest corners of the mind"

→ *Labyrinth of Nightmares* from
collection *Murky* by Grace Rubaduka

← *Asphalt* from collection *Concrete*
by Bettina Blomstedt

Here, a stiff plasticky black polyurethane-
coated yarn and a shiny, grey mercerised
cotton yarn alternate on both sides of the
horizontally pleating waffle ridges, thus
forming a three-dimensional texture with a
colour-shift effect. Depending on the angle,
the grey or black colour dominates.

*"This collection explores
the appearance of concrete.
Density and softness represent
the material that is often
perceived as rough. The names
of the samples come from the
various ingredients used in
mixing concrete"*

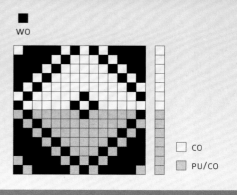

■
WO

☐ CO
☐ PU/CO

Concrete is a complementary collection to
the collection *Glass* (p.196)

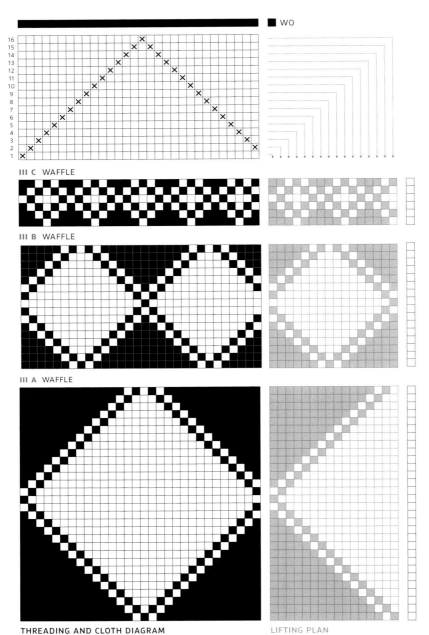

■ W0

16
15
14
13
12
11
10
9
8
7
6
5
4
3
2
1

III C WAFFLE

III B WAFFLE

III A WAFFLE

THREADING AND CLOTH DIAGRAM

LIFTING PLAN

MAXIMUM 3D-DRAMA

The pointed draft on this page demonstrates combining several waffle weaves in one set-up (III). The sixteen-shaft pointed-draft set up for waffle weave enables even longer floats compared to the straight-draft version (p.273), and **maximal three-dimensionality** in the raised and sunken honeycomb squares (III A). The twenty-nine-end or -pick floats are the weak point in this structure and, depending on yarns used, might result in great instability. This phenomena, and the possible collapse of the three-dimensional loom-tensioned structure into a loose pile of yarns, can be studied and thereafter prevented by using a more rigid, thick, or hairy pick, by weaving in rows of smaller waffle weaves or plain weave, or by adding some extra binding points in the middle of the longest floats, as exemplified in *Maku–Finland* and *Taste–Taiwan* (pp.280–281).

PU (ALTERNATING COLOURS BLACK AND WHITE)

■ WO

□

In this vivid texture, bands of small waffle structures are arranged between the large waffle squares to stabilise the fabric. Irregularly alternating rubbery black and white polyurethane-coated flat-pressed picks create an expressive meander of brushstrokes on the surface. Doubling the picks per shed in one of the waffle squares with maximally long floats further exaggerates the dramatic grooved effects.

→ *Finnish Oil Painting* from collection *Finland* by Lu Zeng

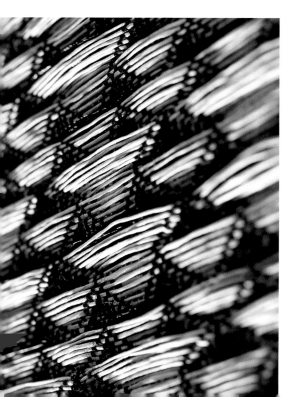

■ WO

□

PI (PAPER YARN)

"Complex, Brisk, Distant."

← Here, the rigidity of the paper yarn pick helps stabilise the long floats into neat rows and allows the contracting wool ends to pull these bands into ridges when released from loom tension. Smaller waffle structures texturise and stabilise the fabric.

The image-driven design process behind the *Heavy–Light* collection is described by Salla-Maaria Syvänen on pp.110–111.

← *Play* from collection *Light* by Salla-Maaria Syvänen

COLLECTION
MAKU / TASTE

Maku–Finland / Taste–Taiwan
Colour and woven fabrics design course
assignment 2014

by Nina Chen

"One of the easiest ways to understand a culture is through its food! To further explore this view, I created the two collections, Taste–Taiwan *and* Maku – Finland, *to portray the differences between Taiwanese culture and Finnish culture through the taste of food.*

In my experience, Finnish food is rich, creamy, heavy, rough, bland, smooth, strange, and new. While on the other hand, Taiwanese food is flavourful, textural, mixed, chewy, sticky, familiar, spiced, and tossed.

The above-mentioned words served as the basis for weaving the samples for these collections. From the pattern to the material choice, everything in the collections was thoughtfully chosen to represent the texture of food in one's mouth."

WO

KALAKUKKO ☐ WO
ANGUGUI ☐ PU/CV/CO

→ Woven with the exact same structure used in *AnGuGui*, in this fabric the pick is replaced with a soft and thick woollen carpet yarn. These two samples showcase how the choice of weft yarns with opposing qualities can lead to completely different textures.

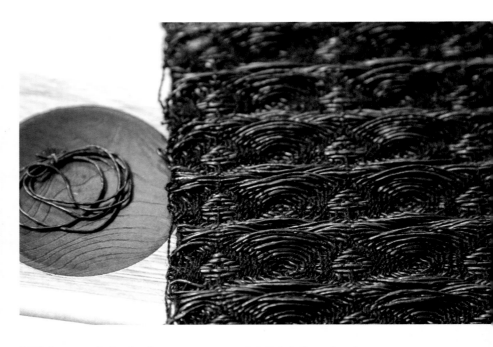

↑ This **honeycomb** structure is woven on **sixteen shafts** with a rubbery polyurethane cotton viscose blend yarn as pick. Extra binding points in the form of a heart shape have been integrated into the structure to stabilise the longest honeycomb floats.

↑ *AnGuGui–Chewy, Sweet, Sticky and Springy* from collection *Taste–Taiwan* by Nina Chen

→ *Kalakukko– Strange, Full and Packed* from collection *Maku–Finland*

BACK TO BASICS

Going **back to basics**, this **plain weave** sample is a smooth and shiny fabric with golden pinstripes. The piece is woven on the same worsted wool warp as the two other fabrics on this page, with a raffia-type viscose background pick and a thin metallic polyester combination pick for the stripes.

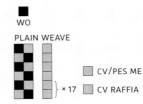

WO

PLAIN WEAVE

□ CV/PES ME

} × 17   □ CV RAFFIA

← *Jiangyougao–Rich, Salty, Smooth and Shiny* from collection *Taste–Taiwan*

See more tasty fabric stories by Nina Chen on pp.248 and 261.

"Putting on that glittery jacket when you get dragged to the club. You say yes because you do not want to be the boring one."

↑ *Clubbin* from collection *Murky* by Grace Rubaduka

PATTERNING WITH WAFFLE

The waffle weave is a textured weave, but the structure can be used in a more decorative fashion when woven with weft yarns contrasting to the ends, or by utilising fancy yarn picks. As the samples on this page demonstrate, the structure remains flat and less textured when the floats are not exceedingly long, the warp is woven slack, the picks are soft and slippery, and are either loosely or very densely sett.

POINTED PATTERNS

↑ Rows of triangles pattern this eight-shaft honeycomb variation. The fabric, woven with a black polyurethane-coated chenille pick plied with a metallic slit-film yarn, has a similar appearance to pointed twill.

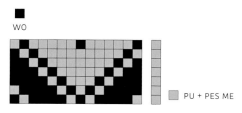

WO

PU + PES ME

DISTORTING THE DIAMOND SHAPE

A pick sequence of two contrasting yarns, seven thin viscose yarns for the lower triangle and seven broad flat polyester tape yarns for the upper triangle of the structural draft, distort the diamond shape of the waffle weave to a pointed crystal-like pattern.

WO

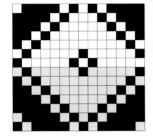

☐ PES (TAPE YARN)

☐ CV

↑ *Mineral Section* from collection *Hard Surfaces* by Pei-Nung Lee

For Worse
Kaisa Kantokorpi

At the Cemetery

It was my favourite place in that town.
Especially in the morning when the fog
cleared and revealed the gravestones.
It always reminded me how lucky
I was just to be alive.

← *At the Cemetery* from collection *For Worse* by Kaisa Kantokorpi

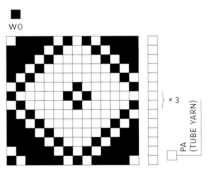
WO

} × 3

PA (TUBE YARN)

In this fabric a transparent polyamide knitted-tube yarn pick highlights the cross motif of the ornaments generated by the black wool warp. The waffle weave has been modified by repeating the rows with stitchers for the longest floats, thus forming a double-layered structure in between the bands of black crosses, resulting in rows of looser sett plain weave on the face of the fabric and floating ends on the reverse.

"Over the past few years, I have received traditional Finnish handmade wool socks each Christmas as a gift. They keep me warm during the Finnish winter and remind me of family and friends."

↑ *Temperature – Wool Socks* from collection *Finland* by Tong Ren

↑ This grainy modified waffle texture woven with a black woollen pick is developed on the sample warp **SET-UP II** (p.273) on a computer-assisted loom. The coarse wool pick secures the floats in place. For woollen yarns, refer to pp.132 and 187.

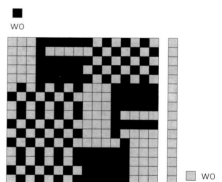

WO

WO

STRUCTURAL EXPLORATIONS–MODIFYING WAFFLE

The three-dimensional textural effects familiar to waffle weave are created by the disparity of tension between opposing structural areas. Interesting waffle modifications can be developed by arranging groups of warp and weft floats on a plain weave ground. These examples are an encouragement to delve into generating your own weaves. The distinct structural concept of the waffle weave offers excellent ground for explorations.

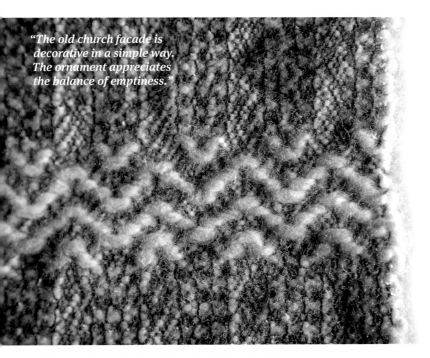

"The old church facade is decorative in a simple way. The ornament appreciates the balance of emptiness."

↑ *Ornament* from collection *Finland* by Yuki Kawakami

← In this striped fabric woven with a white wool pick, decorative bands of diagonally arranged modified waffle run on a mock-leno type ground. Similarly to *Temperature–Woollen Socks*, the texture has been created on a computer-assisted loom.

WO

MOCK-LENO VARIATION

 } × 9

MODIFIED WAFFLE

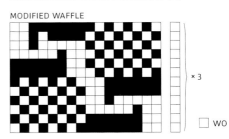 } × 3

☐ WO

← This fabric, produced on the treadle loom with sample warp **SET-UP I** (p.272), interweaves plain weave with waffle weave. Two plain weave units woven with a thin golden pick alternate with a thick black cotton tube pick weaving the triangle-shaped waffle variation. The result resembles a grouped weft distortion, with plain weave notches woven with a thin golden pick twinkling behind rows of bulging thick black cotton tube yarn pick. Unlike waffle weave and similar to the grouped weft distortion, the backside of this sample is dissimilar to the front. This sample exemplifies how creative combining of weave structures can lead to limitless and surprisingly beautiful new designs.

"Once the sunlight passed through the windows, I was mesmerised by the shine of the surfaces."

■
WO

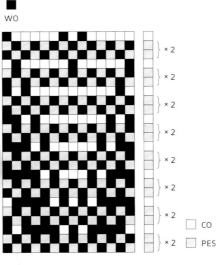
} × 2
} × 2
} × 2
} × 2
} × 2
} × 2
} × 2
} × 2
} × 2

☐ CO
☐ PES

← *Filtered Light* from collection *Excess* by Leonardo Hidalgo-Uribe

IX Wool Silk Blend Yarn and Cotton Yarn Warp

PIQUÉ
VARIATIONS WITH THE STITCHING PATTERN
AND WADDING PICK

FIBRE AND YARN INFO:
MERINO WOOL
MERINO WOOL SILK BLEND YARN
MERCERISED COTTON YARN

2.9 Quilted Layers

This section explores the furrowed, three-dimensional effects of **piqué**. This patterned double-cloth structure (p.206), belongs to the group of **matelassé** weaves in which the stitching forms the pattern. The sample warp consists of two sets of ends: a **face warp**, or **ground warp**, of soft and adaptable wool silk blend yarns, and a **stitching warp**, or **backing warp**, of mercerised combed cotton yarns. The two-ply wool silk blend yarn makes an ideal ground warp for the plain-weave face of the piqué fabric. This silky and malleable yarn emphasises the quilted effects, while the thicker stitching ends of strong four-ply mercerised cotton offer a reliable backing warp for the face cloth to slide along. The divided draft in the sample warp is a combination of **straight draft** for the face warp and **pointed draft** (p.272) for the stitching ends.

Warp yarns The two sets of warp yarns, a fine and supple **two-ply Merino wool silk blend spun yarn** for the face warp and a strong **four-ply mercerised combed cotton** yarn for the stitching ends, offer fertile ground for exploring the piqué weave.

The wool silk yarn combines desired properties of both fibres—silk increases strength and stability of the yarn while merino wool increases the bulk and loft properties. This relatively fine yarn can be woven to form a dense plain-weave piqué face layer. The strong and smooth mercerised cotton yarn makes for a reliable stitching warp.

Merino wool is derived from Merino sheep, known for their fine, soft wool and their ability to thrive in extreme climates. The breed originates from Spain and is now grazing highlands around the world, from New Zealand and Australia to South Africa and South America. Merino staples are exceptionally long and thin. The natural crimp of the fibre increases the resilience and loft of the yarn and fabric, adding to their insulation properties. Merino fibre is used to make strong high-quality worsted and woollen yarns with unique properties suitable for a wide range of applications

from light-weight next-to-skin wear to functional sports clothing and fine suiting. With today's spinning technology and fibre treatments, merino wool makes for outstanding fabrics that have replaced cotton and synthetic fabrics on many fronts.

For further information on yarns and fibres refer to: wool (p.187), silk (p.303), blend yarns (p.227), cotton (p.129) and the mercerisation process (p.417).

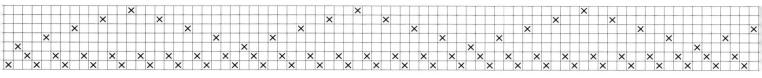

Merino wool silk yarn and mercerised cotton yarn warp
Warp yarns:
Merino wool silk blend yarn, Nm 2/20 (tex 50 × 2) | 75% WO 25% SE
Mercerised combed cotton yarn, Ne 8/4 (tex 74/4) | 100% CO
Yarn sett: 7 ends per cm
Reed: 70: 1 (stitching warp), 2 (face warp)
Divided draft on seven shafts on a double beam loom

A **divided draft** is used to incorporate different draft types in separate groups of shafts. This type of drafting is often employed for weaving interwoven double warp fabrics such as double weave (p.188) and piqué weave, where the face and back threads are drawn on separate groups of shafts. The featured threading combines **straight draft** and **pointed draft**.

All samples in this section are woven with the featured **divided-draft** set-up on a treadle loom. Similarly to the double-weave (p.188), exploring the **double-cloth** structure on a treadle loom can help novice weavers better understand the complexities of these **interwoven fabrics** (p.206). Variations are easily created by altering the pedalling sequences and exploring different yarn qualities.

Both warps are wound onto separate beams to allow the stitching warp to be woven under greater tension than the face warp, resulting in a heightening of the quilted effect. Hence the more heavily tensioned backing warp pins the plain weave face down according to a **stitching pattern**, thus letting the unstitched areas of the fabric rise. The bulging effects can be further adjusted by regulating the difference of tension between the two warps.

In addition to the two sets of warp yarns, two sets of weft yarns are used in the piqué weave. The **ground pick** (white pick) weaves the plain weave fabric face and on the back of the fabric a **wadding pick** (blue pick), inserted under the face fabric and supported over the **stitching ends**, adds padding to enhance the raised three-dimensional effect of the unstitched cloth cushions. In the sample warp, the ratio of the ground picks and ends to the wadding picks and stitching ends is two-to-one. For pronounced cushioned effects a thick and soft pick–such as bulgy wool yarn, or **roving**–should be used for the wadding. It is advisable to use a finer yarn in the face than for the backing.

The stitching motif–with the backing ends threaded in a pointed draft–can be varied in ways similar to twill (p.251), either by forming a pointed zigzag pattern (B) or, with

pointed treadling, a diamond pattern (A). The length, and consequently the visibility of the stitches on the face of the fabric, can also be altered. The stitches can be long floats or they can disappear in the furrows. In the cross pattern (C) the backing ends which form the motif are visible on the fabric face while the shorter stitches remain hidden. It must be noted, that all yarns in the backing warp should be interwoven in some way, even with short stitches to the face of the fabric. Such explorations with patterns can push learning further, as can be seen in the samples on the following pages. This sample warp set-up also offers the possibility for adding in layers of 2:1 rib weave (D) to tie the two layers together, and to study more complex double-cloth structures.

Altering the ratio of the ground picks to wadding picks or varying the type of yarns used for the two sets of weft yarns results in novel interpretations of the weave. Typically, the wadding pick is not visible on a piqué fabric face. However, letting the wadding show through a loosely woven plain weave face layer results in interesting effects. Furthermore, by weaving with a flat and stiff yarn instead of the typical bulgy wadding yarn or leaving the wadding pick out entirely can bring surprising effects. Some effects can be intensified by shrinking the yarns after weaving.

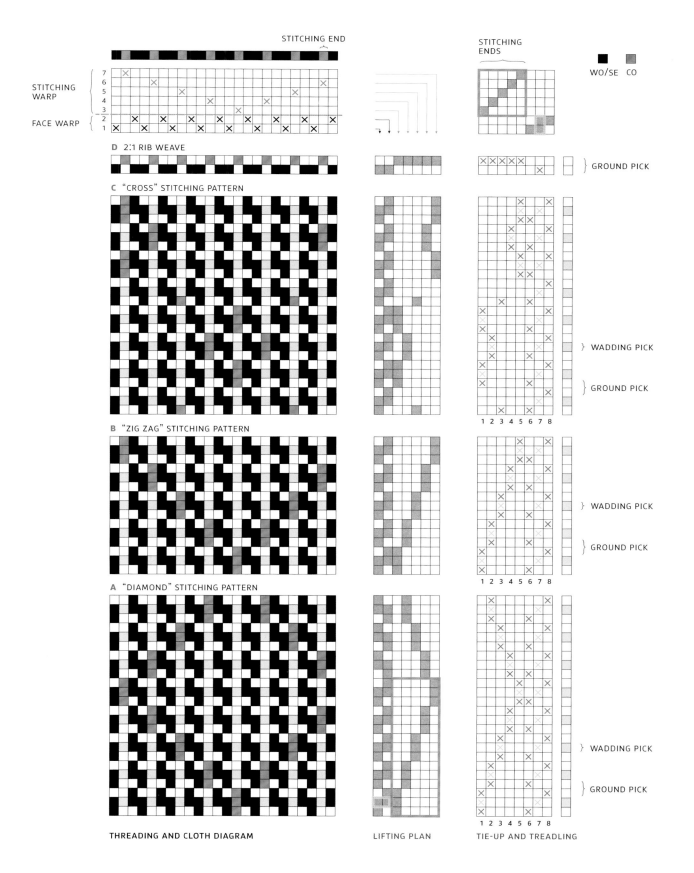

STITCHING END

STITCHING ENDS

WO/SE   CO

STITCHING WARP
7
6
5
4
3
FACE WARP
2
1

D 2:1 RIB WEAVE

} GROUND PICK

C "CROSS" STITCHING PATTERN

} WADDING PICK

} GROUND PICK

1 2 3 4 5 6 7 8

B "ZIG ZAG" STITCHING PATTERN

} WADDING PICK

} GROUND PICK

1 2 3 4 5 6 7 8

A "DIAMOND" STITCHING PATTERN

} WADDING PICK

} GROUND PICK

1 2 3 4 5 6 7 8

THREADING AND CLOTH DIAGRAM   **LIFTING PLAN**   **TIE-UP AND TREADLING**

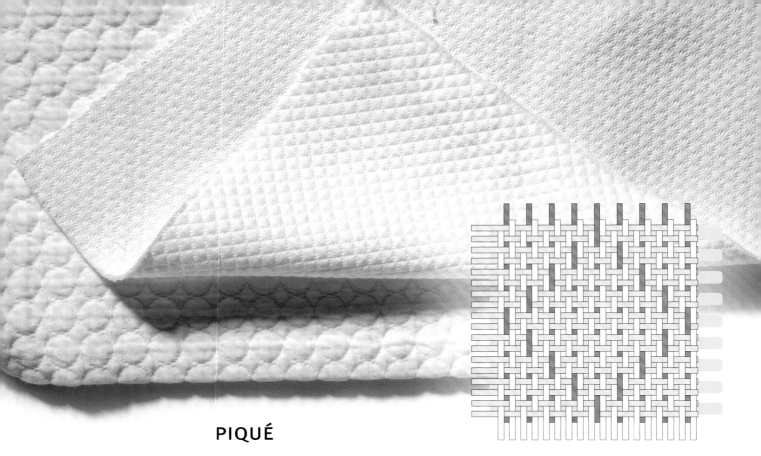

PIQUÉ

↑ Industrially woven cotton
piqué bedspread fabrics,
Lauritzon

Piqué is a **matelassé** weave, a padded structure in which the stitching forms the pattern.
The name **piqué** derives from the French word
for "quilted". Piqué weaves are **double-cloth**
structures with two warps, one for forming the
face weave and the second one for stitching,
each wound onto separate beams (see p.206).
Often the face of the piqué fabric is **plain weave**
or **basket weave**, but also **twill weave** or **satin**
are used to achieve a smoother and denser
fabric face.

The **stitching warp**, also called **backing
warp**, is held in greater tension while the **face
warp**, or **ground warp**, made from finer yarns,
is woven under less tension. Alternatively, one
or two sets of picks can be used: the **ground
pick** for forming the face weave and an option-
al filling, or **wadding pick**, which is only visible
on the reverse side of the fabric. The tensioned
backing warp forms floats on the reverse and
stitches form decorative furrows on the face of

the fabric thus creating the three-dimensional
look typical for piqué. The three-dimensional
effect can be enhanced by further tensioning
the stitching warp and by adding a thick, fluffy
wadding pick. As opposed to double weave or
pleats (p.198) piqué weave does not feature a
full layer of interwoven cloth on the back of the
fabric. Wadding runs between the face layer
and the layer of floating stitchers in the back.

Piqué weaves are closely related to **corded
weaves**, structures with vertically running
ridges. In fact, piqué constructions with the
floating ends forming straight weft-wise ribs
are sometimes called horizontal cords. In
contrast, **Bedford cord** – a corded weave with
floating picks on the back of the fabric – has
vertically running ridges. Bedford-cord fabrics
are often woven with woollen yarns, which
shrink after washing to form soft warp-wise
cords. A similar construction is used to make
weft-pile fabrics such as **corduroy** (p.210).

STITCHING AND WADDING

The plain weave face of this shimmering fabric is woven on the silk wool ground warp with a fine silvery polyamide lurex combination yarn. The wadding, a fluffy plied mohair pick, adds soft three-dimensionality to the delicate texture. The stitches merge to form the diamond shaped grooves on the fabric face. The mohair yarns are visible under the layer of floating cotton backing yarns.

SI/WO   CO

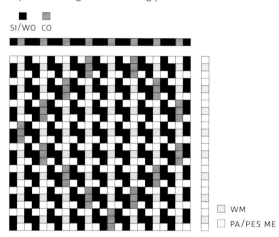

WM
PA/PES ME

Here, a thin cotton polyester marl yarn pick creates melange colour effects on the plain weave face cloth. Undulating waves are formed by the mercerised cotton stitching ends. A rigid polyurethane coated cotton viscose yarn wadding pick fills up the ridged ripples.

→ *Hum* from collection *Have the Courage for New* by Lotta Köhler

SI/WO   CO

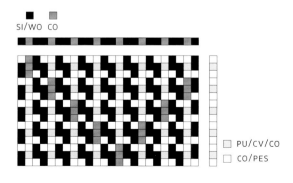

PU/CV/CO
CO/PES

↑ *Silver – Gentle and Charming* from collection *Party Time* by Anna Sorri

REVEALING THE WADDING— DISTORTING THE PICKS

The gauze-like fabric face, loosely woven on the wool silk warp with a thin black wool yarn, reveals the wadding of thick linen bouclé. The rough, looped wadding yarn distorts the picks on the face adding texture to the surface.

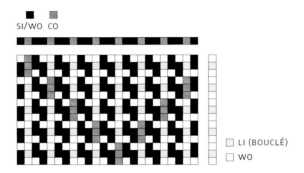

SI/WO   CO

☐ LI (BOUCLÉ)
☐ WO

"Göteborg is for me the most familiar place of the unfamiliar places in the collection. It's thick and soft, a bit brushy. It's not too intimidating, just like most Swedish things. I think I would like the city. Still, it's a part of the unknown. That's why the texture is rough and a little hazy."

↓ *Göteborg* from collection *On the Way to Unknown Grounds* by Kajsa Hytönen

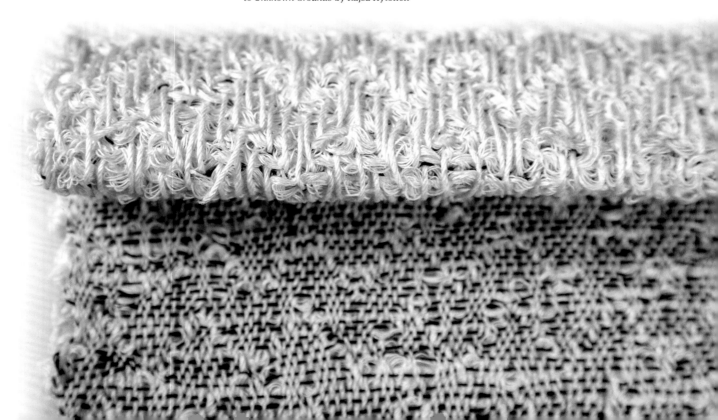

↑ *Home* from collection *Morphology– Human metaphors* by Erin Turkoglu

"*Home is a piqué weave with a metallic surface. The soft wadding behind the silver yarn symbolises a protective layer.*"

A loosely woven metallic pick adds contrasting sparkle to this soft, wavy piqué texture padded with bulgy cotton mop yarn. The distorted-yarn effect on the fabric face comes from varying the treadling sequence–two ground picks woven in the same shed are separated by succeeding stitching ends thus trapping the yarns into undulating paths on the fabric face.

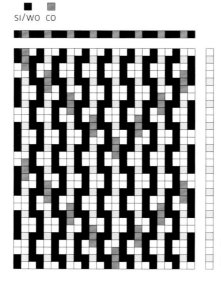

SI/WO CO

CO

CV/PA ME
(COVERED YARN)

↑ *Kakekotoba* from collection *Japan* by Yuki Kawakami

SHIFTING BLACK AND WHITE STRIPES

This three-dimensional texture plays with the shifting effect of the two contrasting colours woven on the two sides of the piqué ridges. The thicker, plied black viscose yarn forms wider stripes while the thinner white viscose yarn interlaces into narrow furrows.

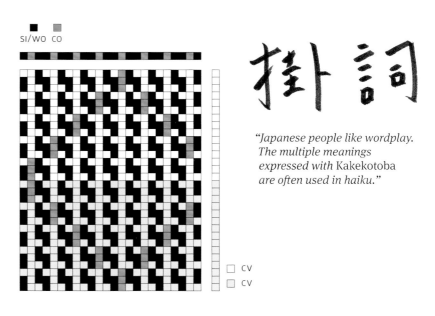

"Japanese people like wordplay. The multiple meanings expressed with Kakekotoba are often used in haiku."

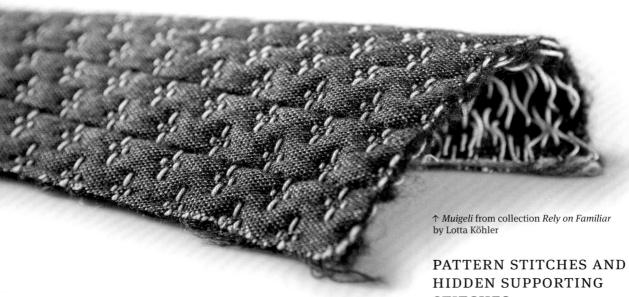

↑ *Muigeli* from collection *Rely on Familiar*
by Lotta Köhler

PATTERN STITCHES AND HIDDEN SUPPORTING STITCHES

In this piqué fabric the length of the **pattern stitches** varies from over-four to over-two plain-weave units. The face layer is woven on the wool silk ends with thin, soft worsted wool yarn and a soft brown wool **roving** is used for wadding pick. **Supporting stitches**, ends not involved in patterning, interlace with the face layer in short over-one-pick interlacement. These supporting stitches are required in order to join all stitching warp ends in the construction. Grooves are formed where the stitches of pattern floats and supporting ends lie dense next to each other.

Roving is produced by preparing fibres for making spun yarns from wool sliver, cotton, or other staple fibres. A loose assemblage of fibres is carded to lie roughly parallel to each another forming a **sliver**. This long narrow bundle is then drawn out and slightly twisted to form roving lengths suitable for spinning. Refer to p.132 for more information on spun yarns.

In this section wool roving is used as the wadding pick in *Muigeli*, *City in Finland*, *Incipient Winter*, *First Encounter* and *Moonlight*.

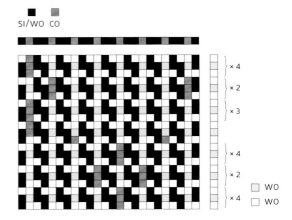

SI/WO   CO

×4
×2
×3

×4
×2
×4

☐ WO
☐ WO

VARIATIONS WITH — OR WITHOUT — THE WADDING PICK

A glimmering polyamide slit-film ground pick accentuates this mountainous relief. The raised effect is further heightened by the contrast of the thick wadding, which undulates against an enclosed area woven without a wadding pick. The wadding is a bunch of surplus yarns found in the weaving studio.

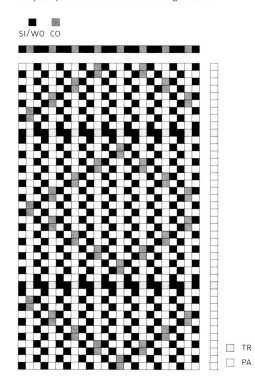

SI/WO CO

TR
PA

VARIATIONS WITH THE STITCHING PATTERN AND WADDING PICK

↑ *Alpi – Alps* from collection *Italy* by Tiina Paavilainen

Piqué can be varied in multiple ways. *Talisman* (p.91) highlights the effects of the unconventional choice of a metallic slit-film ground pick. A loosely woven ground layer results in the wadding pick showing on the face, thus adding textural effects seen in fabrics *Home* and *Göteborg*. The stitching pattern can be altered by changing the treadling sequence or by varying the length of some of the stitches as in *Muigeli*. The wadding pick can also be partly left out to create partial cushioned effects as in *Alp* and *City*, or pulled up to dot the fabric face as in *Incipient Winter*.

In this ribbed relief, bands of soft cotton picks and the padding of bulgy white wool roving enhance the raised effect of the patterned tracks running on an unpadded zigzag ground which is further flattened by the stiff paper yarn pick. The addition of a silvery metallic yarn highlights the icy trails.

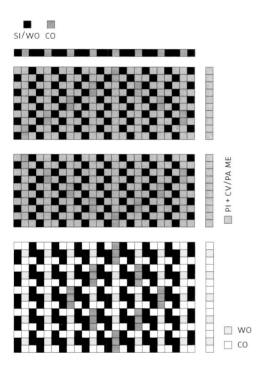

→ *City in Finland* from collection *Finland* by Lu Zeng

WEAVING THE LAYERS TOGETHER

Rows of elliptical shapes decorate this metallic fabric woven with bundles of silvery covered yarn. The pattern is formed by adjusting the lifting sequence of the stitching ends and adjusting the length of the floats. A padding pick of fluffy white wool roving cushions the soft ovals. The chains are separated by a dent formed by weaving both the ground ends and stitching ends together to form a flat two-to-one rib weave strip.

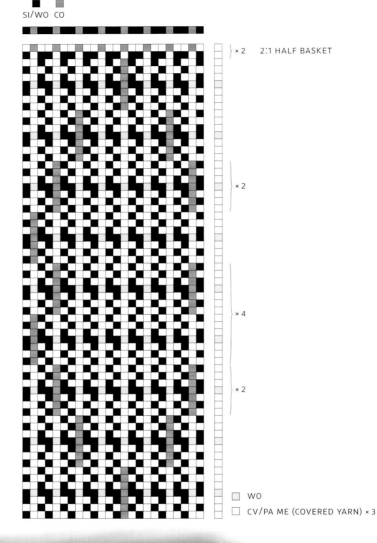

SI/WO   CO

} × 2   2:1 HALF BASKET

× 2

× 4

× 2

☐ WO

☐ CV/PA ME (COVERED YARN) × 3

↓ *First Encounter* from collection
Space by Ilona Hackenberg

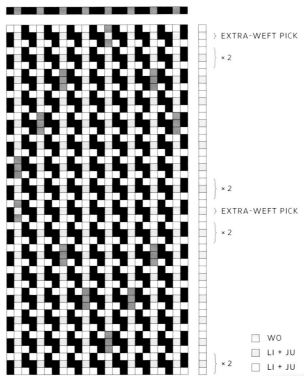

SI/WO ■ **CO** ■

} EXTRA-WEFT PICK

} × 2

} × 2

} EXTRA-WEFT PICK

} × 2

} × 2

□ WO
□ LI + JU
□ LI + JU

PIQUÉ VARIATION
WITH EXTRA-WEFT
PATTERNING

Extra-weft patterning with fluffy dark brown
wool roving dots the face of this piqué
variation. The extra-weft pick is raised onto
the face of the fabric by leaving the stitching
ends down in the middle of the patterning
sequence. A coarse linen jute combination
is used both for the ground pick and the
wadding pick.

↓ *Incipient Winter* from collection
Finland by Tiina Teräs

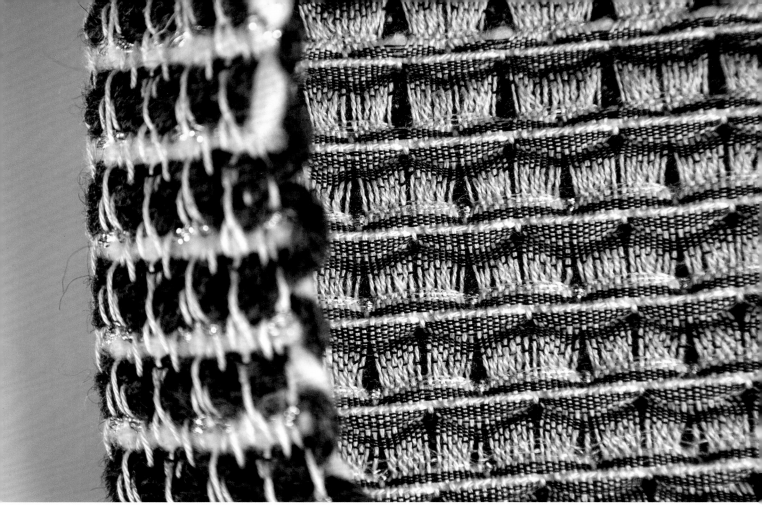

↑ *Moonlight* by Hanna-Maaria Sinkkonen

EXPLORING DOUBLE CLOTH

With this brilliant weave we challenge the reader to sit at the shaft looms with an open mind, and to explore the unforeseen.

The inventively textured **double-cloth** (p. 206) is an excellent example which pushes the boundaries of the sample warp and its tie-up. The fabric is woven with a selection of seven different picks ranging from thin cotton and viscose yarns to thick woollen yarn and roving. The clever selection of weft yarns in different sizes and types, each with its dedicated position in the structure, enables vast possibilities for texturing by grouping, distorting, hiding and revealing the yarns, resulting in an intriguing web full of details. Both cloth layers are stitched together with care taken to avoid overlong floats. The thick brown woollen pick, the white wool roving and the bundle of metallic slit-film yarns are woven on top of the plain weave ground and stitched down with the cotton warp. The ground warp of wool silk ends is woven with bands of thin black viscose thread, thin metallic and cotton picks and mercerised cotton yarn.

Silk Yarn Warp

SATIN WEAVES
DAMASK
COMBINING WEAVES—
FROM TEXTURES TO PATTERNS

FIBRE AND YARN INFO:
SILK
MULBERRY SILK, SILK FILAMENT YARN, SILK SCHAPPE YARN

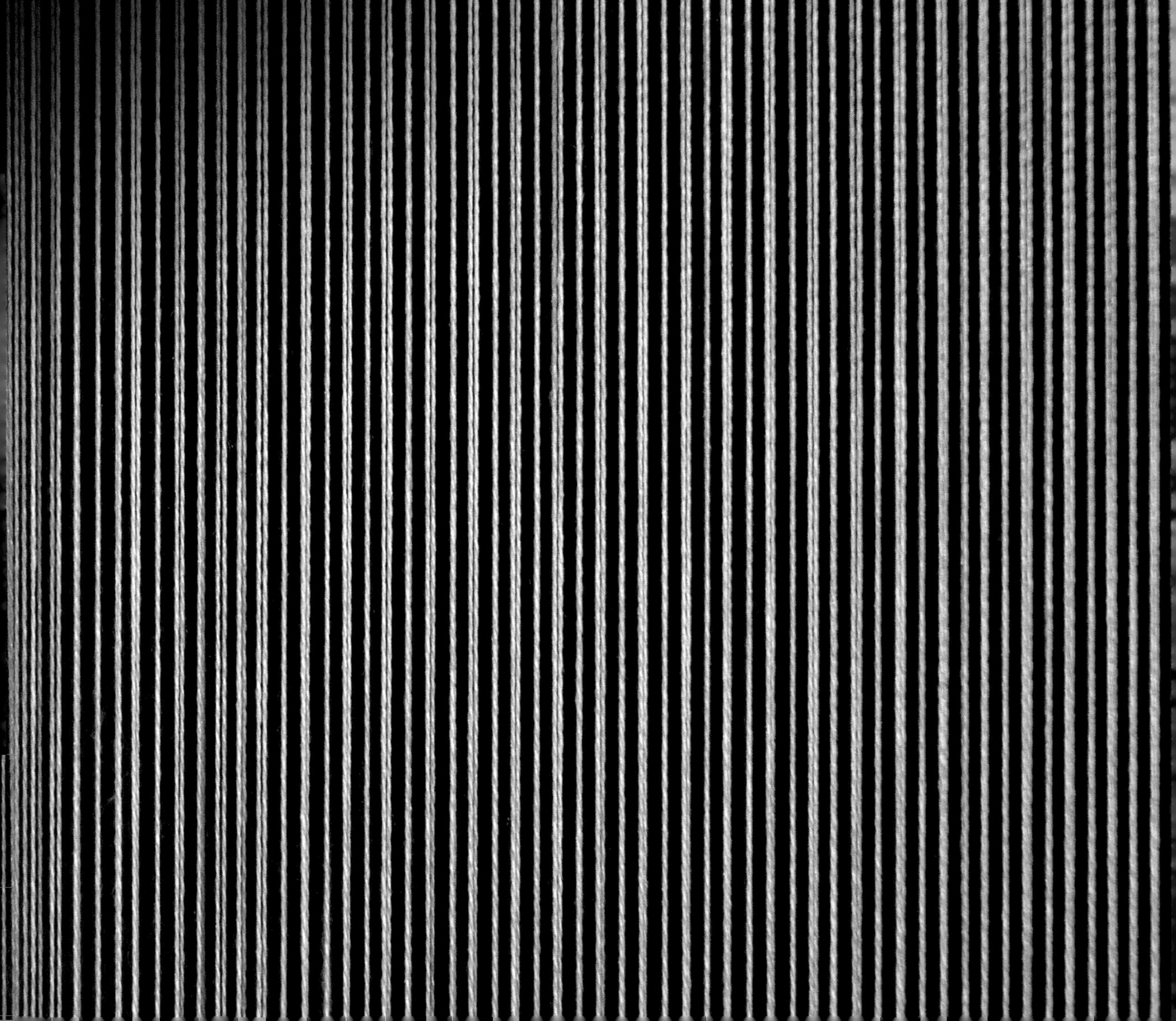

2.10 Smooth and Silky Freestyling to Patterns

This section introduces **satin weave**, one of the three basic weaves alongside plain weave (p.129) and twill weave (p.243). Satin weaves create a dense, smooth surface of yarn **floats** (p.130), with one side of the fabric warp-faced and the other side weft-faced. Hence, the weave allows for a distinctly different fabric face and back. The **stitchers**, points of yarn intersections, are scattered throughout the repeat in a uniform pattern as far as possible from each other, and the fabric thus lacks the distinct diagonal line characteristic of twill. Increasing the overall float length enables a tight yarn sett resulting in a densely woven lustrous fabric with an enhanced drape–the yarns float on the surface of the fabric, presented in all their beauty.

Damasks are patterned fabrics which combine warp-faced and weft-faced satin weave or twills on the face. Damask is often woven in a single colour to highlight the delicate effects of reflecting light on the warp-faced pattern against the weft-faced ground. It is the interplay of light and the floats in opposing directions which brings the damasks to life. Here, damask patterning is explored on shaft looms by using a block draft. Jacquard damasks are discussed on p.354.

The tightly sett silk warp is set up for 8-end satin. According to availability and preference,

B

Silk / SE is a natural protein fibre secreted by various moth larvae (p.28). It is the only natural continuous filament fibre. Sericulture, the production of cultivated silk started in China (p.54). Throughout its history, silk has played an important role in the advancement of weaving technology (p.66). Recent developments in weaving machines enable silk weaving not only on shuttle looms, but also modern shuttleless looms (p.73). Artisanal silk weaving however still remains a notable sector (pp.83 and 397).

Although several species of silkworm exist, most silk used in the commercial silk industry is derived from the cocoon spun by the larvae from cultivated **mulberry silk moths**. The mulberry silkworm feeds on the leaves of the white mulberry tree and then spins a cocoon shell around its body from liquid silk and **sericin** secreted by glands on its head. After some days it will have spun a thread two to four denier in size with the length of the solid fibre around 1500m. In order to keep mulberry silk in filament form, most cocoons are heated using hot air or steam to kill the silkworms before they mature into moths and emerge from the cocoon. Sericin, a water-soluble gum, is softened in hot water after harvesting the cocoons to enable the continuous filaments

to be unwound as yarns. The filaments are then **reeled** from cocoons by combining and winding them. Typically, filaments from four to twenty cocoons are combined and slightly twisted together to form a uniform raw silk filament thread. In addition to these more valuable filament yarns, **schappe silk**, or **spun silk** yarns, are made from broken silk filaments, fibre material from outer or inner parts of the cocoon, or cocoons where moths have emerged.

Silk has outstanding natural properties due to the fibre's high tensile strength, good moisture absorption, elasticity and ability to bind chemical dyes. Despite competition from man-made filaments, silk has maintained its position in luxury and high-quality items. Silk products are soft and comfortable to wear in both warm and cold climates. They are lustrous and have an excellent drape, which make silk products desirable not only for clothing, but also home textiles. Due to its biocompatibility and mechanical properties, silk is increasingly used in biomedical applications. Waste silk is used as a reinforcing material for composites thus ensuring strength and good deformability. Silk is a renewable and biodegradable natural fibre. Environmental impacts of silk cultivation include use of pesticides and

fertilisers in growing of the mulberry trees. Water and chemicals are used throughout the silk production process. To reduce environmental harm, waste water management is essential.[27]

← Mulberry silk schappe yarn warp

Warp yarns Lustrous silk yarn provides ground for exploring the smooth, nearly unbroken surface of yarn floats in satin weave. Two alternative yarns are suggested for the warp: a fine **mulberry silk filament yarn** (A) and a spun yarn, low-twist two-ply **mulberry silk schappe yarn** made from staple silk from the outside layers of the cocoon (B). The filament yarn provides a more shiny, classic satin surface. However, for novice weavers, the latter alternative might prove an easier warp to handle.

A

Silk yarn warp

Warp yarn: Mulberry silk yarn, Nm 1/33 (tex 30) silk filament or schappe, spun silk yarn Nm 2/60 (tex 17 × 2) | 100% SE
Yarn Sett: 14 ends per cm
Reed: 70:2

SET-UP I: DOBBY LOOM
Straight draft on sixteen shafts. The set-up is for 8-end **satin** woven weft-dominating side up (A) and striped **damask** (B). The damask can be mirrored on the computer-assisted loom for a chequered design (p.310). It is important to note that when warp-faced satin and weft-faced satin are combined, sharp breaking of the two weaves is an essential feature. This is achieved by using the alternative **rising number** (see pp.307 and 310). An example motif is provided for **extra-weft patterning** (p.83) on plain-weave ground (C). More small-scale patterns can be created on the computer. Weave combinations are explored by weaving lustrous bands of satin weave (A) against a matte taffeta plain-weave ground (D).

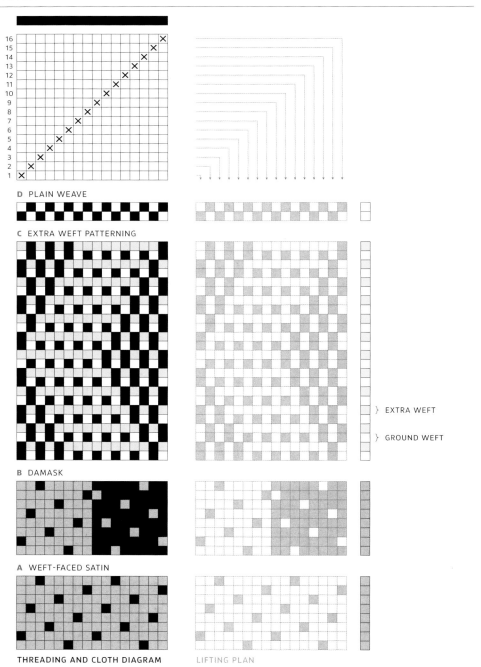

SE

D PLAIN WEAVE

C EXTRA WEFT PATTERNING

} EXTRA WEFT

} GROUND WEFT

B DAMASK

A WEFT-FACED SATIN

THREADING AND CLOTH DIAGRAM   LIFTING PLAN

SET-UP II: TREADLE LOOM

Straight draft on sixteen shafts. The set-up is for 8-end **satin** woven weft-dominating side up (A) and striped **damask** (B). Both arrangements I and II can also be expanded to a block draft (grouped draft) with shafts 1 to 8 assigned for the first block and shafts 9 to 16 for the second block (p.190), thus enabling variations to the scale of the stripe (B) or the dotted pattern (A+B). The tie-up for shafts 1 to 8 can also be changed to mirror the tie up of shafts 9 to 16 resulting in a checked damask pattern (p.310). Note the sharp breaking of the two weaves both horizontally and vertically (see p.310).

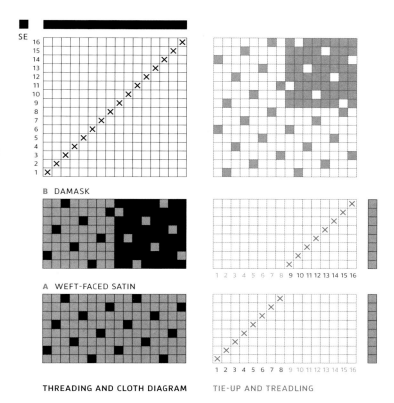

B DAMASK

A WEFT-FACED SATIN

THREADING AND CLOTH DIAGRAM   **TIE-UP AND TREADLING**

either silk filament yarn or spun silk yarn can be used. On the warp-faced side of the fabric–with floats over seven picks–the silk ends enhance the shimmering effects of the weave. Weft yarns are similarly highlighted. The uniform surface of satin brings out the full character of any yarn, be it shiny, furry or fancy. A satin plain is great for balancing out a collection of busy textures and elaborate patterns. Satin weave also works well for colour stripe designs, enabling clear juxtaposition of the coloured yarns.

The sample warp is set on a sixteen-shaft loom with a straight drawing-in draft. A warp set-up for 8-end satin, weft-faced side up, and damask is provided for both a sixteen-shaft dobby loom (SET-UP I) and treadle loom (SET-UP II). The set-up can be altered according to the availability of shafts. Satin can be woven with as few as five shafts, with a block draft on ten shafts providing ground for studying the effects of damask.

For technical reasons satins, as well as other prominently unbalanced weaves, are usually woven with the weft-dominating side up, regardless of the fabric face of the final product. Although exceptions exist, this generally applies to jacquard looms as well as dobby looms, and industrial weaving as well as hand-weaving. Lifting fewer ends helps control the process and makes weaving lighter.

The section also provides information on **combining weaves** and elaborates on the overall impact of the **threading draft** in shaft loom patterning. The path from textures to patterns discussed on p.314 paves the way to jacquards and designing more elaborate ornamental and floral damasks in Chapter 3. *Jacquards–Boosting the Patterns*.

Studying satin weaves on a computer-assisted dobby loom, rather than on a treadle loom with its restricting tie-up, encourages flexible switching between the variations and damasks as well as combinations of different weaves. The samples in this section have been woven on a sixteen-shaft dobby loom with a straight draft (I). Other lifting plans are for treadle looms with 16 or 8 shafts. Depending on the amount of shafts available on the loom, any other satins can be used. A two-block striped damask for a 5-shaft satin would only require ten shafts and ten treadles.

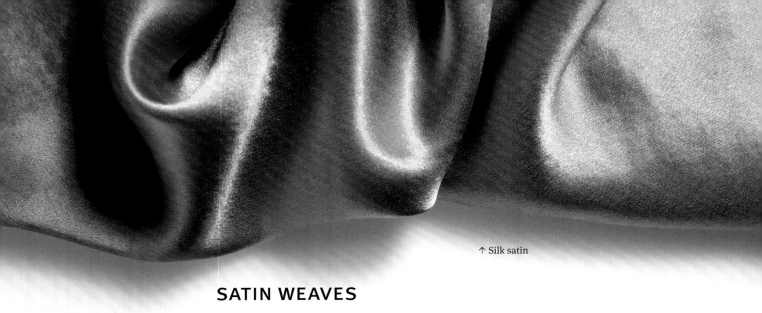

↑ Silk satin

SATIN WEAVES

8-END SATIN

**Fabric names:
satin weave**

*antique satin,
baronette, charmeuse,
double-faced satin,
duchesse satin,
façonne, Venetian
cloth, gattar,
messaline, sultan,
sateen*

Satin weave is formed of densely sett yarn floats – with one side dominated by the ends and the other side by the picks. A **warp-faced satin weave** is formed of densely sett warp yarn floats and **weft-faced satin weave** or **sateen** is a satin fabric with the picks floating on the face of the fabric. As the satin weave allows long floats of threads to run on the face of the fabric, the colour as well as the material characteristics of the floating yarns become a prominent feature of the fabric. Silk and other lustrous filament yarns with little or no twist are frequently used for satin fabrics. For spun-yarn satins, spun silk yarn, smooth mercerised cotton yarns (p. 417), fine line linen yarns (p. 243) and high-quality worsted wool yarns are preferred. Smooth, silky yarns floating on the fabric face capture light and enhance the appearance and drape of satin weave.

Generally, increasing the overall float length enables a higher yarn density, or sett, than used in more closely bound weave structures. Hence, satins are woven with a **close sett**, or high density, in contrast to **normal sett**, which is the yarn sett based on a plain-weave structure. In contrast to the twill weave, the thread **intersection points**, or **stitchers**, of satin weave are generally longer and scattered as far apart as possible in a non-directional pattern. The result is a seemingly unbroken,

flat and lustrous surface and a compact, flexible and well draping fabric.

The preferred draft to use for a satin fabric is influenced by the yarn sett as well as the size and type of the warp and weft yarns. The longer the floats, the more widely scattered the stitches, and the more possibility for yarns to lie densely next to each other forming a smooth, lustrous face. However, a satin draft with too widely placed intersection points results in shifting yarns, overall sponginess and weakness of the fabric, snagging and seam-slippage problems. On the other hand, a draft for a high-density warp with inadequate float length does not allow for sufficiently closely sett picks and results in a ribbed surface. For the above mentioned reasons, developing satins for production requires multiple rounds of weaving and testing to find the optimal balance between the sett and design of the weave. Although generally in satins the abrasion resistance and seam slippage are compromised compared to more closely bound structures, its lustre, smooth silky hand, flexibility and wonderful drape make satin popular for many applications from fashion to interiors. Due to their high density, satin fabrics have good thermal retention and wind resistance properties, and perform well as functional fabrics such as black-out curtains.

Drafting satins

Satin weaves require at least five shafts. The intersection points of the satin weave can be scattered in an optimal way by using **rising numbers**, also called **move numbers** or **satin intervals**. The rising number defines the sequence of the intersection points in succeeding picks. It is calculated by dividing the basic repeat unit into two so that both numbers add up to this unit's yarn count but do not share common prime factors. The satin is drafted by marking the first intersection point in the left corner of the basic repeat. The following stitches are marked based on the chosen rising number.

Satin	Rising numbers
5-end	2 or 3
6-end (irregular satin)	–
7-end	2 or 5 and 3 or 4
8-end	3 or 5
9-end	2 or 7 and 4 or 5
10-end	3 or 7
12-end	5 or 7

↑ Examples of rising numbers for a selection of satins

← Silk satin and cotton satin

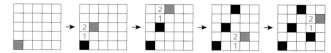

A 5-END SATIN: RISING NUMBER 2

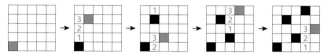

B 5-END SATIN: RISING NUMBER 3

Determining the order of progression for the stitchers in a 5-end satin. The number 5 can be divided into 2 and 3. Either of these numbers can be used as a rising number. The first row is an example of drafting the 5-end satin using number 2 as the rising number (**A**). Beginning with the first intersection point in then left corner of the draft with the first end and first pick and progressing 2 picks up, the second end is stitched on the third pick, the third end on the fifth pick etc. until all ends are stitched. The second exam-

ple demonstrates use of number 3 as rising number (**B**). In designing satins, the order of progression can also be carried sideways instead of upwards.

Due to the small repeat size, a 5-end satin features an unavoidable twill line and is sometimes called satin twill. The only difference between the 5-end draft with rising numbers 2 and 3 is the reversing of the diagonal line. The 5-shaft satin is used for both warp-faced and weft-faced weaves.

C 6-END SATIN

This draft features a frequently used order for the 6-end **irregular satin** (**C**). There is no regular order of progression for the stitchers in a 6-end satin, as according to the rule for defining rising numbers the number 6 can only be divided into 2 and 4 and thus share the common prime factor 2. However, it is possible to construct a so-called irregular satin which has a slightly pebbly look in contrast to the smooth appearance of regular satins.

D 7-END SATIN   8-END SATIN

The 7-end satin and the 8-end satin are **regular satins** (**D**). Here, the rising number used for the 7-end satin is 4, and for the 8-end satin 3 has been used as the rising number.

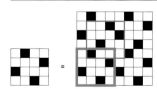

E 4-END "SATIN", BROKEN TWILL

E The minimum number of shafts for a satin weave is five, as the intersection points cannot be distributed evenly with less ends. Despite this, frequently the 1/3 broken twill (p.252) is called a satin.

UNIFORM SURFACES:
HIGHLIGHTING YARN CHARACTER

Satin weave creates a dense, smooth surface of yarn floats. These 8-end satin fabrics are featured with the weft-faced side up. The character of the fabric greatly changes with the choice of the weft yarns. The fabrics from collection *Skin* are woven on the silk filament sample warp. In *Old Skin*, the mohair wool blend pick plied with thin wire creates a dense, furry surface with scratchy metal loops, whereas *Young Skin* is characterised by a luminous, smooth mercerised cotton pick and a soft hand. *Nights in White Satin* is woven on the schappe silk warp with a wool polyester combination pick.

"*This piece reminds me of the mineral shine in a rock. I found a lovely shimmering wool polyester combination yarn and wanted to give it the main role in one sample, so I chose the satin weave and used the yarn in the weft. The satin weave is wonderful in the way it presents the yarn at its best. It lets the yarn shine. But weaving dense satin takes time. It is about finding the right rhythm.*"

From left to right: *Nights in White Satin* from collection *Minerality* by Marjo Hanhisalo, and fabrics *Young Skin* and *Old Skin* from collection *Skin* by Laivi Suurväli

SE

NIGHTS IN WHITE SATIN	☐ WOOL POLYESTER COMBINATION YARN
YOUNG SKIN – SCRATCHES	☐ MERCERISED COTTON YARN
OLD SKIN – HAIRS	☐ MOHAIR WOOL BLEND YARN PLIED WITH THIN METAL WIRE
MEMORY OF A MIDNIGHT	☐ FLAT-PRESSED YARN (PU/CO/PA)

The image reveals the distinctly different fabric face and back of the satin weave fabric. A lustrous wool polyester combination yarn pick on the weft-faced side is highlighted against the matte sheen of the spun-silk ends on the warp-faced side.

← *Nights in White Satin* from collection *Minerality* by Marjo Hanhisalo

A densely packed polyurethane coated flattened chenille pick forms the thick, furrowed surface of this 8-end satin fabric. The white silk filament warp remains all but hidden from this weft-faced side of the fabric, only small specks of the white warp flicker on the dark surface.

"When I was a child, one night, my sister and I lay down on the grass in the park and counted the stars in the dark sky."

→ *Memory of a Midnight* from collection *China* by Tong Ren

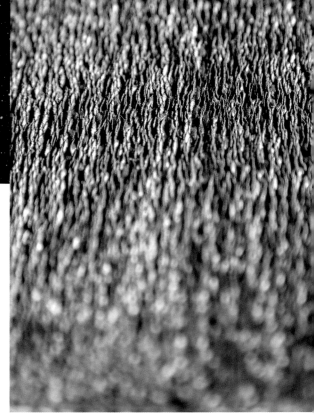

CONTRASTING SATIN STRIPES

Shiny cross stripes of viscose filament yarns are set against matte wool blend spun yarns in this 8-end satin woven on the schappe silk sample warp.

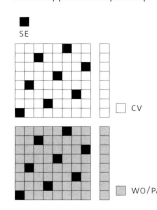

SE

CV

WO/PA

← Fabric from collection *Moonlight* by Hanna-Maaria Sinkkonen

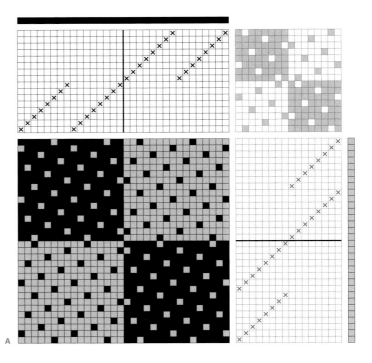

A Example of a block draft for an 8-end satin chequerboard damask. This style of drawing-in is used on shaft looms for the production of striped and chequered designs. In these combination weaves, a sharp breaking of the weaves is an essential feature. This is achieved in satins by using the alternative rising-number (3 for the weft-faced and 5 for the warp-faced satin) and twills by running weft-faced and warp-faced weaves in opposite directions. Variation comes from the endless potential to vary the amount, sequence and width of the blocks. More on the impact of threading drafts appears on p.320. See also p.264 for information on elaborate patterning through drawing-in patterns.

A

DAMASK

Damask is a reversible fabric woven with one set of weft yarns and one set of warp yarns, and patterned by combining warp-faced satin and weft-faced satin or twills on the face. The interplay of light and the floats in opposing directions bring the damasks to life. Damasks are often woven in a single colour to highlight this contrasting luster, the effects of reflecting light on the warp-faced pattern placed against the weft-faced ground. In two-colour damasks, with contrasting colours for warp and weft, the colours reverse on either side. Colourful damasks can be woven on multicoloured striped warps (see scarf on p.327).

The invention of the **drawloom** (p.66) enabled the creation of elaborately patterned silk fabrics. Alongside the development of weaving technology, fine damasks were further embellished with brocade patterns. These fine fabrics were introduced to Europe via the Silk Road and the trading and manufacturing centre Damascus, which gave them their name. Today the term refers to a broad group of jacquards or shaft-loom fabrics with ornate botanical or geometric patterns, manufactured of linen, cotton, wool and man-made fibres such as viscose, acetate and polyester, in addition to the traditional silk. Ornamental and floral damasks are woven on jacquard looms, whereas on shaft looms a **block draft** (A) is often used to create geometric damask patterns such as stripes and checks (B, C). Damasks have remained popular for centuries, especially for furnishings such as ornamental upholstery fabrics and draperies, as well as for home-textile applications such as tablecloths, bedspreads, and towels. Silk damasks have endured as favourites in formal dress historically as well as in today's accessories, such as scarves, often embellished with a logo pattern.

Fabric names: damask

damas, damas chine, damas de Lyon, damas lisére

B Chequerboard damask tablecloth woven in a single colour on a linen warp with cotton weft

C Damask kitchen towel woven in a single colour with the same cotton linen blend yarn for both warp and weft

↑ The interplay of light and the floats in opposing directions, on an ornately patterned jacquard damask table linen

SMALL-SCALE
TWO-COLOUR DAMASK

Here, 8-end weft-faced satin and 8-end warp-faced satin alternate according to a chequer draft. The fabric is woven on the white mulberry silk filament warp with a black two-ply worsted wool pick. The soft, closely woven weft yarns completely cover the warp and partly slide on the warp-faced areas thus distorting the pattern to diagonal stepped lines.

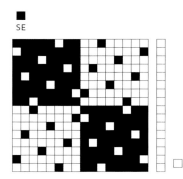

→ *Journey* from collection
The Moments by Ali Zamiri

VARIATIONS WITH PICK

Bands of stiff metallic pick and slippery viscose filament pick alternate in the chequered stripes of this glittering chequer design woven on the silk filament warp. Altering the length of the pattern blocks forms the illusion of three-dimensionality.

SE

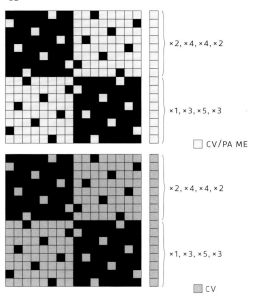

×2, ×4, ×4, ×2

×1, ×3, ×5, ×3

☐ CV/PA ME

×2, ×4, ×4, ×2

×1, ×3, ×5, ×3

☐ CV

← *Dishonest* from collection *China* by Tong Ren

→ A collection of woven fabrics and prints inspired by space travel. The small-scale textures and patterns are woven on different warps and set-ups on dobby looms. *Trapped* by Kajsa Hytönen

↑ Damask with warp-faced and weft-faced satins. The fabric is woven with silvery slit-film yarn on a white mercerised cotton warp on a jacquard loom. *Diagonal* from collection *Memphis Blues* by Miisa Lehto

COMBINING WEAVES—FROM TEXTURES TO PATTERNS

Examining the process of **combining weaves** and pattern design on shaft looms sets the stage for jacquard fabrics and digital design, the focal points of the following Chapter 3, *Jacquards—Boosting the Patterns*. The surface texture of a woven fabric can be observed as a small-scale pattern. A twill fabric has a distinctive diagonal texture that can also be seen in satins. Even a simple plain weave woven with contrasting yarns in warp and weft, could be regarded as a chequered texture. Stripe patterns can be woven on a striped warp or by altering the pick colours. However, a woven fabric is generally considered patterned when the colour-and-weave effect (pp.154 and 258) or a combination of two or more weaves forms a design or distinctive motifs, on its surface.

The term combining weaves is used to describe two different processes in woven fabrics design. Firstly, the process of combining any two or more weaves with different appearances to form a pattern. As an example, damasks (p.310) are patterned **combination weaves** with warp-faced and weft-faced satins or twills in one fabric. Secondly, combining weaves also refers to the process of

constructing a **compound weave** (p.144), such as used in the fabrics *Crosswalk* (p.143) and *Old Town* (p.145) which combine two weaves each with a dedicated set of weft yarns. The essence of a compound weave is that the picks and ends or both are divided into several sets, which have different functions in the structure. The sets of picks are often referred to as **weft systems**, and the sets of ends are labelled as **warp systems**. In the examples *Crosswalk* and *Old Town*, plain weave acts as a supporting weave, stabilising the fabric.

A further example of compound weave structures is **interwoven fabrics** (p.206), such as double-faced structures—with either one warp system and two weft systems, or one weft system and two warp-systems—or double cloth and double weave, integrating two sets of weft yarns and two sets of warp yarns.

Combination weaves and compound structures are woven on both shaft-looms and jacquard looms. Their role is essential to the design of complex patterned jacquard fabrics in particular. Techniques for creating various compound weaves are described in the context of jacquard design on p.364–400.

FREESTYLING SMALL-SCALE DESIGNS

"Time to unleash your creativity and start drafting dobby patterns!"

This small-scale dobby pattern is woven with a metallic pick on the silk filament sample warp with straight draft on sixteen shafts. The symmetric pattern forms lines of inverted interlacements in warp- and weft direction similar to mock leno (p.218). As a result, units of picks and ends group together to create the perforated, geometric lacy design. The size and density of the picks and ends affects the appearance of the final woven pattern. Here too, the outcome of the final woven pattern may differ from the proportions of its draft (p.360). However, this deviation can also provide the weaver with unexpected and delightful discoveries.

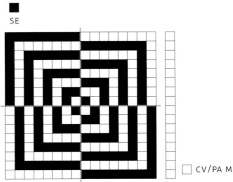

SE

CV/PA ME

← Sample from collection *Malaysia* by Jonathan Ho

Here too, a graphic take is applied to drafting the lifting plan of a dobby design woven on the white silk warp on sixteen shafts. The geometric pattern inspired by optical illusions is woven with a smooth viscose filament pick. Here the density and size of the picks and ends is similar, and thus the appearance of the woven design resembles the draft.

"*The pattern in this fabric is an optical illusion of a box that changes its direction. The fabric reminds me of snake skin and bankers' ties.*"

↑ *Banker* from collection *Manhattan* by Saara Louhensalo

SE

☐ CV

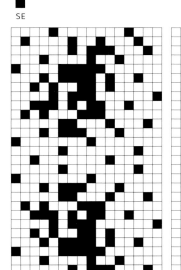

SE

WO/PES + PES/PA + CA/PA/PES

"The multitude of colours and fragments reflected on the walls capture this very sacred moment."

The stitches of the design appear as speckles thrown on the draft, scattered and grouped at random. The fabric is woven warp-facing side up on a silk sample warp with a straight draft. It is woven with a unit of black wool yarn combined with a bunch of shimmering golden and bronze hued synthetic filament yarns.

↓ *Cathedral Glass* from collection *Excess* by Leonardo Hidalgo-Uribe.

CATHEDRAL GLASS

EARTH / SPACE

Earth / Space

Woven fabrics studio course assignment 2014

by Ilona Hackenberg

My two collections, *Earth* and *Space*, are designed to function not only as independent collections but also in conjunction with one another. The collections are inspired by the 1960s and each consists of ten woven designs.

The *Earth* collection is influenced by the fun and colourful aspects of the decade, and particularly by the ceramic art of Birger Kaipiainen. *Earth* aims to convey a safe, fun, and familiar feeling. Hence, the collection is woven with soft, structured, and toned yarns while employing polished and smooth weave structures such as satins.

The inspiration for the *Space* collection is drawn from the space-age style and minimalistic trends of the 60s. Here I aim to portray a feeling of solitude and unfamiliarity. The work expresses a cold, clean, and serene place in zero gravity. This collection integrates numerous graphic elements with strong contrasts; dense and stiff weave structures, and flat and shiny yarns.

I worked very intuitively throughout the process by first trying out a structure and reflecting on the feelings it evoked in me, and then choosing the materials and making the final design.

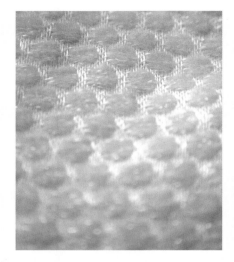

Peach from collection *Earth*

↑ This patterned satin damask is woven with a furry wool polyamide combination yarn plied with an iridescent slit-film yarn as pick. Due to the pick density versus sett of the warp, the ellipse shape in the draft is translated to a dot in the final woven fabric.

Fruit Basket from collection *Earth*

↑ In this sample a three-dimensional satin stripe bulges against the plain weave background. The fabric is woven with a wool yarn plied with an iridescent slit-film yarn. As well, a supporting weft in plain weave is integrated between the satin stripes.

← Fabrics from collection *Earth*

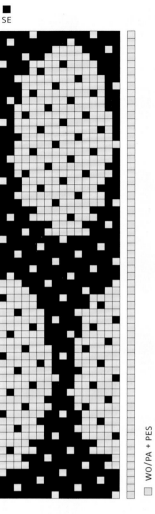

■
SE

WO/PA + PES

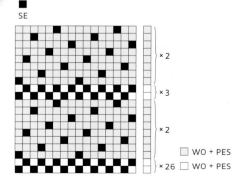

■
SE

× 2
× 3
× 2

☐ WO + PES

× 26 ☐ WO + PES

↑ Moodboard for collection *Space*

← Fabrics from collection *Space*

Radio from collection *Space*

↑ This two-weft system sample with vertical wavy stripes features **extra-weft patterning** with a 3-ply pattern pick on a plain weave ground. Two contrasting pattern weft yarns, a hairy black acrylic yarn and a shiny viscose raffia yarn identical to the pick in *Take-off*, are woven in block stripes of varying width. The texture difference between the two picks results in a blurring pattern effect in the stripes woven with the acrylic yarn.

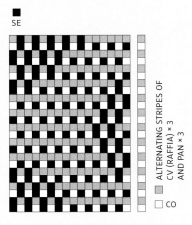

SE

ALTERNATING STRIPES OF CV (RAFFIA) × 3 AND PAN × 3

CO

Take-off from collection *Space*

↑ Floats of shiny black viscose raffia pick create the elliptic patterns in this design. A thin white cotton pick woven in a weft-packed structure on the face of the fabric forms rows of vertical stripes with the white silk ends. The raffia picks, alternating with the silk picks, float on the reverse side and generate narrow black stripes on the face when intersecting with the silk ends.

SE

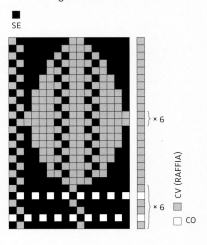

× 6

× 6

CV (RAFFIA)

CO

The impact of the drawing-in draft in shaft-loom patterning
by Maija Fagerlund

**Pattern design for dobby looms:
the impact of threading**

This section discusses the impact of a straight draft, a pointed draft, a block draft and a divided draft on patterning. The effects of the drawing-in draft in designing twills are featured on p.251.

Furthermore, decorating woven surfaces through unique threading patterns on a limited number of shafts is discussed on p.264. A prehistoric point of view on patterning through threading is offered in *The story of early European wool fabrics* on p.58.

Designing patterns on dobby looms is dependent on the number of shafts as well as the threading and the sett used. However, the width of the repeat is determined by the threading and the sett. With a **straight draft**, the horizontal pattern repeat equals the number of shafts. As an example, when designing a pattern to be woven on a loom with sixteen shafts using a straight draft, the available repeat width is 16 ends. With a sett of 8 ends per cm, the available repeat would be 2 cm wide. A narrow repeat is a typical feature of fabrics woven using straight threading. To compensate for the small repeat size of the width, more variation can be added to the repeat height by variations to the lifting plan. Though in principle, there are no limitations to the height of the pattern repeat, in practice long pattern heights may be cumbersome.

→ Industrially woven fabric made on a dobby loom with a straight draft on twelve shafts. The sett of the warp is 10 ends per cm resulting in a relatively narrow repeat. The designer has compensated for the restrictions of the horizontal repeat by utilising the lifting plan to create more variation in the vertical repeat. The fabric is woven using black cotton yarn as warp and grey silk yarn as weft.

→ *Shiny* from collection *Harlequin* by Eveliina Netti

↑ *Mosaic* and *Leaves* from collection
Parc Güell by Christine Valtonen

A **pointed draft** results in mirrored patterns.
This type of draft can be used to scale up
the repeat size and add variation to the
design. With a pointed order of drawing-
in, diagonal lines transform into zigzag
patterns and semicircles into circles. This
type of threading has been used widely from
prehistoric times until today. Examples of
the use of pointed draft in Bronze Age fabrics
can be seen on p.59. Further examples can
be found on p.251 and p.272.

↑ Damasks presenting symmetrical patterns
woven on a dobby loom with a pointed draft
on sixteen shafts. The fabrics are woven
using polyester yarn as warp and cotton
yarns as wefts.

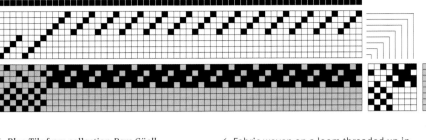

← *Blue Tile* from collection *Parc Güell* by Christine Valtonen

← Fabric woven on a loom threaded up in two blocks. The wider block consists of four rows of 3/1 broken twill and four rows of weft floats. The structures used in the narrow block include a plain weave that is implemented to secure the long floats in place, and a 1/3 broken twill. The fabric is woven using viscose yarn as warp and cotton yarn as weft.

↓ Fabric woven on a loom using block draft threading. The background of the design is woven in plain weave and the structure used in the pattern is a weft faced satin. The fabric is woven using black wool viscose blend yarn for the warp and white polypropylene yarn for the weft.

Office (MF)

A **block draft** (p.190) can be used to enable larger repeat sizes and more versatile patterning. In this threading, a group of warp ends is threaded into one set of shafts, while another group of ends is threaded into a different set of shafts. Thus, entirely different weave structures can be used for each group of ends. Based on the number of shafts available, three, four or more varying threading blocks can be created. Block threading can be used for designing vertical stripes or blocks with different width. A skilful designer can use this type of drawing-in to create complex patterned fabrics, reminiscent of jacquards, especially when 16 or 24 shafts are available and multiple blocks can be drafted.

Examples of complex patterning on a loom set up using block threading. It is challenging to recognise the original lifting plan used and to identify which parts of the design are repeated in different blocks. Both fabrics are woven on a dark grey wool lyocell warp. The weft materials in *Rhythm* are light blue polyester and gold viscose, and *Red Curtain* is woven using red mercerised cotton and black viscose chenille as wefts.

↖ *Rhythm* (top) and *Red Curtain* (bottom) from collection *Harlequin* by Eveliina Netti

When designing woven structures with two sets of ends, these two warps can also be threaded in their own sets of shafts in a **divided-draft** arrangement as demonstrated in the sample warp for double weave on p.188. The threading for both warps can be similar, but using a different drawing-in draft for each warp allows for additional variations to the design. For example, one warp can be used as a ground warp, which only requires a few shafts, while the second warp can be composed of more complex threading using several shafts (see p.288). To amplify the pattern design possibilities further, the threading for this **extra warp or supplementary warp** can be pointed or in blocks.

↑ In this extra-warp patterned design, the beige cotton ground warp is threaded on four shafts and the white lyocell supplementary warp uses point threading for 12 shafts. The weft material used is a black thin worsted wool yarn. Fabric by Maria Huusko

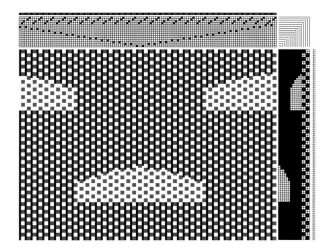

Patterned dobby fabrics can be designed using several techniques such as sampling on treadle looms or drawing the structures by hand on paper. **Weave design software**, such as Weave Point, is an effective tool in the design process and allows the designer to quickly design and test the effects of various structures woven with different types of threading. The use of Adobe Photoshop software as a tool in the design process of jacquard fabrics is explained in Chapter 3. *Jacquards – Boosting the Patterns*. This method can also be used to design woven structures on shaft looms.

↓ In addition to colourful graphics, patterns can be used to create structural effects. The face side of this double-weave fabric is woven on a cotton warp with a cotton pick. A polyester elastane pick weaves the lyocell warp of the back cloth. The weft yarns in the back cloth shrink through steaming, creating a puckering effect in the fabric.

Find more information about double weave structures in the section *Layers, Pleats and Blocks* on p.187. The topic is discussed in the context of jacquard weaves on p.380. Information on steaming and other finishes can be found in Chapter 4.

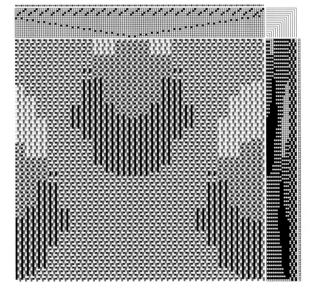

↑ This fabric is woven with the same divided-draft arrangement as the fabric above, but it has a more complex structure due to the two different weaves used for the first and second pick. The black lyocell supplementary warp is woven into the ground in most parts of the design and is only left to float in details of the pattern on the face or back side of the fabric. The outcome is a colourful pattern with various structures mixing the two warps with green and blue cotton picks.

↑ *Fence* by Anna Semi

↓ *Cuddly* by Anna Semi

Designing coordinated colour-ways for industrially woven fabrics woven on a white linen warp. The colouration of the fil coupé fabric and yarn-dyed plain-weave fabric is guided by the colour story and moodboard. Collection *Hyper Fusion* 2021, Vanelli (MS)

2.11 Adding Colour

Colour in a **yarn-dyed fabric**—a fabric in which the hues of the interwoven yarns define the colour of the final product—is rarely uniform. As demonstrated by this chapter's ten sample warps and the fabrics woven on them, colour can appear as a blend, or a combination of the yarn shades used, or the hues can form clear patterns. How and in which proportions the yarn colours are mixed on the surface of the fabric depends greatly on the yarns, yarn sett and weaves used. The colour of a woven fabric can differ on the face and the back of the cloth. Different yarn types and weaves create shadows and variations in the luminosity, saturation and tone of the final textile.

Even the limited colour palette of black, white and unbleached neutrals used in the fabrics woven on the sample warps provides enough colour contrast for exploring colour effects with different weave structures and materials. The variety and richness of the textiles presented in this chapter demonstrate how materials and structures influence colour.

Yarn-dyed fabrics are woven or knitted with yarns that have been dyed prior to fabrication of the cloth.[28] The final colouration of a yarn-dyed fabric is generally planned before and achieved during the weaving or knitting process.

Piece-dyed fabrics are woven or knitted in the **greige**, generally using unbleached, undyed yarns. The fabricated goods then undergo the dyeing and finishing process in larger batches. Piece-dyed fabrics are usually in solid colours. They can be plains or patterned through texturally contrasting areas.[29] For more on colouration finishes see p.424.

A **colourway** is any of a range of combinations of colours in which a design is available.[30]

The teaching approach of this book first introduces the ways in which materials and structures influence colour, before delving into the topic of **colouration** of yarn-dyed woven fabrics more deeply (p.121). Colour is an important element which greatly influences the appearance of the weave and with it the final cloth, but it can also overpower more subtle design elements. Understanding the role of colour in a woven fabric develops alongside the practice-led exploration of the interplay of materials and structures. Achieving the desired **colourway** is not only a matter of selecting suitable shades for the yarns, but understanding how the weave structure, yarn sett and yarn type come together to form the final appearance of the fabric. Introducing a more versatile colour palette is recommended after a basic understanding of the concepts behind woven fabric design has been established.

→ A silk scarf by the UK-based design studio Wallace & Sewell. The colourful chequered damask woven with dense warp-faced satin and weft-faced satin features masterful play with weaves and colouration.

← A colouration concept along-side a mood board is created to outline the premises of the design and development work of a new collection. As preparation for the following sampling phase, weft yarns are selected, and in case new shades are needed, new yarn colours are sourced from yarn producers or dyed.

Creating the colour story, colouration, along with the mood board kickstart the initial concept creation phase of the commercial collection design process. However, once the initial concept reaches the actual textile design phase within the textile industry, the colourways are generally introduced to the design at a later stage, after the yarns, the yarn sett, the weaves and all other elements of the woven product have been fixed and tested. Professional weave design software is often used to support **digital prototyping** in the colouration phase and to reduce pre-production sampling costs. Dyeing yarns and finding the correct shades from commercial yarn colour cards often requires advance preparation. Through the subsequent colouration, the final product, its appearance and concept, are defined. Nevertheless, colour plays a smaller role during the development of the actual fabric, reappearing in the main role only in the final phase.

See more on concept creation and mood boards in the section *Visual Research – creating and narrating a concept* on pp.112–117.

← Planning a range of colour-ways for a linen blend hound-stooth upholstery fabric. The weft yarn colours are coordi-nated with the collection's colouration concept.

→ Generally more than one warp colouration needs to be used in order to achieve a full colourway of shades ranging from light to dark. Colour sampling in the industry is done on colour range warps, with warp sections dedicated to the warp colours. Here a colour range warp with a section of dark, medium and light ends is woven with a selection of pick colours. The selected colourways are cut out from the sampling warp for later reference. Vanelli (MS)

Learning about woven fabric colouration

The *Colourways and woven fabrics design* course focuses on the topic of colouration of yarn-dyed woven fabrics and deepening the understanding of shaft-weave design, including complex compound structures and patterned weaves (p.314) and the impact of the drawing-in draft in shaft-loom patterning (p.320).

During the initial *Woven fabrics studio course* (pp.80–83 and 120–123) students have learnt to understand basic weaves, combination weaves and a number of compound structures including double weave. Limited to a restricted colour palette of black, white and unbleached neutral colours, the students have focused on building their understanding of the interplay of an array of different yarn materials and weave structures, and their expressive and performative qualities. Building on this, in the *Colourways and woven fabrics design* course they are ready to use a wider palette of hues as a further design element and a means of expression and storytelling in woven fabrics.

Rather than having warps set-up with the intent of studying specific weaves, as during the basic course, during the *Colourways and woven fabrics design* course the students predominantly weave on pre-arranged warps on computer-assisted dobby looms with simple, versatile threadings on sixteen or more shafts. On the computer-assisted looms, the students are expected to draft the lifting plan for their samples, and design fabrics using the skills learned during the basic course and advance to compound weaves, patterns and more complex structural explorations. The students explore the impact of the threading in shaft-loom patterning on looms set up with block draft, pointed draft and divided draft. Treadle looms are available for plains and textural material explorations to complement the collection. The colour range of the warps is versatile, including reliable neutrals as well as one or two warps with bolder hues. The students are encouraged to select from a wide palette of coloured weft yarns to build a coordinated and coherent colour concept for their collection.

During the course, students develop a textile collection intended for interior or fashion use. Mood boards are used as a tool and they play an important role in narrating the concept and defining the colours and atmosphere of the collection. The mood boards are developed through an assignment of making an imaginary journey to search for colour inspirations and patterns in a city, country, continent or any other geographically defined location of their choice. For students working on other long-term projects such as a fashion collection, visual research for their specific project can also be used as a starting point for the course assignment. Collection coordination is enhanced using a mood board, presenting the desired balance between main colours and accent colours, as well as patterned and plain fabrics. See more on concept creation and mood boards in the section *Visual Research – creating and narrating a concept* (pp.112–117).

Students can further expand their colouration skills through the task of designing alternative colourways for their woven collections. Weave design software or Adobe Photoshop software can be used to change the colour combinations for this second colourway. In addition, a further assignment related to commercial woven fabrics design can be integrated within the course. For this group work assignment, students weave colourways for a simple plain-weave fabric or twill on a **colour range warp** similar to the ones used in colour sampling in the industry. The set of colourways is targeted at a particular customer segment or market and is presented as a waterfall fabric sample set.

The following pages feature examples of students' work from the *Colourways and woven fabrics design* course.

As the students' curriculum, especially during short Master's studies, is often crowded, students are in principle equipped to proceed directly to the *Jacquard fabrics studio course* (p.338) after the basic *Woven fabrics studio course*. However, especially at an undergraduate level, the type of content – including learning the colour design process – and a slower path to advancing to jacquards are of advantage to the learning process.

↑ *Colourways and woven fabrics design* course assignment: fabrics from collection *New York* by Emmi Pakkanen

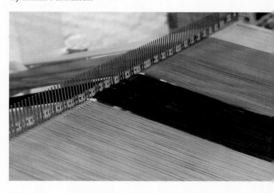

↑ Colour range warp being set up on the loom. Another colour range warp, with more neutral hues, including black, and neutrals: white, ecru, grey and beige-tones is also available for the students.

↑ Colourways of 2/2 cotton twill for segmented target groups presented in waterfall fabric sample sets.

New York
Colour and woven fabrics design course assignment 2012
by Emmi Pakkanen

As long as I can remember, I have always wanted to travel to the Big Apple. My woven collection is a portrayal of the fantasy of this city that I have never been to. In my mind, it is a place where everything is possible. It is a place where I would wear high heels and drink colourful cocktails in a skyscraper.

In these woven fabrics, I played with flashing images and scenes that I had envisioned, and combined different colours, materials, and structures to depict this playful mood.

Some of the samples are more practical while others lean towards artistic expression. They are a combination of simple blue jeans and shiny glitters.

Designing for me is all about manifesting what I feel inside. Often thoughts make more sense and feel more real after making them tangible. Looking back, this longstanding collection still feels like a real souvenir from the city of my dreams.

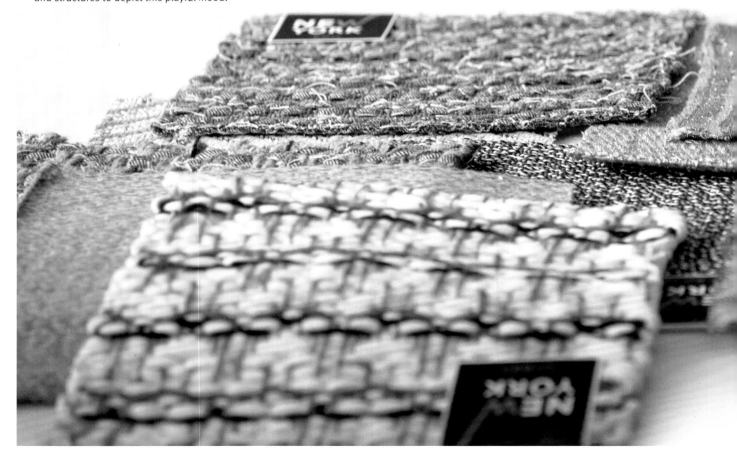

South Korea
Colour and woven fabrics design course assignment 2014
by Anna Sorri

Looking for a country or city to serve as inspiration behind my woven collections, I decided to choose a country that I had visited before. South Korea was an intuitive choice, since I had spent some time there as a tourist and was left with a lively and layered impression, which provided rich background to draw inspiration from.

To me, South Korea is a place where old and new collide; a place of high contrasts.

For instance in Seoul one can encounter modern, sleek skyscrapers standing right next to traditional houses with intricate roof patterns. However, some contrasts are more disguised in nature as the cultural developments of the past decades have been so fast that the traditional and contemporary cultures are still wrestling for balance. I wanted to bring some of these notions into my collection and include references from

both the traditional and the modern aspects of the country. Each sample in the collection holds a memory while the story is conveyed with colour, material, and structure. The storytelling approach, essential to many textile design processes, opened my eyes to how extensively it can broaden and enhance the design process.

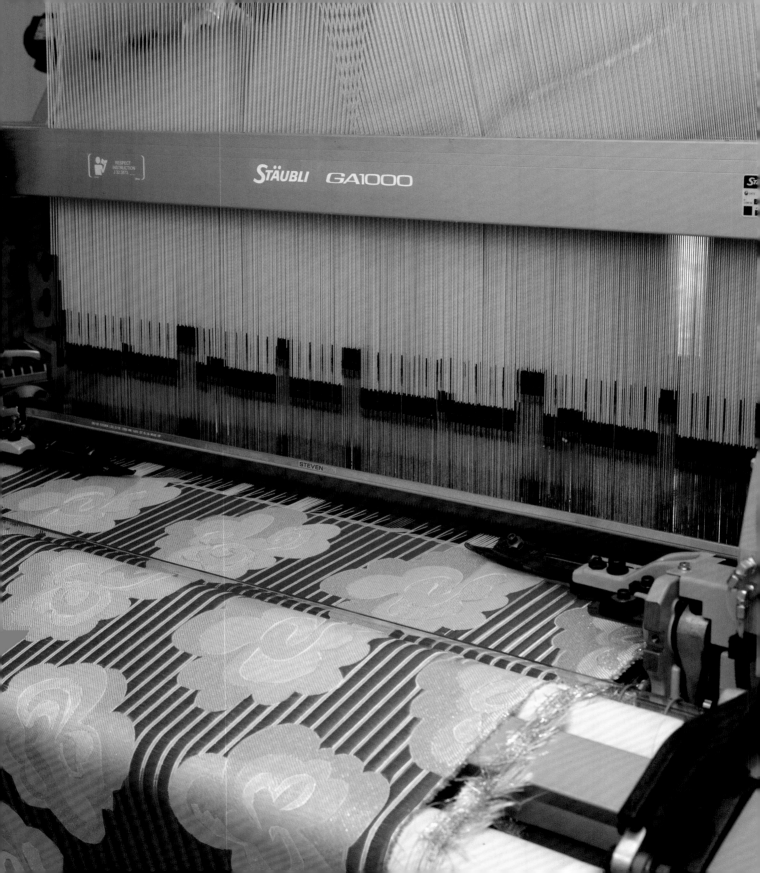

3. Jacquards— Boosting the Patterns

by Maija Fagerlund

Combinations of woven structures and textile materials provide a myriad of possibilities for a designer. This chapter introduces the jacquard technique which further broadens this potential. As described in the section *Combining Weaves—from Textures to Patterns* (p.314), the surface of a woven fabric always has a texture that can be observed as a small scale pattern. However, a woven fabric is generally considered patterned when the colour-and-weave effect (p.258) or the combination of two or more weaves form a more distinctive design on the surface.

Jacquard fabrics are patterned textiles woven on a jacquard loom. Invented by Joseph Marie Jacquard in the early 19th century, the jacquard loom simplified the process of manufacturing patterned woven fabrics, allowing for almost unlimited variations in their designs (pp.67–68). The examples presented in Chapter 2. *To the Looms—Weaving and Experimenting* are woven on shaft looms, which pose many restrictions on the patterning of the fabric. Unlike in shaft looms, in jacquard machines each warp end in one repeat unit of the machine can be controlled separately. This allows for more elaborate use of patterns and larger repeat sizes.

← Jacquard fabric being woven on an industrial weaving machine (left) and finished fabric with cut fil coupé stripes, presented on the catwalk (above). Master's thesis collection 2019 by Netta Törmälä

↑ This collection is inspired by the wonders of nature. The third fabric from left, *Serendipity*, is a jacquard design; all other fabrics are woven on shaft looms. *Serendipity* is introduced in more detail on p. 344. Collection *Marvel* by Oldouz Moslemian 2014

Although weaving large-scale patterns was possible before Joseph Marie Jacquard's invention, it was a rather slow process and a special assistant, a draw boy, was required to lift the warp ends needed to form the pattern. Several inventors worked on the automatic production of patterned fabrics during the 18th century.

Therefore, although Joseph Marie Jacquard patented the final jacquard machinery, some parts of the mechanism were most probably influenced by other inventors' work. However, as described in Chapter 1 (p.69), Jacquard's invention led to the development of the computer and to the birth of modern informa-

→ Student sampling on a hand-operated digital jacquard loom

tion technology.[i] The development circled back to weaving in the 1980s when the introduction of electronic jacquard machines marked a major improvement in looms. Before this advancement, a punch card was necessary to weave a design, but an electronic machine only requires a digital file of the design to weave it, making the design process significantly faster.

In this chapter, the reader is introduced to the design process for jacquard fabrics, from the sketching process to the generation of the final digital production file. The computerised design process of jacquard fabrics does not facilitate the tactile aspects such as materials and the feel of the fabric that are crucial in textile design. Therefore, creative sketching methods for woven fabrics are also introduced in this chapter. Sketching with fabrics is an advisable method for keeping the design process creative and tangible.

Conventional weave design software such as WeavePoint or PointCarré is utilised for designing weaves for shaft looms and in loom control of computer-assisted dobby looms (pp. 80 and 121). This type of software is essential when the impact of the drawing-in draft needs to be taken into account. However, in jacquard design it does not play a similar role.

This chapter introduces digital design of woven fabrics using Adobe Photoshop software. The weaving mills use professional jacquard design software such as EAT, NedGraphics and Arahne instead of Photoshop, but these special programmes are often out of reach for freelance designers and artists due to their high prices. Many designers are already familiar with and have access to Photoshop which makes it a practical solution for freelance designers collaborating with industry.

The key aspects of designing surface patterns for jacquard fabrics are also introduced in this chapter. The reader will learn the restrictions the technique makes on the repeat and composition of the design, as well as about colouration of jacquard fabrics and rules governing the drafting of the surface

↑ Maija Fagerlund at an industrial jacquard loom

pattern. Detailed instructions for making a pattern design in repeat are not included in this book, but recommendations for study material on this area can be found in the list of supplementary literature at the end of this book. (See *Further Reading*, p. 484.)

This chapter does not focus on introducing jacquard looms in detail. Here, the difference is drawn between industrial jacquard looms (pp. 67 and 77) and hand-operated electronic jacquard sampling looms (pp. 80 and 82). Industrial jacquard machines are generally used in weaving mills to manufacture patterned fabrics on an industrial scale, although having one in a design school provides great opportunities for learning. Hand-operated digital jacquard looms, excellent for sampling and production of unique pieces, are mainly used by individual designers and artists as well as educational institutions. Requirements of industrial production of fabrics are briefly discussed in this chapter with insights into the learning process of developing handwoven samples that can be further adapted and produced on an industrial machine.

↑ A collection of woven fabrics
2014, Niina Vilppunen

Learning jacquard design

In the pedagogical method introduced in this book, the most advanced course in woven fabrics concentrates on jacquard structures and industrial production of woven fabrics. The course begins with an introductory section regarding the technical and theoretical aspects of jacquard design. After that, the students concentrate on developing their individual design projects. During the theoretical part, students learn about the process of digital design for jacquard fabrics and sample their designs on hand operated jacquard looms using a variety of materials. A significant portion of the design process of jacquard fabrics proceeds digitally. Therefore, more theory is needed in this course compared to other woven fabrics courses. However, even in this advanced course most of the learning occurs through sampling and practical work. After sampling on hand-operated electronic jacquard looms, the designs are adjusted and developed to conform to industrial production requirements and are woven on industrial weaving machines. Even though the basic principles of function in hand-operated looms and industrial ones are similar, the processes are considerably different. Many designs and materials that are easily woven using handlooms are not suitable for fast and automated industrial machines. The best way to understand the difference between these two production methods is through practice.

After weaving, students are encouraged to finish their fabrics with methods such as dyeing, printing, brushing, steaming, and washing. *The textile collection design course* (pp.434–435), where students learn to use finishes, is often taken before this *Jacquard fabrics studio course*. Another option is to offer a separate studio course on dyeing and finishes and link the lessons timewise.

The outcomes of each student's individual design projects range from fashion fabrics to upholstery and from individual fabric collections to collaborative projects. For example, textile design and fashion design students use this opportunity to design fabrics for their thesis collections. Projects in which fashion and textile design students collaborate with one another are common. Textile design students also collaborate with interior design students to create upholstery or other interior fabrics. Many interior design students and industrial design students study textile design as a minor to be able to pursue their own projects. Textile design students frequently design jacquard fabrics in collaboration with the industry. Students tailor their own projects within the course and are encouraged to combine their ideas with other projects at hand, which highly motivates them to learn and develop fabrics and collections that suit their areas of interest and future plans.

Assignment:
Jacquard fabrics studio course

Design a collection of woven fabrics. The focus and use of the collection can be linked to your other courses and projects. The fabrics could be a part of a collection of interior fabrics, or for other applications such as clothing. The fabric's usability should be taken into account in each design. In addition to patterned jacquards, your collection should include samples of plains and textures. Your collection presentation should include a relevant illustration of how the fabrics would be used, especially if the fabrics are not presented in a product form. In addition, you should submit a product card for each design.

You are welcome to employ finishing methods to further process your fabrics. In particular, students taking a course in the dyeing and finishing studio are encouraged to link the course to this weaving studio course and also finish, dye, and print their own woven fabrics.

The practice-led design process in the woven fabrics studio

Start by selecting yarns best suited for your collection and continue by test weaving the structures:
- Weave a test sample of a damask structure.
- Weave a test sample of a double-faced structure (two or more weft systems).
- Weave a test sample of a multi-layered structure (two or more layers).

Combine the new acquired knowledge with your previous understanding of woven structures:
- Select two interesting shaft loom samples from one of your previous courses, and develop them to be woven on a hand-operated jacquard loom.

Get acquainted with industrial weaving:
- Select one or more of the samples, and develop them further to be woven on an industrial jacquard loom.

Repeat the process of weaving test samples on hand-operated looms, developing them and finally trying them out on industrial machines. You can also sketch the designs with the material collage method prior to weaving.

Follow the processes of your colleagues and share your findings with your peers at group meetings.

The content of the product cards

- The titles of your sample and collection.
- Material information. This should include the composition of the material e.g. 100% CO, yarn count e.g. Nm 50/2 and the pick density and warp yarn sett.
- The structures used in the fabric, submitted in a similar fashion to the way that jacquard structures are presented in this chapter.

One copy of each product card and a small sample of the fabric should be handed in for inclusion in the weaving workshop archives. They will be used as reference material for future courses.

3.1 Pattern Design for Jacquard Fabrics

SKETCHING WITH MATERIALS

Working with jacquards is exceedingly inspiring for a designer. A skilled jacquard designer requires both excellent surface pattern design expertise and thorough understanding of textile materials and woven structures. A jacquard design is generally a large and complex woven structure. Hand drawing the entire design with weave structures is a rather time-consuming process; hence a computer is often used to speed up the process. The digital design process allows for more flexibility, which can be considered an advantage, but it does not necessarily encourage the designer to concentrate on the use of materials, three-dimensional structures and the hand of the fabric. To keep the sketching process creative, it is important to take advantage of the tactile world of materials and not solely work on the computer screen.

Fabric sketching, using fabrics and other materials to generate a design, is a noteworthy method for this purpose. The aim of this technique is to develop a sketch that readily resembles a woven fabric. The materials employed are suggestive of the various structures and materials that are utilised in the final woven fabric. Starting the design process with material sketching frees the designer of only using structures familiar to them and challenges them to attempt new constructions. Additionally, material sketching is a suitable technique for jacquard design for freelance designers with no access to a loom. The benefits of the technique are illustrated in the section *Floating and Clipping* (pp. 460–463) where a project for designing fil coupé jacquards using creative material sketching is shared.

This collage technique is especially appropriate for designing jacquards, as jacquards can also be perceived as collages of various structures. In a fabric collage, elements of the design are created from fabric cut-outs, while in a jacquard fabric motifs are generated through different structures and materials. Making a fabric collage is technically simple. Motifs are cut out using scissors, or if possible, a laser cutter or blade cutter, and are then adhered onto a base fabric. Double-sided fusible webbing can be used to achieve polished results. Selection of the materials is the most important aspect of collage sketching. Multi-coloured fabric swatches result in a radically different design outcome than fabrics of similar colour with various shines, feels, and structures. The application of fabric is not obligatory and the design could be made from yarns, loose fibres, and other inspiring materials. In addition or instead of the collage technique, the designer can utilise fabric manipulation, embroidery, beading, hand stitching, painting and other means to achieve the desired effects.

← Fabrics, yarns and sketches used in the design process of the garments and fabrics for a 2015 Master's thesis collection. The final collection is presented on pp. 364–365, Ilona Hackenberg.

↓ Painted with opaque paste with white pigment and black ink on dark grey wool; Woven jacquard fabric based on the sketch. The structure of the woven fabric is presented on p. 372 *Lily* (MF).

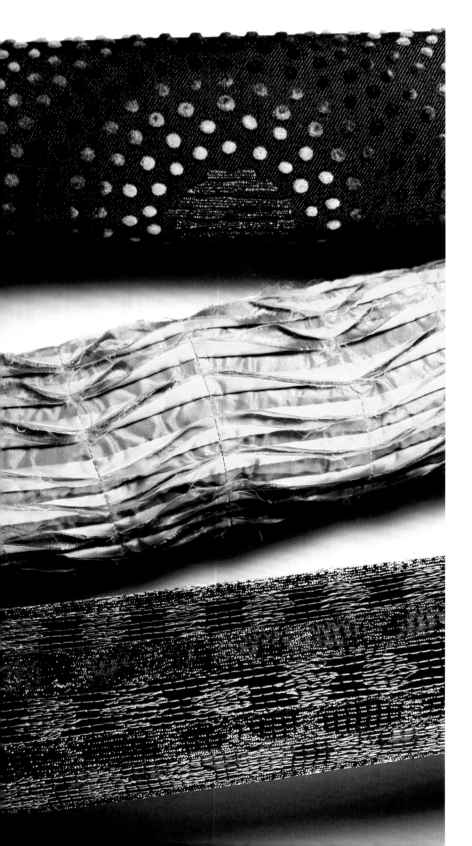

Painting on fabric can generate interesting effects. Relatively similar to the process of painting on paper, watercolours, inks, or reactive dyes appropriated for textiles do not generally alter the feel or structure of the background fabric. However, using contrasting materials, such as applying acrylic paint on woolly fabric, modifies the surface structure of the background fabric and could result in intriguing ideas for material variations.

Material sketching can also be used to generate 3D-surface and texture ideas. Fabric manipulation techniques such as sewing, pleating, folding, and stuffing can be utilised to develop a three-dimensional design (A). These methods could be used for all types of pattern design, but especially suit well for making otherwise plain designs such as simple stripes and geometries. However, it is important to bear in mind that the aim of this method is to create a sketch for a woven fabric rather than an independent piece of artwork. Therefore, the final outcome should be viable for weaving.

Sketches made using the collage technique can be realised as a jacquard fabric by using weft and warp yarns and weave structures resembling the materials used in the collage. The velvet fabric in a collage could be replaced with chenille yarn in the final jacquard or a shiny piece of silk can be represented using a warp-faced satin. A three-dimensional quilted material collage (B) could inspire the designer to design a fabric using multilayered structures, such as pocket weave or piqué variations. An excellent example of using material sketching to generate ideas of complex textural and multilayered 3D jacquards is presented in the section *Floating and Clipping* pp. 460–463.

← A Employing various collage and fabric manipulation techniques for design studio Affabre in Vienna. This studio largely concentrates on fabric collage designs; the designs are purchased by jacquard weaving mills and further developed into jacquard fabrics. Mari Heinonmäki.

↑ B In the picture above is a material sketch combining painting, quilting, and fabric manipulation at the top, and below the final woven fabric. The woven fabric is introduced in more detail on pp.398–399, *Form* (MF).

Technical aspects of pattern design for jacquards

From a technical point of view, the two necessary steps in jacquard design are to design a surface pattern and replace each colour area of the design with a weave structure. Although the issues are often more complex in an industrial set-up, as the production process depends on the available materials and machinery, the points discussed over the following pages are the initial principles that should be considered when designing a jacquard pattern.

A

B

Drafting the Surface Pattern

The surface pattern, in terms of style and texture, plays a pivotal role in determining the appearance of the woven fabric. Whether an amorphous or geometric design, both can result in striking jacquards. Varying weave structures and materials in a surface pattern with well-defined colour areas (F) adds finesse to the fabric (D, E). On the other hand, using a selection of weaves to fill the amorphous colour areas of a rough, painterly surface design (A) creates an intriguing, irregular mixture of textures (B). A process of painterly jacquard design is exemplified in the story of the fabric *Daisies and Friends – Scraping a path to a jacquard design* on pp. 376–379.

↑ The original surface pattern design (A) and the woven fabric (B). The textural surface of the fabric is created by inserting various satin structures onto the colour areas of the painterly design. Inspired by the light reflections and water movements on a lake, the design was generated by brush ink sketching. The design conveys the depth, magic, and mystery of what is underneath the surface. *Serendipity* from the collection *Marvel* 2014 by Oldouz Moslemian.

→ Example of a jacquard fabric collection created from simple geometric surface patterns. The inspiration behind this collection was to create the illusion of three-dimensionality in fabrics with flat surfaces. Collection *Illusions* by Emmi Pakkanen, 2012.

D

← Comparison of the outcome based on fabric sett. The industrially woven curtain fabric *Dilli* (left) is woven on a fine polyester warp with 80 ends per/cm. The high-density warp enables fine lines and intricate details. Even though the design *Alex* (right) presents the finest lines possible with the materials used, the lines are much thicker. The sett of the silk warp is only 24 ends per/cm, and the pick density is even less. The weft materials of *Alex* are silk and stainless steel for the background and black wool for the lines. *Alex* (MF) and *Dilli* from the 2011 collection *Chandni Chowk* for F&F (MS).

C

← The woven fabric (E) and the original surface pattern design (F). The optical illusion in this design is achieved by using four slightly different structures that make a subtle gradient from the blue weft to the silvery one. When seen from certain angles, the gradations generate an impression of shadows that resemble a three-dimensional pattern. The fabric is woven on a wool acrylic blend warp, and the weft material is polyester-coated viscose with a metallic shine. *Illusion 5* from the collection *Illusions* by Emmi Pakkanen.

E   F

The influence of yarn sett and pick density

The properties of the final fabric, such as density and materials, should be considered already at the stage of designing the surface pattern. Warp densities of the production warps at weaving mills are generally predetermined. The warp density is essential information as the fineness of the lines and scale of the details in a jacquard design greatly depend on the yarn sett (C). This is comparable to the resolution of an image on a computer screen: the higher the number of pixels per cm, the more intricate the details of a design can be. Furthermore, understanding the impact of the warp density on weave structures is crucial when selecting weaves. For instance, a particular weave results in a compact structure when woven on a high-density warp, while the same weave woven on a low warp density creates longer floats and a loose structure. The yarn materials, weave structures, planned fabric's end-use and desired hand determine the pick density. See examples on pp. 362, 372, 373, 397 and 398.

Jacquard repeat sizes

When designing a pattern for a jacquard, one needs to be aware of the available repeat size and number of repeat units per width of the fabric. The number of hooks in the jacquard control unit defines the repeat size – the number of individually controlled warp ends. Each harness cord is connected to a heddle and controls the movement of the warp end drawn through its eyelet. The harness cords transfer the movement of the hooks to the individual warp ends by either lifting them or leaving them down, depending on the design (A–D). See p. 67 *Jacquard Shedding*.

The harness divides the warp into identical repeat units–sets of harness cords–thus multiplying the pattern defined by the number of hooks in the jacquard system. Attaching the harness in a way that mirrors the pattern is also possible. According to the size of the jacquard control unit on the weaving machine, the warp is divided into two (B, D), three, four (C) or any other number of repeat units. Jacquard control units with fewer hooks (C) are most common in the industry since the number of hooks affects the machinery's cost, and attractive patterns can generally be achieved without large repeats.

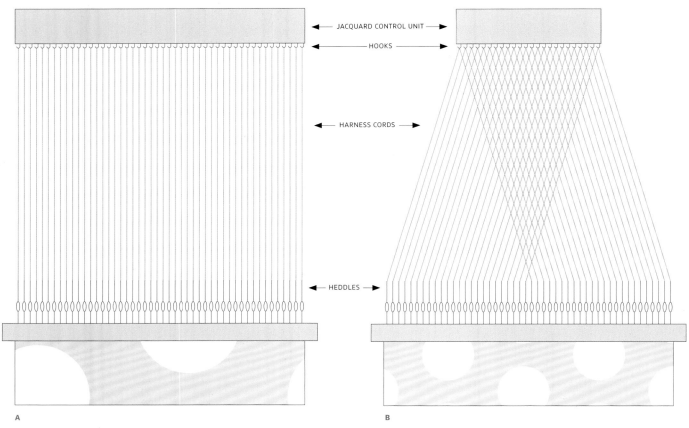

JACQUARD CONTROL UNIT

HOOKS

HARNESS CORDS

HEDDLES

A

B

↑ In a full-width jacquard repeat system, the harness cords connect the control unit's hooks to the individual heddles and the warp ends drawn through them, thus controlling each warp yarn independently and giving the designer complete control over the formation of the shed. This type of jacquard system opens up a world of possibilities, enabling the creation of fabric-wide designs or designs with smaller repeat sizes.

↑ In this jacquard system, each hook in the control unit is connected to two heddles, each controlling a warp end. This means that the warp is divided into two repeats. On this type of loom, the largest possible repeat width is half the width of the fabric. The repeat could also be smaller as long as it divides evenly into the repeat unit defined by the number of hooks.

With the warp divided into two units, the width of the pattern repeat is half of the width of the fabric, typically 70 to 80 cm (B). In warps divided into four repeat units, the width of the pattern repeat is a quarter of the width of fabric, commonly 35 to 40 cm, the most frequent jacquard repeat size at weaving mills producing fabrics for fashion and interiors (C). Naturally, the repeat can also be smaller as long as it divides evenly into the repeat unit's measurements, determined by the number of hooks. Each warp end can be controlled separately with a full-width jacquard control unit, allowing a pattern repeat as wide as the fabric width (A). Similar to shaft looms, there are, in principle, no restrictions to the height of the repeat in jacquards.

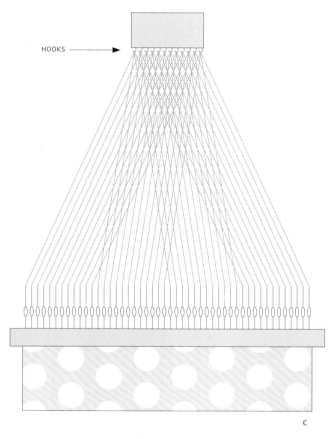

HOOKS

C

↑ This image features a jacquard system where one hook connects to four harness cords and heddles, each controlling a warp end. In essence, the harness of this loom divides the warp into four repeats. On this type of loom, the largest possible repeat width is a quarter of the width of the fabric.

D

↑ Jacquard fabric on an industrial weaving machine. The harness of this loom divides the warp into two identical pattern repeats, similar to graph B. More information on the fabric design is on p. 335.

The correlation between the composition of the design and warp take-up

When designing the composition of a jacquard pattern, it is essential to consider the warp take-up of the weaves used in the design. The term take-up refers to the measure of warp yarn consumed during weaving. If the ends frequently intersect with the weft, the take-up of the structure is high. Plain weave has the highest take-up, with its over-one under-one construction encompassing the maximum number of intersections (p. 134). Conversely, the take-up is lower in weaves, which consist of longer floats and fewer intersections, such as satin weaves. (A)

A PLAIN WEAVE HAS
THE HIGHEST TAKE-UP

SATIN WEAVE HAS
LOWER TAKE-UP

The overall take-up of the design should be kept relatively even; otherwise, some warp ends will become tenser than others, which could result in warp breakage during production. Even if it might seem possible to weave a short length with irregular take-up, complications occur in a longer piece, especially on industrial looms in the production phase. Hence, weaves with the same take-up should be used in designs with uneven composition and vertical stripes. Damask (pp. 310, 354), combining warp-faced and weft-faced satins or twills, is an excellent option. However, should the designer opt for a fabric with variations in the take-up of weaves, the overall take-up should be carefully balanced by creating an even composition of motifs (B).

This jacquard fabric combines five different weave structures with slightly different take-ups. The balanced repeat spreads the structures evenly onto the fabric to balance the overall take-up of the fabric. Fabric designed by Tiia Sirén for *The Voice of the Unheard* collection inspired by studying contemporary urban gangs as modern tribes, 2013 by Tiia Sirén, Siiri Raasakka, and Elina Laitinen.

B

C

↑ Jacquard woven upholstery fabrics with all-over repeat patterns running in four directions. *Paratiisi* (left) and *Koivu* (right), Lauritzon 2006 (MF)

D BRICK REPEAT

E HALF-DROP REPEAT

F ALL-OVER REPEAT

G PLACEMENT DESIGN

Repeat types

Brick, **half-drop**, and **all-over repeats** can be used to balance the warp take-up of the design. Furthermore, these types of repeats are often visually pleasing and do not generate any distracting repeat stripes or blocks. **All-over patterns** (F) are favourable for many purposes. For example, in fashion and upholstery fabrics, it is an advantage to be able to cut the patterns anywhere in the fabric without the need to align the motifs. Fabric waste can be reduced when it is not necessary to be concerned with the direction of the design while cutting the fabric. Hence, if possible, design motifs should be arranged to run in all four directions instead of only one (C).

Historically, brick and half-drop repeats have been widely implemented in fabrics such as classical damask patterns. A **half-drop repeat** (E) is created by shifting the repeat unit vertically by half of its height relative to the neighbouring unit. A repeat where the units are shifted horizontally is referred to as a **brick repeat** (D), built similarly to a wall of bricks. A brick repeat doubles the height of the entire design repeat, while the half-drop repeat doubles the width of it. Therefore, in most cases the brick repeat is more suitable for jacquard fabrics, as the width of the repeat is defined by the settings of the loom, but the height of the repeat can be chosen freely.

In addition to continuous patterns, **placement designs** (G) are used in products such as towels, cushions and tablecloths. It is essential to consider the take-up of the weaves with these design compositions. Again, damask (pp. 310, 354), combining warp-faced and weft-faced versions of satins and twills, is an excellent option.

→ This industrially woven upholstery fabric is a good example of colouration of a jacquard fabric with one warp and two weft systems. The fabric is woven with three yarn types with different colours. The yarns include black polyester ends, and the white viscose and grey chenille as weft materials. *Pi* from 2014 collection *Facett*, F&F (MS)

COLOURATION OF JACQUARD FABRICS

The colouration of jacquards differs from that of printed fabrics, but is similar to the colouration in all other woven fabrics. Each clearly distinctive colour used in jacquards requires its own specific weft or warp system. Therefore the more colourful the fabric is, the thicker it becomes. However, as all warp and weft yarns are interlaced in the structures, it is easy to achieve mixtures of colours that create an illusion of additional colours existing in the design.

If two motifs of a surface pattern never intersect in the same horizontal line, they can be coloured with two different weft colours without adding more weft systems. One weft system could be simply woven in two different colours according to the pattern. As an example, a simple polka dot design would look quite different if every other row of dots was woven with a varying weft colour. In a more complicated pattern a skilled designer can almost hide these weft stripes and create patterns that form an overall colour surface. In today's industry these types of stripes are often woven as wefts, but using striped warps can create similar effects.

→ In this design the green cotton pick is used throughout the fabric, but the red and yellow mercerised cotton picks are never used in the same horizontal line. Hence, adding the yellow weft to green and red does not add thickness to the fabric and can be woven using the same weft system. The black and white warp colours also help create a more colourful look. Inspired by the Arab textile culture, here the designer has aimed to create a textile as rich in colour and varying structures as possible. *Arabia Rug* 2013 by Aoi Yoshizawa

The fabric is woven using petrol coloured mohair and copper coloured mixed quality yarns as wefts. While some of the weave structures show a mixture of these yarns, other structures only show the mohair weft or the copper coloured weft. A white cotton lyocell blend is used as warp, but warp-faced structures are not used in the design. Therefore, there are no clearly visible white areas in the fabric. This fabric is part of a Master's thesis collection from 2016 that was inspired by research into structural or aesthetic changes stemming from external forces. *Magma* from collection *Forces* by Teija Vartiainen

3.2 Structures in Jacquard Fabrics

What distinguishes jacquard design from graphic surface design is the combination of the creative pattern design process with the technical process of designing weave structures. Once the idea of a design, its motifs, repeat, and colours are finalised, knowledge of yarns and structures needs to be implemented to realise it as a fabric. Indeed the combination of the choice of materials and structures will influence the fabric's surface and three-dimensional effects.

In this book the structures of jacquard fabrics are divided into three categories according to the number of weft and warp systems used. **Damasks** only use one weft and one warp system. **Structures with multiple weft systems** can be used to create more variations in the colours and materials of a jacquard fabric. **Multilayered structures** are used when separate fabric layers in one structure are needed. These three structure types are introduced separately, but several of these techniques are often combined in one jacquard fabric.

Adobe Photoshop in Jacquard Design

Most weaving mills use professional software made for jacquard design, such as EAT Design-Scope Victor, NedGraphics or Arahne Jacquard. This type of software is optimal for mill use, allowing fast modification of designs and structures as well as directly linking the parameters of the weaving machine to the design process. However, Photoshop's relatively affordable price and the general familiarity that most designers have with the program, has made it a popular software for jacquard design, especially among freelance designers, artists, and universities. The cost of professional jacquard software is prohibitive for most freelance designers. Building and modifying weave structures in Photoshop is reasonably simple, but it is not an automatic procedure and requires

a systematic thinking process. This can be an advantage for novices, as designing the structures themselves gives beginners a deeper understanding of the weaves and provides knowledge that can be applied to any other software later in their career.

Making a design with a single layer structure in Photoshop is relatively easy, as it only requires drawing the weaves, saving them as patterns, and inserting them into the design. In more complicated designs the compound structures should be created first. The key factors of building compound structures in Photoshop are the "base units" used to define the number of weft and warp systems in the structure. For example, a base unit for a structure with two weft systems and one warp system is one pixel wide and two pixels high. The two pixels stand for the two weft systems, and therefore, must be coloured with two distinguishable colours. This base unit is saved as a pattern and filled into a new structure file, which now becomes striped. A separate layer is made for each stripe colour and each layer is then filled with a specific weave.

The advantage of this technique is the flexibility it allows to modify the structures. For an experienced designer, the process described above can at first seem time consuming, compared to simply drawing the compound structure. However, once the structure file with layers is made, it is easy and quick to change the weaves in it. For a beginner, the technique makes the start of jacquard design easier, as the method is simple to follow using the instructions. After a couple of weaving trials the jacquard structures are easier to understand. For all designers, whether experienced or beginners, the ability to easily make, weave, and modify a jacquard design is essential for mastering the technique and developing new and interesting designs.

← Process books record the design process of the collection, including design of the surface patterns, colours, materials and woven structures. The finished collection from 2015 is introduced on p. 386. (Above) *Cool Beans* and (below) *Sunny Blocks*, *Chunky Salt & Pepper*, and *Diagonal* from collection *Memphis Blues* by Miisa Lehto

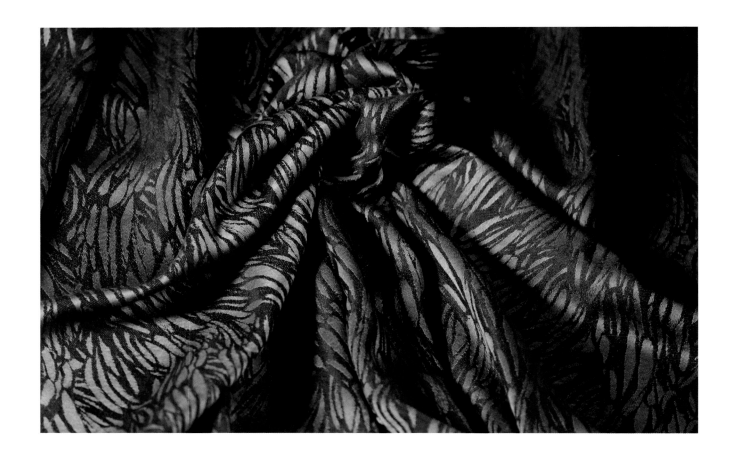

JACQUARDS WITH ONE WARP AND ONE WEFT SYSTEM

↑ An example of a damask
fabric in which two weave
structures are used in
the design. A warp-faced
satin reveals the turquoise
mercerised cotton warp, and
a weft-faced satin shows
the blue wool weft yarn.
This design is inspired by
the underwater world and
Baroque style. *Seagrass* from
the 2013 collection *Seirên* by
Helmi Liikanen.

Damasks (p. 310) are patterned fabrics
constructed with one warp and one weft
system. They are technically the simplest
patterned fabrics. In this type of fabric only
one set of weft yarns and one set of warp
yarns is interlaced in each pattern area.
These structures can be warp-faced, weft-
faced, balanced or between these extremes.
This means that two clearly distinctive yarn
qualities can be utilised in the design – those
of warp and of weft. In addition, different
mixtures of these two yarns can be used.
Stripes, in warp or weft or in both of them,
can be employed in the design.

It is simple to prepare a file for a damask
design. Each colour area in the pattern is
simply replaced with a different weave. As long
as the differences in the take-up (p. 348) of the
structures do not create problems during the
weaving process, any structures can be used.
Satins and twills and variations of them are
suitable for surface patterning as both warp-
faced and weft-faced versions and gradations
between them can be constructed. These
gradations between warp-faced and weft-faced
weaves are called shaded twills and satins,
and are often used in classical damasks. The
drawing of the satin structures is introduced
in Chapter 2 (p. 306) and different twills are
described on pp. 246–267.

→ Using striping weft yarns in a damask design. The fabric is woven using white mercerised cotton as ends and various cotton and wool materials in different shades of blue and white as picks. *Rippling* from 2016 by Kaisa Karawatski

→ This curtain fabric is designed to interact with light. Satin and shaded satin structures are used to create a damask pattern in the background of the design. This pattern can be seen when light does not pass through the curtain. However, a new pattern of lamps is revealed when the light passes through. The weave used in the lamp pattern is mock leno (p.218). This type of weave groups together sets of warp and weft floats that create an open structure, which becomes visible with the presence of light.

The fabric is woven using white mercerised cotton as warp and weft, and it is later piece dyed into black.

This fabric is part of the designer's Bachelor's thesis from 2014 exploring two-sided curtains that display different patterns when seen from the outside or inside of the house. Walking on the street and looking into people's homes from outside inspired this design. *Out-In* by Outi Lehto

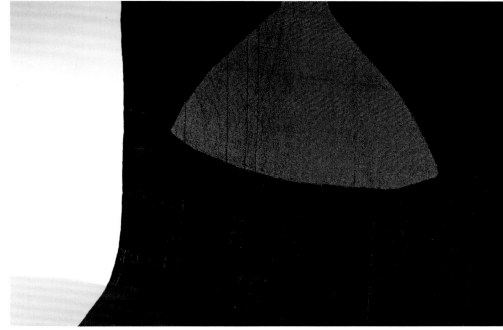

→ An experimental jacquard design process without using any actual weave structures. A greyscale image is converted into black and white pixels in Photoshop, using tools usually employed for making screen print rasters. The resulting digital file is used to weave a jacquard on a cotton lyocell blend warp using linen yarn as weft. More comprehensive tools for converting an image directly into a woven structure without separating the colours are included in some professional jacquard design software. *August* (MF)

Basics of Jacquard Design in Photoshop: Drawing Weaves and Inserting Them into the Design

Instructions in this section provide information on the basics of making a jacquard design in Photoshop. By following these instructions you can make a single layered jacquard design with one weft system and one warp system. The same basic settings and system of drawing the weaves, and using them to fill in a design will be also used for jacquards with more complex structures.

This section does not provide information on creating a repeating design, but the repeat could be designed in Photoshop or Illustrator, or made by hand. Recommendations for study material on this topic can be found in the list of supplementary literature at the end of this book.

Working with woven structures requires some adjustment to the settings of Photoshop. Photoshop by default attempts to soften the edges of selected image areas, which results in new colour tones in the design. This should be avoided when designing jacquards, as it could cause mistakes in the structure. By implementing the settings listed below, you can prevent Photoshop from adding new colour tones in the design.

- Work in RGB Color Mode
- Adjust how Photoshop calculates the colours for new or altered pixels when the design is scaled or transformed:
  In Edit → Preferences → General (Windows) or Photoshop → Preferences → General (Mac), change Image Interpolation into Nearest Neighbor.
- With selection and drawing tools, never tick Anti-Alias and put 0 for Feather.
- When drawing, use hard edged pencil instead of soft edged brush.

Drawing the structures

① Make a new file, with the same size in pixels as the repeat size of the weave you intend to draw.
For example, to draw a 6-end satin, as in this example (2A), make a file size 6 px × 6 px. **For Background Content, select White.**

The Grid will make it easier to draw the structure.
Select View → Show → Pixel Grid and View → Show → Grid.
Pixel Grid will show as a white grid on a dark background, and Grid will show as a black grid on a white background.
Adjust the size of the Grid.
Select Edit → Preferences → Guides, Grid & Slices and choose: Gridline every 1 pixels, Subdivisions: 1, Color: Black.

② With black colour and pencil size 1 px, draw the weave (2A). When drawing the structures, use only #00000 black and #FFFFF white.

2A WEFT-FACED
6-END SATIN

③ A warp-faced structure can be converted into a weft-faced structure, and vice versa:
Do Image → Adjustment → Invert (3A).

3A WARP-FACED
6-END SATIN

④ Draw as many weaves as needed for the design, one per each colour in the pattern.
(see p.358: Separating the colours)
You can use any kind of basic or derivative weaves that suit your idea of the design such as satins, twills, honeycomb, panama or mock leno. Plain weave has a very high take-up compared to other structures and can easily create an uneven take-up in the fabric if used as a structure for large or unevenly placed elements.

There are seven colours in this flower design (4A); two in the background and five in the flowers and leaves. Therefore, seven varying weave structures are needed for it. In order to preserve the watercolour appearance of the original sketch, shaded satins that gradually change from weft-faced to warp-faced were selected for this design (4B–H).

⑤ In order to be able to fill the design with your structures, save them as Pattern Presets: Do Edit → Define Pattern.

4A DESIGN

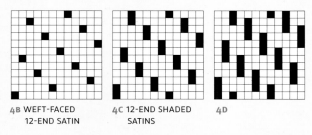

4B WEFT-FACED
12-END SATIN

4C 12-END SHADED
SATINS

4D

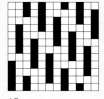

4E

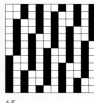

4F

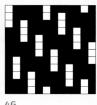

4G

4H WARP-FACED
6-END SATIN

Preparing the design

① **Open one repeat of the design** (4A). Convert the size of the design to match the properties of the future fabric. The pixel dimensions of the design should be the same as the number of ends and picks in (one repeat of) the fabric, as each pixel in a design file corresponds to an intersection of one pick and one end in the design. **Select: Image → Image Size. Resample should be ticked and Constrain Aspect Ratio selected. First, change the resolution into the yarn sett of upcoming fabric** (in this example 40 ends p/cm) **and then the width in pixels into the number of ends in it** (in this example 2400 ends). In the first trial you can keep the number of picks, the height of the design, as it is. In the section Fixing Proportions of a Design (p.360) you will learn to adjust the height of the design according to the weft density of the fabric. Check how the design looks with these new dimensions. You might need to do some corrections to the drawing if some details or fine lines are removed in the process.

② **Compare the height of the design repeat with weave repeats. The repeat height of the design (in pixels) should divide evenly into the repeat height of the weaves used in it.** (If the height of the design is 400 pixels, you can use weaves with the repeat height of 4, 5, 10, 8 or 16 pixels, but structures with height of 6 or 7 pixels cannot be used). **You can change the height of the design to the nearest value dividing evenly into all structures intended to use.** If the structures do not repeat evenly in the design, there will be a mistake on the edge of the repeat, as a structure not repeating entirely would be cut there. When weaving a design on a loom that repeats the design horizontally, the width of the repeat should also be divided evenly into the width of the weaves.

Separating the colours

The colours used in a design draft for jacquard do not need to have any correlation to the final colouring of the fabric. Colours of the fabric come from the colours of warp and wefts, and colours in the design draft are only technical colours used to define the locations of different structures. A weave structure will fill the place of each colour of the design. In a photograph or a scanned sketch, there are usually thousands of colours that must be reduced before converting an image into a jacquard design. The design has a reduced number of colours if it is made in a vector format and multi-coloured effects such as gradients are not used.

A large variety of tools and functions in Photoshop could be used for colour separation. In this section, the simple technique of converting an image into Indexed Color mode is introduced. Colour reduction could be done before or after finishing the repeat design.

1. Before colour reduction (A), consider if you want the design to be neat and clean with solid colour areas, or if you prefer to keep it painterly. If you wish to achieve a design with clean and solid colour areas, the design could be smoothed before colour reduction by blurring it. You can use Blur functions such as Surface, Smart or Gaussian Blur with a small Radius (0.5–1 px). Surface Blur only alters the surface, while preserving the outlines of the design. For example, blurring can be used to reduce the undesired structure of the paper from the sketch. Increasing the contrast can also help in colour reduction and functions such as Levels or Curves can be used.

2. **Reduce the colours by converting the image into Indexed Color mode** by selecting Image → Mode → Indexed Color.
Note that the design must be in RGB Color mode before converting.

An Indexed Color window opens:

For Palette, select: Local Perceptual, Selective OR Adaptive (these functions count all the colours in the image, and determine, in the colour palette, the colours that appear most often or are easiest for the human eye to see. When working with woven fabrics, you can simply test different options and select the one giving the best visual result to your design).

OR: Exact (this palette can be selected, if the exact desired number of colours in the image is already present).

For Colors, select: The lowest number of colours needed for the design to look good is approximately 2–20 colours. The amount can be reduced later.

For Forced, select: Usually None (for black and white sketches, you could select Forced: Black and white)

Ticking Transparency leads to a transparent background behind the image. (if you clear or erase parts of the image, you will see the transparent background underneath) For jacquard design, Transparency is usually not needed.

For Dither select: None, Noise or Diffusion. Selecting None will give neat and clean edges between the colour areas, and Noise or Diffusion create a fine pixel mesh on the edges.

Keep the Preview ticked to follow how changing the settings affect the result. When satisfied, click OK to reduce the colours (B).

3. **After reducing the colours select Image → Mode → Color Table**. Here you can see all the colours left in the design. You can change similar shades into the same colour: Click a colour swatch, and select a colour close to it from the design, using the Color Picker. You can also select several colours at once if they are next to one another in the Color Table, and change them to a new colour. To ensure the combining of the swatch colours in the Color Table into one, **convert the design to RGB Color mode (Select Image → Mode → RGB). Then change back to Indexed Color mode (Select Image → Mode → Indexed Color). Photoshop should now suggest the right number of colours in the design (Exact →).**

Note that the number of colours in the design defines the number of weaves in the final jacquard design. A suitable number to start with is between 2–8 colours.

Filling the design with structures

Set the Magic Wand tool for this step: Tolerance 0, do not tick Anti-Alias, Contiguous, or Sample All Layers.

1. Select a colour in the design with the Magic Wand and select Layer → New Fill Layer → Pattern. In the New Layer Window select Color: None, Mode: Normal and Opacity: 100%. Name the layer clearly (e.g background or lightest tone of flower). Click OK. In the Pattern Fill Window, select the desired structure from the Pattern Presets. Scale 100%. You can tick Link with layer. Do not select Snap to origin. Click OK (c).

2. Repeat until you have replaced all the colours in the design with a weave (D). To later change a structure, double click the Pattern Fill icon in the Layers panel and you will get back to the Pattern Fill window. Then select a new structure from the list of Pattern Presets.

3. The file is now ready for weaving. For some looms, it is better to flatten the layers first and/or convert the file into Indexed Color mode.

4. Select Window → Patterns. In here weave patterns can be saved, organised, and deleted. Organise the patterns and save them as sets according to type. Make, for example, one folder for twills and another folder for satins and so on. Saving the weave patterns is important, as the pattern memory of Photoshop can be automatically emptied when a new version of software is updated.

A DESIGN BEFORE COLOUR SEPARATION

B DESIGN AFTER COLOUR SEPARATION

C ONE STRUCTURE FILLED IN THE DESIGN

D ALL STRUCTURES FILLED IN THE DESIGN

Fixing proportions of a design

If the densities of weft and warp in a fabric are not exactly the same, the proportions of design will get stretched or flattened when woven. In this case, you will need to stretch or flatten the original design file in height to fix the proportions. (You cannot change the width of the design file, because the width of the design is defined by the width of the warp.) With the method introduced in this section you can calculate how much you need to stretch or flatten the design to fix the proportions.

(1) To recognise how much the proportions will change, weave a test sample of the design with the desired warp and weft materials (1B, 2B). **From the woven sample, calculate the weft density, the number of picks per/cm. (Count first the number of picks per 10 cm and then divide it by 10). Then calculate the ratio between pick density and warp yarn sett: picks/cm | ends per cm.**

(2) **Open the design file (1A, 2A) in Photoshop. Check the height of the design in pixels from Image → Image Size.**

(3) **Multiply the height with the ratio. This number or a value closest to it, in** which all structures used in the design can be divided evenly, should be the new height used in the design.

(4) **Change the height of the design in the Image Size window. Resample should be ticked and Constrain Aspect Ratio should not be selected.** After changing the height of the file, the design will look stretched or flattened on the computer screen (1C, 2C). However, when woven with the same properties as the test sample, the proportions will be corrected (1D, 2D).

1A ORIGINAL DESIGN

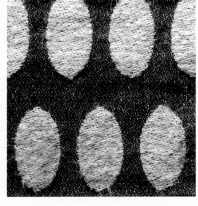

1B TEST SAMPLE WOVEN WITH MOHAIR YARN

1C DESIGN AFTER FIXING THE PROPORTIONS

1D FABRIC WOVEN WITH MOHAIR YARN

Examples of correcting the proportions

① In this design woven with mohair yarn, the pattern is supposed to be a polka dot (1A). However, in a test sample (1B) the dots are elongated vertically, therefore the proportions should be fixed before weaving the final piece. The weft density of the sample is only 12 picks/cm, and the yarn sett is 24 ends per cm. The pick density and warp sett is thus 12/24 = 0.5. Height of the design is 200 px. To fix the proportions, 200 px must be multiplied with 0.5. This makes 100 px and hence the height of the design must be changed into 100 pixels (or a value closest to 100, in which all structures used in the design are divided evenly).

The design file (1C) appears flattened after fixing the proportions, but when the sample is woven using this file the proportions of the outcome are correct (1D).

2A ORIGINAL DESIGN

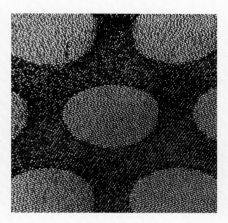

2B TEST SAMPLE WOVEN WITH METAL LAME YARN

2C DESIGN AFTER FIXING THE PROPORTIONS

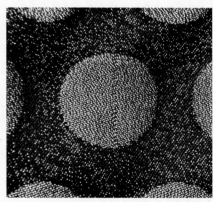

2D FABRIC WOVEN WITH METAL LAME YARN

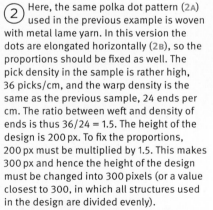

② Here, the same polka dot pattern (2A) used in the previous example is woven with metal lame yarn. In this version the dots are elongated horizontally (2B), so the proportions should be fixed as well. The pick density in the sample is rather high, 36 picks/cm, and the warp density is the same as the previous sample, 24 ends per cm. The ratio between weft and density of ends is thus 36/24 = 1.5. The height of the design is 200 px. To fix the proportions, 200 px must be multiplied by 1.5. This makes 300 px and hence the height of the design must be changed into 300 pixels (or a value closest to 300, in which all structures used in the design are divided evenly).

The design file appears stretched after fixing the proportions (2C), but when the sample is woven using this file the proportions of the outcome are correct (2D).

If the weft density of a fabric is already known before weaving a sample, these corrections can be made without making any trials. However, the designer can only know the exact weft density when working with materials, structures, and densities familiar to them. When weaving with new materials and structure combinations, it is always best to weave a test piece first.

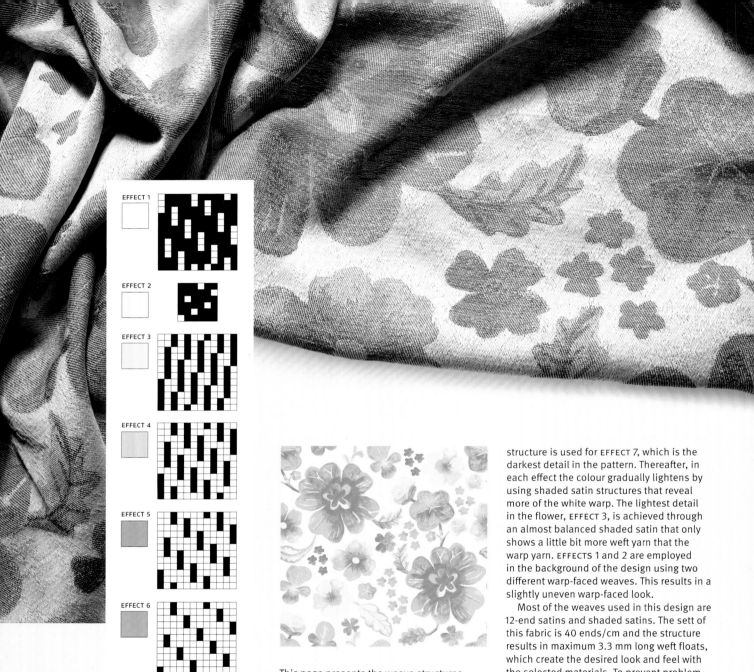

EFFECT 1

EFFECT 2

EFFECT 3

EFFECT 4

EFFECT 5

EFFECT 6

EFFECT 7

This page presents the weave structures used in the design *Flora* (MF), a fabric inspired by wildly blooming gardens. The fabric structure is designed with one warp system and one weft system and is woven using white mercerised cotton yarn as ends and dark green linen as picks.

As the colour of the weft yarn is darker than the warp yarn colour, a weft-faced satin structure is used for EFFECT 7, which is the darkest detail in the pattern. Thereafter, in each effect the colour gradually lightens by using shaded satin structures that reveal more of the white warp. The lightest detail in the flower, EFFECT 3, is achieved through an almost balanced shaded satin that only shows a little bit more weft yarn that the warp yarn. EFFECTS 1 and 2 are employed in the background of the design using two different warp-faced weaves. This results in a slightly uneven warp-faced look.

Most of the weaves used in this design are 12-end satins and shaded satins. The sett of this fabric is 40 ends/cm and the structure results in maximum 3.3 mm long weft floats, which create the desired look and feel with the selected materials. To prevent problematic long warp floats, 6-end satin is used in the warp-faced background of the design. As the repeat sizes of all the structures used in the design are either the same or can be divided evenly, it is easy to find a size for the design repeat that can also be divided evenly into the size of the weave repeats.

Ori from 2019 collection *Nukuness* by Elisa Defossez—This page presents the weave structures used in the design *Ori*. The fabric structure is designed with one warp system and one weft system and it is woven using off-white mercerised cotton as ends and navy blue wool as picks. 14 different weft-faced, warp-faced, and balanced left and right-hand twills are used as structures in this fabric. The collection concept *Nukuness* is aimed at creating warm and cosy interiors with sophisticated yet playful fabrics.

EFFECT 1

EFFECT 2

EFFECT 3

EFFECT 4

EFFECT 5

EFFECT 6

EFFECT 7

EFFECT 8

EFFECT 9

EFFECT 10

EFFECT 11

EFFECT 12

EFFECT 13

EFFECT 14

JACQUARDS WITH MULTIPLE WEFT SYSTEMS

↑ This jacquard fabric is designed using two weft systems. Three different compound structures are used in this design. The first structure reveals the black wool elastane pick and black lurex pick on the face of the fabric. The second structure shows the shiny golden lurex yarn. The third one exposes the white cotton lyocell blend warp. *Cloud Flower* by Ilona Hackenberg

To create jacquards with more colour and material variation in the pattern, two or more weft systems can be utilised. Employing multiple weft systems enables the use of different yarns in separate elements of a design. Structures with two or more warp systems could be used for similar purposes but generally require a warp set up on two beams with varying yarns. However, fabrics that use several sets of weft threads can be woven on any type of warp. As described in Chapter 2 (p. 207) these types of structures using one set of warps with multiple sets of wefts, or one set of wefts with multiple sets of warps result in two-sided fabrics and are referred to as **double-faced** fabrics.

The basic principle of building structures with two weft systems is to combine the weaves of the two alternating picks into one structure. One typical double-faced structure shows one set of weft threads on the face of the fabric and hides the other set on the reverse side. In this type of structure, two weaves are combined; a

weft-faced weave is created for the picks on the face of the fabric and a warp-faced weave is intended for the wefts that are hidden. Structures with two weft systems can also be created using a weft-faced weave for both alternating picks. This results in a structure that reveals a mixture of the two weft materials on the surface. Using a warp-faced weave for both picks would naturally create a structure that reveals the warp.

In other words, in a jacquard fabric woven with two weft systems three varying yarns can be used in the pattern; the material of the warp, the material of the first set of weft threads, and the material of the second set of weft threads. In addition, mixtures of these yarns can be created. For example, the colours red, blue, and black can be used in a design when weaving in the black warp with red and blue weft yarns. Furthermore, combinations of these colours such as shades of purple (mixture of red and blue), dark blue (mixture of blue and black), and dark red (mixture of red and black) can be achieved. In this structure, using different coloured yarns helps students to understand the principle of the structure when weaving the first trials. Instead of or in addition to the colour, the difference in the yarns could also be in the type of materials used. Creating a surface pattern with similar tones but with different materials can create intriguing jacquards.

Structures with multiple weft systems are mainly designed to exhibit the material of the weft on the face of the fabric, and thus often cover the warp almost entirely. Satins are often used in this kind of compound structure, as their nature is to merely reveal or hide the picks without any distinctive pattern. All types of twills are also suitable, and plain weave can be used as a structure for tightly interwoven ground picks. Through testing and practice, other types of weaves can also be used.

Warp-faced and weft-faced versions of the same weave such as weft-faced 8-end satin and warp-faced 8-end satin, or different weaves such as weft-faced 8-end satin with warp-faced 16-end satin could be combined in one structure. Weaves belonging to the same class are often combined in one structure, but it is also possible to combine weaves from different classes such as satins with twills or twills with plain weave. (Refer to p. 371 for more information and examples about compatibility of weaves).

When using contrasting weft materials in one design, a structure that best suits each material type should be selected. Loose structures with long floats can be selected for heavy and textured yarns such as chenille or mohair, but if a finer yarn is used in the same fabric it probably needs to be interwoven more firmly. Moreover, varying weaves can be used in compound structures in order to alter the feel and hand of the fabric. To make a fabric stiffer without changing the look of the face side, a weave with shorter floats for the picks hidden on the reverse side can be used. Using weaves

↑ This collection from 2015 is inspired by the imagery and visual language of medieval tapestries. Most of the colourful and ornamental jacquards in the collection are woven using double-faced structures. Master's thesis collection by Ilona Hackenberg

→ This design is part of the designer's Master's thesis collection from 2013 in which notions of familiar and sweet are entangled and blended with the themes of the unknown and surreal. In this fabric the designer has combined soft pastel colours and long free floats with metallic shine and a strict geometric pattern.
Hazy Plaid by Anna Alanko

with longer floats on the reverse side of the fabric can produce a softer fabric. On the other hand, longer floats on the reverse side allow for packing more weft threads into the fabric structure, and are often used in structures consisting of three or four weft systems.

In a compound structure with picks woven with the same or similar weaves, the weft systems have equal functions, as they are each interwoven as firmly as the other. When alternating picks have different functions in the structure, the picks generating a tighter weave are referred to as ground wefts, and the picks woven with longer floats and looser structure are called supplementary or **extra wefts**. The advantage of this type of structure is the possibility to experiment with different yarn effects and loose structures without weakening the base construction of the fabric. An extra weft can even be left to float without binding it at all. Long weft floats can be cut away after weaving to create fil coupé fabrics, or can be partially cut to create fringes. Floats that are intended for cutting should be surrounded by a border of a tight structure such as plain weave to prevent the yarn from detaching.

Though complicated to build in Photoshop, a varying number of weft systems can be incorporated into one fabric. Refer to p.150 for extra-weft patterning on shaft looms, and for fil coupé jacquard designs to p.460.

← The structure of this jacquard fabric is designed using two weft systems. The materials in the fabric consist of white mercerised cotton yarn as ends and light pink cotton and silver viscose polyester yarns as picks. In this structure, the polyester viscose yarn functions as an extra weft and is left to float, while the cotton weft yarn functions as a ground weft. The double weave areas reveal either the viscose polyester pick or the cotton pick on the face of the fabric. Due to the vertical stripes running across the fabric, it is important that all the structures used in this design have very similar take-ups.

↑ This upholstery fabric is industrially woven by the Backhausen weaving mill in Austria. This two weft systems fabric has three different structures. One of the structures shows the first set of picks using brown cotton yarn on the face of the fabric and the second one shows the second set of picks in golden polyester yarn. The third structure used is a warp-faced rib weave that reveals the black viscose warp yarn. *Carmen*, Lauritzon 2005 (MF)

→ The fabric structure of the fil coupé *Tiles* is designed using two weft systems and is woven with white linen and light blue mohair weft yarns. In certain parts of the design the mohair weft is left floating. The floats are cut after weaving and reveal the white linen weft underneath them. Mohair floats are left on the fabric to create fringes.

Honeycomb is a fabric with interesting tactile properties which result from the woven structures of the fabric. The two different weaves integrated in the fabric are a weft-faced satin that creates an even surface and a waffle weave that results in a three dimensional surface.

These fabrics are inspired by theories of colour interactions, the first hippie commune of Drop City and the Futurist art movement, and are part of the designer's Bachelor's thesis collection. This work examines the potential of textiles in demonstrating the different theories of colour mixing such as transparency effects, and optical colour fusion techniques. (left to right) Transparent *White*, fil coupé *Tiles* and *Honeycomb* from the 2016 collection *Drop City Revisited* by Miisa Lehto.

Building Structures using Multiple Weft Systems in Photoshop

Designing a jacquard structure with two or more weft systems requires the ability to combine two or more weaves into one structure in Photoshop. By following these instructions you can make compound structures with two weft systems. The same method is also used for designing jacquards with three or more weft systems and is briefly presented at the end of this section.

Structures with two weft systems

① **Make a base unit: Create a new file, size 1 × 2 px. Colour the file with two colours (1A) (not black and white, as the colours must differ from the black and white weave structures).** Save the file as a Pattern Preset: Select Edit → Define Pattern. **Name it: Base unit for structures with two weft systems.** This file is not a weave structure, but rather a base unit used for building a structure with two weft systems. The two rows of colour represent the two alternating picks in the structure. The width of the file is one pixel, which defines that one warp system is used in the structure.

☐ 2ND WEFT SYSTEM
☐ 1ST WEFT SYSTEM **1A BASE UNIT**

② **Draw two basic weaves to be used in a compound structure (2A, 2B).** You can use a weft-faced weave to show one set of weft threads on the face of the fabric and a warp-faced structure to hide the alternating set on the reverse side. Weaves used in the structure should be compatible with each other. The repeat sizes of weaves should be either the same, or of sizes that can be evenly divided into one another. If the repeat sizes of weaves cannot be evenly divided, the final size of the compound structure should be determined so that both weaves can be divided evenly into it. For example, when combining 5-end satin and 8-end satin, the final size of the compound structure would be 40 × 40 px. In this example, weft-faced 5-end satin (2A) and warp-faced 10-end satin (2B) are used. (Refer to p.371 for more information about compatibility of weaves).

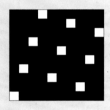

2A WEFT-FACED 5-END SATIN   **2B WARP-FACED 10-END SATIN**

③ **Double the height of the weaves: Select Image → Image Size. Resample should be ticked and Constrain Aspect Ratio should not be selected.** Change the Height of 5-end satin to 10 px (3A) and the height of 10-end satin to 20 px (3B). Click ok. If you do not stretch the structures at this stage, every other pick of the weaves would be lost in the next step. **Save the files as Pattern Presets: Edit → Define Pattern.**

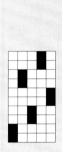
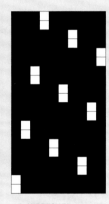

3A STRETCHED WEFT-FACED 5-END SATIN   **3B STRETCHED WARP-FACED 10-END SATIN**

④ **Make a base grid: Make a new file with a size that both stretched weaves can divide into evenly.** In this example the sizes of weaves divide evenly into one another. Therefore, the size of the new file can be the same as the weave structure with a bigger repeat (warp-faced 10-end satin) after stretching, 10 × 20 px.

Fill in the base grid with the base unit made during the first step: Select Edit → Fill → Use: Pattern, and select the base unit from Custom Pattern. (4A) Make a separate layer for each weft system (= stripe colours): Choose a stripe colour with the Magic Wand tool and select Layer → New → Layer via copy (Ctrl + J). Repeat the same process for the second stripe colour. Name the layers: 1st weft system and 2nd weft system. Change the Blending Mode of layers to Multiply.

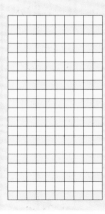

4A BASE GRID

5 Fill in the weaves in layers: First, select a layer. Then select the contents of the layer (click Ctrl – Command on Mac – and Layer Thumbnail in the Layers Window) and select Edit → Fill → Use: Pattern, and select a weave structure (5A). **Repeat the process for the second layer** (5B). As a weft-faced satin was used for the first pick (blue), and a warp-faced for the second pick (beige), consequently, the compound structure shows the first set of picks on the face of the fabric and hides most of the second set on the reverse side.

In this compound structure, the binding points of the warp-faced and weft-faced satins are aligned. (5B) It is better to hide these conflicting binding points between long weft floats on the face of the fabric. To do so, **select one of the layers and choose Filter → Other → Offset. Shift the weave horizontally. Wrap Around should be ticked** (5C). In this example, binding points can be completely hidden, as the weaves are compatible. (Refer to p.371 for more information about compatibility of weaves)

Although in this structure it might seem that there are many warp threads on the face of the fabric, when woven the weft threads will pack together and thus hide the warp. The extent to which the weft will conceal the warp depends on the materials and the density used.

6 Save the new compound structure as Pattern Preset: Select Edit → Define pattern.

Note: Pattern Fill Layers can also be used when building compound structures.

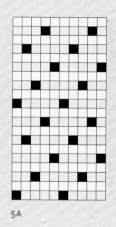

5A

5B

5C FINISHED COMPOUND STRUCTURE SHOWING 1ST WEFT SYSTEM ON FACE

7 In order to reveal different weft materials in different elements of a jacquard design, structures showing the first set of weft threads on the face of the fabric and structures showing the second set of weft threads on the face of the fabric are needed. **To make the latter compound structure, fill a weft-faced weave for the second pick (beige), and a warp-faced one for the first pick (blue).** (7A) Changing the structures in the layers can be done following the instructions previously explained.

First, select a layer. Then select the contents of the layer (click Ctrl – Command on Mac – and Layer Thumbnail in Layers window) and select Edit → Fill → Use: Pattern, and select the structure.

7A STRUCTURE SHOWING 2ND WEFT SYSTEM ON FACE

CONTINUES ON THE NEXT PAGE →

8 To create a structure showing a mixture of both weft materials, fill a weft-faced weave for both sets of picks (8A). Note that if only 5-end weaves are used in the compound structure, as in this example, the repeat size of the structure does not need to be larger than 5 × 10 pixels. The take-up of this structure is slightly higher than the previous structures in which 10-end satin and 5-end satin were combined.

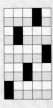

8A STRUCTURE SHOWING BOTH WEFT SYSTEMS ON FACE

9 To make a structure showing only ends, fill a warp-faced weave for both sets of picks (9A). Here, a warp-faced 5-end satin was used instead of the warp-faced 10-end satin, as combining two warp-faced 10-end satins would result in a structure with relatively long warp floats. However, the final length of the floats depends on the weft density. The take-up of this structure is similar to the previous structure with weft-faced 5-end satins.

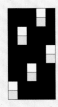

9A STRUCTURE SHOWING ONLY ENDS = BOTH WEFT SYSTEMS ON REVERSE SIDE

10 To create a structure in which one set of weft threads is floating, fill any tightly interweaving structure with one set of picks, and fill the second set of picks with white colour (10A). First, select a layer. Then select the contents of the layer (click Ctrl – Command on Mac – and Layer Thumbnail in Layers window) and choose Edit → Fill → Use: White.

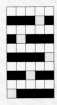

10A STRUCTURE IN WHICH 2ND SET OFF PICKS IS FLOATING

11 Make as many compound structures with two weft systems as needed and fill the design with them. Compound structures are filled in the pattern draft using the same basic system as in jacquard structures with one weft system. Before saving the file for weaving, flatten the layers and change all of the weft colours to white (this applies to most looms): Select Image → Mode → Indexed Colors. Photoshop should suggest:

Palette → Exact: 3 (one warp colour and two weft colours). Click OK.
Select Image → Mode → Color Table, and change all weft colours to white.

In addition to warp-faced and weft-faced weaves, balanced weaves such as shaded satins and twills can also be used. Using this type of weave would result in showing a set of weft threads partially on the face of the fabric and

partially hiding them on the reverse side. Although derivative weaves such as crêpe weave could create interesting results as they possess other structural properties beyond merely hiding or showing weft or warp, they could lead to unexpected results. Thus, they are likely to require further altering and developing after the first weaving trials.

8A

5C

7A

9A

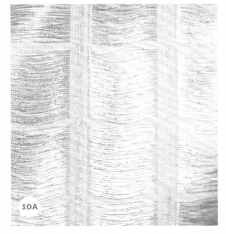

10A

Compatibility of weaves

When using compatible weaves in a compound structure, it is possible to hide the weft binding points of the warp-faced weave between the weft floats of the weft-faced weave. If the weaves are not compatible, the binding points cannot be hidden and always conflict in some parts of the structure (A). Conflicting binding points would prevent the weft picks from packing together and hiding the warp. Binding points in satin do not conflict if the two satins use the same move number. The same applies to twills with the same angle in diagonal. Please note the difference in drafting satins for damasks (p.310).

Examples of compatibility of weaves:

A COMPOUND STRUCTURE WITH CONFLICTING BINDING POINTS (IN PINK)

 Because these satins (1A and 1B) are both constructed with move number 3, combining them creates a flawless result (1C).

1A 5-END SATIN CONSTRUCTED WITH MOVE NUMBER 3

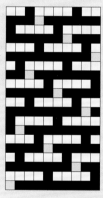

1B 10-END SATIN CONSTRUCTED WITH MOVE NUMBER 3

1C FLAWLESS COMPOUND STRUCTURE

 Twills with the same angle of diagonal (2A and 2B) are compatible (2C).

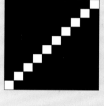

2A 1/4 TWILL WITH A 45° ANGLE OF DIAGONAL

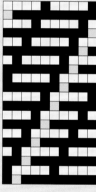

2B 9/1 TWILL WITH A 45° ANGLE OF DIAGONAL

2C FLAWLESS COMPOUND STRUCTURE

It is however often possible to combine weaves that do not seem compatible based on the requirements of the design look. Conflict of the binding points is not always a problem and can be used as an effect. Plain weave can be combined with most structures, as it spreads the conflicting points evenly within the structure.

One technique to combine different types of weaves is to adjust the binding points manually. It is usually better to modify the weave on the reverse side of fabric, so the look of the face side is not altered. The structure on the reverse side can even be drawn entirely by hand. Make sure to weave a test piece for all structures of this type, as they do not always present the expected results, and might need some developing after the initial weaving trials.

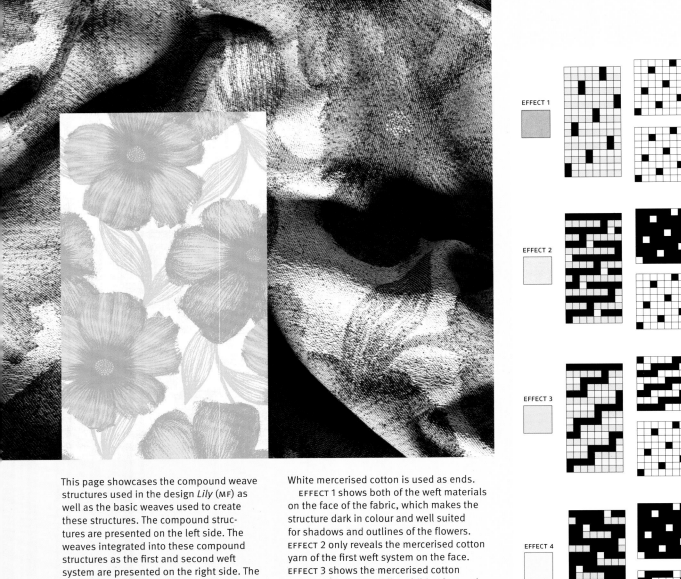

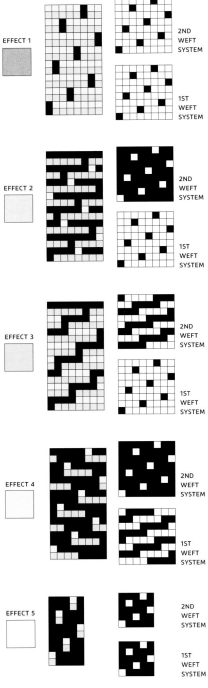

EFFECT 1

2ND WEFT SYSTEM

1ST WEFT SYSTEM

EFFECT 2

2ND WEFT SYSTEM

1ST WEFT SYSTEM

EFFECT 3

2ND WEFT SYSTEM

1ST WEFT SYSTEM

EFFECT 4

2ND WEFT SYSTEM

1ST WEFT SYSTEM

EFFECT 5

2ND WEFT SYSTEM

1ST WEFT SYSTEM

This page showcases the compound weave structures used in the design *Lily* (MF) as well as the basic weaves used to create these structures. The compound structures are presented on the left side. The weaves integrated into these compound structures as the first and second weft system are presented on the right side. The fabric structure is designed using two weft systems and one warp system. The sett of the warp is 40 ends/cm and the weft density is 24 picks/cm.

8-end satins and shaded satins are mainly used in this design. Based on the density of this fabric, combination of two warp-faced 8-end satins would result in long warp floats. Therefore, 5-end satins are used for the only entirely warp-faced structure in the fabric. The material of the first set of picks, marked in the compound structures as blue, is a dark grey mercerised cotton and the material of the second set of picks, marked as beige, is a black wool boucle.

White mercerised cotton is used as ends.

EFFECT 1 shows both of the weft materials on the face of the fabric, which makes the structure dark in colour and well suited for shadows and outlines of the flowers. EFFECT 2 only reveals the mercerised cotton yarn of the first weft system on the face. EFFECT 3 shows the mercerised cotton and in addition partially exhibits the wool boucle yarn of the second weft system on the face of the fabric. In the digital compound structure file of EFFECT 3, the first set of weft threads seems to be more visible than the second set. However, the thicker and more textured wool boucle is more visible than the fine cotton in the woven fabric. EFFECT 4 is mainly showing the warp and the EFFECT 5 is entirely warp-faced.

Lily is from a series of fabric designs that study the relation between fabric collage sketches and jacquard woven fabrics. The fabric collage sketch of this design is presented on p. 341.

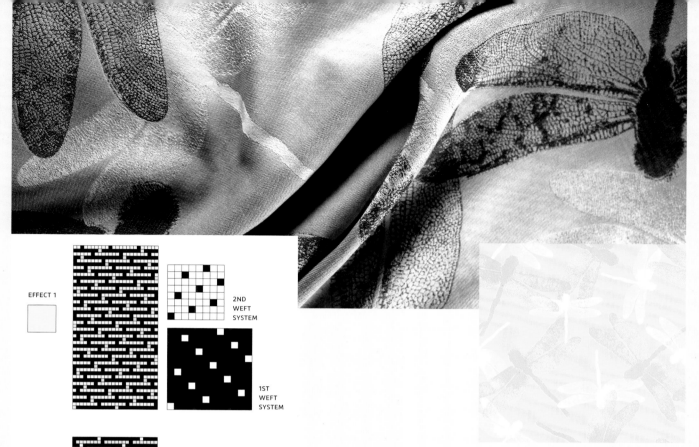

EFFECT 1

2ND
WEFT
SYSTEM

1ST
WEFT
SYSTEM

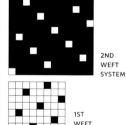

EFFECT 2

2ND
WEFT
SYSTEM

1ST
WEFT
SYSTEM

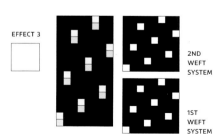

EFFECT 3

2ND
WEFT
SYSTEM

1ST
WEFT
SYSTEM

Korento from 2013 collection *Zoom* by Teija Vartiainen. Similar to *Lily*, this fabric structure consists of two weft systems and one warp system. The sett of the warp is 30 ends/cm and the weft density is 34 picks/cm.

Three different compound structures are used in the design. In EFFECT 1, the second set of picks in peach coloured cotton can be seen on the face of the fabric. EFFECT 2 shows the first set of picks in indigo coloured cotton and EFFECT 3 presents the white mercerised cotton warp material. The weft-faced compound structures consist of 8-end and 12-end satins. As both of these satins should divide evenly into the compound structure, the repeat size cannot be smaller than 24 × 48 pixels.

The 8-end satin is used on the face side of the structure as it shows the weft material well. The resulting 2.5 mm weft floats are not too long for the intended use. 12-end satin is selected for the reverse side of the fabric to make the fabric slightly softer. However, only 8-end satins are used in the entirely warp-faced structure to prevent the warp floats from getting too long.

The fabric was woven with a horizontal repeat of 80 cm, which repeats twice within the width of the fabric. The vertical repeat is approximately the same. The elements of the design pattern are evenly distributed and the various structures are uniformly spread in the fabric. The *Zoom* collection and *Korento* fabric are inspired by magnified images of the wings of a dragonfly.

Structures with three weft systems

The method of building structures with three weft systems is similar to the construction of structures with two weft systems.

① To begin, make a base unit: Create a new file, size 1 × 3 px and colour it with three colours (1A) (not black or white). Save the file as a Pattern Preset: Select Edit → Define Pattern. Name it: Base unit for structures with three weft systems.

1A BASE UNIT

② **Draw the basic weaves to be used in a compound structure.** In this example weft-faced, warp-faced and shaded 8-end satins are used (2A, 2B, 2C). When making the compound structure, the weft-faced satin is used for the picks intended to be shown on the face of the fabric, the warp-faced for the picks intended to be hidden on the reverse side, and the shaded satins are meant for the picks that are partly visible on the face and partly hidden on the reserve side.

2A WEFT-FACED 8-END SATIN

2B WARP-FACED 8-END SATIN

2C 8-END SHADED SATIN

③ **Triple the height of the weaves (3A, 3B, 3C). Save the files as Pattern Presets: Define Pattern.**

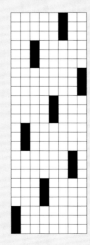

3A STRETCHED WEFT FACED 8-END SATIN

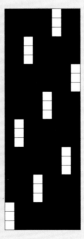

3B STRETCHED WARP-FACED 8-END SATIN

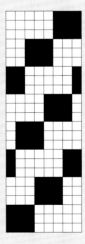

3C STRETCHED 8-END SHADED SATIN

④ Make a base grid: Fill the base unit in a new file (4A), and make a separate layer for each stripe colour.

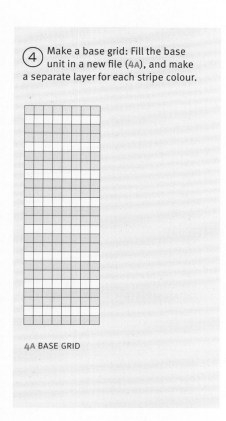

4A BASE GRID

⑤ Name the layers and fill in the weaves. Shift the weaves if needed (5A, 5B, 5C).

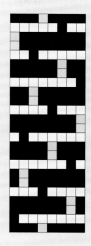

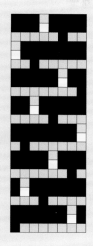

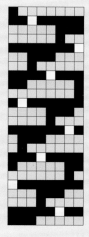

5A STRUCTURE SHOWING 2ND WEFT SYSTEM ON FACE, 1ST AND 3RD WEFT SYSTEMS ON REVERSE SIDE

5B STRUCTURE SHOWING 1ST WEFT SYSTEM ON FACE, 2ND AND 3RD WEFT SYSTEMS ON REVERSE SIDE

5C STRUCTURE SHOWING 3RD WEFT SYSTEM ON FACE 1ST WEFT SYSTEM PARTLY ON FACE AND PARTLY ON REVERSE SIDE, 2ND WEFT SYSTEM ON REVERSE SIDE

Structures with an uneven ratio of picks

The ratio of picks in weft systems does not have to be equal. If weft yarns with contrasting thicknesses or textures are used, the uneven ratio of picks could balance the difference in materials.

1 To begin, make a new base unit defining the ratio of picks (1A). In this example the ratio is 1:2. Save the base unit as a Pattern Preset: Select Edit → Define Pattern. Name it: Base unit for structure with ratio of picks 1:2

1A BASE UNIT

2 Make a base grid: Fill the base unit in a new file (2B) and make layers for each stripe colour and name them.

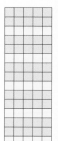

2B BASE GRID

3 When building an uneven structure, it is often easier to draw the weaves in layers than to define them as patterns and fill. In this example (3C) a warp-faced 5-end satin (3A) is used for the first weft system (beige) and weft-faced 1/4 twill (3B) is used for the second weft system (blue).

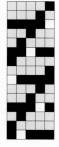

3A WARP-FACED 5-END SATIN

3B WEFT-FACED 5-END TWILL

3C STRUCTURE WITH RATIO OF PICKS 1:2

DAISIES AND FRIENDS—
SCRAPING A PATH TO
A JACQUARD DESIGN

by Hanna-Kaisa Korolainen

During my jacquard design process, I am interested in testing different sketching methods in order to achieve varying results. In this fabric, *Daisies and Friends* from 2015, I have employed the scraping technique. Many remember scraping with oil pastels from elementary school. There was a strange looking metallic tool included in the colour box. I still have a vivid memory of how that device, half fork and half knife, hurt my fingers as I worked. The grattage technique plays with light; first an image is composed just to be covered with a darker layer of colour that resembles a shadow. Afterwards the dark layer is scraped off to partly reveal the image underneath.

Scraping can be done only in a few areas of the canvas in order to create new figurative elements or it can be done thoroughly to reveal as much of the original image as possible. I mostly use the latter option. The end result looks different than the original; it gains an instant patina. I find similarities between the scraping technique and developing photographs in a dark room. When you scratch the dark surface, the image seems to (re)appear as if it were magic.

I have tried various scraping methods. At the beginning, I directed the movement in a neutral way; horizontally or vertically. As a tool, I used either a fine and sharp, or a thick and blunt needle. I scratched in the shapes of arcs or fans, creating new patterns on top of my flowery subjects. Sometimes I scraped the same image twice, crossing my own markings. This created a very structural effect, almost resembling a woven fabric. The more I scratched and scraped, the more the image

underneath became visible. Scratching as an act felt almost violent; there was a feeling of breaking something. The process proved to be physically exhausting, and it was difficult to compose more than two to three sketches during the same session.

Chance played a great role in the process. Each shade of colour absorbed other colours and was affected by the surface differently. The covering layer left its own shadows, almost like some wandering souls in Asian horror movies. The scraping technique creates a strong impression of light and shadow. The original image seems to be deeply embedded in dark light, where colours seem more vivid and luminous, and this creates an almost three-dimensional effect. There is an illusion of space between the image and the surface, as if the subjects such as flowers, trees, or scenery, were contemplated upon through a glass window. During the sketching process, I, once again, fell under the spell of this unusual technique.

After completion of the sketching phase, a digitised version of the drawings was necessary for further development. Scanning was not an option as the machine could not capture the two-layered depth of the work and flattened its appearance. Only after properly photographing the sketches, I could further develop my ideas into textiles. This kind of excessively detailed visual material proved to be challenging to work with and the final choices were made after many trials and errors. However, every now and then these failures made space for new beginnings.

The jacquard design for *Daisies and Friends* was finalised in Photoshop. To be

able to create a file for jacquard I reduced the number of colours from hundreds down to nine, using one for each weave structure. I love this phase of the work; I go forward and back again to find the best balance in the reduced number of colours. The final result can still be greatly altered. For weaving this design, I used a three-weft system. I selected one of the weft colours to be similar to the warp, which made the design look fresher. The warp was an off-white cotton, and the wefts included a dusty blue and white mohair, mixed with a straw yellow wool-silk. The *Daisies and Friends* jacquard was scraped horizontally and this made the weave structures vary frequently on the surface of the fabric. Lines created an effect that resembles old tapestry.

Understanding the role of sources of inspiration is central to my textile design process, which was the topic of my doctoral research *The Making of Inspiration – From Monet to Warhol and beyond* [1]. *Daisies and Friends* draws inspiration from Flemish still-life masterpieces, in which lighting plays an important role – with strong colours vividly glowing in the dark. It seems almost as if these paintings were created at night. Objects are depicted as an imitation of reality and as detailed as possible. Mysterious lights, however, make their appearance unreal; almost too accurate, more real than reality. I find that the scraping method brings the floral motifs in my work close to the ambience of such artworks, and lines that seem to break the design create an effect that my textile could have been made in the faraway past.

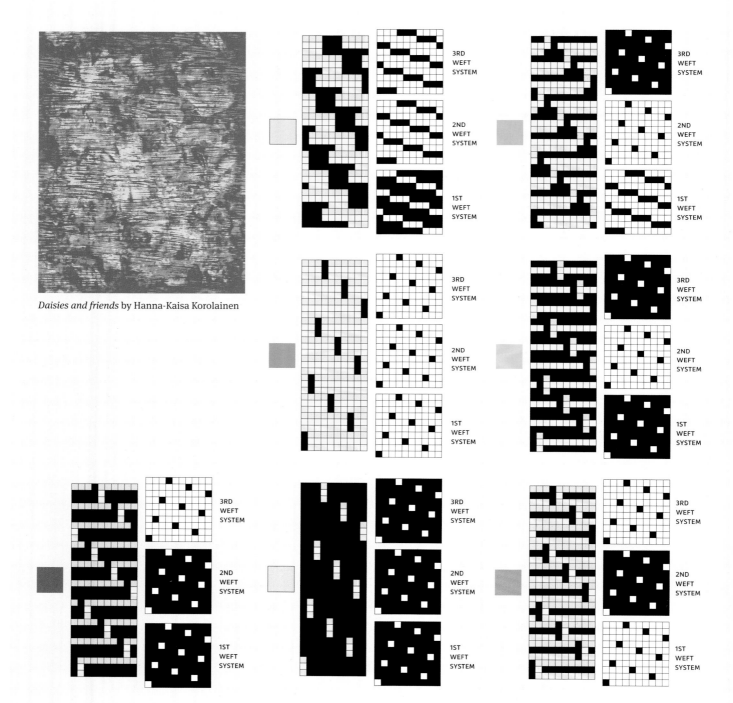

Daisies and friends by Hanna-Kaisa Korolainen

3RD
WEFT
SYSTEM

2ND
WEFT
SYSTEM

1ST
WEFT
SYSTEM

3RD
WEFT
SYSTEM

2ND
WEFT
SYSTEM

1ST
WEFT
SYSTEM

3RD
WEFT
SYSTEM

2ND
WEFT
SYSTEM

1ST
WEFT
SYSTEM

3RD
WEFT
SYSTEM

2ND
WEFT
SYSTEM

1ST
WEFT
SYSTEM

3RD
WEFT
SYSTEM

2ND
WEFT
SYSTEM

1ST
WEFT
SYSTEM

3RD
WEFT
SYSTEM

2ND
WEFT
SYSTEM

1ST
WEFT
SYSTEM

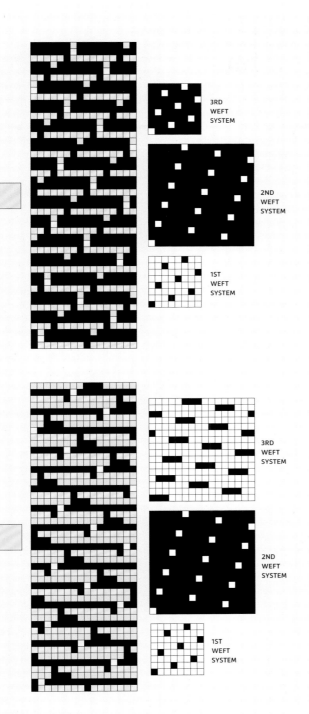

3RD
WEFT
SYSTEM

2ND
WEFT
SYSTEM

1ST
WEFT
SYSTEM

3RD
WEFT
SYSTEM

2ND
WEFT
SYSTEM

1ST
WEFT
SYSTEM

→ There are only two woven structures used in this black and white design. The fabric is a twill double weave revealing either the black weft and the black warp, or the white weft and the white warp on its face. Solid white stripes are printed on the surface of the woven pattern. *Security Tape* from 2015 collection *Pack-Age-Day-Dream* by Aamu Salo

JACQUARDS WITH MULTILAYERED STRUCTURES

Using multilayered structures in jacquard design provides a myriad of possibilities for a designer. As described in Chapter 2 (p. 206), in these structures not only are multiple weft systems employed, but also warp threads are divided into two or more sets. These separate sets of ends and picks allow the weaving of several layers of fabric at once. The fabric structure could be divided into three, four or even more layers, but the most common example of a multilayered structure is **double weave** that consists of two separate layers of fabric. Because of the pockets formed between the fabric layers, double weave is also known as **pocket weave**. The two layers of double weave are referred to as **face cloth** and **back cloth**.

The section *Layers, Pleats and Blocks* (pp.186– 213) described how using contrasting colours in each set of ends enhances colouration possibilities. Multilayered structures allow for creation of solid colour areas in the jacquard patterns by using matching colours in weft and warp. Additionally, the different

colours in weft and warp sets enable the use of more versatile colour combinations. For example, the combinations of first end and first pick, second end and first pick, first end and second pick, or second end and second pick can be presented in the face cloth. A weft-faced weave, a warp-faced weave, or a balanced weave can be used in any of them. If more sets of ends and picks with varying yarn qualities are used, an almost endless amount of colour and material combinations can be created. A number of weaving mills use this type of jacquard warps, referred to as **multicoloured jacquard warps** or **tapestry warps**.

A double-weave jacquard is always **stitched** together at the edges of the design motifs, where the face and back cloths interchange. However, large sections of open pocket weave are not very durable, and depending on the application can create problems because of the two layers hanging apart from one another. It is also possible to stitch together the two layers of one double-weave structure throughout the fabric. This enables design of a durable fabric structure, in which the designer can still play with the varying colours and yarn types of the separated weft and warp systems. Tight stitching is often used in the structures of industrially woven fabrics that need to withstand abrasion, such as upholstery. Stitching can be done by lifting a pick or end from the back cloth to the face, or alternatively, lowering a pick or end from the face cloth to the back. Adding only one binding point in the area of several weave repeats can provide looser stitching. The stitching can be done tightly by adding one or more binding points in one weave repeat. As described in Chapter 2 (p. 206), this type of interwoven fabric is referred to as **double cloth**. Refer to this section for more information on stitching the multilayered structures.

→ This colourful jacquard fabric represents the vast possibilities of colour combinations in a double weave by using only two warp and two weft systems. More than ten different double-weave structures are used in this design, which show different combinations of the two sets of warp and weft threads in warp-faced, weft-faced and balanced structures in the face cloth. Black and white silk yarns are used in the two warp systems. The fabric is woven with six wefts with various colours and materials. The weft stripes match the geometric pattern of

the design that creates an illusion of an even more complex structure.
For the Forgotten Architecture is a collection of interior fabrics intended to be used in vacant buildings, to liven up these bare constructions with one simple piece of fabric. Thus, the fabrics are designed to be warm and welcoming, and include both colourful and peaceful compositions. Many of the designs in this collection reflect back on the Japanese heritage of the designer.
Joy (below) from 2013 collection *For the Forgotten Architecture* (above) by Nanako Tani

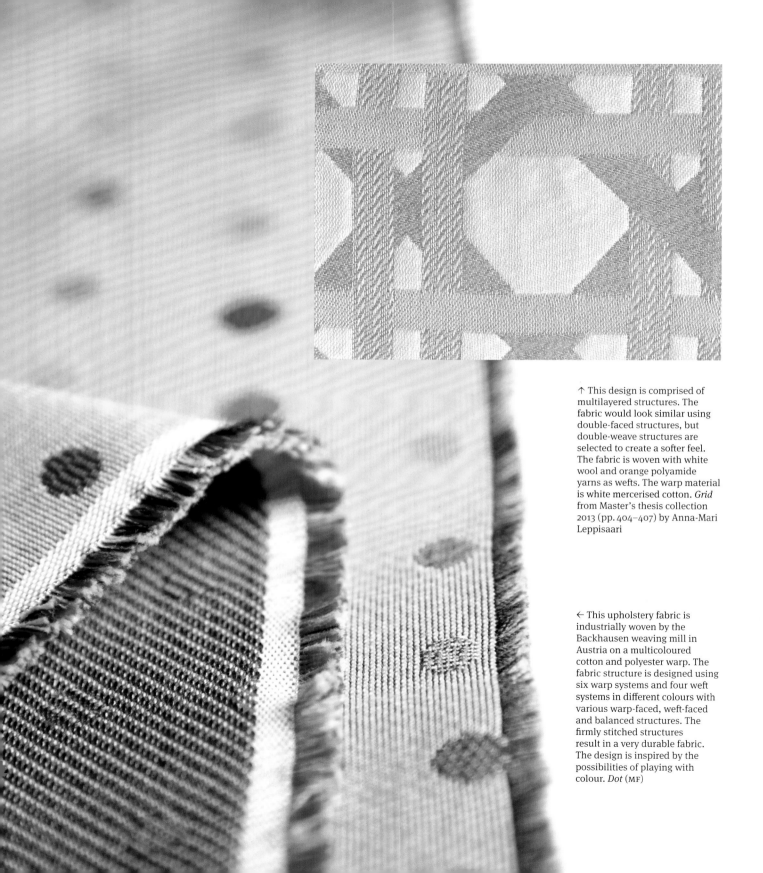

↑ This design is comprised of multilayered structures. The fabric would look similar using double-faced structures, but double-weave structures are selected to create a softer feel. The fabric is woven with white wool and orange polyamide yarns as wefts. The warp material is white mercerised cotton. *Grid* from Master's thesis collection 2013 (pp. 404–407) by Anna-Mari Leppisaari

← This upholstery fabric is industrially woven by the Backhausen weaving mill in Austria on a multicoloured cotton and polyester warp. The fabric structure is designed using six warp systems and four weft systems in different colours with various warp-faced, weft-faced and balanced structures. The firmly stitched structures result in a very durable fabric. The design is inspired by the possibilities of playing with colour. *Dot* (MF)

When woven on a single coloured warp, a fabric with double-weave structures (A p.206) can look very similar to a design with double-faced structures with two weft systems and only one warp-system (p.207). The double weave will be softer and perhaps more three dimensional as its materials are dispersed within two layers of interchanging lighter fabrics, while in a double-faced structure all the materials are stitched together within one layer.

More three-dimensionality in double-weave fabrics can be created by using different types of materials in face cloth and back cloth. Using materials with different shrinking properties can result in interesting outcomes with finishes such as steaming or washing (see Chapter 4 p. 416). Using highly shrinking materials like elastane or high-twist yarn in the back cloth can create puckering effects in the fabrics. Employing weaves with higher take-up, more picks or ends, or thicker material in the face cloth can create similar effects. The pockets formed between the fabric layers can be filled with a free-floating yarn, referred to as wadding yarn. For example, loosely twisted polyester can be used as a wadding yarn, which takes little space when stitched tightly but expands to fill the pocket when floating loosely. For these effects to have an influence on the fabric's structure only some elements of the design should be pockets, while the background is interwoven tightly.

↓ This soft multilayered jacquard fabric is made using thick orange coloured mohair and burgundy coloured wool as picks and light blue mercerised cotton as ends. The loosely bound structure of 16-end satin is used for the thick mohair picks on the face cloth to generate a soft feel in the fabric. This weft floats between the face and back cloth in other parts of the design. *The Voice of the Unheard* collection is designed by Tiia Sirén, Siiri Raasakka and Elina Laitinen. Fabric below by Siiri Raasakka

↑ This fabric, woven with a white linen silk elastane combination yarn and a grey silk metal pick, mimics the spongy look of the moon's surface. The soft lustre of the silk metal yarn resembles space dust. Two different structures generate the effect of moon rocks and craters. A double-faced structure stitches together all the wefts in the flat parts and a double weave creates the puckering surface. In the double-weave pattern areas, combinations of linen and silk metal yarns are used in the face cloth and silk elastane in the back cloth. The texture is further accentuated with steaming to finish. The shrinkage of the elastane in the back cloth results in pleats and wrinkles on the face cloth. Space, its colours and objects, and the wonders of other planets inspire this collection. *Moon* (above left) from 2014 collection *Beyond The Boundaries* (above right) by Mariia Elizarova

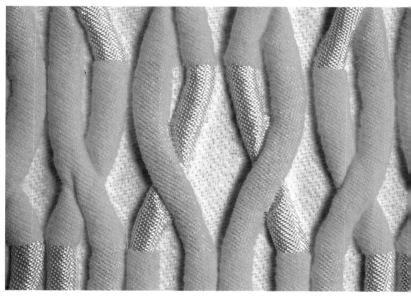

← This jacquard design uses two weave structures, a double-faced structure for the background and a double-weave structure for the pattern. The fabric is woven with a black wool elastane pick, a grass green cotton pick, and an acrylic lurex pick. The white cotton lyocell blend warp is barely visible on the face of the fabric.

The double-faced structure shows the first weft system of black wool elastane picks on the face of the fabric and hides the second weft system of green cotton and acrylic lurex combination yarns on the reverse side. In the pattern area, the double-weave structure shows the second set of picks, the green yarns, on the face and hides the black wool elastane picks at the back. Steaming shrinks the wool elastane yarn at the back, resulting in the green pattern puckering. The double-faced structure in the background emphasises the puckering effect, as it binds both layers of the fabric.

The industrially woven fabric, inspired by the early stages of information technology and 90s techno music, is designed by Kajsa Hytönen for a fashion collection by Maria Korkeila, Emilia Kuurila and Satu Rauhamäki. *Technology*, 2015

←← The three-dimensional multilayered fabric *Cables* is inspired by cable knits. A tightly interweaving double-faced structure in the background creates a contrast with the bulging double-weave cable pattern. A shrinking wool elastane pick weaves the back cloth of the pattern areas. A polyester wadding yarn floats between the fabric layers and adds padding to the design.

← In this *Cables* version, instead of a double weave, a double-faced structure was used in some of the cable-pattern areas. These areas remain flat. *Cables*, 2012 by Anna-Mari Leppisaari.

For more information on the fabrics and finishes used to achieve the final look, see Chapter 4, p.416.

→ This jacquard fabric is soft and thick with subtle three-dimensional effects. Firmly interwoven double-faced structures are used in the lilac and silver coloured pattern areas of the design that create contrast with the more loosely bound three-layered structures in the blue parts of the fabric. The weaves used in all three layers of this multilayered structure are loose, allowing the blue mohair yarns to stand out from the surface. To further emphasise this effect, a polyester wadding yarn is inserted to float between the layers. *Cool Beans* (right) from the collection *Memphis Blues* (below) 2015 by Miisa Lehto.

↓ *Diagonal* is a damask fabric made of white mercerised cotton yarn as ends and silver lurex yarn as picks. The structure of the pink and yellow *Barbie Insect* is designed using three weft systems. In some parts of the design one of the wefts, the silvery lurex, is left floating and these floats are partly cut after weaving.

This collection is inspired by the Italian *Memphis* group and its aesthetic, which was criticised for being a shotgun wedding between Bauhaus and Fisher-Price. Expressive, glittery and unashamedly kitsch things serve as the main inspirations. Imagining a fling between luxury and clutter, this dizzy, colourful and carefree collection is created for fashion use.

densities can be utilised to balance the use of different thicknesses of yarns in the fabric layers. Additionally, varying densities could be used to create different looks. Interesting effects can be achieved when the face cloth has a more open structure, allowing back or middle layers to be seen through it. This effect can be further accentuated through material choices such as selecting a light or even transparent material for the face cloth.

Most of the ideas and techniques introduced in this section can be combined with one another, or can be integrated in one fabric with other types of structures. The possibilities of using and modifying multilayered structures in jacquards are endless. However, the more complex the fabric structure becomes, the more important it is to keep in mind that the overall take-up of the fabric should be kept even.

↑ This three-layered jacquard represents different patterns and yarns on each side of the fabric. The back cloth is a damask woven using grey silk yarn as warp and weft. The other two fabric layers are woven in patterned double weave using grey silk yarn as warp and black and white mohair yarns as wefts. The back cloth is loosely stitched together with these two layers. The stitching is done by lifting a grey silk back pick thread over a face end, as the stitches can be best hidden between long mohair floats. *Silent Immersion* from the 2011 collection *You Were Here* by Emmi Pouta

Double-cloth structures can be used to make reversible fabrics that are completely different on the face and back side. To achieve this effect, only one weft and warp system should be used on each side of the double-cloth fabric. In this type of design it is necessary to stitch the fabric layers together, as otherwise the layers would not be attached at all or would be attached only at the edges of the fabric.

The sett of the fabric layers does not need to be equal. Double weave with uneven fabric

← In this double-weave jacquard, the back cloth is woven with damask pattern using black cotton lyocell warp and brown viscose weft and can be seen through the face cloth. The density of the face cloth is lower than that of the back cloth and the weft material used in the face is a transparent lurex yarn. The brownish viscose weft used in back cloth has been shrunk through washing and creates a puckering effect in the fabric. Bachelor's thesis collection *Under Wraps* 2016 by Maria Korkeila. For more information on the collection and finishes used in it see pp. 426 and 444.

Building multilayered structures in Photoshop

Instructions in this section provide information regarding the design of multilayered structures in Photoshop. By following these instructions you can make double-weave structures with two separate fabric layers on top of one another. The same method can also be employed to design structures with more layers of fabric, as presented at the end of this section.

6B

Double weave

① **Make a base unit: Create a new file: size 2 × 2 px. Colour all the four pixels of the file with different colours (1A) (not black and white, as the colours must differ from the black and white weave structures). Save the file as a Pattern Preset: Select Edit → Define Pattern. Name it: Base unit for structure with two warp systems and two weft systems.** This file is not a weave structure, but rather a base unit for building a structure with two warp systems and two weft systems. The two rows of pixels stand for the two alternating picks, and the two pixels in width define the two warp systems in the structure (1B).

1A BASE UNIT

	1ST WARP SYSTEM	2ND WARP SYSTEM
2ND WEFT SYSTEM	1ST WARP SYSTEM AND 2ND WEFT SYSTEM INTERSECTING	2ND WARP SYSTEM AND 2ND WEFT SYSTEM INTERSECTING
1ST WEFT SYSTEM	1ST WARP SYSTEM AND 1ST WEFT SYSTEM INTERSECTING	2ND WARP SYSTEM AND 1ST WEFT SYSTEM INTERSECTING

1B

② **Draw basic weave(s) to be filled into the double-weave structure.** You can use the same or different weaves in the two fabric layers of the structure. Note that constructing a double weave doubles the length of both weft and warp floats of the original weave. Hence, weaves with short floats, including plain weave, suit multilayered structures well. When using two weaves with different repeats, the sizes of the repeats should divide evenly into one another, or into the final size of the double-weave structure. In this example, weft-faced 5-end satin (2A) is used in both fabric layers. Using a weft-faced weave in both face and back cloths will naturally result in a weft-faced weave in both fabric layers and thus, the face side of the entire structure is weft-faced. The weft-faced right side of the back cloth will be hidden inside the structure, and the reverse side of the fabric will be warp-faced.

2A WEFT-FACED
5-END SATIN

③ **Double the size of the basic weaves: Select Image → Image Size. Resample Image should be ticked.** Change the Height and Width of 5-end satin to 10 px (3A). Click ok. If you do not stretch the structure at this stage, every other pick and end of the weaves would be lost when filled into double-weave structure. **Save the stretched weave as a Pattern Preset: Select Edit → Define Pattern.**

3A DOUBLED WEFT-
FACED 5-END SATIN

④ Make a base grid: Create a new file with a size that both stretched weaves divide evenly. In this example 10 × 10 px. Fill in the base grid with the base unit made in the first step: Select Edit → Fill → Use: Pattern, choose the base unit in Custom Pattern (4A). Then, make a separate layer for all pick and end intersections (= four colours). Select a colour with the Magic Wand. Create layer → New layer via copy (Ctrl+J). Repeat for all colours. Name the layers according to pick and end intersections as followed: First weft system and first warp system, First weft system and second warp system, Second weft system and first warp system, Second weft system and second warp system.

4A BASE GRID

⑤ Before filling the structure with weaves, decide which ends and picks will be bound together into one fabric layer. In this example the 2nd weft system and 2nd warp system will make one fabric. Hence, the 1st weft system and 1st warp system are left for the second fabric layer. **Use a weave to fill the layer where the 2nd weft system and 2nd warp system are intersecting (pink), (5A) as well as in the layer in which the 1st weft system and 1st warp system are intersecting (blue) (5B).** To do this, select the layer. Then select the contents of the layer (click Ctrl – Command on Mac – and Layer Thumbnail in Layers window) and choose Edit → Fill → Use: Pattern, and select the structure.

5A

5B

⑥ The next step is to define which fabric layer is the face cloth and which one is the back cloth. In this example the fabric with the 2nd weft and warp systems is defined as the face cloth, and the fabric with the 1st weft and warp systems is the back cloth. To keep the two fabric layers separate, the ends and picks of each fabric should only intersect with the ends and picks assigned to them. Notice that the ends of the face cloth should always stay on top of the picks of the back cloth, and the picks of the face cloth should always stay above the ends of the back cloth. **To lift up the ends of the face cloth so that they do not intersect with the picks of the back cloth, fill in the layer in which the 2nd warp and 1st weft systems are intersecting (green) with the colour black. Select the layer and then select the contents of the layer and choose Edit → Fill → Use: Black. (6A) To lift up the picks of the face cloth in order for them not to intersect with the ends of the back cloth, fill in the layer in which the 2nd weft and 1st warp systems are intersecting (beige) with the colour white. Select the layer and then select the contents of the layer and choose Edit → Fill → Use: White (6B).**

6A

6B FINISHED DOUBLE-WEAVE STRUCTURE SHOWING IN FACE CLOTH 2ND WEFT AND 2ND WARP SYSTEMS

Changing the weaves in fabric layers

(1) Using a weft-faced 5-end satin in the face cloth, and a warp-faced 5-end satin in the back cloth (instead of filling weft-faced in both layers), would result in a structure like this (1A). The face of the fabric will look the same as the previous version and the difference is only visible in the back cloth.

1A DOUBLE WEAVE WITH WEFT-FACED 5-END SATIN ON THE FACE CLOTH AND WARP-FACED 5-END SATIN ON THE BACK CLOTH

(2) Using a warp-faced 5-end satin structure in the face cloth and a weft-faced 5-end satin in the back cloth, would result in a structure like this (2A). The face of the double weave will be warp-faced.

2A DOUBLE WEAVE WITH WARP-FACED 5-END SATIN ON THE FACE CLOTH AND WEFT-FACED 5-END SATIN ON THE BACK CLOTH

The use of technical colours in structure files

(1) Black and white structure files can be difficult to read, especially without long experience in the design of woven fabrics. In structures with multiple weft systems, changing the Blending Mode of layers to Multiply reveals the colours on the face of the fabric. This could also be done in a double-weave structure, but the results will not be as clear (1A). However, using this method can help understand which picks will be visible on the face of the fabric in each structure.

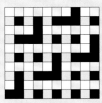

1A DOUBLE WEAVE, BLENDING MODE OF LAYERS CHANGED TO MULTIPLY

(2) Another colouring method can also be used. The following method will not help in defining which weft or warp colours will show on the face of the fabric in each structure, but it aids understanding of the double-weave structure in general. In this method, use the normal Blending Mode, but change the opacity of the layer with the weave for back cloth (in this example blue) to 50% (2A). The picks of back cloth can now be seen in light blue, and the ends of back cloth are visible in dark blue. The picks of face cloth are shown in white, and the ends of the face cloth are in black.

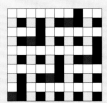

2A DOUBLE WEAVE, OPACITY OF THE BLUE LAYER CHANGED TO 50%

Double weave structures showing different weft and warp systems in face cloth

In all the previous structures in this section, the same picks and ends were used in the face cloth. Even though the structures were different, the same weft and warp materials will show on the face of the fabric. For a jacquard design, structures showing various ends and picks in the face are usually needed. If only one yarn type and colour is used in the warp, then it can be enough to make two kind of double-weave structures; one that shows the 1st weft system (B and C) and another one that shows the 2nd weft system on the face of the fabric (A and D). If two alternating yarn types are used in the warp, one for each warp system, then various material combinations can be achieved by using four types of structures in the face of the fabric; structures with 1st weft and 1st warp systems (B), 1st weft and 2nd warp systems (C), 2nd weft and 1st warp systems (D), and 2nd weft and 2nd warp systems (A).

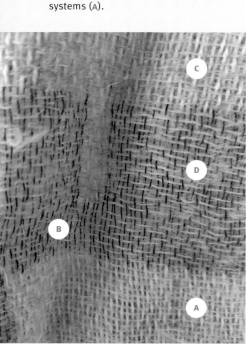

The image features broken twill-weave versions of the presented structures.

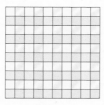

BASE GRID

A DOUBLE WEAVE
SHOWING IN FACE CLOTH
2ND WEFT AND
2ND WARP SYSTEMS

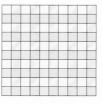

BASE GRID

B DOUBLE WEAVE
SHOWING IN FACE CLOTH
1ST WEFT AND
1ST WARP SYSTEMS

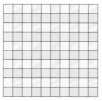

BASE GRID

C DOUBLE WEAVE
SHOWING IN FACE CLOTH
1ST WEFT AND
2ND WARP SYSTEMS

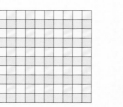

BASE GRID

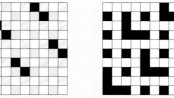

D DOUBLE WEAVE
SHOWING IN FACE CLOTH
2ND WEFT AND
1ST WARP SYSTEMS

Stitching the fabric layers together

Fabric layers in double weave can be stitched together if an open pocket structure is not needed. Stitching can be achieved by lifting one of the back ends over a face pick, or one of the back picks over a face end. These binding points or stitchers are usually intended to be hidden throughout the structure. A weft stitcher is best hidden in a weft-faced structure (1A) between the weft floats (1B), and a warp stitcher in a warp-faced surface (2A) between the warp floats (2B). It is not possible to hide the stitchers in a plain weave, as there are no long floats in the structure. It is not always necessary to hide the stitching points and they can be used as effects. When using stitchers as effects, it is important to pay attention to the arrangement of the stitchers throughout the structure.

① To stitch the fabrics with weft stitchers, lift a back pick over a face end = change the colour of one or more pixels of the black coloured layer into white (1B).

② To stitch the fabrics with warp stitchers, lift a back end over a face pick = change the colour of one or more pixels of the white coloured layer into black (2B).

There are many ways of arranging the binding points. Here are some examples:

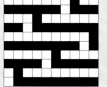  

1A DOUBLE WEAVE

1B STITCHED DOUBLE CLOTH, A WEFT STITCHER (PINK) IN ONE REPEAT HIDDEN BETWEEN WEFT FLOATS OF THE FACE CLOTH

2A DOUBLE WEAVE

2B STITCHED DOUBLE CLOTH, A WARP STITCHER (GREY) IN ONE REPEAT CONCEALED BETWEEN WARP FLOATS OF THE FACE CLOTH

← This double-sided mohair blanket has a plain weave double-cloth structure with weft stitchers. The binding points in brown mohair are visible on the otherwise pink face cloth. *Nella*, Lauritzon (MS)

(3) To bind the fabrics more loosely, repeat the structure several times before adding the stitchers (3A). In this structure there are two weft stitchers in four repeats (3B).

(4) Stitching can also be done by using a weave structure. To stitch the fabrics with warp, use a weft-faced structure to fill the white coloured layer. The warp binding points of the structure will stitch the fabrics together (4B).

This example represents a double weave with warp-faced 5-end satin in the face and weft-faced 5-end satin in the back, which is repeated four times (4A). The stitchers are added using a weft-faced 10-end satin (4B). All the satins in this double cloth use move number 3.

(5) To stitch the fabrics with weft, fill a warp-faced structure into the black coloured layer. The weft binding points of the structure will stitch the layers together.

For stitching, use a weave that is compatible with other weaves used in the double cloth.

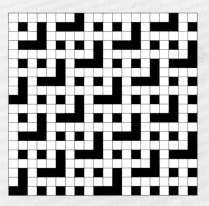

3A DOUBLE WEAVE, FOUR REPEATS

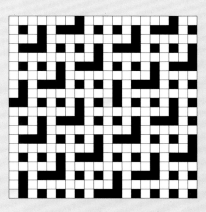

3B STITCHED DOUBLE CLOTH, TWO WEFT STITCHERS (PINK) IN FOUR REPEATS

4A DOUBLE WEAVE, FOUR REPEATS

4B STITCHED DOUBLE CLOTH, TEN WARP STITCHERS (GREY) IN FOUR REPEATS

Three-layered structure

By following these instructions you can create fabrics with three-layered structures. The method is similar to constructing double-weave structures and can be used to create structures with four or even more layers of fabric.

(1) **Make a base unit: Create a new file, size 3 × 3 px. Colour all the 9 pixels of the file with nine colours (1A)** (not black and white, as the colours must differ from the black and white weave structures). **Save the file as a Pattern Preset: Select Edit → Define Pattern. Name it: Base unit for structure with 3 warp systems and 3 weft systems.** This file is not a weave structure, but rather a base unit for building a structure with three warp systems and three weft systems. The three rows of pixels stand for the three alternating picks, and the three pixels in width define the three warp systems in the structure (1B).

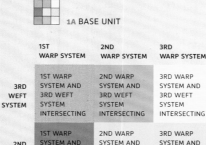

1A BASE UNIT

	1ST WARP SYSTEM	2ND WARP SYSTEM	3RD WARP SYSTEM
3RD WEFT SYSTEM	1ST WARP SYSTEM AND 3RD WEFT SYSTEM INTERSECTING	2ND WARP SYSTEM AND 3RD WEFT SYSTEM INTERSECTING	3RD WARP SYSTEM AND 3RD WEFT SYSTEM INTERSECTING
2ND WEFT SYSTEM	1ST WARP SYSTEM AND 2ND WEFT SYSTEM INTERSECTING	2ND WARP SYSTEM AND 2ND WEFT SYSTEM INTERSECTING	3RD WARP SYSTEM AND 2ND WEFT SYSTEM INTERSECTING
1ST WEFT SYSTEM	1ST WARP SYSTEM AND 1ST WEFT SYSTEM INTERSECTING	2ND WARP SYSTEM AND 1ST WEFT SYSTEM INTERSECTING	3RD WARP SYSTEM AND 1ST WEFT SYSTEM INTERSECTING

1B

(2) **Draw weave(s) to fill in the three-layered structure.** In this example weft-faced 1/3 broken twill (2A) and warp-faced 3/1 broken twill (2B) are used.

(3) **Select Image → Image size, and triple the size of weave(s).** (Weave size 4 × 4 px into 12 × 12 px) (3A, 3B) **Save these as Pattern Presets: Select Edit → Define Pattern.**

2A 1/3 BROKEN TWILL

2B 3/1 BROKEN TWILL

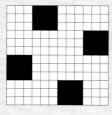

3A TRIPLED 1/3 BROKEN TWILL

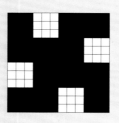

3B TRIPLED 3/1 BROKEN TWILL

(4) **Make a base grid: Create a new file with a size in which all stretched weaves divide evenly. In this example 12 × 12 px. Fill in the file with the base unit made in the first step: Select Edit → Fill → Use: Pattern, select base unit in Custom Pattern (4A).** Then, **make a separate layer for all pick and end intersections (= 9 colours). Select a colour with the Magic Wand. Choose layer → New layer via copy (Ctrl+J). Repeat for all colours. Name the layers according to pick and end intersections.**

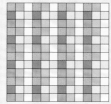

4A BASE GRID

(5) Before filling the weaves in the structure decide which warp and weft systems will be bound together into one fabric layer.
Here, the 1st weft and 1st warp systems will make the first layer of fabric. The 2nd weft and 2nd warp systems make the second layer of fabric. Thus, the 3rd weft system and 3rd warp system are left for the third layer of fabric.

In this example 1/3 broken twill fills the layer where the 1st picks and 1st ends are intersecting (red). To do this, select the layer, and then select the contents of the layer (click Ctrl – Command on Mac – and Layer Thumbnail in Layers window) and choose Edit → Fill → Use: pattern, and select the structure. The same structure also fills the layer where the 2nd picks and 2nd ends are intersecting (blue). A 3/1 broken twill fills the layer where the 3rd picks and 3rd ends are intersecting (beige). (5A)

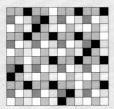

5A

⑥ The next step is to define which fabric layer is the face cloth and which ones are the middle cloth and the back cloth. In this example the fabric with 1st weft and 1st warp systems is defined as the face cloth, the fabric with 2nd weft and 2nd warp systems is the middle cloth, and the fabric with 3rd weft and 3rd warp systems is the back cloth. Notice that to keep these three fabric layers separate, the ends and picks of each fabric should only intersect with the ends and picks assigned to them.

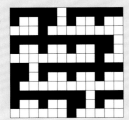

6A FINISHED THREE-LAYERED STRUCTURE

To lift up the ends of the face cloth so that they do not intersect with the picks of the back or middle cloths, fill in the layers in which the 1st warp, 2nd weft, and 3rd weft systems are intersecting (purple and grey) with black. Select the layer and then select the contents of the layer (click Ctrl – Command on Mac – and Layer Thumbnail in the layers window) and select Edit → Fill → Use: Black. As well, to lift up the ends of the middle cloth in order for them not to intersect with the picks of the back cloth, fill in the layer in which 2nd warp and 3rd weft systems are intersecting (brown) with black.

To lift up the picks of the face cloth so that they do not intersect with the ends of the back or middle cloths, fill in the layers in which 1st weft, and 2nd warp, and 3rd warp systems are intersecting (salmon and pink) with white. Select the layer and then select the contents of the layer (click Ctrl – Command on Mac – and Layer Thumbnail in the layers window) and select Edit → Fill → Use: White. As well, to lift up the picks of the middle cloth in order for them not to intersect with the ends of the back cloth, fill in the layers in which 2nd weft and 3rd warp systems are intersecting (green) with white (6A).

Stitching the fabrics of a three layered structure together

To stitch multilayered structures, you should decide which layers you want to be bound together; the face cloth and middle cloth or the middle cloth and back cloth. Naturally, stitching the face cloth and back cloth results in stitching all three layers together, but the stitchers would not be hidden. To avoid this, the stitchers should be added on the middle layer as well.

As an example, to stitch the back, middle and face cloths together, stitchers should be inserted into the layer in which 2nd warp and 3rd weft systems are intersecting (originally brown) as well as on the layer in which 2nd warp and weft systems are intersecting (originally blue).

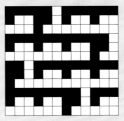

THREE-LAYERED STRUCTURE

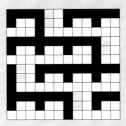

STITCHED THREE-LAYERED STRUCTURE, BACK, MIDDLE AND FACE CLOTHS STITCHED TOGETHER, FOUR STITCHERS (PINK) IN ONE REPEAT IN BOTH LAYERS.

Multilayered structures with uneven ratio of fabric densities

The ratio of fabric densities can be defined in the base unit. In the previous examples, a fabric ratio of 1:1 – one pick and end per one pick and end – was used in each fabric layer, but other ratios such as 2:1 – one end and one pick in the back cloth per two ends and two picks in the face cloth – could be used as well. An uneven ratio can be used to balance the distribution of fine and heavy materials in the same fabric, or to achieve variation in the densities of fabric layers.

(1) **To begin, make a new base unit defining the ratio.** Here are some examples (1A, 1B, 1C, 1D):

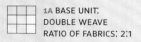

1A BASE UNIT:
DOUBLE WEAVE
RATIO OF FABRICS: 2:1

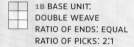

1B BASE UNIT:
DOUBLE WEAVE
RATIO OF ENDS: EQUAL
RATIO OF PICKS: 2:1

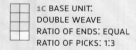

1C BASE UNIT:
DOUBLE WEAVE
RATIO OF ENDS: EQUAL
RATIO OF PICKS: 1:3

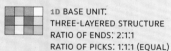

1D BASE UNIT:
THREE-LAYERED STRUCTURE
RATIO OF ENDS: 2:1:1
RATIO OF PICKS: 1:1:1 (EQUAL)

(2) **Save the base unit as a Pattern Preset:** Select Edit → Define Pattern. Fill the base unit in a new file. Then, create separate layers for each colour and name them. When constructing multilayered structures with different ratios of fabrics, it is often easier to draw the weaves in the layers than to define them as Patterns and use Fill.

Double weave with wadding

Pockets created between the layers of double weave can be filled with wadding yarn.

(1) **Start by making a base unit for two warp systems and three weft systems** (1A).

1A BASE UNIT

(2) **Make a base grid and fill it in with the base unit** (2A).

2A BASE GRID

(3) **Then, build a double-weave structure for two warp systems and two of the weft systems** (3A). In this example, plain weave is used in both fabric layers.

3A

(4) **For the third weft system, construct a structure for the wadding yarn:** Select the layer with face cloth ends (purple) and fill it in with black. Select the layer with back cloth ends (brown) and fill it in with white (4A).

The wadding yarn will not be stitched to anything and will float in the pocket between the two fabric layers.

4A FINISHED DOUBLE-WEAVE STRUCTURE WITH WADDING YARN

The wadding yarn should also be used in all other structures of the design. In those structures the wadding yarn can be stitched on the reverse side of the fabric.

Double cloth with binder thread

A similar base construction to do double weave with wadding can be utilised to create double-cloth structures with binder thread, as both of these structure types consist of two warp systems and three weft systems.

(1) **Repeat the steps 1–4 of creating double weave with wadding,** but instead of one repeat, repeat the structure several times. In this structure there are four repeats (1A).

1A

(2) **The third weft system floating between the fabric layers will act as a binder thread and so needs to be stitched in both face and back layers** (2A).

2A

↓ The photo features a twill-weave version of the structure 2A. When twill is used, the binding points should be hidden between the weft floats as described in p.392, but the stitchers cannot be completely hidden in plain weave.

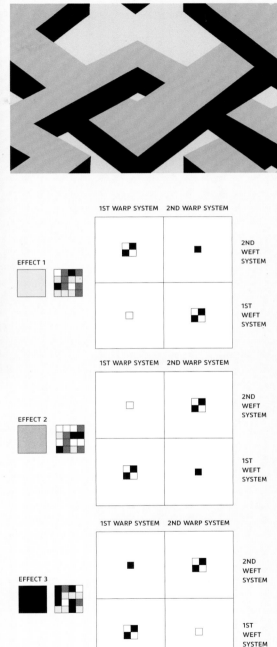

Illusion 6 from 2012 collection *Illusions* by
Emmi Pakkanen. This fabric is an example of
a double-weave jacquard that is woven on a
end and end warp with two sets of picks in
different colours. The warp material is wool
acrylic blend and the colour of the first warp
system is black and the second warp system
is grey. The two picks are viscose polyester
blend yarns, and the first pick in the structure
is blue, and the second is silvery. The sett of
the warp is 24 ends/cm and the weft density is
30 picks/cm.

Three plain weave double-weave structures
are used in this design. EFFECT 1 shows the
background of the design in the face cloth and
is a combination of the blue weft with the grey
warp. The lighter grey appearance of EFFECT
2 is made of the grey warp and silvery weft in
the face cloth. EFFECT 3 is the only structure
that shows the black warp in the face cloth
and is combined with the blue weft. The entire
Illusions collection is presented on p. 345.

1ST WARP SYSTEM 2ND WARP SYSTEM

EFFECT 1

2ND WEFT SYSTEM

1ST WEFT SYSTEM

1ST WARP SYSTEM 2ND WARP SYSTEM

EFFECT 2

2ND WEFT SYSTEM

1ST WEFT SYSTEM

1ST WARP SYSTEM 2ND WARP SYSTEM

EFFECT 3

2ND WEFT SYSTEM

1ST WEFT SYSTEM

Form (MF) – This three-dimensional jacquard is part of a series of fabric designs that study the relation between fabric collage sketches and woven jacquard fabrics. The sketch for this design, presented on p. 343, was created by means of quilting and painting on fabric. The structure of the woven fabric is constructed using five weft systems and two warp systems to imitate the quilting effect. The sett of the warp is 24 ends/cm and the weft density is 50 picks/cm.

The fabric is woven using beige silk yarn as warp and three different viscose and polyester yarns as wefts. The material of the first, second and third pick in the structure is black viscose (marked in the structures with different shades of grey). The fourth pick is white viscose raffia (marked in the structures as blue) and the fifth pick that functions as wadding yarn is a white loosely twisted polyester yarn (marked in the structures as beige).

The structures used in EFFECTS 1 and 2 are quite similar. In both effects, the 2nd warp system and the 2nd and 4th weft systems are used in the face cloth, and the 1st warp system and the 1st and 3rd weft systems are hidden in the back cloth. Double-faced structures are used in both the back and face cloths. In effect 1 the second pick, black viscose, is showing on the face of the fabric, and in effect 2 the 4th pick, white raffia, is showing on the face of the fabric. The fifth pick, the wadding yarn, is floating between the fabric layers in both effects.

In EFFECT 3, all weft systems are bound together in a double-faced structure to imitate the quilted lines of the original sketch. To achieve the black colour in the effect, black viscose wefts are present on the face of the fabric and the white raffia and wadding yarn are hidden on the reverse side.

To achieve the quilted effect, all possible means of supporting the three-dimensionality of the structure are taken into account. The fabric structure is comprised of tightly bound double-faced areas with open pockets, in which the wadding yarn is inserted to float in the pockets. While the raffia yarn used in the face cloth is very stiff, the viscose yarn used in the back cloth is soft and elastic. Hence, the overall take-up of the face cloth is higher than the take-up of the back cloth which results in further puckering on the fabric surface.

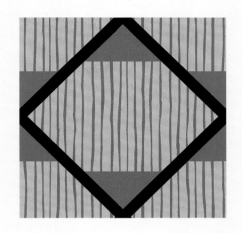

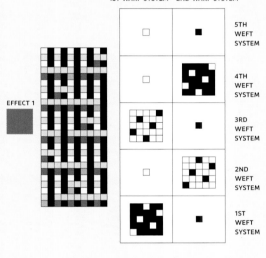

1ST WARP SYSTEM   2ND WARP SYSTEM

☐	■	5TH WEFT SYSTEM
☐	(grid)	4TH WEFT SYSTEM
(grid)	■	3RD WEFT SYSTEM
☐	(grid)	2ND WEFT SYSTEM
(grid)	■	1ST WEFT SYSTEM

EFFECT 1

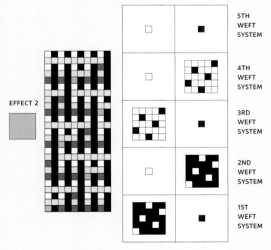

1ST WARP SYSTEM   2ND WARP SYSTEM

☐	■	5TH WEFT SYSTEM
☐	(grid)	4TH WEFT SYSTEM
(grid)	■	3RD WEFT SYSTEM
☐	(grid)	2ND WEFT SYSTEM
(grid)	■	1ST WEFT SYSTEM

EFFECT 2

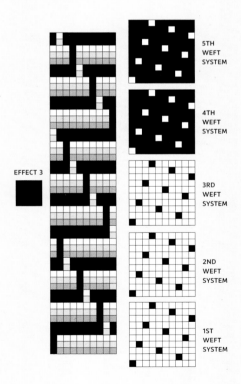

EFFECT 3

(grid)	5TH WEFT SYSTEM
(grid)	4TH WEFT SYSTEM
(grid)	3RD WEFT SYSTEM
(grid)	2ND WEFT SYSTEM
(grid)	1ST WEFT SYSTEM

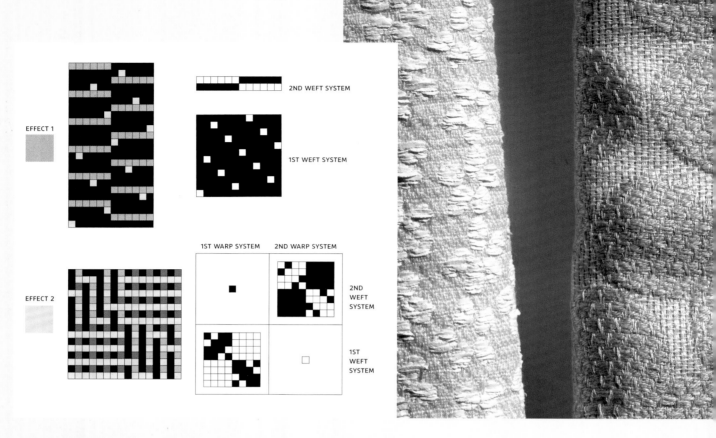

EFFECT 1

2ND WEFT SYSTEM

1ST WEFT SYSTEM

EFFECT 2

1ST WARP SYSTEM   2ND WARP SYSTEM

2ND WEFT SYSTEM

1ST WEFT SYSTEM

Ciottoli and *Flora* from 2019 collection *Spiaggia* by Riikka Piippo. Both fabrics are woven using double-faced structures in the background and double weave in the patterned areas. This page presents the weave structures used in the design *Ciottoli*. EFFECT 1 presents the double-faced structure used in the background, and EFFECT 2 is the double weave.

The fabric is woven using white mercerised cotton as ends and two types of linen as picks. The material of the first set of picks, marked in the compound structures as beige, is natural coloured linen and the material of the second set of picks, marked as light grey, is finer white linen. *Flora* on the other hand is woven using wool and polyurethane coated cotton as wefts, as the designer wanted to play with the contrast of shiny and matt yarns in this collection.

The structure in EFFECT 1 shows the first set of picks on the face of the fabric woven in a half panama weave, and hides the second weft system on the reverse side with a satin weave. In contrast, the double-weave

structure in EFFECT 2 displays the second set of picks on the face cloth woven in a broken twill variation, and hides the first weft system in the back cloth. Baskets served as an inspiration for the interesting structure choices, and the aim of the designer was to make textural surfaces with an interesting hand-feel.

The contrast between the double-faced structures that bind all the materials together and the open double-weave pockets creates a subtle three dimensionality in both of the fabrics. However, due to the materials used, they are not as three dimensional as the design *Technology* with similar structures presented on p. 385. *Ciottoli* and *Flora* are designed to be used in accessories such as bags, and the materials are accordingly selected to create durable fabrics capable of withstanding abrasion.

The theme of the collection *Spiaggia* is an idea of a serene beach holiday in Italy and reflects the aesthetic memories related to that mindscape.

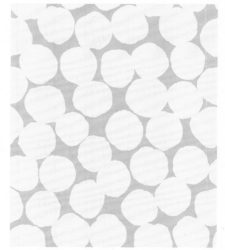

SIMULATING JACQUARD FABRICS

It is not always possible for a designer to sample on a loom during the design process. Using the fabric collage method can be beneficial in these cases. However, if the design is already in digital format, the designer can make a fabric simulation to anticipate the outcome of the pattern as a woven fabric. Most professional jacquard design software include a function to make a simulation based on the weave structures, but reliable simulations for sketching and presentation purposes can also be generated in Photoshop.

This process begins by scanning woven fabrics with basic weaves. These images are developed into seamless patterns and inserted into the digital draft of the design in a similar manner as the weave structures. This idea is analogous to fabric collage, but instead of scissors and glue, Photoshop is used in the process. The structure images should be coloured according to the number of existing weft and warp systems in the simulated fabric. For instance to make a design with one warp system and two weft systems, the warp should be coloured with the same tone in each image, and two varying colours or yarn types should be used for the wefts. Keeping the materials and scales of the structures similar throughout the design generates a more reliable simulation.

↖ This simulation is generated in Photoshop by inserting scanned images of fabrics with satin structures into the digital draft of the design. Samples of this design as a painted sketch and a jacquard woven fabric are presented on p. 341. *Lily* (MF)

←↓ These images showcase an upholstery fabric as a Photoshop simulation (below) and as a woven fabric (left). The scale of this pattern design is relatively large and the pattern includes a number of different vertical, horizontal, and diagonal elements. The simulation technique has provided the designer with an opportunity to visualise the outcome of the design with different woven structures before weaving. In this fabric, the designer has focused on the pattern making process by systematically placing the stripes in random directions. *Patch* from collection *Random Order* (pp.464–465) for the Swedish weaving mill Ludvig Svensson. Master's thesis 2014 by Aoi Yoshizawa

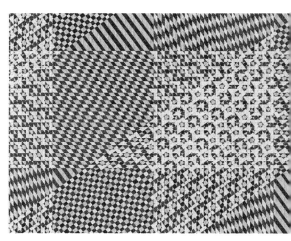

3.3 From Sampling to Weaving on Industrial Looms

With an understanding of jacquard structures with single or multiple weft and warp systems, it is possible to create any woven structure. When the designer has gained the knowledge to construct structures with two weft systems, they can also create structures with three or four weft systems. With the understanding of how to divide the warp into multiple systems and with knowledge of the principles of compound structures, the designer can generate a myriad of multi-coloured, two sided, or three-dimensional structures. When this knowledge is combined with the understanding of materials and colours, any fabric can be created.

The information provided in this chapter and the understanding of the jacquard structures is only a starting point for mastering the jacquard design techniques. More complex jacquard structures can lead to potentially more technical challenges in weaving, especially on industrial looms. One of the most important aspects of designing jacquard fabrics for industrial looms is to make sure that the overall take-up of the fabric including the selvedges is even. Long warp floats and large warp-faced areas in a design are more challenging for the machine to weave and need to be taken into consideration. Lastly, the materials of warp and weft strongly influence the success rate of the weaving process.

Envisaging in advance which design can or cannot be woven on industrial looms is generally challenging. Small differences in machine setup and equipment, as well as small changes in the material and structure of the design, can greatly influence the weaving success rate. Therefore, proficiency and deeper understanding of the principles of jacquard design lead to greater possibilities for development and design of successful jacquard fabrics.

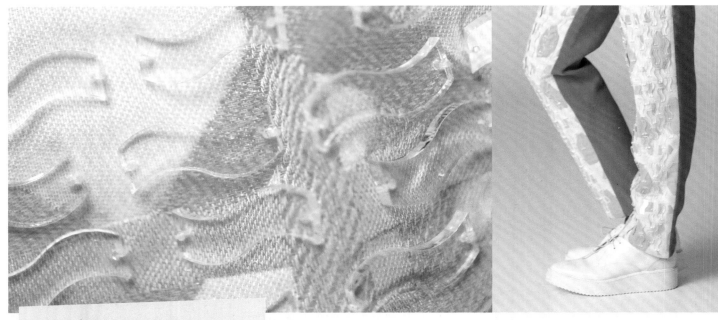

TWISTS AND GRID –
PATTERN TO STRUCTURE,
STRUCTURE TO PATTERN

by Anna-Mari Leppisaari

My womenswear collection is an exploration of fashion through textile and surface design, where form and aesthetics follow the woven and embroidered fabric. I was inspired by Alinka Echeverria's photographs of Mexican pilgrims carrying colourful and vivid self-crafted shrines on their backs. The experimental use of multiple handcraft techniques and combinations of materials was an inspiration in the design of the woven fabrics for this 2013 Master's thesis collection (see p. 440).

As the woven fabrics were a starting point for the collection, the weaving methods and the restrictions of the loom have strongly affected the style and form of the clothing. The garments were designed on the loom with the aim of creating as little waste as possible. The ability to steer the entire design process and qualities of a garment from yarn to finished product was an important part of the design process.

The theme of material appreciation in the collection also extended to the design of the woven fabrics. The patterns represent woven structures and play with contrasting scales. I find the relationship between a pattern and a structure fascinating. At what scale does the structure become a pattern and at what scale the pattern a structure?

For me, weaving is a compelling technique as it enables bringing a pattern to life and creating interesting textures with a clever combination of structures and materials. I feel that geometric patterns in particular make it possible to really experiment with and control different properties.

In the research phase of my design process, I sketched some ideas for the patterns by hand. Due to the geometric nature of my designs, I chose to recreate my sketches with Illustrator. From the outset, I had an idea of the functions and materials I would like to "insert" into my patterns. I knew that I wanted to experiment with pocket weaves and try very clear colour areas with fancy yarns in my designs. For this reason, I kept the lines of my designs very

sharp and designed the patterns in reduced colours from the start.

The pattern design phase was rather quick and resolute. My first pattern, called *Grid*, was made of a simple design with overlapping lines, and a relatively small repeat. Only the joints of the lines required some fixing to get the lines in the design look as if they go under and over one another naturally.

The second design, *Twisted*, is a variation of the first pattern. I repeated the first pattern for a large background, making sure that the background was also in repeat. Then I started to distort the design, displacing parts of the design and experimenting with different filters. In Illustrator, I was able to easily control the thickness of the lines and the proportions of the pattern.

When the patterns were ready, I started to make the digital files for weaving in Photoshop. I enjoy the process of making sense of the black and white pixels and multiple weft systems and layers in Photoshop, and made several versions from the same design. I worked mainly with satins and a few of my own weaves. My favourite phase in the whole process was testing the designs with a hand-operated jacquard loom to create test samples, as I wanted to experiment with finishing techniques such as felting,

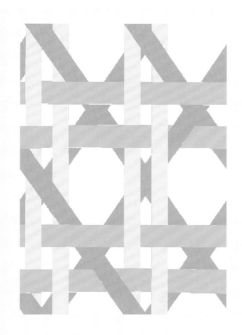

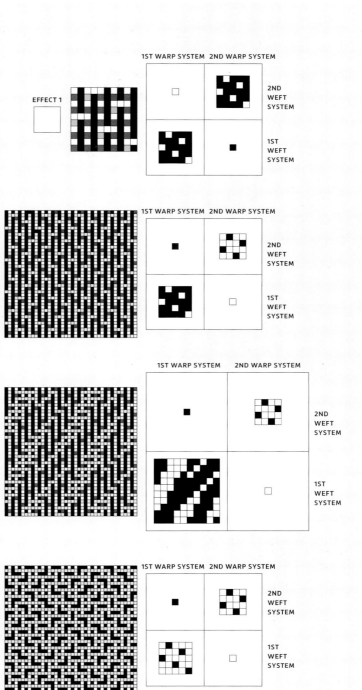

shrinking and combing. Then, I returned to using Photoshop to create more files based on the observations I had made during the weaving, and to test some new ideas I got from the trials. The pocket weave allowed me to achieve multiple effects from the same fabric structure depending on the elasticity and thickness of the yarn, the density of the fabric, and the finishes used. I tried filling the pockets with a wadding yarn, using wool with elastane to shrink some parts of the designs, and used very contrasting materials such as shiny plastics and hairy mohair yarns.

Ultimately, I chose to execute the *Grid* design as pocket weave. A thin, shiny, bright orange polyamide pick and a white wool pick were woven on a white cotton warp. At the first glance, the textile looks like a very simple single layered fabric. However, by implementing two layers, I was able to achieve a fabric which without any special finishes is lightweight and falls nicely. The fabric becomes very three-dimensional, soft, and heavier in quality with some tumble-drying and felting, due to the felting properties of the wool and the utilised structures. In my clothing collection, I used both versions of the fabric. I also appliquéd some laser cut plexiglass adornments to the final garments made from this fabric.

In the *Twisted* jacquard, I used three weft systems for a two-layered weave structure. The weft yarns are purple mohair, neon orange wool blend, and a thin, transparent polyamide slit-film tape yarn. The warp is a white cotton as in the *Grid*. The fabric was finished with some gentle combing and it was bonded with double-sided cashmere wool in order to give it more body.

My original idea for the *Twisted* jacquard was to pack the white warp-faced area of the design with candy wrapper-like, wide and transparent polyamide slit-tape yarn. I wanted to create a very three-dimensional, distinguishable, and crispy effect, and have the other colours of the design visible under the plastic layer. Unfortunately, while producing the fabric it became evident that industrial production with the polyamide tape yarn was not possible even after several test runs. Therefore, I had to swiftly come up with a different solution. Instead of the wide tape, I worked with a very thin transparent tape-yarn, which from a distance looks almost invisible. I altered the weaves so that the 5-end satin repeats each binding point twice. This makes the warp floats longer while still keeping the weft floats short and stable. In the final fabric, the warp yarns in those areas float beautifully, creating a similar wavy movement present in the pattern. This was a fortunate accident and it created

a much more sophisticated look compared to the original material choice. In my opinion, these unexpected elements in the behaviour of the material, combined with structures and imaginative large-scale patterns, are what makes jacquard weaving so exciting.

For more on finishes, please refer to the section *Searching for the Final Look and Hand* on pp. 411–433.

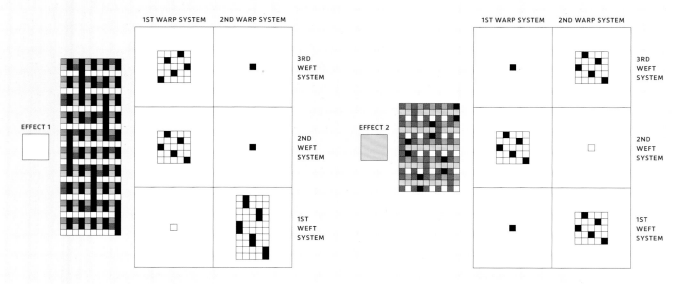

EFFECT 3

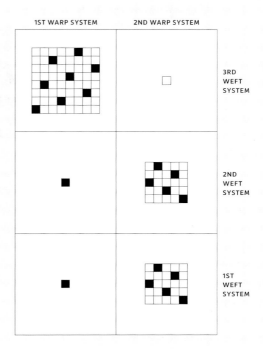

	1ST WARP SYSTEM	2ND WARP SYSTEM	
			3RD WEFT SYSTEM
			2ND WEFT SYSTEM
			1ST WEFT SYSTEM

EFFECT 4

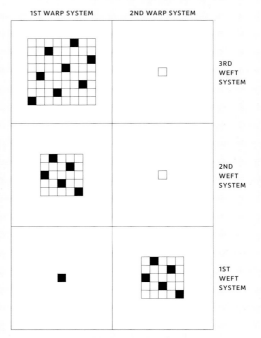

	1ST WARP SYSTEM	2ND WARP SYSTEM	
			3RD WEFT SYSTEM
			2ND WEFT SYSTEM
			1ST WEFT SYSTEM

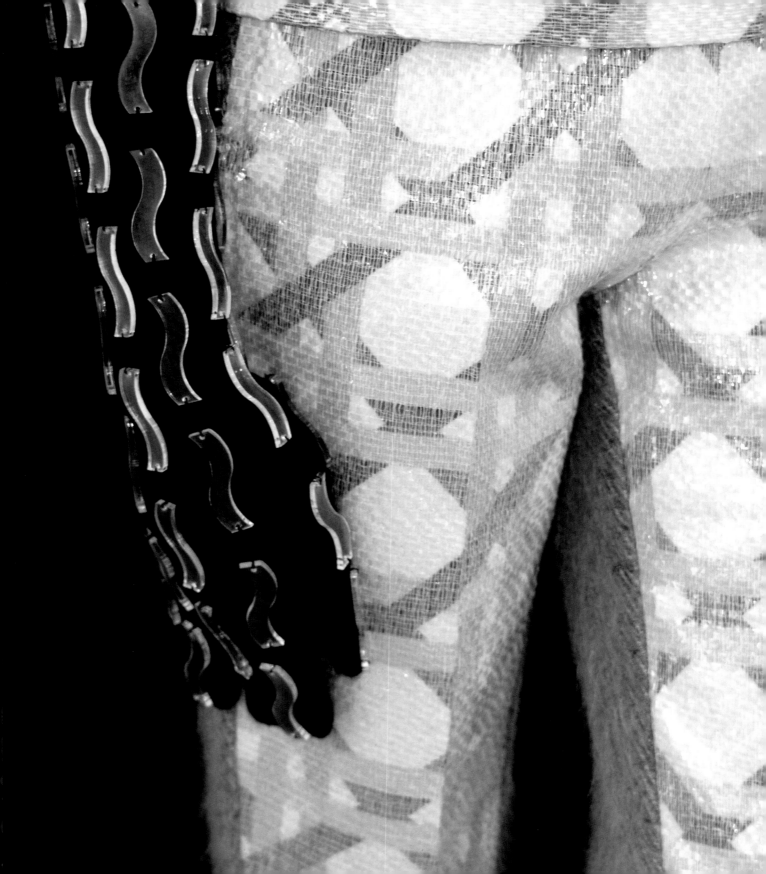

4. Finished Fabrics— into Fashion, Interiors and Beyond

This chapter expands the design skills for woven fabrics acquired in earlier chapters into finishes and onwards to designing for fashion, interiors and commercial collections. It explains the evolution from samples to practical applications of textiles as well as introduces case studies of exciting new applications, illustrating the ever-expanding field of textile design. The chapter advises on how to develop woven samples with different textile finishing methods, integrate the techniques into collections, and apply this knowledge to industrial collaborations in clothing and interior contexts.

Understanding how textile materials and structures affect the form and function of a garment, interior textile application, or other product is essential for textile designers. Obtaining haptic knowledge through hands-on experience with fabrics plays an important role in this process. As illustrated in the case studies, engaging with textile design is an asset for fashion, product and interior designers alike. Recognising the potential of textiles provides designers with additional tools for realising the desired aesthetic, expressing ideas and experimenting with materials.

The broad scope of textiles invites collaboration between professionals across specializations. Textile structures can be applied on architectural as well as microscopic scales. Textile materials and structures are widely implemented for technical purposes in fields such as medicine, the automobile industry and construction just to name a few. An intriguing glimpse into multidisciplinary concepts for new applications is included at the end of this chapter, exploring the possibilities of combining materials and structures in woven textiles beyond their present use and weave the way to sustainable and multidisciplinary textile futures.

↖ Multilayered fabric with an integrated woven sensor matrix. Emmi Pouta

← Fabrics and outfit from Master's thesis collection 2013 by Anna-Mari Leppisaari

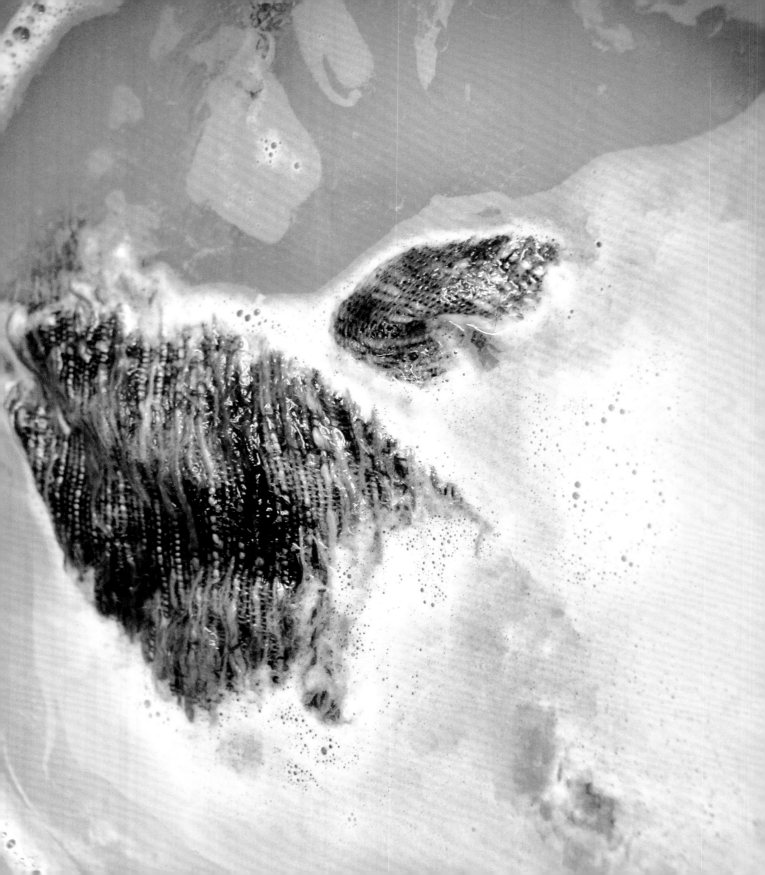

4.1 Searching for the Final Hand and Look

by Anna-Mari Leppisaari

The textile industry is a process industry where finishes play an important role in transforming the woven fabric into an applicable material and improving the look, performance, quality, and the hand of the fabric. An appropriate finishing process can turn raw and rough material into a desirable product.

Today's consumer demand has driven manufacturers to develop new materials and finishes to make textile products increasingly comfortable, easy to clean and care for, and simultaneously improve their look.[1] A large number of finishes were initially developed for functional, high-performance textiles, but have since been adapted by the fashion and interior textile industry.[2] New finishing solutions are researched and tested constantly, and are often considered big secrets in the industry.

Designing by means of finishing techniques is an essential part of textile design. The textile design process often starts from the visual aspects. However, the haptic qualities and performance of fabrics are equally important. Unpleasant hand or impractical qualities can render the most beautiful fabrics unusable. Conversely, great comfort or high-performance alone do not make unattractive textiles appealing. A favourable combination of aesthetic and functional qualities is important, and finishes can address both.

Experimenting with different types of finishes provides fascinating design opportunities. It helps designers better understand the role of this step in the production process. In addition to testing established finishing techniques, one is encouraged to explore and generate new and innovative finishing methods. Broadening the designer's imagination can lead to novel finishing solutions. Many brands and designers, such as Prada, Issey Miyake and Iris van Herpen, are continuously

← Final dyed, printed and brushed fabric

collaborating with engineers and scientists to push the boundaries of the final look and hand.

Although today's finishing processes are an essential part of producing textiles to meet the required look and functionality, they are also the cause of some of the biggest environmental challenges of producing textiles. Innovations are needed as finishing processes require large quantities of energy and water, and can contain hazardous chemicals.[3] Consumer awareness is moving the market towards finding multi-functional solutions that meet aesthetic, functional, and sustainability requirements. Many of the new finishing solutions are developed as sustainable alternatives in response to one of the textile industry's most pressing issues. For more information on sustainability see pp. 36–39.

Industrial finishes and categorisation

The textile finishing field is an intriguing mix of traditional craftsmanship and innovative

← Woven fabric in finishing solution. Fabric by Eeva Suorlahti

textile science and technology, where designers, scientists, and engineers work hand in hand to develop new fabrics. It consists of a broad range of techniques and processes that can be carried out at various stages of textile production, ranging from fibre to finished garment production. Finishes that a textile designer can influence are often executed at the fabric stage, as is the case in most examples presented in this section.

Techniques vary from basic washing to highly specialised processes such as nano-finishes, which benefit from the use of nanotechnology. Although some weaving mills have their own finishing department, finishing is commonly outsourced. Many finishes are specific to certain fibres or based on distinct application requirements, and often finishing mills specialise in a particular range of finishing services.

Finishes can be categorised in multiple ways. Based on the life cycle of a particular finishing application, they can be divided into **temporary**, **durable**, or **permanent**. Based on the mode of action, finishes can be categorised as **mechanical** or **chemical**. On the grounds of the achieved results, they can be divided into **basic**, **special** or **functional**, and **colouration finishes**.[4] Based on the procedure, sometime finishes are also divided into wet or dry. This section follows the categorisation of basic, special, and colouration finishes. Some of the most common finishes are introduced in A. For further information on finishes and their categorization, please refer to the literature list at the end of this book.

Basic finishes are common processes that the majority of industrially produced fabrics undergo. These include both chemical finishes, which are based on chemical reactions, and mechanical finishes that are carried out by machines or by hand. Many of the basic finishes are also pre-treatments for special or colouration finishes, which ensure uniform absorption of dye and chemicals.[5] After undergoing one or several of the basic procedures, the finishing process can advance to special finishes for aesthetics, functional finishes for performance, and colouration finishes. Colouration finishes include various dyeing and printing methods, and in their simplest form refer to applying colour to fabric and fixing it.

Implementation of finishes on a non-industrial scale

It might be difficult for students and freelance designers to gain access to industrial finishing machines. However, plenty of techniques can be explored within the workshop facilities available in design schools and small studios. Many finishes can also be performed by hand or with chemicals available at shops. Detailed guidance about appropriate finishing processes and suitable chemicals for each material can be found in the literature list. Safety instructions should be carefully followed when planning the finishing steps. It is advisable to take sustainability aspects into account by choosing chemicals and techniques that minimise the environmental impact. Some finishing processes, such as dyeing and fulling, can be merged and conducted during the same processing stage which results in better environmental practices.

It is important to consider the interrelatedness of finishes and the order of the finishing processes to make sure that the result of one finishing does not nullify the outcome of another.

Generating a test sample before applying the finishes to a final piece is always advisable. Fabrics with the same composition can react differently to the same treatment, depending on their yarn type, density and structures used in the fabric.

Fabrics intended for use in products should always be finished before cutting and assembly to prevent the distortion of the planned design. If finishes are applied at the garment or product stage, the effects of the finishing process in relation to the shape and size of the garment or product should be taken into consideration.

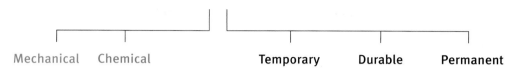

Common industrial finishes

Mechanical Chemical

Temporary Durable Permanent

Basic finishes

INSPECTION
SINGEING
BASIC CALENDERING
TENTERING
CRABBING
DECATING
FULLING
HEAT SETTING
STEAMING
TUMBLE-DRYING
DESIZING
SCOURING
BLEACHING
STIFFENING
WEIGHTING
MERCERISATION
CARBONISATION

Special/functional finishes

For appearance

SPECIAL CALENDERING:
· SCHREINERING
· MOIRÉ
· EMBOSSING
· FRICTION CALENDERING
RAISED SURFACE FINISHES:
· NAPPING
· GIGGING
· SUEDING
· EMERISING
· FLOCKING
· BRUSHING & SHEARING
CLIPPING
SANFORISING
SPECIAL HEAT-SETTING:
· PLEATING
· CRUSHING

DELUSTRANTS
OPTICAL BRIGHTNING AGENTS
ACID FINISHES
ALKALI FINISHES (PLISSÉ)
SOFTENING FINISHES
STIFFENING FINISHES
FADING FINISHES

For performance

ABSORBENT FINISHES
ANTISTATIC FINISHES
ANTISLIP FINISHES
STAIN & SOIL RESISTANT
DURABLE PRESS FINISH
SHRINK RESISTANT (ALSO MECHANICAL)
FLAME RESISTANT
WATER-REPELLENT & WATERPROOF
ANTIPESTICIDE FINISHES
LIGHT REFLECTANT FINISHES
MOTH PROOF FINISHES
ANTIMICROBIAL FINISHES
MICROENCAPSULATION FINISHES:
· FRAGRANT
· MOISTURISING
· VITAMINS
· DEODORANTS

Colouration finishes

Dyeing

FIBRE, YARN, FABRIC OR GARMENT DYEING
RESIST DYEING
· TIE AND DYE
· BATIK
RESERVE DYEING
CROSS DYEING
SHADOW DYEING
SPACE DYEING
OMBRÉ DYEING

Printing

DIRECT PRINTING
RESIST PRINTING
DISCHARGE PRINTING
TRANSFER PRINTING (SUBLIMATION)
DEVORÉ
FLOCK & FOIL PRINTING
CLOQUE PRINTING
DIGITAL PRINTING

A

→ Students working in the
dyeing and finishing studio

Dyeing is applied to the entire fabric, whereas printing is applied locally to produce a pattern. Special finishes include techniques that alter the appearance or introduce a new aesthetic feature, such as producing wavy **moiré** fabrics by **special calendering** or flannel fabrics by **napping**. Functional treatments in turn affect the safety, comfort, and after-care properties of fabrics. Functional finishes are especially important in specialised fields such as sportswear, work-wear, and textiles for public spaces which must adhere to high safety and quality standards.

The process of designing through finishes

It is possible to boost different elements of the textile such as drape, weight, texture, colour, and pattern through finishes. While the word *finishes* refers to the final stages of the textile production process, one of the first choices, the choice of the fibre type of the yarn, is extremely important. The **material composition** should be chosen keeping the desired qualities and the end use in mind, as the fibre properties greatly affect the behaviour and modification possibilities of the fabric. Using blends, combinations and mixtures (p.227) can create compelling effects but requires knowledge of material behaviour. Understanding specific **fibre properties** is crucial for the finishing process, as procedures that suit some fibres could severely damage others. A good example is sodium hydroxide solution: used on cotton it shrinks the material for a crêpe finish, but on wool it destroys the fibres and may be used for a devoré finish.

As described in Chapter 2, yarn type and weight, weave structure, and the density of picks and ends form the defining qualities of a fabric. These properties also greatly affect the results achieved from the chosen finishing method. Soft and fluid dress fabric, heavy and fluffy winter coat fabric, or a durable carpet all call for very different materials, structures, and finishes. A carefully selected combination of materials and structures lay the foundation to achieving the desired outcome and allow the application of appropriate finishes. By employing different finishing techniques, the same fabric can be developed for distinctly different end uses.

When selecting yarns, it should be considered that they may have been treated at the yarn stage, which could affect the results of fabric-stage finishes. For example, some wool yarns are treated to enable machine washing, preventing them from felting and thus making them not suitable for fabric fulling or felting finishes.

Basic finishes

The focus of this section is on durable and permanent **finishes**. Some examples of basic, special, and colouration finishes are introduced through samples. To demonstrate the finishing possibilities in a small scale, in studio circumstances, the examples are mainly from student projects.

Washing and **steam ironing** are great standard procedures for all samples. They usually improve the hand and emphasise the texture of the fabric. They also release the tension of the yarns generated during the weaving process and allow the yarns to shape and shrink into their final relaxed form. The washing process, also called **scouring** in the industry, removes impurities that are either naturally occurring, or caused during the weaving process or from the treatments in the yarns. It also prevents unwanted shrinkage after making the fabric into a product.

If the fabric contains yarns intended for shrinking effects, such as elastane or over-twisted yarns, high-temperature steaming or hot washing usually results in three-dimensional effects.

Interesting textural effects are achieved by **combining Z-twist and S-twist yarns** in one fabric. The effects are emphasised with wash treatments. A fabric can be woven with weft yarns twisted in a direction opposite to that of the warp ends, or the yarns can be alternated in either the warp or weft direction. **Over-twisted yarns** further emphasise the textural effects. Elastic and adapting wool yarns are well suited to experiments with twist combinations. The grainy hand of wool crêpe, as well as the light-weight plain-weave fabric **georgette**, is made by alternating over-twisted S and Z filament yarns in both warp and weft directions. The results emerge in the finishing washes.

The fabrics combining S-twist and Z-twist yarns before the finish

The steamed fabrics

← This material research project demonstrates how S-twist and Z-twist wool yarns combined with diverse weave structures affect the results of steaming, washing, and wetting treatments in the fabric. The twist of the yarn, length of yarn floats and denseness of the stitches in the weaves result in significant differences in the finished outcome. Dense structures, such as plain weave, do not allow the fabric to shrink or reform during the steam finish in the same way that looser weaves, such as the 16-end satin (second sample from the bottom) or pocket weave (lowest sample) used in this example do. The different reactions of S- and Z-twist yarns to steaming are also clearly visible in the steamed 16-end satin sample, where the steam has caused the S-twist yarn to twist strongly and shrink thereby forcing the Z-twist yarns to rise up.

← *The Effects of the Twist* by Ia Kähkönen

HIGH-TEMPERATURE WASH

This sample is woven with a shrinking wool yarn ground pick, while grey tape yarn picks float on the surface, loosely stitched to the ground. The wool yarn shrinks significantly as a result of high-temperature washing, making the surface very three-dimensional. The unfinished piece on the left helps illustrate the effect that the finishing has had on the final sample.

← *Sample* by Teija Vartiainen

STEAM IRONING

In this sample, the combination of a double-weave structure and cleverly selected materials—a polyester wadding pick inside the pockets and a shrinking wool pick at the back of the fabric—form a prominently three-dimensional surface when steamed at high temperature. More information on the fabric can be found on p.385.

← *Cables* (AL)

WOVEN PLEATS AND TUMBLE DRYING

The pleated effect of this woven fabric is due to a combination of mixed-material composition, structure bindings, and the finish. The weave structure combines viscose wool blend picks with thermoplastic polyester ends. The *Airo* treatment, washing with softeners and drying with a high-temperature airflow, softens the fabric and shrinks the viscose wool blend weft floats. The shrinkage on the fabric reverse results in a sharply pleated surface on the fabric face.

← *Frill* for Lodetex (AL)

↑ *Outfit* from Bachelor's thesis collection 2018 by Eetu Kemppainen

PLEATED GARMENTS

This hand-painted silk fabric is pleated using large cardboard pleating patterns. The fabric is stuffed into the cardboard pattern and bound as a tight package before being fixed into shape in an industrial steamer at high temperature. Pleated silk has to be handled with care as it is not as durable as pleated polyester.

Tumble-drying is a process that uses airflow and heat to improve the volume and richness of the fabric. It also helps open up fluffy yarns like mohair and soften the hand of the fabric. The fabric should be gently wetted before tumble-drying and checked regularly during the process to prevent felting or shrinking of the fabric due to high temperature or prolonged tumbling time.

Calendering is an ironing process in which the textile is pressed between rotating cylinders at high temperature, increasing its density and providing lustre. Many sewing or printing facilities own a heat-press, with which the combination of compression and heat can be used for calendering.

Tentering is a drying process in which the fabric is stretched onto a tenter frame, secured with clips and passed through a heated chamber. It is used to straighten the warp and weft yarns and set the desired dimensions of the fabric. In addition to stretching, removing creases and drying, fixing and condensing can also take place at once.[6] This process is referred to as **crabbing** when used for wet wool fabrics. Thermoplastic fibres, such as polyester and nylon, require **heat setting** at very high temperatures to stabilise the dimensions of the fabric, prevent future shrinking, and to provide crease-resistance.[7] Heat setting can also refer to setting special surface effects, such as permanent pleats.

Bleaching is a chemical finish that culminates in a white fabric and is typically used to remove colour from natural fibres.

Mercerisation is an alkali finish applied to cotton threads and fabrics, but applicable also to cotton blends and other cellulose fibres. This treatment improves the strength and lustre of the yarn, and increases its absorbency, which makes dyeing and finishing of the yarn easier. Mercerisation is done either after spinning on yarns or after weaving on fabrics. During the treatment, the fabric is stretched to keep its original dimensions.

Fulling, also called **milling** and **felting,** is a wool-specific finish, which makes the wool fabric denser and stronger, and improves its insulation properties. Felting wool yarns should be used for this finish. The fulling process requires a combination of mechanical friction and hot moisture to allow the fibres to migrate and entangle with one another for the fabric to felt. Soap may be used to speed up the finishing by hand. Fulling is often applied to wool fabrics to make them more compact, and increase their waterproofing and suitability for clothing applications.[8] After fulling, the fabric needs to be set, steamed and stretched to its correct dimensions. The softness of the hand of the fabric may be improved by gentle brushing. *I Weave Dogs and Clothes* by Venla Elonsalo on pp. 442–443 showcases an intriguing project involving fulling.

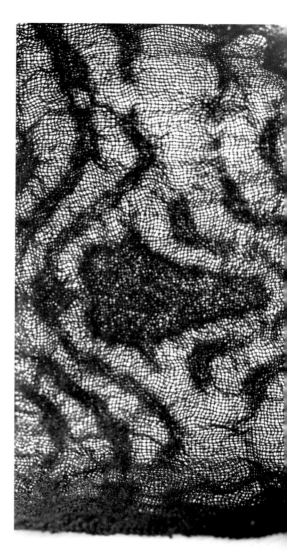

↑ *Sample* by Ida-Sofia Tuomisto

RESIST FELTING

A pattern may be introduced by fulling, often called resist felting or partial felting. This sample is initially printed with the thickening agent alginate and then treated with alum, which resists entanglement of the fibres during the felting process and as a result forms the pattern. A water softener agent is applied to remove the alginate after the felting process has been carried out.

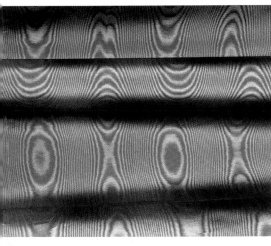

← In this rib-weave silk fabric, the moiré pattern is created utilizing the traditional moiré calendering process instead of imitating it through the print or jacquard technique.

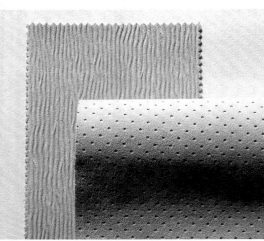

← Non-woven *Alcantara* polyester upholstery fabrics which feature wavy, embossed, and perforated dot patterns.

Special finishes

Calendering treatments include special variations, such as **moiré** and **embossing**. In the traditional **moiré calendering** process, ribbed fabrics are crushed together by two heated cylinders under a high pressure. When the fabrics are separated, a wavy moiré pattern appears on both fabrics. Embossing is a special calendering method in which a three-dimensional pattern is embossed onto the fabric by pressing it through metallic rollers that are engraved with the design.

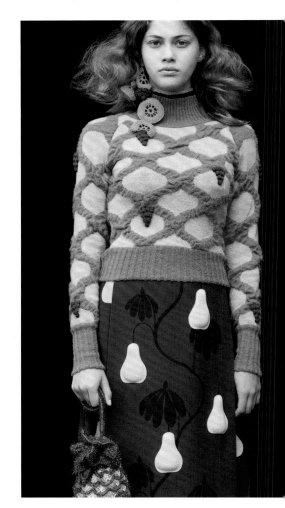

COMBINING DIGITAL PRINT AND CREATIVE EMBOSSING

The digitally printed pear designs on this skirt are transformed into three-dimensional surfaces using an embossing technique. The effect is achieved through innovative use of tailored moulds and heat setting the thermoplastic polyester fabric at high temperature.

→ *Outfit* by Ilona Hackenberg, 2014

Clipping, or **fil coupé**, is a mechanical finish that is done by cutting the floating extra wefts of woven fabrics to obtain partly transparent or lighter patterns or fringes. The fil-coupé technique can be used to imitate handwoven **brocade** effects (p. 83). The appearance may in some cases look similar to the devoré effect (p. 432).

FIL COUPÉ

This curtain fabric is woven with an additional weft system that covers parts of the design while floating over the transparent areas, from which the floats have been mechanically clipped away. In order to facilitate clipping, it is important to keep the minimum length of the floats to approximately a few centimetres and to add plain weave around the edges of the clipping areas to prevent the yarns from slipping.

→ Industrially woven fil coupé fabric by Tiina Paavilainen for Lodetex. See p. 460–463 for more information on the *Floating and Clipping* Master's thesis collection

FRINGING BY CLIPPING

Clipping can also be used to create fringes in woven designs. Here floats are cut from one corner and ironed outwards for a three-dimensional effect.

← Bachelor's thesis collection 2017 by Netta Törmälä

FRINGES AND LONG FLOATS

This fabric is designed to include different float lengths. Floats are cut into fringes. The reactive dyeing process lets the viscose yarn floats open and expand.

→ Bachelor's thesis collection 2018 by Anna Semi

BRUSHING

This jacquard design is woven with long-haired wool mohair picks that are brushed from the back of the fabric using a metal brush. Brushing blurs the lines of the design resulting in a soft, smooth, and hairy surface.

← Sample from Master's thesis collection 2016 by Teija Vartiainen

INTRODUCING PATTERNS THROUGH BRUSHING

The fabric, woven with a long-haired wool mohair blend, is partially brushed to create a gradient design.

← Master's thesis collection 2013 by Anna-Mari Leppisaari

Brushing is a raised surface finish which pulls loose fibres from the fabric structure creating hairy and soft surfaces. In a studio setting metallic brushes, such as those found in pet shops, work well for this purpose.

In the **flocking process**, small fibre particles, called flocks, are applied onto the fabric surface with adhesive and are then cured. In the industry, the flock fibres are spread mechanically or through an electrostatic process. Both natural and man-made flock fibres are used.

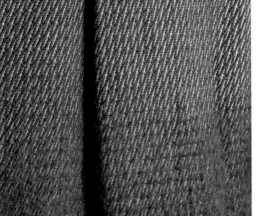

FLOCKING

This design creates a three-dimensional velvet-like texture. The adhesive is screen printed and heat-pressed with a sheet of flock, which only remains in the printed areas.

→ Sample by Heta Vajavaara

Crêpe finish, also called **plissé finish**, is a mercerisation treatment with a sodium hydroxide solution on fabrics made of cellulose fibres. In **cloqué printing**, the mercerising solution is printed on the material. Untreated cotton fabrics with a loose weave structure work best for this treatment. The textile is not stretched during the finish, thus allowing the treated areas to swell, densify and shorten to create three-dimensional effects. Furthermore, treating a fabric woven with a mixture of cellulosic and synthetic fibres – not affected by the treatment – may intensify the three-dimensional puckering. A mercerised fabric is not affected by the crêpe finish, as the yarns have already undergone the treatment with the sodium hydroxide solution.
See also **seersucker** (p.172).

CRÊPE FINISH ON MIXED-MATERIAL WARP

The warp of this double-weave fabric is designed for experimentation with the plissé finish. It consists of bands of red polyester ends and white cotton ends. The polyester ends are woven with yellow polyester pick and the cotton ends with black cotton pick. The plissé finish builds tension between the two fibre material areas. The finished sample on left features puckering effects on the polyester stripes that contrast with the shrinking cotton stripes.

The top and bottom samples are woven on the same mixed-material warp. In the top sample, the white cotton warp yarns are dyed red using reactive dyes.

→ Samples by Yuki Kawakami woven on mixed-material warp

LAYERED CLOQUÉ PRINTING

This fabric contains a base layer of thin cotton gauze and a top layer of digitally printed polyester. The two fabrics are bonded together by screen printing a puff binder on them, and finished by treating the whole fabric in a sodium hydroxide solution. The finishing process shrinks the cotton gauze layer in areas where the fabrics are not bonded together resulting in the polyester layer puckering up.

← Bachelor's thesis collection 2018 by Anni Salonen

Fading effects have been very fashionable, especially in denims, and can be obtained by stone-washing, washing with enzymes or ozone, or applying chemicals onto fabrics or directly onto the garments. Due to health and safety issues as well as the high environmental impact related to stone washing, bio-stoning with enzymes or ozone treatments are preferred options in the industry.[9] A great variety of techniques and chemicals have been developed for finishing denims to achieve worn-out looks and fancy effects.[10] CO_2 **laser treatment** is a common sustainable alternative.

On non-industrial scale, fading effects can be obtained through discharge printing (see colouration finishes p.432), or by using mechanical abrasion, for example with sandpaper.

A SUSTAINABLE ALTERNATIVE TO FADING FINISHES

The patterns on this garment are created by placing objects on the garment and leaving it under the sun for a long period of time. The colour of the unblocked areas of the fabric fades due to exposure to sunlight, introducing patterns to the fabric.

↑ *Pyhävaatteita* (Sunday Clothes) Master's thesis collection 2016 by Elina Laitinen

FINISHING WITH ADHESIVE PASTE

The delicate silk fabrics in this outfit are finished using a thick layer of thermal adhesive paste to attach the pleats, stiffen the fabric, and glaze the surface. The adhesive is screen printed using an open screen and finished by heat-pressing it with silicone paper, which polishes the adhesive.

→ Master's thesis collection 2018 by Emilia Kuurila

Softening finishes are used to alter, relax, and soften the hand of a fabric. Commercially available fabric softeners function well for softening purposes. Experimenting with the amount of softener and the length of washing or tumbling process will produce different results.

For **stiffening**, there exists a wide range of textile lacquers and thermosetting resins used to coat the fabric or print on it, altering the fall and the surface of the fabric.

Bonding has great potential to alter and enhance the appearance of fabrics, particularly their fall. An adhesive web fabric can be placed between two layers of fabric to bond them together using a heat press.

BEESWAX COATING

Waxed fabrics are generally used for water-resistance, but in this project the beeswax was chosen for its smell and its tactile properties on the transparent material. Melted beeswax is applied onto this reactive-dyed silk organza fabric using a soft paint-roller. To make the waxed surface as even as possible, the fabric then is placed in a ceramic oven for a few minutes at approximately 70° C. The excess wax melts off and a smooth result is achieved.

← Beeswax treated coat from Master's thesis collection *Triggers* 2018 by Mira Järvinen

TRANSPARENT WOVEN FABRIC BONDED WITH DIGITAL PRINT

In this design, a transparent hand-woven wool and polyamide mixture is bonded with a digitally printed cotton fabric. The end result improves the durability of the delicate handwoven fabric while resembling a multi-layered, textural jacquard design.

← Fabrics from Master's thesis collection 2013 by Anna-Mari Leppisaari

CREATIVE COATING

Fake grass blades are attached to the green fabric featured in this outfit by screen printing an adhesive onto the fabric. The fabric is then coated with a textile lacquer. The result generates an interesting texture on the fabric, stiffens it, and gives body.

↑ Master's thesis collection 2012 by Satu Maaranen

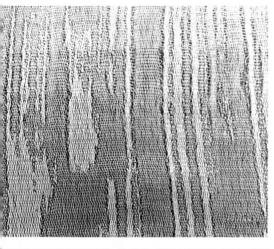

The images on this page showcase the same fabric (CO, CV, PA) with different reactive dye colouration finishes and a heat press finish.

← The original undyed jacquard fabric that is mainly warp-faced. The fabric is woven on a cotton warp with a combination yarn pick consisting of 90% viscose and 10% polyamide.

← Reactive dyeing with light grey dye demonstrates how the weft has twisted and relaxed, typical for this specific yarn, during the dyeing process resulting in vertical folds.

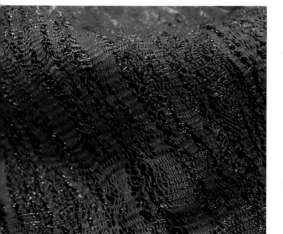

← Reactive dyeing and heat press. The fabric is heat pressed at 160 °C for 20 seconds after dyeing to straighten and polish the crinkled surface.

→ The final outfit features the fabric dyed light blue.

→ Outfit from Bachelor's thesis collection 2018 by Anna Semi

Colouration finishes

Colouration finishes offer the potential to design coloured and patterned fabrics without the limitations of available yarn colours, types of looms, and repeat sizes. Yarns or samples can be **dyed**, **painted**, or **printed** in the desired colour, and patterns can be printed on top of various structures and material combinations.

The term **print ground** refers to a fabric used as a base for printing. Undyed fabrics are referred to as **greige** cloth (p. 327). The fibre and yarn materials and structures in the ground greatly influence the appearance of the surface pattern and colour of the final dyed or printed fabric. Designing special woven fabrics and jacquards with fibre mixtures and intriguing textures to be used as grounds for **piece-dyeing** and **printing** offers exciting potential for unique textiles, especially in high-end fashion and interior fabrics.

The following samples
feature ways in which
a variety of printing
processes and dyes
are used to introduce
large-scale patterns
and textures onto plain
fabrics.

Here a jacquard look is
achieved on wool mohair
fabric with reactive dye
printing.

→ Sample by Ida-Sofia Tuomisto

Films or foils, such as
featured in this sample,
can be attached to
fabrics using a heat
press after first applying
an adhesive.

→ Sample by Tiia Sirén

Mixed-material woven fabric
is dyed with black tea

← Sample by Maria Korkeila

A dye can be applied at the fibre, yarn, fabric, or product stage. Various classes of dyes are available, depending on the material composition of the fabric and the desired outcome, from either an aesthetic point of view or according to the demands of the end product. Like all other finishes, suitable dyes, fixing agents, and their utilisation methods must be carefully selected case by case. In addition to industrially produced **synthetic dyes**, many creative and natural colouration methods can be used. Some of these include **rusting**, **earth staining**,[11] and **natural** dyeing.

Plants, fungi, algae, and insects have been used as sources of dyes by cultures around the world for centuries. Today, research projects worldwide aim to revive the use of **natural dyes** and bring forgotten dyeing practices on a broader, industrial scale.

In this double-cloth jacquard fabric, a shrinking-yarn pick is woven into the base structure in order to trigger the top layer consisting of polyamide and cotton yarns to pucker up. The fabric is finished with tea dyeing.

←Fabric from Bachelor's thesis collection 2016 by Maria Korkeila. For more information on the collection and techniques, see pp. 387 and 444

Natural dyes cause less environmental impact than synthetic dyes as the process generally utilises fewer harmful chemicals. However, natural dyes pose challenges of uneven colour appearance and inferior colour fastness when compared to the dyeing result achieved with synthetic dyes. In addition to improving these qualities in natural dyes, a change in attitude regarding colour is much needed—embracing a new kind of diversity and uniqueness in colours instead of aiming for flawlessly replicable results in standardised industrial production.

Popular plants for natural dyeing include onion skins, madder roots, indigo plants, and tea. When selecting the source for natural dyes and planning the dyeing process, it is essential to find solutions that do not damage the ecosystem. Attention must also be paid to selecting the mordants or fixatives needed to fix the colour to the fibres.

DYEING WITH NATURAL INDIGO

The outfit is dyed with Finnish-harvested dyer's woad, a natural indigo plant with several species found worldwide. The woven fabrics and knit pieces are a mixture of cellulose and polyamide fibres. The different materials absorb the natural dye differently, resulting in a lively colour surface. The fabrics' combinations of materials and structures are designed to dissolve the unevenness of natural dyes and include this aspect in the design.

→ *Changing Seasons* knitwear (AL),
Spring to Autumn woven fabric (MF)

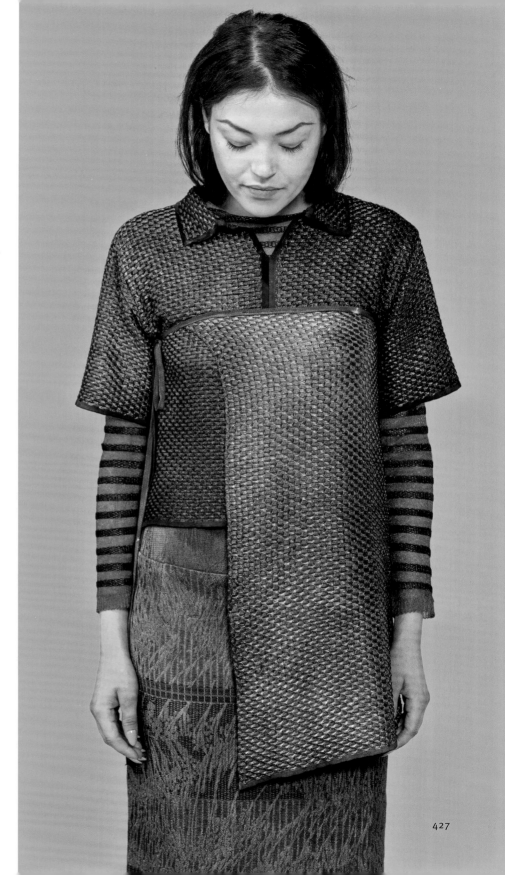

Dyeing or printing the weft or warp yarns before weaving allows the designer to gain the precise colours needed for the woven design, and allows the application of patterns or special effects to yarns. The warp yarns can be dyed, painted, or printed before the warp is set up, or can be hand-painted after the warp set-up. Resist-dyeing methods may be used to create **ikat** or **tie-dye** designs, both in yarn and fabric stages.

WEAVING AND CREATIVE COLOURATION

In this project, reactive dye painting is combined with weaving during several stages of the design process. The final finished fabric can be seen on p.411.

→ Collection *Dark Light* 2010 by Eeva Suorlahti

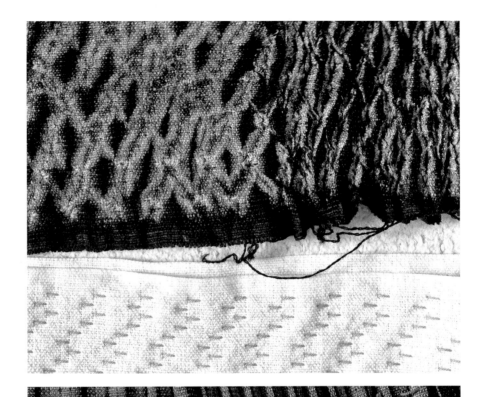

PATTERNING THROUGH WOVEN PLEATING YARNS FOR RESIST DYEING

Pleating yarns are woven in instead of being stitched. Pulling the yarns crushes the fabric, consequently preventing the dye from colouring the fabric evenly, thus forming patterns. The images show the fabric with pleating yarns prior to indigo-dyeing, as well as the resulting effect after the resist tie-dye process.

→ Samples from Master's thesis collection 2019 by Ma Jiayi

The images on this page feature a cotton, thermoplastic polyester and silk mixture fabric with two different reactive dye colouration finishes.

← The original undyed ground

Yarn and fabric blends, combinations and mixtures (p.227) allow designers to generate various effects and textured surfaces. As fibres have different dye-uptake properties, colouration effects and patterns can be created by deliberately choosing fibres, yarns, and dyeing agents, targeting specific components. These options include **reserve, cross**, and **shadow effects**.[12] In reserve dyeing one fibre component is kept undyed, while the other is dyed. In cross dyeing both fibres are dyed in different hues to obtain a contrasting effect. Whereas, in the shadow effect both fibres are dyed to different depths of the same hue. All of the above-mentioned effects can also be obtained through printing, and would work well with blends, combinations and mixtures consisting of very different dye-uptake properties, such as cotton and polyester mixture fabrics. Experimentation with reserve, cross, or shadow effects is a great way to broaden the available patterning and colouration possibilities, to personalise samples, and to learn about material properties. Simple alterations like mixing different natural fibres will most likely result in different shades through dyeing.

RESERVE DYEING WITH CRUSHING

The fabric is tied and scrunched around a plastic tube before dyeing. The achieved three-dimensional surface is durable to some extent, but not permanent. High-temperature treatments can undo this effect. Increasing the amount of thermoplastic fibres to more than 65 % increases the durability of the crush.

COLOURED RESIST PRINTING WITH RESERVE EFFECT

In this sample the reserve effect is clearly visible. The white polyester yarn used in the fabric has remained undyed as it is not affected by reactive dyes.

Samples (AL)

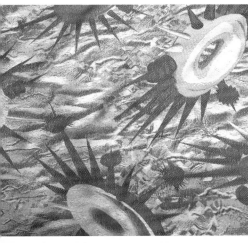

The samples featured on this page demonstrate the variety of ways in which painting with reactive dyes can be used to alter the appearance of a 1-weft system jacquard fabric.

← Damask jacquard fabric before colouration finishes. The fabric is woven on a white cotton warp with orange polyester pick.

↓ A fil coupé design with cross printing effect. The polyester cotton mixture double-cloth structure is initially finished using a clipping technique. Then, the blue square design is printed on using reactive dyes. As polyester is not substantive to reactive dyes, the areas with only polyester in warp and weft have stayed undyed while cotton is printed.

↓↓ Here, a black and white sublimation print is added to the polyester ground.

Samples (AL)

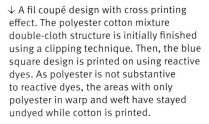

← White cotton ends are painted with bright reactive dye colours. The orange polyester pick remains undyed due to the reserve effect.

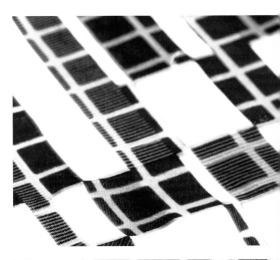

← White cotton ends are painted with dark colours. As in the brightly coloured sample, the orange polyester pick remains undyed.

Samples by Leevi Ikäheimo

← The original woven fabric

WHITE DISCHARGE PRINTING ON JACQUARD FABRIC

↙ A discharging agent of varying intensity is printed on the jacquard ground and bleaches the yarn.

In addition to direct printing, special printing styles such as resist printing, discharge printing, and devoré can also be used to further develop the woven samples. Interesting surfaces could be designed by hand-painting or printing woven grounds for discharge printing with different colours or hues. Some dyes, which will not be affected by the chosen discharge agents, could also be added for further effects.

Devoré, also called **burnout**, is a printing technique in which chemicals are applied to mixed fibre materials to dissolve and remove one of the fibre components. Devoré may be used to create a semi-transparent pattern, a relief-like surface, or holes in the fabric. Man-made fibres polyester and polyamide, and protein fibre silk are not affected by the chemicals applied in devoré, and hence can be used as the remaining component in mixed-fibre materials. The acquired result is dependent on the fabric structure and the percentage of each fibre in the composition. When designing a woven fabric for devoré, it is important to construct the textile in a manner that ensures the remaining fibres retain a durable structure.

DEVORÉ PRINTING AND REACTIVE DYEING

This silk viscose blend velvet is dyed with a red reactive dye. The flower pattern is then screen printed using chemicals which burn the viscose pile off while the silk ground remains. See p. 449 for another devoré fabric example.

Fabrics and outfits from Bachelor's thesis collection 2016 by Emilia Kuurila

Digital printing has gained popularity due to its flexibility, diversity, and speed. The benefits of digital textile printing include the ability to print patterns with numerous colours and details, printing photographic images, and producing designs with no constraint in repeat height. Product customization and the ability to combine CAD patternmaking for engineered prints create a high demand for digital printing. Additionally, improvements to the design software and development of the printing heads[13] provide the possibility to print on textured surfaces such as knits and three-dimensional jacquards.

Combining weaving and digital textile printing offers exciting possibilities. In recent years, some traditional weaving mills have invested in digital printing machines to develop designs that combine both techniques. Mixed-material grounds are very important for digital printing and these blends are used to create a variety of effects.

There are different methods for **digital printing**, and **reactive dye** and **sublimation** have been traditionally popular. However, developments in pigment inks have made **digital pigment printing** a feasible and sustainable alternative. The process consumes less energy and water during production and is suitable for both natural and synthetic materials.

BLENDS AS DIGITAL PRINT GROUNDS

Cotton and polyester dye differently, causing colour variation. Printing on cotton polyester spun-yarn blends creates textural and vintage effects.

→ Industrially woven and digitally printed fabrics for Lodetex (AL)

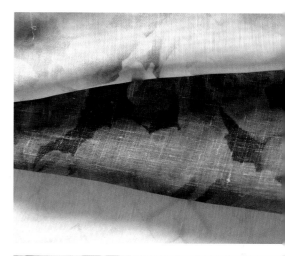

DIGITAL PRINTING ON MIXED-MATERIAL GROUND

The satin ground of this jacquard velvet upholstery fabric is woven with a yarn-dyed grey cotton pick on a white polyester warp. The velvet pile consists of adjacent areas with light grey yarn-dyed viscose pile and white polyester pile. The fabric is digitally printed with dyes suitable for polyester which after the finishing, result in only the polyester pile being printed while the cotton ground and viscose pile maintain their original colour.

→ *On Repetition*, industrially woven velvet by Kaisa Karawatski for GM Fabrics

→ *Fleur de Sel*, digital pigment print on ground woven with alternating S- and Z-twist wool yarns by Ilkhe du Toit.
See p. 415 for information on how S-twist and Z-twist yarns combined with diverse weaves affect the results of finishes.

Learning to combine techniques, use finishes and build collections

The visual research and storytelling-driven teaching method for woven textile design introduced in Chapters 1 and 2 can also be adapted for teaching the process of designing through finishes, printed fabrics design and knitwear design. Students deepen their skills in woven, knitted, and printed fabrics as they learn to use finishes to achieve the final hand and look they desire and coordinate the samples made in different textile studios into versatile and cohesive textile collections.

Students are introduced to the foundations of collection design and guided in directing the design work towards a selected target group. They create a concept and mood board based on visual research methods, and explore and experiment with their concept using a variety of textile techniques. This pedagogical platform teaches students to take into account the visual and technical requirements of the various textile techniques, as well as to consider the aspects related to finishing processes, the textiles' use and maintenance. They will be able to use various design and manufacturing processes, and to creatively implement their ideas within collections. The information and hands-on experience of the textile production process, including finishes, enables students to understand sustainability issues.

This pedagogical platform encourages students to start their work by targeting it towards a specific project. For fashion students, the project might be their fashion collection. For textile students, the project might be an interior textile collection. Designing for a specific function guides the students to think about the practical and use-specific aspects of the fabric. After identifying their project and concept through thorough visual research, students select suitable yarns and start designing textiles in the weaving and knitting studios. Students experiment with both knitted and woven textile techniques. During this time, they also acquire new skills in computer-aided design.

In addition to weaving on the standard warps in the studio or tailored warps prepared by the instructor, the students can team up in pairs or small groups according to the looks required for their collections, design a warp, and set up the loom. These tailored warps can include special features, such as layers or stripes of natural and man-made fibres (see example woven on the mixed-material warp p. 421), and further enable learning about material properties, especially linked to various finishes.

After work in the constructed textiles studios, the students continue to develop their woven and knitted samples in the printing, dyeing and finishing studios. They may also work with industrially manufactured fabrics that suit their collection. In addition to dyeing and other finishing techniques, students explore printing methods such as screen printing and digital printing.

Specific learning tasks are assigned to students to help them accomplish the learning goals. The following list of course requirements describes the variety of materials, structures, and techniques to be experimented with during the course. However, for the final collection the students can choose samples that best suit their individual concept. Other techniques such as laser cutting, crochet, and embroidery may also be implemented in the collection. Similar to the other learning platforms described in this book, a product card with technical information is made for each sample. The product cards are an important part of the learning process, in which the students learn to mark down structures, materials, recipes, and processing steps. Subsequently, they will be able to reproduce the samples in larger quantities when needed. To conclude, the students organise a fabric fair in order to present their collections in a professional setting.

↑ *Africa Goes to Space*, a collection of finished woven fabrics, knits and prints by Aamu Salo

Assignment: Textile collection design course

A textile collection of 16 swatches based on visual research/storytelling, either for interiors or fashion.

- Mood board/concept/visual research book based on the student's creative interests.
- From all the swatches made during the course, 16 carefully selected samples will be chosen for the final textile collection. Product cards are made for each selected sample.

PART 1
Preparatory tasks
(if course schedule permits)
- Designing and setting up a loom (group work)

12–14 samples, which should include:

1) Woven:
- 1 swatch for colouration finishes with either cellulose or protein fibres
- 1 swatch with combined weaves
- 1 jacquard sample

2) Knitted:
- 1 swatch for colouration finishes with either cellulose or protein fibres
- 1 swatch with combination of various knit structures
- 1 jacquard or intarsia sample

3) Knitted or woven:
- 1 swatch with mixed fibres for reserve, shadow, or cross-colouration effects
- 1 swatch from which cellulose or protein fibres can be discharged (Think about the materials, will all the yarns be dischargeable or not?)
- 1 swatch with felting wool, which can be felted or resist felted
- 1 swatch in which cotton and polyester are mixed for a plissé finish or cloqué printing
- 1 swatch with shrinking yarns
- 1 swatch to implement mechanical finishing techniques of your choice (For example fil coupé or brushing)

(Note: One swatch can contain several features)

PART 2
Requirements for printing and finishing:
- Exposing a screen
- Reactive dye painting, dyeing, or printing with natural dyes
- Discharge printing
- White resist printing and coloured resist printing
- Plissé finish or cloque printing
- Devoré
- Felting or resist felting

You may also use:
- Folio and flock printing, coating with adhesives
- Pigment and special pigment printing (Puff-paste etc.)
- Digital printing
- Sublimation printing
- Other mechanical and chemical finishing techniques

Product cards should include:
- Names of the techniques and structures used
- Structural draft of the weave or knit
- Material composition
- The recipe if colouration finishes or chemical finishes have been used
- Flow chart of all the steps
- Picture of the final sample
- Name of the sample

Note: industrially manufactured fabrics may also be used as grounds for printing and finishing in addition to woven and knitted samples from part 1.

← Anna-Mari Leppisaari
and Maarit Salolainen
instructing a student

COMBINING TECHNIQUES CREATIVELY

In her collection, Pialot was inspired by the floral ceramics of her hometown in Southern France and the photographs of her rebellious mother in the 70s. With the aim of embodying her heritage in the design, the Montpellier ceramics are turned into elegant silkscreen prints, knits, and laser-cut leathers.

Collection Faïence 2015 by Lucille Pialot

4.2 The Hybrid Practice of Combining Textile and Fashion Design
by Anna-Mari Leppisaari

Textiles and fashion are inevitably interconnected. The shift towards a textile focus is a growing trend, with experimental textile design having developed into a trademark for many designers and brands. A strong bond between creative textile design and fashion design has always existed especially in couture, but due to recent technological developments, innovative textiles have reached all levels of the fashion industry.[14] Moreover, the new advances in fibres, textile finishing, and technologies such as computer-aided design and digital textile printing have influenced the way in which designers work with textiles.

Despite this interrelationship, the design and use of fashion fabrics are often seen as different skill sets, drawing a divide between textile and fashion designers[15]. Although collaborations are common, they are not always acknowledged in public, which in many cases has led to an unequal relationship between fashion and textile professionals, and has kept the development and manipulation of textiles as "the hidden art of fashion"[16]. Simultaneously, the production of textiles has largely moved overseas and the level of knowledge in textile materials and techniques in our society is alarmingly decreasing. The renowned trend forecaster Li Edelkoort[17] has talked about the importance of reinstating textile knowledge, and she recognises textiles as a core field in future developments. A more comprehensive integration of textile and fashion design practices can introduce interesting design directions and novel aesthetics, and offer the possibility to rethink how garments are produced.

The growing emphasis on sustainable and functional, yet aesthetically appealing, products calls for interdisciplinary collaborations and designers with compound skills whom are capable of combining artistic expression and deep technical knowledge. Technological developments and advances in computer-aided design tools make combining textile and fashion design practices more accessible. The methods introduced in this book illustrate how textile design studies may be integrated with fashion design, with the aim of supporting textile-led approaches to fashion design.

The following section examines the role of textiles in fashion design practice from the point of view of a designer, and presents a selection of examples from both industry cases and student projects, in which various textile-led approaches are utilised. The student projects are examples of explorative artisanal cases which illustrate the results of the teaching methods in this book. The emphasis of the text is on the fashion designer as the designer of textiles, while correlations with material appreciation and sustainable design are also addressed.

Historical point of view

A textile-led approach, although nowadays often empowered by modern technology, is by no means a new phenomenon. Its roots lie in our past when textiles were appreciated, cherished, and mended due to the scarce resources and time-consuming methods of spinning and weaving[18]. The Indian sari and Japanese kimono are examples of traditional textile-led clothing and material appreciation, using the entirety of the fabric as garment. The simple shapes of a kimono, which are not disrupted by cutting, offer a great platform for a variety of exquisite textile techniques and complex surface designs. In fact, the focus on textiles and surface decoration has kept the cut of kimono away from undergoing almost any changes over the years[19].

The kimono and sari can also be seen as examples of Zero Waste Fashion practices (ZWF) that concentrate on waste-minimizing garment shapes and construction methods, with the aim of using the whole material without off-cuts.[20] The correlation between dimensions, quality of the textile, and silhouette greatly affects the look of the garment. Although the main focus of ZWF practices is on patternmaking, it can be linked to textile-led practices, as the textile material and its value are the starting point of the design process. In fact, there can be an added artistic value to combining unique textile design with ZWF practices,[21] as the woven shibori-project by Sanna Ahonen (p. 440) demonstrates.

The role of textiles in fashion design process

A fashion designer can approach the design process from many perspectives. Textiles can offer a starting point of inspiration, connected to the designer's philosophy and values, or to their preferred ways of working. The role of textiles is also defined by the restrictions of the design process such as the availability of resources, the design brief or concept, accessibility of facilities, or predetermined price points. Townsend and Goulding[22] define three approaches to fashion design, labelled as 'garment-led', 'textile-led', and 'simultaneous' design methods, which all underline different roles for the textile and the shape of a garment in the design process. The wearer's body creates an additional element to this combination[23], as there is always a bodily aspect in fashion design.

While in the garment-led approach, the shape and volume of the garment are at the core of the design and the textile is designed or selected to support the shape, the textile-led approach emphasises the features of textiles.[24] There exists a range of working methods that could be labelled textile-led. The common factor in textile-led practices is identifying or designing the textile, its appearance, and texture prior to designing the shape, or letting the design of the fabric and its placement, direction, fall, or repeat size inspire the form and construction of the garment.[25] The term could as well be used to describe clothing where the use of special fabrics or surface decoration is the dominant feature of the garment in comparison to the shape. Designers and brands can be well-known or even more recognised for their textiles rather than the cut of the clothing. This is the case with brands such as Marimekko and Missoni.

In the industry, it is common for high-end designers or brands to design and develop exclusive fabrics with textile mills. Dries van Noten and Prada are among brands known for their high-quality custom-made textiles. Textile-led fashion is often practiced collaboratively with in-house or freelance textile designers and mills. Collaboration can be exceedingly fruitful as the partnership between textile designer Yuki Kawakami and fashion designer Rolf Ekroth showcases (pp. 448–449).

Meanwhile, there are a growing number of fashion designers that design and even generate their own textiles.

Fashion designer as the designer of both textile and garment

Niinimäki sees a "renaissance in material appreciation" among fashion designers.[26] She argues that there are benefits to fashion designers engaging with self-made approaches to textile design, as it can deepen their knowledge and appreciation of materials and textiles, as well as creating unique aesthetics. A self-created material can become extremely valuable for the designer, both figuratively and literally, and it affects the way of working with the material. The significance of a unique textile leads to the desire to minimise the waste of the precious fabric and to design clothing to support and enhance its features. Exclusive prints, weaves, and knits become a competitive asset and are essential in differentiating the designer or brand from others, and enforcing their design identity. Aakko calls combining skilful materiality and the designer's integrated role a possibility for materializing values.[27]

In a simultaneous design approach both the textile and the garment are considered and designed in unison for the desired purpose. Knitwear and print designs tailored to the garment shapes are examples of simultaneous design approaches, where the designer needs a sensitivity to both textile and garment design.[28] However, examples of fashion designers simultaneously engaging with the design of woven textiles have been rare in the industry. Many designers work in close collaboration with weaving mills, but usually rely on the in-house designers at the mill regarding the textile quality and yarn choices. To successfully collaborate with a weaving mill to create new looks, adequate understanding of technique is essential.

By following the methods introduced in this book, fashion design students learn the basics of woven textile design and develop an understanding of how to design and collaborate with weaving mills. As the examples in this text illustrate, the integration of knowledge of woven textile design and textile finishing with garment design can support the work of the designers and lead to a more holistic approach.

Guided by concept

When designing the textile and the garment simultaneously, emphasis should be placed on strong concept development at the beginning of the design process. Concept guides the entire chain of design decisions and empowers meaningful integration of both practices. It also helps enforce the unique aesthetics and better express the storyline. Fashion designer Emilia Kuurila's design process always starts from visual research. For her, a good story and mood are most important, both in supporting the design process and in the final collection.

Kuurila's collection from 2016 is an example of strong and unique looks created through the combination of textile and fashion design. She is the designer of both the garments and the textiles, which in her case are a combination of jacquard weaving and industrial knitting with artisanal textile printing and finishing methods. Her collection was inspired by early Nick Cave and the Bad Seeds, Victor Vasarely's optical art, Dario Argento's horror film *Suspiria* (1977), and flowers in still life paintings. Kuurila's collection is a great example of how the same motifs can be implemented into the collection through various textile techniques and materials. The importance of a strong concept in both practices is evident in her work. The result is a striking and yet balanced collection, in which both textile and fashion design play an equal role in communicating the story.

→ Bachelor's thesis
collection 2016
by Emilia Kuurila

← Collages from the
visual research book

↑ Master's thesis collection 2013
by Anna-Mari Leppisaari

Material appreciation and sustainable design

The ability to design customised textiles for fashion allows the designer to express their ideas and convey their messages in novel ways. These messages not only support the visual concept of the collections, but also transmit deep meanings and values from within their design philosophy. Values such as material appreciation and utilisation of self-created high-quality and durable textile materials can be the focal point of textile-led design. Anna-Mari Leppisaari and Sanna Ahonen's collections explore material appreciation and value creation through the textile-led fashion design process.

Anna-Mari Leppisaari's collection is an exploration of fashion through textile and surface design, where form and aesthetics follow the woven and embroidered fabric. The collection is inspired by Alinka Echeverria's photographs that portray Mexican pilgrims carrying colourful and vivid handcrafted shrines that were built using a variety of techniques and materials. The experimental use of materials and techniques, as well as the collision of contemporary style and folklore motifs in these images became an inspiration for the mixing and bonding of materials and patterns in the collection. An essential element in the project is sustainability, which is approached through the appreciation of high-quality, unique materials. The weaving methods and restrictions of the loom strongly affect the style and form of the clothing. Garments are designed on the loom with the aim of creating as little waste as possible. The ability to control and influence the entire design process and the qualities of a garment, from yarn to finished product, creates strong individual aesthetics and a value base.

Being involved in the design and production process of both the textile and garment, starting from yarns to design and manufacturing, enables the designer to affect and rethink several aspects of the life-cycle of a garment. Decisions can be made keeping in mind the ethical and environmental impacts of the garment, while taking into account its overall quality, durability, and aesthetic appeal. Unique high-quality materials and their sustainable values can also help build an appreciation for the garment and influence the degree of care and the consumption habits of consumers.

Recycling and repurposing materials are topical themes in the fashion industry. More and more companies are offering an increasingly wide range of options for sustainable and recycled yarns and fabrics. For some designers and brands, repurposing is part of the design process and aesthetics. Reinvention of recycled garments is by no means a new phenomenon in fashion. For many designers, such as Martin Margiela whose Artisanal-line upcycles found materials and objects, it has been a long-standing approach and aesthetic. For many students and young designers, using or making their own sustainable, recycled or vegan textiles and garments is inherently important, and materials are used very innovatively.

Digital impacts

The development of digital technologies and **computer-aided design** (CAD) has had a significant impact on creative integration of textile and fashion design practices and production. Computer-aided design and manufacturing allow designers to combine a multitude of concepts and aspects, such as textile

Woven Shibori and Zero Waste Clothing

Sanna Ahonen explores how wearable garments can be designed and implemented through structural textile design, using traditional dyeing processes in a new way. Her project shifts the emphasis of the clothing design process to the textile itself, avoiding traditional garment design techniques such as pattern cutting and sewing. In her work, woven shibori is applied in a novel way to zero-waste clothing design. This new approach to zero-waste design is inspired by past artesans, who developed innovative techniques for transforming rectangular fabrics into clothes that appreciated and utilised the properties of the fabric. For example, the ends of the warp threads were used to tie pieces together and selvages were used in the hem of the garment, reducing the need to finish the edges by sewing. Sanna Ahonen's background as a textile designer informed her approach to fashion

← Master's thesis collection *Slow Unfolding – Woven Shibori in the Context of Zero-Waste Clothing* 2023 by Sanna Ahonen

design, as she used her knowledge in structural textile design to construct garments.

The collection consists of five garments, through which she explores how to use the woven shibori technique in combination with finishes, such as dyeing and felting, to give shape to rectangular pieces of fabric created on the loom. The woven pieces of fabric are formed into garment shapes by pleating – pulling the woven threads. In the conventional shibori technique, the fabric is pleated or knotted as preparation for resist dyeing. The tightly gathered areas remain undyed, decorating the finished fabric. The traditional indigo dyeing process creates compelling contrasts in the folds and emphasises the three-dimensional texture of the fabric. Traditionally, the pulling yarns are removed from the fabric at the end of the dyeing process, as they are primarily used to create the surface pattern (see example on p. 429). In Ahonen's garments, the pulling yarns are not removed but take on a central role in constructing the garments' shape. These yarns are also used to assemble the garment pieces by knotting them together to form the seams.

The pulling yarns and their placement transform the simple loom-woven rectangular fabrics into garments and open up a world of possibilities in their shaping. Adjusting the gathering of the cloth makes it possible to modify the shape and size of the clothes. Therefore the same piece can be customised and adjusted to changes of the wearer's body over time. This approach also cleverly addresses the challenges of sizing often associated with zero waste designs.

Ahonen's collection is a great example of using the design possibilities of textile finishes and advanced jacquard weaving knowledge in holistic thinking, which integrates textile and fashion design practices. The project builds on knowledge of traditional textile techniques and combines the hands-on process of manipulating fabrics with high-tech 3D jacquard weaving in a novel way.

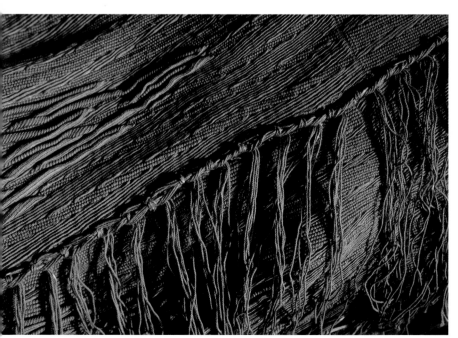

← Detail of the indigo-dyed woven shibori fabric and the seam of knotted pulling yarns

surfaces, structures, and 3D garment shapes within one scheme.[29] Virtual sampling on various kinds of **3D modelling software** makes it possible to instantly visualise variations of designs and plan the integration of textile and garment shapes quickly and easily. Many companies use 3D fashion design software, such as CLO3D or Browzwear, to simulate their garment designs and streamline and digitalise the design and production process to eliminate unnecessary sampling. The development of 3D features in textile software makes it possible to import structural textile designs to 3D fashion design software.

Knitwear design is an area of textile design in which developments through digital technologies and computer-aided design have been very progressive. The leading flat knitting machine producers, Stoll and Shima Seiki, have developed 3D design features in their software, which allow realistic fabric simulation and 3D virtual sampling of knitwear. Digital yarns with realistic features can be scanned and created to be shown in different colourways, and structures can be simulated in different gauges. Flat-knitting machine producers and circular-knitting machine producers have also created their own systems for **seamless-knitting technology**. In seamless knitting (whole-garment knitting), the entire garment can be knitted seamlessly in one go, and the technology produces less waste in the production process as it does not require any traditional cutting or sewing of garment pieces. The advantages of seamless knits are also enhanced comfort, fit and motion range, which makes them especially popular in activewear.

Companies such as EAT and Shima Seiki have also developed 3D design

systems that support the virtual modelling of woven fabrics. Yarns can be scanned to create accurate simulations, and three-dimensional weaves visualised. The fabric simulations can also be further enhanced with print and embroidery designs.

This type of software can have a positive impact on sustainability in the product development process and can help designers to holistically combine different aspects of the design process and product features. The A-POC (A Piece of Cloth) garment developed by Issey Miyake and Dai Fujiwara in 1997 is a great early commercial example of this integration. In an A-POC product, the textile and the garment are simultaneously knitted from a single thread with the support of computer-aided design and manufacturing technologies. The innovations of A-POC include waste-minimising in complete garment production processes and a concept that allows customisation for each customer.[30]

Using both manual and virtual modelling is beneficial when combining textile and fashion design processes. The haptic knowledge and hands-on experimentation emphasised in this book are a perfect foundation for meaningful utilisation of these technologies. Computer-aided weave design enables complex explorations with three-dimensional textile surfaces that can be transformed into garment shapes. Combining computer-aided 3D pattern-making with weaving facilitates designing garments on looms, featured in the design project by and Venla Elonsalo. The groundbreaking project offers new pathways into a future of **woven textile form**, which combines computer-aided 3D patternmaking with expertise on the loom.

I WEAVE DOGS AND CLOTHES
by Venla Elonsalo

My interest in whole-garment weaving and its possibilities started when I challenged myself to construct a 3D-woven plush toy. I was intrigued by how complex forms could be woven using layered, interwoven fabric structure variants (pp. 206–207). Once I succeeded in creating a 3D toy dog design, I decided to test the concept further by designing a complete 3D-woven clothing collection.

Each piece of the collection—a plush toy dog (p. 46), a suit jacket, pants, and a pleated skirt—interweaves four

↑ Suit jacket and pleated skirt. Master's thesis project *I Weave Dogs and Clothes* 2024 by Venla Elonsalo

A map showcasing the construction of the 3D-woven suit jacket and dog by Venla Elonsalo. The numbers and slashes (/) refer to the layers of the jacquard fabric and how they are separated (/) or interwoven.

↑ Stuffing the 3D-woven dog. The stuffed, finished 3D-woven dogs are presented on p. 46.

fabric layers in specific ways, forming a three-dimensional product without sewing. The fabric is woven with wool yarns on a fine, 80 ends/cm, polyester filament warp and fulled (see p. 417) after weaving to prevent the fabric and its interwoven seams from fraying during cutting. After the fulling process, the fine polyester ends remain hidden within the shrunk wool surface.

The collection was woven at the Turkish weaving mill Vanelli on industrial looms with a jacquard repeat width of 150 cm. Combining the factory's facilities and expertise with my creative pattern-cutting and textile design skills made this experimental collection possible. Specialists at Vanelli handled the weave programming and weaving based on my structural drafts, while I did the post-weaving finishes, including fulling, steaming, cutting, and stuffing.

In addition to the design experimentation, *I Weave Dogs and Clothes* explores the role of digital technology in the design processes. CAD software and physical modelling are equally integral to my work process. I use CLO3D and Shima Seiki's ApexFiz alongside Adobe Photoshop and Illustrator. The digital tools provide quick and reliable results before moving on to physical prototypes. In contrast, physical modelling provides essential tactile knowledge. The scale of prototypes extends from structural weave samples to prototypes on a 1:1 scale. The physical models include paper mock-ups, sewn toiles, and samples woven with industrial and hand-operated digital jacquard looms. Furthermore, digital

simulations and process pictures were key in communicating the design to collaborators, especially when working remotely with the weaving mill.

When designing 3D-woven garments, designers must understand and visualise the connection between textile and form.[1] The weaving process imposes certain constraints on the designs. One notable constraint is the two-dimensionality of standard weaving machines, which requires the garments to lay flat. Additionally, the fabric's rectangular shape restricts the garment's size, volume, and efficient use of the fabric area.[2]

The design needs to be adjusted to the properties of the loom. The cloth diagram is created by placing the weave structures onto a two-dimensional map that showcases the construction of a product with differently coloured areas.

I Weave Dogs and Clothes thrives on pushing the boundaries of conventional garment production and inspiring further development of 3D-woven garments. Even though post-weaving cutting is required, there is a significant reduction in manual construction steps compared to the industry standard cut-and-sew production.

Render of the 3D-woven garments in CLO3D (A). The jacquard simulation of the featured suit jacket, pleated skirt and pants has been created on Shima Seiki's Apex Fiz simulation software (B). The garments' colours visualise the four-layered construction process. Each layer is presented with a different colour, which helps highlight the garments' structural complexity, while exaggerated seams further emphasise the form. The top is turquoise, the two middle layers are yellow, and the bottom is orange.

As demonstrated by these examples, there are many ways of meaningfully integrating textile and fashion design practices, whether it is through material appreciation, handcraft, or combining the latest technologies and computer-aided design. These approaches are not in opposition to one another but are best when creatively merged.

"Being able to mix and match fashion and textiles, integrating textile design and manipulation as part of my fashion collections, is a big factor in what makes my work stand out." – Maria Korkeila

Mixing and matching fashion and textiles

The *Under Wraps* collection by Maria Korkeila was awarded the special prize of the jury, sponsored by Schiaparelli, at Hyerès International Fashion and Photography Festival in 2017. The theme of Korkeila's collection is concealment and disclosure, the act of covering and revealing. The inspiration includes Christo and Jeanne-Claude's artwork of wrapped mundane objects, magazines that were covered in transparent materials, as well as 70's adult magazines. Korkeila's design process starts with visual research, and then moves forward to developing materials and designing garments. In order to express the ideas behind her research, she mixes woven, printed, and knitted fabrics with embroidery and material manipulation techniques. The collection features several clever ways of representing the idea of plastic wrapped magazines through different techniques, such as multilayered woven jacquard with a transparent lurex layer on top with an image of a body beneath, and combining silk screen printing with plastic layers.

"Studying textiles extensively alongside my core fashion design studies has been essential in shaping my work. It has opened up more career opportunities as well. It has given me the tools to truly be able to design a garment or collection from scratch, meaning that I am not limited to existing materials, and even when using existing materials, I have a broader set of skills to manipulate them to my liking. Incorporating knitwear, woven jacquards, printing, and embroidery has become an important part of my design process." – Maria Korkeila

Under Wraps, Bachelor's thesis collection 2016 by Maria Korkeila

444

↑ Lookbook and final products: a fil coupé fabric with cotton and cupro, a wool-linen-cotton double weave jacquard, and a partially felted wool-linen fabric. Master's thesis collection *Life of Garments* 2018 by Heta Vajavaara

↑ Camouflage jacquard fabric with pocket weave and filling. Polyester warp woven with cotton, acrylic wool and cupro. Textile design by Yuki Kawakami for Rolf Ekroth's fashion collection 2017

Fashion, Textiles and Collaboration

The following texts expand upon the theme of combining textile and fashion design practices. Furthermore, both cases illustrate skillful material modification through textile finishing.

Heta Vajavaara examines in her text *Life of Garments* the materiality of clothing, and the significance and purpose of the relationship humans have with textiles through everyday clothes. It has a reflective sensitivity to both textile and clothing design, which is realised in a collection of unique woven textiles made into six identical suits.

In her text, Yuki Kawakami introduces her collaboration with fashion designer Rolf Ekroth. It showcases how supportive dialogue between a textile designer and a fashion designer, both of whom have their own strengths and roles, can lead to compelling and successful results. Their cooperation is an excellent example of how meaningful collaborative design work requires encouraging interactions and most importantly, mutual respect.

↖ Selecting yarns and colours
↑ Experimenting with colour finishes

LIFE OF GARMENTS
by Heta Vajavaara

Life of Garments is an exploration into the significance, purpose, and materiality of clothing. It ponders two fundamental questions: what is the everyday life of clothes like, and how do fashion and textile designers influence the world. In its tangible form, it is a collection of unique woven textiles made into six identical suits.

In order to tackle such complex questions, I looked at clothing from five different viewpoints: through the specific lens of traditional Japanese aesthetics, the context of our mundane and normal everyday life, the material of a garment and its tactility, the physical purpose of a garment and how it is connected to a biological, living body, and finally the social function of a garment and how the shape of clothing acts as a signifier in society.

In 2016 I spent six months in Kyoto and traditional Japanese aesthetics influenced my thinking immensely. The aesthetic concepts of *wabi* and *sabi* encourage humility, modesty, and acceptance of change. They urge humans to acknowledge objects as our equals and appreciate the materials that surround us. These thoughts and visual cues served as the starting point for the mood, colours, and materials of the collection. My aim was to use finishing techniques to create variations in the colour, structure, or surface of each fabric.

The paradox between how clothes are presented and thought of, and how they actually look, feel, and behave in normal daily use is interesting. I explored this by photographing clothes in my home, concentrating only on situations where they are not in contact with a human being, and are not folded or hanging nicely on hangers. In the end, I mostly had pictures of garments piled up on different kinds of furniture. Looking at the pictures, I see piles of textiles. I know they are clothes, but in some pictures there are no identifying features relating them to the human body. The form of the garment is completely lost. When observed at home and in everyday situations, the most important and visible feature of a garment is its material. The fabric retains its qualities even when the garment is not worn.

The material of a garment determines a considerable deal of its character. The relationship between a piece of clothing and a human is essentially a relationship between textile and human. Although visual aspects of textiles are important in carrying messages and conveying status and power in societies, on a personal level the foremost qualities of textiles are protection and tactility. Touch is essential for a person to understand the surrounding reality, which

↑ Kanjiro Kawai's home in Kyoto is a prime example of traditional Japanese aesthetics

446

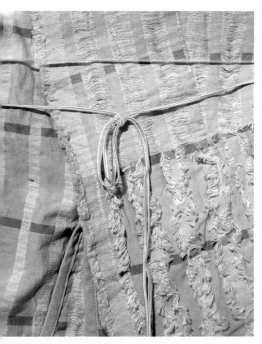

↑ Cut and uncut floats of a cotton-cupro blend

is why tactile surfaces have the ability to arouse powerful emotions and ground us to reality. I designed the textiles as stimulants to our sense of touch and explored different finishing techniques and materials to create interesting haptic surfaces.

Clothes exist in relation to the human body and act as tools for our survival. We often separate purely functional clothes from casual or fashionable garments, even though social signalling and protection are equally relevant human needs. I investigated how to make casual garments better suited to face the demands of thermoregulation by concentrating on weaving techniques and structures. I developed a specific jacquard weaving technique with body-mapped see-through areas for moisture release and elastic areas to create form.

To consider the meaning of a garment through history—the tradition, conventions, how the form of clothing can shape our society and culture—I chose to look at the men's business suit. I came to understand that instead of creating something completely new, we as humans prefer to modify and develop an existing form, be it a physical object or a custom, in order to establish connotations and create meanings around it. This is one of the reasons that the men's suit has survived through the ages and has been used to define masculinity. I used the form of a suit to define my idea of modern femininity. The shape of a two-piece suit is so iconic and recognizable that it served as a good platform to demonstrate how fabrics with different drape alter the shape of a garment, and the significant role of the textile in creating form.

Fashion and textile designers shape the world. We are creators of atmospheres and values, and we shape the everyday life of others. We are creators of tactility and sensations. We can design a person's nearest environment and define human relationships, social organisation, and hierarchies.

→ A mix of cotton and cupro, this fabric was inspired by common Japanese bamboo fences

→→ A see-through mock leno weave reveals a diagonal stripe running underneath in this wool-linen-cotton fabric. Master's thesis collection *Life of Garments* 2018 by Heta Vajavaara

TEXTILE COLLABORATION FOR A FASHION COLLECTION

by Yuki Kawakami

Rolf Ekroth and I met at Aalto University in 2014 when he was looking for a collaborator to design textiles for his second-year fashion collection. At the time I was an exchange student visiting from Japan. Rolf's collection was inspired by mountain climbers of the 30s and 40s, and the documentary *Chasing Ice*. My inspiration for the custom-made textiles were the glaciers and landscapes of the documentary. In order to turn abstract images of glaciers into rich textures, I created a special woven fabric with very long and fluffy mohair floats. The print I designed for the collection also played with textures and was executed by three-dimensional puff printing on felted wool.

The collection went on to win the Designer's Nest Award in 2015, and according to the judging panel was admired for its "great colours and great manipulation of material". This feedback helped us recognise what a great team we make. Working together was so inspiring that it became the starting point for a creative collaboration that has spanned many years. We continued working together after graduation when Rolf established his own brand and I started work at a weaving mill in Kiryu, a textile district in Japan. Rolf's collections have received international acclaim and have been shown at the Hyerès Fashion Festival and in Florence at Pitti

Uomo. Throughout the collections I have combined various industrial and artisanal weaving and finishing techniques in the custom-made textiles. In Kiryu, we have a network of local textile companies, whose expertise I have been able to utilise in textile development, for example on a special needle punched fabric.

This type of collaborative design work between fashion designer and textile designer requires above all mutual respect. I appreciate the way my inspiration and vision has always been respected and trusted. At the beginning of each collaboration Rolf would share his mood board and colour scheme with me, and let

←← Jacquard fabric inspired by glaciers. Woven on a mercerised cotton warp with mohair, lamé yarn and wool.

← Woven fabric with polyamide warp and weft. Textile design by Yuki Kawakami for Rolf Ekroth's collection 2014.

→ Devoré (p. 432) and pigment print on cotton polyester mixture fabric. Textile design by Yuki Kawakami for Rolf Ekroth's Bachelor's thesis collection, finalist in Hyerès Fashion Festival 2016

me come up with fresh ideas for the textiles. Sometimes Rolf would even design the garment based on the fabric I developed. Being able to think and experiment so freely and creatively is refreshing amid all the commercial textile design work I do. Our collaboration has always been an interaction and that is why I value and enjoy it so much.

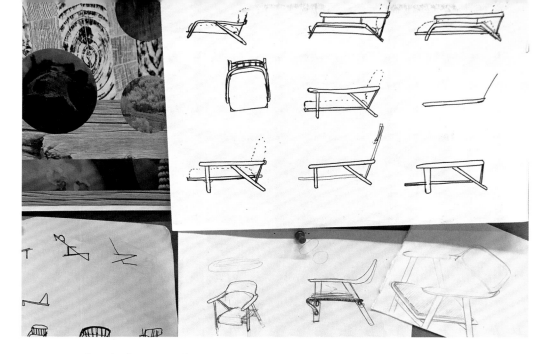

4.3 Hybrid Explorations – Bringing Together Wood and Textile

The multidisciplinary nature of textiles is emphasised throughout this book. By inviting the reader into the world of textile practices, materials and structures, and introducing the concept of *textile thinking*, the book advocates the development of designers with hybrid skills. These hybrid skills allow designers to apply their textile knowledge to other fields of design, art and craft. For designers, artists and makers new to textile practices, immersion into the unexplored world of textiles can offer new perspectives and awareness which inform and expand upon familiar design practices. Conversely, this interaction also brings new knowledge and ideas to the field of textiles.

The following example offers an intriguing continuation of the insights on hybrid textile and fashion design introduced in the previous sections of this chapter. **Josh Krute**, a furniture designer with a minor in Textile Design, describes how being introduced to textiles lead to realising the interrelatedness of the types of joinery in both textiles and woodwork,

A carefully planned and compact **Textile Design minor** study module offers a good way to integrate textile content into the curriculum of students from other disciplines. Plunging into a field with new techniques and materials broadens the students' thinking and gives new perspectives to already acquired practices. The text below offers an example of how minor Textile Design studies can be integrated into further studies. Here, new knowledge is reflected upon and used in the student's Master's thesis project by examining the design processes behind the development of an upholstered chair prototype with practice-led research methods.

reorienting and deepening his thinking on materials and structures. Moreover, the text demonstrates how embodied immersion into textile-making can expand design practices and thinking. In his text Krute also reflects on hand-knowledge, the notion of tacit, **embodied thinking**, introduced previously in *Embodied thinking in the hand-weaving practice* pp. 84–85.

← Chair and upholstery fabric *Kuulas* by Josh Krute

← In his project Josh Krute examined the design processes behind the development of an upholstered chair prototype with practice-led research methods. Chair *Kuulas*, Master's thesis project 2019 by Josh Krute

END-GRAIN

by Josh Krute

When I compare structures in woodworking and textiles, the principle of combining overlapping and interlocking components to provide strength and support is the same. There are different types of joinery applied in woodworking that connect and make furniture components rigid and stable, just as there are many types of structures in woven textiles that make up the qualities and aesthetic of a fabric. I find that structure is one of many parallels between making a chair and weaving a fabric.

My background is in furniture design, woodworking and printmaking. When working, the qualities of the material often guide how I use my hands and body. This familiar "hand-knowledge" adapts to the physicality of wooden forms; my hands know what to do when ripping a board on the table saw. However, with yarns, fabrics, bobbins, or shuttles, it has been challenging to adopt different ways of working and thinking. I believe that is what draws me to textile design the most. Being immersed in a new field that emphasises colour and tactility while learning to combine these using specific techniques, gives newness to my

practice that is both exciting and innovative.

Maarit Salolainen once told me that the jacquard loom is essentially the oldest computer; weaving structures can be thought of as an analogue system that is both systematic and mathematical, yet allows for countless structural and pattern possibilities. When I started to weave I considered my own engagement with furniture design, woodworking and printmaking. Regardless of the obvious differences, traditional weaving follows similar parameters and principles to those of woodworking and printmaking. These include structure, material knowledge, and process-driven practices – the foundation of each discipline.

I developed a collection of handwoven fabric samples inspired by wooden end-grain patterns. I remember standing in a room filled with ten old wooden shaft-looms, each having different warp yarns, treadles and tie-up charts. With instruction and practice, weaving on each loom became more intuitive. I learnt how coordinating the shaft loom's tie-up and treadle sequences with specific weft yarn qualities resulted in structural effects that mimicked the

texture, colour and grain pattern of wood. Additionally, I realised that my physical movement became synchronised with the loom's components; a person operating the shaft-loom becomes a part of the entire mechanism. This is similar to the process of hand-printing wooden forms; another parallel between practices.

I continued working with the concept of wood grain in the industrial woven upholstery fabric *End-grain*. Using traditional hand-printing techniques as a starting point, I recorded the grain patterns of twenty-five inked oak blocks onto paper. Each oak block is square in dimension and has a unique grain pattern. The hand-printing technique requires careful distribution of pressure to burnish each block's surface qualities. This results in sharp contrasting lines. Once printed, the wood block's grain pattern was represented in a uniform grid composition that is in pattern-repeat. The design was then digitised for industrial weaving while retaining its original aesthetic. The white and black areas of the print were translated into pixels according to the amount of ends in the repeat of the industrial jacquard machine,

→ Cotton-wool mix upholstery
fabric *End-grain*. Master's thesis
project 2019 by Josh Crute

then applied to a double cloth structure and
woven with black wool picks of contrasting
colour to the white cotton ends. The utilised
structure created a dense and durable
upholstery fabric.

I used *End-grain* to upholster the seat
of my wooden chair prototype and for an
accompanying woven blanket. The fabrics
utilise different scales and structures but
feature the same motif. Different combinations of the wood grain pattern highlight the
story of the wooden material's visual, tactile
and functional qualities. The similarities of
woodworking and printmaking are present,
and have been woven into a textile form.

4.4 Creative Textile Design for the Industry

Textile designers working in the industry often take part in demanding product development projects that involve new production techniques, machinery, or materials. In these cases, the design process starts from understanding the technical framework behind the production process as well as both the capacities and limitations of the machineries involved. Specialised knowledge of industrial production, especially of design-driven development of yarns, material constructions and finishes is required. Simultaneously, the designers must be able to collaborate in a multidisciplinary research and development team, find solutions, and push the boundaries of creative and innovative approaches to generate novel textiles. The creative concept development process, as well as communication between the engineer and designer, needs to start before the initial sampling. The main challenge is taking into consideration the manufacturing processes and controlling the technical parameters whilst maintaining creativity throughout the design process.

This section introduces three product development projects that have navigated these challenges. In her project *Floating & Clipping* (p.460), **Tiina Paavilainen** demonstrates a strategy for managing the design process of technically challenging industrially-woven fil coupé jacquards which involve complex structures and multiple finishes. The initial inspiration for the collection is drawn from structures with floats and the technique of clipping them, and it illustrates new approaches to designing fil coupé fabrics while exploring their past frameworks. The project, conducted in collaboration with the Italian weaving mill Lodetex, employs a practice-led research method. The design process utilises an idea portfolio in which innovative sketching methods are used to demonstrate the appearance of fabrics and assist in the dialogue between the designer and the technician.

In her text *Restrictions as Inspiration* (p.464), **Aoi Yoshizawa** contemplates fostering creativity despite the limitations of industrial design and manufacturing processes. Her design work is bound by the strict performance regulations of contract fabrics, textiles used in public spaces. Yoshizawa's commitment to using restrictions to propel problem-solving and inspire creativity resonate with the overall ethos of this book. The technical and creative are inseparable in textiles. Hence, ideally the creative design process is a perfect balancing act between the functional and aesthetic, whilst at the same time maintaining high quality and overarching demands of sustainability.

Petra Haikonen introduces her development project of curtain fabrics designed to improve the sound environment of indoor spaces. In her text *Woven Sounds – Design Exploration and Experimentation with Acoustic Curtain Fabrics* (p.456) Haikonen demonstrates the ways in which designing functional fabrics is a combination of disciplined research and creativity. Acoustics for Haikonen is not only a parameter guiding her design process from the technical point-of-view. She was intrigued by the thought of using the concept of sound on multiple levels. Accordingly, sound permeates the textiles on all levels: in technical qualities, as visual inspiration and method of sketching.

← Fabrics from collection *Woven Sounds*. Master's thesis collection 2016 by Petra Haikonen

← Digital print *Electronic Gradient* on polyester Trevira and lurex slit-film yarn print ground. The design is created with audio-visual programming. The program creates a colour gradient where the dark shades are low tones and light shades are high tones of a song. Acoustic test group 2 (4–7 dB attenuation from 700Hz and up).

All fabrics, Master's thesis project 2016 by Petra Haikonen for Lodetex

"Giacomo Puccini's opera classics—soprano's singing. I don't understand what."

→ Polyester Trevira and lurex slit-film yarn curtain fabric *Soprano*. The fabric cover and surface area are the key features of acoustic curtain fabrics. Acoustic test group 4 (2–6 dB attenuation from 700Hz and up)

WOVEN SOUNDS—DESIGN EXPLORATION AND EXPERIMENTATION WITH ACOUSTIC CURTAIN FABRICS

by Petra Haikonen

"What a funny crunchy squeaking sound snow makes when you walk on it."

My work involves the development of jacquard-woven sheer and lightweight curtain fabrics that improve the sound environment of indoor spaces. Acoustic curtain fabrics are considered functional textiles, since they have the appearance of conventional lightweight curtains but are able to absorb medium and high frequency sounds. There are many advantages to using woven acoustic curtains: their easy application and maintenance, relatively low costs, and adjustable nature. Acoustic curtains can easily replace conventional curtains in interiors without the need for adding vast quantities of extra acoustic elements. By changing the draping of the curtains or their placement, it becomes easy to adjust the acoustics of the interior.

Acoustic curtain fabrics belong to a group of functional textiles in which a particular function is integrated as a primary design criterion for adding value to otherwise conventional textiles. Designing functional fabrics is a combination of disciplined research and creativity. The basic considerations—whether the fabric hangs and drapes well, how it feels, and how heavy or lightweight the fabric is—have to be recognised during the design process of acoustic fabrics. But there are several factors that influence acoustic performance, and those factors need to be researched and considered as a priority. The performance requirements have to be tested and fulfilled as a part of the design process. Therefore, the design process should be a productive balance between the function and the look of a fabric, while at the same time maintaining high quality.

Design Experiments

I explored these themes in my work for the Italian weaving mill Lodetex and their international clients. A textile designer working for a manufacturing company can usually work freely when it comes to innovating new design ideas. It is common to work with a broad idea collection that includes a wide range of fabric qualities and styles for diverse clients. During my time as an intern at Lodetex I realised that the company has a notable demand for acoustic curtain fabrics. The majority of the acoustically functioning woven curtain fabrics on the market are plain fabrics, so I decided to emphasise jacquard weaving and digital printing in my work, creating an acoustically performing and yet visually appealing collection of fabrics. As a designer, I felt that this collection should stand out in the market of sound absorptive curtain fabrics with its versatile look.

For this project I created an applied interior textile product development model with two development cycles, where the actual prototyping, testing, analysing and developing phases appeared. The first prototype development cycle was an experimental try-out round for testing and developing different structures and material combinations. The second development cycle was then more focused on the advanced technical solutions and visual aspects. The design process for functional products has to include a round of tests after each prototyping phase, and therefore all of the fabrics were tested either by myself or by a certified test laboratory. The collection fabrics are still considered prototypes, since the tests I was able to carry out were only preliminary. Acoustic fabrics on the market have to pass a sound absorption coefficient test, which gives a comparable acoustic classification value between A to E (A being the most absorbing fabric and E the lowest).

The design process for woven acoustic fabrics aims to create a balanced fabric cover. The surface of the fabric should be dense

"Sine waves are humming and buzzing while oobleck is dancing around the ink"

← Digital print design *Sine Wave Marble* on polyester Trevira and lurex slit-film yarn print ground created with cymatics sketching. When oobleck (corn starch and water) is exposed to low frequency sine waves, it starts to move mixing ink with itself creating a marble effect. Acoustic test group 4 (2–6 dB attenuation from 700Hz and up)

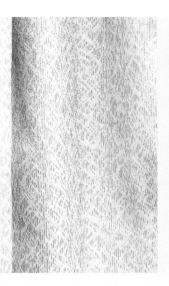

↑ Woven polyester Trevira curtain fabric *Loons* created with audio-visual programming. Acoustic test group 5 (1–5 dB attenuation from 700Hz and up)

↑ *Loons* (left) and polyester Trevira and lurex slit-film yarn curtain fabric *Walking on Snow* (right) created with audio-visual programming. *Walking on Snow* acoustic test group 8 (0–3 dB attenuation from 700Hz and up) materials PES and Lurex film yarn (PES)

"Loons call each other on a lake – kuui-ko-kuui-ko-kuui-ko – creating a beautiful wave pattern."

enough for the sound wave to absorb but not too dense, otherwise the sound wave just reflects from the surface. The microstructural surface area should also be as large as possible. There are several factors that affect the fabric cover and the surface area such as density, woven structures, used materials, fabric thickness, and layering. Different finishes also affect the absorption ability. For example, air blow-drying increases the microstructural surface area of the fabric because it opens the fibres more. Due to the research and my own discoveries, I ended up using mainly two weft system structures where a transparent flat slit-film yarn (p.156) is woven on the backside with plain weave for providing an efficient covering, and a more porous and hairy yarn is woven on top of the fabric for creating an increased microstructural surface area.

Layers of Sound

I was intrigued by the thought of using the same concept of sound on many levels. Therefore, sound is featured as an inspiration, as a technical tool, and eventually

as a sketching method in the visual design process as well. The sound concept appears as woven and digitally printed patterns and as structural inspiration. I used two pattern sketching methods for versatile looks: material cymatics sound vibration and audio-visual coding. Both of the methods worked in a way that a played sound generated the visuals independently through either a material medium or an algorithm capturing the essence of that particular sound. Visuals vary from wave drawings and colour gradients to cellular structures. The designed fabrics do not only take in excessive sound, but they also include visual sound stories, for example a moment on a lake when loons are calling each other.

Designing acoustically functioning fabrics proved to be complex work requiring sensitivity to all factors of the fabric construction acting both independently and in conjunction. Even though I was able to control the factors during the design process, the results were never quite how I expected them to be. And moreover, the performance of acoustic curtains is not only based on

the designer's technical skills in creating a perfect sound absorbing surface, but there are also external factors that appear with the use of the acoustic curtains which affect the ability to absorb excessive noise. These external factors include the amount of draping, the airspace behind the curtain, and the curtain's placement within the room. A textile designer cannot influence application of the curtains that much, though simple mounting instructions could result in efficient use of acoustic curtains.

My design practice combines thorough technical exploration and creative experimentation. Through experimentation I was forced to let go of the constraints of trying to achieve all goals at once, and instead I was able to find the optimal solutions through several try-outs. It is essential to understand the possibilities and boundaries while working with a new product development process, but I also believe that indulging in experimentation and learning from flaws are effective ways to gain a deeper design knowledge.

FLOATING AND CLIPPING

by Tiina Paavilainen

↑ The portfolio of handmade material sketches consists of three themes. These themes offer a starting point for visual inspiration and serve as a tool for studying the requirements and production phases at the weaving mill. These pages feature the organic and harmonious surfaces from the theme *After Rain*.

Advancements in the textile industry continuously influence weaving techniques and provide new opportunities for design and production. Inspired by the unique aesthetics of clipped designs, I delved into fil coupé fabrics to explore the potential and limitations of industrial production of this technically challenging textile. Fascinated by the origins of fil coupé, my aim was not to reinvent the fabrics' essential features but rather to push the boundaries of their design, appearance, and performance through a novel approach.

Fil coupé and Brocade Fabrics

Fabrics using weft floats in which the floats have been cut out, are commonly referred to as **fil coupé**, de coupé, or clipped designs (p.419). Fil coupé fabrics are woven with a ground weft and a supplementary weft (see extra-weft patterning p.150). The function of the ground weft is to construct a cohesive ground structure and the body of the fabric, while allowing for the supplementary weft to generate the figuring on the surface of the fabric and to travel loosely creating intervals or floats between the decorative motifs of the pattern. These floats are usually cut to create a fringed look or to generate a lighter appearance and hand. The plain weave on the edges of motifs ensures that the yarn does not unravel or slip from the ground after clipping. The advanced application of the supplementary weft is to duplicate it. This provides latitude for designers but also increases material consumption. Similar to all industrially manufactured fabrics, certain requirements regarding the quality of

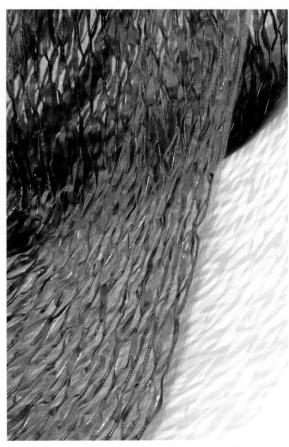

↑ This polyester fabric from the collection *After Rain* is digitally printed before clipping. The floats are cut in the fabric reverse and brushed in front to create a fringed look.

→ A thin shrinking polyester ground pick forms the base weave. While the base fabric shrinks during finishing, the fancy yarn (lurex and tape yarn) supplementary weft floats rise and pucker.

materials and structures must be met for the application of the product. Other technical requirements, such as the length of the float, depend on the available resources and facilities of the weaving mills and the finishing companies.

Fil coupé represents a luxurious and sophisticated style in dressing and dwelling, and settles within a higher price category. Today, fil coupé fabrics are primarily used in mid-range and high-end products and appear prominently in clothing and furnishing markets. The variety in industrially produced fil coupé products resembles the handwoven brocades of the past. **Brocade** (p. 83) is a detailed decorated fabric that was used for drapery and upholstery, especially in church textiles, as well as men's waistcoats and women's skirt flounces. These patterned textiles were originally hand-embellished with a true brocading weft using precious materials such as gold, silver, and silk. Brocading was used to reduce material consumption and to avoid adding extra weight to the fabric. Clipping techniques today are not used for conserving material but rather to add value to the product with the highly decorated appearance of the cloth. Obviously, replacing the true brocading weft by a supplementary weft travelling from selvedge to selvedge and clipping the floats is a feasible and more efficient method of patterning in the industry. The treatment increases the cost of manufacturing and produces leftovers from the supplementary weft floats that have been cut.

Sketching Methods and Idea Portfolio

While researching the historical and technical aspects of clipped designs, I created sketches for my collection. Although initially I found the fil coupé technique restrictive, it inspired me to strive to find novel solutions for the creative process to overcome its limitations and technical challenges. I began by developing new sketching methods in order to create an idea portfolio of designs. The idea portfolio consisted of handmade material sketches that represented prototypes of woven fabrics and demonstrated the structure, texture, and appearance of each final fabric. Transparency, fringed and frayed effects were essential features in my designs.

Silk paper and tulle created light and transparent effects, while yarns and slashed fabrics provided a fringed look. The most expressive and efficient sketching methods were rolling yarns around cardboard, partly gluing them onto a light fabric, and cutting the unglued yarns. Tearing and creasing silk paper or combining it with other materials, as well as cutting and layering tulle provided interesting results. This creative process

fostered new approaches to design and technical solutions for final fabrics, each sketch offering new ways to work and improve the idea.

Design and Production Process

To translate these sketches into textiles, I worked in collaboration with the Italian weaving mill Lodetex. The collaboration allowed me to adapt my ideas into production, gain new influences for sketching, and familiarise myself with the production process. Working together with experts at Lodetex and visiting the clipping company Vibe provided me with knowledge of the production processes, and helped me explore the distinct possibilities of the clipping technique. This enhanced understanding of the technical aspects of the production process allowed me to examine more advanced three-dimensional structures.

The design process for industrial fil coupé fabrics requires a level of abstract thinking as the various materials, structures and industrial processes cannot be trialled on a handloom. This challenge ultimately opened up new ways of thinking about clipped designs and gave birth to new ideas. Most importantly, the idea portfolio with hand-made fabric sketches helped me to overcome this challenge. It provided visual and tangible information about the designs and helped me to communicate with the production team regarding their technical implementations.

This experience taught me that although the facilities at the weaving mill impose certain limits, they also open up new possibilities for exploration. As I gained a deeper understanding of the technical requirements and phases of production, the limitations and restrictions of industrial weaving guided me towards *textile thinking*, new approaches in design thinking and processes. Additionally, researching the historical background and the current standing of clipped designs and their production methods made me consider the industrial design process as artistic work, where aesthetics and techniques advance hand-in-hand. Industrial textile design and discovering new solutions is a creative practice. Thus, learning from practice complemented the experimental design process.

← In this polyester-linen double-cloth fabric the three-dimensional structure is achieved by simultaneously weaving two separate fabric layers and interlacing these with a supplementary weft. This extra-weft system alternately interlaces in plain weave on both fabric face and back, fills the pockets between the layers, and floats on the fabric face and back. After the floats are clipped and the fabric is set under tension, the structure transforms into a bold three-dimensional construction.

All fabrics, Master's thesis project 2016 *Floating and Clipping* by Tiina Paavilainen for Lodetex

→ Fabrics from collection *After Rain*. Master's thesis collection 2016 by Tiina Paavilainen

RESTRICTIONS AS INSPIRATION

by Aoi Yoshizawa

Having lived abroad from my native country Japan for more than ten years, I have faced a number of culture and language barriers. However, these limitations have motivated me to solve problems in my everyday life, and I have come to believe that restrictions can inspire creativity. In my work I have investigated how the restrictions of the industrial textile design process can foster creativity.

Contract fabrics are a category of functional interior textiles that are used in public spaces such as hospitals and hotels. In the contract textile industry, higher quality standards are implemented to ensure safety and pass the strict performance regulations for textiles used in public premises. These quality specifications restrict not only the manufacturing process but also the design process of these textiles. Contract textile designers face the challenge of developing new products with a limited choice of woven structures and yarn materials. I took on this challenge to investigate how the quality criteria affects the design process. I aspired to take the limitations and restrictions of the contract textile design process as a source of inspiration in my creative process.

I began designing a collection of contract textiles as a form of practical research while simultaneously researching the topic theoretically, challenging myself to apply this research to my design process. The resulting collection of upholstery and drapery textiles titled *Random Order* draws inspiration from the structural patterns of architecture and random movements of people. The design process initially began by creating surface patterns that suited the collection theme and weaving a number of sample swatches with different structural bindings. The collection gradually developed by testing out different woven samples and adjusting the technical aspects, such as weave structures and scales of patterns. During the final prototyping phase at the Swedish weaving mill Svensson, the designs were adapted to accommodate the materials and yarn colours available at the mill.

↑ Collection *Random Order, colourway 2*. Designs from left: *Order, Vertical, Patch, Diago, Parallel*. The curtain fabric *Diego* is flame-retardant polyester Trevira CS, all upholstery fabrics wool polyamide mix. Designing colourations is an important part of a textile designers work in the context of commercial collections. The images show additional colourways from the collection.

→ Designing colourways is an integral part the work of textile designers. On these pages you can see three different colourways in the collection *Random Order*.

→→ Collection *Random Order*, colourway 1. All fabrics, Master's thesis 2014 by Aoi Yoshizawa

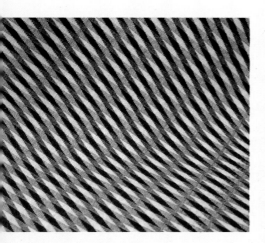

↑ *Opt* wool-polyamide mix upholstery fabric from the collection in *Simulating Jacquard Fabrics* (p. 401).

The design process involved generating sample swatches before the final prototyping stage. The challenge then became to adapt the design ideas and samples made in the studio into industrially woven fabrics. Tackling this issue involved a series of preparatory steps including using alternative processes such as textile simulation methods. As the plan for weaving the final textiles at Svensson's factory was settled, the factory facilities became my design tools. Access to materials, looms, and colours became limited to those available at the factory. However, these limitations did not affect my design process negatively but served as a helpful boundary for my creative design work. In fact, it proved much more efficient to work with a number of fixed design parameters.

At first, some of the criteria hindered my creativity as I concentrated on the limitations of the design process. However, through exploration and better understanding of the principles, I was able to find new ideas and solutions. The best way forward was first to experiment with little consideration of the technical restrictions in order to develop ideas and create the samples freely. Then, with more focus on the technical limitations, I could look through all the samples and figure out what could work as contract textiles and what could not. Thus, even though limitations at first imposed restraints on my creativity, they contributed positively to the collection design at the latter stages of the process.

The technical limitations of contract textiles affect the overall design process as well as the aesthetic features of the textiles. On the other hand, these restrictions motivate designers to find innovative solutions to design challenges and serve as a driving force for creativity by allowing freedom within a framework of technical limitations.

4.5 Textile Thinking towards Multidisciplinary Futures

As discussed throughout this book, textiles have an internal twisted, interwoven, inter-meshed, intertwined, bonded or interlocked structure. These constructions can incorporate a wide variety of fibres and raw materials. As the Bauhaus textile pioneer Anni Albers emphasised in her writing, there is an inherent interdependence between weave structures and materials.[31] Grasping this relationship demands analytical structural thinking, technical textile construction skills, and a keen tactile and aesthetic sensibility. These are the essential elements at the core of **textile thinking**, the potential of which lies in the constant rethinking of the interrelation of materials and structures and in the creative adaptation of textile practices and manufacturing processes. *Textile thinking*, the synthesis of tactile and sensory knowledge combined with aesthetic creativity and technical skills,[32] can substantially contribute to how we experience technology.

In recent decades, textile design scholars have sought to delve deeper into the distinctive traits of this particular mode of thinking associated with textile design practices. The work of Elaine Igoe[33] has greatly contributed to understanding the inner workings of textile designers. This exploration of *textile thinking* and the inclusion of textile practice-based approaches has extended into interdisciplinary research fields, inspiring new research questions and methodologies in domains such as functional materials, biomaterials, technical textiles, eTextiles, and wearable electronics, among others.

This section introduces two points of view on how textile thinking can shape the trajectory of innovative eTextile development. **Sandra Wirtanen** introduces her multidisciplinary collaboration project on integrating energy-harvesting technology into woven textiles in "Prototyping on a Loom – Weaving the Futures" (p. 468). She focuses on working on a loom and celebrates the possibilities of hands-on practice-based research through the process of weaving.

Emmi Pouta, in her piece "Layered Approaches – Woven eTextile Explorations Through Applied Textile Thinking" (pp. 470–473), delves into how technological advancements open up new perspectives in textile design. Drawing from her doctoral research, she discusses how electrical functionalities, alongside textile qualities evoking associations, emotions, and tactile desires, can be considered equally in woven eTextile development. Pouta approaches woven eTextiles as electrically functional material systems, where the hierarchical textile structure intersects with circuit design principles, laying the groundwork for a hierarchical model for woven eTextile design.

← Woven pressure sensor integrated within a three-layer double-cloth structure

PROTOTYPING ON A LOOM — WEAVING THE FUTURES

by Sandra Wirtanen

↑ Testing a textile with a solar simulator

Textiles protect the human body and serve our need for beauty, expression, and belonging. By integrating electronics into textiles and using engineered fibres, it is possible to enhance the existing properties of materials and expand their performance and functionality into more complex and intelligent directions. In the future, these materials can transform the way we communicate with our surroundings, and interact with our bodies and other beings. Autonomous self-charging systems may one day adjust our clothes to a perfect temperature, guide us through a foreign city, or help us recover from injuries. Nowadays, in various fields ranging from healthcare to entertainment, there is great interest in using textiles as interfaces. Current advancements in technology, from nanoscale engineered yarns to complex weave structures that allow embedding electronics, provide a great platform for endless exploration in the field of textiles.

I believe that rethinking the potential of textiles opens up new opportunities on both the creative and technical sides of the field. Aesthetic and tactile features are often neglected in the development of smart textiles or wearable technology, and harnessing material and design knowledge in the field could result in better products. On the other hand, novel materials and their technical restrictions challenge designers to find new directions for their artistic expression.

Developing complex textile materials requires hybrid knowledge in a variety of fields such as chemistry, electrical engineering, and advanced weaving. Sharing our knowledge and ideas with professionals from different fields allows us to find creative solutions for future materials. During and after my studies at Aalto University, I have had the opportunity to work in such interdisciplinary teams. In collaboration with a group of physicists and designers, we researched

the possibilities of integrating the technology of energy harvesting from the sun into our clothes and accessories. This process involved various methods ranging from lab measurements to prototyping with textile techniques. Later, the ideas were translated into woven textiles. The outcome was a collection of textile prototypes that allow integration of flexible solar cells within the weave structure.

Hands-on work with different materials and techniques is an essential part of my design process. Weaving as a technique is suitable for the creation of futuristic textile concepts as it allows bringing together storytelling and technical knowledge in a tangible form. Conductive, transparent, and textured yarns as well as insulating or shrinking materials can be integrated in the structure. Multilayered weave structures enable incorporation of sensors, actuators, and other electronics within the textile structure. The

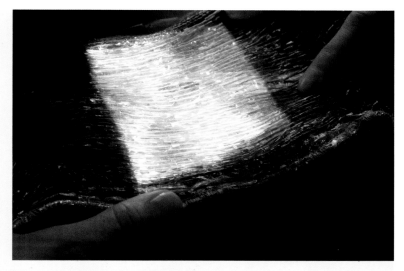

→ A textile prototype woven on a shaft loom

↘ Integration of solar cell within the woven textile

↘ Working at the Aalto University Department of Applied Physics solar cell measurement laboratory. Master's thesis project 2018 by Sandra Wirtanen

properties and aesthetics of the fabric are designed by altering and controlling these factors. It is difficult to predict the outcome of a new combination and intuitive trial and error often leads to further unique discoveries. To me this kind of learning by doing approach is key to innovation. In addition, the act of weaving allows the mind to wander and lets the imagination run wild. This is why I love prototyping on a loom. Interest in smart textiles is growing and rapid technological developments present exceptional opportunities for textile designers. It is enthralling to recognise the extent to which we can still learn about and progress in weaving.

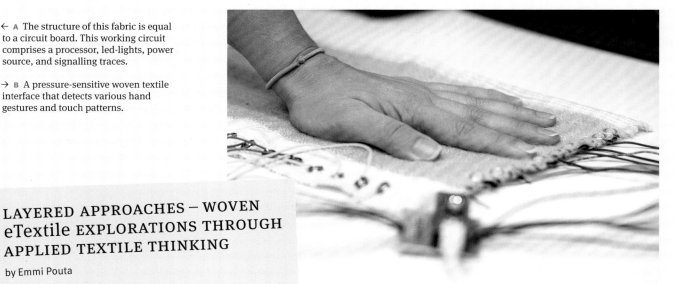

← A The structure of this fabric is equal to a circuit board. This working circuit comprises a processor, led-lights, power source, and signalling traces.

→ B A pressure-sensitive woven textile interface that detects various hand gestures and touch patterns.

LAYERED APPROACHES – WOVEN eTextile EXPLORATIONS THROUGH APPLIED TEXTILE THINKING

by Emmi Pouta

Over the past thirty years, advancements in material science and flexible electronics have revolutionised the integration of interactive functionalities into woven textiles. The emergence of electrically conductive yarns and components tailored for textile incorporation has shifted the focus from merely using textiles as a base for attaching electronic elements to embedding functionality directly within textile structures. This evolution has opened up new opportunities for textile designers, allowing them to leverage their technical expertise, deep understanding of textile structures, and tactile sensitivity in the interdisciplinary realm of electronic textiles, known as eTextiles. At the same time, managing electrically active materials and exploring their newfound interactive capabilities has expanded the conventional textile design process, encouraging interdisciplinary approaches and collaborative methods.

In the interdisciplinary eTextile domain, initially dominated by scientific and engineering disciplines, the inclusion of textile practice-based approaches has greatly influenced the research landscape. This shift has redefined the research questions being asked, the methodologies employed, and the stakeholders involved. By observing challenges within electronics engineering and addressing and exploring these issues through textile expertise, new research

avenues have been uncovered, driving novel technical innovations and enriching the field of eTextiles.

Woven eTextile Explorations Through Applied Textile Thinking

In my doctoral thesis titled "Layered Approaches: Woven eTextile Explorations Through Applied Textile Thinking"[1], I explored how practices and thinking associated with woven textile design can drive new directions in eTextile development. This exploration took shape through practice-based design research, primarily through weaving. The study embraced a material-centric and exploratory approach, aiming to tacitly grasp the properties of electrically active materials, often outside the usual material repertoire of textile designers. Engaging with these materials provided firsthand experiences, fostering a deeper, embodied understanding of their design potential.

My thesis framed woven eTextiles as electrically functional material systems, where the woven textiles' structural architecture intersects with electronic circuit design. This idea stemmed from the observation that multilayer circuit boards and interconnected multilayered weave structures share underlying structural similarities. This realisation sparked an inquiry: could woven textile structures be viewed on par with circuit boards, serving as holistic electrically

functional systems for circuit integration? Moreover, the research aimed to investigate whether the inherent qualities of textile materials—those that evoke associations, emotions, and a desire for tactile interaction—could contribute to crafting more meaningful and emotionally engaging ways to interact with technology.

These aspects were explored via a series of design experiments organised into three distinct phases. Initially, the study delved into understanding how the orthogonal yarn arrangement in woven structures facilitates the integration of electrical circuitry (A). The second phase focused on aligning electrically functional structures with the visual and tactile qualities of textile surfaces, exemplified by the creation of a textile-based tactile user interface. The third phase revolved around an exploratory weaving process aimed at uncovering the potential of multilayered weaves in advancing woven eTextile development (B). Through iterative design experimentation, each phase of the process contributed to an enhanced comprehension of feasible functional structures, a knowledge base progressively applied to more versatile woven samples. The newfound understanding of materials allowed for integrating functional capabilities as an equal factor alongside the attributes inherent in conventional woven textile design processes.

↑ C The Rose-sensor fabric

Merging Electrical and Sensorial Properties

The research uncovered new perspectives on how versatile weaving techniques can be harnessed to craft intricate electrically functional weaves. These revelations underscored the significance of fundamental textile characteristics, such as appearance and tactile feel, as pivotal elements shaping the expressive nature of eTextiles. The synthesis of electrically functional fabric architecture and versatile tactile and visual surface attributes is made possible by combining several weaves and weaving techniques, such as multilayered structures, weft and warp patterning techniques, and double-faced layers. These techniques allow for a balanced focus between the internal electrically functional structure and the outward-facing surface layers, enabling relatively independent design considerations for both. Liberating the outer surfaces to accommodate diverse textures and materials contributes significantly to the comfort, aesthetics, and durability of woven eTextiles, especially in applications like interactive clothing. Moreover, there's potential for deeper interlinkage between surface characteristics and the electrically functional structure. The findings suggest that embedding visual cues, indicating touch-sensitive sensor locations within the textile's surface pattern, can support gestural interaction and enhance the experiential aspects of textile interfaces (C). See also the woven pressure sensor integrated into a three-layer fabric on p. 466.

While incorporating additional functional materials and complex structures may impact fabric thickness and texture, applying *textile thinking* from the early stages onward can mitigate these effects. By concurrently designing visual, tactile, and functional properties, surface characteristics can be tailored to encompass desired sensorial attributes— such as specific material feels, colours, and textures—without compromising the overall look and feel of the final product.

Hierarchical Approach for Interdisciplinary Woven eTextile Development

As Anni Albers has noted, a woven textile is a sum of its structure, materials, and the interdependency of those two.[2] The weave can either downplay or accentuate specific material characteristics of yarns and fibres and vice versa. Essentially, a woven textile can be viewed as a hierarchical structure composed of various components within its architectural framework. Textile design researcher Lynn Tandler proposed a structural hierarchy model for deeply responsive woven textiles, delineating four levels: polymers and macromolecules, fibres and filaments, yarns, and the woven structure—each level building upon the previous one.[3] Drawing from the insights of design experiments, my thesis proposes augmenting this structural hierarchy with additional levels tailored to eTextile circuit design. This expanded model aims to facilitate a deeper understanding of the interdisciplinary dimensions inherent in woven eTextile development.

When electrically active materials are introduced, woven textiles' structural hierarchy collides with circuit design principles. Viewing woven eTextiles as electrically functional material systems introduces new hierarchical levels pertinent to multilayer structures and circuit layout design (D). These hierarchical levels are shaped by the specific demands of the intended application level. In practice, within multilayer composites, each layer's weave pattern, yarn densities, and material combinations can be adjusted according to specific requirements. For instance, outer surfaces can prioritise visual aesthetics and durability against wear, while the internal layer architecture aligns with circuit design principles. Additionally, weaving allows for the creation of distinct weave structures and material combina-

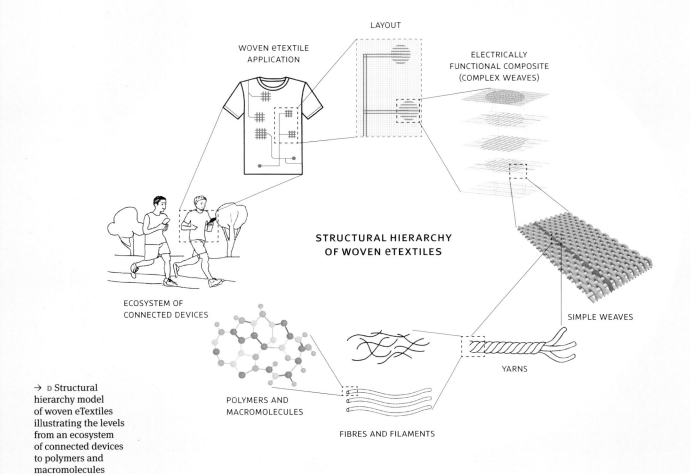

LAYOUT

WOVEN eTEXTILE
APPLICATION

ELECTRICALLY
FUNCTIONAL COMPOSITE
(COMPLEX WEAVES)

STRUCTURAL HIERARCHY
OF WOVEN eTEXTILES

ECOSYSTEM OF
CONNECTED DEVICES

SIMPLE WEAVES

YARNS

→ D Structural
hierarchy model
of woven eTextiles
illustrating the levels
from an ecosystem
of connected devices
to polymers and
macromolecules

POLYMERS AND
MACROMOLECULES

FIBRES AND FILAMENTS

tions across different pattern areas within a broader textile, which is particularly evident in Jacquard woven fabrics. This enables the design of circuit layouts across the textile surface based on intended interface specifications. Ultimately, the woven textile can be perceived as an amalgamation of electrically functional composite units and traditional textile elements, designed akin to any tangible user interface layout.

Through this model, woven eTextiles are approached as hierarchical material systems that have the potential to foster interdisciplinary collaboration across diverse fields. This model offers a framework that could assist researchers from various disciplines in comprehending how their contributions align with different hierarchical levels, from initial material development to the production of interactive garments. For textile designers, adopting this hierarchical approach could furnish valuable tools to navigate the integration of electrical properties and functional structures as additional variables within the woven textile design process. This approach aids in visualising the design variables and circuit layout prerequisites while considering their intricate connections across both single-layer woven structures and multilayer composite levels. Moreover, it provides textile designers with a platform to intertwine aspects like figurative pattern design with the internal functional structure and its layout design, thereby considering the three-dimensional form of the envisioned interactive textile application.

The eTextiles domain is constantly evolving, reshaping the role of textile designers from innovating materials[4] to purpose-led design of eTextile products[5]. As Maarit Salolainen mentions in the preface of this book, these shifts in design methodologies necessitate textile designers to cultivate hybrid skills and investigate novel ways of deploying what is already within the core of our knowledge (pp. 16–19). I believe that we can design more meaningful and emotionally resonant interactions with technology by harnessing our combined tactile and technical expertise. We are well-positioned to explore the vast potential of weaving, pioneering new innovations, and demonstrating how *textile thinking* can guide exploration in these uncharted territories.

List of Warps from Chapter 2. *To the Looms*

plain weave basket weave unbalanced plain weave weft-faced rib weave crêpe weave extra-weft patterning	**I Cotton twine warp** p.128 **Warp yarn:** Cotton seine twine, Ne 12/18 (tex 50 × 6 × 3) **Yarn sett:** 3 ends per cm **Reed:** 30:1 Straight draft on **six shafts**
unbalanced plain weave warp-faced rib weave	**II End and end fancy yarn warp** p.152 **Warp yarns:** Viscose polyester combination spiral yarn, Nm 15 (tex 66) Viscose polyamide combination tape yarn, Nm 4.6 (tex 217) or any tape yarn of similar size **Yarn sett:** 10 ends per cm **Reed:** 50:2 Straight draft on **four shafts** on a double beam loom
seersucker plain weave basket weave weft-faced plain weave	**III Striped monofilament and spiral yarn warp** p.168 **Warp yarns:** Polyamide monofilament, den 750 (tex 83) Viscose polyester combination spiral yarn, Nm 6.8 (tex 147) **Yarn sett:** monofilament yarn: 10 ends per cm spiral yarn: 5 ends per cm **Reed:** 10 yarns monofilament 50:2 | 5 yarns spiral yarn 50:1 Straight draft on **four shafts** on a double beam loom
double weave double cloth backed weave woven-pile fabric plain weave	**IV End and end spun yarn warp** p.186 **Warp yarns** **Warp 1:** Worsted wool yarn (white), Nm 2/36 (tex 28 × 2) or Nm 2/40 **Warp 2 Alternatives:** Worsted wool yarn (black), Nm 2/36 (tex 28 × 2) or Nm 2/40 Mercerised combed cotton yarn, Ne 8/2 (tex 76 × 2) or Nm 2/34 (tex 30 × 2) **Yarn sett:** 14 ends per cm **Reed:** 70:2 **Alternative set-ups:** **I:** Block draft on **eight shafts** on a double beam treadle loom, with the two units in a divided-draft arrangement in warp-wise groups **II:** Block draft on **eight shafts** on a double beam computer-assisted dobby loom
skip-dent plain weave mock leno	**V Paper yarn warp** p.214 **Warp yarn:** Paper yarn, Nm 3.9 (tex 256) **Yarn sett:** 4 ends per cm **Reed:** 20: 4,0 Straight draft on **eight shafts**
grouped weft distortion plain weave	**VI Tape yarn warp** p.226 **Warp yarn:** Viscose polyamide combination tape yarn, Nm 45 (tex 22) or any tape yarn or tube yarn of similar size **Yarn sett:** 4.5 ends per cm **Reed:** 45:1 Block draft on **eight shafts**

VII Striped wool and line linen yarn warp p.242

Warp yarns:
Unbleached line linen yarn, Nel 16/1 (tex 103)
Worsted wool yarn, Nm 2/36 (tex 27 × 2)
Yarn sett: 10 ends per cm
Reed: 50:2
Alternative set-ups:
  I: Straight draft on **eight shafts** on a double beam treadle loom
  II: Straight draft on **sixteen shafts** on a double beam computer-assisted dobby loom

twill weave
broken twill
pointed twill
diamond twill
combined twills
undulating twill
corkscrew twill
diagonal ribs
plain weave
seersucker

VIII Worsted wool yarn warp p.270

Warp yarn: worsted wool yarn, Nm 2/18 (tex 55 × 2)
Yarn sett: 8 ends per cm
Reed: 40:2
Alternative set-ups:
  I: Pointed draft on **eight shafts** on a treadle loom
  II: Straight draft on **sixteen shafts** on a computer-assisted dobby loom

waffle weave (honeycomb)
diamond twill
plain weave

IX Wool silk blend yarn and cotton yarn warp p.286

Warp yarns:
Merino wool spun silk blend yarn, Nm 2/20 (tex 50 × 2)
Mercerised combed cotton yarn, Ne 8/4 (tex 74 × 4)
Yarn sett: 7 ends per cm
Reed: 70: 1 (stitching warp), 2 (face warp)
Divided draft on **seven shafts** on a double beam loom

piqué weave
matelassé
double cloth

X Silk yarn warp p.302

Warp yarn alternatives:
Mulberry silk filament yarn Nm 1/33 (tex 30)
Spun Mulberry silk yarn Nm 2/60 (tex 17 × 2)
Density: 14 ends per cm
Reed: 70:2
Straight draft on **sixteen shafts** on a computer-assisted dobby loom

satin weave
damask
plain weave
extra-weft patterning
combination weave
compound weave
extra-warp patterning

Yarn number calculator: http://www.swicofil.com/companyinfo/manualyarnnumbering.html
See also mobile phone apps: Yarn Converter, Yarn Count

**The yarns for the sample looms have been
sourced from the following companies:**
Avia (II, III)
Fomast (III)
Garnindköbsforeningen af 1998 (V, VI)
Grignasco (IX)
Gruppo Tessile Industriale spa Risignolo (IV, VII)
Hasegawa (X)
Luigi Boldrini (II)
Papi Fabio SpA (III)
Lankava (I, VII, IX)
Wetterhoff Oy (VIII)
Schoeller (II)

Cotton twine warp

PLAIN WEAVE
BASKET WEAVE
WEFT-FACED PLAIN WEAVE
WEFT-FACED RIB WEAVE
CRÊPE WEAVE

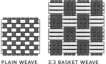

PLAIN WEAVE   3:3 BASKET WEAVE   2:4 RIB WEAVE

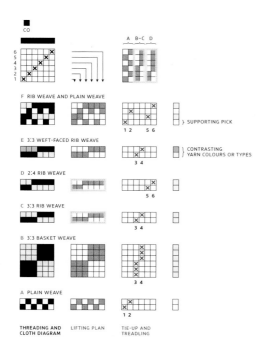

CO

6
5
4
3
2
1

A B—C D

F RIB WEAVE AND PLAIN WEAVE

1 2   5 6

} SUPPORTING PICK

E 3:3 WEFT-FACED RIB WEAVE

3 4

} CONTRASTING
   YARN COLOURS OR TYPES

D 2:4 RIB WEAVE

5 6

C 3:3 RIB WEAVE

3 4

B 3:3 BASKET WEAVE

3 4

A PLAIN WEAVE

1 2

THREADING AND   LIFTING PLAN   TIE-UP AND
CLOTH DIAGRAM   TREADLING

Cotton twine warp

Course	**Woven Fabrics Studio**
Set-up	Straight draft on six shafts
Weaves	plain weave / basket weave / weft-faced plain weave / weft-faced rib weave / crêpe weave
Warp length	11 m
Yarn sett	3 yarns per cm
Width on reed	21 cm
Reed	30:1
Warp yarns	Cotton seine twine, Ne 12/18 (tex 50 × 6 × 3)	100% CO
Weft yarns	
Pick density	Picks per cm
Width in reed	20 cm

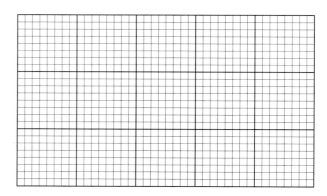

Example of a warp card (warp I) for treadle looms. General information on each warp can be found on warp cards at the looms. The information on treadle looms includes a structural draft with suggestions for treadling sequences. The warp cards on computer-assisted dobby looms include suggestions for the lifting plan. On the back, additional information is provided, such as the composition and size of the warp yarns, the sett, the reed, the width of the warp on the reed, a grid and blank space for taking notes. Copies of the sheets are provided to the students.

Similar warp cards can be easily compiled for the other nine sample warps by using the detailed information provided at the beginning of each warp introduction in Chapter 2.

See pp.80–81 and pp.121–123 for information on more practical arrangements for the *Woven fabrics studio course.*

Endnotes

Preface 14–17

1 Fagan, B. M. *Cro-Magnon: How the Ice Age Gave Birth to the first Modern Humans* (New York, NY: Bloomsbury Press, 2010), 161, 167.

Introduction 20–23

1 Pallasmaa, J. "Drawing with the mind – Thinking with the Hand – pen, hand, eye, and brain," Art of Research 2014 Conference, Aalto University School of Art, Design and Architecture, Helsinki, Finland. Paper, 2014. Also available: http://artofresearch2014.aalto.fi/keynotesJP.html

1. Interwoven–On Textiles and Humans 24–117

1 Long, A. C. ed. *Design and Manufacture of Textile Composites* (Cambridge: Woodhead, 2005).

2 Räisänen, R., Rissanen, M., Parviainen, E. and Suonsilta, H. *Tekstiilien materiaalit* (Helsinki: Finn Lectura, 2017).; Yu, C. "Natural Textile Fibres: Vegetable Fibres," in *Textiles and Fashion. Materials, Design and Technology*, ed. Sinclair, R. (Cambridge: Woodhead Publishing, 2015), 29–56.

3 Babu, K. M. "Natural Textile Fibres: Animal and Silk Fibres," in *Textiles and Fashion. Materials, Design and Technology*, ed. Sinclair, R. (Cambridge: Woodhead Publishing Limited, 2015), 57–78.

4 Räisänen, R., Rissanen, M., Parviainen, E. and Suonsilta, H. *Tekstiilien materiaalit* (Helsinki: Finn Lectura, 2017), 70.

5 Chen, J. "Synthetic Textile Fibers: Regenerated Cellulose Fibers," in *Textiles and Fashion. Materials, Design and Technology*, ed. Sinclair, R. (Cambridge: Woodhead Publishing Limited, 2015), 79–95.

6 https://ioncell.fi

7 Lawrence, C. "Fibre to Yarn: Filament Yarn Spinning," in *Textiles and Fashion. Materials, Design and Technology*, ed. Sinclair, R. (Cambridge: Woodhead Publishing Limited, 2015).

8 https://infinitedfiber.com/

9 https://spinnova.com/

10 Räisänen, R., Rissanen, M., Parviainen, E. and Suonsilta, H. *Tekstiilien materiaalit* (Helsinki: Finn Lectura, 2017).; Deopura, B. L. and Padaki, N. V. "Synthetic Textile Fibers: Polyamide, Polyester and Aramid Fibres," in *Textiles and Fashion. Materials, Design and Technology*, ed. Sinclair, R. (Cambridge: Woodhead Publishing, 2015), 97–114.

11 Duhoux, T et al. *Study on the technical, regulatory, economic and environmental effectiveness of textile recycling.* Final Report. (Luxenbourg: European Comission, 2021).

12 Materials Market Report, December 2023, TextileExchange, accessed July 13, 2024, https://textileexchange.org/app/uploads/2023/11/Materials-Market-Report-2023.pdf, 9–11.

13 Ibid. 10, 14, 32.

14 Ibid. 57–59.

15 Ibid. 51–55.

16 Räisänen, R., Rissanen, M., Parviainen, E. and Suonsilta, H. *Tekstiilien materiaalit* (Helsinki: Finn Lectura, 2017), 95.; Chen, J. "Synthetic Textile Fibers: Regenerated Cellulose Fibers," in *Textiles and Fashion. Materials, Design and Technology*, ed. Sinclair, R. (Cambridge: Woodhead Publishing Limited, 2015), 83–93.

17 Räisänen, R., Rissanen, M., Parviainen, E. and Suonsilta, H. *Tekstiilien materiaalit* (Helsinki: Finn Lectura, 2017).; Young, D. *Swatch Reference Guide for Fashion Fabrics.* 2nd revised edition. (London: Fairchild Books, 2013).

18 Sinclair, R. ed. *Textiles and Fashion. Materials, Design and Technology* (Cambridge: Woodhead Publishing Limited, 2015), 3–24.; Räisänen, R., Rissanen, M., Parviainen, E. and Suonsilta, H. *Tekstiilien materiaalit* (Helsinki: Finn Lectura, 2017).

19 Behery, H. *Effect of Mechanical and Physical Properties on Fabric Hand* (Cambridge: Woodhead Publishing Limited, 2005).

20 Rast-Eicher, A. "Bast before Wool: The First Textiles," in *Hallstatt Textiles: Technical Analysis, Scientific Investigation and Experiments on Iron Age Textiles*, ed. Bichler, B., Grömer, K., Hofmann-de Keijzer, R., Kern, A. and J. Reschreiter, J. (Oxford: Archaeopress, 2005), 117–131.

21 Long, A. C. ed. *Design and Manufacture of Textile Composites* (Cambridge: Woodhead, 2005).

22 Gong, R. H. "Yarn to Fabric: Specialist Fabric Structures," in *Textiles and Fashion. Materials, Design and Technology*, ed. Sinclair, R. (Cambridge: Woodhead Publishing Limited, 2015), 337–339.

23 Schoeser, M. *Textiles: The Art of Mankind* (New York, NY: Thames and Hudson, 2012), 162.

24 Gong, R. H. "Yarn to Fabric: Specialist Fabric Structures," in *Textiles and Fashion. Materials, Design and Technology*, ed. Sinclair, R. (Cambridge: Woodhead Publishing Limited, 2015), 344–345.; Schoeser, M. *Textiles: The Art of Mankind* (New York, NY: Thames and Hudson, 2012), 168.

25 Turnau, I. "Knitting," in *The Illustrated History of Textiles*, ed. Ginsburg, M. (London: Studio Editions Ltd., 1991), 148.

26 Power, E. J. "Yarn to Fabric: Knitting," in *Textiles and Fashion. Materials, Design and Technology*, ed. Sinclair, R. (Cambridge: Woodhead Publishing Limited, 2015), 289–302.

27 Russell, S. J. ed. *Handbook of Nonwovens* (Cambridge: Woodhead Publishing Limited, 2006).

28 Harris, S. "Flax fibre: Innovation and Change in the Early Neolithic – A Technological and Material Perspective," Textile Society of America 2014 Biennial Symposium Proceedings: New Directions: Examining the Past, Creating the Future, Los Angeles, California, September 10–14, 2014. Paper 913, 2014. http://digitalcommons.unl.edu/tsaconf/913

29 Turnau, I. "Knitting," in *The Illustrated History of Textiles*, ed. Ginsburg, M. (London: Studio Editions Ltd., 1991), 147.

30 Schoeser, M. *Textiles: The Art of Mankind* (New York, NY: Thames and Hudson, 2012), 167.

31 Hearle, J. W. S. "Introduction," in *Advances in 3D Textiles*, ed. Chen, W. (Cambridge: Woodhead Publishing, 2015), 1–18.

32 Nilsson, L. "Textile Influence: Exploring the Relationship between Textiles and Products in the Design Process", Paper 3 Designing with Textiles (Doctoral Thesis, University of Borås, Faculty of Textiles, Engineering and Business, 2015), 12–14.

33 Ibid.

34 Liu, Y. et al. "Interlacing molecular threads," *Science*, vol 351 Jan 2016 Vol 361 http://science.sciencemag.org/content/351/6271/336?utm_campaign=email-sci-toc&et_rid=35359318&et_cid=226053

35 Ibid.

36 Ovid, "Methamorphoses 6," in *Greek and Roman Technology: A Sourcebook of Translated Greek and Roman Texts*, eds. Sherwood, A. N., Nikolic, M., Humphrey, J. H. and Oleson, J. P. (London: Routledge, 2019).

37 Rast-Eicher, A. "Bast before Wool: The First Textiles," in *Hallstatt Textiles: Technical Analysis, Scientific Investigation and Experiments on Iron Age Textiles*, ed. Bichler, B., Grömer, K., Hofmann-de Keijzer, R., Kern, A. and J. Reschreiter, J. (Oxford: Archaeopress, 2005), 117–119.

38 Metropolitan Museum of Art, accessed June 7, 2021, https://www.metmuseum.org/art/collection/search/253348

39 Adovasio, J. M., Soffer, O. and Page J. *The Invisible Sex: Uncovering the True Roles of Women in Prehistory* (New York, NY: Harper Collins, 2009).; Gordon, B. *Textiles the Whole Story: Uses, Meanings, Significance* (New York, NY: Thames & Hudson, 2013).

40 Barber, E. W. *Women's Work: The First 20,000 Years – Women, Cloth and Society in Early Times* (New York & London: W. W. Norton, 1995).

41 Kvavadze, E. et al. "30,000 Years Old Wild Flax Fibers – Testimony for Fabricating Prehistoric Linen," *Science* 325(5946), 2009: 1359. http://nrs.harvard.edu/urn-3:HUL.InstRepos:4270521

42 Adovasio, J. M., Soffer, O. and Page J. *The Invisible Sex: Uncovering the True Roles of Women in Prehistory* (New York, NY: Harper Collins, 2009), 86, 161–192.; Gordon, B.

Textiles the Whole Story: Uses, Meanings, Significance (New York, NY: Thames & Hudson, 2013), 82.

43 Schoeser, M. *Textiles: The Art of Mankind* (New York, NY: Thames and Hudson, 2012), 96.

44 Harris, S. "Flax fibre: Innovation and Change in the Early Neolithic–A Technological and Material Perspective," Textile Society of America 2014 Biennial Symposium Proceedings: New Directions: Examining the Past, Creating the Future, Los Angeles, California, September 10–14, 2014. Paper 913, 2014. http://digitalcommons.unl.edu/tsaconf/913; Zohary, D., Hopf, M. and Weiss, E. *Domestication of Plants in the Old World: The origin and spread of domesticated plants in Southwest Asia, Europe, and the Mediterranean Basin* (New York: Oxford University Press, 2012), 3–4.

45 Rast-Eicher, A. "Bast before Wool: The First Textiles," in *Hallstatt Textiles: Technical Analysis, Scientific Investigation and Experiments on Iron Age Textiles*, ed. Bichler, B., Grömer, K., Hofmann-de Keijzer, R., Kern, A. and J. Reschreiter, J. (Oxford: Archaeopress, 2005), 119.

46 Leuzinger, U. and Rast-Eicher, A. "Flax processing in the Neolithic and Bronze Age pile-dwelling settlements of eastern Switzerland, " *Vegetation History and Archaeobotany* 20(6), 2011: 535–542.

47 Mellaart cited in *5000 Years of Textiles*, ed. Harris, J. (Washington: Smithsonian Books, 2010), 50.; McDowell, J. A. "The Ancient World: Introduction," in *5000 Years of Textiles*, ed. Harris. J. (Washington: Smithsonian Books, 2010), 54–55.

48 Rast-Eicher, A. "Bast before Wool: The First Textiles," in *Hallstatt Textiles: Technical Analysis, Scientific Investigation and Experiments on Iron Age Textiles*, ed. Bichler, B., Grömer, K., Hofmann-de Keijzer, R., Kern, A. and J. Reschreiter, J. (Oxford: Archaeopress, 2005), 119–121.

49 Morris, W. "Textile Fabrics," pamphlet of a lecture given on July 11, 1884 at the International Health Exhibition at the South Kensington Museum, London, accessed July 25, 2015, https://www.marxists.org/archive/morris/works/1884/fabrics.htm

50 Barber, E. W. *Prehistoric Textiles: The Development of Cloth in the Neolithic and Bronze Ages with Special Reference to the Aegean* (Princeton: Princeton University Press, 1991), 26.

51 Rast-Eicher, A. "Bast before Wool: The First Textiles," in *Hallstatt Textiles: Technical Analysis, Scientific Investigation and Experiments on Iron Age Textiles*, ed. Bichler, B., Grömer, K., Hofmann-de Keijzer, R., Kern, A. and J. Reschreiter, J. (Oxford: Archaeopress, 2005).; Grömer, K. and Saliari, K. "Dressing Central European prehistory–the sheep's

contribution: An interdisciplinary study about archaeological textile finds and archaeo-zoology," *Annalen des naturhistorischen Museums in Wien*, Serie a 120. (January 2018)

52 Beckert, S. *Empire of Cotton–A Global History* (New York: Alfred A. Knopf, 2015), 7–10.; Conklin, W. J. "Textiles and Their Messages: Perspectives from the Central Andes: An examination of structure as ‚message' in the Chavin textiles," Approaching Textiles, Varying Viewpoints: Proceedings of the Seventh Biennial Symposium of the Textile Society of America, Santa Fe, New Mexico, 2000. Paper 821, 2000. http://digitalcommons.unl.edu/tsaconf/821; Moulherat, C., Tengberg, M., Haquet, J.-R. and Mille, B. "First Evidence of Cotton at Neolithic Mehrgarh, Pakistan: Analysis of Mineralized Fibres from a Copper Bead," *Journal of Archaeological Science* 29(12), 2002: 1393.

53 Barber, E. W. *Prehistoric Textiles: The Development of Cloth in the Neolithic and Bronze Ages with Special Reference to the Aegean* (Princeton: Princeton University Press, 1991), 31–32.

54 Wilson, V. "The Far East: China," in *5000 Years of Textiles*, ed. Harris. J. (Washington: Smithsonian Books, 2010), 133–134.

55 Barber, E. W. *Prehistoric Textiles: The Development of Cloth in the Neolithic and Bronze Ages with Special Reference to the Aegean* (Princeton: Princeton University Press, 1991), 9.

56 Grömer, K. *The Art of Prehistoric Textile Making* (Vienna: Natural History Museum Vienna, 2016), 81.

57 Grabundžija, A., Schlichtherle, H., Leuzinger, U., Schier, W. and Karg, S. "The interaction of distant technologies: bridging Central Europe using a techno-typological comparison of spindle whorls," *Antiquity*, 95 (381), 2021: 627–647. https://doi.org/10.15184/aqy.2021.6

58 Grömer, K. *The Art of Prehistoric Textile Making* (Vienna: Natural History Museum Vienna, 2016), 76.

59 Harris, J. ed. *5000 Years of Textiles* (Washington: Smithsonian Books, 2010), 8.

60 Grömer, K. *The Art of Prehistoric Textile Making* (Vienna: Natural History Museum Vienna, 2016).

61 Grömer, K. "Textile Materials and Techniques in Central Europe in the 2nd and 1st Millennia BC," Textile Society of America 2014 Biennial Symposium Proceedings: New Directions: Examining the Past, Creating the Future, Los Angeles, California, September 10–14, 2014. Paper 914, 2014. http://digitalcommons.unl.edu/tsaconf/914

62 Grömer, K. *The Art of Prehistoric Textile Making* (Vienna: Natural History Museum Vienna, 2016), 127–138.

63 Rast-Eicher, A. "Bast before Wool: The First

Textiles," in *Hallstatt Textiles: Technical Analysis, Scientific Investigation and Experiments on Iron Age Textiles*, ed. Bichler, B., Grömer, K., Hofmann-de Keijzer, R., Kern, A. and J. Reschreiter, J. (Oxford: Archaeopress, 2005).

64 Grömer, K. *The Art of Prehistoric Textile Making* (Vienna: Natural History Museum Vienna, 2016), 93–107, 171–189, 450–454.

65 Grömer, K. "Textile Materials and Techniques in Central Europe in the 2nd and 1st Millennia BC," Textile Society of America 2014 Biennial Symposium Proceedings: New Directions: Examining the Past, Creating the Future, Los Angeles, California, September 10–14, 2014. Paper 914, 2014. http://digitalcommons.unl.edu/tsaconf/914

66 Grömer, K. "Textile Materials and Techniques in Central Europe in the 2nd and 1st Millennia BC," Textile Society of America 2014 Biennial Symposium Proceedings: New Directions: Examining the Past, Creating the Future, Los Angeles, California, September 10–14, 2014. Paper 914, 2014. http://digitalcommons.unl.edu/tsaconf/914; Rast-Eicher, A. and Bender Jörgensen, L. "Sheep wool in Bronze and Iron Age Europe," *Journal of Archaeological Science* 40(2), 2013: 1224–1241.

67 Grömer, K. *The Art of Prehistoric Textile Making* (Vienna: Natural History Museum Vienna, 2016), 171–172.

68 Grömer, K., Kern, A., Reschreiter, J. and Rösel-Mautendorfer, H. *Textiles from Hallstatt–Weaving Culture in Bronze Age and Iron Age Salt Mines* (Natural History Museum, Vienna. Budapest: Archaeolingua, 2013), 398.

69 Ibid., 416.

70 Ibid., 534.

71 Ibid., 512–513.

72 Grömer, K. *The Art of Prehistoric Textile Making* (Vienna: Natural History Museum Vienna, 2016), 93–100.

73 Grömer, K., Kern, A., Reschreiter, J. and Rösel-Mautendorfer, H. *Textiles from Hallstatt–Weaving Culture in Bronze Age and Iron Age Salt Mines* (Natural History Museum, Vienna. Budapest: Archaeolingua, 2013), 451.

74 Grömer, K. *The Art of Prehistoric Textile Making* (Vienna: Natural History Museum Vienna, 2016), 101–107.

75 Ibid., 104.

76 Rast-Eicher, A. "Bast before Wool: The First Textiles," in *Hallstatt Textiles: Technical Analysis, Scientific Investigation and Experiments on Iron Age Textiles*, ed. Bichler, B., Grömer, K., Hofmann-de Keijzer, R., Kern, A. and J. Reschreiter, J. (Oxford: Archaeopress, 2005), 119.

77 Harris, J. ed. *5000 Years of Textiles* (Washington: Smithsonian Books, 2010), 16.

78 Harris, J. ed. *5000 Years of Textiles* (Washington: Smithsonian Books, 2010), 16–17.; Geijer, A. *The History of Textile Art*

(London: Sotheby Parke Bernet Publications, 1982), 23–25.

79 Brunton, G. *Badarian Civilisation and the predynastic remains near Badari*, PlXXXVIII, C70K. (London: British School of Archeology in Egypt, 1928).

80 Harris, J. ed. *5000 Years of Textiles* (Washington: Smithsonian Books, 2010), 16–17.; Geijer, A. *The History of Textile Art* (London: Sotheby Parke Bernet Publications, 1982), 25–29.

81 Hilden, J. *Bedouin Weaving of South Arabia and its Neighbours* (Surbiton, UK: Arabian Publishing Ltd, 2010).

82 Petzold, A. "The dawn of the modern era 1550–1780," in *The Illustrated History of Textiles*, ed. Ginsburg, M. (London: Studio Editions Ltd., 1991), 44.

83 Geijer, A. *The History of Textile Art* (London: Sotheby Parke Bernet Publications, 1982), 96–125.; Harris, J. ed. *5000 Years of Textiles* (Washington: Smithsonian Books, 2010), 18–20.

84 Geijer, A. *The History of Textile Art* (London: Sotheby Parke Bernet Publications, 1982), 96–103.

85 Essinger, J. *Jacquard's Web: How a Hand-loom Led to the Birth of the Information Age* (New York: Oxford University Press, 2007).

86 Allen, R. C. *The British Industrial Revolution in Global Perspective* (Cambridge: Cambridge University Press, 2009).

87 Ibid., 182–216.

88 Allen, R. C. *The British Industrial Revolution in Global Perspective* (Cambridge: Cambridge University Press, 2009), 182–208.; Beckert, S. *Empire of Cotton–A Global History* (New York: Alfred A. Knopf, 2015), 65–67.; Petzold, A. "The dawn of the modern era 1550–1780," in *The Illustrated History of Textiles*, ed. Ginsburg, M. (London: Studio Editions Ltd., 1991), 43–45.

89 Beckert, S. *Empire of Cotton–A Global History* (New York: Alfred A. Knopf, 2015), 65.

90 Ibid., 66.

91 Ibid., 66–69.

92 Ibid., 29–30.

93 Ibid., 36–37.

94 Ibid., 102–103.

95 Ibid., 102.

96 Gordon, B. *Textiles the Whole Story: Uses, Meanings, Significance* (New York, NY: Thames & Hudson, 2013), 170–172.; Beckert, S. *Empire of Cotton–A Global History* (New York: Alfred A. Knopf, 2015), 94–103.

97 Beckert, S. *Empire of Cotton–A Global History* (New York: Alfred A. Knopf, 2015), 50.

98 Beckert, S. *Empire of Cotton–A Global History* (New York: Alfred A. Knopf, 2015), 56–82.; Gordon, B. *Textiles the Whole Story: Uses, Meanings, Significance* (New York, NY: Thames & Hudson, 2013), 170–173.

99 Pallasmaa, J. *The Thinking Hand: Existential and Embodied Wisdom in Architecture* (Chichester: John Wiley & Sons, 2009), 47–48.

100 Tuckle, S. *The Second Self. Computers and the Human Spirit*. Twentieth Anniversary Edition (London & Cambridge, MA: MIT Press, 2005).

101 Schoeser, M. *Textiles: The Art of Mankind* (New York, NY: Thames and Hudson, 2012), 23.

102 Weiner, A. B. and Schneider, J. eds. *Cloth and Human Experience* (Washington, DC: Smithsonian Institution Press, 1989).

103 Boyd, B. *On the Origin of Stories: Evolution Cognition and Fiction* (Cambridge: Belknap Press, 2009), Kindle.

104 Pallasmaa, J. *The Thinking Hand: Existential and Embodied Wisdom in Architecture* (Chichester: John Wiley & Sons, 2009), 15.

105 Kapur C. R. and Singh, M. eds. *Saris of India–Tradition and Beyond* (New Delhi: Lustre press, Roli Books, 2010).

106 https://www.harristweed.org/

107 https://www.fondazionelisio.org/en/

108 Gordon, B. *Textiles the Whole Story: Uses, Meanings, Significance* (New York, NY: Thames & Hudson, 2013), 167.

109 Weiner, A. B. and Schneider, J. eds. *Cloth and Human Experience* (Washington, DC: Smithsonian Institution Press, 1989).

110 Volkmann, H. *Purpurfäden und Zauberschiffchen: Spinnen und Weben in Märchen und Mythen* (Göttingen: Vandenhoeck & Ruprecht, 2008), 8.

111 Scheid, J. and Svenbro, J. *The Craft of Zeus: Myths of Weaving and Fabric*, trans. C. Volk (Cambridge: Harvard University Press, 2001), 10.

112 Weiner, A. B. and Schneider, J. eds. *Cloth and Human Experience* (Washington, DC: Smithsonian Institution Press, 1989), 2.

113 Ibid. 1.

114 Harris, J. ed. *5000 Years of Textiles* (Washington: Smithsonian Books, 2010), 11.

115 Weiner, A. B. and Schneider, J. eds. *Cloth and Human Experience* (Washington, DC: Smithsonian Institution Press, 1989) 1–2.

116 Harris, J. ed. *5000 Years of Textiles* (Washington: Smithsonian Books, 2010), 11.

117 Ibid., 12.

118 Bean, S. "Gandhi and Khadi, the Fabric of Indian Independence," in *Cloth and Human Experience*, eds. Weiner, A. B. and Schneider, J. (Washington, DC: Smithsonian Institution Press, 1989), 355–365.

119 Davis, W. *One River–Explorations and discoveries in the Amazon Rain Forest* (New York: Simon & Schuster Paperbacks, 1996), 59.

120 Scheid, J. and Svenbro, J. *The Craft of Zeus: Myths of Weaving and Fabric*, trans. C. Volk (Cambridge: Harvard University Press, 2001), 2.

121 Gordon, B. *Textiles the Whole Story: Uses, Meanings, Significance* (New York, NY: Thames & Hudson, 2013), 38–39.

122 Scheid, J. and Svenbro, J. *The Craft of Zeus:*

Myths of Weaving and Fabric*, trans. C. Volk (Cambridge: Harvard University Press, 2001), 12–13.

123 Weiner, A. B. and Schneider, J. eds. *Cloth and Human Experience* (Washington, DC: Smithsonian Institution Press, 1989), 5–9.

124 Davis, W. *One River–Explorations and discoveries in the Amazon Rain Forest* (New York: Simon & Schuster Paperbacks, 1996), 58–59.

125 Scheid, J. and Svenbro, J. *The Craft of Zeus: Myths of Weaving and Fabric*, trans. C. Volk (Cambridge: Harvard University Press, 2001), 5.

126 McLerran, J. ed. *Weaving is Life: Navajo Weavings from the Edwin L. and Ruth E. Kennedy Southwest Native American Collection* (Athens, OH: Kennedy Museum of Art, Ohio University, 2006).; Patterson-Rudolph, C. *On the Trail of Spider Woman: Petroglyphs, Pictographs and Myths of the Southwest* (Santa Fe, NM: Ancient City Press, 1997).

127 Gordon, B. *Textiles the Whole Story: Uses, Meanings, Significance* (New York, NY: Thames & Hudson, 2013), 44.

128 Scheid, J. and Svenbro, J. *The Craft of Zeus: Myths of Weaving and Fabric*, trans. C. Volk (Cambridge: Harvard University Press, 2001), 1–3.

129 Ibid., 87–88.

130 Weiner, A. B. and Schneider, J. eds. *Cloth and Human Experience* (Washington, DC: Smithsonian Institution Press, 1989), 22–23.

131 Scheid, J. and Svenbro, J. *The Craft of Zeus: Myths of Weaving and Fabric*, trans. C. Volk (Cambridge: Harvard University Press, 2001), 82–90.

132 Gordon, B. *Textiles the Whole Story: Uses, Meanings, Significance* (New York, NY: Thames & Hudson, 2013), 12.

133 Schneider, J. "Rumpelstiltskin's Bargain: Folklore and the Merchant Capitalist Intensification of Linen Manufacture in Early Modern Europe," in *Cloth and Human Experience*, eds. Weiner, A. B. and Schneider, J. (Washington, DC: Smithsonian Institution Press, 1989), 177.

134 Gottschall, J. *The Storytelling Animal: How Stories Make Us Human* (Boston & New York, NY: Houghton Mifflin Hartcourt Publishing Company, 2012), preface.

135 Scheid, J. and Svenbro, J. *The Craft of Zeus: Myths of Weaving and Fabric*, trans. C. Volk (Cambridge: Harvard University Press, 2001), 68–69.

136 Boyd, B. *On the Origin of Stories: Evolution Cognition and Fiction* (Cambridge: Belknap Press, 2009), Kindle.

137 Scheid, J. and Svenbro, J. *The Craft of Zeus: Myths of Weaving and Fabric*, trans. C. Volk (Cambridge: Harvard University Press, 2001), 106–112.

138 Boyd, B. *On the Origin of Stories: Evolution Cognition and Fiction* (Cambridge: Belknap Press, 2009), Kindle.

Kirsi Niinimäki:
Environmental Impact of Fibres 36–39
1 Niinimäki, K. ed. *Sustainable Fashion: New Approaches* (Espoo: Aalto ARTS Books, 2013), available: https://aaltodoc.aalto.fi/handle/123456789/13769
2 Orzada, B. and Moore, M. A. "Environmental Impact of Textile Production," in *Sustainable Fashion; Why Now?*, eds. Hethorn, J. and Ulasewicz, C. (New York: Fairchild Books, 2008), 299–325.; Kalliala, E. and Nousiainen, P. "Life cycle assessment environmental profile of cotton and polyester-cotton fabrics," *AUTEX Research Journal*, 1(1), 1999.
3 Anguelov, K. *The Dirty Side of the Garment Industry: Fast Fashion and Its Negative Impact on Environment and Society* (Boga Raton, FL: CRC Press, 2016).
4 Baugh, G. "Fibers: Clean and Green Fiber Options," in Sustainable Fashion; Why Now?, in *Sustainable Fashion; Why Now?*, eds. Hethorn, J. and Ulasewicz, C. (New York: Fairchild Books, 2008), 326–357.
5 Krüger, H., Himmestrup Dahl, E., Hjort, T. and Plathinn, D. *Guide Lines II: A Handbook on Sustainability in Fashion* (Sustainable Solution Design Association, SSDA, 2012).
6 Black, S. *Eco-Chic: The Fashion Paradox* (London: Black Dog Publishing, 2011).
7 Baugh, G. "Fibers: Clean and Green Fiber Options," in Sustainable Fashion; Why Now?, in *Sustainable Fashion; Why Now?*, eds. Hethorn, J. and Ulasewicz, C. (New York: Fairchild Books, 2008).
8 Anguelov, K. *The Dirty Side of the Garment Industry: Fast Fashion and Its Negative Impact on Environment and Society* (Boga Raton, FL: CRC Press, 2016).
9 Ibrahim, N. A., Abdel Moneim, N. M., Adbel Halim, E. S. and Hosni, M. M. "Pollution prevention of cotton-cone reactive dyeing," *Journal of Cleaner Production*, 16(12), 2008: 1321–1326.
10 Kant, R. "Textile Dyeing Industry: An environmental hazard," *Natural Science*, 4(1), 2012: 22–26.
11 McDonough, W. and Braungart, M. Cradle to Cradle (New York: North Point Press, 2002).
12 See https://newcottonproject.eu/
13 https://ioncell.fi/
14 Baugh, G. "Fibers: Clean and Green Fiber Options," in Sustainable Fashion; Why Now?, in *Sustainable Fashion; Why Now?*, eds. Hethorn, J. and Ulasewicz, C. (New York: Fairchild Books, 2008).
15 https://biocolour.fi/en/frontpage/

Helmi Liikanen: Embodied Thinking in the Hand-Weaving Practice 84–85
1 Pallasmaa, J. *The Thinking Hand: Existential and Embodied Wisdom in Architecture* (Chichester: John Wiley & Sons, 2009), 50.
2 Pallasmaa, J. *The Thinking Hand: Existential and Embodied Wisdom in Architecture* (Chichester: John Wiley & Sons, 2009).
3 Merleau-Ponty, M. *Phenomenology of Perception* (London: Routledge, 2002).

2. To the Looms–Weaving and Experimenting 118–333
1 Tortora, P. G. and Johnson, I. *The Fairchild Books Dictionary of Textiles*, 8th edition (London: Bloomsbury Publishing, 2014).
2 Description by American society for testing Materials (ASTM) in Elsasser, V. H. *Textiles: Concepts and Principles* (London: Fairchild Publications, 2010).
3 Alagirusamy, R. and Das, A. "Conversion of Fibre to Yarn: An Overview," in *Textiles and Fashion. Materials, Design and Technology*, ed. Sinclair, R. (Cambridge: Woodhead Publishing Limited, 2015), 162–169.; Kadolph, S. J. *Textiles: Basics* (New Jersey: Pearson, 2013), 124–125.; Young, D. *Swatch Reference Guide for Fashion Fabrics*. 2nd revised edition. (London: Fairchild Books, 2013), 31–33.; Elsasser, V. H. *Textiles: Concepts and Principles* (London: Fairchild Publications, 2010), 116–135.
4 Lawrence, C. "Fibre to Yarn: Filament Yarn Spinning," in *Textiles and Fashion. Materials, Design and Technology*, ed. Sinclair, R. (Cambridge: Woodhead Publishing Limited, 2015), 215.; Kadolph, S. J. *Textiles: Basics* (New Jersey: Pearson, 2013), 123.
5 Yu, C. "Natural Textile Fibres: Vegetable Fibres," in *Textiles and Fashion. Materials, Design and Technology*, ed. Sinclair, R. (Cambridge: Woodhead Publishing, 2015), 29–40.; Kadolph, S. J. *Textiles: Basics* (New Jersey: Pearson, 2013), 50–56.
6 Behery, H. *Effect of Mechanical and Physical Properties on Fabric Hand* (Cambridge: Woodhead Publishing Limited, 2005).
7 Alagirusamy, R. and Das, A. "Conversion of Fibre to Yarn: An Overview," in *Textiles and Fashion. Materials, Design and Technology*, ed. Sinclair, R. (Cambridge: Woodhead Publishing Limited, 2015), 161–164.; Elsasser, V. H. *Textiles: Concepts and Principles* (London: Fairchild Publications, 2010), 116–135.
8 Tortora, P. G. and Johnson, I. *The Fairchild Books Dictionary of Textiles*, 8th edition (London: Bloomsbury Publishing, 2014), 463.
9 Swatch reference guides for fabric names: Young, D. *Swatch Reference Guide for Fashion Fabrics*. 2nd revised edition. (London: Fairchild Books, 2013).; Cohen, A. C. and Johnson, I. *J.J. Pizzuto's Fabric Science: Key to Fabric Swatches* (New York: Fairchild Publications, 2012).
10 Alagirusamy, R. and Das, A. "Conversion of Fibre to Yarn: An Overview," in *Textiles and Fashion. Materials, Design and Technology*, ed. Sinclair, R. (Cambridge: Woodhead Publishing Limited, 2015), 170–175.; Kadolph, S. J. *Textiles: Basics* (New Jersey: Pearson, 2013), 126–127.; Elsasser, V. H. *Textiles: Concepts and Principles* (London: Fairchild Publications, 2010), 116–135.
11 Deopura, B. L. and Padaki, N. V. "Synthetic Textile Fibers: Polyamide, Polyester and Aramid Fibres," in *Textiles and Fashion. Materials, Design and Technology*, ed. Sinclair, R. (Cambridge: Woodhead Publishing Limited, 2015),.; Räisänen, R., Rissanen, M., Parviainen, E. and Suonsilta, H. *Tekstiilien materiaalit* (Helsinki: Finn Lectura, 2017), 74–78.; Kadolph, S. J. *Textiles: Basics* (New Jersey: Pearson, 2013), 99–101.
12 Materials Market Report, December 2023, TextileExchange, accessed July 13, 2024, https://textileexchange.org/app/uploads/2023/11/Materials-Market-Report-2023.pdf, 51.
13 https://ioncell.fi, https://www.aalto.fi/en/give-for-the-future/sustainable-ioncell-fibre, accessed June 16, 2019.
14 Chen, J. "Synthetic Textile Fibers: Regenerated Cellulose Fibers," in *Textiles and Fashion. Materials, Design and Technology*, ed. Sinclair, R. (Cambridge: Woodhead Publishing Limited, 2015), 79–95.; Räisänen, R., Rissanen, M., Parviainen, E. and Suonsilta, H. *Tekstiilien materiaalit* (Helsinki: Finn Lectura, 2017), 92–94.
15 Deopura, B. L. and Padaki, N. V. "Synthetic Textile Fibers: Polyamide, Polyester and Aramid Fibres," in *Textiles and Fashion. Materials, Design and Technology*, ed. Sinclair, R. (Cambridge: Woodhead Publishing Limited, 2015), 102.; Boncamper, I. *Tekstiilioppi: kuituraaka-aineet* (Hämeenlinna: Hämeen ammattikorkeakoulu, 2004), 261–273.; Young, D. *Swatch Reference Guide for Fashion Fabrics*. 2nd revised edition. (London: Fairchild Books, 2013),.; Räisänen, R., Rissanen, M., Parviainen, E. and Suonsilta, H. *Tekstiilien materiaalit* (Helsinki: Finn Lectura, 2017), 78–81.
16 Shenton, J. *Woven Textile Design* (London: Laurence King Publishing Ltd, 2014), 132–135.; Young, D. *Swatch Reference Guide for Fashion Fabrics*. 2nd revised edition. (London: Fairchild Books, 2013), 64–70.
17 Poem by Ahmad Shamlou, accessed July 4, 2019, http://www.thanalonline.com/en/page.asp?ID=296
18 Elsasser, V. H. *Textiles: Concepts and Principles* (London: Fairchild Publications, 2010), 34–61.; Babu, K. M. "Natural Textile Fibres: Animal and Silk Fibres," in *Textiles and Fashion. Materials, Design and Technology*, ed. Sinclair, R. (Cambridge: Woodhead Publishing Limited, 2015), 57–78.; Boncamper, I. *Tekstiilioppi: kuituraaka-aineet* (Hämeenlinna: Hämeen ammattikorkeakoulu, 2004), 148–174.; Kadolph, S. J. *Textiles:*

Basics (New Jersey: Pearson, 2013), 61–66.

19 Johnson, I., Cohen, A. C. and Sarkar, A. K. *J.J. Pizzuto's Fabric Science*, 11th edition (London: Fairchild Books, 2015), 102–104.; Elsasser, V. H. *Textiles: Concepts and Principles* (London: Fairchild Publications, 2010), 136–161.; Alderman, S. *Mastering Weave Structures: Transforming Ideas into Great Cloth* (Loveland, CO: Interweave Press, 2004), 173–176.; Räisänen, R., Rissanen, M., Parviainen, E. and Suonsilta, H. *Tekstiilien materiaalit* (Helsinki: Finn Lectura, 2017), 144.; Silpala, E. *Sidoksia kankaisi-in–Vipupuilla, vetopuilla ja poimien* (Helsinki: Opetushallitus, 2005).

20 More in: Johnson, I., Cohen, A. C. and Sarkar, A. K. *J.J. Pizzuto's Fabric Science*, 11th edition (London: Fairchild Books, 2015), 102–104.; Elsasser, V. H. *Textiles: Concepts and Principles* (London: Fairchild Publications, 2010), 136–161. Young, D. *Swatch Reference Guide for Fashion Fabrics*. 2nd revised edition. (London: Fairchild Books, 2013), 71–92.; Alderman, S. *Mastering Weave Structures: Transforming Ideas into Great Cloth* (Loveland, CO: Interweave Press, 2004), 189–200.; Shenton, J. *Woven Textile Design* (London: Laurence King Publishing Ltd, 2014), 151–152.; Räisänen, R., Rissanen, M., Parviainen, E. and Suonsilta, H. *Tekstiilien materiaalit* (Helsinki: Finn Lectura, 2017), 145–147.

21 https://www.fondazionelisio.org/en/

22 Tortora, P. G. and Johnson, I. *The Fairchild Books Dictionary of Textiles*, 8th edition (London: Bloomsbury Publishing, 2014), 368.; Elsasser, V. H. *Textiles: Concepts and Principles* (London: Fairchild Publications, 2010), 136–161.; Johnson, I., Cohen, A. C. and Sarkar, A. K. *J.J. Pizzuto's Fabric Science*, 11th edition (London: Fairchild Books, 2015), 86–117.; Kadolph, S. J. *Textiles: Basics* (New Jersey: Pearson, 2013), 158.

23 Kadolph, S. J. *Textiles: Basics* (New Jersey: Pearson, 2013), 57–58.; Sinclair, R. ed. *Textiles and Fashion. Materials, Design and Technology* (Cambridge: Woodhead Publishing Limited, 2015), 43–46, 54.; Räisänen, R., Rissanen, M., Parviainen, E. and Suonsilta, H. *Tekstiilien materiaalit* (Helsinki: Finn Lectura, 2017).; Fletcher, K. *Sustainable fashion and textiles: design journeys* (London: Earthscan, 2008).

24 Anderson, F. *Tweed* (London: Bloomsbury Academic, 2017), 7–9.

25 Ibid., 15–18.

26 Ibid.

27 Elsasser, V. H. *Textiles: Concepts and Principles* (London: Fairchild Publications, 2010), 34–61.; Babu, K. M. "Natural Textile Fibres: Animal and Silk Fibres," in *Textiles and Fashion. Materials, Design and Technology*, ed. Sinclair, R. (Cambridge: Woodhead

Publishing Limited, 2015), 62–71.; Räisänen, R., Rissanen, M., Parviainen, E. and Suonsilta, H. *Tekstiilien materiaalit* (Helsinki: Finn Lectura, 2017), 62–66.; Kadolph, S. J. *Textiles: Basics* (New Jersey: Pearson, 2013), 69–73.

28 Tortora, P. G. and Johnson, I. *The Fairchild Books Dictionary of Textiles*, 8th edition (London: Bloomsbury Publishing, 2014), 694.

29 Ibid., 456.

30 Oxford Dictionary of English

3. Jacquards–Boosting the Patterns 334–407

1 Essinger, J. *Jacquard's Web: How a Hand-loom Led to the Birth of the Information Age* (New York: Oxford University Press, 2007).

Hanna-Kaisa Korolainen:
Daisies and Friends – Scraping a Path to a Jacquard Design 376–379

1. Korolainen, H-K. *The Making of Inipiration–From Warlhol to Monet and Beyond* (Espoo: Aalto ARTS Books, 2022).

4. Finished Fabrics–into Fashion, Interiors and Beyond 408–473

1 Sekhri, S. *Textbook of Fabric Science: Fundamentals to Finishing* (Delhi: PHI Learning, 2011), 224, Kindle.

2 Braddock Clarke, S. E. and O'Mahony, M. *Techno Textiles 2: Revolutionary Fabrics for Fashion and Design* (New York: Thames & Hudson, 2005), 76.

3 Wulfhorst, B., Gries, T. and Veit, D. *Textile Technology* (Munich: Hanser Publishers, 2006), 216.; Fletcher, K. *Sustainable Fashion and Textiles: Design Journeys* (London: Earthscan, 2008), 49.

4 Sekhri, S. *Textbook of Fabric Science: Fundamentals to Finishing* (Delhi: PHI Learning, 2011), 207, Kindle.

5 Wulfhorst, B., Gries, T. and Veit, D. *Textile Technology* (Munich: Hanser Publishers, 2006), 216–217.

6 Ibid., 228.

7 Hauser, P. "Fabric Finishing: Pretreatment/Textile Wet Processing," in *Textiles and Fashion: Materials, Design and Technology*, ed. Sinclair, R. (Cambridge: Woodhead Publishing, 2015), 465.

8 Willman, L. and Forss, M. *Kudontakirja* (Helsinki: Taideteollinen korkeakoulu, 1996), 77.

9 Nielsen, P. H., Kuilderd, H., Zhou, W. and Lu, X. "Enzyme biotechnology for sustainable textiles," in *Sustainable Textiles: Life Cycle and Environmental Impact*, ed. R. S. Blackburn, R. S. (Cambridge: Woodhead Publishing, 2009), 114–115.

10 Chakraborty, J. N. "Designing through dyeing and finishing," in *Textile Design: Principles, Advances and Applications*, eds. Briggs-Goode, A. and Townsend, K. (Cambridge: Woodhead Publishing Limited, 2011), 162–167.

11 Irwin, K. *Surface Design for Fabric* (New York: Fairchild Books, 2015), 18–25.

12 Chakraborty, J. N. "Designing through dyeing and finishing," in *Textile Design: Principles, Advances and Applications*, eds. Briggs-Goode, A. and Townsend, K. (Cambridge: Woodhead Publishing Limited, 2011), 153.

13 Stegmaier, T. "Recent Advances in Textile Manufacturing Technology," in *The Global Textile and Clothing Industry: Technological Advances and Future Challenges*, ed. Shishoo, R. (Cambridge: Woodhead Publishing, 2012), 119–120.

14 Black, S. *Fashioning Fabrics: Contemporary Textiles in Fashion* (London: Black Dog Publishing, 2006), 17.

15 Gale, C. and Kaur, J. *Fashion and Textile: An Overview* (Oxford: Berg Publishers, 2004), xii.

16 Black, S. *Fashioning Fabrics: Contemporary Textiles in Fashion* (London: Black Dog Publishing, 2006), 7–8.

17 Edelkoort, L. "Anti-Fashion: A Manifesto for the Next Decade," Lecture, BoF Voices 2016, The Business of Fashion, February 9, 2017. Video: 30:44. https://www.youtube.com/watch?v=LV3djdXfimI.

18 Rissanen, T. "Zero-waste Fashion Design: A study at the intersection of cloth, fashion design and pattern cutting," (PhD thesis, University of Technology Sydney, 2013), 46.

19 Iwao, N. "Introduction: Clad in the aesthetics of tradition: from kosode to kimono," in *Kimono: The Art and Evolution of Japanese Fashion*, ed. Jackson, A. (London: Thames and Hudson Ltd., 2015), 10.

20 Rissanen, T. "Zero-waste Fashion Design: A study at the intersection of cloth, fashion design and pattern cutting," (PhD thesis, University of Technology Sydney, 2013), 46.

21 Niinimäki, K. "Renaissance of Appreciating Material; Case study in Zero Waste Fashion," *Journal of Textile Design Research and Practice*, 1(1): 2013, 77–92; 84.

22 Townsend, K. and Goulding, R. "The interaction of two and three dimensional design in textiles and fashion," in *Textile Design: Principles, Advances and Applications*, eds. Briggs-Goode, A. and Townsend, K. (Cambridge: Woodhead Publishing Limited, 2011), 303.

23 Ibid., 288.

24 Ibid., 304–307.

25 Ibid., 304.

26 Niinimäki, K. "Renaissance of Appreciating Material; Case study in Zero Waste Fashion," *Journal of Textile Design Research and Practice*, 1(1): 2013, 77–92; 78, 84.

27 Aakko, M. *Fashion In-between: Artisanal Design and Production of Fashion* (Helsinki: Aalto ARTS Books, 2016), 98.

28 Townsend, K. and Goulding, R. "The interaction of two and three dimensional design in textiles and fashion," in *Textile Design:*

Index

Principles, Advances and Applications, eds. Briggs-Goode, A. and Townsend, K. (Cambridge: Woodhead Publishing Limited, 2011), 309.

29 Ibid., 312.

30 Miyake, I. and Fujiwara, D. *A-POC Making: Issey Miyake & Dai Fujiwara*, eds. Kries, M. and von Vegesack, A. (Weil, Germany: Vitra Design Museum; and Tokyo: Miyake Design Studio, 2001), 92. Exhibition held at Vitra Design Museum, Berlin, 1 June to 1 July 2001.

31 Albers, A. *On Weaving: New Expanded Edition* (Princeton NJ: Princeton University Press, 2017). Albers, A. *On Designing* (Middletown, CT: Welseyan University Press, 1961).

32 Salolainen, M., Leppisaari, A-M. and Niinimäki, K. "Transforming Fashion Expression through Textile Thinking." In Arts, 8:(3), 2018.

33 Igoe, E. (2021). *Textile Design Theory in the Making*. (London: Bloomsbury, 2021).

Venla Elonsalo: I Weave Dogs and Clothes 442–443
1 McQuillan, H. *Zero Waste Systems Thinking: Multimorphic Textile-forms* (Doctoral Thesis, University of Borås, 2020).
2 Piper, A. *Material Relationships: The Textile and the Garment, the Maker and the Machine. Developing a Composite Pattern Weaving System.* (Doctoral Thesis, Nottingham Trent University, 2019).

Emmi Pouta: Layered Approaches: Woven eTextile Explorations Through Applied Textile Thinking 470–473
1 Pouta, E., *Layered Approaches: Woven eTextile Explorations Through Applied Textile Thinking* (Doctoral Thesis, Espoo: Aalto University Publication Series, 2023), available: https://aaltodoc.aalto.fi/items/2e17341b-246d-4f26-a760-b6cc5725cfb0
2 Albers, A. *On Weaving: New Expanded Edition* (Princeton NJ: Princeton University Press, 2017), 41–43.
3 Tandler, L. *The role of weaving in smart material systems* (Doctoral Thesis, United Kingdom: University of Northumbria, 2016).
4 Pouta, E., Vidgren, R., Vapaavuori, J., and Mohan, M. *Intertwining material science and textile thinking: Aspects of contrast and collaboration*, in Lockton, D., Lenzi, S., Hekkert, P., Oak, A., Sádaba, J., Lloyd, P. (eds.), DRS2022: Bilbao, 25 June – 3 July, Bilbao, Spain, 2022 available: https://doi.org/10.21606/drs.2022.525
5 Wickenden, R. *Rethinking E-textile design: Process, purpose and sustainability* (Doctoral Thesis, United Kingdom: Nottingham Trent University, 2021).

Featured Student Works from Aalto University

Samples and industrially produced work for commercial purposes designed by the book contributors are marked with initials:
   Maija Fagerlund (MF)
   Anna-Mari Leppisaari (AL)
   Tiina Paavilainen (TP)
   Maarit Salolainen (MS)

All uncredited quotes presented alongside fabrics are attributed to the designers who have created them.

Further Reading

Woven Fabrics Design and Textile Design
- Albers, A. *On Designing*. Middletown, CT: Wesleyan University Press, 1961.
- Albers, A. *On Weaving: New Expanded Edition*. Princeton, NJ: Princeton University Press, 2017.
- Alderman, S. *Mastering Weave Structures: Transforming Ideas into Great Cloth*. Loveland, CO: Interweave Press, 2004.
- Behera, B. K. and Hari, P. K. *Woven Textile Structure: Theory and Applications*. Cambridge: Woodhead Publishing, 2010.
- Black, S. *Fashioning Fabrics: Contemporary Textiles in Fashion*. London: Black Dog Publishing, 2006.
- Bowles, M and Isaac C. *Digital Textile Design*. 2nd edition. London: Laurence King Publishing Ltd, 2012.
- Braddock Clarke, S. and O'Mahony, M. *Techno Textiles 2: Revolutionary Fabrics for Fashion and Design*. London: Thames & Hudson, 2005.
- Coxon A., Fer, B., & Müller-Schareck, M. *Anni Albers*. London: Tate Publishing, 2018.
- Elsasser, V. H. "Woven Fabrics and Their Properties." In *Textiles: Concepts and Principles*, edited by V. H. Elsasser, 136–161. New York: Fairchild Books, 2010.
- Gale, C. and Kaur, J. *Fashion and Textile: An Overview*. Oxford: Berg Publishers, 2004.
- Grosicki, Z., ed. *Watson's Textile Design and Colour: Elementary Weaves and Figured Fabrics*. 7th ed. Cambridge: Woodhead Publishing, 1975.
- Harjumäki, U. et al. *Kankaankutojan sidosoppi*. Helsinki: Kustannusosakeyhtiö Otava, 1985.
- Holyoke, J. *Digital Jacquard Design*. New York: Bloomsbury Visual Arts, 2019.
- Hume, R. *Fashion and Textile Design with Photoshop and Illustrator – Professional Creative Practice*. New York: Fairchild Books, 2016.
- Igoe, E. *Textile Design Theory in the Making*. London: Bloomsbury, 2021.
- Irwin, K. *Surface Design for Fabric*. London: Bloomsbury Publishing, 2015.
- Kaur, J. and Gale, C. *The Textile Book*. Oxford & New York: Berg Publishers, 2002.
- Larsen, J. L. and Freudenheim, B. *Interlacing: The Elemental Fabric*. New York: Kodansha, 1986.
- Ng, F. and Zhou, J. *Innovative Jacquard Textile Design Using Digital Technologies*. Cambridge: Woodhead Publishing, 2013.
- Nilsson, L. "Designing with textiles." In *Textile influence: exploring the relationship between textiles and products in the design process*, edited by L. Nilsson. Doctoral thesis. Bårås: University of Borås, Faculty of Textiles, Engineering and Business, 2015.
- Oelsner G. H. *A Handbook of Weaves*. New York: MacMillan Company, 1915. Unabridged and unaltered republication of the original edition. New York: Dover Publications, 2015.
- Pellonpää-Forss, M. *Contemporary Colour Methods*. Espoo: Aalto ARTS Books, 2018.
- Schlein A and Ziek B. *The Woven Pixel: Designing for Jacquard and Dobby Looms Using Photoshop*. Westport: Bridgewater Press, 2006.
- Shenton, J. *Woven Textile Design*. London: Laurence King Publishing Ltd, 2014.
- Silpala, E. *Sidoksia kankaisiin – Vipupuilla, vetopuilla ja poimien*. Helsinki: Opetushallitus, 2002.
- Stankard, S. "Yarn to Fabric: Weaving." In *Textiles and Fashion: Materials, Design and Technology*, edited by R. Sinclair, 255–288. Cambridge: Woodhead Publishing Limited, 2015.
- Steed, J. and Stevenson, F. *Sourcing Ideas: Researching Colour, Surface, Structure, Texture and Pattern*. Lausanne: AVA Publishing, 2012.
- Sutton, A. and Collingwood, P. *The Craft of the Weaver: A Practical Guide Spinning, Dyeing and Weaving*. London: British Broadcasting Corporation, 1982.
- Sutton, A. *Structure of Weaving*. Loveland, CO: Interweave Press, 1982.
- Trocmé, S. *Fabric*. London: Mitchell Beazley, 2002.
- Udale, J. *Textiles and Fashion: Exploring Printed Textiles, Knitwear, Embroidery, Menswear and Womenswear*. New York: Fairchild Books, 2014.
- MA theses by Nora Bremer, You-Chia Chen, Victoria Fislage, Petra Haikonen, Leonardo Hidalgo-Uribe, Kaisa Karawatski, Emilia Kuurila, Elina Laitinen, Anna-Mari Leppisaari, Helmi Liikanen, Jiayi Ma, Mithila Mohan, Oldouz Moslemian, Tiina Paavilainen, Laivi Suurväli, Netta Törmälä, Sandra Wirtanen, Aoi Yoshizawa, and Zuzana Zmatekova. Available online at aaltodoc.aalto.fi.

Textile and Fashion Technology
- Behery, H. *Effect of Mechanical and Physical Properties on Fabric Hand*. Cambridge: Woodhead Publishing Limited, 2005.
- Boncamper, I. *Tekstiilioppi: kuituraaka-aineet*. Hämeenlinna: Hämeen ammattikorkeakoulu, 2004.
- Chakraborty, J. N. "Designing through dyeing and finishing." In *Textile design. Principles, advances and applications*, edited by A. Briggs-Goode & K. Townsend, 146–169. Cambridge: Woodhead Publishing Limited, 2001.
- Elsasser, V. H. *Textiles: Concepts and Principles*. London: Fairchild Publications, 2010.
- Essinger, J. *Jacquard's Web: How a Handloom Led to the Birth of the Information Age*. New York: Oxford University Press, 2006.
- The European Technology Platform for the Future of Textiles and Clothing (Textile ETP) https://textile-platform.eu
- Frumkin, S. and Weiss, M. (2012). "Fabrics and New Product Development. " In *New Product Development in Textiles. Innovation and Production*, edited by L. Horne, 65–79. Cambridge: Woodhead Publishing Limited, 2012.
- Hauser, P. (2015) "Fabric Finishing: Pretreatment/Textile Wet Processing." In *Textiles and Fashion: Materials, Design and Technology*, edited by R. Sinclair, 459–473. Cambridge: Woodhead Publishing Limited, 2015.
- Hearle, J. W. S. "Introduction" In *Advances in 3D Textiles*, edited by W. Chen, 1–18. Cambridge: Woodhead Publishing, 2015.
- Johnson, I., Cohen, A. C., & Sarkar, A. K. *J.J. Pizzuto's Fabric Science*, 11th edition. London: Fairchild Books, 2015.
- Kadolph, S. J. *Textiles: Basics*. New Jersey: Pearson, 2013.
- Kozlowski, R. M. and Mackiewicz-Talarczyk, M., ed. *Handbook of Natural Fibres. Volume 2: Processing and Applications*. 2nd edition. Cambridge: Woodhead Publishing, 2020.
- Kozlowski, R. M., ed. *Handbook of Natural*

Fibres. Volume 1: Properties and Factors Affecting Breeding and Cultivation. Cambridge: Woodhead Publishing, 2012.
- Lewin, M., ed. *Handbook of Fiber Chemistry.* 3rd edition. Boca Raton, FL: CRC Press, 2007.
- Long, A. C., ed. *Design and Manufacture of Textile Composites.* Cambridge: Woodhead, 2005.
- Markula, R. *Tekstiilitieto.* Porvoo: WSOY, 1999.
- Mather, R. R. and Wardman, R. H. *The Chemistry of Textile Fibres.* 2nd edition. Cambridge, UK: The Royal Society of Chemistry, 2015.
- Russell, S. J., ed. *Handbook of Nonwovens.* Cambridge: Woodhead Publishing Limited, 2006.
- Sekhri, S. *Textbook of Fabric Science: Fundamentals to finishing.* Delhi: PHI Learning, 2011.
- Sinclair, R., ed. *Textiles and Fashion. Materials, Design and Technology.* Cambridge: Woodhead Publishing Limited, 2015.
- Stegmaier, T. "Recent advances in textile manufacturing technology." In *The Global Textile and Clothing Industry. Technological Advances and Future Challenges*, edited by R. Shishoo, 113–130. Cambridge: Woodhead Publishing, 2012.
- Thompson, R. *Manufacturing Processes for Textile and Fashion Design Professionals.* New York: Thames & Hudson Inc, 2014.
- Tortora, P. G. and Johnson, I. *The Fairchild Books Dictionary of Textiles.* 8th edition. London: Bloomsbury Publishing, 2014.
- Watkins, S. M. and Dunne, L. E. *Functional Clothing Design: From Sportswear to Spacesuits.* New York and London: Bloomsbury, 2015.
- Woodings, C., ed. *Regenerated Cellulose Fibres.* Cambridge: Woodhead Publishing, 2000.
- The Woolmark Learning Centre: online educational platform. https://www.woolmarklearningcentre.com
- Wulfhorst, B., Gries, T. & Veit, D. *Textile Technology.* Munich: Hanser Publisher, 2006.
- Yu, C. "Natural textile fibres: Vegetable fibres." In *Textiles and Fashion. Materials, Design and Technology*, edited by R.

Sinclair, 29–56. Cambridge: Woodhead Publishing, 2015.

Sustainablilty, Environmental Impact of Fibres
- Anguelov, K. *The Dirty Side of the Garment Industry: Fast Fashion and Its Negative Impact on Environment and Society.* Boga Raton, FL: CRC Press, 2016.
- Baugh, G. "Fibers: Clean and Green Fiber Options." In *Sustainable Fashion; Why Now?*, edited by J. Hethorn and C. Ulasewicz, 326–357. New York: Fairchild Books, 2008.
- Black, S. "The role of nanotechnology in sustainable textiles." In *Sustainable Textiles. Life Cycle and Environmental Impact*, edited by R. Blackburn, 302–328. Cambridge: Woodhead Publishing Limited, 2009.
- Black, S. *Eco-Chic: The Fashion Paradox.* London: Black Dog Publishing, 2011.
- Fletcher, K. *Sustainable fashion and textiles: design journeys.* London: Earthscan, 2008.
- Gullingsrud, A. *Fashion Fibers: Designing for Sustainability.* New York: Fairchild Books, 2001.
- Ibrahim, N. A., Abdel Moneim, N. M., Adbel Halim, E. S. & Hosni, M. M. "Pollution prevention of cotton-cone reactive dyeing." *Journal of Cleaner Production,* 16(12), 2008: 1321–1326.
- Kalliala, E. and Nousiainen, P. "Life cycle assessment environmental profile of cotton and polyester-cotton fabrics." *AUTEX Research Journal,* 1(1), 1999.
- Kant, R. "Textile Dyeing Industry: An environmental hazard." *Natural Science,* 4(1), 2012: 22–26.
- Krüger, H., Himmestrup Dahl, E., Hjort, T. & Plathinn, D. *Guide Lines II: A Handbook on Sustainability in Fashion.* Sustainable Solution Design Association, SSDA, 2012.
- McDonough, W. and Braungart, M. *Cradle to Cradle.* New York: North Point Press, 2002.
- Nielsen, P. H., Kuilderd, H., Zhou, W. & Lu, X. "Enzyme biotechnology for sustainable textiles." In *Sustainable Textiles. Life Cycle and Environmental Impact*, edited by R. Blackburn, 113–138. Cambridge: Woodhead Publishing Limited, 2009.

- Niinimäki, K., ed. *Sustainable Fashion: New Approaches.* Espoo: Aalto ARTS Books, 2013. https://aaltodoc.aalto.fi/handle/123456789/13769
- Niinimäki, K., ed. *Sustainable Fashion in a Circular Economy.* Espoo: Aalto ARTS Books, 2018.
- Orzada, B. and Moore, M. A. "Environmental Impact of Textile Production." In *Sustainable Fashion; Why Now?*, edited by J. Hethorn and C. Ulasewicz, 299–325. New York: Fairchild Books, 2008.

Fabric Reference Guides
- Cohen, A. C. and Johnson, I. *J.J. Pizzuto's Fabric Science: Key to Fabric Swatches.* New York: Fairchild Publications, 2012.
- Young, D. *Swatch Reference Guide for Fashion Fabrics.* 2nd revised edition. London: Fairchild Books, 2013.

Textiles Early History and Archaeology
- Adovasio, J. M., Soffer, O. and Page J. *The Invisible Sex: Uncovering the True Roles of Women in Prehistory.* New York, NY: Harper Collins, 2009.
- Barber, E. W. *Prehistoric Textiles: The Development of Cloth in the Neolithic and Bronze Ages with Special Reference to the Aegean.* Princeton: Princeton University Press, 1991.
- Barber, E. W. *Women's Work: The First 20,000 Years – Women, Cloth and Society in Early Times.* New York & London: W. W. Norton, 1995.
- Grabundžija, A., Schlichtherle, H., Leuzinger, U., Schier, W. & Karg, S. "The interaction of distant technologies: bridging Central Europe using a techno-typological comparison of spindle whorls." *Antiquity,* 95(381), 2021: 627–647. https://doi.org/10.15184/aqy.2021.6
- Grömer, K. "Textile Materials and Techniques in Central Europe in the 2nd and 1st Millennia BC." *Textile Society of America 2014 Biennial Symposium Proceedings: New Directions: Examining the Past, Creating the Future, Los Angeles, California, September 10–14, 2014.* Paper 914, 2014. http://digitalcommons.unl.edu/tsaconf/914
- Grömer, K. *The Art of Prehistoric Textile*

Making. Vienna: Natural History Museum Vienna, 2016.
- Grömer, K., Kern, A., Reschreiter, J. & Rösel-Mautendorfer, H. *Textiles from Hallstatt – Weaving Culture in Bronze Age and Iron Age Salt Mines*. Natural History Museum, Vienna. Budapest: Archaeolingua, 2013.
- Harris, S. "Flax fibre: Innovation and Change in the Early Neolithic – A Technological and Material Perspective." *Textile Society of America 2014 Biennial Symposium Proceedings: New Directions: Examining the Past, Creating the Future, Los Angeles, California, September 10–14, 2014*. Paper 913, 2014. http://digitalcommons.unl.edu/tsaconf/913
- Hurcombe, L. M. *Perishable Material Culture in Prehistory: Investigating the Missing Majority*. New York: Routledge, 2014.
- Kvavadze, E. et al. "30,000 Years Old Wild Flax Fibers – Testimony for Fabricating Prehistoric Linen." *Science* 325(5946), 2009: 1359. http://nrs.harvard.edu/urn-3:HUL.InstRepos:4270521
- Langlois, G. *How Textile Communicates: From Codes to Cosmotechnics* (1st ed.). London: Bloomsbury Publishing USA, 2024.
- Leuzinger, U. and Rast-Eicher, A. "Flax processing in the Neolithic and Bronze Age pile-dwelling settlements of eastern Switzerland." *Vegetation History and Archaeobotany* 20(6), 2011: 535–542.
- Moulherat, C., Tengberg, M., Haquet, J.-R. & Mille, B. "First Evidence of Cotton at Neolithic Mehrgarh, Pakistan: Analysis of Mineralized Fibres from a Copper Bead." *Journal of Archaeological Science* 29(12), 2002: 1393.
- Rast-Eicher, A. and Bender Jörgensen, L. "Sheep wool in Bronze and Iron Age Europe." *Journal of Archaeological Science* 40(2), 2013: 1224–1241.
- Rast-Eicher, A. "Bast before Wool: The First Textiles." In *Hallstatt Textiles: Technical Analysis, Scientific Investigation and Experiments on Iron Age Textiles*, edited by B. Bichler, K. Grömer, R. Hofmann-de Keijzer, A. Kern & J. Reschreiter, 117–131. Oxford: Archaeopress, 2005.
- Zohary, D., Hopf, M., & Weiss, E. *Domestication of Plants in the Old World: The origin and spread of domesticated plants in Southwest Asia, Europe, and the Mediterranean Basin*. New York: Oxford University Press, 2012.

Textile History and Culture, Social Studies
- Allen, R. C. *The British Industrial Revolution in Global Perspective*. Cambridge: Cambridge University Press, 2009.
- Anderson, F. *Tweed*. London: Bloomsbury Academic, 2017.
- Barthes, R. *The Fashion System*. Translated by M. Ward and R. Howard. Berkeley: University of California Press, 1990.
- Beckert, S. *Empire of Cotton – A Global History*. New York: Alfred A. Knopf, 2015.
- Conklin, W. J. "Textiles and Their Messages: Perspectives from the Central Andes: An examination of structure as 'message' in the Chavin textiles." *Approaching Textiles, Varying Viewpoints: Proceedings of the Seventh Biennial Symposium of the Textile Society of America, Santa Fe, New Mexico, 2000*. Paper 821, 2000. http://digitalcommons.unl.edu/tsaconf/821
- Dormore, C. *A Philosophy of Textile – between practice and theory*. London & New York: Bloomsbury, 2020.
- Essinger, J. *Jacquard´s Web: How a hand loom led to the birth of the information age*. Oxford & New York: Oxford University Press, 2004.
- Fagan, B. M. *Cro-Magnon: How the Ice Age Gave Birth to the first Modern Humans*. New York, NY: Bloomsbury Press, 2010.
- Geier, A. *The History of Textile Art*. London: Sotheby Parke Bernet Publications, 1982.
- Ginsburg, M. *The Illustrated History of Textiles*. London: Studio Editions Ltd., 1991.
- Gordon, B. "The Fiber of Our Lives: A Conceptual Framework for Looking at Textiles' Meanings." *Textiles and Settlement: From Plains Space to Cyber Space, Textile Society of America 12th Biennial Symposium, Lincoln, Nebraska, October 6-9, 2010*. Paper 18, 2010. http://digitalcommons.unl.edu/tsaconf/18
- Gordon, B. *Textiles the Whole Story: Uses, Meanings, Significance*. New York, NY: Thames & Hudson, 2013.
- Harris, J., ed. *5000 Years of Textiles*. Washington: Smithsonian Books, 2010.
- Hemmings, J., ed. *The Textile Reader*. London & New York: Berg, 2012.
- Hilden, J. *Bedouin Weaving of South Arabia and its Neighbours*. Arabian Publishing Ltd, 2010.
- Jeffries, J., Wood Conroy, D. & Clark, H. *The Handbook of Textile Culture*. London & New York: Bloomsbury Publishing, 2015.
- Kapur Chisthi, R. and Singh, M., eds. *Saris of India – Tradition and Beyond*. New Delhi: Lustre press, Roli Books, 2010.
- McLerran J., ed. *Weaving is Life: Navajo Weavings from the Edwin L. and Ruth E. Kennedy Southwest Native American Collection*. Athens, OH: Kennedy Museum of Art, Ohio University, 2006.
- Patterson-Rudolph, C. *On the Trail of Spider Woman: Petroglyphs, Pictographs and Myths of the Southwest*. Santa Fe, NM: Ancient City Press, 1997.
- Plant, S. *Zeros + Ones: Digital Women + The New Technoculture*. London: Fourth Estate, 1998.
- Scheid, J. and Svenbro, J. *The Craft of Zeus: Myths of Weaving and Fabric*. Translated by C. Volk. Cambridge: Harvard University Press, 2001.
- Schoeser, M. *Textiles: The Art of Mankind*. New York, NY: Thames and Hudson, 2012.
- St. Clair, F. *The Golden Thread – How fabric changed history*. London: John Murray Publishers, 2018.
- Tuckle, S. *The Second Self, Twentieth Anniversary Edition: Computers and the Human Spirit*. London & Cambridge, MA: MIT Press, 2005.
- Volkmann, H. *Purpurfäden und Zauberschiffchen: Spinnen und Weben in Märchen und Mythen*. Göttingen: Vandenhoeck & Ruprecht, 2008.
- Weiner, A. B. and Schneider, J., eds. *Cloth and Human Experience*. Washington, DC: Smithsonian Institution Press, 1989.

Journals
- *Craft Research*. Intellect.
- *Journal of Textile Design Research and Practice*. Taylor and Francis.
- *Textile: The Journal of Cloth and Culture*. Taylor and Francis.

Storytelling
- Boyd, B. *On the Origin of Stories: Evolution Cognition and Fiction*. Cambridge: Belknap Press, 2010.
- Gottschall, J. *The Storytelling Animal:*

How Stories Make Us Human. Boston & New York, NY: Houghton Mifflin Hartcourt Publishing Company, 2012.
- Heckman, A. M. *Woven Stories: Andean Textiles and Rituals*. Albuquerque, NM: University of Mexico Press, 2003.
- Prain, L. *Strange Material. Storytelling through Textiles*. Vancouver: Arsenal Pulp Press, 2014.
- Silverman, G. P. *A Woven Book of Knowledge: Textile Iconography of Cuzco, Peru*. Salt Lake City, UT: University of Utah Press, 2008.

Practice-led Research
- Ings, W. 2014. "Into the realm of unknowing: Immersive drawing, imagination and an emerging fictional world." *Art of Research Conference 2014, Aalto University School of Art, Design and Architecture, Helsinki, Finland*. http://artofresearch2014.aalto.fi/papers/WelbyIngsforAOR.pdf.
- Korolainen, H.-K. *The Making of Inspiration – From Monet to Warhol and beyond*. Espoo: Aalto ARTS Books, 2022.
- Mäkelä, M. A. and Nimkulrat, N. "Reflection and Documentation in Practice-led Design Research." *Conference: The 4th Nordic Design Research Conference, At School of Art and Design, Aalto University, Helsinki, Finland 2011*. https://www.researchgate.net/publication/277309368_Reflection_and_documentation_in_practice-led_design_research
- Mäkelä, M. A., Dash, D. P., Nimkulrat, N. & Nsenga, F. "On Reflecting and Making in Artistic Research." *Journal of Research Practice*, 7(71), 2011.
- Mäkelä, M. A., Heikkinen, T. & Nimkulrat, N. "Drawing as a Research Tool: Making and understanding in art and design practice." *Studies in Material Thinking* 10, 2014, 1–12.
- Merleau-Ponty, M. *Phenomenology of Perception*. London: Routledge, 2002.
- Pallasmaa, J. "Drawing with the mind – Thinking with the Hand – pen, hand, eye, and brain." *Art of Research 2014 Conference, Aalto University School of Art, Design and Architecture, Helsinki, Finland*. Paper, 2014. http://artofresearch2014.aalto.fi/keynotesJP.html
- Pallasmaa, J. *The Thinking Hand: Existential and Embodied Wisdom in Architecture*.

Chichester: John Wiley & Sons, 2009.

Textile Design for Interiors
- Elsasser, V. H. and Sharp, J. *Know Your Home Furnishings*. 2nd edition. New York: Fairchild Books, 2016.
- Godsey, L. *Interior Design Materials and Specifications*. 3rd edition. New York: Fairchild Books, 2017.
- Koe, F. T. *Fabric for the Designed Interior*. 2nd edition. New York: Fairchild Books, 2017.
- Larsen, J. L. and Weeks, J. G. *Fabrics for Interiors: A Guide for Architects, Designers, and Consumers*. New York: Van Nostrand Reinhold Co., 1975.
- Yates, M. P. and Concra, A. *Textiles for Residential and Commercial Interiors*, New York: Fairchild Books, 2024.
- Young, D. E. *Swatch Reference Guide for Interior Design Fabrics*. New York: Fairchild Books, 2017.

Software
- Adobe Photoshop https://www.adobe.com/photoshop
- Apex Fiz by Shima Seiki (simulation: knitwear, dobby, jacquard, embroidery) https://www.shimaseiki.com/product/design/software/
- CLO3D (simulation: garments) https://www.clo3d.com/en/clo
- Arahne (ArahWeave) https://www.arahne.si
- EAT – The DesignScope Company (Dobby and Jacquard) https://www.designscopecompany.com
- NedGraphics (Woven CAD software: Dobby and Jacquard) https://nedgraphics.com
- PointCarré (Dobby and Jacquard) https://www.pointcarre.com
- WeavePoint https://www.weavepoint.com

- Digital Weaving Norway: a department of Tronrud Engineering Moss manufacturing hand-operated digital jacquard loom, Thread Controller 2 (TC2). Vibeke Vestby from Digital Weaving Norway has developed study material for jacquard design in Photoshop to be used in their workshops. https://digitalweaving.no

Photo Credits

All photograps by Eeva Suorlahti unless stated otherwise.

All diagrams and illustrations on pp. 30–319 by Tiina Paavilainen and on pp. 321–407 by Maija Fagerlund unless stated otherwise.

8, 14, 16–18, 24, 26, 27B, 35, 48 lower right and lower left, 75D, 76G, 76J Photograph by Eeva Suorlahti, courtesy of Vanelli https://vanellitextile.com

15, 42B, 43, 61A, 74B, 76F, 76H, 76I, 77K, 83 upper, 123 upper, 328 right, 392 Maarit Salolainen

28D Ilya / Adobe Stock Images

29F, 29G Aalto University / Adolfo Vera

36 upper RecycleMan / Shutterstock

36 lower Maximum Exposure PR / Shutterstock

38 upper, 471 Aalto University / Mikko Raskinen

42D basket The National Museum of Finland, Seurasaari Open-Air Museum Collection, CC BY 4.0, shoes Museum Centre Vapriikki, Cultural Historical Collection, CC BY 4.0

46, 443 Venla Elonsalo

47 You-Chia Chen

49 left Cover of *Science* vol 351, issue 6271 (22 Jan 2016). Illustration: C. Bickel / *Science*

49 right Mithila Mohan

50 Niina Vilppunen

52 Met Museum, image in public domain, attributed to the Amasis Painter

53 NsdPower / Shutterstock

54, 68 left, 70A–F Pictorial Gallery of Arts by Charles Knight, New York Public Library

55 upper Amt für Archäologie Thurgau, www.archaeologie.tg.ch, Daniel Steiner

55 lower Tiina Paavilainen. Partly drawn from photograph by Karina Grömer in *The Art of Prehistoric Textile Making*, by Karina Grömer, Natural History Museum Vienna, 2016.

57 lower Martin Rottler / 123RF

59–60 Photograph by Andreas Rausch, from the book *The Art of Prehistoric Textile Making*, by Karina Grömer, Natural History Museum Vienna 2016, © Natural History Museum Vienna

60H Kordula Gostencnik

60I Photograph by Rauno Träskelin, The National Museum of Finland / Finno-Ugric collection, CC BY 4.0

61B, 63F Karina Grömer, *The Art of Prehistoric Textile Making*, Natural History Museum Vienna 2016, © Natural History Museum Vienna

62C Tiina Paavilainen. Illustration is based on an image in *A History of Textile Art*, by Agnes Geijer, Pasold Research Fund Ltd in association with Sotheby Parke Bernet, 1982.

62D University College London, Petrie Museum of Egyptian Archaelogy

63E Image from the book *Bedouin Weaving of Saudi Arabia and its Neighbours*, by Joy Totah Hilden, Arabian Publishing Ltd. / Medina Publishing 2010.

64 Photograph by Aino Oksanen (1925), Finnish Heritage Agency / Ethnographic Picture Collection, CC BY 4.0

66 upper Past Art / Alamy Stock Photo

66 lower The History Collection / Alamy Stock Photo, image in public domain

67L Ivan-96 / iStock

68O National Museums Scotland

69I M-Production / Alamy Stock Photo

69K, 121 left, 295 lower left, 419 upper right, 433 left and lower right, 460, 461 right, 462 right Tiina Paavilainen

71D Lewis Hine, Wikimedia Commons, image in public domain

74A, 75C, 75E, 77L, 77M, 86, 100, 112, 113, 326, 328 left Photographs courtesy of Vanelli https://vanellitextile.com

78, 84, 85 Helmi Liikanen

82 upper Lapuan Kankurit

82 lower Pilvi Waitinen

83 middle left, 83 middle right, 83 lower left, 83 lower right, 213 Photograph by Stefano Casati, Fondazione Arte della Seta Lisio

87 Ateneum Art Museum, CC 0

88 upper Wikimedia Commons, image in public domain

94 left Russ Bishop / Alamy Stock Photo

94 right Granger Historical Picture Archive / Alamy Stock Photo, photograph by Edward Curtis

95 Granger Historical Picture Archive / Alamy Stock Photo

97 right, 99 right, 209 upper middle, 223 middle right, 255 upper middle, 283 lower middle Kaisa Kantokorpi

107–109 Reference photographs from family album of Tiina Teräs

110–111 upper left, middle right, and lower left Salla-Maaria Syvänen

110 upper right James Burns

110 middle left FabrikaSimf / Shutterstock

110 lower right Lestoil advertisement in *Life* magazine, 1968

111 upper right Astronaut scene, 2001:

A Space Odyssey, Stanley Kubrick, 1968 / Photographer: All Star Picture Library / copyright of MGM

111 middle left Futuro houses designed by Matti Suuronen. Photograph is most likely taken by Mauri Korhonen in 1969.

111 lower right Nicolas Obéry

114–115 Leonardo Hidalgo Uribe

116 Linda Lehtovirta and Emilia Pennanen / Aalto University 2021, Sun-Powered Textiles, funded by Business Finland

138 Sameli Rantanen

140 upper right, 184 left Anna Sorri

140 middle right, 180 upper right, 185 middle right, 199 middle left, 219, 300 upper left Family album of Tiina Teräs

143 upper Pedro Antonio Salaverría Calahorra / 123RF

145 upper right Karasev Victor / Shutterstock

145 middle left Yiu Tung Lee / 123RF

162 upper left NASA, CC BY-NC 2.0

163 upper right Aimo Kinnas / Shutterstock

166 middle right K009034 / Shutterstock

172B Kaufmann Mercantile

173 lower right Robsonphoto / 123RF

175 upper left Dndavis / 123RF

183 lower left "Nest of milk" by Tom MacDonald, www.tommac.photography

195 middle right F_y_b / Shutterstock

197 upper left, 283 upper middle Unknown

197 upper right Max5128 / 123RF

199 lower left Tiina Teräs

203 upper right Venars.original / Shutterstock

209 upper left Andrejs Zavadskis

223 middle left Fanny Gustafsson / Unsplash

224 upper right David Abbet

233 upper right, 285 upper right Yuki Kawakami

236 middle right Zhu difeng / 123RF

238 middle right Cult of Mac / Cultomedia Corp

239 upper right Jose L. Vilchez / Shutterstock

255 upper left photograph by Dorothea Lange (1938), J. Paul Getty Museum, image in public domain

264 Courtesy of Pollin Piha, Taivassalo, Finland, Maarit Salolainen

265 Tampere Historical Museums

277 upper right Eduard Zayonchkovski / 123RF

279 upper middle Ruth Vilmi

297 lower Unknown, photograph possibly by Lu Zeng

309 upper left Martinfredy / 123RF

319 upper left Ilona Hackenberg

331 right Pexels / Pixabay

332 right Jackmac34 / Pixabay

335, 364 upper right, 387 lower right, 416 right, 421 left, 422 lower, 432 right, 436 left, 439 upper right and lower right, 444 Guillaume Roujas

344 upper left surface design Oldouz Moslemian

345 lower right surface design Emmi Pakkanen

348 upper Tiia Sirén

348 lower right Courtesy of Lauritzon, photograph by Juho Huttunen

359, 370 lower left, 391 Maija Fagerlund

366 upper Sanna Lehto

382 upper, 421 upper right, 423 middle, 431 lower right Anna-Mari Leppisaari

383 lower left Tiia Sirén and Siiri Raasakka

385 upper left Maria Korkeila

404 upper right, 408, 423 lower left, 440 right Sara Riikonen

415 Ia Kähkönen

418 right, 423 right, 440 left Chris Vidal Tenomaa

419 left Bryan Saragosa

419 lower right, 424 upper left, middle left, and lower left Anna Semi

422 upper left Elina Laitinen

422 upper right, 445 right, 447 lower left and lower right, 448 right Sofia Okkonen

424 right Juho Huttunen

429 Mia Jiayi

431 upper left, middle left, and lower left Leevi Ikäheimo

433 middle right Kaisa Karawatski

433 lower right Nora Bremer

439 left Emilia Kuurila

441 upper Jaakko Kahilaniemi

441 lower Sanna Ahonen

442 Paavo Lehtonen

443 diagrams and renders Venla Elonsalo

446 Heta Vajavaara

448 left, 449 Niklas Kullström

450–453 Josh Krute

454, 457, 459 left Petra Haikonen

456, 458, 459 right Ilkka Saastamoinen

464, 465 Aoi Yoshizawa

473D Emmi Pouta

Thank you to everyone who gave us permission to use their photographs in this book. We have tried to reach out to all the copyright holders. If you notice your photograph is used without permission in this book, please contact us at Thames & Hudson.

Contributors

 Maarit Salolainen is Professor of Textile Design at Aalto University and Head of the MA Major in Fashion and Textile Design. She is a textile expert and creative director with extensive international experience across the textile industry, passionate about bringing textile knowledge to interdisciplinary platforms. At Aalto University, Professor Salolainen has developed higher education studies in textile design, focusing on renewing studio pedagogy and linking textile studies to fashion education and other design disciplines. As a creative director within the global textile manufacturing industry, she has led the design and development of fabrics and interior textile collections for international textile editors and brands, from research and initial concept through technical and creative development to final quality decisions and colour coordination.

 Maija Fagerlund is a Lecturer in Textile Design at Aalto University and a freelance textile designer. She holds an MA in Textile Design. Her main areas of interest in the field are the design of woven fabrics and surface design. Designing jacquard fabrics combines both of these and is especially close to her heart.

 Anna-Mari Leppisaari is a Lecturer in Textile Design at Aalto University and works internationally as a freelance textile and knitwear designer. She holds an MA in Fashion and Clothing Design and is especially interested in combining textile and fashion design practices. She has worked as an in-house designer at an Italian weaving mill and collaborated with Japanese, Dutch and Finnish textile and knitwear manufacturers. Her works range from experimental artistic collaborations to commercial designs, which have been exhibited at various international exhibitions and fairs.

 Kirsi Niinimäki is a leading scholar in the field of sustainable fashion. She is Doctor of Arts and Professor of Design and Fashion Research in Aalto University where she leads the Fashion/Textile FUTURES research group. The research done in this group integrates closed loop, bio-economy and circular economy approaches in fashion and textile systems and extends the understanding of strategic sustainable design. Professor Niinimäki has published widely in top scientific journals, and she has authored and edited several books about sustainable design and fashion, and biobased colours.

 Eeva Suorlahti is a textile designer and photographer who works in the fashion textile industry in Switzerland. She previously taught textile courses at Aalto University. Her area of interest lies in design research, embellishment techniques and experimental material compositions. She holds an MA in Fashion textiles from Central Saint Martins London.

 Tiina Paavilainen is a Lecturer in Textile Design at Metropolia University of Applied Sciences. She holds an MA in Textile Design. Her main areas of interest in textiles are collection design and woven textures. Previously, she worked as an in-house designer at Italian weaving mills, creating woven fabrics for interior textiles. As Designer in Residence at Aalto University, she taught woven structures and developed learning materials for textile studio courses.

 Minna Luoma is a multi-award winning graphic designer who studied both textile design and graphic design at the University of Art and Design (Aalto University).

First published in the United Kingdom in 2025
by Thames & Hudson Ltd, 181A High Holborn, London WC1V 7QX

First published in 2025 in the United States of America
by Thames & Hudson Inc., 500 Fifth Avenue, New York, New York 10110

Interwoven – Exploring Materials and Structures © 2025 Thames & Hudson Ltd, London
Text © 2022 and 2025 Maarit Salolainen, Aalto University and the authors

Originally published in 2022 by Aalto ARTS Books, Espoo, Finland
Illustrations and Photo Editor: Tiina Paavilainen
Editor: Essi Viitanen
Photographs: Eeva Suorlahti (unless otherwise specified)
Graphic design: Minna Luoma
Reproductions: Kari Lahtinen

Cover: *Wings*, from collection *Party Time* by Anna Sorri. Photo by Eeva Suorlahti

This revised edition published 2025

British Library Cataloguing-in-Publication Data
A catalogue record for this book is available from the British Library

Library of Congress Control Number 2023942887

ISBN: 978-0-500-02780-6

Impression 01

Printed in China

Be the first to know about our new releases, exclusive content
and author events by visiting
thamesandhudson.com
thamesandhudsonusa.com
thamesandhudson.com.au